Magdalena de Cao

An Early Colonial Town
on the North Coast of Peru

**Peabody Museum of
Archaeology and Ethnology**

Harvard University

Cambridge, Massachusetts, U.S.A.

PAPERS

VOLUME 87

Magdalena

PAPERS • VOLUME 87

de Cao

An Early
Colonial Town
on the North
Coast of Peru

Jeffrey Quilter
EDITOR

PEABODY MUSEUM OF ARCHAEOLOGY AND ETHNOLOGY

HARVARD UNIVERSITY • CAMBRIDGE, MASSACHUSETTS, U.S.A.

PEABODY MUSEUM PRESS
PEABODY MUSEUM OF ARCHAEOLOGY AND ETHNOLOGY
HARVARD UNIVERSITY
11 Divinity Avenue
Cambridge, Massachusetts 02138
peabody.harvard.edu/publications

Editorial direction by Joan Kathryn O'Donnell
Cover and interior design by Melissa Tandysh
Copyediting and composition by Westchester Publishing Services
Proofreading by Bridget Manzella
Printed and bound in the USA by Sheridan Books, Inc.

ISBN: 978-0-87365-2162

LIBRARY OF CONGRESS CATALOGING-IN-PUBLICATION DATA
Names: Quilter, Jeffrey, 1949- editor.
Title: Magdalena de Cao : an early colonial town on the North Coast of Peru / Jeffrey Quilter, editor.
Other titles: Magdalena de Cao (Peabody Museum Press) | Papers of the Peabody Museum of Archaeology and Ethnology, Harvard University; vol. 87.
Description: Cambridge, Massachusetts : Peabody Museum of Archaeology and Ethnology, Harvard University, [2020] | Series: Peabody Museum of Archaeology and Ethnology; volume 87 | Includes bibliographical references and index.
Identifiers: LCCN 2020001416 | ISBN 9780873652162 (hardcover)
Subjects: LCSH: Archaeology and history—Peru—Magdalena de Cao. | Excavations (Archaeology)—Peru—Magdalena de Cao. | Acculturation—Peru—Magdalena de Cao. | Indians of South America—Peru—Magdalena de Cao—Antiquities. | Magdalena de Cao (Peru)—Antiquities. | Magdalena de Cao (Peru)—History.
Classification: LCC F3429.1.M335 M34 2020 | DDC 985/.16—dc23
LC record available at https://lccn.loc.gov/2020001416

Dedicated to the people
of Magdalena de Cao,
past, present, and future

Contents

List of Figures   ix

List of Tables   xv

Acknowledgments   xvii

1. Past and Present: The Contexts of Magdalena de Cao Viejo   1
   Jeffrey Quilter

2. Overview of the Research Project   23
   Jeffrey Quilter and Régulo Franco Jordán

3. Plants and Animals   77
   Victor Vásquez Sánchez, Teresa Rosales Tham, and Jeffrey Quilter

4. Bioarchaeology   107
   Catherine M. Gaither and Melissa S. Murphy

5. An African Cranium   147
   Catherine M. Gaither, Raul Y. Tito, Cecil M. Lewis Jr., Brendan J. Culleton, George H. Perry,
   Douglas J. Kennett, John Krigbaum, Victor Vásquez Sánchez, Teresa Rosales Tham,
   Rocío Delibes Mateos, Régulo Franco Jordán, and Jeffrey Quilter

6. Textiles and Clothing   163
   Carrie Brezine

7. Beads   189
   Alexander Menaker

8. Colonial Ceramics: Commerce and Consumption   209
   Parker VanValkenburgh

9. Indigenous Pottery   231
   Jennifer Ringberg

10. Metals   269
    Andrew Z. Lorey and Jeffrey Quilter

11. Colonial Period Coins   303
    Richard L. Burger

12. A Historical Approximation of Santa María de Magdalena de Cao
    Through the Written Sources   317
    Rocío Delibes Mateos

13. Papers   351
    Jeffrey Quilter, Karen Spalding, and Nicholas E. Brown

14. Playing Cards   383
   Sarah McAnulty Quilter

15. Other Inscriptions: Gourds, Marked Adobes, and Burial Textiles   401
   Jeffrey Quilter

16. Concluding Thoughts   427
   Jeffrey Quilter

   Volume Appendix   433
   Jeffrey Quilter

   Contributors   439
   Illustration Credits   443
   Index   445

Figures

1.1 Colonial Peru   4

1.2 Map of the Chicama Valley   6

1.3 Ruins of the church complex in Chicama   9

1.4 The Ascope Aqueduct, looking west   10

1.5 Sugar cane fields with the Huaca Rosario in the distance   10

1.6 Chronological chart of prehistoric cultures of the North Coast of Peru   11

1.7 The El Brujo terrace seen from the Huaca Prieta   12

1.8 Aerial photo map of the El Brujo terrace   12

1.9 Looter holes   14

1.10 The Huaca Cortada (Huaca El Brujo), looking north   15

2.1 Quincha wall remains in the colonial town   24

2.2 Raimondi's 1868 sketch map of the El Brujo huacas   26

2.3 The Huaca Prieta   27

2.4 The ceremonial well   28

2.5 The bundle containing the Señora de Cao   29

2.6 Excavations in the interior eastern wall of the church nave   30

2.7 A fragment of fallen wall plaster   30

2.8 Excavation of the northwest corner of the church atrium   31

2.9 The church compound from the top of the Huaca Cao Viejo, 2005   34

2.10 The east wall of 2005 excavations in Unit 4 at the atrium   36

2.11 Unit 12-2005 under excavation   36

2.12 Jaime Jiménez in Unit 14, eastern compound sector   37

2.13 Conducting ground-penetrating radar studies in the colonial town   38

2.14 Photo map of the colonial town   40

2.15 Map of the town with major excavation units numbered   41

2.16 Early excavations in Unit 2   43

2.17 Excavating the nave in 2006   43

2.18 Fragment of painted wall plaster on the east wall of the nave   44

2.19 Aerial view of the sacristy under excavation   45

2.20 Eastern exterior wall of the sacristy   46

2.21 The baptistry, looking east   47

2.22 Exterior western wall of the baptistry with *chicha* paddle   48

2.23 Searching for an entry into the church compound   49

2.24 Objects on floor of Unit 1 house excavations   50

2.25 Gourd bowl filled with cloth scraps and seeds   50

2.26 Gabriel Prieto and Parker VanValkenburgh in Unit 19 excavations   51

2.27 Venetian-style bead found in Unit 19 (detail)   52

2.28 Interior of Unit 19 showing the waterborne deposit   53

2.29 Indigenous-style burial of an adult woman   55

2.30 Top: Bag that accompanied the woman's burial; bottom: contents of the bag   56

2.31 Wall fall in the eastern church complex   58

2.32 Detail of adobe bricks   58

2.33 Long trench running from the church compound to the town   59

2.34 Unit 2 in early excavation, view to northeast   60

2.35 Leather object found in Unit 26   62

2.36 Aerial photograph of 2007 excavations in eastern sector of church complex   63

2.37 Bench in church complex   64

2.38 The milling station as found, seen from above   65

2.39 Aerial photograph of Unit 28 early excavations   67

2.40 Adobe walls in central excavation in Unit 28   68

2.41 Composite photograph of the church complex walls   70

2.42 Photo montage of main areas of central church complex   71

3.1 Complete net bag found in Unit 1   78

3.2 Scrub brush found in Unit 1   79

3.3 Small hand broom found in Unit 1   80

3.4 Popular fish: Peruvian banded croaker and Peruvian grunt   90

3.5 Top: looter hole; bottom: strata   93

3.6 Kitchen area in Unit 28   97

4.1 Burial excavations in Unit 12 east   108

4.2 Burial excavations in Unit 12, church nave   109

4.3 Burial 5   110

4.4 Mat and textile remains under head of Burial 5   111

4.5 Stacked burials under the church floor   115

4.6 Achondroplastic and normal radius; achrondroplastic and normal first metatarsal   122

4.7 Healed fracture of the achondroplastic radius head and normal radial head   123

4.8 Lumbar vertebra showing lesions consistent with tuberculosis   124

4.9 Portion of an eye orbit showing periostosis consistent with vitamin C deficiency   125

4.10 Tumor on pelvis of a young individual from the nave interior   126

4.11 Deformed humeral head and normal humerus   126

4.12 Colonial or Republican Period burial   127

5.1 Two views of the African cranium   148

5.2 Radiocarbon date for cranium   149

5.3 Light isotope analyses of Magdalena and other burials   152

5.4 Illustration showing Africans or African Peruvians   156

6.1 Examples of textile seams found at Magdalena   168

6.2 Andean cotton tunic   172

6.3 Linen fabrics found at Magdalena   174

6.4 Silks found at Magdalena   175

6.5 Three-part cotton shawl   176

6.6 Incomplete two-part shawl   177

6.7 Buttons excavated at Magdalena   178

6.8   European-style garment fragment   180

6.9   Cotton sock   181

6.10 White cotton scarf or shawl   182

6.11 Mid-eighteenth-century illustration of man using European-style loom   184

7.1   *Spondylus* shell beads   195

7.2   European glass beads   199

7.3   Beads from Magdalena de Cao   200

8.1   Panamanian majolica   213

8.2   Kraak ware and porcelain   216

8.3   Sherds of Early Green Glazed (EGG) Ware   217

8.4   Tin oxide and lead oxide composition in EGG Ware and tin-enameled wares   219

8.5   Calcium oxide and magnesium oxide concentrations in EGG Ware   220

8.6   Principal-components analysis of EGG Ware   220

8.7   Calcium oxide and magnesium oxide concentrations in tin-enameled wares   221

8.8   Principal-components analysis of tin-enameled wares   222

8.9   Distribution of wares by sector and major town units   223

8.10 Distribution of functional types within site sectors and major domestic units   224

9.1   Mid-eighteenth-century image of Indian women using pottery vessels   233

9.2   Reconstruction of common indigenous vessel forms   234

9.3   Olla subtypes   238

9.4   Boxplot of orifice diameters for four olla forms   239

9.5   C-rim olla forms   240

9.6   Whole c-rim olla from house floor, Room 2, Unit 28   241

9.7   Neckless olla forms   242

9.8   Vessel fragments with interior yellow-green glaze from Units 1, 2, and 28   243

9.9   Angled-neck olla forms   244

9.10 Convex-neck olla forms   245

9.11 A possible lid form   246

9.12 Large bowl forms and small, individual serving bowls   246

9.13 Vessel fragments with yellow-green glaze   247

9.14 Tinaja forms   248

9.15 Cántaro forms   249

9.16 Jarra and bottle forms   250

9.17 Whole jarra from clerical residence   251

9.18 Reduction-fired bottle fragment and oxidized bottle fragment   252

9.19 Rayador rim and body fragments   253

9.20 Rayador forms from house compounds   254

9.21 Figurine fragment   255

9.22 Figurine fragment, Unit 1, Level 1   255

9.23 Indigenous vessel function bar graph   256

9.24 Bar graph of olla subtypes   257

9.25 Box plot of orifice diameters for olla subtypes   257

9.26 Bar graph of liquid storage and serving forms   259

9.27 Bar graph of liquid storage and serving forms, Units 1, 2, and 28   259

9.28 Bar graph of bowls categorized by orifice diameter 260

9.29 Common decorative techniques on Magdalena ollas 262

10.1 Straight pins 273

10.2 Bells 276

10.3 Ornaments 279

10.4 Iron objects 280

10.5 Possible horseshoe and fragment 281

10.6 Two views of a bent wire artifact 282

10.7 Possible hammer of a flintlock gun 282

10.8 Copper alloy box on rod 283

10.9 Copper alloy objects 288

10.10 Copper knife or ingot 289

10.11 Folding knife 290

10.12 Crescent knife 290

10.13 Three cubes of lead 291

10.14 Candlestick 292

10.15 Views of triangular base 293

10.16 Andean-style tweezers 294

10.17 Detail of finger rings 295

10.18 Needle fragment 296

10.19 Mid-eighteenth-century illustration showing a couple working metal 298

11.1 Silver 2-real coin 304

11.2 Silver half-real coin 304

11.3 Rendering of Hapsburg shield on obverse of 2-real coin 306

11.4 Half-real coin 308

11.5 Spectra of elements in two *macuquina* coins 311

11.6 Silver 1-real coin produced in Lima in 1776 312

12.1 Letter fragment 326

12.2 1682 map showing Magdalena de Cao 333

12.3 Map commissioned between 1780 and 1790 showing Magdalena de Cao 334

13.1 Page from book on Spanish invasion of the Netherlands 355

13.2 Two examples of print of St. Martin of Tours 357

13.3 Fragment of print of the Ascension 358

13.4 Page of missal with print of Jesus washing disciples' feet 359

13.5 Fragment of upper section of an indulgence 360

13.6 Fragment of lower section of an indulgence 361

13.7 Fragment of page from the Bravo Thesaurus 362

13.8 Fragment of page from confessionary with Quechua and Aymara 363

13.9 Two sides of fragment of religious musical text 364

13.10 Examples of musical scores 365

13.11 Two sides of the letter and number list 367

13.12 Examples of cutouts 369

13.13 Papers with dates 371

13.14 Cigarette ends 372

13.15   Name list   375

13.16   Examples of writing practice   377

13.17   Folded and pierced papers   378

13.18   Scratch paper   379

13.19   Letter fragment addressing curate of Magdalena de Cao   380

14.1   Examples of Latin Deck cards from Copacabana, Bolivia   385

14.2   Unit 4 card fragments   387

14.3   Unit 8 card fragment, a three of swords   388

14.4   Unit 1 playing card fragments   389

14.5   Single card fragment found in Unit 2, likely a *sota*   390

14.6   Card from Unit 28, a sota of cups   390

14.7   Comparison of sword pommels from Sevillian deck and card from Magdalena   392

14.8   Cards from Huaca Tres Palos, Lima   393

14.9   Guaman Poma's 1615 rendering of a card game between a priest and a corregidor   397

15.1   Vessels in the food preparation area of Unit 28   402

15.2   Gourd vessel found on a floor in Unit 1   403

15.3   Complete pyroengraved gourd vessel   404

15.4   Gourd vessel fragments showing various techniques   405

15.5   Shallow gourd bowl with exterior wandering line design   406

15.6   Gourd fragments and gourd bowl with tocapu design elements   407

15.7   Gourd fragments with images of animals   408

15.8   Gourd fragments with images of birds   409

15.9   Fragments of a repaired gourd engraved with images of birds and fish   410

15.10   Gourd fragment with fine-line depiction of human figures   411

15.11   Three fragments of a gourd bowl showing animals and human figures with a stacked tocapu border   412

15.12   Gourd bowl fragment depicting a human and a quadruped in a tree   414

15.13   Marked adobes in the collapsed wall found east of the church nave   418

15.14   The two adobes with the most elaborate markings   419

15.15   Section of a painted burial shroud   420

15.16   Section of a burial shroud with a blue glass bead   421

15.17   Section of another painted burial shroud   422

15.18   Underside of a Lambayeque handled plate from burial M-U1412   424

16.1   Magdalena de Cao under excavation in 2007   428

16.2   Four examples of footwear   430

Tables

3.1   Animal and plant remains at Magdalena de Cao Viejo   82

3.2   Percentages of animal remains in Magdalena church and town   89

3.3   Faunal and plant remains from a column sample, Magdalena town   94

3.4   Plant and animal remains from ashes in Unit 28   98

3.5   Summary of starch grain analyses of Unit 28 vessels   98

3.6   Starch grain analyses from dental calculus of Colonial burials   99

4.1   Sample composition of intact and partially intact burials   116

4.2   Ancestry classification results   116

4.3   Frequency of pathological lesions other than NSIS (adults)   118

4.4   Nonspecific indicators of stress   118

4.5   Actual and expected counts of porous cranial lesions in adults   119

4.6   Porous cranial lesions in adults   120

4.7   Actual and expected counts of porous cranial lesions in non-adults   120

4.8   Porous cranial lesions in non-adults   121

4.9   Comparison of D^{30+}/D^{5+} ratios   130

9.1   Raw count, MNV, and metric data assemblage counts for pottery   235

9.2   Indigenous vessel forms in town units and clerical residence   236

9.3   Indigenous vessel mouth complex categories in church and town   237

10.1   Metal objects   271

10.2   Straight pins   274

10.3   Bells   277

10.4   Results of pXRF analysis   286

11.1   Coins   307

12.1   Caciques of Magdalena de Cao during the sixteenth and seventeenth centuries   319

12.2   Population and tribute payers (adult men)   321

12.3   Preachers of Magdalena de Cao   327

12.4   Annual tribute required of Indians of the Chicama repartimiento, 1549   332

13.1   Distribution of papers in church and town   354

Acknowledgments

THE AUTHORS AND I thank a multitude of people and institutions who helped support this work. We are extremely grateful to the Fundación Wiese of Lima, Peru. It has supported research at the El Brujo Complex for more than twenty-five years and continues to safeguard its treasures. It has offered many resources to us during the course of our work at Magdalena de Cao Viejo. We want to especially thank Marco Aveggio of the Fundación for his long-term interest in our work and the warm friendship we have developed with him over many years.

We thank the National Science Foundation for the awarding of the grant The Archaeology of Sta. Magdalena de Cao Viejo: Cultural Encounters in Early Colonial Peru (2005; Award No. 0514330) and the National Endowment for the Humanities for the grant Interpreting the Colonial Experience at Magdalena de Cao Viejo, Chicama Valley, Peru, 1578–1770 (2010; RZ-51150-10). Support also was provided through leave time and funds from Dumbarton Oaks and the Peabody Museum of Archaeology and Ethnology, Harvard University: for these I am also sincerely grateful.

The National Library of Peru is thanked for permission to use the photograph of Raimondi's sketch of El Brujo in his journal. Many other institutions gave us permission to use images, for which we are grateful, and their kindnesses are noted through citations in figure captions. Very special thanks to Gilda Corgorno Ventura of the Instituto Riva-Agüero, Lima. Gilda was extremely generous with her time and trouble in sharing her knowledge of the playing cards found at Huaca Tres Palos during a very pleasant time with Jeffrey and Sarah Quilter at the Institute. Staff at the John Carter Brown Library at Brown University, the Patrimonio Nacional de España, the Proyecto Arqueológico San José de Moro, and Stanford University Press also were generous in their help and support and in the granting of permission to use images under their care, as noted in relevant figure captions in this book

There are many individuals who helped make this project and book possible. We would like to place Elio and Margarita Barriga Sanchez at the top of the list. They were in charge of taking care of us in the Casa Wiese, the residence owned by the Fundación Wiese's Marco Aveggio and so generously offered to us while we worked on the project. Elio handled everything from small mechanical issues to providing fresh vegetables from the garden, while Margarita's cooking skills made us the must-visit place for every hungry archaeologist on the North Coast of Peru, particularly for her outstanding *alfajores* (filled shortbread cookies).

Conservators Without Borders helped us in working on a variety of materials. Its members at our site were Christie Pohl, Judith Jungels, and Diana Medellin.

Catherine Gaither wishes to thank the Metropolitan State University of Denver, where she was employed during the work she conducted at El Brujo. Many field school students from that institution made valuable contributions to the bioarchaeological studies, which would have taken much longer to accomplish without their aid and would have been far less enjoyable without their company. Cathy Gaither, Melissa Murphy, and I also wish to thank John Verano and Maria Fernanda Boza for the help and support in matters relating to bioarchaeology.

Parker VanValkenburgh gives special thanks to Deysi Parades, Jima Portal, and Katina Tarazona for assistance with ceramic analysis and to Laure Dussubieux and Sarah Kelloway for help with analysis of chemical data.

I wish to give thanks beyond words to Régulo Franco Jordán, the co-director of this project and a constant source of help. Régulo is one of the finest field archaeologists I have ever met. I am constantly astounded at how, walking across the El Brujo terrace, he can spot the tiniest bead on a dazzling desert surface, and his skill as well as his instincts in excavation are second to none. He has been a very fine colleague and friend for many years, for which I am deeply grateful. In the early years of the Magdalena project, Cesár Gálvez and Segundo Vasquez were serving as co-directors of the El Brujo Archaeological Complex, and I thank them for their support. Augusto E. Bazán Peréz and Ingrid Claudet Lascosque of the Fundación Wiese provided important support in the final stage of the project and the preparation of this volume.

Many thanks are due to the two associate field directors of the project, Jaime Jiménez Saldaña and Merly Rosas Jimenez. Jaime mostly supervised excavations in the church sector, while Merly mostly supervised excavations in the town. They are outstanding archaeologists and very fine colleagues and friends. I especially appreciated Jaime's passion for our project and for archaeology in general and Merly's steady-on attitude to getting the work accomplished. Merly also has been of tremendous help to the project in post-excavation laboratory work.

Thanks also to Carmen Gamarra and Arabel Fernández, successive former directors of the Museo de Cao laboratory. Thanks to Denis Vargas, former director of investigations at El Brujo. Augusto Bazán, his successor, has been most helpful in some of the final work in producing this book, for which we are extremely grateful. Carlos Araujo Calvanapón was vital for his cartography and aided the project in numerous ways, and Luís De la Vega provided excellent aid in photography and various computer issues.

I wish to give special thanks to William Doonan, professor of anthropology at Sacramento City College. It was Bill who first encouraged me to consider excavations in the colonial sector of the El Brujo Complex, and it was very good advice indeed. Bill brought his friend and colleague Hal Starratt to participate in the work for many years as well, and he added greatly to our work, especially in photography. Many of the aerial photographs in this book were taken through the use of balloon or kite photography that he and Bill supervised during the period in which most of the fieldwork was carried out, between 2004 and 2008. Andrew Gordon also helped in the project, including providing excellent service in dealing with balloon photography, which eventually was abandoned in favor of kites, due to the steady wind at the site.

I offer my sincere thanks to Larry Conyers, now of the Department of Anthropology at Denver University. Larry is a longtime friend and came to Peru early in the project to employ his ground-penetrating radar (GPR) at the site. He also brought along with him two students, Jennie Sturm and Richard Busch, who were of vital assistance. As a side project, however, Larry employed his GPR on the Huaca Cao Viejo and basically discovered the tomb of the Señora de Cao, noting that there was a space below the patio that turned out to be her tomb.

My many Peruvian colleagues other than El Brujo staff deserve deep thanks. Chief among them is Luis Jaime Castillo, who used his drones to map the site after the main fieldwork was done. Without the many kindnesses extended by Luis Jaime, my work would never have been done. The late Santiago Uceda also was a true friend, and his kindnesses to me in so many ways will never to be forgotten. Enrique Vergara is a true friend and a lot of fun, and my visits with him in Trujillo always have been delightful.

There are many others who contributed to the research, but chief among them are R. Jeffrey Frost and Gabriel Prieto. Jeff was involved with early work at the site and has been a source of friendship and support from way before this project to the present day. I have had the pleasure of watching Gabriel Prieto transform himself from an enthusiastic student to a young colleague who is doing outstanding research in the vicinity of his home, Huanchaco, and in the region, in general.

The same is true for Carrie Brezine, Ari Caramanica, Michele Koons, Lisa Trever, and Parker VanValkenburgh, graduate students at Harvard who contributed to the project while they pursued their own scholarly interests in the region. Harvard undergraduates Andrew Lorey, Maryum Jordan, Danielle Olga Mirabal, and Jo Osborn were all at the site and involved in various ways: Andrew became an author in this volume, and Danielle's work found its way into Chapter 3.

I thank Gary Urton and Tom Cummins, my two Andeanist colleagues at Harvard who constantly supply me with ideas and inspirations. Gary was generous of his time to come and visit us while we were excavating, and Tom has provided ideas and references, especially in regard to some of our paper fragments, as the work has progressed. Matthew Liebmann invited me to participate in a School for Advanced Research (SAR) Seminar in Santa Fe, New Mexico, before he had fully arrived at Harvard. I thank him and SAR for the opportunity as the seminar was very useful to me in numerous ways. His co-organizer of the session, Melissa Murphy, has become a very fine colleague and friend and a most valuable contributor to research on the Magdalena collections, as well.

Steven LeBlanc, former director of collections at the Peabody Museum and a very fine archaeologist, has been of enormous help to me in many different ways. He visited El Brujo and has been of great benefit to this project and to me in innumerable ways, and I thank him heartily.

There are many people at the Peabody Museum who deserve my thanks. I have worked on this book mostly by myself and mostly on weekends and in the evenings, as my duties at Harvard tend to fill my days. Nevertheless, I wish to thank my close associates Catherine Cezeaux, Pamela Gerardi, and Kara Schneiderman for helping me to administer the Peabody Museum well enough to allow me to spend my free time on this book. Linda Ordogh, my administrative assistant, deserves my praise and thanks for all her support beyond measure. Castle McLaughlin, curator of North American ethnology, provided useful information on some of the metal objects, especially bells and equine shoes.

Personnel at the Harvard Herbaria were generous with their time and support, particularly Dr. Gustavo Romero, who identified the contents of some of the cigarette ends as tobacco. Thanks to Sabine Hyland (University of St. Andrews) and Byron Hermann for advice on some of the paper fragments and to David Earle (Antelope Valley College) for his help with the playing cards.

I am particularly grateful to the skilled professionals behind the publication of this volume. Director Kate O'Donnell and publications coordinator Bridget Manzella of the Peabody Museum Press shepherded the project from its early manuscript days into print. At

Westchester Publishing Services, senior production editor Melody Negron and her team have expertly undertaken the editing, indexing, and typesetting of the book. Melissa Tandysh created the beautiful and elegant design.

And, of course, thanks to the authors of the chapters in this book. It has been a lot of work, but I hope you will be glad we went through all of the work to make it happen. You are all good friends and colleagues for having come all this way.

There are many more people to thank, and I do not doubt that I have forgotten some of them. If so, I am sorry. I offer my closing thanks to my family: my two daughters, Susanna and Elizabeth, and especially my wife, Sarah. It is impossible to fully express my appreciation for their love and support. I also am delighted that Elizabeth came to the site for a field season and helped to clean and process paper fragments and that Sarah became so interested in the playing cards that she became an author of a chapter in this book.

Last but definitely not least, we sincerely thank the many townspeople of Magdalena de Cao and neighboring communities for their work at the site and the ways in which they generously welcomed the research team to live among and work with them over the years. In addition to the help they provided us in accomplishing our goals, it was a lot of fun to befriend such kind, generous, intelligent, and enthusiastic people. It was mostly those townspeople who excavated the town where the ancestors of some of them had lived. The names of many of our fieldworkers, combined, over the years, are listed below, in recognition and thanks for their work:

Iban Alzugaray Galarreta
Alberto Asencio Villegas
Claudia Barriga Vizcarra
Hipólito Chamache Barrantes
Rubí Calderón Chamache
Enrique Cisneros
Nery Escobedo Alzugaray
Oscar Gamarra de la Cruz
Shirley García Ávila
Rodolfo García Sifuentes
José Jiménez
Jesús Loayza Barrientos
Alberto Marchena Salcedo

Claudia Martínez Chamache
Wilson Morillas Yep
Carlos Paredes Solano
Joni Santos Paredes Escobedo
Renato Rodríguez Baca
Héctor Torres Alzugaray
Tomas Silva Escobedo
Domingo Torres Flores
Bruno Torres Silva
Tito Vásquez Leiva
Oscar Vásquez Lozada
Wilson Villar Sánchez

— Jeffrey Quilter

Past and Present

The Contexts of Magdalena de Cao Viejo

Jeffrey Quilter

Conquest to Colony

BY 1578, THE GENERATION in Peru that had endured the first clash of the Old and New Worlds was almost gone. A few old men and women still remembered life before Francisco Pizarro and his Spanish conquistadors had come in 1532, but most people had been raised amid the conflicts of the Conquest Period. Political and social systems had been turned upside down like earth and rocks in an earthquake—a *pachacuti*, in Andean terms. Yet life went on despite the turmoil: people still fetched water, made and tended fires, sought spouses, bore and reared children, buried the dead. The troubles and uncertainties brought by foreigners were piled onto all the other troubles and uncertainties of life.

Peru had changed, and the world beyond it was changing as well. Moors and Jews had been driven from the Iberian Peninsula in 1492 by royal edict, four decades before Pizarro. In those two generations, Spain had emerged as a nation and grown to become a world power, prized by the Vatican as the champion of Christendom. Spain's ascendency, however, was complicated by the rise of Protestantism, which embroiled Europe in centuries of strife. European intrusions into the New World were carried out in the immediacy of concerns for God, gold, and glory but also in the context of a grand struggle in that larger world, one into which Peru and its inhabitants had been pulled.

In November 1532 Spaniards seized Atahualpa, the Sapa Inca, in the highland city of Cajamarca. A year passed before the head of state was executed, native allies were secured, and the campaign to seize the Inca capital of Cuzco was launched. In the following decades the Spanish looted temples and graves for gold and silver, established cities and estates on top of ancient temples and sacred gardens, and petitioned the royal court in Spain for rights and privileges to exploit local peoples officially.

The smoldering embers from the sack of Cuzco had barely cooled when the two leading generals, Pizarro and Diego de Almagro, fell into dispute over how to share victory's spoils. After failing to find an equally rich land to conquer in Chile, Almagro returned to make war against Pizarro, losing the Battle of Salinas and his head in 1538. Three years later Pizarro himself was killed in Lima by a sword through his throat, delivered by the hands of Almagro loyalists seeking revenge.

Pizarro's death did not mark the end of the troubles. In the next three decades, frequent and severe conflicts arose among Spaniards in Peru, between conquistadors and agents sent from Spain, and between indigenous peoples and foreigners. Of the last set of conflicts, three events were critical in the process of the transition from the Conquest Period to the Colonial Period: the Manco Inca Rebellion of 1536–1544, the Taki Onqoy movement of circa 1564 to the early 1570s, and the crushing of the last Inca resistance in 1572.[1]

Manco Inca was a native aristocrat installed by the Spanish as a puppet leader, but disrespect and maltreatment impelled him to flee Cuzco, establish an independent community at Vilcabamba, in Peru's tropical zone, and make war upon his enemies. His greatest campaign mustered perhaps as many as 100,000 warriors to attack Lima, but the promising plan failed. Manco retreated to the jungle, where he was eventually murdered by Spaniards who had sought refuge with him as a ruse. Despite Manco's death, Vilcabamba resisted outright conquest for some years to come (Bauer et al. 2015).

As in Mexico and elsewhere, Spanish successes in Peru were due partly to local conflicts among native peoples. The Andeans did not realize that the few Spaniards on their shores were the tip of a sharp and long rapier—the people and resources of Europe—that would soon drive deep into them. The Andes were home to hundreds of language groups, ethnic communities, and polities with deep historical legacies, many of whom had felt much pain from the yoke of the Inca Empire; many peoples had revolted more than once against the lords of Cuzco. Consequently, Pizarro had quickly found native allies to aid him in his conquest, although many remained loyal to the Inca. Thirty years after Cajamarca, however, many Andean people thought that the Spanish god had successfully triumphed over the Inca deities that had been imposed on them (Stern 1993). At the same time, local disputes and concerns were muted by the growing sense of a common Andean identity that was neither Inca nor Spanish and both local and pan-Andean.

The *huacas*, the local deities of the rocks, streams, and springs; the towering ancestor *apus* of great mountains; and the shriveled remains of grandparents in grottos and caves were called upon to rise up and cast out the foreigners. This millenarian movement, known as the Taki Onqoy (Dancing Sickness), resembled many similar efforts at other times and places, such as the Ghost Dance movement in the North American plains three hundred years later, and met with the same fate: dancing, chanting, and calling on the huacas failed to drive the Spaniards away.

A further blow to the Andean cause came with the arrival of the fifth Viceroy of Peru, the Count of Oropesa, Francisco de Toledo, in 1572. Unlike Crown representatives before him, he was a master administrator, and he effectively stamped out native resistance, but he also ended many abuses by conquistadors and their heirs. He introduced the Inquisition to the viceroyalty, yet he also reduced the manipulation of the ancient labor tax, the *mita* of the Inca, that Spaniards had used to virtually enslave Indians. During Toledo's viceroyalty, any hope for a reestablishment of the Inca dynasty ended with the successful capture of the Inca sovereign, Tupac Amaru, from Vilcabamba. To the consternation of most natives and even many Spaniards, the last Inca was beheaded in the Plaza de Armas in Cuzco.

Toledo also reformed the *encomienda* system, under which conquistadors had been granted lifetime rights to the labor and produce of native communities in a given area, and in return were supposed to provide protection and care to the Native Americans under their control. Most *encomenderos* preferred to live in towns, letting caretakers maintain (and often abuse) their estates, and some encomenderos acted as if they owned the land as well as the native labor, attempting to bequeath both land and laborers to their sons. Although the New Laws of 1542 were intended to check these abuses, the problems lingered because of the difficulty of enforcing the laws over long distances. But when Toledo arrived as viceroy, he quickly put into place a system that had been employed in the Caribbean since the early days of the Spanish presence there: the forced resettlement of native people into new towns of Spanish design. Known as *reducciones*, they were intended to keep indigenous people under control and to Christianize and civilize them (Mumford 2012). This resulted in one of the largest forced population movements in history.[2] By the 1570s, the Conquest Period in Peru had ended and the Colonial Period had begun (Figure 1.1).

Circa 1578

In 1571, a Crimean khan, supported by the Ottomans, burned Moscow and planned a full conquest of the Russian state, though he would be repulsed by Ivan the Terrible's army a year later. Also in 1571, Ottoman expansion was checked dramatically in the massive sea battle at Lepanto, in which Spaniards led combined forces to victory, an event sometimes equated with the Battle of Marathon when Greeks halted Persians. That same year also saw the establishment of the Spanish settlement of Manila, as treasure galleons increasingly plied the Pacific with Asian goods for the West. The Spanish Empire also had reached out to North America with settlements in what is now Florida, Georgia, and South Carolina in the late 1560s and early 1570s.

In the 1570s, Europe was embroiled in religious wars between French Protestants and Catholics. The St. Bartholomew's Day Massacre of Huguenots took place in 1572, one incident among many involving religion, politics, and violence. Tens of thousands of copies of Martin Luther's German-language New Testament were being printed each year. Sebastian I of Portugal was killed in the Battle of Three Kings, in Morocco, in 1578; because he lacked an heir, a succession crisis soon loomed over the kingdom. In 1580, Spain seized Portugal, uniting the Iberian Peninsula for 60 years.

In 1578, a child emperor sat on the throne of China; in Japan, samurai deployed the first artillery. Mary, Queen of Scots, was in prison; her sister, Queen Elizabeth I, financed a Dutch rebellion against the Spanish. William Shakespeare was a schoolboy in Stratford-upon-Avon, and Cervantes was a galley slave in the Mediterranean.

It was a world lit only by fire, and in which the few people who lived past age 60 were considered ancient.[3] Disease was thought to be caused by ill humors, and for Christians a bath once a year was enough, maybe excessive. Tycho Brahe was challenging the Aristotelian belief in an unchanging universe, but most people believed that the celestial spheres were moved by the will of God. William Harvey was discovering blood circulation, but barbers still handled surgery along with cutting hair and shaving clients. Although at odds over issues of faith, all good Christians, Jews, and Muslims believed in dragons, mermaids, astrology, and alchemy. God and the devil were active in a world moved by spirits, not by the clockworks of Descartes and Newton, yet unborn.

In late 1577, Francis Drake struggled to find favorable winds to take his ship, the *Pelican*, northward from the Straits of Magellan to begin a campaign of attacking Spanish colonial cities

Figure 1.1   Colonial Peru. Detail from Bowser 1974.

and ships on the west coast of South America. He was to gain a reputation as a pirate, capturing a Spanish treasure ship worth millions, and the distinction of being the second circumnavigator of the globe and the first captain of such a voyage to make it home alive.

While pirates and potentates across the world intrigued, warred, and made grand gestures, poorer folk struggled for their daily bread. Yet Drake and the poorest farmers and fisherfolk shared a common concern: the weather. It is quite likely that Drake's long struggle to free his ship from contrary winds was due to a disruption of the cold Humboldt Current by a mass of warm water overriding its northward flow. And in valleys along the Peruvian shoreline, in one of the driest deserts of the world, people grew anxious at portents for bad weather ahead as 1577 turned to 1578.

A World Turned Upside Down

Pizarro had landed on the far north coast of Peru and traveled down it before turning eastward and heading up the Jequetepeque Valley to his destiny in Cajamarca. The deserts and valleys through which he rode had been occupied for millennia. His horse's hooves trod on the chipped stone tools of people who had hunted the last of the ice age mammals; his group passed the ruins of temples shrouded in myth even to the Inca. Many of those temples were known to contain hoards of gold and other precious items in the tombs of ancient lords and ladies.

It was no accident that the Spanish city of Trujillo, founded in 1534, was located in the Moche Valley between some of the most impressive prehistoric monuments in the region; the Spaniards' choice of site symbolically inserted them into a mighty lineage. Trujillo, named after Pizarro's birthplace, lay between the great centers of Huacas de Moche, with its massive adobe pyramids occupied by the Moche archaeological culture (ca. A.D. 350–900), and Chan Chan, the vast, sprawling ruin of the capital of the Kingdom of Chimor of the Chimu (ca. A.D. 1000–1450), the great opponents of the Inca.[4] It also was a convenient location from which to loot treasure from those ancient centers.

About 32 km north of Trujillo was Chicama, where the Dominicans had established a base. From there the order's missionaries ministered to the populations of several reducciones that had been established in the 1560s, before the Toledan reforms (Figure 1.2).

One of those towns was Santa María de Magdalena de Cao. The people who lived there had been gathered together from elsewhere in the Chicama Valley and possibly from places farther afield. Although torn from their traditional homes, decimated by European diseases, and pressed under the demands of their European masters, much of what they did to make a living and pass the days was not greatly different from what they had done for generations.

In the old order, coastal communities specialized in fishing and inland groups in agriculture. These distinctions were so strong that these two populations spoke different languages, though likely there was a common tongue as well.[5] In all communities there were people who could read the stars, the clouds, and the waves, observing small changes in the environment that offered portents about the future: whether water would be abundant in the rivers for irrigating crops, and whether the seas would continue to offer up dense schools of anchovies, sardines, and larger fishes. Such interpretive practices had been refined over the thousands of years that people had lived in the area.

In normal years the cold Humboldt (or Peru) Current runs parallel to the coast of northern Chile and Peru, from south to north. The upwelling of cold waters brings nutrients from the ocean's depths that feed a chain of life, producing one of the richest marine biomes on the planet.[6] The cold waters are also responsible for the coastal desert, as moist air from the oceans is first cooled by the current and then expands over the warmer landmass, withholding rain until it cools again in the highlands in the summer or rolls in as fog in the winter. On occasion warmer waters overwhelm the Humboldt Current in a phenomenon commonly known

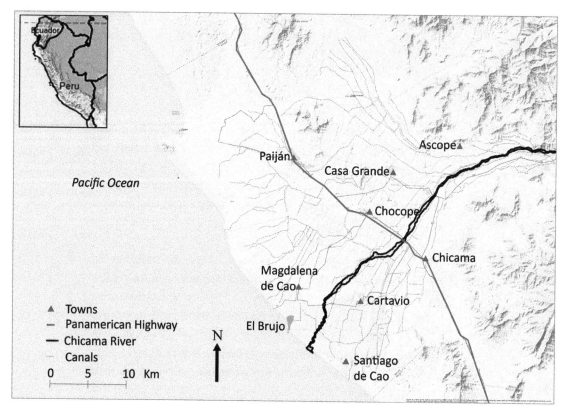

Figure 1.2   Map of the Chicama Valley with towns mentioned in the text.

as El Niño, and the coastal ecology is pushed into a different pattern, with rains on the coast, drought in the highlands, and dramatic changes in the behavior of animals.

At precisely which point in 1577 the people of the North Coast first became alarmed at changes in the weather is unknown. Perhaps the worries had started as early as in the austral winter, in June, July, or August, with warm, sunny days instead of chilly, gray, and damp ones. As summer turned to fall, more signs were in evidence: fish and mollusks more common to Ecuador began to be found by the shore; the cold waters were being replaced by warmer ones; sea lions and flocks of seabirds were leaving the region in droves, heading south to colder waters.

It had happened many times before. Andean belief systems are founded on concepts of dualism, in which opposing forces and beings are necessary to keep the world in balance: sun and moon, male and female, night and day, wet and dry. Generations of people whose lives depended on understanding the forces of nature had accumulated knowledge of what to expect when they saw signs of changes in those forces.

El Niño events are highly variable, as we know from the ones that have occurred in historical times. Sometimes one valley will be inundated with torrents of rain while others receive little, and even within a particular valley, rainfall patterns can vary from spot to spot. Sometimes El Niños are light or fail to come at all despite apparent warning signs. Occasionally, however, El Niño events are so strong that many valleys over a vast region are affected. In some cases the disruption to the Humboldt Current extends far to the south, even beyond Lima. In 1577–1578 the residents of the North Coast surely were alarmed at the numbers of animals migrating southward and other signs of an impending event of great magnitude.

The severity of the 1578 El Niño is hard to assess on an absolute scale, but it was clearly devastating to the North Coast—indeed, a pachacuti. Heavy rains quickly eroded adobe architecture, and the associated floods damaged irrigation systems and obliterated entire villages. Not only were the deserts and coastal valleys filled with rain, but coastal torrents were paired with highland droughts. Another inversion occurred as fertile agricultural bottomlands were washed away even as the deserts bloomed in herbs and grasses from seeds that had lain dormant for years. Some opportunities could be made of these changes, such as catching different kinds of fish, grazing animals in the greening deserts, or planting crops in moistened patches of normally dry soil, but overall, the disruption to normal life was disastrous. The cosmos may have been operating on the pulse of opposition, but a powerful El Niño pushed that whirling balance far out of order.

Two years after the 1578 El Niño, Spanish agents were sent on fact-finding missions to the North Coast to record what had happened in the disaster. In the city of Chiclayo in the Lambayeque Valley, one of the northernmost and therefore most humid of Peru's coastal population centers, the average annual rainfall is 83.6 mm, mostly from heavy fog (*garua*) in February (accounting for 20.2 mm of rain) and March (17.5 mm).[7] In 1578, it rained every day from February 24 to March 3, stopped a day, and then continued until April 5 or 6. The rivers overflowed their banks, causing massive destruction. The rain was so torrential that people said it was as if barrels of water had been dumped from the sky.[8]

In the Chicama Valley, south of Lambayeque, Don Juan de Mora, the *cacique* (chief) of Chocope, did not state how long it had rained but provided a dramatic narrative of the culmination of the devastation, especially what had befallen the people of Magdalena de Cao:

> At the time of the rains in the town of Cao . . . which was next to the river of this valley and due to the rains, [the river] sprang from its natural course, as had never been seen before, and extended itself throughout the entire valley and the Indians of this town left it, in fear, and found refuge at an ancient town next to the ocean on a height where they remain today and the rains were so intense that the Indians said that it was the universal flood and the end of the world and the town of Cao underwent ruin and destruction.[9]

Responses to the investigators' questions repeatedly made clear that the aftermath of the flood brought additional hardships and that severe suffering continued two years after El Niño:

> The Indians of this valley lost their foods of maize, wheat, and beans that they had guarded . . . and thus suffered great hunger and they left this town and sought food as far as Guañape and the mountain and other places. . . .
>
> The Indians of this valley do not have livestock . . . and almost all the birds were killed because of these rains and the moving of towns; even up to today food is lacking. . . .

After the rains had passed there came a great quantity of crickets and other insects and rats ... and the crickets ate much of [the food] in the fields and store-houses such that [the Indians] suffered great hunger and want for a year.[10]

The town of Cao, mentioned in the chronicle, was the 1560s community of Magdalena de Cao, and the "ancient town next to the ocean on a height" is the site where the town of Magdalena was reestablished in 1578 (today's El Brujo archaeological complex). Despite great hardships, the Magdaleneros stayed at their refuge for the following two centuries. Eventually, however, that settlement was abandoned as well, and the community relocated 4 km north, to the site of the present Magdalena de Cao.[11]

Even before the first excavations took place there, it had long been generally believed that the colonial artifacts and architecture easily visible on the surface were the remains of the Magdalena refuge community. Such a claim derived from the fact that no other place matches the requisite features: colonial remains on a prehistoric site, on a height, next to the sea.[12] Our research began with this information and proceeded through both archaeology and further historical studies.

The Chicama Valley

The Chicama is one of the largest valleys on the North Coast of Peru, although its population is relatively small. Conversely, the Moche, south of Chicama, is a relatively small valley, yet it holds Trujillo, now one of the largest cities in Peru, with a steadily growing population. The Chicama, however, has no large city or town today. People are concentrated in settlements that mostly were established in the Colonial or Republican Period, such as Chicama itself and Chocope, both along the Panamerican Highway, which once was an Inca road and probably was first developed in even earlier times. Indeed, some of those colonial towns were ancient ones as well, despite the dictates of the colonial reducción policy (Cummins 2002; Mumford 2012). Even when colonial settlements were built away from native settlements, the past was always present in the remains of large huacas clustered in various locales in the valley.[13]

Some contemporary towns are former haciendas, such as Casa Grande, the hacienda of the Gildemeister family, and Chiclín, that of the Larco family, although they too are at or near locations favored in prehistory. It is probably no accident that the town of Chicama is at the southern margins of the irrigated fields, Chocope in its center, and the town of Paiján at its northern boundary. All three of these places are very old settlements. Chocope was a major town in prehispanic times, with a small huaca on its southern edge, and likely was associated with the nearby archaeological site now known as Mocollope. Chicama was a *tambo*, a way station on the Inca royal road, and later became the center of the Dominican missionary presence in the valley, complete with a church and convent (Figure 1.3). In colonial times Magdalena de Cao and Santiago de Cao were reducciones; Ascope likely is ancient, near a key point in ancient canal systems. Modern Cartavio, however, is built around a rum distillery.

Today's landscape is radically different than it was in centuries past in terms of both people and plants. By the nineteenth century, the descendants of the Spanish encomenderos who received grants of land and labor had sold out their holdings to foreigners: the tombstones of the Gildemeisters in the cemetery near Casa Grande are in German. Similarly, a foreign plant,

Figure 1.3
The ruins of the church complex in the town of Chicama. The cemetery, on the far side of the church from the viewer, remains in use.

sugar cane, came to dominate the valley around the turn of the eighteenth century. Now most of the Chicama Valley floor is filled with vast tracts of sugar cane (about 860 km^2), and the sugar produced is largely for national consumption, much of it going to make Cartavio rum. Sugar cane is planted and harvested on an eight- to nine-month cycle, with fields going in and out of production. Most of the water to irrigate the sugar cane is now supplied by pumps introduced in recent times, although the water still is channeled to fields by short canals. In the past, for three millennia or more, canals brought water from the highlands to the coast. Control over those waters was one of the main issues in the politics of the valley for equally as long (Figures 1.4 and 1.5).

Gaining an understanding of former physical and other features of the valley is a difficult task because of the great transformations wrought by sugar production. Enough traces remain, however, that we know that there were brackish marshes, freshwater ponds, and woodlands. Before agroindustry, more diverse subsistence practices resulted in a varied landscape; sheep, goats, cattle, and horses were raised, and crops were more diverse than today, including both native and introduced European plants.

Areas of the valley that have been least affected by modern agricultural uses are those that were never irrigated. They include the valley margins above the level of agricultural fields as well as small and large hills that protrude here and there from the valley floor. The Pampa de Mocan, an extensive plain on the northern edge of the lower valley, is another area that has been found to be filled with ancient occupations, although it seems likely that those remains soon will be eradicated by plans to expand sugar cane fields in the valley (Caramanica 2018). In these places there often are extensive remains of prehistoric dwellings, canals, and other structures, usually signaled by alignments of low stone walls and other rocky features that served as the foundations of prehistoric adobe structures or lined the canals. The extent of such features indicates that in antiquity the Chicama Valley supported great numbers of people.

Figure 1.4   The Ascope Aqueduct, viewed here looking west, is 1.15 km in length and dates to Chimu times (ca. A.D. 1370–1470).

Figure 1.5   Sugar cane fields now dominate a landscape once filled with temples, towns, and fields of maize. The Huaca Rosario, dating to the Middle Horizon, still stands in the distance.

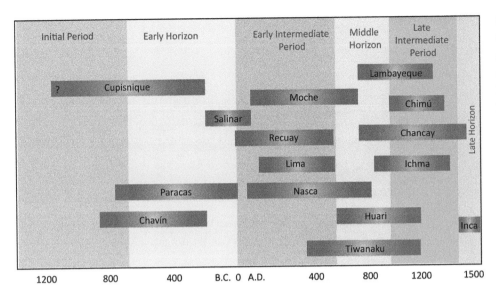

Figure 1.6
Chronological chart of prehistoric cultures of the North Coast of Peru.

The sugar cane fields are the most obvious changes to the landscape since the sixteenth century, but they are not the only ones. The 1578 El Niño flood scoured the valley, and although such floods are rare events, similar strong El Niño floods no doubt greatly affected the landscape before and after the Colonial Period event. In addition to the effects of El Niños, earthquakes rearranged the landscape by lifting up sections of the land surface, flattening others, and producing landslides of loose rocks and gravel. One theory suggests that sediments loosened by earthquakes were swept down to the seashore by El Niño rains and were eventually blown back inland, creating sand dunes that often force land out of agricultural production (Manners et al. 2007; Moseley 1983, 1987; cf. Wells and Noller 1999).

The resources of the desert and valleys were rich and abundant enough that a succession of prehistoric cultures prospered in Chicama and its vicinity. The people now represented by one of the earliest archaeological cultures in South America, Paiján, hunted, gathered, fished, and foraged in the late Pleistocene environment, which supported grasslands in what is now desert. They were succeeded by later preceramic cultures that advanced fishing technologies and domesticated many of the key Andean plants. In the Initial Period ceramics and true weaving were adopted, and distinctive regional cultures based mostly on pottery styles appear, such as Guañape and Cupisnique. The Moche culture left one of the strongest marks on the landscape, with numerous huacas and its distinctive ceramic style. It was followed by the Lambayeque and Chimu cultures, the latter of which was conquered by the Inca, who had little time to make a strong mark in the region before the arrival of the Spanish (Figure 1.6).

El Brujo

As previously noted, it has long been believed that the colonial occupation at El Brujo is the site of the 1578 reestablishment of Magdalena de Cao, for no other site conforms to the historical descriptions (Figures 1.7 and 1.8).

The El Brujo terrace is a triangle of land almost exactly 1 km² in area, rising 9 m above the beach to the west, a dried-up lagoon to the north, and irrigated fields to the east and south. The

Figure 1.7 The El Brujo terrace as seen from the Huaca Prieta at its southern tip, looking northward to the Huaca Cortada, left, and the Huaca Cao Viejo, right.

Figure 1.8
Aerial photo map of the El Brujo terrace from Google Earth Pro. The terrace is a little less than 2 km in length, 1 km at maximum width, and 1 km² in area. 1. Huaca Cao Viejo and Magdalena Church; 2. Huaca Cortada; 3. Paredones; 4. Huaca Prieta and the Cupisnique Mound.

triangle is a remnant of a Sangamon terrace (Pino 2017), from the Pleistocene land surface. When the ice age ended, extensive glaciers in the Andes melted and the resulting floodwaters scoured away valley floors in floods that would have made the 1578 inundations seem minor. Apparently, however, and for reasons still unclear, a relatively small wedge of the old valley floor, the El Brujo terrace, remained unaffected by those floods.

In various places on the El Brujo terrace a considerable amount of the land is not natural soil but the remains of human residences, particularly adobe bricks, that have eroded and melted back into unformed clay. Indeed, this square kilometer is one of the most intensively and longest occupied places in the New World (Dillehay 2017). Although we cannot be certain that El Brujo always had a resident population directly on or near it, the terrace has been the site of consistent human activity for at least 5,000 years and possibly for as long as 14,000 years. To this day, a small hamlet of fisherfolk is on the beach in the shadow of Huaca Prieta. If we consider this community as part of El Brujo, then close to continuous occupation is quite likely.

At the southern tip of El Brujo is a large mound known as Huaca Prieta (Dark Huaca) because charcoal and ashes from centuries of occupation turned the soil there a dark gray color. The site is famous in the history of archaeology because in 1944 Junius Bouton Bird of the American Museum of Natural History camped at its base with his family for eleven months as he carried out excavations (Bird et al. 1985). The research was part of the equally famous Virú Valley Project, which mostly took place two valleys to the south of the Chicama. Rafael Larco Hoyle, the *hacendado* of Chiclín, a supporter of the project, and a scholar of antiquities in his own right, suggested that Bird dig at Huaca Prieta, however.

Although there had been much speculation and a growing consensus that the prehistory of Peru extended much further into the past than had previously been considered, Bird's work definitively demonstrated that there was indeed a long Preceramic Period. Bird never returned to the site but spent subsequent years conducting detailed laboratory research on many of his finds. Those studies clarified that the materials he had uncovered dated to the Late Preceramic Period (ca. 2500–1500 B.C.). Recently Tom Dillehay and a team of archaeologists conducted additional research at Huaca Prieta. The results of that work indicate that the first occupation at Huaca Prieta may be one of the earliest known sites in the New World, dating to circa 12,000 B.C. (Dillehay 2017; Dillehay et al. 2012). Very early occupations are known for the North Coast in general in the remains of the Paiján archaeological culture of early hunter-gatherer-fisherfolk (Chauchat 2006).

Huaca Prieta is abutted on its northern end by another artificial hillock, known as the Cupisnique Mound because excavations there recovered dark, polished, and incised ceramics and other remains typical of this Initial Period (ca. 1500–200 B.C.) culture. Although Bird placed a large excavation trench that ran from Huaca Prieta into the Cupisnique Mound, no other large-scale, systematic research has been carried out at the site. Bird did recover a great number of ceramic artifacts, however, as well as houses, burials, and other features.

Moving northward, there are areas that appear to have relatively light occupations. Four hundred meters north of Huaca Prieta there is a large feature running east-west cutting across a relatively narrow section of the terrace. Again, no extensive research has been done here, but Peruvian archaeologists believe that this is a Chimu wall associated with a nearby huaca (Montículo 5) that also has been little studied.

Farther north, on the seaward side of the terrace, is Paredones, a sprawling complex of mounds, walls, and courts; it may have been a disembarkation point for long-distance maritime trade in Moche times. Looters in the early 1990s were seen to haul large quantities of *Spondylus princeps* shells out of the mound. The closest source of *S. princeps*, which had ritual importance that made it more precious than gold in late prehistory, is Ecuador, and long-distance voyages to obtain the shell are well documented. One arm or extension of the Paredones complex stands out from the rest of the complex due to its dark midden deposits. The project at El Brujo led by Tom Dillehay determined that this area also was a Preceramic Period occupation, although other sectors appear to be much later.

From Paredones northward virtually the entire ground surface manifests intensive human activity. Much of that activity involves looting (Figure 1.9). The degree to which graves and abandoned temples were left untouched before the arrival of the Spaniards is uncertain, but evidence suggests that ancient remains were respected most of the time and in most places. Eventually, however, people came to see grave goods and temple treasures not as part of their own history but as resources to be mined. Huacas were used as sites for picnics and honoring the dead on Good Friday in Colonial and Republican times, but a close association between the living and the dead was not considered; the ancients were *gentiles* (meaning roughly "pagans"), the moderns good Christians. Looting might be done casually, by a family on a weekend outing, or professionally, with large-scale excavations in search of gold to sell or textiles and ceramics that eventually made their way to the international art market. These attitudes are not entirely gone in Peru despite legislation to prevent looting, and many who consider themselves model citizens may be weekend *huaqueros* (those who excavate in huacas).

Looting has been so common that the northern sector of El Brujo is filled with overlapping holes, commonly a meter or so in depth and twice as wide. The greatest looting activity

Figure 1.9   Looter holes are highlighted by early morning light while excavation of Unit 28 proceeds. View to the northwest.

Figure 1.10 The Huaca Cortada, also known as the Huaca El Brujo, viewed looking north. The cut was made into what was probably a lateral (southern) side of the structure in the Colonial Period or in the Early Republican Period by unknown individuals. The cobbles in the foreground are the deflated remains of a prehispanic structure.

can be seen at the northernmost huaca at El Brujo, itself called both El Brujo and the Huaca Cortada (Cut Huaca) because of the huge trench cut into its southern side (Figure 1.10). No one is sure exactly when this cut was made, but the name "El Brujo" supposedly derives from the claim that at one point in the past the huaca was the gathering place for grand meetings of all the North Coast shamans.[14]

There are at least two other huacas, small ones, on the western edge between Huaca Cortada and Paredones, again with little research conducted on them. On the northern edge of the terrace, spot finds and small areas have revealed evidence from the Preceramic and Initial Periods. The majority of archaeological remains, however, date to an early Moche occupation (ca. A.D. 350–650) and are flanked by the Huaca Cortada on the west and by the Huaca Cao Viejo, 500 m to the east on the landward terrace edge.

Moche huacas were solidly built, with layers of adobe bricks placed over earlier structures, thus gaining in height and area as each new building phase occurred. Around these main temples were built secondary structures that included smaller shrines, courtyards, plazas, and buildings to house temple staff. Such complexes appear to lie under the surface to the east and northwest of the Huaca Cortada.

Abandoned or "decommissioned" temples often were used as cemeteries for later peoples, as evidenced by the numerous Lambayeque burials found in the talus slope of the Huaca Cao Viejo when it was excavated in the 1990s. The same seems to be the case for the east side of the Huaca Cortada, based on artifacts excavated but not taken by huaqueros, suggesting that this is the front of the structure.

Most of the half kilometer between the two huacas consists of a large residential area, as revealed by lines of cobbles that once served as the foundations of adobe houses. Despite intensive looting, some areas preserve enough of these foundations intact that the outlines of house compounds and streets between them can clearly be seen today. Until fairly recently, these remains were associated with the Gallinazo culture, antecedent to Moche, but revisions in ceramic chronologies and evidence for a town at Huacas de Moche, in the neighboring Moche Valley, which shares many similarities in layout and other features with El Brujo, suggest that the occupation is Moche in date. As with Paredones, some research has been carried out in the El Brujo town, but detailed reports have not yet been published.

The northeastern sector of El Brujo is where Huaca Cao Viejo and Magdalena de Cao are located and where most of the field research described in this book took place.

This Book

The 150 years during which Magdalena de Cao Viejo was occupied is a very short period for most archaeologists, especially prehistorians. For historians, however, that time span runs from the Late Renaissance to the Age of Enlightenment, from a time when the divine right of kings was still a serious proposition to an age of revolution against such ideas. In Peru, an aged Spaniard who passed through the North Coast when the Magdaleneros were recovering from the El Niño flooding could have been born the year Ferdinand and Isabella united his home country. And one of the last children born in Magdalena de Cao Viejo before the site was completely abandoned might, if long-lived enough, have heard the bells of liberation ringing out colonial times and ringing in the republic.

This book offers a report on our investigations of the colonial sector at El Brujo and, through them, views of what life was like at Magdalena de Cao Viejo during the Colonial Period. It does so by presenting information on archaeological and historical research carried out at the site and in other places as far away as Spain and the United States. It is both a site report, presenting the logic and rationale for what was done, how the excavation was carried out, and the data it produced, and a narrative of how the pieces of information may be interpreted to offer insights into the daily life of Magdaleneros.

This book also offers views on colonialism, cultural hybridity, resistance, assimilation, and many other theoretical issues in anthropology and history. For the most part, it discusses them not directly but within the context of reports and discussions of the specifics of the site, its artifacts and documents, and what researchers understand happened there. The authors of this volume believe that at this stage of investigation their most important duty is to present information on what was found and offer early interpretations, and this more than fills the present book.

While mostly avoiding deep theoretical issues and concentrating on discoveries about our site and the region, we authors consider our work and this book as a means of drawing attention to the importance of the Colonial Period as a subject worthy of archaeological and other investigation. Scholars in Latin America, Spain, and other European countries are deeply engaged in studying the period, and they are joined by many devoted historians in the United States. In archaeology, however, investigation of the time period started to grow only in the last decade and, beyond a few key historic sites along the sea coasts and selected sites of high touristic value, arguably still doesn't quite garner the interest or recognition it deserves.

An example of the subaltern status of colonial archaeology in the anglophone world is manifest in the style guide for *American Antiquity* and its companion journal, *Latin American Antiquity,* the premier journals for publishing in anthropological archaeology in the United States, in which "colonial period" goes uncapitalized as a common noun. In this volume, however, we have chosen to capitalize the name of this period as a recognition of its importance in the face of concerns about the political and ethical implications of how to deal with this painful but fascinating era (see Oland et al. 2012).

For now, at least, for the purposes of clarity and consistency in this book, I establish the following general chronology. The Conquest Period is from 1532 to 1572 (the arrivals in Peru of Pizarro and Toledo, respectively). The early Colonial Period is from 1572 to 1700 (the establishment of the Bourbons in Spain occurred in 1700). The late Colonial Period is from 1700 to 1824 (the latter being the date of the Battle of Ayacucho, which freed Spanish America from Spain). More succinctly, for heuristic purposes in discussing the archaeology and history in Peru, the early Colonial Period mostly is the seventeenth century and the late Colonial Period mostly is the eighteenth century.

The story of how the project came to be and how it was carried out is presented in Chapter 2. It is appropriate to note here, however, that projects have shelf lives of limited duration. Despite investigators' best intentions, as field and laboratory studies move farther into the past and as new work and life events take up their time and attention, scholars' ability (and often willingness) to write reports, chapters, and books on that old research often declines. This is why we have decided to publish this book now, while our studies are still relatively fresh. That said, the quantity of the data from Magdalena is so great and its quality so high that significant research remains to be done.

We have assembled key project members to write chapters on major aspects of the work and some minor ones as well. The combination is due partly to the need to present basic information on what was done and found and partly to the interests of the researchers. Thus we provide overviews of the research project, the main features of the site, ceramics, textiles, two categories of paper, metal objects, and beads.

A draft manuscript of this book was sent to two anonymous reviewers, who wrote very kind comments on the book as a whole and the individual chapters in it. Both raised two issues, however, that merit consideration. The first was that there is not a lot of context provided for artifacts—neither the archaeological contexts of their discovery at the site nor their cultural and social contexts. This is a valid critique. Indeed, the book has largely been constructed as an account of the research program followed by chapters that review different categories of artifact and bioarchaeological discoveries. As volume editor, I weighed two factors in my decision to follow this path. One is that because the site was so badly looted and materials have been strewn and moved about, in many cases reliance on find location is dubious at best. There are still plenty of well-documented find locations, however, and the second reason simply was expediency in getting a book published on the research. Our website (https://www.peabody .harvard.edu/Magdalena) provides more detailed descriptions of find locations and opens the possibility for discussion of how different materials relate to one another in their use lives at the site, and we hope this will address the issue.

The second issue was the placement in the middle of the book of Rocío Delibes's fascinating and important chapter on what the documentary sources tell us about Magdalena de

Cao. Both reviewers suggested that this chapter be the first or second in the volume. I placed it where I did because historians' accounts of the past always seem to trump archaeological ones. The project I began was to examine a Colonial Period site archaeologically—literally and figuratively from the ground up. I had presumed that all of the data we would retrieve would be the remains of the material culture of the Magdaleneros and that the interpretations, in turn, would be archaeological, serving as a narrative of early colonial life that is different from written accounts. Of course, as is often the case in archaeology, things did not turn out the way I had expected. Still, I want the reader who decides to read this book in sequence to retain a sense of the archaeological investigation of the site for several chapters.

The book thus begins in typical archaeological fashion, with this chapter presenting the larger cultural and social contexts of the world of the late sixteenth century. Then follows an overview of the research project in Chapter 2. Chapters 3 through 10 proceed through archaeological materials: the plants and animals that served to feed, house, and otherwise support or engage the Magdalena community (Chapter 3), the remains of the Magdaleneros themselves (Chapter 4), the clothes they wore (Chapter 5), beads (Chapter 6), ceramics (Chapters 7 and 8), metals (Chapter 9), and the few coins found at Magdalena (Chapter 10). Chapter 11, a presentation of what documents tell us, serves as a pivot for the book, for all the following chapters are related to various kinds of inscriptions, especially (though not exclusively) on paper. In Chapter 15 I offer some concluding thoughts on the project and how the results might be considered in various ways.

This book is not the last word on any of these topics. Indeed, I and the other authors believe that the Magdalena materials will be scholarly resources for many years to come, particularly because collections of Colonial Period materials—indeed, of late sixteenth- and seventeenth-century everyday objects in general—are so rare. This book is a start, however: a statement about one particular place at a time between a prehistoric past and a colonial present, and also a glimpse of past research and a hint of research to come.

NOTES

1 The general events of the conquest are not cited in detail in this chapter because they generally are well known and not controversial. The reader desirous of an introduction to the topic may consult Hemming 2003 or McQuarrie 2008.

2 See Cummins 2002 and Mumford 2012 on reducciones. The observation that this forced resettlement was one of the earliest and largest was first made in VanValkenburgh 2012.

3 See Manchester 1993.

4 These are modern names for ancient sites.

5 Quilter et al. 2010.

6 There is an extensive literature on El Niño events. The interested reader may refer to Sandweiss and Quilter 2009 for an introduction and other sources.

7 Compiled from http://www.worldweatheronline.com/Chiclayo-weather-averages/Lambayeque /PE.aspx.

8 Huertas 2001:78: "que se derramba cántaros de agua." *Cántaros* are large earthenware jugs the size of and equivalent to European barrels.

9 Huertas 2001:200–201: "Al tiempo de las dichas lluvias en el pueblo de Cao . . . de Chicama el qual estaba poblado junto a un rio deste valle el qual con las dichas lluvias salio de su madre . . . y se estendio

por todo el valle . . . los yndios del dicho pueblo . . . se fuero huyendo a un su pueblo antiguo questa junto al mar en un alto a donde se an quedado y estab poblado del dia de hoy."

10 The text uses *grillos*, the term for crickets. In Spanish, *langostas* refers to grasshoppers and locusts (a form of swarming grasshopper), although, as in English, these terms are not always used with precision. We thus do not know the precise animal in question.

11 Throughout this book, "Magdalena" and "Magdalena de Cao" will refer to the archaeological site unless the context makes it clear that the terms refer to the contemporary town; sometimes a modifier will be used to clarify that the modern town is under discussion. The term "Magdalena de Cao Viejo" (Old Magdalena de Cao) also will be used to specifically reference the site at El Brujo. Technically, the first Magdalena de Cao Viejo is the 1560 reducción, but its location is unknown, so that label falls to the refugee community at El Brujo. The full name of Santa María Magdalena de Cao was sometimes used at the time of its occupation, but the shorter version was equally common.

12 The residents of the modern town of Magdalena believe that their town was established in 1534. No evidence supports this claim.

13 *Huaca* has a number of different meanings. It can refer to significant features in a sacred landscape or to spiritlike entities that are thought to be in those features or separate from them. The term is often used to refer to an archaeological site, usually one with a pronounced vertical dimension, such as the eroded adobe temples on the coast of Peru.

14 Based on conversations with local people, the Huaca Brujo's role as the shamanic conference center of the North Coast was in the late Colonial and early Republican Periods, after Magdalena de Cao Viejo was abandoned.

REFERENCES CITED

Bauer, Brian, Javier Fonseca Santa Cruz, and Miriam Araoz Silva
  2015 *Vilcabamba and the Archaeology of Inca Resistance.* Los Angeles: Cotsen Institute of Archaeology, University of California, Los Angeles.

Bird, Junius B., John Hyslop, and Milica Dimitrijevic Skinner
  1985 *The Preceramic Excavations at the Huaca Prieta, Chicama Valley, Peru.* Anthropological Papers Vol. 62, Pt. 1. New York: American Museum of Natural History.

Bowser, Frederick
  1974 *The African Slave in Colonial Peru.* Stanford, CA: Stanford University Press.

Caramanica, Ari
  2018 Land, Labor, and Water on the Ancient Agricultural Pampa de Mocan, North Coast, Peru. Unpublished Ph.D. dissertation, Department of Anthropology, Harvard University.

Chauchat, Claude
  2006 *Prehistoria de la Costa Norte del Perú.* Translated by Santiago Uceda. Trujillo, Peru: Instituto Francés de Estudios Peruanos.

Cummins, Tom
  2002 Forms of Andean Colonial Towns, Free Will, and Marriage. In *The Archaeology of Colonialism,* edited by Claire L. Lyons and John K. Papadopoulos, pp. 199–240. Los Angeles: Getty Research Museum.

Dillehay, Tom D. (editor)
  2017 *Where the Land Meets the Sea: Fourteen Millennia of Human History at Huaca Prieta, Peru.* Austin: University of Texas Press.

Dillehay, Tom D., Duccio Bonavia, Steven Goodbred, Mario Pino, Victor Vásquez Sánchez, Teresa Rosales Tham, William Conklin, Jeff Splitstoser, Dolores Piperno, José Iriarte, Alexander Grobman, Gerson Levi-Lazzaris, Daniel Moreira, Marilaura Lopéz, Tiffiny Tun, Anne Titlebaum, John Verano, James Adovasio, Linda Scott Cummings, Phillipe Bearéz, Elise Dufour, Olivier Tombret, Michael Ramirez, Rachel Beavins, Larisa DeSantis, Isabel Rey, Philip Mink, Greg Maggard, and Teresa Franco

2012 Chronology, Mound-Building and Environment at Huaca Prieta, Coastal Peru, from 13 700 to 4 000 Years Ago. *Antiquity* 86:48–70.

Hemming, John

2003 *The Conquest of the Incas.* Boston: Mariner Books.

Huertas, Lorenzo

2001 *Diluvios andinos: a través de las fuentes documentales.* Lima: Fondo Editorial, Pontificia Universidad Católica del Perú.

McQuarrie, Kim

2008 *The Last Days of the Incas.* New York: Simon and Schuster.

Manchester, William

1993 *A World Lit Only by Fire: The Medieval Mind and the Renaissance: Portrait of an Age.* New York: Little, Brown and Company.

Manners, R. C., F. J. Magilligan, and P. S. Goldstein

2007 Floodplain Development, El Niño, and Cultural Consequences in a Hyperarid Andean Environment. *Annals of the Association of American Geographers* 97(2):229–249.

Moseley, Michael E.

1983 The Good Old Days Were Better: Agrarian Collapse and Tectonics. *American Anthropologist* 85(4):733–779.

1987 Punctuated Equilibrium: Searching the Ancient Record for El Niño. *Quarterly Review of Archaeology* 8:7–10.

Mumford, Jeremy

2012 *Vertical Empire: The General Resettlement of Indians in the Colonial Andes.* Durham, NC: Duke University Press.

Oland, Maxine, Siobhan M. Hart, and Liam Frink (eds.)

2012 *Decolonizing Indigenous Histories: Exploring Prehistoric/Colonial Transitions in Archaeology.* Tucson: University of Arizona Press.

Pino, Mario

2017 Stratigraphy, Sedimentology, and Chronology at Huaca Prieta. In *Where the Land Meets the Sea: Fourteen Millennia of Human History at Huaca Prieta, Peru,* edited by Tom D. Dillehay, pp. 617–630. Austin: University of Texas Press.

Quilter, Jeffrey, Mark Zender, Karen Spalding, Régulo Franco Jordán, César Gálvez Mora, and Juan Castañeda Murga.

2010 Traces of a Lost Language and Number System Discovered on the North Coast of Peru. *American Anthropologist* 112(3):357–369.

Sandweiss, Daniel H., and Jeffrey Quilter

2009 *El Niño, Catastrophism, and Culture Change in Ancient America.* Washington, DC: Dumbarton Oaks Library and Collections.

Stern, Steve J.

1993 *Peru's Indian Peoples and the Challenge of Spanish Conquest: Huamanga to 1640*. Madison: University of Wisconsin Press.

VanValkenburgh, Nathaniel Parker

2012 Building Subjects: Landscapes of Forced Resettlement in the Zaña and Chamán Valleys, Peru, 16th and 17th Centuries C.E. Unpublished Ph.D. dissertation, Department of Anthropology, Harvard University.

Wells, Lisa Esquivel, and Jay Stratton Noller

1999 Holocene Coevolution of the Physical Landscape and Human Settlement in Northern Coastal Peru. *Geoarchaeology: An International Journal* 14(8):755–789.

2

Overview of the Research Project

Jeffrey Quilter and
Régulo Franco Jordán

General Research Strategies

IN THIS CHAPTER WE will first cover some general considerations of work at the site and the broad theoretical questions addressed by our studies. This will be followed by a history of research at the El Brujo complex, a discussion of our methods of study, and then summaries of what our fieldwork revealed in the church and town sectors of Magdalena de Cao.

The general aim of the project at Magdalena de Cao was to gain an understanding of the organization and nature of the colonial occupation and to document changes that occurred there through time—very basic approaches to field archaeology. Two related features made this research unique, however.

First, a great deal of the site organization could be easily interpreted from visual inspection alone. Large sections of the walls of the nave of the church were still standing, in some places more than 2 m in height, and other walls in the church complex were visible to greater or lesser degrees. The same held true for the town. Stumps of cane from wattle-and-daub (known in Peru as *quincha*) walls delineated large blocks of occupation areas and streets between them; even the town plaza was clearly in evidence by absence of these features (Figure 2.1).

A second feature is one shared by many coastal Peruvian sites: the high quality of preservation of organic materials. Ceramic fragments, textiles, and human and other bone remains made up the majority of these materials. They littered the ground surface because of past looting activities. The destruction to archaeological contexts is lamentable, but the abundance of materials offered both a wealth of easily retrieved data and, at the same time, a challenge to proper documentation of its collection.

The goal of understanding a particular place in its temporal and sociocultural contexts influenced the way in which we approached archaeological investigations of the site. Of course, understandings of the events that transpired in Peru after the arrival of the Spanish in 1532 vary according to who considers the issue. And while a common approach decades ago was to assume that indigenous beliefs and practices (except for basic subsistence) had been completely swept away, today more nuanced perspectives predominate. For example, religion has received much attention in both Peru and Mexico, and earlier views in which

Figure 2.1 Quincha wall remains in the colonial town. The Huaca Cao Viejo is in the distance, to the south. The Moche plaza that supported the church complex is the rise in front of it.

Roman Catholicism was thought to have replaced indigenous beliefs have shifted to notions of syncretism and hybridity that see Catholicism blending with indigenous beliefs to create new religious systems or, going further, even being absorbed by the fundamental theologies of indigenous peoples.

Studies of native and foreign religious systems have been carried out mostly by ethnohistorians and were mostly based on documentary sources. Very few similar studies have been done regarding realms of life other than religion, and when they have, such as with economics, these too have been based on documentary sources, often relatively late in the history of colonization.

The opportunity to examine issues of resistance or accommodation of Spanish practices and beliefs through archaeology opens up a field of inquiry into the colonization process completely different from the historical program of relying on documents. Archaeology offers a view of the "small things forgotten"—the everyday life of ordinary people, something that often is not available in the archives of civil and religious institutions (Deetz 1977). This project and this book, then, provide scholars and other interested readers with an opportunity to explore not only what we know about the past but also how we come to know it.

Historical studies can tack between the general laws and proclamations made by elites in urban centers and the particulars of individuals at specific times and places as revealed in court cases or probate records. In archaeology, by contrast, the fineness of detail provided by the remnants of people's material world offers a special kind of view not found in any other discipline.

This project began as a study in what archaeology could say about the past in the absence of documentary sources, for we assumed that the remains to be found would be solely the kinds of artifacts found at prehistoric sites, such as tools, food remains, and the trash of long ago. But this assumption didn't last long: only a few hours into the first day of excavations in 2004, we discovered fragments of paper documents. Although we had always planned to investigate what archival sources could tell us about Magdalena de Cao and its world, we had assumed that such research would run parallel to the archaeology. The discovery of the paper resulted in a multidimensional project that brought together archaeology and documentary studies via the study of paper documents both as sources of information (in the manner of archival records) and as artifacts.

History of Research Prior to Our Project

The ancient ruins at the edge of the sea in the Chicama Valley were little known to most outsiders throughout most of the eighteenth and nineteenth centuries. Various national, regional, and local authorities wrote on matters pertaining to the area, however, as will be discussed in more detail in Chapter 12 by Rocío Delibes. One notable commentator was Miguel Feijoo de Sosa (1718–1791), *corregidor* (local administrative official) of Trujillo from 1757 to 1760. Another was Baltasar Jaime Martínez Compañón (1737–1797), bishop of Trujillo, who produced an extensive treatise on the region, most of which has been lost, although a volume of remarkable paintings of daily life was preserved and is a valuable resource to this day.

The only person known to have commented on the ruins specifically was the Italian-born Antonio Raimondi, who, in addition to serving as one of the founding professors of the medical school of the National University of San Marcos, in Lima, undertook 18 extensive trips through his adopted country and wrote a large tome that described his observations from natural history to ethnography to archaeology. In April and May 1859, while traveling between Trujillo and Cajamarca, he visited La Caleta del Brujo (Brujo Cove) and drew a sketch map of the "artificial hills called Huacas" there (Figure 2.2).[1] His map, made in ink with a quill-tip pen in his notebook, clearly shows the "Huaca prieta" at the southern end of the complex. He also drew a linear form at the northern side of this map and rather confusingly labeled it "Huaca redonda" (round huaca). Between the two he drew a mound labeled "Huaca blanca" (white huaca), which likely refers to the site sector now known as Paredones. Inland from these three huacas he drew a large mound and labeled it "Garita" (shelter). To its north, short L-shaped marks apparently indicate the remaining walls or outlines of them in the town of Magdalena de Cao, for above them he wrote "Pueblo viejo" (old town).

The relationships of the four mounds and town in Raimondi's sketch are incorrect, or at least quite distorted. Perhaps Raimondi wrote his notes at the end of the day, with his impressions of the walk from one mound to the next distorting his representation of their relationships in space. Whatever the case, Raimondi links the "pueblo viejo" with the contemporary town of Cao in his published account of his visit. Indeed, he makes the point that neither Feijoo de Sosa nor any other previous author mentioned a "pueblo viejo," thus indicating

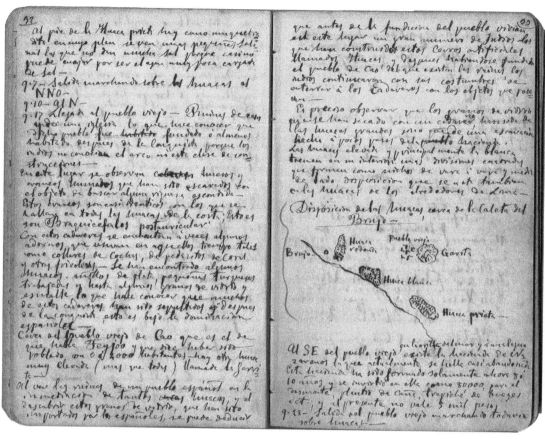

Figure 2.2 Pages from Antonio Raimondi's 1868 notes showing his sketch map of the El Brujo huacas.

that the modern town was established after 1760, the date of Feijoo's publication, and making Raimondi the "discoverer" of the archaeological site, at least in regard to the outside world (Raimondi 1942:190).

The next person known to have engaged with the ruins at El Brujo was the American archaeologist Junius B. Bird, as noted in Chapter 1. Bird and his family lived near the Huaca Prieta for 11 months (Figure 2.3). Subsequently, he made the site famous through his definitive identification of its occupation as the Late Preceramic Period (ca. 3000–1500 B.C.) with a later Initial Period (ca. 1500–1000 B.C.) occupation overlapping part of it. He never noted the colonial occupation at El Brujo in print, however.

In 1991, another Italian-born Peruvian, the financier Guillermo Wiese de Osma, led a group of friends and colleagues on a tour of the North Coast of Peru. They stopped at the El Brujo terrace and discovered murals on the mound that Raimondi had labeled "garita" but which by then was called the Huaca Blanca.[2] At the time this huaca was thought to date to the Lambayeque Culture (ca. A.D. 800–1370), but work funded by Wiese identified it as Moche, and so it was renamed the Huaca Cao Viejo—"Cao" being the old name for the area as well as for the nearby town of Magdalena de Cao. Wiese committed funds for a long-term investigation of the site in cooperation with the National Institute of Culture of Peru and local

Figure 2.3 The Huaca Prieta is at the southern tip of the El Brujo terrace. The mound to its right is a later, Cupisnique site.

authorities. That support and research continued after Wiese's death, in 1999, through to the present day via the Fundación Wiese, which has helped support the work reported in this book.

Many important finds have been made by Peruvian archaeologists, most notably the tomb of the Señora de Cao, a high-ranking Moche lady, and the colorful wall murals on the front of the Huaca Cao Viejo (Mujica 2007). The site also has been developed for tourism. In 2006, the wooden roof protecting the murals on the front of the huaca was replaced with a fabric awning; shortly thereafter, old laboratories and offices were demolished to make way for a modern facility that includes laboratories, offices, and the Museo de Cao, which houses the mummy of the Señora as well as displays of recovered artifacts, including some of the Colonial Period remains discussed in this book.

The Magdalena de Cao Project

Through a series of events Jeffrey Quilter became aware of the archaeological project at El Brujo and was invited by Marco Aveggio of the Fundación Wiese and Régulo Franco Jordán, César Gálvez, and Segundo Vásquez, codirectors of the archaeological research, to become involved with research at the site. Quilter developed two projects of modest scale at El Brujo. Both involved further work on research that had been started by the Peruvian archaeologists and was generously supported by the National Geographic Society.

Figure 2.4 The ceremonial well. Restoration has consolidated the loose cobbles of the spiral ramp. Maximum width is about 5 m.

The first project was the excavation of the area around a well with a spiral ramp located 470 m from the Huaca Cao Viejo in a Moche residential area (Figure 2.4). Previous work had concentrated on the well itself, which was filled with artifacts and human remains. The subsequent work helped to contextualize the well within the El Brujo complex and contributed to understanding the changing uses of the site (Quilter et al. 2012).

The second project involved excavations on the northwest corner of the huaca, revealing colorful Moche murals in a small ceremonial precinct, known as a *recinto*. Ground-penetrating radar studies carried out by Larry Conyers (University of Denver) as part of Quilter's research suggested that there was something of interest buried below the floors of that precinct. Later excavations carried out by the site archaeologists discovered the Señora de Cao (Figure 2.5).

The research at the well and preliminary studies of the recinto of the Señora de Cao took place in 2002 and 2004. Excavations at the well, the primary focus of the North American contingent, finished with about a week to spare in the field season, and so thought was given to conducting a small project that would aid the general goal of understanding the El Brujo complex better. At this point, William Doonan (Sacramento City College), co–field director of the excavations at the well, suggested to Quilter that the Colonial Period remains at the site offered a rare opportunity for study, given that such remains were often difficult to find without later occupations, including contemporary ones, on top of them. The fact that the remains of the colonial church were within the boundaries of the Huaca Cao Viejo plaza,

Figure 2.5   The bundle containing the Señora de Cao under excavation.

less than 100 m from the painted façade, was an added incentive, for its study would help in development of the site for tourism.

There were, of course, important intellectual reasons for an archaeological project on the Colonial Period. Perhaps the most important reason, as previously noted, is that we know very little about the Colonial Period in Peru except through historical records written by Spaniards or, somewhat later, by native people who had learned to write or had access to someone who could write for them. Although written documents are a tremendously rich source of information about past events, they commonly do not offer much information about the everyday lives of ordinary people. Archaeology, by contrast, does offer views on those lives. Relatively little Colonial Period archaeology had been carried out in Peru, and so it seemed an opportune time to develop such a project.

The fieldwork done in 2004 consisted of cleaning out several small excavation units that had been placed by the El Brujo archaeologists at various locations in the church complex within the walls of the old Huaca Cao Viejo plaza (Figure 2.6). This work revealed the presence of painted walls and fragments that had fallen from them in the church as well as some details of the architecture that already had been noted in the earlier work (Figure 2.7). The 2004 research also included the placement of small (mostly 1 × 1 m) excavation units in the flat area immediately in front of the northern perimeter wall of the Moche plaza, which also had served as the limits of the church complex. That work revealed the presence of colonial-era remains as well as some prehistoric materials.

Figure 2.6
Cleaning out
excavations near
the southern end of
the interior eastern
wall of the church
nave. The work
revealed an entry
space between
the nave and the
sacristy that was
later excavated.

Figure 2.7
A fragment of
fallen wall plaster
found while
cleaning the old
excavation near
the passageway
between the nave
and the sacristy.

Figure 2.8
Excavation of the
north face of
the northwest
corner of the
church atrium.

The U.S. team also placed a new excavation unit (1×2 m) on the northern side of the northwest corner of a small plaza that was later determined to be the church atrium, an open forecourt where congregants could gather before or after services. This work noted that a series of wooden posts had been placed along the top of the wall, probably to support a screen of woven mats. The outer face of the wall retained traces of a mural in white paint of a line of squares with a large dot in each, presumably a colonial decorative treatment (Figure 2.8). If the U.S. team had any remaining doubts about working in the colonial sector, they were dispelled when these excavations also uncovered a dense deposit of colonial trash in which were found numerous paper fragments dating to the colonial era.

Funds were raised from the National Endowment for the Humanities to conduct archaeological investigations of the colonial sector at El Brujo—the remains of Magdalena de Cao Viejo. Large-scale excavations took place in 2005 and 2008, with less intense field studies in 2012. Laboratory analyses were ongoing beginning in 2004. The National Science Foundation, Dumbarton Oaks, and the Peabody Museum of Archaeology and Ethnology at Harvard University provided additional financial support through the years of the project. The Fundación Wiese offered a great deal of in-kind support though the generous provision of the time and talents of staff to aid the North Americans in numerous ways. Free use of the Casa Wiese and Fundación Wiese vehicles also greatly aided the project.

The Field Research and Other Studies

The field investigations began with very basic questions regarding the nature of the site and its history of occupation. As in all archaeological projects, control of our understanding of data in the dimensions of space, time, and form was paramount throughout the investigations but played the greatest role early in our study. As research continued and we came to know the site better, we were able to refine some of our questions, which in turn led to new questions.

The following subsections are organized on the basis of a general chronological narrative of the history of our studies. During any one field season, investigations were undertaken on more than one issue and then were carried through to later field seasons, allowing us to revisit certain topics, revise our approach, and sometimes remarkably clarify our understanding of what had transpired at the site.

Spatial references are critical in conducting field archaeology. In excavating at Magdalena de Cao we followed a system already employed by the El Brujo archaeologists, who had established a grid system over the entire site complete with concrete markers for major points along north and south axes. That system was based upon the Universal Transverse Mercator (UTM) system, employed worldwide. In the first few field seasons the Peruvians used the letters *R* and *Y* to indicate east-west and north-south coordinates, respectively, and using the last several digits of the UTM accordingly. In later years the *R*s and *Y*s were dropped from record keeping.

In addition to the UTM system, we designated excavation units by numbers. In order to use the North American team's time in the field efficiently, we would send a list of planned excavations to our Peruvian colleagues in advance of our arrival. This resulted in many more units being planned than we were able to excavate, and so the numbers of the units actually excavated do not follow a sequential order. Another difficulty that had to be corrected was the repetition of the same unit numbers in more than one year. Using a numerical designation to distinguish one field season in a unit from the next rectified this problem. Thus "07-12" indicates excavations in Unit 12 in 2007, and "08-12" signals work in the same area the following year.

Excavations within the town were controlled by reference to the meter-square unit in which the work took place, which was noted by reference to the coordinates of the unit's southwest corner. In cases of units larger than 1 × 1 m, all relevant southwest corners or the range between them were noted for spatial control. When working inside clearly recognizable structures, such as rooms in the town or the nave or atrium in the church, a notation referring to that location was commonly made.

Natural stratigraphic units were followed in all excavations. Thick strata were sometimes subdivided by using an arbitrary control in centimeters within them, but this was rarely employed, as in most cases the natural strata appeared to have been deposited within a relatively short period.

The overwhelming majority of excavated soils were sifted through hardware cloth (¼ in) nailed to wooden frames. In the rare cases where there were dense deposits of overburden, such as windblown soil or thick deposits of straw and animal dung, screening was not done. When excavating occupation surfaces, finer hardware cloth (openings of less than ¼ in) was employed as well.

Many different units were excavated during our multiyear investigation. The greatest amount of work in the town was done in Units 1, 2, and 28. In Units 1 and 28, detailed photographs and drawings were made when living surfaces and in situ artifacts were encountered. In Unit 2, excavated by Parker VanValkenburgh as part of the research for his doctoral dissertation, a system of elements and detailed piece plotting were employed. Numerous excavation units were placed in the church compound, with particularly intensive work carried out in Units 7 and 12.

As every archaeologist knows, fieldwork is an early stage in research; many more hours are commonly devoted to processing recovered materials, and even more should be spent in studying them. We had a team to immediately receive bags of excavated materials during and at the end of each workday. The quantity of materials was so great that simply keeping track of their field numbers and temporarily storing them took a considerable amount of effort. When time permitted during the excavation season, and after the season was over, laboratory assistants cleaned, documented, catalogued, and stored the materials for eventual analysis. Analysis of the materials began with the start of the project. Such studies varied depending on the time available and the interests and concerns of project members. The field season of 2008 saw the last large-scale field investigation, with laboratory and archival studies increasing since that time. We believe that the assemblage of artifacts from Magdalena de Cao represents not only the largest collection of items of quotidian material culture in Peru but also perhaps the largest collection of such remains from a single site of the late sixteenth and seventeenth centuries anywhere. The Magdalena materials likely will be a source of study for many years to come.

A Narrative of the Research

The 2004 Field Season

Our first work was carried out in 2004, when we placed an excavation unit on the north side of the northwestern corner of the atrium as well as two small pits on the ground below the north atrium wall. That work revealed a mural on the wall exterior and postholes spaced along the top of the wall. The identification of dense deposits of trash, including paper fragments, on top of the wall and on its northern face, however, is what drew the most attention and spurred us to develop a project for the site. We also cleaned out a number of small (usually 1×1 m) pits previously placed by the Peruvians in the church nave. These proved of little interest except for a pit on the interior eastern wall of the nave near its front. In cleaning this unit, we learned that there was a passageway from the nave to a room, later determined to be the sacristy, where the priest would have kept his garments for the Mass. In addition, we found several fragments of brightly painted wall plaster that further demonstrated the rich potential of more work at Magdalena de Cao Viejo.

The 2005 Field Season

The Church

In 2005 we came back to Magdalena with more funds and more time for our work.[3] Most of our field season focused on the church complex in order to identify its basic architectural features and general characteristics. Peruvian archaeologist Jaime Jiménez Saldaña served as codirector for all fieldwork in general as well as the chief supervisor of excavations in the church compound (Figure 2.9).

We returned to the northwest corner of the atrium and placed a small excavation unit inside it in order to investigate the source of the rich midden that we previously had uncovered on its exterior. That midden was a thick mantle covering the top of the wall and extending down in front of it. The excavation in the interior corner of the atrium, however, revealed very little midden. This suggests that the midden did not originate from the interior of the atrium— an unlikely place for it anyway, as the atrium would have been kept clean and few people would have occupied it except before and after church services.

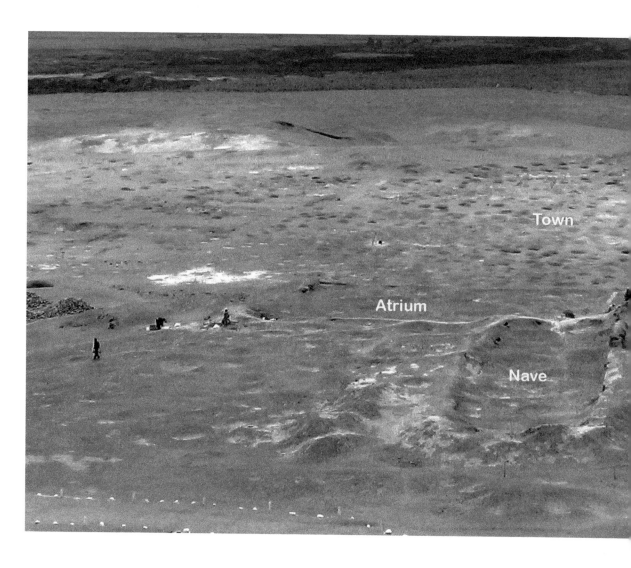

Town

Atrium

Nave

Figure 2.9
The church
compound as it
appeared in 2005
from the top of the
Huaca Cao Viejo.
View to the north.

The profile of the cut midden was layered, but not so much as to suggest that the midden had been deposited sporadically (Figure 2.10). Rather, it looked as if its contents had been thrown over the wall. Also, the nature of the materials suggested that they had been there a long time; the initial assessment is hard to justify, but there was a quality to the deposits that suggested great age, and indeed all recovered materials turned out to be old, with no items that might indicate deposition had taken place in the nineteenth or twentieth centuries. We also observed that the midden extended along the rest of the walls, thinning out along the northern wall but thick along the western one; subsequent excavations confirmed this observation.

A second area of study was the northern end of the nave. Unit 12 covered the area from the midpoint of the church doorway up to the higher eastern sector of the complex and from 1 m in front of the door to behind the church bell tower. Because there was a considerable amount of overburden, work mostly involved clearing down to the floor levels of the colonial occupation, which revealed various features of interest (Figure 2.11).

The entry to the church was beveled, wider on the exterior than the interior. The ground surface during the last occupation of the complex was sloped, higher in the east than the west.

There was a north-south containment wall against the higher bulk of the eastern complex sector, with no clear access from one level to the next. There was, however, a short stairway made of adobe bricks two or three levels in height, abutting the north face of the bell tower. Although the remains of the bell tower were only 1 m in height from the present ground surface, it was clear that it had been a solid structure set apart from the nave. It almost certainly was a section of freestanding wall with one or more apertures at its summit for the bell or bells rung by ropes running to the ground. Great amounts of straw and other plant remains were compacted within a narrow space between the rear of the bell tower (to the south) and a structure behind it.

The entire eastern sector of the church complex was our third major area of study in 2005. This sector had the most severely damaged architecture in the church complex, with numerous looter holes, piles of backdirt, fallen adobe wall fragments, and other detritus. We placed 12 excavation units in the area, mostly along the edge of the complex in a line with the better-defined wall of the western sector as well as units in the interior of this square sector.

The results of this work did not bring much greater clarity regarding details of the structures that had once stood in this place. We were able to find enough of the southern wall of

Figure 2.10   The east wall of the 2005 excavations in Unit 4 at the northwest corner of the atrium. The width of the unit is 1 m. Note the compacted deposits and layers of vegetal matter.

Figure 2.11   Unit 12-2005 under excavation. The view is from the higher eastern sector of the church compound looking westward.

Figure 2.12   Jaime Jiménez cleaning the patch of undisturbed floor in Unit 14, eastern compound sector. View to the northeast.

the compound to be confident that it had been present and was of the same two-course adobe form as that on the edge of the atrium. No clear indications of a similar wall on the eastern edge of the compound could be found, however, because looting had been intense, although we think it likely that such a wall was once present, based on some adobes that we found in the area. In the interior of this sector little of interest could be found. The area was so badly looted that the largest section of floor we uncovered was an irregularly shaped patch less than 2 m in length and barely 50 cm in width in Unit 14 (Figure 2.12).

One curious feature that struck our attention was the presence of quincha wall remnants at various places in this eastern sector. The remains were so fragmentary that we could not discern the shape of the original structures. Three possibilities might explain these quincha walls. First, quincha may have been part of the original Colonial Period architecture in the compound. Second, squatters or similar folk may have built and used the quincha structures not too long after the church was abandoned. Third, the quincha may be the remains of huts built in even later times by people who visited huacas on Good Friday, a common practice in the region. Based on later work, as will be discussed, the second of these possibilities seems most likely, although a definitive conclusion on the matter has not been reached.

It seems least likely that the original occupants of the church complex made the quincha architecture that we observed in the eastern sector of the compound. They may have used the quincha technique in some part of their buildings, but the remains we saw likely would not have withstood the extensive looting in this area. Most likely this area was so severely looted because it was the residential area for friars, a priest, and perhaps novitiates of the Dominican order; there were enough walls and other fragments of architecture to suggest that dormitories, administrative offices, and the like probably had occupied this space, and this would have attracted looters looking for items associated with those activities. In addition, subsequent work nearby revealed other architectural features of everyday life suggesting that the eastern site sector was reserved for the quotidian activities of the members of the religious order who once occupied and worked in the church compound.

The Town

The use of ground-penetrating radar had produced good results at the huaca in detecting the tomb of the Señora de Cao, so Larry Conyers employed it over a large section of the western area of the town, near the plaza (Figure 2.13). This research produced good results, but we soon came to realize that a much simpler method could quickly identify and delineate the structures occupying the town blocks.

Most of the quincha structures in the town had decayed. The adobe melted and puddled on the old ground surface, building up linear mounds where the walls had stood. This phenomenon highlighted the roads between town blocks, which were slightly lower than the mounded adobe. Even more useful than adobe, however, were the remnants of the cane component of the quincha. The wattle was constructed in a grid pattern with horizontal elements interwoven with the vertical ones, like a textile, and tied for further support. In some places the preservation was so good that the entire structure of horizontal and vertical elements, tied together, was preserved. This mostly occurred in areas covered by substantial midden, such as

Figure 2.13 Conducting ground-penetrating radar studies in the colonial town. Pictured are (left to right) Jennie Sturm, Richard Busch, and Larry Conyers (seated).

in places that became trash dumps. Elsewhere, the horizontal cane had either decayed or been removed for other uses, but the vertical elements remained. Over time, most of the vertical canes deteriorated, but their stumps, buried in the linear mounds of melted adobe, were preserved. In some places the stumps were already visible, with no work required to reveal them. In other locales, especially where adobe did not puddle in lines, russet-colored soil indicated where the walls had been, and a little digging soon revealed the stumps.

We were thus able to quickly follow old walls by scraping away soil in areas where stumps, red-brown lines of soil, or linear mounds of adobe were present, and following the remnants of the vertical canes into areas that were less well defined. We often gave this task to young, inexperienced workers because it was so easy to do. This process revealed many of the walls of the town residences. The picture is less than complete because of circumstances such as irregular ground surfaces, midden piles, looter holes and, possibly, removal of cane for use elsewhere while the site was still occupied.

It is worth noting here that the looter holes not only impeded our ability to follow quincha walls in many places but also were obstacles in other work as well, often having destroyed Colonial Period floors that would have been exposed in excavations. In many places the ground surface was thoroughly pockmarked, with only narrow ridges of soil separating holes as big as cars. Despite the extensiveness and intensity of looting in the colonial sector of the site, relatively little is to be found there that has value in the art market. Those who damaged the site rarely ever reached the Moche occupation levels below Colonial Period strata.

The church and town offered strikingly different archaeological features, reflecting the difference in their uses during Magdalena's occupation. The church was a three-dimensional jumble of standing adobe walls and fragments within the confines of the old Moche plaza. The town, however, was relatively flat, with less visible architecture apparent at first glance. It was situated in relation to the large *montículos* (mounds) from the Moche occupation. Their irregular surfaces would have made them unattractive as places to settle.

Simply by the observation of artifacts that littered the ground surface, we saw that the colonial occupation consisted of an area stretching from the eastern edge of the El Brujo terrace to the contemporary site access road on the west. The colonial town was mostly south of Montículo 2. We never established the precise eastern and western boundaries of the town, but on its eastern side the town occupation appeared to be relatively light for about 10 m in from the terrace edge. On the west, we noted a patch of colonial occupation west of the road, close to the northern limits of the contemporary parking lot of the Museo de Cao.

The southern town limit was the wall of the church compound, the same wall as the northern limit of the Moche plaza. Although we detected Colonial Period activity in our 2004 test pits in this area, such as miscellaneous ceramics and other artifacts, we found no dwellings there. Instead, the large colonial plaza began immediately in front of the church complex, with house compounds arranged around the other three sides of the square. Conceptually, then, if the Colonial Period occupation of Magdalena de Cao was conceived on a European model (see Cummins 2002), the church compound could be thought of as one side of a large quadrangle fully incorporating the prehispanic base on which it rested. That base consists of layers of successive plazas of the Huaca Cao Viejo constructed on top of one another, except in the plaza's northeast corner. That area, directly under the eastern sector of the church compound, was a prehispanic structure that has not been extensively investigated, mostly because of its

Figure 2.14 Photo map of the colonial town. 1. Church complex; 2. Town plaza; 3. Unit 1; 4. Unit 2; 5. Unit 19; 6. Unit 28; 7. Column sample; 8. Montículo 3; 9. Montículo 2. Drone photo taken in 2017.

location underneath the church compound. Given that the architectural organization of the Huaca Cao Viejo resembles that of the Huaca de la Luna, in the Moche Valley, and that the equivalent space there is occupied by a Moche temple, it is likely that a similar edifice is at Cao Viejo. The presence of such a structure at Cao also likely explains why the eastern sector of the church compound is higher than the western sector, because the Moche building underneath the eastern sector was higher than the plaza.

Aerial photos (both from Google Earth and older images) and our inspections on the ground (Figures 2.14 and 2.15) revealed that the town covered 5.43 ha. In one direction it extended from close to the front (north) side of the church compound north to the base of Montículo 2, a distance of between 150 and 155 m. The town's eastern boundary was the edge of the terrace; the town extended across it and around Montículo 3, ending just on its other side, for a distance of between 320 and 370 m.

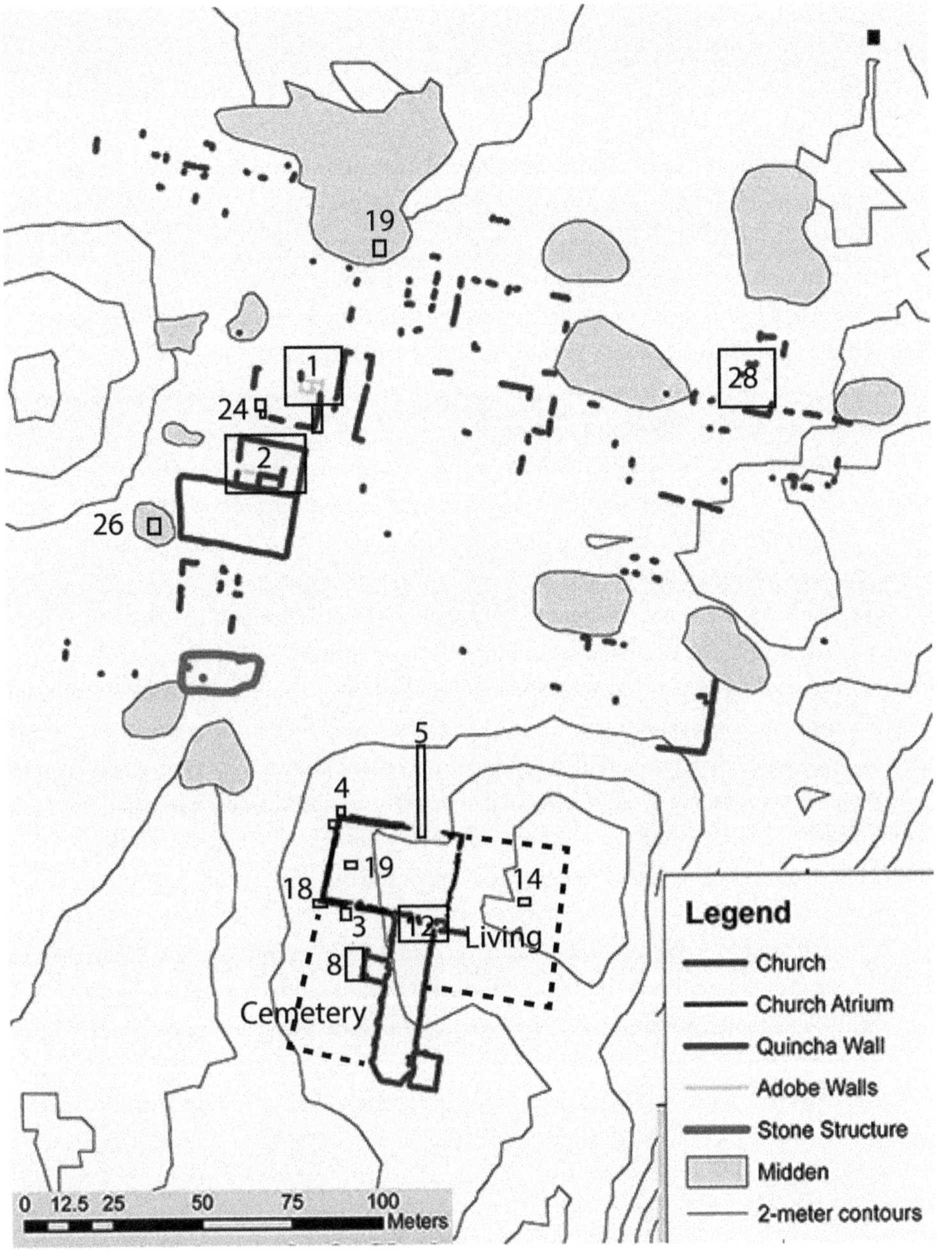

Figure 2.15
Map of the town
showing major
excavation units.

The plaza was a square, measuring about 60 m on a side, about the same as that in present-day Magdalena de Cao. There were two avenues flanking the eastern and western sides of the plaza. The plaza is somewhat offset in relation to the church compound, rather than centered, with the street flanking the plaza's eastern side aligned with a possible entry to the compound on its northern face (discussed at greater length in the section on the 2007 field season). There may have been an east-west street directly abutting the north side of the church compound; there is a clearly defined street parallel to it on the plaza's northern side. There is a short east-west street separating Units 1 and 2, but no other streets were clearly observable. The streets running along the northern and western sides of the plaza were among the best-defined thoroughfares in the town, as was the short street that ran from Montículo 3 to intersect the western avenue next to the plaza. We began work in this area to clarify the nature of the street surface, finding that it had no distinctive features other than being a compacted surface.

Documentary sources refer to an "entry" to the town (see Chapter 12), but we could not discern where this might be. It is quite possible that the current road from Magdalena de Cao follows an earlier route. An alternative is that one of the major east-west streets led into the town, although that would have required a steep climb up the eastern side of the terrace.

We excavated in the approximate center of the plaza but did not find any signs of a central architectural feature, nor was a prepared surface encountered. A sprinkling of water on the natural ground surface would have produced a relatively hard, dust-free surface, forming a crust (caliche) from the calcium carbonate in the soil. If present, this should have been detected, but we did not find such a surface.

Great amounts of household midden, in piles that were sometimes several meters in length and more than a meter in height, covered large sections of the town. It is quite likely that these are deposits made in the waning years of the occupation of Magdalena de Cao as the size of the resident population shrank, and old homes were abandoned.

The search for the town residences quickly aided us in outlining the basic format of Magdalena de Cao Viejo. Residences during the late occupation of the site consisted of large rectangular compounds. Although we have only studied three compounds in detail, all seem to be relatively equal in size, about 15 × 40 m. Most of the space in them was devoted to a large open-air patio where food was prepared and other domestic chores were carried out. Two or three sheltered areas usually were placed in a corner of the compound near the entrance, which seems to have been located on the southern side, facing the church (Figure 2.16). Presumably the enclosed spaces were used for sleeping and for staying out of the chill when winter winds and fog were bothersome.

In 2005, we put most of our workforce in the church compound. A smaller contingent of young, inexperienced workers was placed in the town working with trowels to expose quincha compound walls so that we could develop a map of the town. We spent much of our time in Unit 1 following the eastern wall of the compound, which paralleled the north-south avenue. In later field seasons we extended our excavation pits westward, revealing a number of rooms, as will be discussed later in this chapter.

The 2006 Field Season

The Church

The 2006 field season built on the research of the previous year and included significantly more work in both the church and town sectors. In the church, we began with a systematic surface collection of human bones in the nave, an activity that was repeated more than once during our work, as every year new fragments were exposed.[4]

We spent much of the 2006 season cleaning and excavating the walls of the church nave, which had been preserved in outline at their bases (Figure 2.17). We also stabilized the highest standing wall section on the west side of the nave by propping up the upper portion of the wall and inserting modern adobe bricks in the lower section, which had been undermined through erosion.[5] Church walls left exposed after excavation were capped with a new layer of adobe bricks, thus helping to preserve the original portions of the wall.

Figure 2.16 Early excavations in Unit 2, showing one of the sheltered areas in the southeastern sector of the compound. View to the west.

Figure 2.17 Excavating the nave in 2006. View to the southwest.

Figure 2.18
Fragment of
painted wall plaster
(about 23 cm in
length) on the
inner face of
the east wall of
the nave.

In working to support the eastern wall we encountered a patch of painted plaster. It was white with red bands on it, suggesting that the last mural on this wall included a horizontal red band of unknown length, likely with vertical bands extending down from it (Figure 2.18). We have no way of knowing whether this design was used to frame an image on the interior of the defined space or was a geometric motif. It is worth noting, however, that geometric motifs are quite common in churches in the region, such as in the roughly contemporary church at Santiago de Cao.

Our work in exposing the nave wall consisted of clearing soil in some places and excavating in other locales where the walls were deeply buried. One such excavation took place immediately to the south of the remains of what may have been an engaged column that had served to demarcate the nave proper from the chancel or sanctuary, where the priest performed the Mass. Only a few centimeters below the floor level in this area we encountered the remains of a small coffin covered in red fabric. This was the interment of an infant, probably dating to the nineteenth or twentieth century (see Chapter 4).

We excavated in the large room (8.8 m N-S × 7 m E-W) on the eastern side of the southern end of the church where we had cleared out a passageway in our brief 2004 excavations. This appears to have been the sacristy, a room where the vessels, plates, and other articles for celebrating the Mass were kept and in which the priest prepared himself for the service. Its location conforms to the usual placement of sacristies in relation to naves in European churches (Figure 2.19).[6]

Three features of particular interest were found in the sacristy excavations. First, a *Spondylus princeps* valve was found in dust immediately above the sacristy floor. It was lying at an angle, almost vertical, on the southern side of the room. Whether the shell was accidentally interred in the room during a period of looting or was deliberately placed in position is hard to assess.

Figure 2.19 Aerial view of the sacristy under excavation. Note the entrance to the nave, at left, and the deteriorated altarlike adobe construction on the middle of the wall at right. North is top of photo.

Another feature of interest was the remains of a large block of adobe attached to the inner eastern wall of the room. This feature was damaged, probably by looters, but originally seems to have measured about 2 m in length and about 1 m wide. A large section of its smoothed, flat plaster surface was preserved. This may have served as a table on which the priest could lay out his vestments, a typical feature in sacristies, though it also might have served as a personal altar.

As excavations continued on the outside of the structure we found a human foot with an attached lower leg stuck into the adobe wall directly opposite the adobe table inside (Figure 2.20). The lower leg had been placed into the wall so that the foot faced outward. Although we cannot be entirely certain, it appears that the foot had been covered by the adobe

Figure 2.20
A skeletal foot may be seen in the lower left-hand area of the photograph of the eastern exterior wall of the sacristy. The inset at top right shows the removed foot and lower leg.

mud facing of the exterior wall, so it would not have been visible when the sacristy was in use. Unlike the *S. princeps* shell, there is no doubt that the foot was intentionally placed in the wall, although interpreting its significance is a challenge.

We encountered another room on the northern end of the western wall of the nave. It measured 5 m on a side and had entrances on its southern, western, and eastern sides (Figure 2.21). The eastern entry connected the room directly to the nave, and the western and southern entries, with their steps leading down to the floor of the room, would have provided easy access to an area we later determined was the town cemetery. A notable feature of the entry was a large, thick, round baulk of adobe that had to be surmounted to get from the nave to the interior of the room. Fairly substantial wooden poles lay in the room. And there were clear signs that water had run through this space—something that only could have occurred during an El Niño event, likely after the abandonment of the church.

The room had preserved fragments of wall plaster with the remains of mural painting on them. We noted two different superimposed mural styles, which implies at least two significant stages in the use life of the space. We had been working under the assumption that this room had been a chapel. When the entire space was excavated down to the floor, however, we noticed a curious low adobe feature, a few centimeters in height, in the middle of the room. Nearby, pressed into the floor, were large pieces of a smashed decorated ceramic.

The adobe feature in the center of the room was in the form of a heptagon, a seven-sided polygon. We were quite puzzled by this odd shape, but when Padre Ricardo of the Trujillo Cathedral came for a visit, he remarked that it was quite apparent to him that this was the base of a baptismal font, with the seven sides symbolizing the seven sacraments, of which baptism is one. Thus the room was a baptistry, a logical feature for a church with a missionizing agenda.

Excavation of the exterior of the western wall of the baptistry uncovered loose straw as well as paper document fragments. One large paper fragment had been soiled by bird dung.

Figure 2.21 The baptistry, looking eastward. Note the steps in the centers of the western and eastern walls and the seven-sided base for the font in the middle of the room.

This was significant because it indicated that the paper had lain exposed to the elements for some time before being covered by straw and soil.

Below the straw and paper, we found fragments of a gourd bowl and a large wooden paddlelike object that clearly had been placed flush against the exterior western wall at ground level (Figure 2.22). This object almost certainly was a paddle used in brewing chicha (maize beer). It is likely that the blade originally had been symmetrical, was broken, and then continued to be used for a while, as the broken edge was smoothed, presumably from use. The interpretation of the object as a chicha paddle makes sense in relation to the gourd remains next to it, as similar gourd bowls were used in preparing and serving chicha. Although it clearly was deliberately placed against the wall, the reasons for doing so are unclear: was this a reverential deposit—a "decommissioning" of the paddle—or a simple act of disposal? Furthermore, do these remains signify that chicha production occurred at colonial Magdalena? The answer to that question could hinge on exactly when the paddle was placed against the baptistry wall; a few decades one way or the other, undetectable through any current dating method, could make all the difference to such an interpretation.

The final major work conducted in the church in 2006 was the search for the entryway into the compound from the town plaza. As noted previously, in 2005 we had attempted to locate the compound's perimeter wall by following the well-preserved atrium section eastward and then placing small excavation units in relevant places in the eastern sector of the compound, but we did not gain any understanding of the features because of the heavy looting that had taken place there.

Figure 2.22
The exterior
western wall of
the baptistry with
the chicha paddle
laid on the ground
against it.

To see if there had been a ramp, a formal entry, or other features along the perimeter wall, we located the central point of the perimeter wall and placed a large pit, 4 × 4 m, directly over the area where the entry should be if it was oriented on the central axis of the church nave. We found only a prepared floor, with no signs that a wall or ramp had been part of the compound (Figure 2.23). We extended a section of the unit another 5 m westward along the line of the perimeter wall, eventually encountering that wall, but there were no signs that it had been finished in any special way; it just stopped. The only interpretation we could draw from this is that the compound had an open access point, without a door or gate, and that the natural talus slope of the deteriorated adobe from the prehistoric structures underneath the compound had served as the ramp that connected the town and religious sectors.

The Town

Most of the workforce was concentrated in the church compound in 2006. A small crew continued to work on Unit 1, however. Much of that work consisted of defining and following the eastern perimeter wall of the compound. When we reached the northern end of the compound the excavations proceeded inward, and we worked in an area 3 × 3 m in size for the first deep excavations in the town.

The upper layers of the excavations included surface dust and lots of straw. Immediately below this there was a four-course line of adobe bricks that indicated a large wall. Unfortunately, the wall did not extend very far; the bricks in it may have been removed for use later in the

Colonial or Republican Period. Next to the wall we found numerous objects that appeared to have been left in situ on a very poorly preserved floor of powdery soil (Figure 2.24).

The objects were within a small space, confined by the wall to the east and fallen adobe bricks on the sides. They consisted of a strip of blue cloth, a swath of coarse cloth, a short stick pointed at one end, a fan-shaped flat copper alloy object, and what appeared to have been a scrubbing brush with a string attached to it. Nearby, wedged under an adobe brick, we found a section of a small, bell-shaped bottle gourd that had been cut to serve as a container and filled with small pieces of textiles, seeds, and other plant remains (Figure 2.25; see also Figure 15.2 in Chapter 15).

Why these objects came to be in this place is unclear. We might assume that the metal object would have had some value, but it was next to scraps of cloth and a scrubbing brush. Did the fact that these objects were left in the floor signify that the house's inhabitants left in a hurry? The filled gourd was probably a household offering. Why was it, too, left in the house?

Unit 19

Students Gabriel Prieto and Parker VanValkenburgh carefully excavated Unit 19, a pit that we placed at the end of the street on which Unit 1 was located (Figure 2.26). Where the street apparently ended there was a distinct rise of the terrain into a mounded area that appeared to be one of the trash piles we had noticed. But we only had been assuming that such mounds were trash piles, so we excavated here to confirm our conjecture.

We were also concerned with issues of the duration of the site occupation and changes in the nature of that occupation through time. By the later weeks of the 2006 field season we

Figure 2.24 Objects on the floor of the Unit 1 house excavations included a scrub brush, a piece of blue cloth, other scraps of cloth, cane fragments, and a fanlike thin metal object (see Chapter 10).

Figure 2.25 A gourd bowl filled with cloth scraps and seeds had been tucked into the corner of a room in Unit 1. (See Figure 15.2 for another view.)

Figure 2.26 Gabriel Prieto, left, and Parker VanValkenburgh, right, during initial excavations of Unit 19. View to the south.

concluded that the artifact-rich trash found outside the church complex perimeter wall likely had been deposited there in the Colonial or early Republican Period. What we had thought was the collapsed roof on the height to the east of the nave was actually, upon closer inspection, more compressed backdirt from old excavations in and around the church complex, and we found no materials that might suggest that the looting had occurred relatively recently; all indications suggested that the looting or mining had taken place in the Colonial or early Republican Period. Furthermore, we found paper throughout our excavation units in both the church and the town, and some of the paper fragments found in town had been cut into fanciful shapes such as a butterfly or a spearhead (see Figure 13.12 in Chapter 13). Since we assumed that clerics would not have freely given documents to the townspeople, we inferred that something had happened to the church, likely an abandonment by its religious occupants, while the townspeople had stayed on. While this may seem like a rather grand interpretive leap, it was based on our changing understanding of the church. Our work on the large piles of midden there and discoveries such as the chicha paddle placed next to the baptistry had led us to start thinking that the religious area of the site had been abandoned but that local folk, presumably the residents of the town, had subsequently mined the collapsed and abandoned church complex. We decided that the excavation of a trash deposit in the town itself might shed some light on these issues of duration and use.

We picked a looter hole on the rise at the (northern) end of the street that ran by our Units 1 and 2 and laid out an excavation unit 1 m wide and 2 m long. As the looter hole provided a profile of the strata buried elsewhere, we could accurately control our excavations to examine the sequence of soil and refuse deposition as we excavated. We began by straightening the

Figure 2.27 Detail of a Venetian-style bead found in the middle of ashes under an inverted gourd found in the trash deposit excavated in Unit 19.

southwestern wall of the unit for better control in our work, although eventually we converted the irregular looter hole into a squared-off unit.

Excavations in Unit 19 were done following natural levels. The deposit consisted of layers of trash of varying composition, some with more shells, cinders, and food remains and others with more layers of straw. Some levels had the remnants of upright posts in the midden; perhaps people had built a structure in the area, or maybe the upright posts were simply a consequence of how trash was disposed of in a particular moment. We could not easily expand the excavations to clarify this situation, as we were near the end of our field season and the work was already very slow because of the great amounts of materials we had to sort in the screens.

It was clear, however, that this was not simply a trash dump but rather a midden that had been an occupational surface at various times during the life of the town. In one of the levels we found an inverted gourd bowl lying on an occupation level. When we removed it we found that the bowl had been filled with a smoldering vegetal material that had not fully burned and that a multicolored, mostly blue millefiori Venetian bead had been placed in the center of the smoldering mass before the gourd had been inverted (Figure 2.27). As there were no signs of burning on the bead, it must have been placed in the bowl just before it was inverted on the ground. It is true that archaeologists are prone to explain odd phenomena as "ritual," but that may in fact be the case in this instance. We found other examples of inverted bowls with ashes in them but without beads, likely also ritual elements that would have gone uninterpreted as such if no bead had been found in this instance.

Figure 2.28   View of the interior of Unit 19 showing the waterborne deposit at bottom. The excavation unit was oriented off the grid to take advantage of the profile of a looter's pit, and the wall in view is thus on the southwestern end of the excavation.

In the last several levels of Unit 19, the quantity of items of everyday life dropped dramatically, with few artifacts amid plant remains and soil. Finally, at a depth of 1.3 m, we encountered a very different kind of deposit (Figure 2.28). It consisted of a fine-grained sediment with no cultural remains in it whatsoever, nor were there any plant parts or other remains that could be interpreted as trash. Upon close inspection we noticed that there were insects embedded in the surface of this layer. We found no colonial-era materials below it, only prehistoric deposits. This layer, then, was physical evidence of the 1578 El Niño. The rains had washed fine sediments into what was then a low-lying area. The damp soils had trapped some insects that commonly hatch in profusion during and immediately after El Niño rains. Seeing the physical manifestation of the 1578 El Niño gave us goose bumps.

The 2007 Field Season
The Church

Field research starts out with general or specific questions to be addressed; as the work proceeds, those questions sometimes are answered and sometimes are not. Sometimes they become irrelevant, and sometimes new questions arise, occasionally on different theoretical planes than the initial ones. The 2006 field season at Magdalena de Cao made us focus more intently on a set of interrelated questions that we had had at the start of our work and which over time came to loom large in our research. These questions had to do with interpreting the archaeological record in relation to changes in the nature of the site occupation, including eventual abandonment of the locale.

The ubiquity of paper fragments was remarkable; we seemed to find them almost everywhere we dug, although we only fully came to this realization in 2006 as both our experiences and the papers themselves accumulated. This was brought home most strikingly in our excavation of Unit 19, where we found paper fragments in the deposits in all but the last few layers of the pit. As mentioned previously, we found paper in both the town and the church, and of course these fragments were highly noticeable in the trash deposits we had encountered first along the perimeter wall of the church compound.

The church walls were standing in only a few places, so it seemed possible that the church had collapsed, and the friars had left without spending much time retrieving items that had been buried. Then again, maybe the collapse occurred much later, after the site had been abandoned for decades. But clearly something had happened that resulted in church materials being accessed by townspeople, and the most logical explanation seemed to be that a catastrophic event had taken place in the church but that the town had survived, and afterward the townspeople had mined the ruins for useful or interesting things there, including paper. The bird dung on the paper we found outside the baptistry indicated that paper had been lying around exposed to the elements, while human excrement on another scrap of paper suggested that not everyone in the town was impressed by the written word.

We know that books and manuscripts were rare and hard to come by in early colonial Peru, and we could easily see that some of the scraps were from liturgical works, some even bearing decorations in gold leaf (see Chapter 13). Even though we could not explain why the ecclesiastics had left behind such presumably valuable materials, we could investigate what had taken place afterward. To do so, though, we needed a clearer idea of the chronology of events in town and church, and especially how they linked together, both archaeologically and historically.

At this point in our research we also realized we needed a better understanding of the way in which the built spaces of the church complex and the town related to one another and also to the huaca, which clearly was a factor in how the church had been oriented in the landscape. We thus began the 2007 field season by clearing the surface sand in the center of the atrium toward its western end, where we had found a patch of original floor surface, taking a reading of its altitude with our total station. We then compared that reading with the height of the plaza floor in the last major construction phase of the huaca, the base of the Prisoner Frieze on its front.[7] We

Figure 2.29 The indigenous-style burial of an adult woman. The trowel points to the north. See Chapter 4 for a discussion.

found them to be the same, allowing us to conclude that the atrium and the western section of the compound more generally had been built directly on the ancient Moche plaza surface.

We also placed two pits to clarify the nature of the atrium walls, one in the middle of the west wall of the atrium and another at the middle of the southern atrium wall with the pit mostly on the exterior of the southern wall face. The pit at the corner revealed that the atrium wall did not continue southward but rather joined the east-west wall. This work uncovered what at first appeared to be an unusual artifact: a wooden swordlike object roughly 1 m in length. Further work in Unit 18 revealed an odd feature that resembled a bin, made of adobe, next to a vertically placed stick. Jaime Jiménez determined that the swordlike object was a hide scraper, and the other features likely also had been used for hide processing. We assumed that this activity occurred after the church compound had been abandoned for religious use.

The excavation outside of the southern atrium wall also yielded interesting finds. In an upper level, but one that we ascertained was the ground surface at the time the atrium was in use, we found a small cloth bundle that contained the remains of a badly decomposed but still recognizable infant. Further work at a slightly lower level revealed the remains of a woman who had been buried in native style: in a flexed position, on her side, and wrapped in a plain cloth outer covering followed by painted textiles (Figure 2.29). The body was fairly well preserved (see Chapter 4), and she was buried with a small bag containing balls of twine and other items associated with textile work (Figure 2.30).

The baby and the woman were buried in prehispanic style and not in the church but close to it, directly next to the atrium wall. Later work identified this area, immediately south of the atrium, as the town cemetery. The area had been very badly looted, and we speculated that

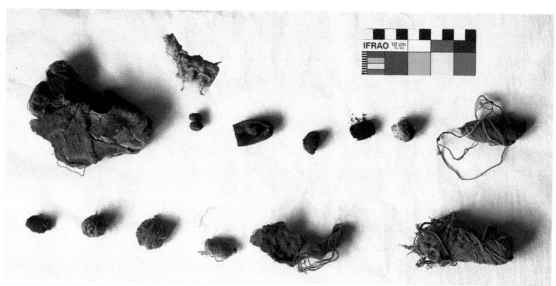

Figure 2.30 Top: the bag that accompanied the woman. It had been sewn shut. Bottom: the contents of the bag included small skeins of thread, possible coloring agents such as seeds, and a wadded-up strip of decorated textile.

the burials of the woman and infant had been spared probably because they were so close to the church walls, an awkward spot in which to excavate.

Another area on which we focused attention was a large looter hole in the northeastern corner of the church nave. As we consistently found great numbers of human bones in the nave every year, we suspected that there were burials under the floor, and so we conducted excavations there, supervised by Catherine Gaither.

The looter hole in the corner of the nave provided an easy way for us to search for them. The hole had been filled with soil over the years, but once it was cleaned out we quickly saw that burials were indeed present below the church floor (see Chapter 4). The interred individuals were lying on their backs in extended positions, following Christian practice, so they were clearly Colonial Period burials even though they were entombed amid the bricks of the prehispanic structure on which the church stood. These individuals were not Spanish but indigenous people who had converted to Catholicism. They likely were town leaders who were accorded the honor of burial in the nave of the church because of the pious works they had carried out on behalf of the community. Some likely were members of a *cofradía* (confraternity), a voluntary organization that was devoted to a particular saint and that carried out good works for their neighbors (see Chapters 4 and 12).

The main excavation work in the church compound in 2007 was on an axis running from behind the bell tower to in front of it and then along the slope of the northern side of the church complex down to the level of the town. As we had a basic understanding of the atrium and nave, which were to the west, and of the looted northeastern section of the complex, this area between them was of importance, as it included a high area immediately behind the bell tower and adjacent to the east nave wall. We also dug a narrow (1 m) trench running from the area immediately in front of the bell tower northward along the edge of the retaining wall that supported the mass of the higher eastern sector of the complex. Although this wall had been exposed to the elements for four centuries, it still retained remnants of fine mud plaster with traces of red paint on it.

Late in the season we came upon some important discoveries that allowed us to reach significant understandings about the site. These discoveries occurred at the opposite ends of the long axial study we were conducting. At the south end, up on the high area behind the bell tower and next to the east nave wall, we uncovered a jumble of adobe bricks whose pattern clearly indicated that there had been a major wall collapse in the area (Figure 2.31).

Within this jumble we found marked adobe bricks, including one that had the word *cho* inscribed into it when the clay was wet—perhaps this was a variant of *Cao*, the name of the town (Figure 2.32; see Chapter 15). The indication of a wall collapse was especially significant in confirming our suspicions that the church building had undergone a catastrophic event with the townspeople subsequently mining the ruins for materials.

We also conducted more work on the northern edge of the church compound, digging a trench 3 m wide that ran from there down to the town area. This was done because we had not been completely satisfied with our search for some kind of formal entrance into the church complex from the town. We simply maintained an assumption that there would have been such a formal entrance, perhaps with a ramp, an arched portal, or another architectural feature on the compound wall. But if a formal entryway ever existed at the site, it was not on the northern edge of the church compound. The trench confirmed that there had been an open, wide entry, because this area contained no traces of the perimeter wall; if there had ever been any posts or pylons defining the ends of the walls or the sides of the entry, the remnants had long vanished (Figure 2.33).

Although we failed to find a ramp or gate, our extension of the trench down the talus slope of the mound was quite revealing in an unexpected way. Beneath the surface dust we found a thick layer of *tara*, running the entire 3 m length of our trench. *Tara* or *taya* is the Quechua word for a small leguminous tree or shrub (*Caesalpinia spinosa* [Molina] Kuntze) that has high tannin content and is cultivated for use in tanning hides. The discovery of great quantities of

Figure 2.31 The wall fall in the eastern church complex. View to the southeast.

Figure 2.32 Detail of some of the adobe bricks. Note the *cho* on the brick at right and markings on other bricks. See Chapter 15 for a discussion of marked adobe bricks.

Figure 2.33 The long trench running from the northern edge of the church compound down to the town area. Photo taken from the church compound looking northwest.

the plant on the slopes of the church complex explained the swordlike hide scraper and other features we had encountered earlier in the field season in Unit 18. It also clarified the final stages of the Colonial Period use of the site: in the last phases of its occupation, after the abandonment of the church complex, the area had been used by goat and sheep herders who kept and slaughtered them and processed their hides nearby. This interpretation was aided by work in the town, as will be discussed shortly.

The long trench also clarified the later history of the prehispanic use of the area. Below the Colonial Period occupation we found large, open-mouthed jars, commonly known in local archaeology as *paicas*, and occupational surfaces next to them that suggested that chicha had been prepared, briefly stored, and consumed in the final prehistoric use of the area, which was immediately outside of the Moche plaza. This pattern also has been found at one of the most extensively excavated Moche sites on the North Coast, San José de Moro (Castillo 2003). There, in front of huacas, in a space equivalent to the one at El Brujo, an extensive cemetery was found that had been used over centuries, mostly by the Moche. Excavations revealed a "party level" (*nivel de fiestas*) with the same features we found. The interpretation of the level at San José de Moro, backed by extensive and intensive studies, is that during Moche times people from the surrounding region came to this site to bury their dead and then returned at various intervals (perhaps on a yearly or seasonal basis) to feast their ancestors by preparing food and chicha, which they also consumed in honor of the dead. Our work strongly suggests that the same pattern took place at El Brujo in prehistory. The import of this for our study of the Colonial Period is that it is very likely that the people who reestablished Magdalena de Cao at El Brujo and continued to live there knew that they were living on top of the burial places of their ancestors and that the church of the foreigners was within the confines of a temple of their ancestors.

The Town

Excavations in Unit 1 continued to expose rooms at the northern end of the compound, and we added another excavation, Unit 2 (Figure 2.34), in the town. This was a large compound south of Unit 1 and separated from it by one of the town streets. The primary reason for excavating another compound was to have a comparison with Unit 1. We chose the area immediately south of Unit 1 for two reasons. First, the area appeared to be higher and in a rectangular form, as if there might be a prehispanic platform extending off Montículo 3, which was due west. We wondered whether the colonial occupation had built a compound directly on top of a prehispanic platform, and if so, how the structures may have related to each other.

Another important reason for choosing this location was the relatively light amount of straw and grasses in surface dust and upper stratigraphic levels. The great quantities of this material in Unit 1 impeded us from clearing the entire compound, as it would have consumed too much labor and time. In Unit 2, by contrast, there appeared to be less of this material, and the general outlines of the rooms and other features could be seen without much excavation. Our work bore out this assessment, and much of the compound with its various features was well documented, especially thanks to Parker VanValkenburgh, who was in charge of the excavations there. Although the amount of straw was less in Unit 2 than in Unit 1, it still had to be removed. This material was a combination of bedding and fodder from the later occupation of the site, when, we inferred, sheep and goat herding was the main activity of the villagers, and the remains of insulation of the quincha houses. As straw was being excavated along one

Figure 2.34   Unit 2 in early excavation. Note the smaller rooms defined by the cane stumps close to the viewer. View to the northeast.

quincha wall in Unit 2, a worker found a folding knife with an iron or steel blade and an intricately carved wooden handle (see Figure 10.11, Chapter 10).

Once the straw was removed, details of the compound began to come to light. On the south side of its southeastern corner was a single entryway—a fairly elaborate one, with spaces in front and immediately inside that might have imparted a sense of formality to visitors entering and leaving, despite the entry being made of humble quincha. The short wall of the entry on the compound interior also defined the first of three adjoining rooms or spaces that ran along the compound's southern wall. This first room, closest to the entry, was a kitchen, an interpretation based on ashes, carbon, and a hearth found there; the room probably had an open side facing into the compound. The other two rooms had fewer features that might indicate their uses. One or both could have been for sleeping or storage.

The majority of the space in the compound was in the form of a large patio. Although looting had been fairly intense in this area, there were clear indications that large ceramic vessels had been buried in the ground to serve as storage. These vessels had been relatively close to the kitchen and other rooms and absent to the north and west of them. There also were lenses of ash, cinders, and different soils, indicating that many activities took place in the courtyard—a common practice in farming communities, especially in mild climates. In addition to storage and processing of food, these activities probably included the repair of fishing and farming equipment and the penning of animals.

Although Unit 2 was closer to the church compound and the huaca, it appeared to be a poorer household than Unit 1. Fewer metal objects, imported porcelains, and other items of the colonial economy were found in it.[8] It might be noteworthy that although we found a small, hand-carved wooden cross and most of a copper alloy crucifix pendant in Unit 1, few clearly Christian items were found in Unit 2.

Excavation on the southeastern edge of what appeared to be the platform of Unit 2 failed to reveal clear signs of a prehispanic or colonial constructed platform: we found no features that showed deliberate construction to raise up the area from the original ground surface. We did, however, find evidence of a colored soil below the colonial occupation, which suggested that there may be prehispanic burials below Unit 2. The possibility that the area was part of a prehistoric burial platform has not been completely eliminated.

The plans of reducciones published in colonial times were highly specific about where the church, plaza, and the residences of various functionaries were to be located. The residence of the highest-ranking native resident (*curaca* in Quechua) was supposed to be located directly across the plaza from the church. As we now knew both the location of the entrance to the compound and the church nave, we followed a line from that access across the plaza and placed an excavation unit at the first evidence of quincha on the north side of the plaza. Our excavation unit there was relatively small, 3×3 m, but it was where the entrance to the curaca's house should have been. Excavation there did reveal a house, but the work we carried out revealed no features of the structure that suggested it was significantly different from other houses in terms of the materials used or the elaboration or ornamentation of the entrance facing the plaza. Further work in the area might have located a house suggesting higher than normal status, but we decided that what we had done in the area was sufficient to indicate that Magdalena did not always follow the strictures of reducción plans dictated from far away.

Figure 2.35
The leather object
found in Unit 26.

There was a small mound, measuring only about 3 m in diameter, situated on the corner of the supposed platform and outside of Unit 2. We excavated it (Unit 26) and found the bottom of a small rectangular (4 × 6 m) structure. Few artifacts were associated with this structure, although a thick white leather cutout in the form of a fleur-de-lis was recovered (Figure 2.35). The artifact resembles a decorative piece of a bandolier or other piece of military dress. Given this item and the fact that the structure appeared too small to be a storage shed, we speculated that it might have been a sentry post, watchtower, or similar facility. This is not a very satisfactory inference, however. If such a guard post had been deemed necessary, whether to express control over the villagers or to guard against intruders from the sea, it would have been more logical to establish it on top of nearby Montículo 3, where it would have commanded a much better view in all directions. Also, in general, there are few signs of a military presence at the site.

The 2008 Field Season
The Church

The 2008 field season was the last period of major excavation work at Magdalena de Cao. Catherine Gaither continued to excavate burials below the floor of the church, shifting to a looter's pit in the northwest corner of the nave. Other than the subfloor burials, the atrium, nave, baptistry, and sacristy had all been fairly well documented at this point, so we decided to turn our attention to a more detailed look at the eastern sector of the church complex. Our

Figure 2.36 Aerial photograph of 2007 excavations in the eastern sector of the church complex. 1. Subfloor burials on west side of nave entrance; 2. Subfloor burials on east side of nave entrance (backfilled); 3. Bell tower remains; 4. Room with long bench; 5. Area of heat-reddened floor; 6. Milling station patio; 7. Kitchen hearth; 8. Passageway; 9. European-style ovens; 10. Unexcavated baulk. The wall fall had covered all of 5 and 6.

2005 work had followed the compound perimeter wall and investigated places on the interior of this area, but mostly in its far eastern and central sectors. The work we had done to the south of the bell tower, however, strongly suggested that the area immediately to the east of the nave was much better preserved than the location in which we had worked in 2005. This turned out to be quite true (Figure 2.36).

There were several well-preserved rooms and spaces running parallel to the church from just behind the bell tower to about halfway down the nave. In the northwestern part of this complex was a rectangular room with a long adobe bench built into its eastern wall (Figure 2.37). The underside of this bench, which presumably would have been flat when first built, was eroded into a concavity, most likely undercut by the heels of restless feet. This, then, may have been a schoolroom, though whether for novitiates or children is uncertain. We have evidence in the form of scraps of paper with writing practice on them that more than one person learned to write at Magdalena; perhaps it was in this room that such lessons were given and learned.

Figure 2.37   The bench in a room in the northwest area of the eastern sector of the church complex. The patch behind it covered by a thin layer of soil is the heat-reddened floor.

A food preparation area was at the southern end of the room complex. Closest to the nave wall was a room with a small kitchen to its east. A large hearth had been made of adobe bricks stood on end to serve as pot stands. There was a great amount of charcoal and ash throughout this area, suggesting that it was the main kitchen for the occupants of the complex. Two large European-style ovens were east of the kitchen but accessible from it. We found a thin wooden stick, about 1 m long, set to run across the passageway between the kitchen and the ovens. The stick was a symbolic barrier rather than a physical one, and examples of this device have been found at prehistoric sites. Perhaps this one was meant to warn people not to disturb the cook. One of the domed ovens was slightly larger than the other, but both were built against a wall running east-west that formed the boundary of this part of the complex. These ovens were not enclosed within a room but could be accessed from a patio to the east and north (as best could be determined, given looting activities there).

North of the bakery and thus in the center-east of the complex was a large space that may have been an open-air patio, although it is hard to assess how high the surrounding walls may have risen and where roofs were located. The exact size of the patio is undetermined because we left a large baulk of unexcavated materials at its southern end. The patio was at about 5 m in width and at least double that in length. More likely it extended farther south for a length of about 20 m.

A milling station on the interior west wall of the patio consisted of a low adobe bench or platform, 20 cm in height (Figure 2.38). The surface of a hard, flat passive grinding stone, known as a *batán* in Peru, was flush with the top of the adobe bench, and an active grinding stone of the "rocker" variety still rested on its surface. The rocker-grinder was a large quartzite

Figure 2.38 The milling station as found, view from above. The blue-colored rectangular object is a passive grinding stone, a batán, embedded in an adobe surround. The active grinding stone and wooden objects were found as seen. Note the large whale vertebra at the upper end of the adobe surround, which served as a seat. Top of the photograph is to the east.

cobble; the batán was of a different, harder stone. As we did not want to destroy the adobe platform in which the passive stone was set, however, we were not able to examine this element in great detail. The adobe platform that held the grinding stones continued out from this workstation to surround a large whale vertebra that served as the seat for the person working at grinding. To the south of the grinding station but within easy reach of someone working at it was a small gourd plate, and farther along the wall was a piece of cut and split cane. These items may have been associated with the last person to sit on the whale vertebra and grind grain, probably maize.

The patio likely was a central communal space and place of transit between the bakery and kitchen, to the south, and the classroom, to the north. We did not have enough time or resources to extend our excavations farther east, but our impression was that this might have been a large courtyard; no architecture was visible or hinted at from surface remains. There were indications of structures east of the ovens, and these likely were built onto the southern perimeter wall of the church compound. These remains were in a poor state of preservation, as previously determined, but their appearance suggests they may have been storage sheds or similar facilities.

Immediately to the north of the patio with the grinding station was a great pile of fallen adobe bricks that we had probed in the previous field season and where we had found marked bricks. We now opened up this area to find a large pile of adobe bricks; the arrangement indicated that they were all part of a collapsed wall, although the date of its collapse could not be ascertained. The orientation of the bricks suggested that the wall had been to the south or west of the pile and thus either a barrier at the north end of the grinding patio or, more likely, part of the nave wall to the west. Upon removing the bricks we came upon a large, well-made puddled adobe floor that showed intensive signs of burning: a large, bright red stain more than 2 m in diameter and ash on the floor's surface. It seems unlikely that the burning episode took place during the active use of the church compound. Consequently, we infer that the wall collapsed after the fire and thus after the abandonment of the site by the friars. As noted earlier in this chapter, when Antonio Raimondi visited the site in the late nineteenth century he reported many walls still standing, including some at the south end of the nave, that are not known from living memory, so it is quite possible that the wall represented by the bricks collapsed after his visit.

We investigated two other areas in the church compound before the 2008 field season was finished. The first investigation consisted of a systematic surface collection in a rectangular area defined by the southern wall of the atrium and the western wall of the nave—more generally, the area just west of the main church building. This area was where the infant and woman buried in native style had been found outside but next to the southern atrium wall. We traversed this area many times during the day walking to and from the site offices and laboratories to the nave and other compound areas under study, and Quilter noticed that there were many fragments of cloth just below the surface dust. Furthermore, it was an area where human bones constantly were coming to the surface. During our surface collection we uncovered a substantial number of large textiles, many of which were decorated with painted designs and numerous human bones. The textiles were burial shrouds (see Figures 15.16 and 15.17, Chapter 15) and the area was the town cemetery.

In the last week of the 2008 field season, as work was winding down throughout the site, Quilter decided that it would be worthwhile to place a small excavation unit abutting the exterior of the church compound perimeter wall, at the northwest corner of the compound. Our research for the prior two years had concentrated on defining architectural features in the church. As we knew that the area immediately outside the perimeter wall was particularly rich in artifacts, an excavation there would increase our sample of the material culture of the church residents. This work yielded many artifacts of interest, the most important of which was a complete letter regarding a financial transaction (see Figure 13.11, Chapter 13). The letter had been later folded and its reverse side used to write down the words for basic numbers in a language that may be Quingnam, a native tongue spoken over a great area of the North Coast and about which we know very little at present. This find was made on the last day of excavations.

The Town

Work continued in Unit 2, as described in the discussion of the 2007 field season. Work in Unit 1 was done as well. We followed the outer walls of Unit 1 and confirmed that it was a large compound of roughly the same size as Unit 2, but we did not clear the entire area down to an occupation level.

When the Unit 1 excavation team was available for new work, we searched for another compound in a different area of the town, seeking a comparison to the two adjacent units on the western side of the plaza. We decided on a compound located on the long east-west street that bordered the northern side of the plaza, though this compound was not on the plaza itself

Figure 2.39 Aerial photograph of Unit 28 early excavations. The pit at right is the kitchen area. The central pit was aligned correctly to the site grid at a later stage of work.

but farther east. This area had been noted previously and given the designation of Unit 28 (Figures 2.39 and 2.40).

Unit 28 offered the promise of yielding good data, for two reasons. First, there was relatively little sign of looting, with only a few looter holes visible at the surface (although sometimes superficial appearances can be deceiving). Second, there appeared to be relatively light

Figure 2.40   Adobe walls in the expanded central excavation unit shown in Figure 2.39. The red and white arrow at left points northward.

amounts of straw in the upper layers of the area, suggesting that we could get to early Colonial Period occupation levels relatively efficiently. We therefore laid out a series of excavation units and began work.

The overall form of the compound followed the same plan as Units 1 and 2, with rooms and activity areas on its southern and eastern sides. Perhaps because it was less looted, we found many more adobe walls in Unit 28 than in the other two units. We did not get to excavate very deep in these spaces, however, as our time was running out. On a floor in a central room, however, we encountered several interesting objects. These included a fragment of an indigenous-style textile, another piece of indigenous-style fabric in the form of a tassel, two large finger rings, and the best-preserved playing card that we had encountered to date.

We also found a number of jars sunk into a puddled adobe floor in what appeared to be a kitchen area on the east side of the compound (see Figure 3.6, Chapter 3). Some of these jars still had gourd bowl covers and rags stuffed into their mouths, so the chance of finding undisturbed residues of their contents was high. The temptation to remove the coverings and take samples was great, but we chose to close the excavation unit and wait until we could return to work on these remains with care.

Research in 2009–2013

No fieldwork was conducted from 2009 through 2011, as our efforts were focused on laboratory analyses. There were still a number of issues remaining that could only be cleared up with further excavations, however, so in 2012 we conducted a short field season to address them.

The Church

Although we believed that we understood most of the church compound fairly well at this point, we were still uncertain about features on its southern side. There were three matters to be addressed. First, as we had determined that the space south of the atrium and west of the nave was the town cemetery, we wanted to see if a wall had enclosed it. Second, we had never discovered a clear southern limit of the church complex, in general, so we wished to find it if one was present. Third, Jaime Jiménez, co–field director of the project, suspected that there might have been a ramp on the southeastern side of the complex as a rear entrance to it, and we wanted to explore this possibility.

The most efficient way to approach the issue of the town cemetery wall was to place a fairly large excavation unit at the spot likely to have been the corner of the rectangular cemetery area. By extending the line of the western wall of the atrium to the south and then running a line west from the southern end of the nave, we identified where the corner likely would be located. This location was also at the southwestern limit of the area in which we had found the great concentration of human bones and shrouds on the ground surface.

We found no perimeter walls for either the cemetery or the complex in this area. Instead, we came across the remains of poorly preserved cane and fiber structures, perhaps windbreaks or small huts. These likely are the remains of the camps of goat herders who used the area on a short-term basis after the church and, probably, the town had been abandoned.

Regarding the southern limit of the church complex, we again assumed that a wall might have run from the southern end of the nave or the sacristy eastward to join with a north-south perimeter wall. If the remains of such a wall were present, a north-south trench (1×20 m) laid across the area should have uncovered it. This trench revealed a large section of adobe bricks but no wall foundations. It is likely that the bricks are part of a collapsed wall oriented in a different direction not found in our narrow trench. In short, there was no clear evidence of a perimeter wall.

To explore the question of whether there was a ramp as a rear entrance, we laid a 2×15 m east-west trench from the eastern edge of the church complex across the likely route of a ramp. This excavation did encounter a double-coursed adobe wall that ran north-south and that could have been a significant wall in defining the church complex boundary. A smoothly plastered surface on the eastern side of the wall also could have been part of a ramp. Two 10×2 m trenches running north-south were placed to follow this wall, and work in them revealed a rather complicated building sequence that included clearly prehistoric walls and other features below and adjacent to the first discovery (Figure 2.41). This work was extensive, but it complicated our view so much that we are uncertain if the double-coursed wall first found is colonial or earlier in date. Human remains and artifacts in a deep pit next to the wall clearly dated to the Lambayeque culture, but there were no artifacts associated with the large wall to date it.

The scale of the building complex is so large that it would have taken another set of very large trenches placed next to the other excavations to uncover, with luck, diagnostic artifacts that would securely date the walls or to clear a space large enough to definitively identify the presence of a ramp. Unfortunately, however, by this point our field season was at its end, so we never could fully determine if a ramp was present or not. We did have a much better idea of the nature and history of the town and the church complex than when we started, however (Figure 2.42).

Figure 2.41 Composite photograph of the complex walls uncovered in our search for a ramp on the southeastern side of the church complex. North is to the viewer's right.

The Town

Research in the town in 2012 was restricted to expanding excavations in Unit 28 and removing the buried jars found there in 2008 so that their contents could be analyzed and identified. The four vessels in the northeastern sector of the excavation were cleared and the area around them carefully excavated before they were removed. Two jars still had gourd bowl lids on them; a third vessel was not ceramic but rather a large gourd (Figure 2.42; see also Chapter 3). The area in which the jars were found was a kitchen, as large patches of ashes and cinders were found around the vessels. Samples were taken of both the contents of the vessels and the ash deposits on the floor surrounding them. The vessels were then removed and they and the samples were sent to the Arqueobios laboratory at the National University in Trujillo for further analysis. Details of the results of those studies are presented in Chapter 3, but it is worth noting here that the remains consisted mostly of basic food staples: fish, maize, manioc, and achira.

This was the last fieldwork carried out at Magdalena de Cao in the project reported in this book. Since that time laboratory work has continued, and the site, including the prehistoric sector, has been developed for tourism, with pathways and interpretive signs.

Time and Change at Magdalena de Cao

Chronological control of events is critical to archaeological and historical work. Each discipline (and its subdisciplines) faces unique challenges in working out chronologies. Furthermore, historical archaeology is very different from prehistoric archaeology. A century or two is barely a consideration for many prehistoric archaeological projects, but for the historical period such a span is tremendous. Indeed, Peru saw radical changes in economics, politics, and society over periods of less than 100 years. How to successfully work with chronologies of this scale as we sought to understand what happened at Magdalena de Cao became one of our greatest challenges.

Figure 2.42   Photo montage of the main areas of the central church complex.

Though we know nothing of the location or occupation of the first Magdalena, the date of the establishment of Magdalena at El Brujo is secure. We are confident that the Magdalena we excavated was established in 1578. There is no place anywhere else in the Chicama Valley that matches the features of the refuge place as described by Fray Bartolomé de Vargas in his account of the disasters brought on by the El Niño that year. But it is hard to discern the changes that took place at the site during its occupation. We might assume that the refugee community was impoverished and so built only rudimentary shelters at first. We do not know how quickly structures were built for long-term residence, nor do we know when building the church complex was initiated. The church at Mansiche, on the main highway from Trujillo to Chan Chan and northward, shares many architectural features with the Magdalena nave; we know that its construction dates to the late sixteenth century, and thus we might assume that the Magdalena building dates to the same time.

Radiocarbon dating of artifacts from Magdalena has proved of little value for the most part. Early in the project, in 2006, we dated cane, carbon, and similar materials from the town and tobacco from cigarettes rolled in ecclesiastical papers (probably taken from the church after its collapse; see Chapter 13), but the date ranges stretched well into prehistory, and these remains definitely were not prehistoric.[9] We have had better luck with dates taken from burials under the nave of the church, thanks to very careful cleaning and long counting periods performed by Douglas Kennett, then of the Pennsylvania State University (see Chapter 5). These dates strongly suggest that the burials were interred in the first third of the seventeenth century, a dating that conforms to the inferences made from other archaeological remains as well as historical documents.

Historical documents have provided a better understanding of the Magdalena occupation than has archaeology (see Chapter 12). Those documents indicate that while the population diminished in size over the years, Magdalena was occupied until well into the eighteenth century and likely was not completely abandoned until 1760 or thereabouts.

Based on the weight of evidence, we can say that the initial occupation of 1578 consisted of adobe houses lived in by people who followed a mixed subsistence strategy highly dependent on fish and basic Andean crops, especially manioc. Over time, Old World food products such as sheep and goats and a great range of non-Andean plants were introduced. The community was brought into the world economy through taxation (including producing cloth as tax payment) and through consumption of European products (including commodities and religious indulgences). Asian porcelains and exotic textiles also were sought and acquired by the Magdaleneros. We have little comparative information by which to judge, but the impression given by the data is that Magdalena may have prospered for a while, likely from the last two decades of the sixteenth century into the first three decades or so of the seventeenth century.

A significant event in the life of the community was the collapse of the church nave. Research in the nave indicates that the region may have suffered the effects of earthquakes more than once, but a devastating event took place in the seventeenth century. Historical records note that a powerful earthquake struck the North Coast in 1619, supposedly flattening every adobe structure in the region. This seems too early to have caused the church collapse in Magdalena, however, as the dates for the nave burials are later than this. Furthermore, fragments of documents found in in the church complex have dates later than 1619, indicating that the religious community was still in residence there, perhaps as late as 1650. It is possible that the church was damaged by the 1619 event but rebuilt or partly rebuilt afterward and that the Dominicans did not finally leave Magdalena until sometime in the last half of the seventeenth century. If that is the case, however, then some other disaster may have been responsible for the collapse that trapped documents and other materials in the ruins of the church. There was a very large earthquake that mostly affected central Peru in 1690, but there is no record of significant damage from it to North Coast communities.

The archaeological record in the town tells a somewhat different story than the historical documents. There is a consistent depositional sequence in the stratigraphy of the site that serves as the primary source for interpretations. Beginning from the lowest levels, the earliest Colonial Period occupation rests directly on a prehistoric land surface that had had little time to accumulate surface dust on top of it. Several centimeters of accumulated debris, melted adobe, and other remains represent the daily lives of the Magdaleneros over some undetermined time.

Above the household layer but sometimes cutting down into it is another stratum composed of white ashes and black cinders, often in the form of wide but shallow basins. These are the remains of large fire pits, possibly used in hide processing. Above this but blended into it is the dense deposit of straw, cane, and sheep and goat dung with a cap of the relatively recent windblown sand and soil of the modern land surface. For the first few years of the project we interpreted this sequence as representing the initial refugee community and the immediately succeeding generations, followed by a separate community of sheep and goat herders who occupied the site after the townspeople reestablished themselves in modern Magdalena. As work continued, however, we became less sure of this interpretation. It may be that the deposits represent the same community over generations in which they gradually shifted their activities from a diversified subsistence to one specialized in pastoralism.

Horizontal stratigraphy is very likely present at Magdalena. When the large size of the archaeological deposits is compared with the population sizes reported at various times in the past, it seems very likely that houses in some sectors were abandoned over time and not reoccupied. It is thus quite possible that these older residences were used for penning goats and sheep as the community's fortunes and activities changed. Probably in the very latest phases of the colonial occupation there were few people living at the site, and that may be when the abandoned church compound was used for processing goat hides for markets in Trujillo and beyond, as suggested by some of the features found in our excavations.

Having discussed the features of the town and church complex in some detail, it is worth reflecting on what life was like on a day-to-day basis in a general sense. Perhaps the most striking feature concerning Magdalena de Cao is that the group that came there as refugees in 1578 stayed and prospered for two centuries. Why did they choose to stay there, rather than return to the original town site (wherever it may have been) or settle elsewhere?

The El Brujo terrace was close to both sandy and pebbled beaches and thus to fishing and mollusk resources. To the north, a large wetland of fresh-to-brackish water would have offered various kinds of fauna and flora.[10] To the east good agricultural land was present, and to the south was a branch of the Chicama River. All these were good resources. But life on the terrace is not comfortable. The winds are nearly constant and can be fierce in the afternoons. It is cold and damp in the winter and hot in the summer. Although moistening the surface to form a hard caliche (calcium carbonate) layer can reduce the dust, that crust is easily disturbed, so the winds can produce small but irritating dust storms. There are many more places to live than this desolate landscape. Modern Magdalena de Cao, for example, is a mere 4 km away; it is only slightly more inland, but there the winds are less fierce and the environment more pleasant.

Why the Magdaleneros stayed so long at El Brujo is therefore something of a mystery. There seem to be two possible explanations. The first, a practical one, is that there was no place else to move because the colonial system of distributing people across the landscape in reducciones was not easily changed once it was established. And, the church complex was apparently built fairly soon after the refugee community arrived, which would have involved a considerable investment. This explanation is not entirely satisfactory, however, because the community persisted at the site for more than a generation after the church collapsed.

Another reason the community may have stayed on involves the very landscape, which appears to us today as desolate and difficult but which was a sacred place to indigenous people.

The huacas of the ancestors were visible in almost every direction in which the people turned, and those mounds would have linked the community to the past.

Eventually, of course, the community did abandon the El Brujo terrace and moved to modern Magdalena. The main impetus for the move appears to have been one that historians have often told us of: the complete breakdown of ancient management systems that had distributed water equitably, with the result that communities such as Magdalena, at the end of the irrigation systems, could no longer sustain themselves. But if this was the primary reason, why did the Magdaleneros move a mere 4 km away to a locale not that different in terms of access to water?

The archaeological and historical research we have carried out at the site has offered us a new and fascinating view into the story of a community in colonial Peru. We have been able to contribute to a richer, more detailed and nuanced picture of life in one place in a larger colonial world. At the same time, we remain ignorant of the answers to some fundamental questions about Magdalena de Cao and its residents. Magdalena was not a reducción in the classic sense of the term. It began as a refugee community that then became a permanent settlement for two centuries. It does not appear to have been built on a plan that conformed fully to the edicts of planners and administrators in Spain or even Lima. So we know from the start that Magdalena is not typical, yet some of the ideas, daily practices, and material culture of the Magdaleneros, both the indigenous forms and foreign imports, likely were shared across a wide geographic region and for a long period of time, even as those cultural elements were changing in the face of new circumstances. Our work at Magdalena and this book reflect our own evolving understandings.

NOTES

1 The phrase he uses is "cerros artificiales llamados Huacas."

2 It is perhaps worth mentioning that in June 1988 Quilter visited the El Brujo complex, mostly to see Huaca Prieta, in the company of Richard L. Burger, Lucy Salazar, and Segundo Vasquez, a native Magdalenero. The Huaca Cortada at that time was known as Huaca Blanca and thought to be Lambayeque. We did not stop to look at the colonial site.

3 To maximize our time in the field, Quilter sent a map of planned excavation units prior to the arrival of the U.S. contingent. The pits were set up by Peruvian workers before work began. We always proposed more pits than were excavated; given our limited time, we chose some pits for excavation over others. The numbering of units excavated thus does not run in sequence. For example, the three major house structures we investigated in the town were Units 1, 2, and 28, while other numbered pits received less work or were left untouched. Numbers sometimes were duplicated in church and town, but these were distinguished by "P," for pueblo (town), and "I," for iglesia (church). Work in the same unit that carried over two or more field seasons was designated with a year code. So, for example, "P-01-06" and "P-01-07" refer to work in Unit 1 in the town in 2006 and 2007, respectively. We excavated in natural levels: *capas* are thick strata usually subdivided into smaller levels.

4 Quilter once remarked to a worker about the quantity of bones that regularly came to the surface at El Brujo. "Oh yes," he replied, "but there used to be many more before the Wiese project began." "Oh? What happened to them?" "One day a big truck came and collected all of the bones to take to feed to pigs to fatten them up for sale."

5 Adobe walls wick even low amounts of moisture from the ground. Cycles of crystallization and decrystallization of salt as moisture levels change in the adobe deteriorate the wall at the bottom and may lead to the eventual collapse of the wall.

6 In some large churches the sacristy, for the keeping of chalices, patens, and other items used for worship, is a separate room from the vestry, where the priest's robes were kept, but in many other churches the

two functions are combined in a single room. It is likely that at Magdalena the room in question served both functions. When a church faces east, the sacristy is usually on the church's northern side. Because Magdalena faces south, the sacristy is on the eastern side but retains its relationship relative to the sanctuary.

7 Visitors to the Huaca Cao Viejo today stand on a floor level below the final construction phase and look up at the Prisoner Frieze. When the huaca was in use, the feet of anyone in the plaza would have been at the same level as the feet of the depicted prisoners, or slightly lower.

8 This is an impression. A detailed study to compare the material goods of the two units remains to be done.

9 Eight radiocarbon samples were taken of various materials from different areas of the town. Dates ranged from 500 ± 40 B.P. (Beta-223738) with a 2-sigma calibration of A.D. 1400–1450 for Sample 2, carbon from a Colonial Period hearth in Unit 19, to 120 ± 40 B.P. (Beta-224740), subjected to conventional radiocarbon dating (non-AMS) for a 2-sigma calibration of A.D. 1660–1960 for an AMS assay of a fragment of a reed mat from Level 13, also in Unit 19. Other dates were:

> Beta-209244, cane from colonial town, 430 ± 50 B.P.
> Beta-224736, cane from colonial town, 410 ± 40 B.P.
> Beta-224737, vine from Level 10, Unit 19, 170 ± 40 B.P. (AMS)
> Beta-224739, carbon from Element L, Level 11, Unit 19, 430 ± 50 B.P.
> Beta-224735, wood from collapsed baptistry roof, 300 ± 30 B.P.

The eighth date was carried out on the African cranium by Douglas Kennett and is reported in detail in Chapter 5. The dates for the tobacco in cigarettes are reported in Chapter 13.

10 Because the water table is high on the coast of Peru, freshwater ponds and wetlands are fairly common. According to Segundo Vasquez, archaeologist and a native son of the modern Magdalena de Cao, the wetland was still present in the 1980s. The reasons for its demise are not known; its disappearance may be due to coastal uplift or, perhaps more likely, the pumping of groundwater for irrigating cane fields.

REFERENCES CITED

Castillo, Luis Jaime
   2003 Los últimos mochicas en Jequetepeque. In *Moche: hacia el final del milenio* Vol. 2, edited by Santiago Uceda and Elías Mujica, pp. 65–123. Lima: Pontificia Universidad Católica del Perú and Universidad Nacional de Trujillo.

Cummins, Tom
   2002 Forms of Andean Colonial Towns, Free Will, and Marriage. In *The Archaeology of Colonialism*, edited by Claire L. Lyons and John K. Papadopoulos, pp. 199–240. Los Angeles: Getty Research Institute.

Deetz, James
   1977 *In Small Things Forgotten: The Archaeology of Early American Life*. Garden City, NY: Anchor Press/Doubleday.

Mujica, Elias (editor)
   2007 *El Brujo: Huaca Cao, centro ceremonial moche en el Valle de Chicama/Huaca Cao, a Moche Ceremonial Center in the Chicama Valley*. Lima: Fundación Wiese.

Quilter, Jeffrey, Régulo Franco Jordán, César Gálvez Mora, William Doonan, Catherine Gaither, Victor Vásquez Sánchez, Teresa Rosales Tham, Jaime Jiménez Saldaña, Hal Starratt, and Michele L. Koons
   2012 The Well and the Huaca: Ceremony, Chronology, and Culture Change at Huaca Cao Viejo, Chicama Valley, Peru. *Andean Past* 10:101–132.

Raimondi, Antonio

    1942 *Notas de viajes para su obra "El Perú"* Vol. 1. Lima: Torres Aguiere.

VanValkenburgh, Nathaniel Parker

    2012 Building Subjects: Landscapes of Forced Resettlement in the Zaña and Chamán Valleys, Peru, 16th and 17th Centuries, C.E. Unpublished Ph.D. dissertation, Department of Anthropology, Harvard University.

3

Plants and Animals

Victor Vásquez Sánchez, Teresa Rosales Tham,
and Jeffrey Quilter

HOW PEOPLE ACQUIRED, processed, and consumed food and other essentials for survival is of chief concern to archaeologists investigating past societies. For Colonial Period Peru the issue is particularly interesting because the arrival of Europeans brought new foods and foodways and affected old ones. Today, Peruvian cuisine is achieving international status for its distinctiveness and innovation, not only combining European foods with Andean ones but also blending the skills and tastes of Andean, African, Asian, and European cooks and consumers. These trends are not new; they began early in the Colonial Period. If hybridity and syncretism are important research concerns, then no better case study can be found for them than food.

Because procuring food is so essential, there are few chapters in this book that do not interrelate with this one. For the sake of brevity, here we will mostly review the plant and animal remains found at Magdalena de Cao and point to some challenges to interpreting them. We will look at several different data sets, beginning with artifacts and facilities uncovered in excavations and continuing with analysis of both large-scale residues of plants and animals and micro-remains. A separate section will be devoted to a well-preserved storage and cooking area in Unit 28.

Artifacts and Facilities

Some tools for procuring or processing foods are discussed in other chapters, such as those on ceramics (Chapters 8 and 9) and metals (Chapter 10). In general, agricultural and other tools were not present in high numbers in our collections, perhaps because they were valuable and thus carefully kept, reused, or recycled rather than being discarded. Sticks of various sizes that could have been used for a variety of purposes are present, but there are no clear examples of Andean foot plows or European-style agricultural tools.

Distinct equipment for food procurement is present in the form of fishing net fragments, of which there were surprisingly few examples. Only nine fragments of net were found in the

Figure 3.1
A complete net bag
found in Unit 1.

entire Magdalena assemblage. The only complete net was a bag that could have been used for carrying small to medium objects (Figure 3.1). Of the remaining eight fragments, two likely were not from fishing nets, while the rest consisted of two each of small, medium, and large meshes, suggesting that a variety of different kinds of fish were taken. Given that fish were a significant portion of the diet, as will be discussed later in this chapter, the relatively low numbers of net fragments may be a result of careful conservation of nets, with few discards entering trash disposal areas. Only two net weights were found at Magdalena. One of them, a surface find, appears to have been later used as a chopper. Nets likely were abundant, however, as we found several pointed wooden instruments probably used for net repair.

Stone tools are not common in our collections. Nevertheless, it is quite likely that unmodified flakes or simple core tools were used for some activities. For a variety of reasons, including the relative paucity of finished stone tools on the coast of Peru after the Preceramic Period, workers tend not to be trained in identifying simple stone tools, so it is likely that many were not collected during excavations. As discussed in Chapter 10, metal knives, tweezers, and the like were used, although access to steel cutting tools appears to have been relatively low.

Grinding stones were not commonly identified and retrieved for study. Large cobbles that could have been used as active grinding stones also served as foundations for adobe walls. Due to looting activities, some such cobbles can be found on the El Brujo terrace surface, but often not in close or clear association with house compounds. It is highly likely that every house compound had two or more grinding stations, each with an active grinding stone and a passive grinding stone, when the area was occupied. We likely overlooked some grinding stones, while others may have been removed when the town population relocated to modern-day Magdalena. The best example of grinding stones is that found in the church compound: an active rocker stone still lying in place on top of a passive grinding stone (a batán) that had been set into an adobe frame on the ground with a whale vertebra for a seat (see Figure 2.38 in Chapter 2).

Objects for processing foods and for household maintenance are more numerous than implements that would have been taken to fields or sea (Figures 3.2 and 3.3). The largest such item was a wooden paddle for making chicha, found placed alongside the western outer wall of the baptistry (Figure 2.22 in Chapter 2). It appears to have split vertically, as it is missing half of the distal section, which would have stirred the chicha mix. Presumably the paddle would have still been serviceable, however, and the smoothed and rounded edge of the break suggests that it continued in use, so it is interesting to consider whether the paddle was placed next to the church because it was no longer thought of as useful or if it was deliberately decommissioned. A large saberlike wooden implement found in direct association with a facility built on the edge of the western compound wall was used to scrape hides in the late occupation era or after the town was abandoned.

Wooden objects with short handles and rounded, mushroom-shaped heads were fairly common in the town, as we recovered several of them. These may have been pestles or mauls used for mashing relatively small quantities of food such as spices; analyses of any residues on them remain to be done. Many other objects that appear to have been elements of multipart tools are common at the site as well; most of these cannot be identified, although one complete example may have been a bola, useful in catching birds in flocks.

Figure 3.2
A scrub brush found in Unit 1, length ~15 cm (see also Figure 2.24).

Figure 3.3 A small hand broom found in Unit 1, length ~30 cm.

We found hundreds of gourd fragments and dozens of gourd containers during our excavations (see Chapter 15). Shallow gourd bowls were used for a wide variety of purposes and were the everyday wares for eating stews and soups as well as drinking. Ceramics served these purposes too, and also were used for the storage of food and drink.

Transportation equipment was relatively uncommon in our assemblage. Baskets tend not to be found widely in the Andes, with the use of textiles and nets (such as the bag noted earlier) more favored. One example of a sling, probably for transporting bulky dry materials such as firewood, was recovered from Magdalena.

Cooking areas in house compounds were located in or near roofed structures such as light ramadas that offered shade and shelter from wind and damp. This is mostly inferred because we did not encounter well-defined kitchen areas in either Units 1 or 2. An exception was Unit 28, as will be discussed later in this chapter.

We found a cooking and food preparation area in the church in the southwest corner of the compound to the east of the nave. This was quite close to the grinding station already mentioned (see Chapter 2).

We found two dome-shaped ovens outside the kitchen arranged along the back wall of this area of the church compound, one slightly larger than the other. Presumably these served to bake bread for the friars as food and for use in the Mass.

Studying Food Remains at Magdalena de Cao

During our field seasons we collected a great amount of plant and animal remains, a result of the fine preservation at Magdalena. Most of the collection of such materials was made during the normal process of excavating houses and the church. As noted in Chapter 2, a salient feature of the town is the presence of large piles of midden, including mounds of trash more than a meter in height and stretching many square meters in area. Given the large total area of the town and our knowledge of population estimates at various times (Chapter 12), we can conclude that many houses were abandoned and used as trash dumps while people continued to live nearby. In 2007, we selected a midden that had a large looter hole in it (thus providing a clear profile of deposits), choosing this particular midden because its proximity to the atrium, just a few meters to its east, suggested that it could have been a church trash dump. Harvard undergraduate Danielle Mirabal (2008) excavated this deposit and studied its contents, and the sample was further analyzed by Arqueobios as a potential indicator of the foodways of friars and others associated with the church.

Unit 19 was at the northern end of the main north-south street on the west side of the plaza, passing by Units 1 and 2. The entire area appeared to have been a garbage dump in colonial times. We excavated Unit 19 in 2006, with a 1 × 2 m pit placed on the side of a large looter hole to control the removal of observed strata. Excavations revealed a deep pit with a total of 18 depositional units. Levels 14 and below are associated with the earliest town occupation, with lower levels linked to the 1578 El Niño event. Most of the upper layers, however, contained paper fragments, suggesting that this area was a trash deposit after the church collapse. The plant and animal remains in Unit 19 contributed to the general inventory at Magdalena but did not allow us to distinguish between pre- and post-church-collapse occupations.

Plants and Animals of Magdalena de Cao

We analyzed the entire assemblage of recovered faunal and floral macro-remains in order to ascertain the range of plants and animals at the site. We identified a wide array of both native and introduced plants, with the latter including exotic species from tropical areas as well as Europe and possibly Asia. There were 88 identifiable faunal and 71 floral species in the Magdalena collections (Table 3.1).

A number of problems confronted analysts, especially regarding faunal remains. Historical documents (see Chapter 12) suggest that Magdalena de Cao changed over time from a community with a relatively diversified agricultural-fishing subsistence pattern to one that specialized in sheep and goats. We cannot determine if the same people gradually shifted their economy as the fortunes of the town changed or if the Magdaleneros left and were later replaced by a group of sheep and goat herders who camped on the ruins of the town and church. Whatever the case, the faunal assemblage may be distorted due to this later occupation, which would have increased the amount of sheep and goat bones at the site.

An additional problem is the distortion of animal remains due to predation on bones after site abandonment. Mirabal (2008:72) noted significant bone loss in the assemblage due to carnivore chew. The most likely culprits are packs of domestic or feral dogs that had free access to the site until the early 1990s, when the Fundación Wiese began work there and posted guards.

Table 3.1 Animal and Plant Remains Found at Magdalena de Cao Viejo

				FAUNA	

PHYLUM	CLASS	FAMILY	GENUS AND SPECIES	COMMON NAME: SPANISH (ENGLISH)
Mollusca	Polyplacophora	Chitonidae	*Chiton cumingsi*	barquillo (NA)
			Acanthopleura echinata	barquillo (NA)
	Gastropoda	Fissurellidae	*Fissurella peruviana*	lapa (limpet)
			Fissurella maxima	lapa (limpet)
			Fissurella latimarginata	lapa (limpet)
			Fissurella limbata	lapa (limpet)
			Fissurella sp.	lapa (limpet)
		Trochidae	*Diloma nigerrima*	caracolito negro (black snail)
			Tegula euryomphala	caracol negro (black snail)
			Tegula atra	caracol negro (black snail)
			Tegula tridentata	caracol negro (black snail)
		Turbinidae	*Prisogaster niger*	caracolito negro (black snail)
		Potamididae	*Cerithium stercusmuscarum*	caracol (snail)
		Calyptraeidae	*Crepipatella dilatata*	pique (limpet)
		Naticidae	*Sinum cymba*	caracol luna (moon snail)
			Polinices uber	caracol luna (moon snail)
		Muricidae	*Xanthochorus buxea*	NA (sea snail)
		Thaididae	*Thais (Stramonita) haemastoma*	caracol (snail)
			Thais (Stramonita) chocolata	caracol (snail)
			Crassilabrum crassilabrum	caracol (snail)
		Columbellidae	*Mitrella* sp.	caracol (snail)
			Anachis sp.	NA (NA)
		Nassariidae	*Nassarius dentifer*	caracol (snail)
		Olividae	*Olivella columellaris*	olivita (sea snail)
			Oliva peruviana	NA (Peruvian olive, sea snail)

Table 3.1   *continued*

FAUNA

PHYLUM	CLASS	FAMILY	GENUS AND SPECIES	COMMON NAME: SPANISH (ENGLISH)
		Mitridae	*Mitra (Atrimitra) orientalis*	NA (NA)
		Cancellaridae	*Cancellaria urceolata*	NA (sea snail)
			Cancellaria decussata	NA (nutmeg snail)
		Bulimulidae	*Scutalus proteus*	caracol terrestre (land snail)
		Planorbidae	*Helisoma* sp.	caracol de agua dulce (freshwater snail)
		Physidae	*Physa* sp.	caracol de agua dulce (freshwater snail)
	Bivalvia	Glycymerididae	*Glycymeris ovata*	mejillón (mussel)
		Mytilidae	*Choromytilus chorus*	choro zapato (mussel)
			Perumytilus purpuratus	chorito playero (mussel)
			Semimytilus algosus	chorito playero (mussel)
		Pteriidae	*Pinctada mazatlanica*	cocha perlera (pearl oyster)
		Pectinidae	*Argopecten purpuratus*	concha de abanico (scallop)
		Spondylidae	*Spondylus princeps*	mullu (spiny oyster)
			Spondylus calcifer	mullu (spiny oyster)
		Anomiidae	*Anomia peruviana*	NA (mollusk)
		Cardiidae	*Trachycardium procerum*	piconudo (mollusk)
		Veneridae	*Protothaca theca*	almeja (clam)
			Eurhomalea rufa	almeja (clam)
		Petricolidae	*Petricola (Petricolarius) rugosa*	NA (clam)
		Psammobiidae	*Gari solida*	almeja (clam)
		Semelidae	*Semele corrugata*	almeja (clam)
		Mactridae	*Spisula adamsi*	almejita (clam)
			Mulinia edulis	NA (NA)
		Donacidae	*Donax obesulus*	maruchas (clam)

(continued)

Table 3.1   *continued*

FAUNA

PHYLUM	CLASS	FAMILY	GENUS AND SPECIES	COMMON NAME: SPANISH (ENGLISH)
		Mesodesmatidae	*Mesodesma donacium*	macha (macha clam)
		Pholadidae	*Pholas (Thovana) chiloensis*	alas de ángel (angel wing mollusk)
Chordata		Chondrichthyes		
		Rhinobatidae	*Rhinobatos planiceps*	NA (flathead guitarfish)
		Myliobatididae	*Myliobatis* sp.	NA (ray)
		Triakidae	*Galeorhinus* sp.	NA (houndshark)
			Mustelus sp.	NA (houndshark)
	Osteichthyes	Ariidae	*Galeichthys peruvianus*	bagre con faja (banded catfish)
		Cheilodactylidae	*Cheilodactylus variegatus*	pintadilla, páramo (Peruvian morwong)
		Engraulidae	*Engraulis ringens*	anchoveta (anchovy)
		Scorpaenidae	*Scorpaena* sp.	diablico (scorpionfish)
		Sciaenidae	*Paralonchurus peruanus*	coco, suco (croaker)
			Sciaena fasciata	gallinaza (drum)
			Sciaena deliciosa	lorna (delicious drum)
			Sciaena gilberti	corvina (corvina drum)
			Sciaena starksi	robalo (robalo drum)
			Sciaena sp.	NA (drum)
		Labridae	*Semicossyphus maculatus*	NA (goldspot sheepshead)
		Oplegnathidae	*Oplegnathus* sp.	loro (knifejaw)
		Cheilodactylidae	*Cheilodactylus variegatus*	pintadilla (Peruvian morwong)
		Serranidae	*Acanthistius pictus*	cherlo (Peruvian seabass)
		Pomadasyidae	*Anisotremus scapularis*	chita (Peruvian grunt)
		Merlucciidae	*Merluccius gayi peruanus*	merluza (Peruvian hake)

Table 3.1 *continued*

			FAUNA	
PHYLUM	CLASS	FAMILY	GENUS AND SPECIES	COMMON NAME: SPANISH (ENGLISH)
	Aves	Anatidae	*Anas* sp.	pato silvestre (mallard duck)
			Anas platyrhynchus	pato doméstico (domestic duck)[1]
		Laridae	*Larus* sp.	gaviota (seagull)
		Columbidae	*Zenaida asiatica*	cuculi (white-winged dove)
		Strigidae		
		Accipitridae	*Pandion haliaetus*	aguila pescadora (osprey)
		Phasianidae	*Gallus gallus*	gallina (hen)[1]
		Pelecanidae	*Pelecanus thagus*	pelícano (pelican)
		Phalacrocoracidae	*Phalacrocorax bougainvillii*	guanay (Guanay cormorant)
		Sulidae	*Sula variegate*	piquero blanco (Peruvian booby)
		Diomedeidae	*Diomedea* sp.	
	Mammalia	Muridae		
		Caviidae	*Cavia porcellus*	cuy (guinea pig)
		Canidae	*Canis lupus familiaris*	perro doméstico (domesticated dog)
			Lycalopex sechurae	zorro costero (desert fox)
		Otariidae	*Otaria* sp.	lobo marino (sea lion)
Cetacea Order ballena (whale)		Cervidae	*Odocoileus virginianus*	venado de cola blanca (whitetail deer)
		Camelidae	*Lama* sp.	camélido doméstico (domestic camelid)
		Bovidae	*Ovis aries*	oveja (sheep)[1]
			Capra aegagrus hircus	cabra (goat)[1]
			Bos taurus	vaca (cow)[1]
		Suidae	*Sus scrofa domestica*	cerdo doméstico (domestic pig)[1]
	Equidae		*Equus caballus*	caballo (horse)[1]
			Equus sp.	NA (equines)[1]

(continued)

Table 3.1   *continued*

FLORA

PHYLUM	CLASS	FAMILY	GENUS AND SPECIES	COMMON NAME: SPANISH (ENGLISH)
Rhodophyta		Gigartinaceae	*Gigartina chamissoi*	mococho (red algae/seaweed)
Pteridophyta		Equisetaceae	*Equisetum giganteum*	cola de caballo (southern giant horsetail)
Angiospermae	Dicotyledoneae	Juglandaceae	*Carya* sp.	pecana (hickory)[1]
		Salicaceae	*Salix chiliensis*	sauce (pencil willow)
		Nyctaginaceae	*Mirabilis jalapa*	clavanilla (four o'clock flower)
		Caryophyllaceae	*Dianthus caryophyllus*	clavel (carnation)[1]
		Annonaceae	*Annona* sp.	NA (pawpaw)
			Annona muricata	guanabana (soursop)
		Lauraceae	*Persea americana*	palta (avocado)
			Nectandra sp.	NA (NA)
		Capparaceae	*Capparis* sp.	alcaparra (caper)
			Capparis angulata	sapote (caper)
		Rosaceae	*Cydonia oblonga*	membrillo (quince)[1]
			Prunus persica	melocotonera (peach)[1]
			Prunus domestica	ciruelo (plum)[1]
		Leguminosae	*Inga feuilleii*	guaba (pacay, ice cream bean)
			Prosopis sp.	algarrobo (carob tree)
			Acacia sp.	acacia (acacia)
			Acacia macracanta	espino (hawthorn)
			Caesalpinia spinosa	tara (tara)
			Cassia fistula	caña fistula (golden shower tree)[1]
			Parkinsonia aculeata	azote de cristo (Jerusalem thorn)[1]
			Phaseolus vulgaris	frijól (common bean)
			Phaseolus lunatus	pallar (lima bean)
			Arachis hypogaea	maní (peanut)
			Canavalia ensiformis	pallar de gentil (jack bean)
			Canavalia maritima	pallar de gentil (jack bean)
		Euphorbiaceae	*Ricinus communis*	higuerilla (castor bean)[1]
			Jatropha macrantha	huanarpo macho (Peruvian Viagra)[1]

Table 3.1 *continued*

<table>
<tr><td colspan="5" align="center">FLORA</td></tr>
<tr>
<td>PHYLUM</td>
<td>CLASS</td>
<td>FAMILY</td>
<td>GENUS AND SPECIES</td>
<td>COMMON NAME: SPANISH (ENGLISH)</td>
</tr>
<tr><td></td><td></td><td>Rutaceae</td><td>*Citrus aurantium*</td><td>naranja (bitter orange, Seville orange)[1]</td></tr>
<tr><td></td><td></td><td></td><td>*Citrus limon*</td><td>limón (lemon)[1]</td></tr>
<tr><td></td><td></td><td></td><td>*Citrus aurantifolia*</td><td>lima (key lime)[1]</td></tr>
<tr><td></td><td></td><td>Malpighiaceae</td><td>*Bunchosia armeniaca*</td><td>cansaboca (peanut butter fruit)</td></tr>
<tr><td></td><td></td><td>Sapindaceae</td><td>*Sapindus saponaria*</td><td>choloque (wingleaf soapberry)</td></tr>
<tr><td></td><td></td><td>Malvaceae</td><td>*Gossypium barbadense*</td><td>algodón (cotton)</td></tr>
<tr><td></td><td></td><td>Bombacaceae</td><td></td><td></td></tr>
<tr><td></td><td></td><td>Passifloraceae</td><td>*Passiflora edulis*</td><td>maracuya (passion fruit)</td></tr>
<tr><td></td><td></td><td></td><td>*Passiflora foetida*</td><td>granadilla de culebra (passion flower)</td></tr>
<tr><td></td><td></td><td>Cucurbitaceae</td><td>*Cucurbita* sp.</td><td>calabaza (gourd)</td></tr>
<tr><td></td><td></td><td></td><td>*Cucurbita maxima*</td><td>zapallo (squash)</td></tr>
<tr><td></td><td></td><td></td><td>*Cucurbita moschata*</td><td>chiclayo (squash, pumpkin)</td></tr>
<tr><td></td><td></td><td></td><td>*Lagenaria siceraria*</td><td>calabaza, mate (bottle gourd)</td></tr>
<tr><td></td><td></td><td></td><td>*Sechium edule*</td><td>caigua chilena (mirliton)</td></tr>
<tr><td></td><td></td><td></td><td>*Citrullus vulgaris*</td><td>sandía (watermelon)[1]</td></tr>
<tr><td></td><td></td><td>Myrtaceae</td><td>*Psidium guajava*</td><td>guayaba (guava)</td></tr>
<tr><td></td><td></td><td>Onagraceae</td><td>*Punica granatum*</td><td>granada (pomegranate)[1]</td></tr>
<tr><td></td><td></td><td>Sapotaceae</td><td>*Pouteria lucuma*</td><td>lúcuma (lucuma)</td></tr>
<tr><td></td><td></td><td>Oleaceae</td><td>*Olea europaea*</td><td>aceituna (olive)[1]</td></tr>
<tr><td></td><td></td><td>Apocynaceae</td><td>*Cataranthus roseus*</td><td>chabela (periwinkle)</td></tr>
<tr><td></td><td></td><td>Convoluvlaceae</td><td>*Ipomoea batatas*</td><td>camote (sweet potato)</td></tr>
<tr><td></td><td></td><td>Solanaceae</td><td>*Solanum nigrum*</td><td>NA (black nightshade)</td></tr>
<tr><td></td><td></td><td></td><td>*Capsicum* sp.</td><td>ají (chile)</td></tr>
<tr><td></td><td></td><td></td><td>*Capsicum annum* var. *cerasiforme*</td><td>ají (chile)</td></tr>
<tr><td></td><td></td><td></td><td>*Capsicum frutescens*</td><td>ají (chile)</td></tr>
<tr><td></td><td></td><td></td><td>*Nicotiana* sp.</td><td>tabaco (tobacco) [11,22] Acanthaceae Asteraceae</td></tr>
<tr><td></td><td></td><td></td><td>*Helianthus annus*</td><td>girasol (sunflower)[1]</td></tr>
<tr><td></td><td></td><td></td><td>*Tessaria integrifolia*</td><td>pajaro bobo (daisy)</td></tr>
<tr><td></td><td></td><td></td><td>*Spilantes urens*</td><td>turre macho (pigeon coop)</td></tr>
</table>

(continued)

Table 3.1   *continued*

				FLORA
PHYLUM	CLASS	FAMILY	GENUS AND SPECIES	COMMON NAME: SPANISH (ENGLISH)
		Fabaceae	*Acacia* sp.	acacia (acacia)
			Acacia macracanta	acacia (acacia)
	Monocotyledoneae	Amaryllidaceae	*Fourcroya* sp.	cabuya (NA)
		Poaceae	*Zea mays*	maíz (maize, corn)
			Paspalum sp.	NA (paspalum)
			Sporobolus sp.	NA (dropseed grasses)
			Gynerium sagittatum	caña brava (wild cane)
			Phragmites australis	carricillo (common reed)
			Distichlis spicata	grama salada (saltgrass)
			Triticum sativum	trigo (wheat)[1]
			Guadua angustifolia	caña de Guayaquil (bamboo)
		Arecacaea	*Astrocaryum chambira*	chambira (Chambira palm)
		Typhaceae	*Typha angustifolia*	enea (bullrush, cattail)
		Cyperaceae	*Cyperus* sp.	juncia (sedge)
			Eleocharis sp.	juncia (sedge)
			Schoenoplectus californicus	totora (California bulrush)
		Musaceae	*Musa* sp.	platano (banana)[1]

1 Non-native.

2 Only found in cigarettes.

List based on macro-remains.

A similar problem of palimpsest effect exists for plant remains. These and other challenges to analysis will be discussed later in the chapter.

Fauna

Identified faunal species included 23 gastropods, 22 bivalves, 19 fish, 9 birds, and 11 mammals. The majority of shellfish are small varieties. In both the town and the church complex, the overwhelmingly dominant mollusk species by weight, minimum number of individuals (MNI), and number of specimens identified (NSI) is *Prisogaster niger*, a rocky-shore-dwelling gastropod ranging between 10 and 35 mm in maximum dimension. Small rocky-shore mollusks overwhelmingly dominated the assemblage, at 85 percent and higher for all three evaluation criteria. *Tegula atra*, a turban snail, follows in popularity (17.92 percent by weight), and the small clam, *Donax obesulus*, is third (4.96 percent by weight).

Table 3.2 Percentages of Animal Remains in Magdalena Church and Town

	WEIGHT			MNI			NSI		
	FISH	BIRDS	MAM.	FISH	BIRDS	MAM.	FISH	BIRDS	MAM.
Church	0.6	10.2	89.1	11.3	26.7	58.7	3.8	35.3	60.7
Town	1.0	7.0	92	14.3	32.5	52.6	8.0	26.1	65.6

Reptiles: church, 0.02, 1.2, and 0.3; town, 0, 0.6, and 0.4.

El Brujo is in a transition zone where a rocky shoreline changes to a sandy one, but the change occurs at the southern tip of the terrace, near the Huaca Prieta, while rocky shores are close to the middle and upper areas of the terrace. It thus appears that the Magdaleneros spent little effort in procuring sandy-shore shellfish, such as clams, preferring to gather those that were closest to them. This likely is because mollusks played a very minor role in diets. Today, small mollusks commonly are consumed in soups and stews, to which they add flavor, and the same is almost certainly true for Colonial Period foodways.

Both *Spondylus princeps* and *S. calcifer* were found at the site. They came from warm Ecuadorian waters and were highly valued as the "food of the gods," in prehistory (Paulsen 1974). They appear to have retained their value at Magdalena de Cao though whether they were kept in secret by the indigenous population or accepted or ignored by clerics is hard to know.

We studied a total of 1,892 osteological remains in the church compound and 1,595 specimens in the town, identifying 327 and 502 individuals, respectively. The relative proportions of different vertebrate classes are quite similar in both church and town, with mammals at more than 50 percent in each setting, followed by birds and fish (Table 3.2).

We had expected to find the remains of domesticated animals, and they were indeed present, including dogs (*Canis lupus familiaris*), camelids (*Lama* sp.), and guinea pigs (*Cavia porcellus*), as well as introduced sheep (*Ovis aries*), goats (*Capra aegagrus hircus*), cattle (*Bos taurus*), pigs (*Sus scrofa domestica*), chickens (*Gallus gallus*), and equines that included horses (*Equus caballus*), although we believe mules also were present based on found feces that crumbled before identification could be confirmed.

By all three of the evaluation methods, the most common vertebrate species remains in the church, in order of importance, are sheep and goats,[1] Guanay cormorants (*Phalacrocorax bougainvillii*), and Peruvian grunts (*Anisotremus scapularis*). In the town, the most common vertebrates are sheep/goats, Guanay cormorants, camelids, Peruvian banded croakers (*Paralonchurus peruanus*), and cattle (*Bos taurus*) (Figure 3.4). Caution must be employed in considering these remains because of the change of the community's subsistence from an agricultural-fishing community into one focused on sheep and goats either in the late occupation of the town or after the Magdalena community moved to its present location, as previously noted.

Working on a limited sample in 2008, but concentrating only on fauna, Mirabal found that sheep dominated the assemblages in four different excavation units at 49.9 percent or higher, except for excavations in the church, in which goats dominated (44.3 percent). A trash midden near the church, however, had sheep remains at 65.5 percent and goat remains at only

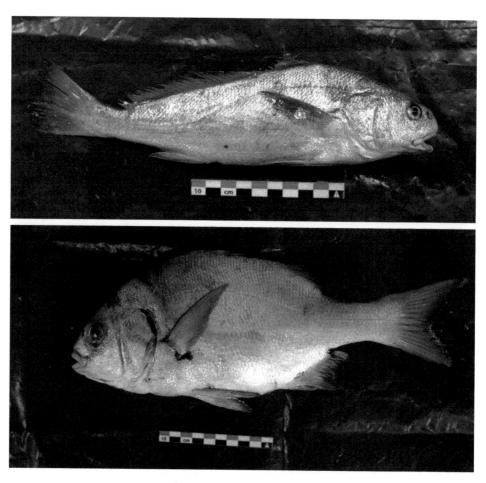

Figure 3.4 Popular fish. Top: Peruvian banded croaker (*Paralonchurus peruanus*). Bottom: Peruvian grunt (*Anisotremus scapularis*).

26.2 percent. The relative importance of these animals in the two different site sectors must be considered with caution, especially given the problem of the late goat-herder occupation. Mirabal's analysis of age ranges indicated that the majority of sheep and goats were killed as juveniles, suggesting meat exploitation. As in so many other aspects of the site, these issues warrant further investigation.

Flora

The majority (71 percent) of plant remains were of industrial nature, such as reeds and grasses used in house construction. Plants for food accounted for 25 percent of the overall assemblage, followed by medicines and stimulants (2 percent), ornamentals (1 percent), oil-producing plants (1 percent), miscellanea (.08 percent), and seaweed (.02 percent). The majority of plants were native to the coastal region (93 percent).

The staples of coastal Andean diets were fully present in the collection, as might be expected: maize, potatoes, sweet potatoes, manioc, squashes, and fruits such as *lúcuma* (*Pouteria lucuma*) and avocado (*Persea americana*). In addition, there were plants from tropical areas of South America that may have been imported from the eastern side of the Andes, Ecuador, or the more humid regions of northern Peru: Chambira palm (*Astrocaryum chambira*), useful for making baskets and similar items; *Nectandra* sp., used in traditional medicine; and *Jatropha macrantha*, another medicine (in recent years sold as "Peruvian Viagra"). There also was a great range of introduced Old World plants: bananas/plantains (*Musa* sp.), bitter/Seville oranges (*Citrus aurantium*), castor beans (*Ricinus communis*), key limes (*Citrus aurantifolia*), lemons (*Citrus limon*), olives (*Olea europaea*), peaches (*Prunus persica*), plums (*Prunus domestica*), pomegranates (*Punica granatum*), quinces (*Cydonia oblonga*), watermelons (*Citrullus vulgaris*), and wheat (*Triticum sativum*). It is of note that the majority of these plants are fruits.

Also, various ornamentals are in the assemblage, most likely grown for their flowers: carnations (*Dianthus caryophyllus*), four o'clock flowers (*Mirabilis jalapa*), periwinkles (*Cataranthus roseus*), Jerusalem thorns (*Parkinsonia aculeata*), and golden shower trees (*Cassia fistula*). The last of these is a native of South Asia.

Finally, there were North American plants, particularly sunflowers (*Helianthus annus*), and hickory (*Carya* sp.), which are known from Canada to Mexico as well as in Asia. Similarly, tobacco (*Nicotiana* sp.) is found throughout various parts of the New World but was not common in coastal and highland regions of the Central Andes in prehispanic times.

Given the bleak, desert conditions of the El Brujo terrace today, it is hard to imagine old Magdalena town filled with flowers, bushes, and trees. There are no indications whatsoever that the terrace was irrigated. But we found not only the seeds of olives but also entire large, leafy olive tree branches. While there are many ways such branches could have arrived at the site, such finds leave open the possibility that bucket irrigation or perhaps more advanced hydraulic systems brought water to Magdalena, although we saw no clear evidence of gardens or fields on the terrace.

No matter how these plants reached the town and church compound, their great diversity likely indicates that our collections consist of a palimpsest of materials from the entire range of site occupation, as previously discussed. Our general assumptions about the difficulties of life on the terrace during the first years of occupation after the 1578 El Niño event make it hard to believe that the early townspeople indulged in planting carnations or golden shower trees, but by the mid-seventeenth century, as domesticates and other goods were more commonly exchanged within the Spanish Empire, such luxuries may have been available to Magdaleneros.

The full inventory of plants and animals is highly informative of social and economic dynamics in the Spanish Empire, especially in the Viceroyalty of Peru, and much may be gleaned not just regarding the grand narrative of trade and commerce but also about tastes and trends. It is interesting to consider, for example, that while many juicy fruits made their way to Peruvian colonial kitchens, there is no evidence that the tomato was one of them. There also is an absence of coca (*Erythroxylum coca*) in the plant remains. It is uncertain whether this is because the leaf was carefully kept and used, leaving no traces, or because the friars banned it, as clerical attitudes toward its use varied widely in practice and theory (Gagliano 1963).

To the best of our knowledge, the El Brujo deposits yielded the earliest known remains of cigarettes in Peru, and possibly the earliest physical evidence of paper-wrapped cigarettes in general.[2] They were found in the church compound area and consisted of finely chopped tobacco rolled in fragments of paper documents presumably taken from the church after its collapse. The tobacco was AMS-dated to 442 +/− 76 RC years. The use of paper from ecclesiastical documents, however, suggests that the cigarettes date to the mid-seventeenth century, after the church collapsed. This is still early for cigarette use.

In order to examine plant and animal uses in these different eras we needed to find chronologically distinctive samples. We were particularly interested in the earliest occupation, when the weight of the conquest was still heavy on the population and the transition from traditional to hybrid foodways was in its early stages. Other avenues of investigation consisted of identification and study of early strata containing food remains, the discovery of a kitchen area with associated ceramics in the town, and the analysis of starch grains and isotopes from the teeth of burials that reflect diet. In addition, the general analyses of burials (Chapter 4) and of ceramics (Chapters 8 and 9) contribute to understanding the subsistence economy of the town and the diets of its people.

A Column Sample in Early Deposits

Because the overall study of plants and animals showed such a diverse array of introduced species, we sought data that might better indicate the nature of foods and other materials consumed by Magdalena's population during the early occupation of the site. Finding such a deposit was challenging, but a means to do so was available based on the presence or absence of paper fragments in strata.

Paper fragments serve as an "index fossil" at Magdalena. While it is possible that paper was in the possession of townspeople early in the occupation of the site, it probably was not common, as it would have been expensive and controlled by friars in the church compound. Papers do appear in strata, however, and we have interpreted these layers as dating to the period after the collapse of the church and the apparent abandonment of the complex by clerics. It is possible that pre-collapse strata might contain paper, and the reverse is also possible: there almost certainly are post-collapse strata with no paper fragments in them. Given the fact that radiocarbon and other commonly employed chronometric techniques are inadequate to distinguish occupational phases at the site, however, discriminating between deposits with and without papers in them offers some hope in identifying phases of the Magdalena occupation.

In 2012, Quilter found a looter hole several meters north of the perimeter wall of Unit 28 that presented a vertical profile from the contemporary ground surface down to prehispanic levels. Exploring this cut, he found a section immediately above the prehistoric level that was distinguished by a sharply different soil consistency and color and capped by a thin layer of compact melted adobe (Figure 3.5). Above this level the deposits contained paper fragments. The intermediate level, however, contained no paper and thus likely was deposited in the early Colonial Period. A 50 × 50 cm block of this material was removed unscreened to be examined in detail for its contents. The block was divided into two stratigraphic units, A and B, although the division was arbitrary.

The resulting analysis (Table 3.3) identified eleven species of mollusks, the distribution of which follows the same pattern as the entire assemblage, with many small gastropods and bivalves. There were crabs as well, including a freshwater variety (*Hypolobocera* sp.). The shellfish came from both sandy and rocky shorelines, with a predominance of rocky-shore species in both levels. *Prisogaster niger* accounted for 13.7 percent (MNI) of species in level A and

Figure 3.5

Top: The looter hole with column sample cut. Unit 28 excavations in the distance. Bottom: Strata. Arrow points to caliche layer above prehistoric deposits.

Table 3.3 Faunal and Plant Remains from a Column Sample in Magdalena Town

				FAUNA
PHYLUM	**CLASS**	**FAMILY**	**GENUS AND SPECIES**	**COMMON NAME: SPANISH (ENGLISH)**
Mollusca	Gastropoda	Fissurellidae	*Fissurella* sp.	lapa (limpet)
		Trochidae	*Tegula atra*	caracol negro (sea snail)
		Turbinidae	*Prisogaster niger*	caracolito negro (sea snail)
		Naticidae	*Polinices uber*	caracol luna (sea snail)
		Muricidae	*Concholepas concholepas*	NA (Chilean abalone)
			Xanthochorus buxea	NA (murex snail, rock snail)
		Thaididae	*Thais (Stramonita) haemastoma*	caracol (rock snail)
			Thais (Stramonita) chocolata	caracol (rock snail)
		Nassariidae	*Nassarius dentifer*	caracolito (mud snail, dog whelk)
		Olividae	*Olivella columellaris*	olivita (sea snail)
		Planorbidae	*Drepanotrema* sp.	NA (ridge ramshorn snail [freshwater])
			Helisoma sp.	caracol de agua dulce (freshwater snail)
	Bivalvia	Veneridae	*Protothaca theca*	almeja (clam)
		Donacidae	*Donax obesulus*	maruchas (surf clam)
		Mytilidae	*Semimytilus algosus*	chorito playero (mussel)
Arthropoda	Malacostraca	Platyxanthidae	*Platyxanthus orbignyi*	cangrejo violáceo (NA)
		Pseudothelphusidae	*Hypolobocera* sp.	cangrejo de río (freshwater crab)
		Portunidae	*Arenaeus mexicanus*	tijeretas (reticulated swimming crab)
Chordata	Osteichthyes	Merlucciidae	*Merluccius gayi peruanus*	merluza (Peruvian hake)
	Aves	Phalacrocoracidae	*Phalacrocorax bougainvillii*	guanay (Guanay cormorant)
		Falconidae	*Falco* sp.	halcón (falcon, hawk)
	Mammalia	Camelidae	*Lama* sp.	camélido (llama, alpaca)
		Bovidae	*Ovis aries, Capra aegagrus hircus*	sheep/goats (sheep, goat)[1]

1 Non-native species.

Table 3.3   *continued*

FLORA

PHYLUM	CLASS	FAMILY	GENUS AND SPECIES	COMMON NAME: SPANISH (ENGLISH)
Rhodophyta		Gigartinaceae	*Gigartina chamissoi*	mococho (red algae)
Angiospermae	Dicotyledoneae	Lauraceae	*Persea americana*	palta (avocado)
		Leguminosae	*Prosopis* sp.	algarrobo (mesquite)
			Phaseolus vulgaris	frijól (common bean)
			Inga feuilleii	huaba (pacay, ice cream bean)
			Pithecellobium sp.	NA (NA)
		Myrtaceae	*Psidium guajava*	guayaba (guava)
		Malvaceae	*Gossypium barbadense*	algodón (cotton)
		Cucurbitaceae	*Cucurbita moschata*	loche (winter squash)
			Lagenaria siceraria	mate (bottle gourd)
		Sapotaceae	*Pouteria lucuma*	lúcuma (eggfruit)
		Solanaceae	*Capsicum* sp.	ají (chile)
		Lythraceae	*Cuphea* sp.	NA (NA)
	Monocotyledoneae	Poaceae	*Zea mays*	maíz (maize, corn)
			Gynerium sagittatum	caña brava (wild cane)
			Phragmites australis	carricillo (common reed)
		Typhaceae	*Typha angustifolia*	enea (bullrush, cattail)
		Fabales Fabaceae	*Acacia* sp.	algarrobo (acacia)
			Acacia macracanta	algarrobo (acacia)
	Magnoliids	Annonaceae	*Annona muricata*	chirimoya[2] (custard apple, soursop)

2 *Annona muricata* is edible, but today the name *chirimoya* usually refers to *Annona cherimola*.

9 percent in level B, making it the dominant mollusk, again matching the overall sample. Tegula is second in frequency, though at much lower percentages, 3.2 percent in A and 1.4 percent in B, with all other species at less than 1 percent each. Crab remains also are below 1 percent.

Only one fish species was found, Peruvian hake (*Merluccius gayi peruanus*); there were two birds, a Guanay cormorant and a falcon (*Falco* sp.), and two mammals, a camelid (*Lama* sp.) and an *ovicaprino* (*Ovis aries, Capra aegagrus hircus*).

The plant remains consisted of gourds, cotton, chiles, cane, and grass. A marine alga (*Gigartina chamissoi*) is present, as well as a single variety of squash (*Cucurbita moschata*) and one form of bean (*Phaseolous lunatus*). Fruits are present (avocado, *guayaba, algarrobo, lúcuma*) as well as *pacay* (*Inga feuilleei*), sometimes known as the "ice cream bean" in English. The pacay tree produces fruits resembling giant bean pods with a sweet fiber surrounding large internal seeds that is still eaten as a treat today.

Chiles predominated (NIS) at 61.1 percent in A and 42.9 percent in B, followed by cotton (4.3 percent and 23.4 percent), maize (3 percent and 3.1 percent), and other plants in single-digit percentages. The high numbers for chiles are most likely due to the great number of small seeds in this pepper, rather than any dominant role in diets. In level B a seed of *Cuphea* sp. was found. This plant is used as an antisyphilitic and a diuretic today.

Except for the ovicaprino, all the remains found in the column sample are native and of known prehispanic origin. Though this is a small sample, the data suggest that the subsistence economy of the townspeople was high in plants, which likely were consumed in stews and soups, with the small shellfish used for flavoring and their contribution of protein. The representation of different fauna and flora in the column sample seems generally similar to that of the overall sample from the town, except, of course, that the range of species in the column sample is narrower and there are fewer introduced species.

If these materials date to a relatively early phase of the occupation of the town, then it appears that diets varied little from those of prehispanic times. How much of a difference sheep and goats made to diets is hard to judge from the column sample alone.

Unit 28

Excavations of the Unit 28 compound, in the northeastern sector, revealed a food preparation and short-term storage area, yielding some of the most distinct evidence for foodways in the town (Figure 3.6). The excavation unit in this area originally was 4 × 2 m, later extended by .5 m on its southeastern side to expose an in situ jar.

In the first clearing of the unit we found two whale vertebrae that may have served as seats. Most of the food-related activity area was in the southern two-thirds of the unit, and the stumps of posts indicate that there may have been a roof over the area to create a ramada. A low adobe baulk running westward from one of these posts and ending at a large looter hole suggests that a low wall might also have demarcated the area.

In a society with few items of furniture, storage was accomplished partly through the use of vessels buried in the ground to serve as storage containers. In Unit 28 we found three relatively complete examples of this practice (Figure 3.6).

Two large ceramic open-mouthed jars were buried side by side to just below their rims, and each was covered with a large shallow gourd bowl. Close by this pair there was a very large gourd that had been similarly buried but had been left covered with a wadded-up large textile. Southwest of the gourd was a gourd bowl resting on the ground surface. These four vessels were west of a large looter hole. At the far end of the looter hole there was a *cántaro* (large earthenware jug) buried only about a third of its length into the clay floor.

There were flecks of charcoal throughout the entire excavation, and pronounced ash lenses and cinders were found on the floor south of the pair of buried jars and east of the buried gourd. If there had once been a proper kitchen in the area, it was no longer present or in a location not excavated.

Separate studies were carried out of the ashes found around the buried vessels in Unit 28 as well as the contents within them. The studies included examination of macroscopic remains as well as the analysis of starch grains.

Figure 3.6 Kitchen area in Unit 28. *P* indicates post stump; lower dashed line indicates ash concentration; upper dashed line indicates adobe baulk. Small unnumbered gourd bowl in lower left corner. View to north.

Five samples were taken in the ash deposits, and will be discussed here in combination (Table 3.4). Macroscopic remains included remnants of the same fish and mollusks found in the column sample: Peruvian hake (*Merluccius gayi peruanus*) and *Prisogaster niger*, respectively. The same is true for the plant remains, with maize, algarrobo, cotton, and chiles present. Starch grain analysis revealed the common presence of maize as well as manioc (*Manihot esculenta*) and potato (*Solanum tuberosum*), neither of which was identified from the macroscopic remains in the entire assemblage nor in the column sample. Some of these starch grains were damaged by heat, indicating that the plants had been cooked.

We analyzed three of the vessels found in the floor of the cooking area of Unit 28 (vessels 1, 3, and 4) and two from other excavation areas. Manioc, potato, and maize were commonly found in these studies. The buried vessels contained sediments that might have been remains of former contents, materials that seeped in after burial, or a combination of both.

Analysis of the vessels' contents revealed interesting histories of use (Table 3.5). Sample 1, from vessel 1, yielded maize and potato starch grains and also a fragment of a frustule (the silica cell wall) of a marine diatom as well as a phytolith of a grass of the subfamily Pooideae, which

Table 3.4 Plant and Animal Remains from Ashes in Unit 28

PLANT REMAINS

Sample 1	*Zea mays, Manihot esculenta, Solanum tuberosum, Merluccius gayi peruanus, Capsicum* sp., *Distichlis spicata*
Sample 2	*Zea mays, Manihot esculenta, Capsicum* sp. (4), *Gossypium barbadense* (3), *Prosopis* sp. (1), *Tegula atra, Donax obesulus*
Sample 3	*Zea mays, Prisogaster niger* (8), *Tegula atra, Semimytilus algosus* (2), *Hypolobocera* sp. (2)
Sample 4 (negative for starches)	*Capsicum* sp., *Gossypium barbadense, Cucurbita moschata, Acacia* sp., *Semimytilus algosus*
Sample 5	*Zea mays, Capsicum* sp. (5), *Gossypium barbadense, Prisogaster niger*

ANIMAL REMAINS

Sample 1	*M. gayi peruanus*, 1 burnt vertebra; *D. spicata*, stem fragment
Sample 5	Eight-row maize cob also recovered

Seeds and mollusks with a count ≥ 1 in parentheses.

Table 3.5 Summary of Starch Grain Analyses of Unit 28 Vessels

Vessel 1: maize, potato, diatom, Pooideae (grass)
Vessel 3: deformed starch grains; black, highly burned sample
Vessel 4: potato, manioc

Complete vessel (Capa C, Unit 28, T1): deformed starches, potato, manioc
Complete vessel (N 0.3/# 0.2; Capa C): manioc, maize, potato

includes many genera. Some of the use history of this vessel, then, is that it once contained maize, either whole or ground, as well as potatoes. At some point it contained salt water, perhaps due to the presence of marine algae, and a grass of some sort made its way into the vessel.

Sample 2 (vessel 3) contained no starches that could be identified because those present had been deformed by high heat. This suggests that the pot had been used to prepare food or drink at high temperature, perhaps a soup, stew, or hot beverage.

Samples 3 (vessel 4) and 4 were similar to sample 2 except that the starches were not as badly damaged. Potato and manioc starches were damaged but identified for both samples. A soup or stew with a potato base likely was made in these vessels.

Sample 5 contained potato and manioc starches and also a high amount of maize. One of the maize starch grains had a hilum (the point around which starch layers are deposited) exhibiting deterioration caused by an enzyme. This suggests that a fermentation process was at work, with the implication that chicha may have been kept in this vessel.

Another approach to examining foodways at Magdalena was followed by examining the dental calculus (tartar) from human burials (Table 3.6). Ten teeth from church burials were analyzed for starch grains. One, a premolar, yielded no calculus, but all others yielded evidence

Table 3.6 Starch Grain Analyses from Dental Calculus of Colonial Burials

SAMPLE NO.	SOURCE	TOOTH	IDENTIFIED SPECIES	SIZE (L × W, μ)	OBSERVATIONS
1	Colonial cemetery, Unit 3, level 4	Central incisor	Unidentifiable	10.4 × 10.4	Partly digested
				18.2 × 10.4	Flattened
			Zea mays	20.8 × 18.2	Faceted
				18.2 × 18.2	Spherical
				20.8 × 15.6	Faceted, digested
				20.8 × 20.8	Faceted, digested
				13 × 10.4	Faceted, digested
				13 × 10.4	Faceted, digested
2	Colonial church, burial 9	Right 3rd molar	Zea mays	26 × 23.4	Fissures in hilum from grinding
				15.6 × 13	Faceted
				15.6 × 15.6	Spherical with cracks
				23.4 × 23.4	Fissures from grinding
				28.6 × 23.4	Fissures from grinding
			Manihot esculenta	20.8 × 19.5	Longitudinal crack
				15.6 × 15.6	Heat-damaged
3	MCV12-06-01, church	Left 2nd incisor	Unidentifiable	26 × 19.5	Heat-damaged
			Unidentifiable	19.5 × 15.6	Rectangular
			Solanum tuberosum	28.6 × 23.4	Typical, preserved
			Zea mays	13 × 10.4	Faceted, polygon
				18.2 × 18.2	Digested, polygon
				13 × 13	Faceted
4	MCV12-22-01, burial 22, church	Right 2nd molar	Zea mays	18.2 × 15.6	Digested, faceted
			Manihot esculenta	18.2 × 15.6	Partly digested, faceted
				20.8 × 18.2	Hemispherical and typical
				15.6 × 15.6	Spherical
			Unidentifiable	18.2 × 15.6	Clustered and heat-damaged
5	MCV12-15-01, burial 15, church	Right 2nd premolar	Unidentifiable	20.8 × 19.5	Heat-damaged
				13 × 10.4	Heat-damaged
			Solanum tuberosum	28.6 × 28.6	Damaged birefringence
				16.9 × 14.3	Preserved in smaller size
				20.8 × 18.2	Typical, preserved
			Zea mays	26 × 20.8	Transversal fissure

(*continued*)

Table 3.6   *continued*

SAMPLE NO.	SOURCE	TOOTH	IDENTIFIED SPECIES	SIZE (L × W, μ)	OBSERVATIONS
6	MCV-12-01, burial 23, church	Right 2nd premolar	*Solanum tuberosum*	28.6 × 23.4	Typical, preserved
				32.5 × 23.4	Typical, preserved
7	MCV12-14-01, burial 14, church	Left 2nd molar	Unidentifiable	13 × 13	Heat-damaged
			Manihot esculenta	15.6 × 15.6	Hemispherical
			Zea mays	20.8 × 20.8	Spherical, perforated hilum
			Solanum tuberosum	73.3 × 44.2	Typical, well preserved
8	MCV12-11-01, church	Left 1st premolar	NA	NA	No calculus
9	MCV12–05-01	Left 1st incisor	Unidentifiable	23.4 × 19.5	Heat-damaged
				23.4 × 20.8	Heat-damaged
			Solanum tuberosum	18.2 × 15.6	Clustered and heat-damaged
10	MCV12-07-01	Left incisor	Unidentifiable	16.9 × 14.3	Heat-damaged
			Manihot esculenta	14.3 × 13	Faceted, typical hilum

of maize, potato, or manioc. Sample 1 (burial 3) also contained starch grains that could not be identified, and six of the nine samples (3–5 and 7–10) had grains that were deformed due to heat and thus could not be identified.

The calculus on each tooth represents about the last two years or so of carbohydrate intake prior to death. Samples 1 through 5 (burials 3, 9, 6, 22, and 15, respectively) had extensive calculus, whereas samples 8 through 10, all loose teeth found in the burial area, had relatively light deposits. While sample 8 lacked calculus altogether, it may be significant that 9 and 10 showed no traces of maize, only potato and manioc. It is possible that these different sets of teeth represent individuals with different diets, maize-eaters versus non-maize-eaters. Vásquez notes that for sample 7 there was a potato starch grain of exceptionally large size that may represent a variety of large potato grown at high altitudes and may possibly indicate that the individual represented by it may have been a *serrano* (an inhabitant of a high-altitude community). It is also noteworthy that burial 15, represented by sample 5, is an African (see Chapter 5) who, at least on the basis of dental calculus, had a diet similar to his Andean contemporaries.

Foodways at Magdalena de Cao

The various studies of plant and animal remains at Magdalena de Cao offer intriguing suggestions concerning foodways and related practices in the colonial town and church complex. Although the complete assemblage we studied includes introduced plants and animals, it and the analyses of the column sample, kitchen ashes, vessel contents, and dental calculus suggest that the subsistence economy of the Magdaleneros was quite similar to that of their prehispanic ancestors.

Diets consisted of carbohydrates supplied by manioc, potatoes, maize, squashes, sweet potatoes, and beans. Fish, shorebirds, peanuts, avocados, and other plants provided protein and fats. Small shellfish, chiles, and probably other plants added extra nutrition and flavor to meals.

One contribution of our research to the study of Andean foodways is our discovery of the importance of manioc in diets. It was found in all of the special, small-scale studies but is completely absent in the general assemblage based on macro-remains. The plant is propagated through cuttings of the edible root, which is high in starch, calcium, phosphorus, and vitamin C, and its leaves are rich in lysine (an amino acid, which is a building block of protein). Consequently, little of the plant itself might remain after use. Its high nutritive value to the people of Magdalena has been borne out by our studies.

It is very likely that manioc was of key economic importance in the Central Andes in prehistory. Because the entire root is consumed, few macro-fossils remain. Furthermore, it is likely that the variety consumed was sweet manioc. The bitter variety of manioc requires leaching of the cyanide it contains, and so special graters and other equipment to process it are often found in tropical areas, where preservation of organic remains is poor. But sweet manioc requires no such special tools or facilities, and so remains of its presence may be scant to nil in places where it was consumed. Manioc is likely drastically underrepresented at many prehistoric sites and likely was a staple crop in most parts of the Central Andes where it can be grown. It has been found in abundance through starch grain analysis at the Initial Period site of Cardal (Burger et al. 2011) as well as many other sites of the same period and the Early Horizon (Richard Burger, personal communication). If it was an important staple during these times and important in the Colonial Period, it is likely that it was important in many places during the intervening centuries as well.

Soups and stews were common not just at Magdalena but throughout the past, and even among people of few means today. These cooking techniques maximize capture of the nutritive value of foods while making them easy to consume and digest. A slowly simmering soup on the fire also offers a meal at any time as well as an ever-ready processor for newly acquired food items. Beyond this general similarity through time, the particularities of the early colonial kitchen, at least as represented at Magdalena, are interesting in terms of what appears to be absent or represented in small quantities as well as what was added by Europeans.

There are no *lomas* plants in the assemblage. Hills that supported fog-fed vegetation are far from the site. Similarly, there are not many riverine species save for a few shellfish and crustaceans. Deer are present but not significant. These absences in combination with the more abundant species indicate that the animals and plants providing the townspeople's diets and other material needs were mostly drawn from the nearby shore, sea, and agricultural fields. Magdalena de Cao was a farming-fishing community.

A critical aspect of the Magdalena diet involves the role of introduced species. Sheep/goats are among the most ubiquitous remains at the site. As already noted, how many of these remains represent activities at the site late in its occupation or after its abandonment is hard to assess. We may presume, however, that sheep and goats were present fairly early in the Colonial Period and that it is quite likely that Magdaleneros would have had access to this meat even if they did not own the flocks. Similarly, we know that cattle were raised in the Chicama Valley starting at an early time. Even though cattle remains do not make up a significant portion of the osteological remains at the site, they may have been more present in the Chicama Valley than as represented in the assemblage. As in the case of sheep/goats, proximity to cattle, even if they were owned by Spaniards, likely would have increased meat and milk intake among the native people charged with tending them. So despite uncertainties about the representation of sheep and goats in the diets of the town and church, it seems quite likely that the community benefited considerably from introduced domesticated animals.

After the general sheep/goats category, the most-represented vertebrate in both the church and town is the Guanay cormorant (*Phalacrocorax bougainvillii*). It is one of the most common shorebirds of Peru, with colonies in the hundreds of thousands, and is named for its production of guano on offshore islands. Before the overexploitation of guano resources in the late Colonial and Republican Periods there probably were extensive colonies on cliffs and other places on the mainland shore, although even island-dwelling birds come to shore to feed.

Cormorants in general and the Guanay in particular were favored food sources from the Late Preceramic Period until recent times. Shorebirds rarely appear to have been primary food sources over the millennia, except in the case of occasional early sites that may represent the end products of specialized hunting forays. But they appear to have been a main source of food after primary sources such as fish and, in the Colonial Period, sheep/goats. They were most commonly prepared by being salted or cooked in stews and are still eaten today by coastal people on traditional festive occasions; in Huanchaco they are referred to as "poor man's turkey" (Prieto 2015).

Anchovies and other small schooling fish do not appear to have played an important role in Magdalena diets. As with most prehistoric and contemporary fisherfolk, fish and other animals higher up the food chain than anchovies were sought (cf. Quilter and Stocker 1983). Conversely, although dolphins and porpoises are abundant in coastal waters and are taken and eaten today, their remains are not present in the Magdalena assemblages. It is likely that Magdalena's fishers considered these animals as allies in fishing, so they were rarely taken or consumed (Oscar Gabriel Prieto, personal communication).[3]

The most numerous fish remains in the church compound were those of the Peruvian grunt (*Anisotremus scapularis*), known as *chita* in Peru today. In the town, however, the most common fish was Peruvian banded croaker (*Paralonchurus peruanus*), referred to as *suco* locally and as *coco* on the Central Coast (Figure 3.4). Both fish have firm white flesh and are mild in flavor. Of the two, however, the near-shore croaker, which feeds on the muddy to sandy bottom, has a more distinctive flavor than the rocky-bottom-dwelling grunt, which is milder in taste.

Today the chita is considered a first-class fish, but it was not popular in prehispanic times. Suco, however, is well represented at prehispanic sites and remains a popular, everyday meal fish on the coast. The high representation of chita in the church compound and the large amounts of suco in the town may thus represent differences in the food preferences of Spanish and native townspeople, differences that are still seen today between urban and rural people.

Similar dietary preference issues arise in relation to plant remains. As in the case of cattle, we know from documentary sources that wheat was grown early in the Chicama Valley. The large dome-shaped baking ovens in the church complex suggest that wheat bread may have been an important part of the diet of the friars but that the townspeople either were not permitted access to it or, more likely, favored their traditional carbohydrates.

What the townspeople do seem to have enjoyed are the various introduced fruits. There already were a great number of native sweet fruits and vegetables that were available to coastal dwellers, some of which were consumed and possibly under cultivation as early as the Late Preceramic Period (Quilter et al. 1991). Apparently Andean folk were quick to include introduced sweet and juicy fruits in their diets: limes, lemons, oranges, peaches, plums, pomegranates, quinces, and watermelons. These were found in the general plant inventory, so we cannot be certain when they were first included in diets, but it seems likely that they were consumed during the main occupation of the town before it became a goat-herding camp. We may thus estimate that these fruits were introduced sometime from about the mid-sixteenth century—potentially even before the abandonment of the first Magdalena—to the end of the seventeenth century, although it is possible that they arrived later in the eighteenth century.

Garcilaso de la Vega (1970) discussed the introduction of European animals and plants in his *Royal Commentaries of the Incas*, written in his old age and published in two parts in 1609 and 1616–1617. His account mostly consists of personal statements as to when he first saw various animals in Cuzco, so these dates must be later than the first arrival of animals and plants in Peru. He saw cows for the first time around 1550, sheep in 1556, and donkeys in 1557. He also notes that a noble lady, María Escobar of Trujillo, first introduced wheat to Peru at the city of Rímac (perhaps Lima), but that in 1547 there was no wheat bread in Cuzco. Goats were still relatively rare in Cuzco at that time as well.

In regard to fruits and vegetables, Garcilaso states that in 1560 Don Antonio de Ribera, of Lima, brought some young olive plants from Seville to his estate, "where he had already produced grapes, figs, pomegranates, melons, oranges, limes and other fruits and vegetables from Spain" (de la Vega 1609:598–599). Garcilaso adds that by the time of his writing, olive oil was imported from Chile because the trees grew better there.

We can surmise that the introduction of the first animals of various kinds that Garcilaso mentions could have been much earlier than when he first saw them: each of his dates is a conservative terminus ante quem for the latest possible introduction. Many animals such as equines, sheep, goats, and cattle presumably would have been of tactical value in the Conquest Period and imported quite early. Conversely, we might assume that agricultural products would have arrived later, in more stable times. And, of course, the relatively difficult growing conditions in the highlands around Cuzco could have delayed the successful introduction of many plants and animals, as Garcilaso occasionally notes, whereas coastal farms could have supported growth much more easily and earlier.

In relation to the Magdalena de Cao inventory of plants and animals, Garcilaso's account supports the general proposition that most of the non-native species found at the site could already have been part of the economy of the town before its reestablishment at El Brujo in 1578. Until tighter dating methods are available, however, we cannot determine precise dates for these species' presence at the site. We might presume that some of the introduced plants did not arrive until fairly late in the life of the town. These might include flowers, some of the plants that may have come from Asia, and the North American plants. We cannot even be certain where some of these plants came from. Bananas and plantains were first domesticated in New Guinea (Lentfer and Boyd 2014) but were present in Europe in the late Middle Ages and cultivated by Portuguese colonists in the Atlantic islands in the fifteenth and sixteenth centuries.

In summary, based on recovered plant and animal remains, the town of Magdalena on the El Brujo terrace between the late sixteenth and late seventeenth centuries supported its food needs through a mixed subsistence economy of agriculture, fishing, and catching shore-birds. At present we cannot fully assess the importance of domesticated sheep and goat in diets because of the change in site use during Magdalena's latest occupation. It may have been significant, however, given the fact that isotopic analyses of the overall intake of protein and plants of the Magdalena population suggest that they had better nutrition than any prehistoric population to which they were compared (see Appendix 4.1 in Chapter 4).

The degree to which there were differences in diets between the native population in the town and the friars in the church is not clear. As Ringberg notes in Chapter 9, the ceramic assemblage in the church compound had more indigenous-style wares than the ceramic assemblage of the town did. This may be due to the fact that the church was abandoned sometime in the seventeenth century, while the townspeople stayed on through at least the first third of the eighteenth century, accumulating more European wares than their ancestors or even the friars of earlier times and becoming more acculturated to European culture in general. Differences between town and church in the kinds of fish eaten and, perhaps, the relative amounts of sheep/goats do suggest, however, that some differences in food culture were in operation in the two sectors.

While many issues remain uncertain regarding food consumption patterns at the site, our work has established some general guidelines for future research. These involve learning more about the differences in patterns of consumption between town and church and changes in them through time, and finding out more about the relative speed of the adoption of exotic plants and animals into the local economy.

In terms of foodways, the detailed studies of diets, especially as revealed in the Unit 28 research but also as augmented by the other studies, suggest a relatively conservative adoption process, with Andean town residents eating meals that likely were not that different from those their ancestors ate before the coming of the Spaniards. In contrast, however, is the presence of many fruits, ornamental plants, and other non-native species that entered the town before its abandonment. Magdalena was not a very important town and was relatively isolated on the shore of the Pacific in the lower Chicama Valley. Despite this, however, it appears to have been linked to the emerging world market economy at a relatively early time. We see this not only in regard to plants and animals, of course, but also through the presence of Asian porcelains (Chapter 8) and European textiles (Chapter 6). These issues too will merit further study as data become available.

If Magdaleneros had hard lives under colonial rule, it was not due to their diets. How Magdalena's population compares to other contemporary populations will only be known when similar work occurs at other sites. Documentary sources and ethnohistorical studies present a picture of extreme hardship in reducción communities, and there is no reason to doubt that life at Magdalena was hard, especially in the early years of colonial rule. The archaeological study of Magdalena de Cao offers a view of one community during a 200-year period that cannot be easily subdivided, so the wealth of our archaeological remains is constrained in what it can tell us. But it offers us a window through which to peer.

NOTES

1 Because sheep and goats are closely related, it is often difficult to distinguish between them when fragmentary or nondiagnostic skeletal remains are found. The Spanish term *ovicaprino*, which combines the genus names for sheep (*Ovis*) and goat (*Capra*), is sometimes used. Here, we use "sheep/goat" when distinctions cannot be made. Mirabal's study, discussed in the following section, distinguished between the two and so is reported here accordingly.

2 See Chapter 13. The earliest cigarettes, of course, are not necessarily the same as the earliest use of tobacco or cigarettelike methods of smoking. The critical distinction of a cigarette from other smoking devices is the use of paper as a wrapper. Cigarettes are generally considered to have been first made in France circa 1830 but did not become widely popular until the twentieth century (Goodman 1993:97). Our case of the expedient use of paper nevertheless seems to register as the earliest cigarettes found to date.

3 Much of the presentation of prehistoric and traditional practices in procuring and consuming maritime resources is drawn from the extensive and informative work of Oscar Gabriel Prieto (2015).

REFERENCES CITED

Burger, Richard L., Lucy C. Salazar, and Victor Vásquez Sánchez
    2011   Rethinking Agricultural Staples for the Initial Period Population of the Lurín Valley: Scraping the Bottom of the Olla. Paper presented at the 77th Annual Meeting of the Society for American Archaeology, April 20, Memphis, TN.

de la Vega, Garcilaso
    1970   [1609] *Royal Commentaries of the Incas and General History of Peru, Part One.* Translated by Harold V. Livermore. Austin: University of Texas Press.

Gagliano, Joseph A.
    1963   The Coca Debate in Colonial Peru. *The Americas* 20(1):43–63.

Goodman, Jordan E.
    1993   *Tobacco in History: The Cultures of Dependence.* New York: Routledge.

Lentfer, C., and W. Boyd
    2014   Tracing Antiquity of Banana Cultivation in Papua New Guinea. The Australia and Pacific Science Foundation. http://www.apscience.org.au/projects/PBF_02_3/pbf_02_3.htm.

Mirabal, Danielle Olga Garner
    2008   Interpretation of Faunal Remains from the Contact Site of Magdalena de Cao Viejo: North Coast of Peru. Unpublished senior honors thesis, Department of Anthropology, Harvard University.

Paulsen, Allison C.
    1974   The Thorny Oyster and the Voice of God: *Spondylus* and *Strombus* in Andean Prehistory. *American Antiquity* 39(1):597–607.

Prieto, Oscar Gabriel
    2015   Gramalote: Domestic Life and Ritual Practices of a Prehispanic Maritime Community. Unpublished Ph.D. dissertation, Yale University.

Quilter, Jeffrey, Deborah M. Pearsall, Daniel H. Sandweiss, Elizabeth S. Wing, John G. Jones, and Bernardino Ojeda E.

　　1991　Subsistence Economy of El Paraíso, Peru, an Early Peruvian Site. *Science* 251(4991):277–283.

Quilter, Jeffrey, and Terry Stocker

　　1983　Subsistence Economies and the Origins of Andean Complex Societies. *American Anthropologist* 85(3):545–562.

Bioarchaeology

Catherine M. Gaither
and Melissa S. Murphy

Introduction

A TOTAL OF 28 intact and partially intact burials were recovered from Magdalena de Cao Viejo, 23 from under the floor of the nave and 5 from the cemetery. In this chapter we present our analyses of these remains within the contexts of research at the site as well as the broader impacts of colonization and forced resettlement. We also discuss remains of note recovered from disturbed contexts as they relate to life, death, physiological stresses, and disease on the North Coast of Peru more generally.

Previous research on the biocultural effects of colonialism reveals that they were considerably more variable and complex than generally believed. Some researchers (Larsen et al. 2001; Verano and Ubelaker 1992) found considerable biological stress resulting in severe population effects, while others have found communities that adapted well (Klaus 2008). At the same time, comparative bioarchaeological studies have been few until recently, limiting our ability to offer conclusive statements about the era. A study of colonial burials in Ecuador found high frequencies of periosteal reactions, dental pathological conditions, and traumatic injuries (Ubelaker and Newsom 2002; Ubelaker and Ripley 1999), but no other studies were available for comparison. Fortunately, however, this situation has changed in the last decade due to growing interest in historical archaeology of South America. Not too far from Magdalena, Haagen Klaus examined burials from two colonial churches, Eten and Mórrope, in the Lambayeque Valley. These two samples presented contrasting outcomes under Spanish colonial rule, with the people of Mórrope suffering higher levels of physiological stress and greater labor demands while those at Eten fared much better (Klaus 2008; Klaus and Alvarez-Calderón 2017; Klaus and Tam 2010). Continuing research on the bioarchaeology of the Colonial Period, such as that presented here, will add to such comparisons and enrich our understanding of the past.

Archaeological Contexts

As noted in Chapter 2, extensive looting scattered human remains on the surface of the El Brujo archaeological complex, with higher bone concentrations in former cemetery areas

Figure 4.1 Burial excavations in 2007 in Unit 12 east, in the northeast corner of the church nave. The thick wall, at right, is the northern wall of the church and the space at the top of the photograph is the threshold to the nave.

than elsewhere. As the church and town rest on prehistoric architecture and burials, we were at first uncertain if human remains in the colonial sector were prehistoric or colonial in age. In addition, after our first field season we returned in subsequent seasons to find more bones on the ground surface, exposed by winds since our previous work. These were systematically collected. As time passed, we noted consistently high quantities of bones in the nave and in the area immediately west of it.

Some of our earliest excavations in the nave focused on its north end, and we soon noticed that there were large and deep looter holes on each side of the interior of the entry to the church. Cleaning out the eastern looter hole revealed the presence of human skeletal parts among the adobe bricks beneath the church (Figures 4.1 and 4.2), and this led to cleaning and slightly expanding as well as deepening first the eastern looter hole in 2007 and then the western one in 2008. Each original hole was 3–4 m long, more than 2 m wide, and more than 1 m deep, and while there were numerous areas of disturbance, excavation revealed several completely or partially articulated human skeletons oriented with heads to the north and feet to the south (i.e., feet toward the altar and the huaca). They were arranged in extended positions side by side and one on top of the other. The matrix consisted of a sandy soil that resulted in decent preservation of the bone; there were no readily visible grave goods, though small artifacts, such a blue glass bead, were uncovered in screened materials.

Sufficiently large sections of the church floor remained to allow us to identify cuts in their surfaces (Figure 4.2), indicating that the bodies were lowered into the graves from inside the church. The bodies were wrapped in textiles, of which little remained (Figures 4.3 and 4.4). The adobe bricks that entombed the burials may have been part of a prehistoric structure,

Figure 4.2 Burial excavations in Unit 12 in the church nave. Top: Eastern unit, 2007. Bottom: Western unit, 2008. Arrows indicate cuts through floor to insert burials. (Sign in bottom photo incorrectly states Unit 7.)

Figure 4.3 Burial 5 in extended Christian position. Note textile fragments underneath the burial.

Figure 4.4
Detail of mat and
textile remains
underneath the
head of burial 5.

but the positioning and orientation of the bodies strongly suggest that they were buried as Catholics.

We also continually found dense quantities of human bones in an area immediately west of the church, especially in the rectangular area defined by the nave on the east and the atrium on the north. A close inspection of the area also noted that in addition to human skeletal parts there were large pieces of painted cotton cloth (see Chapter 6). By 2008, we realized that these cotton fabrics were burial shrouds or wrappings, and that they and the high concentrations of human bones were present because this was likely the town cemetery.

We subsequently conducted a systematic surface collection in the area in 2008. Excavations also were undertaken in 2012 to determine if a wall enclosed the area, as is common for cemeteries, especially in this part of Peru. Although no such walls were encountered, the large quantities of human skeletal remains and textiles that we did find—representing more than 70 individuals—support our interpretation that this was the town cemetery. Unfortunately, due to the great amount of looting in the area, little can be said regarding funeral practices, but a few exceptions are discussed later in this chapter. Of the 28 burials recovered from either the cemetery or under the church floor, 6 were complete or mostly complete, and the remaining 22 presented partial skeletons. Of the 15 adult individuals, only 3 were complete or mostly complete. Of the remaining partial skeletons, 5 presented no sexually dimorphic elements that would permit estimation of sex and 5 presented age estimation features that permitted only a very general age estimation, such as young adult or middle adult (30–50 years). Among the 13 non-adult individuals, 3 were complete or mostly complete and the remainder were partial skeletons. Of the partial non-adult skeletons, only 2 were incomplete enough to prevent age estimation, and of course, sex cannot be morphologically estimated with any degree of accuracy from non-adult skeletal remains.

Analyses

Hypotheses

Based on historical documents, we hypothesized that the individuals from the intact burials at Magdalena de Cao Viejo would show higher levels of physiological stress and disease than prehistoric samples from the El Brujo complex. We also expected that the colonial burials would show the effects of increased labor demands, with high frequencies of antemortem injuries and degenerative joint diseases, particularly osteoarthritis and vertebral osteophytosis. Finally, we believed that our investigations of the burials would reveal syncretism of native Andean and Catholic beliefs. While we expected that the burials would mainly conform to Catholic ideals, we believed that evidence of ideological blending might be indicated by idiosyncrasies consistent with Andean religious ideas and practices.

Methods of Osteological Analyses

Osteological analyses followed standard protocols (after Buikstra and Ubelaker 1994). We estimated sex only for individuals whose skeletal maturation permitted the visual assessment of sexually dimorphic cranial or pelvic characteristics. Additionally, long-bone measurements were utilized to supplement estimation based on morphological features. We estimated adult ages utilizing well-documented age-related changes of specific features, including the auricular surface of the ilium, the sternal rib extremities, the pubic symphyseal face, and cranial suture closure (Bass 2005; Buikstra and Ubelaker 1994; White et al. 2012). These features were assigned a score or phase with an associated age range and mean age. Multifactorial techniques, including the total minimum range, simple average, and statistical equations as outlined in DiGangi and Moore 2013, were then utilized to produce a single age range and mean age from the various scores.

We estimated non-adult age by tooth crown and root formation, tooth eruption, long-bone lengths, epiphyseal union, and skeletal development (Buikstra and Ubelaker 1994; Gaither 2004, 2007; Scheuer and Black 2000; Ubelaker 1999; White et al. 2012). The state of union of the spheno-occipital synchondrosis (i.e., unfused or open basilar suture) and third molar formation and eruption were used to designate an individual as a non-adult.

We accomplished ancestry estimation by utilizing both morphological and craniometric data. We visually assessed traditional morphological characteristics (*sensu* Rhine 1990) and also employed a series of cranial characteristics identified by Hefner (2009) and visually scored in Osteoware 2.4.037, a portable inventory database. Our craniometric data collection followed standard protocols as described in Buikstra and Ubelaker 1994. We also recorded and analyzed evidence of cranial modification (Buikstra and Ubelaker 1994:160–164). In cases where cranial modification was evident, we excluded from statistical analyses any craniometric data involving modified areas of the cranium.

We described and scored the location, severity, and state of healing of cribra orbitalia and porotic hyperostosis according to standard protocols (Buikstra and Ubelaker 1994). Since the underlying etiology is the same for porotic hyperostosis and cribra orbitalia, we pooled the results of these data and report them as porous cranial lesions in the following discussions. We examined all cranial and postcranial elements for evidence of abnormalities in bone loss, bone formation (e.g., periostosis), size, and shape (after Buikstra and Ubelaker 1994). We assessed the pattern of lesion distribution and involvement in order to determine if an infectious process was local or systemic (Buikstra and Ubelaker 1994; Goodman and Martin 2002).

Skeletal evidence of traumatic injuries includes healed calluses from old injuries; remodeling adjacent to joint dislocations; ossification of muscular, tendinous, and connective tissue near injured muscles; and unhealed fractures. We analyzed traumatic lesions in accordance with established methodologies (Buikstra and Ubelaker 1994; Lovell 2008; White et al. 2012). The specific location of the lesion, including the bone, side, and aspect, was recorded, and the timing of the injuries was conservatively determined after careful consideration of the osseous evidence, burial context, and taphonomic processes that might have affected the remains (Berryman and Haun 1996; Berryman and Symes 1998; Buikstra and Ubelaker 1994; Sauer 1998; Sledzik 1998; White et al. 2012).

We identified degenerative joint disease (osteoarthritis and vertebral osteophytosis) by the deterioration of the articular surfaces of bones or the development of osteophytes on joint surfaces or vertebral bodies (Buikstra and Ubelaker 1994). The side and joint location were identified and recorded. These areas of degenerative joint disease were scored according to the severity and nature of the affected bone (Buikstra and Ubelaker 1994).

Carious lesions, inflammatory reactions, and antemortem tooth loss were recorded for all dentitions (following the standards outlined in Buikstra and Ubelaker 1994 and Hillson 2001). The location of the inflammatory reaction or carious lesion was also recorded.

Statistical Analyses

Craniometric data were analyzed utilizing discriminate function analysis performed by the program FORDISC 3.1 (Ousley and Jantz 2005), which is a statistical program that compiles numerous cranial measurements and determines the probability of affiliation of remains to specific ancestral groups based on comparison samples from both modern and archaeological populations. Results are presented as probability statements. Following recommended practices (DiGangi and Hefner 2013), macromorphoscopic analysis of cranial morphological characteristics was done utilizing SPSS (IBM Corp. 2011) and the k-nearest neighbor statistic. As a measure of population adaptation, fertility rates were estimated using a D^{30+}/D^{5+} ratio, where D^{30+} is the number of deaths of individuals over 30 years of age and D^{5+} is the number of deaths of individuals older than 5 years of age (Buikstra et al. 1986; Klaus and Tam 2010). Juvenile mortality was assessed in order to determine its possible impact on the fertility rate. It was measured as the proportion of weaning-age deaths (ages 1–5 years) out of the total number of childhood deaths (ages 1–10 years), a frequency known as the D^{1-5}/D^{1-10} proportion (Buikstra et al. 1986). Significance in the difference of proportions in fertility and juvenile mortality rates between Magdalena and comparative population samples was tested utilizing a difference-in-proportions z-test (Fletcher and Lock 2005). Differences in frequencies of nonspecific indicators of stress between the Magdalena population sample and samples drawn from Late Intermediate Period burials on the Huaca Cao Viejo were tested in SPSS (IBM Corp. 2011) using the ANOVA analysis and the chi square (χ^2) statistic.

Mortuary Analyses

Burial location, position and orientation, taphonomic conditions, and the presence or absence of associated mortuary artifacts were some of the variables we considered in the mortuary analyses. The textile analyses conducted by Brezine (Chapter 6; Brezine 2011, 2012) also helped in our study. We compared mortuary treatments to known practices from the prehistoric remains recovered from the El Brujo archaeological complex, other prehispanic contexts from the Central Andes, and recent studies of Colonial Period burials on the North Coast of Peru and elsewhere.

Results

Mortuary Analysis

A total of 23 individuals (burials 5–27) were recovered from the church. Bodies were wrapped in textiles and stacked one on top of the other. The majority of the bodies were positioned in an extended supine position (i.e., on their back) with their arms crossed over their chest or abdomen and their feet pointed toward the altar—what we call a Catholic position (Figure 4.3). An analysis of the fragmentary textiles found with the burials reveals that they are stylistically indigenous but also demonstrate some European design and technological influences (see Chapter 6). No grave goods were recovered in situ with the burials, although one twisted blue glass bead was recovered during screening, and it too indicates European influence.

Burials 2, 3, 4, and C4.P4.E1 (individuals a and b) were recovered from the cemetery adjacent to the church. Burial 3 and C4.P4.E1 (individual b) were adults, and burials 2, 4, and C4.P4.E1 (individual a) were non-adults. These were wrapped in textiles, and two of the individuals recovered were interred in Catholic position, like the burials under the floor of the church. The position of one adult individual female, burial 3, was distinct from the overall pattern observed. This individual was in a supine position, but semiflexed and with at least one of her arms folded across her abdomen (the other arm had missing parts, which prevented us from determining its exact position). Two fetuses recovered from the cemetery (burials 2 and 4) also were not positioned or oriented in Catholic fashion; rather, they were flexed and lying on one side.

A few other interesting patterns are common to all of the burials recovered at the site. Insect puparia were found associated with all of the bodies, indicating that a full progression of larval development had occurred prior to interment (Anderson 2000). Additionally, there was a case in which articulated portions of a body (burial 15) were stacked on top of another articulated individual (burial 19), indicating these had not been disturbed by looting activities, and when the topmost body (burial 15) was removed, the articulated intact portion of the body beneath it (burial 19) was missing the skull (Figure 4.5).

Intact and Semi-Intact Burials: Osteological Analysis

Of the 28 individuals recovered, we could determine the sex of 9. There were 4 females and 5 males (Table 4.1). The age range for the sample included fetuses to individuals who were more than 50 years old at the time of death. Among the adults, all but three (89 percent) were under 40 years old at death. Forty-six percent of this sample (13 of 28 individuals) were osteologically

Figure 4.5 Stacked burials under the church floor, numbered. Some of the bodies were incomplete when entombed, as was the case for burial 19.

non-adult, meaning there was a lack of or incomplete union of the spheno-occipital synchondrosis and unerupted or incompletely formed third molars. Fourteen percent of this sample (4 of 28 individuals) were fetuses or neonates. Initial ancestral classification of the individuals recovered from Magdalena utilizing only those individuals with crania was consistent with designation as Native Americans, though not all were classified as Peruvian natives (Table 4.2 presents the detailed results). The various possible implications of these results are discussed in more detail later in this chapter.

Fertility, measured using the D^{30+}/D^{5+} ratio (Buikstra et al. 1986; Klaus and Tam 2010), was 0.40. Juvenile mortality for the Magdalena population, measured using the D^{1-5}/D^{1-10}

Table 4.1 Sample Composition of Intact and Partially Intact Burials from Magdalena de Cao

	N	%
Adults	15	53.6
Non-adults	13	46.4
Males	5	33.3
Females	4	26.7
Indeterminate	6	40.0
TOTAL	28	100

Table 4.2 Ancestry Classification Results

BURIAL #	FORDISC 3.1 HOWELLS DATABASE CLASSIFICATION	POSTERIOR PROBABILITY*	TYP F HOWELLS*	TYP CHI HOWELLS*	
6	HAIM (East Asian group—Hainan)	0.715	0.962	0.956	
3	Too dissimilar to all groups to be categorized	NA	NA	NA	
7	PERF (Peruvian)	0.338	0.373	0.286	
9	PERM (Peruvian)	0.748	0.417	0.33	
11	SANM (Native North American group)	0.575	0.164	0.093	
14	SANF (Native North American group)	0.513	0.967	0.957	
15	ESKM (Eskimo)	0.96	0.024	0.007	
23	PERF (Peruvian)	0.962	0.428	0.38	

* Posterior probability should be > 0.70 to accept the classification, and all three typicality statistics (Typ F, Typ Chi, and Typ R) should be > 0.01 in order to accept the classification and > 0.05 to be confidently accepted.

proportion, was 0.60. Forty-three percent of all deaths (12 of 28 individuals) occurred between the ages of 0 and 15 years, and among the osteologically non-adult group 92 percent (12 of 13 individuals) died between the ages of 0 and 15 years, suggesting that juvenile mortality may have affected the fertility rate. A difference-in-proportions z-test (Fletcher and Lock 2005), however, demonstrated no statistically significant differences between the juvenile mortality rate at Magdalena and that of populations with similar fertility rates.

Two males, one female (burials 6, 3, and 9), and two individuals of indeterminate sex (burials 26 and 27) possessed osteoarthritis (5 of 28 individuals, 17.9 percent), but none of these cases was severe. Of the adults examined ($N=15$), a third of them had osteoarthritis. Two individuals had traumatic arthritis associated with antemortem fractures. Four individuals possessed vertebral osteophytosis (burials 15, 26, 27, and C4.P4.E1 [individual b]—one male and three individuals of indeterminate sex) in the form of an elevated ring or curved spicules, which is 14.3 percent of the total sample (4 of 28 individuals) and 26.6 percent of the adults examined (4 of 15 individuals).

Only nine individuals could be examined for dental pathological conditions (burials 3, 5, 6, 7, 9, 11, 14, 15, and 23). Six of nine individuals (67 percent) had dental carious lesions, with a total of 19 affected teeth and an average of 3.2 lesions per individual. Two of nine individuals had dental infections (22 percent), with a total of two affected teeth. Three of nine individuals had antemortem tooth loss (33 percent), with a total of ten affected teeth and an average of 2.7 teeth lost per individual. Moderate to severe dental attrition was also present in at least

TYP R HOWELLS*	HEFNER MACROMORPHOSCOPIC CLASSIFICATION	TRADITIONAL CLASSIFICATION**	COMMENTS
0.913	Native American	East Asian/Amerindian	Male
NA	Not enough characteristics visible for scoring	East Asian/Amerindian	Female
0.143	African	East Asian/Amerindian	Female
0.268	Native American	East Asian/Amerindian	Male
0.115	European	East Asian/Amerindian	Split almost even with Peruvian male
0.962	Native American/Asian	East Asian/Amerindian	Split almost even with Peruvian female
0.019	Native American	East Asian/Amerindian	Male
0.429	Native American/Asian	East Asian/Amerindian	Female

** Traits scored include palate shape, eye orbit shape, suture pattern, nasal bridge shape, nasal aperture width, cheekbone projection, and facial prognathism.

Table 4.3 Frequency of Pathological Lesions Other than NSIS (Adults Only)

	N	%
Antemortem injuries	4/15	26.6
Perimortem injuries	1/15	6.7
Vertebral osteophytosis	4/15	26.6
Osteoarthritis	5/15	33.3
Dental carious lesions	7/9*	77.0
Dental infections	2/9*	22.0

* Only nine individuals possessed dentitions with sufficient teeth to be included in the analysis of oral pathological conditions.

two of these nine individuals (22 percent). Table 4.3 presents the frequencies of these various pathological lesions.

Nearly two-thirds of the sample (61 percent) presented some form of nonspecific indicator of stress (NSIS), with 17 of 28 individuals presenting with porous cranial lesions, periostosis, or linear enamel hypoplasias (Table 4.4). See Appendix 4.1 for information on specific burials, lesion types, and locations. Porous cranial lesions were present in a total of 8 of 28 individuals, or 29 percent, and periostosis was evident in 8 of 28 individuals (29 percent). Taken as a whole, these frequencies are not significantly different from Late Intermediate Period samples (A.D. 1100–1450) from Huaca Cao Viejo (ANOVA results for periostosis, $p = 0.121$; for porous cranial lesions, $p = 0.481$). Only two individuals (7.1 percent) possessed linear enamel hypoplasias, and this was not enough to permit meaningful statistical comparison with the samples from Huaca Cao Viejo.

A closer examination of the NSIS data by age (non-adult versus adult), however, presents slightly different results. For both adults and non-adults, there was no statistically significant difference in the frequencies of periostosis between the samples from Magdalena and those from Huaca Cao Viejo (adult $\chi^2 = 0.024$, $p = 0.877$; non-adult $\chi^2 = 0.279$, $p = 0.598$). All eight individuals with periostosis presented with lesions that were active at the time of death. Three

Table 4.4 Nonspecific Indicators of Stress

STRESS INDICATOR	NUMBER AFFECTED	NUMBER ANALYZED	PERCENTAGE OF INDIVIDUALS WITH CRANIA ANALYZED FOR NSIS
Porous cranial lesions			
Adult	7	9	77%
Non-adult	2	8	25%
Total	9	17	53%
Periostosis	8	28	29%
Linear enamel hypoplasias	2	28	7.1%

Table 4.5 Actual and Expected Counts of Porous Cranial Lesions in Adults in El Brujo and Magdalena de Cao

Cross-tabulation demonstrating actual and expected counts of adults presenting with porous cranial lesions at the sites of El Brujo and Magdalena de Cao.

CROSS-TABULATION

			SITE NUMBER		
			HUACA CAO VIEJO (EL BRUJO)	MAGDALENA DE CAO	TOTAL
Porous cranial lesions	Absent	Count	40_a	2_b	42
		Expected count	36.5	5.5	42.0
	Present	Count	20_a	$7_b{}^*$	27
		Expected count	23.5	3.5	27.0
Total		Count	60	9	69
		Expected count	60.0	9.0	69.0

Each subscript letter denotes a subset of site number categories whose column proportions do not differ significantly from each other at the 0.05 level.

* The count of individuals who present with porous cranial lesions at Magdalena de Cao is higher than expected.

of eight individuals also presented with either separate healed lesions (one individual) or a mixture of healed and active lesions (two individuals) at death. The analysis of porous cranial lesions in adults ($N = 9$) and non-adults ($N = 8$), however, did demonstrate statistically significant differences (adult $\chi^2 = 6.490$, $p = 0.011$; non-adult $\chi^2 = 7.200$, $p = 0.007$) when compared with their predecessors from the Huaca Cao Viejo. The adults at Magdalena demonstrate statistically significantly higher frequencies of porous cranial lesions, whereas the non-adults demonstrate statistically significantly lower frequencies of porous cranial lesions. Tables 4.5–4.8 present the cross-tabulations and chi-square results for these analyses.

Five adults possessed fractures (5 of 15 individuals, 33.3 percent: two males, one female, and two of indeterminate sex, burials 6, 22, 23, 25, and 27), and the majority of these were ante-mortem fractures, with only one instance of a perimortem fracture (17 cases, 16 antemortem fractures, 1 perimortem injury). Of the 16 cases of antemortem fractures, 13 were located on two of the four adults who presented with antemortem injuries (burials 6, 22, 25, and 27). Of the individuals with antemortem fractures, two were male, one was female, and one was of indeterminate sex. One of these individuals, burial 22, had healed fractures to the cranium and multiple ribs, and compression fractures to L1 and L5, for a total of ten healed fractures. Ribs were the most frequently fractured skeletal element (seven cases), followed by vertebrae (six cases). Three individuals possessed healed fractures to their vertebrae, including compression fractures and spondylolisthesis. None of the non-adults presented with any antemortem or perimortem fractures. We observed tumpline deformation on one individual, an adult female (burial 7). Seven individuals (six adults and one non-adult) possessed culturally modified crania, specifically the type known as symmetrical occipital deformation (7 of 28 individuals, 25 percent). Forty percent of the adults (6 of 9 individuals) possessed this type of cranial modification.

Table 4.6 Frequencies of Porous Cranial Lesions in Adults at El Brujo and Magdalena de Cao

Chi-square results demonstrating statistically significant differences at the 5 percent level in the frequencies of porous cranial lesions in adult individuals at the sites of El Brujo and Magdalena de Cao. Adult individuals at Magdalena de Cao demonstrated higher frequencies of porous cranial lesions than would be expected if there were no difference between the two samples.

CHI-SQUARE TESTS

	VALUE	DF	ASYMP. SIG. (2-SIDED)	EXACT SIG. (2-SIDED)	EXACT SIG. (1-SIDED)
Pearson chi-square	6.490[a]	1	.011		
Continuity correction[b]	4.758	1	.029		
Likelihood ratio	6.451	1	.011		
Fisher's exact test				.023	.015
Linear-by-linear association	6.396	1	.011		
N of valid cases	69				

a One cell (25 percent) has an expected count less than 5.00. The minimum expected count is 3.52.

b Computed only for a 2×2 table.

Table 4.7 Actual and Expected Counts of Porous Cranial Lesions in Non-adults at El Brujo and Magdalena de Cao

Cross-tabulation demonstrating actual and expected counts of non-adults presenting with porous cranial lesions at the sites of El Brujo and Magdalena de Cao. Note that the count of individuals who present with porous cranial lesions at Magdalena de Cao is lower than expected.

CROSS-TABULATION

			SITE NUMBER		TOTAL
			HUACA CAO VIEJO (EL BRUJO)	MAGDALENA DE CAO	
Porous cranial lesions	Absent	Count	3[a]	6[b]	9
		Expected count	6.0	3.0	9.0
	Present	Count	13[a]	2[b]	15
		Expected count	10.0	5.0	15.0
Total		Count	16	8	24
		Expected count	16.0	8.0	24.0

Each subscript letter denotes a subset of site number categories whose column proportions do not differ significantly from each other at the 0.05 level.

Table 4.8 Porous Cranial Lesions in Non-adults at El Brujo and Magdalena de Cao

Chi-square results demonstrating statistically significant differences at the 1 percent level in the frequencies of porous cranial lesions in non-adult individuals at the sites of El Brujo and Magdalena de Cao. Non-adult individuals at Magdalena de Cao demonstrated lower frequencies of porous cranial lesions than would be expected if there were no difference between the two samples.

CHI-SQUARE TESTS

	VALUE	DF	ASYMP. SIG. (2-SIDED)	EXACT SIG. (2-SIDED)	EXACT SIG. (1-SIDED)
Pearson chi-square	7.200[a]	1	.007		
Continuity correction[b]	5.000	1	.025		
Likelihood ratio	7.315	1	.007		
Fisher's exact test				.021	.013
Linear-by-linear association	6.900	1	.009		
N of valid cases	24				

a   One cell (25 percent) has and expected count less than 5.00. The minimum expected count is 3.00.

b   Computed only for a 2×2 table.

Special and Disturbed Remains

We collected human remains representing more than 70 individuals from disturbed contexts. They were analyzed in order to document general information about the pathological conditions present on the North Coast of Peru in this archaeological complex. During the course of these analyses, we examined several skeletal elements worthy of discussion despite their lack of archaeological contexts. Among these are a cranium that demonstrates African morphology, the remains of an achondroplastic dwarf, and skeletal elements that demonstrate evidence of interpersonal violence, infectious disease, and neoplastic disease. Additionally, there are several isolated skeletal elements with evidence of nonspecific indicators of stress and nutritional deficiency.

Non-Native Remains: The African Cranium

A cranium with a distinctive morphology was found in 2005. Though recovered from disturbed contexts, its form was noticeably different from the typical Native American morphology seen at the site. After morphological and craniometric analysis, we determined that the cranium was that of a person of African descent. Sex estimations identified it as female, but later DNA analysis revealed it to be a male. This is not surprising, as recent research seeking to validate sex estimation utilizing crania has revealed that the cranium is not nearly as accurate as previously thought, particularly in small-bodied populations (Spradley and Jantz 2011). It appears, in fact, that postcranial measurements are more accurate in these kinds of populations. Unfortunately, there were no postcranial remains found with this individual, but these results present a cautionary tale for bioarchaeologists as well as forensic anthropologists. Age estimation revealed the individual was in his early to mid-20s at death. Subsequent isotopic and molecular analyses further identify this individual as African. The analysis of this cranium is discussed in greater detail in Chapter 5.

Although Africans came or were brought to the New World in the first wave of European exploration in the sixteenth century, this skull is the earliest physical remains of an African in South America and possibly the New World (cf. Price et al. 2012). The find is also evidence of the presence of individuals of African descent early on at Magdalena, which was a reducción, and so contradicted laws in the early seventeenth century that strictly prohibited the coresidence of African and indigenous people in the same community.

Genetic Disorders: The Achondroplastic Dwarf

Also recovered during the 2005 season were two skeletal elements that demonstrate evidence of achondroplastic dwarfism. The elements included a right radius and right first metatarsal (Figure 4.6). Both demonstrate fused epiphyses, abnormally shortened length, and abnormal shape consistent with achondroplasia. The radius was only 71 percent as long as the normal female radius and 63 percent as long as the normal male radius from these populations. The

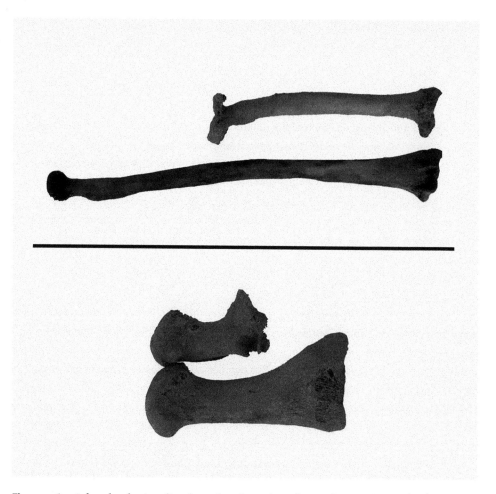

Figure 4.6 Achondroplastic radius shown beside a radius of normal size and shape (top), and achondroplastic first metatarsal shown beside a first metatarsal of normal size and shape (bottom).

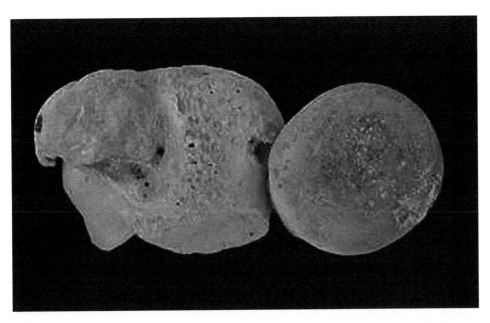

Figure 4.7 Healed fracture of the head of the achondroplastic radius next to a normal radial head (right). Note the visible fracture line and severe arthritis with porosities in the bone of the joint surface.

radius demonstrate well-healed trauma in the form of a fracture of the head (Figure 4.7). Both demonstrate abnormal curvature often seen in cases of achondroplasia (Ortner and Putschar 1981). This case is significant because these bones may represent the first, and perhaps only, recovered physical remains of an achondroplastic dwarf in this region of Peru.

Interpersonal Violence, Trauma, Infectious Disease, and Neoplastic Disease

Numerous remains recovered from disturbed contexts confirm the presence of certain infectious diseases, metabolic disturbances, and neoplastic disease in these populations. Specifically, one lumbar vertebra recovered from Unit 6 (in the Colonial Period church) in 2005 demonstrates large circumscribed lytic defects of the vertebral body consistent with a tuberculosis infection (Figure 4.8). A portion of a left eye orbit recovered from Unit 12 in the church in 2005 demonstrates periostosis consistent with vitamin C deficiency (Figure 4.9) (Brickley and Ives 2008; Ortner et al. 1999). A right ilium from a female individual of young age demonstrate a tumorous growth on the iliac crest (Figure 4.10), indicating not only the presence of neoplastic disease in these populations but also its occurrence in some young individuals. Finally, several remains demonstrate evidence for nonspecific indicators of stress, such as the porous cranial lesions discussed earlier (cribra orbitalia and porotic hyperostosis), which are often associated with anemia (Blom et al. 2005).

In addition to pathological lesions, several remains demonstrate the presence of trau-matic lesions that may indicate interpersonal violence or physically demanding activities. Included among these are several rib fractures, depressed cranial fractures (including one healed fracture on the African skull), a humerus presenting with evidence of long-term

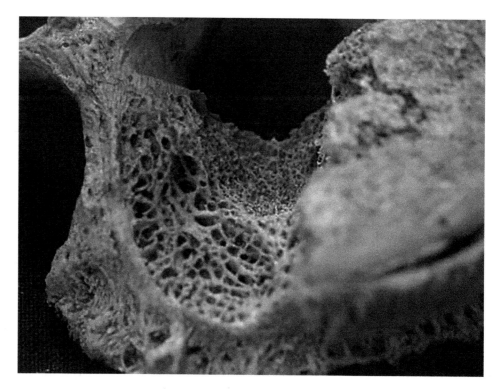

Figure 4.8 Lumbar vertebra recovered from disturbed contexts demonstrating lesions consistent with tuberculosis.

dislocation (Figure 4.11), and spondylolysis (a fracture of the vertebral arch across the laminae resulting in the separation of the arch from the vertebral body). These suggest generally that the populations inhabiting this region of Peru were engaging in physically intense activities.

Ritual Reuse of the Site: A Republican Era Burial

In 2006, a small wooden coffin was recovered as an intrusive burial in the nave of the church (Figure 4.12). The outside of the coffin was covered with red textile and a lace design arranged in the form of a cross over the lid of the coffin. The wood appeared to have been cut by a machine and there were nails present. The body inside the coffin was of a child. It was possible to measure the left femur, which at 79 mm indicates an age between birth and 6 months (Gaither 2004, 2007). It is at the lower end of the range for this age category, suggesting this child was closer to birth than 6 months. Flowers, bound with a green textile material, were lying on top of the body. The body was dressed in several layers of burial clothing and there was a thin organic material similar to bamboo or cane with flowers attached encircling the head, perhaps representing a type of crown. The child was mostly mummified. A small wooden cross had been placed in the child's hands. A string made of cotton or wool was tied around the child's left ankle. The coffin style, burial clothing, and bedding indicate the burial likely dates to the early Republican Period, which began in 1821. The fact that the child was buried in the

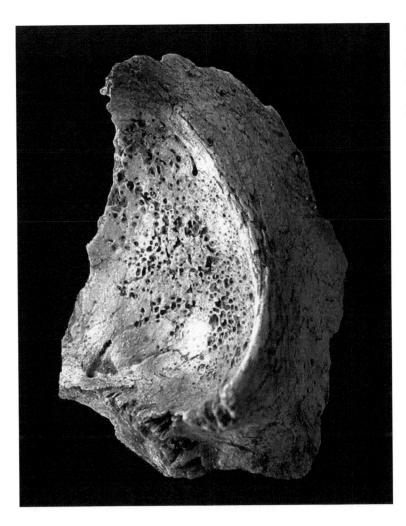

Figure 4.9
Portion of an eye orbit recovered from disturbed contexts demonstrating periostosis consistent with vitamin C deficiency.

location of the old church, as indicated by the evidence of intrusion into the archaeological site, is consistent with ritual reuse of a holy site.

Discussion

Results of the analysis of the intact burials support the hypothesis that the population at Magdalena experienced some biological stress, but the results are mixed and do not offer strong support for the general hypothesis of an overall negative biological impact on the individuals from this community. Our hypothesis regarding culturally blended funerary traditions is supported. A discussion of the mortuary practices as related to this specific sample may help to put these results in context.

The majority of the Magdalena de Cao Viejo sample is composed of individuals buried under the floor of the church, and the burial styles demonstrate clear evidence of Catholic burial tradition, including an extended body position with the feet oriented toward the altar and the arms folded over the chest or abdomen. Catholic practice dictated that parishioners be buried with their feet toward the altar, whereas the priest would be buried with his head

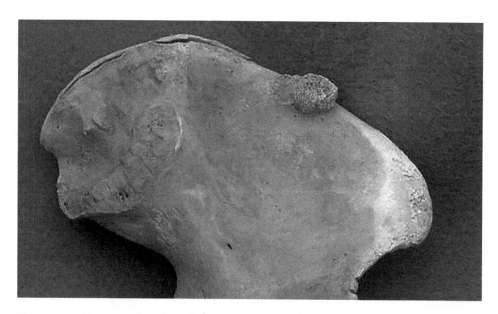

Figure 4.10 Tumor on the pelvis of a young individual from disturbed remains from the central portion of the nave interior.

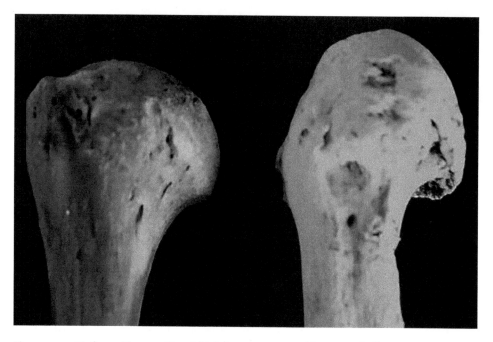

Figure 4.11 Deformed humeral head (right) next to a normal humerus (left). In the deformed humerus note the angular deformation in the neck region and the head flattening and articular lipping consistent with long-term dislocation.

Figure 4.12
Colonial or Republican Period burial, wood coffin in situ.

toward the altar. These positions mimic the positions of the living during church services: the parishioners face the altar, while the priest faces his flock (Eire 1995; Gose 2003, 2008). The burials recovered here were in the nave at the opposite end from where the altar was located, and all were positioned with their feet facing the altar.

These burials demonstrate evidence of native influence as well, as indicated by textile shrouds rather than coffins, the north-south cardinal orientation of the bodies in line with the Huaca Cao Viejo, and possible evidence for ritual reinterment of body parts (i.e., missing skeletal elements). Additionally, the presence of insect puparia indicates the bodies were left exposed for at least two weeks prior to interment (Anderson 2000), a common finding in prehispanic burial contexts. The ongoing practice of some of these native burial traditions was not unknown to the Spanish at the time. An undated document likely written during the vice-royalty of Francisco de Toledo (1515–1582) mentioned, among other issues of noncompliance with Catholic tradition, problems with natives continuing to bury their dead in the "guacas" (Martiarena 2014; Ramos 2010). The problems prompted the implementation in the First Council of Lima in 1551 of strict rules for native burials in order to discourage old customs. Specifically, the rules mandated burial under the floor of the church and the uncovering of the face of the deceased to prevent the native custom of ritual disinterment known as *pacaricuc* (Ramos 2010), something the missing body parts suggest may have occurred at Magdalena de Cao Viejo.

The problem of natives continuing to use the huaca for burials also prompted a call for the destruction of old tombs, something that not all Catholic leaders agreed with and which was banned at the Second Council of Lima in 1557, although the ban was frequently disobeyed (Martiarena 2014; Ramos 2010). Catholic tradition also dictated that the feet of the deceased should be oriented to the east (Thurston 1908). The north-south orientation of the burials at Magdalena, in line with the Huaca Cao Viejo, therefore represents a break with that Catholic tradition. Given the mixed feelings among Catholic leaders about violating old tombs as well as the difficulty in maintaining compliance with Catholic traditions, the pattern seen at Magdalena de Cao Viejo could represent a local conciliation to native traditions, perhaps in exchange for general compliance with Catholic decrees, specifically those against using the huaca as a burial ground. The orientation of the bodies, however, is not the only issue of non-compliance seen at this site.

Despite the rule instituted in the First Council of Lima that mandated burial of natives under the church floor, there are a number of sites where outdoor graveyards are found (Gose 2003, 2008), and Magdalena de Cao Viejo is yet another example. This suggests the likelihood that burial of all parishioners under the floor of the church was not practical in at least some rural parishes, perhaps because of limited space in smaller churches. Given the existence of an outdoor graveyard at Magdalena, and considering the hierarchal nature of Catholic burial traditions, the location of the bodies under the floor of the church likely means these individuals were of a higher socioeconomic status than individuals buried in the associated cemetery (Alvis 2004; Martiarena 2014; Price et al. 2012). The belief was that the dead were still vulnerable to the work of Satan, and therefore salvation could be better ensured if the dead were buried in an area blessed by the church, and the closer one could be to priests and saints, the better (Alvis 2004). Therefore, burial inside the church was better than burial in the associated cemetery, and there was also a hierarchy for burial within the church, with priests and bishops buried closer to the altar or under the altar and lay people buried further away or in an associated ossuary (Alvis 2004; Gose 2003, 2008; Martiarena 2014; Ramos 2010). It appears, therefore, that the burials inside the church of Magdalena de Cao Viejo, while they likely represent lay people of higher status than those buried in the cemetery, are not the burials of bishops or priests.

Regarding the cemetery burials, Emperor Charles V, in the Recopilación de las Leyes de Indias, ordered that all baptized individuals be laid to rest in sanctified ground regardless of age, sex, or place of origin (Price et al. 2012). Both the church and the associated cemetery would be consecrated ground, but cemeteries were most frequently used by families who could not afford burial inside or beneath the church (Muir 2004). Given the significance of burial position for salvation, competition for burial position would not be unexpected. The highest-ranking individuals, very likely the members of a cofradía, would be buried in the church itself. Given their rank, they probably also would have enjoyed better diets and work lives, even if only marginally so. Therefore, the lower frequency of biological indicators of stress in this population may be linked to their higher social standing in the community. This conclusion is of interest given general assumptions about the difficulty of life for indigenous peoples in the Colonial Period and especially in reducciones. Our results underscore the high variability we can expect in the early Colonial Period, a complex time when rules were frequently changed in response to a myriad of local conditions and rapidly shifting circumstances. Given the large variation in local resources and the quickly changing population demographics, it is easy to see how compliance with some rules would be flexible.

The question of the origins of individuals living at the site is of interest given the nature of the reducciones and the possibility that some members of the community were European or from other regions in the Americas. Initial ancestral classification of the individuals with crania was generally consistent with designation as Native Americans (Table 4.2); however, the results are not straightforward, and recent biodistance analyses utilizing dental traits and local comparative samples found possible evidence of Spanish admixture or nonlocal native individuals. Ortiz et al. (2017) found that biodistance dental indicators scored on these remains did not group with any of the comparative samples used from the Chicama Valley, the Lambayeque Valley, the Central Coast of Peru, or the Cuzco region. Instead, these samples grouped more closely with a Spanish comparative sample. The small sample size for the Magdalena individuals, however, prevents any definitive conclusion.

Craniometric analysis utilizing local Chicama Valley comparison samples suggests the individuals from Magdalena de Cao Viejo were not part of the Chicama Valley populations, implying little population continuity in the Chicama Valley after Spanish creation of the town. Several individuals were categorized as native North Americans by FORDISC 3.1 (Ousley and Jantz 2005), which suggests that an appropriate comparison sample was not available within the program; thus, though it is technically possible, it is unlikely that those individuals were North American natives. They could, however, be Native Americans from other areas of the Americas, such as Central America or other parts of South America. Alternatively, this could support a hypothesis of Spanish admixture with local people, though the FORDISC program is not designed to detect admixture. The higher status of individuals buried under the church, as suggested in the mortuary results section, could have resulted from intermarriage between Spanish men and Andean women. It is also possible, though we consider it less likely, that nonlocal native Andean individuals sympathetic to Spanish rule might have been relocated to the site to stabilize the population and/or prevent uprisings from being organized. They likely would have also enjoyed a higher status in this population, given their support of Spanish rule, and this could have been the reason for burial under the church floor.

Yet another possibility is the migration of individuals fleeing less stable regions after conquest. Graubart (2007) and O'Toole (2012) both describe a great deal of mobility in general in the postcontact period, with Native Andeans fleeing their communities in search of better lives in other locations. Thus, some of the individuals buried here could have migrated from other Andean regions (possibly even Central America or other South American regions) and at some point attained a higher status in this community for any number of reasons. Finally, it is possible that some of the individuals are Spanish, though the presence of cranial modification and certain morphological traits suggest otherwise.

The sample is too small and not enough information is available to reasonably discuss mortality rates; however, the fact that the overwhelming majority of individuals from this sample died before the age of 40 years is not surprising for a time period before the advent of antibiotics and modern medical practices. These results are also not inconsistent with what is seen in the prehispanic samples. A high mortality rate among non-adults coupled with a low fertility rate would not be surprising either; however, this site has yielded some unexpected results in that regard.

The fertility rate, based upon the D^{30+}/D^{5+} ratio, is the highest for all of the published cases from the Central Andes (Table 4.9). If the women of Magdalena were under severe nutritional stress or stress from higher workloads, then these conditions would be expected to have negatively impacted fertility (Bogin 2001; Ellison 1994; Ellison and O'Rourke 2000). The Magdalena fertility ratio is higher than ratios calculated from prehispanic sites on the Central

Table 4.9   Comparison of D^{30+}/D^{5+} Ratios

SITE/PERIOD (STUDY)	D^{30+}/D^{5+}
Magdalena de Cao Viejo, Colonial Period (present study)	0.4000
Lambayeque, Late Prehispanic (Klaus and Tam 2009)	0.4397
Mórrope, Lambayeque Postcontact (Klaus and Tam 2009)	0.6028
Eten, Lambayeque Postcontact (Klaus and Alvarez-Calderón 2015)	0.4030
Huaquerones, Late Intermediate Period/Late Horizon (Murphy et al. 2017)	0.5306
57AS03, Late Horizon/Conquest Period (Murphy et al. 2015)	0.4462

Coast of Peru, as well as prehispanic samples from the Lambayeque Valley. Klaus and Alvarez-Calderón (2016) report a fertility ratio similar to Magdalena from the postcontact sample at Eten in the Lambayeque Valley and assert that this community may have fared better under colonialism than the community interred at Mórrope, which demonstrates a much lower ratio.

One indicator of physiological stress, porous cranial lesions, also shows interesting patterns at Magdalena. The adults demonstrate higher frequencies of these lesions than their prehispanic predecessors, whereas the non-adults demonstrate lower frequencies than the non-adults interred on the Huaca Cao Viejo prior to contact. Both of these differences are statistically significant. The Magdalena adults may have experienced greater physiological stress as children, given that, with the exception of one case, all of the lesions recorded in the adults were healed. This indicates that these individuals suffered and then recovered from the conditions that caused these lesions. The lower frequencies in non-adults of the Colonial Period suggest that they suffered less physiological stress than their prehispanic predecessors. While we acknowledge that these children did not survive to recover from these stressors, the fact remains that there were fewer non-adults suffering from NSIS than in the prehispanic period. Perhaps the differences between the adults and the non-adults are due to different life experiences, with the adults having had greater stress when they were children earlier in the Conquest or Colonial Period. The non-adults, on the other hand, might have benefited biologically from being raised in less stressful times or perhaps after the population at Magdalena had successfully adapted to life after the Spanish conquest. Stratigraphic differentiation between the burials under the floor is difficult given the lack of an entirely intact context across the width of the nave, and so it is difficult to ascertain exactly when particular individuals died relative to others; however, surely some of the non-adults died before the adults, and vice versa. The dates of the church indicate a relatively tight time frame for when all of these individuals died and were interred under the floor, and so the suggestion that at least some of the adults may have suffered more biological stress earlier in their lives, during an era that was less distant from the effects of conquest, remains one possibility.

Alternatively, a higher socioeconomic status could offer an explanation for these results. These types of porous cranial lesions (i.e., porotic hyperostosis and cribra orbitalia) are associated with waterborne parasites, malnutrition, or the synergism of the two (Blom et al. 2005). The community of Magdalena contended with poor-quality land, the limited availability of water, the loss of water rights, and the introduction of new cultivars (see Chapter 12), all of which may have contributed to changing environmental conditions, a decline in sanitation, and increasing exposure to pathogens and nutritional stress. The lower frequencies in the children may mean that they were born into a higher socioeconomic status, perhaps suggesting that their parents had recently attained a higher status. If the individuals interred in the church did enjoy overall better health compared to individuals of lower status in the years following conquest, then the increase in frequencies of porous cranial lesions, almost all of which were healed, in the adults could reflect the biological consequences of conquest and the immediate social disorganization and reorganization that ensued, and/or the biological consequences of being part of a lower socioeconomic class during their own childhood.

The frequency of enamel hypoplasias, which would indicate periods of growth interruption, is extremely low at Magdalena (only 2 of 28 individuals, 7.1 percent), which prevents statistically meaningful comparison with prehispanic predecessors. Taken at face value, our hypothesis is not supported by these data on enamel hypoplasias; however, the absence of complete dentitions and a high amount of tooth loss, both antemortem and postmortem, could be impeding our ability to detect any problems with dental development.

In contrast to these typically childhood conditions, the frequencies of periostosis do not statistically differ significantly in either adults or non-adults at Magdalena when compared with prehispanic samples from the El Brujo complex. We hypothesized that the frequency of periostosis would be higher, given increasing work demands under the reducción and the increased likelihood of localized infections, as well as greater exposure to infectious pathogens, but our results do not support these hypotheses. All individuals at Magdalena who demonstrate periostosis had lesions that were active at the time of death (three individuals had areas of healed periostosis as well). These results suggest that the active periostosis may have been associated with failing health near the time of death, versus chronic conditions from higher workloads or previous exposure to pathogens.

The frequencies of degenerative joint disease and vertebral osteophytosis among the colonial burials from Magdalena are low, which is not what we would expect if they were subjected to the heavy workloads experienced by colonial subjects in other regions of the Americas (e.g. Klaus 2008; Klaus et al. 2009) or what has been described in historical and ethnohistorical accounts for the Chicama Valley and the North Coast of Peru (Graubart 2000; see also Chapter 12). This suggests that these individuals did not experience high labor demands, something that may reflect their social standing within the community. The multifactorial etiology of degenerative joint disease (Waldron 2009) and the small sample size, however, make it difficult to further evaluate the nature of the work and activity loads on this community. The low frequency of traumatic injuries, both perimortem and antemortem, supports the interpretation that their lifestyle was not particularly labor-intensive. If these individuals did indeed have a reduced workload because they were of higher socioeconomic status, then these results are likely not representative of the population as a whole.

In sum, results of the osteological analyses can be interpreted in two ways. The first is that the majority of the individuals excavated from Magdalena are higher-status individuals, who were buried in a privileged position within the church. Perhaps they enjoyed overall better lifestyles and did not experience higher workloads and physiological stress. Alternatively, it is possible the individuals from Magdalena are representative of the general population and that the evidence associated with low or stable frequencies of biological stress is indicative of successful adaptive strategies that may have reduced both workload and exposure to parasitic infections and malnutrition while at the same time improving fertility rates. Excavation of more burials from the adjacent cemetery could help to clarify the situation and offer additional support for or a refutation of one of these interpretations. Molecular analysis may shed light on the question of ancestral affiliation and to what degree biological admixture or migration may have played a role in individual status within the population.

Literature on postcontact indigenous populations in the Americas has documented variable impacts of contact on population health and dramatic changes in mortuary practices. Larsen et al. (2001) found severe biological stress in indigenous populations of Florida, which was accompanied by depopulation and cultural collapse. They also recorded cultural transformation as evinced by Catholic-style burials under church floors. Baker and Kealhofer (1996), Larsen and Milner (1994), and Verano and Ubelaker (1992) argued that depopulation and increased morbidity were virtually unavoidable in postcontact populations; however, there was remarkable diversity in the expression of these phenomena at various sites. This variability is exemplified by the results of bioarchaeological research conducted by Haagen Klaus and colleagues at the sites of San Pedro de Mórrope and Eten in the Lambayeque Valley on the North Coast of Peru (Klaus 2008; Klaus and Alvarez-Calderón 2016; Klaus and Tam 2010). The community from Mórrope suffered considerably under Spanish colonial rule, with higher levels of physiological stress, low fertility, and extremely high frequencies of degenerative joint disease affecting younger adults and including severe manifestations of joint breakdown. At Eten, the community fared much better, with lower levels of physiological stress and higher fertility.

Klaus and colleagues also found a mixture of Catholic and native mortuary traditions in their work at Mórrope, with examples of coffin burials, Spanish clothing, and Catholic crosses mixed with native body positions and evidence of ritualized reopening of the tombs in order to remove body parts. They interpreted the data as indicating an atypical postcontact experience, because while the population there did experience increased biological and cultural stress, the biological and cultural hybridization that also occurred served to facilitate their survival (Klaus and Tam 2009).

A mixture of cultural traditions is evident at Magdalena de Cao Viejo, as demonstrated by changes in the mortuary patterns. The culture appears to have retained native mortuary traditions and blended them with Catholic practices. Aside from body positioning and treatment, the presence of individuals with cranial modification may also be an indicator of mixed traditions that included the retention of this native practice despite Spanish opposition to it.

Genetic and isotopic studies of the Magdalena remains are under way, and these may help clarify the preliminary results of the morphological and metric analyses and present additional evidence for biological admixture. Isotopic data may also illuminate the migration patterns and origins of some of the people from Magdalena. The genetic studies will eventually include the modern population of Magdalena de Cao, and this may demonstrate genetic continuity to the present day. Coupled with the evidence for mixed cultural traditions, evidence of biological admixture could offer insight into the biocultural adaptive strategies that facilitated the survival of the population at Magdalena de Cao Viejo in a postcontact world.

Conclusions

We had hypothesized that the population interred at Magdalena would demonstrate evidence of biological stress, reduced fertility rates, an increase in frequencies of trauma, and other biological markers of increased workloads and a physically demanding lifestyle. The results of our analyses of the burials at Magdalena de Cao Viejo indicate that the population of this postcontact reducción did suffer some biological stress, although generally those hypotheses are not well supported. The small sample size and possible sample bias may be skewing the results, preventing definitive interpretations, but the results seem to indicate higher fertility rates, lower labor demands, and mixed evidence for elevated levels of physiological stress when compared with prehispanic populations inhabiting the area. Analyses of the population fertility at Magdalena appear to indicate a fertility rate consistent with populations with similar subsistence strategies in Peru, though significantly higher than at least one other postcontact site in the region (Klaus and Tam 2010). It does not appear that there was an increase in non-adult mortality, as might be expected given the rapidity and fierce nature of the changes that had impacted local populations. In fact, the analyses of biological stressors on the non-adult remains suggest successful adaptive strategies. In contrast, the adult remains may bear the scars of the years immediately following conquest, as indicated by significantly increased frequencies of some biological stressors. The possibility that these remains represent a comparatively elite subset of the population may be skewing the results, however. Future excavation of the cemetery associated with the church may help to clarify which interpretations better characterize the community from Magdalena de Cao Viejo. Our hypothesis regarding cultural transformation, however, is supported as evidenced by a change in mortuary practices that incorporated both Catholic and indigenous funerary traditions. It is possible that mixed cultural traditions as reflected in the blended burial practices ultimately contributed to the survival of this community to the present day.

The sample at Magdalena offers a glimpse into cultural and biological changes that took place in the years following conquest in this region of Peru. While small, this data set presents more evidence for the impact of rapid change on indigenous populations as well as subsequent cultural adaptation responses. The results of these analyses may speak more to the adaptable nature of populations under stress than to the degree of the stress experienced, and they certainly highlight the possibility of variation in the biological impact within subsets of a population and between populations in the same general region.

REFERENCES CITED

Alvis, Robert E.
> 2004 Hallowed Ground, Contagious Corpses, and the Moral Economy of the Graveyard in Early Nineteenth-Century Prussia. *Journal of Religion* 84(2):234–255.

Anderson, Gail S.
> 2000 Minimum and Maximum Development Rates of Some Forensically Important Calliphoridae (Diptera). *Journal of Forensic Science* 45(4):824–832.

Baker, Brenda J., and Lisa Kealhofer (editors)

    1996 *Bioarchaeology of Native American Adaptation in the Spanish Borderlands.* Gainesville: University Press of Florida.

Bass, William M.

    2005 *Human Osteology: A Laboratory and Field Manual.* 4th ed. Springfield: Missouri Archaeological Society.

Berryman, Hugh, and Susan Haun

    1996 Applying Forensic Techniques to Interpret Cranial Fracture Patterns in an Archaeological Specimen. *International Journal of Osteoarchaeology* 6:2–9.

Berryman, Hugh, and Steve Symes

    1998 Recognizing Gunshot and Blunt Cranial Trauma Through Fracture Interpretation. In *Forensic Osteology*, edited by Kathy Reichs, pp. 333–352. Springfield, IL: Charles Thomas.

Blom, Deborah E., Jane E. Buikstra, Linda Keng, Paula D. Tomczak, Eleanor Shoreman, and Debbie Stevens-Tuttle

    2005 Anemia and Childhood Mortality: Latitudinal Patterning Along the Coast of Pre-Columbian Peru. *American Journal of Physical Anthropology* 127:152–169.

Bogin, Barry

    2001 *The Growth of Humanity.* New York: Wiley-Liss.

Brezine, Carrie

    2011 Dress, Technology, and Identity in Colonial Peru. Unpublished Ph.D. dissertation, Department of Anthropology, Harvard University.

    2012 A Change of Dress on the Coast of Peru: Technological and Material Hybridity in Colonial Peruvian Textiles. In *The Archaeology of Hybrid Material Culture*, edited by Jeb J. Card, pp. 239–259. Carbondale: Southern Illinois University Press.

Brickley, Megan, and Rachel Ives

    2008 *The Bioarchaeology of Metabolic Bone Disease.* London: Academic Press.

Buikstra, Jane F., Lyle W. Konigsberg, and Jill Bullington

    1986 Fertility and the Development of Agriculture in the Prehistoric Midwest. *American Antiquity* 51:528–546.

Buikstra, Jane E., and Douglas Ubelaker (editors)

    1994 *Standards for Data Collection from Human Skeletal Remains.* Research Series No. 44. Fayetteville: Arkansas Archeological Survey.

DiGangi, Elizabeth A., and Joseph T. Hefner

    2013 Ancestry Estimation. In *Research Methods in Human Skeletal Biology*, edited by Elizabeth A. DiGangi and Megan K. Moore, pp. 117–149. Boston: Academic Press.

DiGangi, Elizabeth A., and Megan K. Moore (editors)

    2013 *Research Methods in Human Skeletal Biology.* Boston: Academic Press.

Eire, Carlos M. N.

    1995 *From Madrid to Purgatory: The Art and Craft of Dying in Sixteenth-Century Spain.* Cambridge: Cambridge University Press.

Ellison, Peter T.

    1994 Advances in Human Reproductive Ecology. *Annual Review of Anthropology* 23:255–275.

Ellison, Peter T., and Mary T. O'Rourke

    2000   Population Growth and Fertility Regulation. In *Human Biology: An Evolutionary and Biocultural Perspective*, edited by Sara Stinson, Barry Bogin, Rebecca Huss-Ashmore, and Dennis O'Rourke, pp. 553–586. New York: Wiley-Liss.

Fletcher, Mike, and Gary R. Lock

    2005   *Digging Numbers: Elementary Statistics for Archaeologists*. 2nd ed. Oxford: Oxford University School of Archaeology.

Gaither, Catherine

    2004   A Growth and Development Study of Coastal Prehistoric Peruvian Populations. Unpublished Ph.D. dissertation, Tulane University.

    2007   Estudio del crecimiento y desarrollo dental humano en la prehistoria de la costa de Perú: implicaciones paleopatológicas. *Archaeobios* 1:10–14.

Goodman, Alan H., and Debra Martin

    2002   Reconstructing Health Profiles from Skeletal Remains. In *The Backbone of History*, edited by Richard H. Steckel and Jerome C. Rose, pp. 11–60. Cambridge: Cambridge University Press.

Gose, Peter

    2003   Converting the Ancestors: Indirect Rule, Settlement Consolidation, and the Struggle over Burial in Colonial Peru, 1532–1614. In *Conversion: Old Worlds and New*, edited by Kenneth Mills and Anthony Grafton, pp. 140–174. Rochester, NY: University of Rochester Press.

    2008   *Invaders as Ancestors: On the Intercultural Making and Unmaking of Spanish Colonialism in the Andes*. Toronto: University of Toronto Press.

Graubart, Karen B.

    2000   Weaving and the Construction of a Gender Division of Labor in Early Colonial Peru. *American Indian Quarterly* 24:537–561.

    2007   *With Our Labor and Sweat: Indigenous Women and the Formation of Colonial Society in Peru, 1550–1700*. Stanford, CA: Stanford University Press.

Hillson, Simon

    2001   Recording Dental Caries in Archaeological Human Remains. *International Journal of Osteoarchaeology* 11(4): 249–289.

IBM Corp.

    2011   IBM SPSS Statistics for Windows, Version 20.0. Armonk, NY: IBM Corp.

Klaus, Haagen D.

    2008   Out of Light Came Darkness: Bioarchaeology of Mortuary Ritual, Health, and Ethnogenesis in the Lambayeque Valley Complex, North Coast of Peru (AD 900–1750). Ph.D. dissertation, Department of Anthropology, Ohio State University, Columbus.

    2012   The Bioarchaeology of Structural Violence. A Theoretical Model and a Case Study. In *The Bioarchaeology of Violence*, edited by Debra Martin, Ryan P. Harrod, and Ventura R. Pérez, pp. 29–62. Gainesville: University Press of Florida.

    2013   Hybrid Cultures . . . and Hybrid Peoples: Bioarchaeology of Genetic Change, Religious Architecture, and Burial Ritual in the Colonial Andes. In *The Archaeology of Hybrid Material Culture*, edited by Jeb J. Card, pp. 207–238. Carbondale: Southern Illinois University Press.

Klaus, Haagen D., and Rosabella Alvarez-Calderón

2017 Escaping Conquest? Uncovering Regional Variation of Indigenous Experiences of Conquest in Eten, Peru. In *The Bioarchaeology of Contact and Colonialism: Global Visions and New Approaches from Studies of Human Skeletons*, edited by Melissa S. Murphy and Haagen D. Klaus, pp. 95–128. Gainesville: University Press of Florida.

Klaus, Haagen D., Clark S. Larsen, and Manuel E. Tam

2009 Economic Intensification and Degenerative Joint Disease: Life and Labor on the Postcontact North Coast of Peru. *American Journal of Physical Anthropology* 139:204–221.

Klaus, Haagen D., and Manuel E. Tam

2009 Surviving Contact: Biological Transformations, Burial and Ethnogenesis in the Colonial Lambayeque Valley, North Coast of Peru. In *Bioarchaeology and Identity in the Americas*, edited by Kelly Knudson and Christopher Stojanowski, pp. 126–152. Gainesville: University Press of Florida.

2010 Contact in the Andes: Bioarchaeology of Systemic Stress in Colonial Mórrope, Peru. *American Journal of Physical Anthropology* 138:356–368.

Larsen, Clark S., Mark C. Griffin, Dale L. Hutchinson, Vivian E. Noble, Lynette Norr, Robert F. Pastor, Christopher B. Ruff, Katherine E. Russell, Margaret J. Schoeninger, Michael Schultz, Scott W. Simpson, and Mark F. Teaford

2001 Frontiers of Contact: Bioarchaeology of Spanish Florida. *Journal of World Prehistory* 15:69–123.

Larsen, Clark S., and George R. Milner (editors)

1994 *In the Wake of Contact: Biological Responses to Conquest*. New York: Wiley-Liss.

Lovell, Nancy C.

2008 Analysis and Interpretation of Skeletal Trauma. In *Biological Anthropology of the Human Skeleton*, 2nd ed., edited by Margaret A. Katzenberg and Scott R. Saunders, pp. 341–386. New York: Wiley-Liss.

Martiarena, Laurie M.

2014 The Social Life of Death: Mortuary Practices in the North-Central Andes, 11th–18th Centuries, Vol. 1. Unpublished Ph.D. thesis, School of Art History and World Art Studies, University of East Anglia.

Muir, Richard

2004 *Landscape Encyclopaedia: A Reference Guide to the Historic Landscape*. Bollington, UK: Windgather Press.

Murphy, Melissa S., Maria F. Boza, and Catherine Gaither

2017 Exhuming Differences and Continuities: The Interpretation of Shifting and Aberrant Mortuary Patterns after Contact and Colonialism. In *The Bioarchaeology of Contact and Colonialism: Global Visions and New Approaches from Studies of Human Skeletons*, edited by Melissa S. Murphy and Haagen D. Klaus, pp. 43–69. Gainesville: University Press of Florida.

Ortiz, Alejandra, Melissa S. Murphy, Jason Toohey, and Catherine Gaither

2017 Hybridity? Change? Continuity? Survival? A Study of Biodistance and Identity of Colonial Burials from Magdalena de Cao Viejo, Chicama Valley, Peru. In *Colonized Bodies, Lives Transformed: Towards a Global Bioarchaeology of Contact and Colonialism*, edited by Melissa S. Murphy and Haagen D. Klaus, pp. 375–410. Gainesville: University Press of Florida.

Ortner, Donald J., Erin H. Kimmerle, and Melanie Diez

    1999   Probable Evidence of Scurvy in Non-adults from Archeological Sites in Peru. *American Journal of Physical Anthropology* 108:321–331.

Ortner, Donald J., and Walter G. J. Putschar

    1981   *Identification of Pathological Conditions in Human Skeletal Remains.* Smithsonian Contributions to Anthropology 28. Washington, DC: Smithsonian Institution Press.

O'Toole, Rachel S.

    2012   *Bound Lives: Africans, Indians, and the Making of Race in Colonial Peru.* Pittsburgh: University of Pittsburgh Press.

Ousley, Stephen D., and Richard L. Jantz

    2005   FORDISC 3.0. Personal Computer Forensic Discriminate Functions. Knoxville: University of Tennessee.

Price, T. Douglas, James H. Burton, Andrea Cucina, Pilar Zabala, Robert Frei, Robert H. Tykot, and Vera Tiesler

    2012   Isotopic Studies of Human Skeletal Remains from a Sixteenth to Seventeenth Century AD Churchyard in Campeche, Mexico: Diet, Place of Origin, and Age. *Current Anthropology* 53(4):396–433.

Ramos, Gabriela

    2010   *Death and Conversion in the Andes: Lima and Cuzco, 1532–1670.* Notre Dame, IN: University of Notre Dame Press.

Rhine, Stanley

    1990   Non-Metric Skull Racing. In *Skeletal Attributes of Race: Methods for Forensic Anthropology,* edited by George W. Gill and Stanley Rhine, pp. 9–20. Albuquerque, NM: Maxwell Museum.

Sauer, Norman

    1998   The Timing of Injuries and Manner of Death: Distinguishing Among Antemortem, Perimortem, and Postmortem Trauma. In *Forensic Osteology,* edited by Kathy Reichs, pp. 321–332. Springfield, IL: Charles Thomas.

Scheuer, Louise, and Sue Black

    2000   *Developmental Juvenile Osteology.* New York: Academic Press.

Sledzik, Paul

    1998   Forensic Taphonomy: Postmortem Decomposition and Decay. In *Forensic Osteology,* edited by Kathy Reichs, pp. 109–119. Springfield, IL: Charles C. Thomas.

Spradley, M. Katherine, and Richard L. Jantz

    2011   Sex Estimation in Forensic Anthropology: Skull Versus Postcranial Elements. *Journal of Forensic Sciences* 56(2):289–296.

Thurston, H.

    1908   Christian Burial. In *The Catholic Encyclopedia.* New York: Robert Appleton. Retrieved November 30, 2017, from New Advent: http://www.newadvent.org/cathen/03071a.htm.

Ubelaker, Douglas H.

    1999   *Human Skeletal Remains: Excavation, Analysis, Interpretation.* 3rd ed. Washington, DC: Taraxacum.

Ubelaker, Douglas H., and Linda Newsom

    2002   Patterns of Health and Nutrition in Prehistoric and Historic Ecuador. In *The Backbone of History: Health and Nutrition in the Western Hemisphere*, edited by Richard H. Steckel and Jerome C. Rose, pp. 345–375. Cambridge: Cambridge University Press.

Ubelaker, Douglas H., and Catherine E. Ripley

    1999   *The Ossuary of San Francisco Church, Quito, Ecuador: Human Skeletal Biology.* Smithsonian Contributions to Anthropology No. 42. Washington, DC: Taraxacum.

Verano, John W., and Douglas H. Ubelaker (editors)

    1992   *Disease and Demography in the Americas.* Washington, DC: Smithsonian Institution Press.

Waldron, Tony

    2009   *Paleopathology.* New York: Cambridge University Press.

White, Timothy, and Pieter A. Folkens

    2005   *Human Osteology.* 2nd ed. New York: Academic Press.

White, Tim D., Michael T. Black, and Pieter A. Folkens

    2012   *Human Osteology.* 3rd ed. Boston: Academic Press.

Appendix 4.1

Descriptions of Burials Excavated from Magdalena de Cao Viejo

CEMETERY BURIALS (5 INDIVIDUALS)

Burial C4.P1.E1
LOCATION: CEMETERY
MNI: 2 individuals

Present are the incomplete skeletons of at least two individuals: one non-adult (ischium only) and one adult. The adult skeletal elements present include the hyoid and C4, C5, C6, C7, T1, T2, T3, T4, and T5. Vertebral osteophytosis was present on several of the thoracic vertebrae (curved spicules) and degenerative joint disease was noted on the intervertebral joints. Age and sex could not be determined more definitively due to the incomplete nature of the individuals present.

Burial 2
LOCATION: CEMETERY

Present is the complete skeleton of a neonate, aged birth +/− 2 months. Hair, soft tissue, and textile are preserved. Missing elements include both patellae, the left 12th rib, and some of the bones of the hands and feet. Pathological conditions include active periostosis (a nonspecific indicator of biological stress) on the medial aspect of the distal third of the right ulna. No other pathological conditions were seen.

Burial 3
LOCATION: CEMETERY

Present is the complete, mummified skeleton of an adult female, aged 35 +/− 10 years at death. The lower body is the best preserved, with the abdominal region and most of the legs mummified. The upper body has soft tissue preserved but is not as intact as the lower body. The body was covered in textile and this is also preserved. Stature estimation is 145–148 cm utilizing measurements of the humerus, radius, and ulna. Missing elements of this skeleton include some of the bones of the hands and feet. Cranial modification is evident in the form of symmetric occipital flattening. Pathological conditions include healed porotic hyperostosis on the occipital bone, an area of arthritic changes (osteochondritis dessicans, lesion) on the right lateral third cuneiform on the ventral portion of the proximal articulation, and an area of arthritis in the form of coalesced porosities on the left medial femoral condylar articular surface. Dental pathological conditions include a severe periapical abscess associated with carious lesions on the right second and third maxillary molars and linear enamel hypoplasias on the right first and second mandibular molars. The left first molar was lost antemortem, and all teeth demonstrate slight to moderate wear, which is more pronounced on the molars. Anomalies include a septal aperture of the sternum. Also present on the mummified abdominal skin are lesions that appear consistent with welts, perhaps caused by scratching. Adipocere (incompletely decomposed fat) is present in the thoracic cavity of this individual. The body position of this individual is also notable, as it is not typical for either indigenous populations or Spanish colonists. The position is semiflexed with the knees partially drawn up toward the abdomen, but not tightly flexed, and they are skewed to one side. The arms are not flexed but rather are slightly bent, with the hands over the abdomen. Additionally, the textiles that are preserved with the body are consistent with the pattern seen in other individuals at this site.

Burial 4
LOCATION: CEMETERY

Present is the mostly complete skeleton of a fetus/neonate, aged between 8–9 months gestation and birth. Missing elements include most of the cranium (both temporals, part of the right sphenoid, the occipital, and the right side of the mandible are present), the left patella, C1, and some of the bones of the hands and feet. Pathological conditions include active periostosis of the right humerus on the proximal third of the anterior aspect. No other pathological conditions were seen.

NAVE BURIALS (23 INDIVIDUALS)

Burial 5
LOCATION: UNIT 12, NE CORNER OF THE NAVE

Present is a complete skeleton, aged 9 years +/− 12 months at death. Missing elements include some of the bones of the hands and feet. Unintentional cranial modification is evident in the form of asymmetric occipital flattening. Pathological conditions include healed porotic hyperostosis of both parietals and the occipital bone, near the sutures on the former and within the squamous portion of the occipital. Also present is healed periostosis of the right femur on the medioposterior aspect. Healed periostosis is present on the right tibia on the posterior aspect of the middle third of the diaphysis. Active periostosis is present on the left tibia on the posterior aspect of the middle third of the diaphysis. Dental pathological conditions include caries on the mesial aspect of both deciduous second molars. No other pathological conditions were seen. Bone and hair were preserved. Textile was present and appears to have been wrapped around the body. Two additional neural arches of another, younger non-adult were also present, yielding a minimum of two individuals.

Burial 6
LOCATION: UNIT 12, NE CORNER OF THE NAVE

Present is the partial skeleton of an adult male, aged 45 +/− 10 years at death. Cranial modification in the form of symmetric occipital flattening is evident. Hair, textile, and bone are preserved. Missing elements include most of the lower body, including both os coxae, the lower thoracic vertebrae, the lumbar vertebrae, the 11th and 12th ribs on both sides, and all lower limb bones and bones of the feet. Also missing are the upper limb bones with the exception of the right ulna and some of the bones of the hands. An area disturbed by looting found near this individual may contain some of the missing bones. These include a right male os coxae (the age indicators of which are consistent with this individual), left and right femora, a right tibia, left and right fibulae, left and right humeri, a left radius, a sacrum, three thoracic vertebrae, six lumbar vertebrae, and a fragment of a vertebral column. Of the long bones, only the humeri were divergent enough in the measurements to prevent them from being definitively paired. A left os coxae from a younger male was also present, indicating a minimum of two individuals represented in the looted remains. Pathological conditions on the primary individual include healed porotic hyperostosis, lytic areas of bone loss on both clavicles on the medial ends, and an area of bone loss on the sternum where it articulates and fuses with the xyphoid process. Anomalies on the main individual include extremely pronounced scapular notches on both scapulae. Dental pathological conditions include an interesting wear pattern, consistent with holding something in the mouth and then pulling on it in a downward direction. Pathological conditions on the bones possibly associated with this individual include a healed greenstick fracture of the left fibula on the middle third of the diaphysis and a healed fracture of a lower lumbar vertebra (L4 or L5) with complications including deformation of the right inferior pedicle and traumatic arthritis of the joint surface. This vertebra and the one above also demonstrate fused osteophytes on the right side of the vertebral body, possibly a result of complications during healing of the fracture. Another lumbar vertebra (middle lumbar) demonstrates spondylolisthesis (the fracture and complete separation of the vertebral arch from the vertebral body, which then results in the slippage of the vertebral body anteriorly). The area of fracture is completely healed. There is also a cut mark on the right humerus that has the appearance of being perimortem, but given the matrix and looting disturbance present at this site, it is more likely that this damage is postmortem.

Burial 7

LOCATION: UNIT 12, NE CORNER OF THE NAVE

Present is the partial skeleton of an adult female, aged conservatively 25 +/− 5 years at death. Given the age indicators, however, it is likely she was actually between 25–30 years at death. Missing elements include the right humerus, the right radius, the right ulna, both femora, both tibiae, both fibulae, both os coxae, all of the bones of the feet, and most of the bones of the hands. Cranial modification in the form of symmetric occipital flattening is evident. Tumpline deformation is also evident. Pathological conditions include healed porotic hyperostosis on the squamous portion of the occipital. Dental pathological conditions include a large carious lesion of the right 3rd molar. Anomalies include sacralization of L5. A second cervical vertebra of a non-adult is present, yielding a minimum of two individuals. Bone, hair, and textile are preserved.

Burial 8

LOCATION: UNIT 12, NE CORNER OF THE NAVE

Present is the cranium and two cervical vertebrae of a non-adult, aged 2 years +/− 6 months at death. All other skeletal elements are missing. Bone and textile are preserved. Cranial modification is evident in the form of symmetric occipital flattening. Pathological conditions include active periostosis on the left side of the mandible. Copper staining is also evident on the left side of the mandible. Anomalies include split root tips of the incisors and canines. No other pathological conditions or anomalies were seen.

Burial 9

LOCATION: UNIT 12, NE CORNER OF THE NAVE

Present is the cranium, right scapula, and right humerus of an adult male, aged 35 +/− 10 years at death. Bone, hair, and textile are preserved. Cranial modification is evident in the form of symmetric occipital flattening. Pathological conditions include arthritis bilaterally in the temporomandibular joints, healed porotic hyperostosis in the squamous portion of the occipital bone, and a circular, OCD-like area of arthritis on the lateral aspect of the trochlear articular surface of the right humerus measuring 9 mm × 7 mm. Dental pathological conditions include moderate to marked wear on all teeth, particularly severe on the mandibular first molars, which demonstrate a sloping wear on the mesial buccal aspect. No other pathological conditions were seen.

Burial 10
LOCATION: UNIT 12, NE CORNER OF THE NAVE

Present is the partial skeleton of a non-adult, aged approximately 1 year +/− 3 months at death. Missing elements include the cranium and mandible, both of which were present but unable to be excavated because they were situated underneath a floor in the excavation unit. Other missing elements include the hyoid, C1, C2, and C7, several thoracic vertebrae, all lumbar vertebrae, the sacrum, the sternal body, all elements of both os coxae except the left and right pubis, several ribs, the left humerus, the right radius and ulna, both tibiae, both fibulae, all of the bones of the feet, and some of the bones of the hands. Pathological conditions include both healed and active periostosis present on the middle third of the medioposterior aspect of the right humerus. No other pathological conditions were seen. There is a deciduous canine present that appears to be from an older non-adult, yielding a minimum of two individuals.

Burial 11
LOCATION: UNIT 12, NE CORNER OF THE NAVE

Present is the mostly complete cranium of an adult male, aged 28 +/− 10 years at death. The mandible and both palatines are missing, as are all postcranial elements. Cranial modification is evident in the form of symmetric occipital flattening. One extra right maxillary premolar is present, yielding a minimum of two individuals. Pathological conditions include healed porotic hyperostosis of both parietal bones and the occipital bone. Dental pathological conditions include linear enamel hypoplasias on the right maxillary canine, the right maxillary first molar, and the left maxillary canine. There is moderate wear on all teeth and moderate to marked tartar buildup on all teeth.

Burial 12
LOCATION: UNIT 12, NE CORNER OF THE NAVE

Burial 12 was represented by a body situated under a floor in the nave. Two patellae and a distal femoral epiphysis were collected from this individual, and non-union indicates a non-adult. The remainder of the body, however, was never recovered from under the floor. Thus there is no more information available for this individual.

Burial 13
LOCATION: UNIT 12, NE CORNER OF THE NAVE

Present is the partial skeleton of a non-adult, a fetus of approximately 8–9 months gestation at death. Missing elements include both palatines, both patellae, C7, several thoracic vertebrae, several lumbar vertebrae, the sternal body, two right ribs and three left ribs, both tibiae, the left fibula, and several of the bones of the hands and feet. There are a partial left humerus and a second mandibular incisor of an older non-adult present, and there is an adult right maxillary incisor present. This yields a minimum of three individuals. Numerous bones demonstrate periostosis associated with normal growth and development at this age, but no pathological lesions are present.

Burial 14
LOCATION: UNIT 12, NE CORNER OF THE NAVE

Present is the cranium and hyoid body of an adult female, aged 40 +/− 10 years at death. All other skeletal elements are missing. There is one metacarpal of an infant present, which may be associated with burial 13, the location of which was directly above this cranium. This yields a minimum of two individuals. Cranial modification is evident in the form of symmetric occipital flattening. Pathological conditions include healed and active porotic hyperostosis of the parietal bones and the occipital and cribra orbitalia of the frontal bone. Dental pathological conditions include carious lesions on both maxillary central incisors, the first left maxillary premolar, the second right maxillary molar, the first left mandibular premolar, and the third left mandibular molar. The right central maxillary incisor demonstrates a periapical abscess, and the third left mandibular molar is impacted. Additionally, the left second mandibular premolar, first and second mandibular molars, and right second and third mandibular molars were all lost antemortem. All teeth demonstrate moderate wear, and the lower right molar demonstrates marked wear. No other pathological conditions were seen.

Burial 15
LOCATION: NW CORNER OF THE NAVE

Present is the partial skeleton of adult male, aged 35 +/− 10 years at death. Missing elements include the sacrum, coccyx, pelvis, both femora, both humeri, the right scapula, both ulnae, both radii, both patellae, both tibiae, both fibulae, one right rib, and most of the bones of the hands and feet. Remains of textiles were found under the head of this individual. Pathological conditions include vertebral osteophytosis on most of the thoracic vertebrae and L1. The age of this individual and the fact that the osteophytes occur mostly on the thoracic vertebrae suggests activity related and/or pathological changes rather than age indicators. Dental pathological conditions include a carious lesion on the right upper canine and pronounced wear on most teeth suggestive of repetitive paramasticatory behavior.

Burial 16
LOCATION: NW CORNER OF THE NAVE

Present is the partial skeleton of a non-adult of undetermined sex, aged approximately 15–20 years at death. It was not possible to determine sex because of the lack of any sexually dimorphic skeletal elements. Missing elements include the cranium, mandible, all teeth, hyoid, all cervical vertebrae, T1–T3, L3–5, sacrum, pelvis, right clavicle, right scapula, both humeri, left radius, both ulnae, both femora, both patellae, both tibiae, both fibulae, and all of the bones of the hands and feet. Pathological conditions include unhealed periostosis on the anterior aspect of the distal third of the right radius. No other pathological conditions were seen. The bones of a younger non-adult were present (a left clavicle, pars basilaris, and two rib fragments), yielding a minimum of two individuals.

Burial 17
LOCATION: NW CORNER OF THE NAVE

Present is the partial skeleton of a neonate aged between birth and 6 months old at death. The bones present include the right parietal, the right lateral portion of the occipital (pars lateralis), the right temporal, the neural arches of C1 and C2, three neural arches of C3–6, three neural arches of thoracic vertebrae, a sternebra, and nine right ribs. No pathological conditions were observed.

Burial 18
LOCATION: NW CORNER OF THE NAVE

Present is the partial skeleton of a young adult. The bones that are present include the sternal body, a right radius, three right ribs, four left ribs, three right carpal bones, five left carpal bones, ten metacarpals, and 27 manual phalanges. Present also is the distal manual phalanx of a second individual, yielding a minimum of two individuals. No pathological conditions were seen.

Burial 19
LOCATION: NW CORNER OF THE NAVE

Present is the partial skeleton of a non-adult, aged 8 +/− 1 years at death. The bones that are present include C5–7, all thoracic vertebrae, L1–4, eight right ribs, all left ribs, the manubrium, the sternal body, the left scapula, both femora, both patellae, and one metacarpal. All other bones are missing. Present also is the sacral vertebrae of another individual, yielding a minimum of two individuals. A ceramic fragment and piece of wood were found with this individual. No pathological conditions were seen.

Burial 20
LOCATION: NW CORNER OF THE NAVE

Present is the partial skeleton of a non-adult, aged approximately 9 +/− 3 months at death. The bones that are present include the right parietal, right temporal, C1–C5, T1–T7, 11 right ribs, manubrium, sternal body, right clavicle, right scapula, right humerus, right radius, five metacarpals, and 17 manual phalanges. All other skeletal elements are missing. Present also is the left humerus of an older non-adult, yielding a minimum of two individuals. No pathological conditions were seen.

Burial 21
LOCATION: NW CORNER OF THE NAVE

Present is the incomplete skeleton of a young adult aged 27 +/− 10 years at death. The bones present include T10, T11, L1–L4, five left ribs, and one right rib. No craniofacial bones were present. Age estimation was based upon sternal rib end morphology. No pathological conditions were observed.

Burial 22
LOCATION: NW CORNER OF THE NAVE

Present is the nearly complete skeleton of an adult male, aged 42 +/− 5 years at death. The other individuals represented include a non-adult (centrum, cranial fragment, metacarpal or metatarsal) and a rib from a second adult. Missing skeletal elements include the mandible, left innominate, left and right clavicles, right scapula, both humeri, both radii, both ulnae, both patellae, both tibiae, both fibulae, left femur, three right ribs, and most of the hand and foot bones. Few teeth were present, and those present were too worn to score dental enamel defects or to measure the crown dimensions. This individual presented with extensive pathological conditions, many of them associated with age and/or activity-related changes to the skeleton. The right parietal has a well-healed cranial fracture at the temporal line. There is a button osteoma just superior to the left sphenofrontal suture. Barely discernible cribra orbitalia (healed porosity) was present in the left and right eye orbits. Coalescing arthritic porosity was present on the left and right articular eminences of the temporal bones, but the absence of the mandible and mandibular condyles makes further evaluation difficult. Many of the ribs possessed healed rib fractures near or adjacent to the tubercle and along the neck or shaft (RR1, RR2, RR4, RR6, RR8, LR4–7). Many of these fractures are not well aligned. The dens of C2 and the facet for the dens on C1 possess arthritic changes, including surface osteophytes and eburnation (without grooves). The posterior aspect of the lateral condyle on the right femur has coalescing arthritic porosity. The femoral head of the right femur also possesses coalescing arthritic porosity. Vertebral osteophytosis, in the form of elevated rings and curved spicules, is present on many of the thoracic and lumbar vertebrae (T6–T12, L1–L5). The right side of L1 exhibits a compression fracture. The vertebral body has a characteristic wedge shape. The superior aspect of the right side of the fifth lumbar vertebra also possesses a slight compression fracture.

Burial 23
LOCATION: NW CORNER OF THE NAVE

Present is the mostly complete skeleton of an adult female, aged approximately 35 +/− 5 years at death. Missing elements include the hyoid bone and some of the bones of the hands and feet. Stature estimation, based on femoral and tibial measurements and calculated using Genovés (Bass 2005, is 145–150 cm. Pathological conditions include healed porotic hyperostosis on the occipital bone (indicating anemia earlier in life), a perimortem complete fracture of the left 11th rib, and spondylolisthesis of L5, which resulted in a compression fracture of the vertebral body and associated osteophytosis of the inferior rim. Spondylosis, a fracture of the vertebral arch, can result in spondylolisthesis when the arch is broken on both sides and subsequently separates from the vertebral body. The separation of the arch from the body then results in anterior slippage of the vertebral body and frequently an associated compression fracture, as occurred in this individual. A genetic predisposition for this condition has been hypothesized, but it is also known to occur as a result of trauma, including trauma associated with intensive labor activities, such as carrying heavy loads on a regular basis. Dorsal pitting and a preauricular sulcus are present and severe, indicating this woman had given birth. There is also a bony spicule on the inferior demiface of the auricular surface that is likely associated with childbirth. Dental pathological conditions include carious lesions on several teeth: the right first upper incisor, the right upper canine, the left second premolar, the right upper first premolar, the right and left upper second molars, and the lower left third molar. Additionally, several teeth were missing antemortem, including the left maxillary third molar, the right and left second mandibular molars, and the right third mandibular molar. Present with this individual was the humerus and one thoracic vertebra of another adult, yielding a minimum of two individuals.

Burial 24
LOCATION: NW CORNER OF THE NAVE

Present is the partial skeleton of a non-adult, aged approximately 1 year +/− 4 months at death. The bones present include the right parietal, mandible, pars basilaris, both left and right pars lateralis, hyoid, C1–5, one lumbar vertebra, and all mandibular teeth. There is severe endocranial bone deposition on the right parietal, with both woven and healed reactions on more than half of the bone surface.

Burial 25
LOCATION: NW CORNER OF THE NAVE

Present is the partial skeleton of a young adult, aged 22 +/− 5 years at the time of death. Bones present include T4–12, eight right ribs and five left ribs, right clavicle, right scapula, and right humerus. Pathological conditions include a complete healed oblique fracture on the proximal end of the humerus. Deformation of the humerus and a secondary callus are evident. The lateral aspect of the head presents traumatic arthritis and there is healed and woven bone present. A young non-adult sternal body was present as well, yielding a minimum of two individuals.

Burial 26
LOCATION: NW CORNER OF THE NAVE
MNI: 3 individuals

Present is the incomplete skeleton of an adult of indeterminate sex. The skeletal elements present include the vertebral column, the right ribs, some of the left ribs, manubrium, sternum, left clavicle, left scapula, and some of the hand and foot bones. Two additional individuals were represented by the distal epiphysis for the radius and four permanent incisors. Minor vertebral osteophytosis was present on L5. Due to the few skeletal elements present, many of the biological and demographic data could not be collected or analyzed.

Burial 27
LOCATION: NW CORNER OF THE NAVE

Present is the incomplete skeleton of an adult male, aged 42 +/− 5 years. A second individual is commingled with the principal individual and is represented by an adult rib. Skeletal elements present include the thoracic vertebrae, the lumbar vertebrae, the sacrum, both innominates, the coccyx, all of the right ribs, 10 of the left ribs, the clavicles, the scapulae, the left humerus, and several hand phalanges. The bones present exhibit a more youthful appearance than the vertebral elements and pubic symphysis, which may reflect compensatory degenerative changes that resulted from the fusion of both auricular surfaces of the innominates with the sacrum. The sternal rib ends appear much younger than the pubic symphysis. Vertebral osteophytosis is present on T7, T8, and T9. T9 and T10 are fused together, but this is likely a developmental defect rather than the fusion of vertebral osteophytes. L3 has a healed fracture on its right transverse process. The left fifth rib has a healed fracture on its shaft. Pinpoint porosity and surface lipping consistent with arthritic activity are present on the lateral end of the left clavicle.

5

An African Cranium

Catherine Gaither, Raul Y. Tito, Cecil M. Lewis Jr.,
Brendan J. Culleton, George H. Perry, Douglas J. Kennett,
John Krigbaum, Victor Vásquez Sánchez, Teresa
Rosales Tham, Rocío Delibes Mateos, Régulo Franco
Jordán, and Jeffrey Quilter

EARLY IN OUR RESEARCH at Magdalena de Cao, in 2005, a cranium (no. 15) (Figure 5.1) was recovered in loose surface soil in Unit 12, the large excavation unit covering the northern end of the church nave. This was a highly disturbed context, as human skeletal remains were scattered on the surface throughout this section of the site and beyond. The disturbed human remains found in Unit 12 may have been buried initially either in the town cemetery, flanking the exterior western wall of the nave, or within the church. There is no secure way to determine the original location of the Cranium 15 burial.

It became clear once research attention was focused on it that this cranium was the remains of a person of African descent. It is the only physical evidence of Africans at the site, even though we have historical records that discuss an African population at Magdalena and in the region, noting that there were more than 200 slaves in the Chicama Valley by 1594 (see Chapter 12). We therefore subjected the cranium to a number of analytical tests in order to gain the maximum amount of information about this individual.

While Africans were involved in the European entry into the New World from its inception, the physical presence of Africans is scant, and to the best of our knowledge we believe that the Magdalena African cranium represents the earliest physical remains of an African individual found in South America and one of the earliest in the New World. The following sections discuss our research on the cranium and its importance.

Macroscopic Analysis

Our visual assessment of the cranium began with analysis of traditional morphological characteristics (*sensu* Rhine 1990), including a macromorphoscopic analysis utilizing traits identified by Hefner (2009) and a craniometric analysis utilizing FORDISC 3.0 (Ousley and Jantz

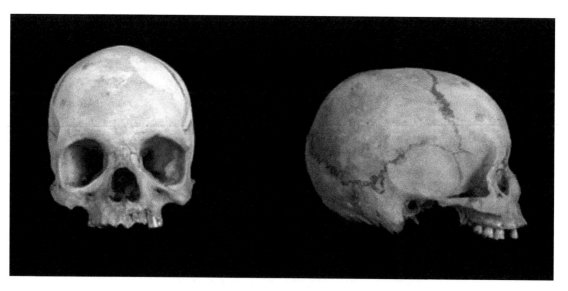

Figure 5.1 Two views of the African cranium.

2005), which performs discriminant function analysis. SPSS and the k-nearest neighbor statistic (IBM Corp. 2011) were used to analyze the macromorphoscopic cranial traits and resulted in the classification of the individual as African. The classification utilizing the FORDISC database of modern comparison samples was equally strong in the classification of the individual as African, as was the use of Howell's database (included in FORDISC) of comparative samples from multiple worldwide cultures and archaeological populations.

The cranium had a small mastoid process and generally appeared gracile. Well-established cranial morphological features identified it as female (Buikstra and Ubelaker 1994; White et al. 2012). Genetic studies, however, identified the individual as male (discussed later in this chapter). This is not necessarily surprising given that sex estimation based only on a cranium can be difficult, especially when samples drawn from the relevant population are not available. Absence of the complete skeleton, lack of comparative specimens, and the young age of the individual contributed to the initial female identification. Additionally, recent validation studies (Spradley and Jantz 2011) have shown that the cranium is less accurate than even postcranial measurements for estimating sex, particularly in individuals from small-bodied populations.

The estimated age at death for this individual is in his early twenties. All teeth were fully erupted and had complete root formation, and there was some dental attrition. All cranial sutures were open with the exception of the spheno-occipital synchondrosis (aka basilar suture), and this suture demonstrated evidence of recent union (Buikstra and Ubelaker 1994). This is consistent with a young adult individual (Scheuer and Black 2000).

Pathological conditions observed on the African cranium include healed and active cribra orbitalia on the superior portion of both eye orbits (pars orbitalis) and healed porotic hyperostosis on both parietal bones as well as the occipital bone, suggesting biological stress during life. There is also a healed depressed cranial fracture on the right side of the frontal bone, indicating antemortem trauma produced by accident or human agency.

Dating

The Pennsylvania State University (Penn State) Human Paleoecology and Isotope Geochemistry Laboratory analyzed a molar from Cranium 15 for AMS radiocarbon dating and stable isotope measurement. After cleaning, bone collagen was extracted from root dentine of an upper first molar. An evaluation of sample quality yielded results indicating good preservation, and carbon and nitrogen concentrations and stable isotopes were measured.

^{14}C ages were corrected for mass dependent fractionation with measured $\delta^{13}C$ values (Stuiver and Polach 1977) and compared with samples of Pleistocene whale bone (background, > 48 ^{14}C yr B.P.), late Holocene bison bone (~1850 ^{14}C yr B.P.), late A.D. 1800s cow bone, and OX-1 oxalic acid standards for normalization.

The conventional ^{14}C age was calibrated with OxCal v4.2.3 (Bronk Ramsey 2009) with the SHCal13 Southern Hemisphere atmospheric curve (Hogg et al. 2013). Recent work has suggested that because of the seasonal southward shift of the Intertropical Convergence Zone (ITCZ) over the Amazon Basin, the IntCal13 Northern Hemisphere curve should be used in the Peruvian Andes and Altiplano (Ogburn 2012). The ITCZ does not diverge as far south in coastal areas, and hence we used the Southern Hemisphere calibration.

Isotopic data indicate a diet relatively low in animal protein, comprising a mix of C3 and C4 plant foods and little or no indication of marine foods (but see later discussion). Therefore, we did not apply a marine reservoir correction or mixed marine/atmospheric curve. To constrain the calibrated age to the postcontact period we applied a terminus post quem of A.D. 1578 using the After command in OxCal. The resulting 2σ modeled calibrated age of the specimen is cal A.D. 1578 to 1633 (Figure 5.2).

Acknowledging the uncertainties with respect to the mixture of Northern and Southern Hemisphere air masses and the potential for a marine contribution to the diet, the Penn State team modeled a series of mixed-reservoir calibrations in OxCal to determine how these factors would affect the calibrated age of the sample. Fifteen calibrations varying the proportions

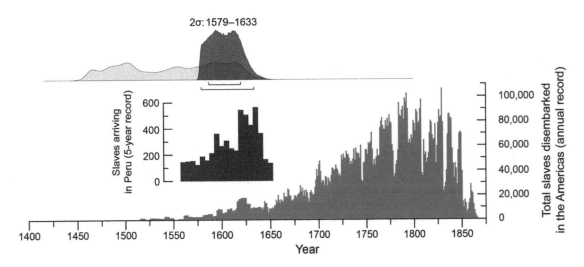

Figure 5.2 Radiocarbon date for the cranium compared to the timing of slave importation to Peru.

of atmospheric mixtures in 25 percent increments from 100 percent Northern Hemisphere (Reimer et al. 2013) to 100 percent Southern Hemisphere (Hogg et al. 2013), and 0 percent, 10 percent, and 20 percent marine (Reimer et al. 2013) were made. The uncertainty in the atmospheric mixes was set at ±10 percent. The local marine reservoir offset, ΔR, was estimated as 146 ± 52 ^{14}C yr from an average of 14 measurements of pre-bomb shells of *Argopecten purpuratus* and *Donax obesulus* collected close to the project area (Etayo-Cadavid et al. 2013; Jones et al. 2007). Calibrated results are plotted in Figure 5.2.

Results of the sensitivity analysis indicate that varying the atmospheric mixture has little effect on the 2σ calibrated distributions, largely because the range is tightly constrained on the older end by the terminus post quem, and the calibration curve drops steeply on the younger end. Larger marine contributions do extend the calibrated range more toward the present, adding 14 and 34 cal yr to the distributions of fully Southern Hemisphere calibrations at 10 percent and 20 percent marine, respectively. The final calibrated results are plotted in Figure 5.2.

Genetics

A first-phase study of DNA extraction, PCR amplification, and mitochondrial DNA (mtDNA) sequencing was carried out in the Ancient DNA Laboratory at the Department of Anthropology, University of Oklahoma, on a tooth root from Cranium 15. This study was followed by independent DNA extraction and mtDNA sequencing, as well as a preliminary analysis of nuclear genome variation, conducted in the Ancient DNA Laboratory at the Departments of Anthropology and Biology at Penn State on the same tooth sample.

The original experiment at the University of Oklahoma used PCR amplification and Sanger sequencing to determine the sequence of the mitochondrial control region following published procedures (Ozga et al. 2015). Based on comparison to the Cambridge Reference Sequence (Andrews et al. 1999), the mitochondrial haplogroup L3e3 was assigned. L3e3 is strongly associated with recent African ancestry (Gonder et al. 2006). Moreover, this haplogroup is associated with Bantu-speakers and West Africa and is quite common in Brazil and the Caribbean as a result of the slave trade (Bandelt et al. 2001).

The University of Oklahoma result was confirmed at Penn State with a different sequencing approach. Specifically, they designed biotinylated, 100 bp RNA "baits" for DNA capture (Gnirke et al. 2009) that were complementary to the complete human mtDNA genome with overlapping, 10x coverage (synthesized by MyCroarray, Inc.). The bait library consisted of five separate mtDNA haplotypes originally selected for use with Native American remains (A2, B2, C1, D1, and X2a), with probes placed at 10 bp intervals around circularized mitogenomic reference sequences. We constructed two barcoded Illumina libraries from the ancient DNA extract using a previously described protocol (Meyer and Kircher 2010). We then used the DNA capture approach to enrich for endogenous mtDNA reads, following a version of the MyCroarray protocol that we modified for aDNA. The enriched libraries were paired-end sequenced (151×151 bp) on part of a multiplexed run of the Illumina MiSeq instrument at the Huck Institutes of the Life Sciences Genomics Core Facility at Penn State. The resulting reads were trimmed, merged, and quality filtered and used to reconstruct a whole mitochondrial genome assembly for this individual. The analysis yielded a 95.7 percent complete mtDNA sequence (with a minimum of two independent reads covering each position) with an average read length of 67 nt and an average of 6.5x non-redundant coverage. For the region of the mtDNA genome that was reconstructed from both the University of Oklahoma and Penn State analyses, the sequences were identical.

Penn State also performed an additional DNA capture and massively parallel sequencing analysis, but in this case with biotinylated RNA baits complementary to DNA sequences surrounding known single nucleotide polymorphisms (SNPs) in the nuclear genome. A total of 10,000 SNPs were systematically subsampled from the Illumina 650Y panel, which are well characterized in the publicly available Human Genome Diversity Project data. Each selected SNP site was targeted with four unique 100 mer RNA probes with the SNP site situated at positions 20, 40, 60, and 80, respectively. Two new sequencing libraries were prepared for nuclear capture, and libraries underwent capture as described for mtDNA. Following DNA capture, the enriched libraries were paired-end sequenced (75×75 bp) on one lane of the Illumina HiSeq 2500 at Penn State. The reads were aligned to the hg18 human genome assembly using BWA with default settings (Li and Durbin 2009), and SNPs at the target sites were called from reads with a minimum mapping quality of 30 using SAMtools (Li et al. 2009).

In total, 909 of the 10,000 SNPs were captured by at least one sequence read. In 163 of these, the Cranium 15 libraries had a unique SNP variant (i.e., neither of the expected variants). Sequence error or aDNA damage driving this proportion of singleton SNP variants could not be ruled out, so these sites were treated as missing data. The remaining SNPs were compared with 346 individuals of African ($N=121$), European ($N=130$), and Native American ($N=95$) descent using Structure (Pritchard et al. 2000). Assuming three populations in the data set ($k=3$), Cranium 15 strongly clusters with other individuals of African descent. Four populations ($k=4$) consisting of two subsets of African populations emerged, one comprising mostly Bantu-speaking agriculturalists and the other consisting of hunting and gathering groups. The Cranium 15 sample is consistent with the former Bantu group. This result is consistent with the cranial and mtDNA haplotype designations. Given the low sequence coverage obtained for this analysis, however, the results from the nuclear genomic analysis should be considered preliminary.

Genetic sex determination of the Cranium 15 individual was carried out as described by Skoglund et al. (2013), using the script distributed with their publication. Although the nuclear capture protocol successfully enriched for the targeted SNP regions (0.5 percent of reads mapping to hg18 were localized to targeted regions, representing > 10x enrichment over background expectation), the majority of the ~500,000 confidently mapped reads originated throughout the genome, including ~15,000 reads assigned to the sex chromosomes. Comparing sex chromosome reads yielded an assignment of biologically male ($R_Y = 0.083$), with 95 percent confidence intervals entirely within the expected male range ($R_Y = 0.0785$–0.0876).

Isotopic Analyses

Isotopic analysis of individual teeth not only can shed light on past diet patterns but also provides a record of geographic origin and potential migration/translocation (Bentley 2006; Price et al. 1994, 2012). Stable isotopes do not undergo radioactive decay; however, such isotopes may themselves be the result of radioactive decay, and they do exhibit natural variation because of mass-dependent fractionation. During fractionation, heavy and light isotopes divide differently between two phases. This division occurs because the energy bond of each

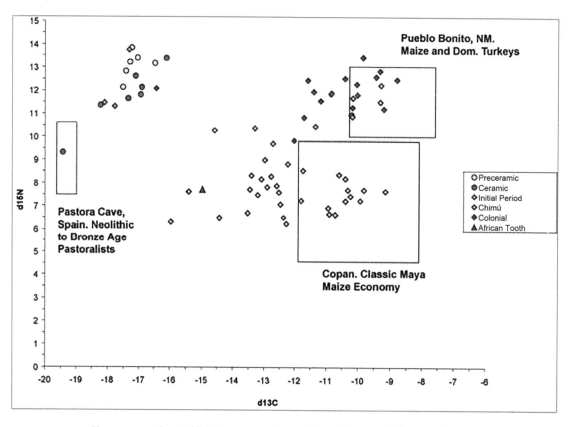

Figure 5.3 Chart of light isotope analyses of Magdalena and other burials. The African cranium is represented by the blue triangle and shows a marked difference from the other colonial samples, which are shown as blue diamonds.

isotope is different. In general, heavy isotopes have stronger bonds and slower reaction rates than light isotopes. That means that light isotopes are more likely to exhibit fractionation. Carbon (δ^{13}C) and nitrogen (δ^{15}N) are among the light isotopes analyzed in the case of Cranium 15, and they can give us specific information about the types of plants the individual was consuming as well as the level of terrestrial versus marine food resources in his diet.

Stable isotope ratios of carbon and nitrogen were measured from different dental tissues associated with Cranium 15. The results yielded a δ^{13}C of −15.0‰ and a δ^{15}N of 7.7‰. Such values seem to reflect a rather poor diet with not much meat protein and (for the New World) very little maize. However, these values were derived from the M1 tooth dentine used for the ^{14}C analysis. Isotopes in tooth dentine are incorporated principally during tooth formation, and there is minimal turnover. Consequently, the dietary components from light isotopes more reflect Cranium 15's childhood diet as opposed to his diet closer to the time of his death. The results of the dental calculus study, as discussed later in this chapter, are likely more consistent with his diet in the last two years of his life.

Cranium 15 was compared with Magdalena colonial burials. As shown in Figure 5.3, the Magdalena colonial individuals had rather good diets with high amounts of protein from terrestrial and marine animals. Their diets also show evidence for ample amounts of maize. This conclusion, however, must be tempered by the fact that we only analyzed skeletons interred within the church, which would include high-ranking members of the community who possibly had better diets than many of the other townspeople.

Based on the isotopic analyses, in his youth the African individual had a radically different diet than any of the church burials, with much less meat and C4 plant foods. Other studies modify this view as will be presented below. The regional comparison also was augmented with data from three individuals identified as enslaved Africans buried in Barbados, some of whom were probably born in West Africa (Schroeder et al. 2009). Those Barbados individuals who were considered to have been born locally, based on their strontium values (discussed in the next section), had δ^{13}C values from −13.5 to −8.5‰ and δ^{15}N values from 9.5 to 14.5‰. These values are considerably different from those of Cranium 15, whose values were −15.0‰ for δ^{13}C and 7.7‰ for δ^{15}N. The δ^{15}N value for Cranium 15 is also significantly lower than the Barbadians who were considered to be African-born. For them, δ^{15}N was 9.6 to 12.4‰. Given that these isotopes are indicators of diet, it is not unexpected to see variation even within regions. The light isotope values for Cranium 15 are much more in line with what was seen in the enslaved Barbadians than in the other burials at Magdalena, which exhibited values of δ^{13}C from −11.75 to −9.0‰ and δ^{15}N values from 11 to 13‰. This, combined with the results of the heavy isotope analyses, strongly supports the hypothesis that the individual represented by Cranium 15 was born in Africa.

Strontium (Sr) and lead (Pb) are two of the heavy isotopes analyzed in the case of Cranium 15, and these give us valuable information about the geographic origin of this individual and the paleoenvironment in which he lived. Radiogenic strontium and lead isotope ratios vary according to the age of bedrock and associated topsoil, and because fractionation is negligible due to such small differences in their mass, these elements become integrated into the biosphere. Bioavailable Sr and Pb thus may substitute for calcium in skeletal tissues as they are integrated into the hydroxyapatite matrix. Thus, individual teeth assayed for Sr and Pb ratios reflect local geological and hydrological sources, associated flora and fauna, and ultimately foods and waters consumed (Bentley 2006; Kamenov and Gulson 2014). When measured in human tooth enamel, Sr ratios (^{87}Sr/^{86}Sr) and Pb ratios (^{208}Pb/^{204}Pb, ^{207}Pb/^{204}Pb, ^{206}Pb/^{204}Pb) reflect a necessarily complex, mixed signal based on weathered geology and bioavailable sources incorporated during the time of enamel formation for the tooth assayed.

There has been considerable use of Sr ratios derived from human tooth enamel to determine whether an individual is local or not (e.g., Bentley 2006; Knudson et al. 2012; Montgomery 2010; Price et al. 2012). Analysis of Pb ratios, however, is less routine, and there is a paucity of comparative data. In particular contexts Pb ratios have been shown to yield consistent patterns that correlate to geology and physiography and help to identify nonlocal individuals within a sample (e.g., Montgomery 2010; Turner et al. 2009; Valentine et al. 2015). Importantly, a number of geological studies help to frame the extent of known Pb ratio variation, including provenance studies of metal ores in Peru to clarify provenance of Pb-containing artifacts (e.g., Kamenov et al. 2002; Macfarlane and Lechtman 2014).

Isotopic assays of Cranium 15's RM^2 tooth enamel included assessment of Sr ratios and Pb ratios to address questions of local (i.e., Chicama Valley, Peru) versus nonlocal status.

M2 tooth enamel formation and mineralization occurs between 3.8 and 6.8 years (Smith 1991). Data from M2 tooth enamel thus reflects a childhood signal that is fixed in time after enamel formation is complete. Two separate assays were conducted from two mechanically cleaned chunks (ca. 20–30 mg) of tooth enamel. Samples were dissolved in precleaned Teflon vials using 8 N nitric acid, and Sr and Pb was separated from single aliquots using ion chromatography and Sr- and Pb-spec resin. One sample was analyzed for $^{87}Sr/^{86}Sr$ using a Micromass Sector 54 thermal ionization mass spectrometer (TIMS) and the NBS-987 standard, with the ratio normalized to $^{86}Sr/^{88}Sr = 0.1194$. A second ratio was measured using a Nu-Plasma multiple-collector inductively coupled plasma mass spectrometer (ICP-MS) against the NBS-987 standard. Pb ratios were measured on the Nu-Plasma ICP-MS with Tl normalization and data reported against the NBS-981 standard.

For Sr, the TIMS result (0.7243652) is quite consistent with the ICP-MS result (0.724634). Such a high $^{87}Sr/^{86}Sr$ ratio falls outside of the Sr range observed in prehistoric Peru, including a recent comprehensive survey of modern soils (Knudson et al. 2014). Further, these ratios are more radiogenic than those typically observed from prehistoric archaeological contexts in the New World; although these results would be consistent with very old (highly radiogenic) rocks such as those associated with the Appalachians, such a scenario seems unlikely. The Sr ratios also exceed data observed in the circum-Caribbean region, including the Yucatan (e.g., Hodell et al. 2004; Laffoon et al. 2012; Price et al. 2012). High $^{87}Sr/^{86}Sr$ ratios have been noted in first-generation African slaves from Cemitério dos Pretos Novos, Rio de Janeiro, Brazil (Bastos et al. 2011) and Campeche, Mexico (Price et al. 2012). Further, high $^{87}Sr/^{86}Sr$ ratios plotted by Goodman et al. (2009:115), which are > 0.720 ($N = 5$), all are from individuals with modified teeth, supporting the suggestion that these individuals were also first-generation Africans. Thus, at several key New World sites, many individuals thought to have origins in Africa have quite heterogenous $^{87}Sr/^{86}Sr$ ratios, including some with ratios > 0.720, such as that exhibited by Cranium 15.

With respect to Pb ratios, two separate assays were conducted on Cranium 15 tooth enamel using ICP-MS; these values are consistent between the two assays, and they are markedly different from published data from Machu Picchu (e.g., Turner et al. 2009). Specifically, when plotted against ore provenance data encompassing known Pb ratio variation across Peru (Macfarlane and Lechtman 2014), Cranium 15's $^{208}Pb/^{204}Pb$ ratios (39.1 and 39.2) and $^{206}Pb/^{204}Pb$ ratios (19.05 and 19.16) are elevated and its $^{207}Pb/^{204}Pb$ ratios (15.88 and 15.94) are markedly elevated compared to published and unpublished values. When Cranium 15's Pb ratios are compared to other New World and Old World contexts, including the Iberian Peninsula, the data do not accord with patterns of isotopic ratios published in the geological, metallurgical, and/or environmental literature (e.g., Álvarez-Iglesias et al. 2012; Santos Zalduegui et al. 2004). There is a paucity of data for Africa with respect to Pb and Sr ratios, such that using these proxies to fingerprint a precise location is untenable. However, the geological history of Africa and the extensive and very old West African Craton suggest that the heterogeneity of Pb values observed in Cranium 15 and two identified individuals at Campeche, 75 and 85.1 (Price et al. 2012), strongly support West Africa as the childhood residence for the Cranium 15 individual.

Microbotanical Analysis

Studies of residues in cooking vessels and ashes from a kitchen area as well as macrobotanical analyses of plant remains indicate that the people of Magdalena had a relatively rich and diverse subsistence economy that included fish and meat from goats and sheep as well as a wide variety of domestic and introduced plant foods (see Chapter 3).

The dental calculus of a premolar from Cranium 15 was analyzed by researchers at Arqueobios, in Trujillo, Peru, and compared with that of eight other individuals from the church burials (See Table 3.6 in Chapter 3). Since dental calculus is built up over short periods of time, it reflects the diet of the last two years or so of an individual's life.

The dental calculus sample from Cranium 15 included starch grains from maize and potato, as well as grains too deformed by heat to identify. The other eight burials only had maize, potato, and deformed grains, with the addition of manioc in some cases. The absence of manioc in the dental calculus sample from Cranium 15 does not necessarily mean that this food was not consumed. The maize and potato grains, however, indicate that he did consume the same New World staples eaten by the rest of the Magdalena population.

The fact that the isotopic analysis of tooth dentin indicates a lack of C_4 plants but that maize starch grains are present in the dental calculus suggests that the individual represented by Cranium 15 spent his childhood in Africa with a different diet than he came to have in Peru. The suggestion that he ate the same general kinds of foods as other townspeople is not an indication that his diet was better, the same, or worse than those of the people buried in the nave, or the rest of the Magdalena population.

Summary and Discussion

Our study of Cranium 15 is one of the most exhaustive, multiple-proxy analyses ever conducted on human remains from South America with scant contextual information. But while our work underscores the power of advanced scientific analyses, it also highlights the difficulty of reaching many definite conclusions in archaeological and even historical investigations.

There are a few things we can say with certainty, and others that are based on some speculation. The individual of Cranium 15 was of African ancestry, he was male, and he died in his 20s. His diet early in life was non-Andean, but toward the end of his life it clearly included Andean foods. He also suffered some physical trauma during his life. He probably was born in West Africa, suggesting that he may have been brought as a slave to the New World. Toward the end of his life, he probably lived at or near Magdalena de Cao, and he may have been a Christian accorded burial in the church. Given this, it is possible that he was a personal servant to a cleric in the church rather than a field laborer.

A common complaint of archaeologists is that they need more data. In the case of the archaeology of colonial Latin America, however, and especially for the case of Africans in that time and place, this is particularly true. There are few comparable cases for our study (cf. Bastos et al. 2011; Price et al. 2012), yet such studies will provide us with considerable new views of the process by which the modern world came to be—both in the New World and the Old.

Africans participated in the exploration and colonization of the New World from the fifteenth century onward; a few were free, but most were slaves. Consequently, our

Figure 5.4 Illustration from Martinez Compañón's book on the North Coast of Peru showing Africans or African Peruvians mining and processing tar at Amotape near Piura.

understandings of even basic circumstances of Africans early in the Colonial Period in Peru are impeded by their low social status and the complex politics of the viceroyalty. An important aspect of those politics was the need for labor due to the dramatic depopulation from diseases, warfare, and disruptions brought by the conquistadors. In 1565, only three decades after the Spanish arrival, sources state that the Chicama Valley was almost abandoned, with a substantial part of its lands uncultivated (Chapter 12).

Initial attempts to enslave Indians were ineffective, and later the Crown felt obliged to protect its native inhabitants and evangelize them; consequently, enslaved Africans and their descendants became the chief sources of labor in many coastal regions of Central and South America. By 1594, more than 230 slaves were working on haciendas and in sugar mills in the Chicama Valley, but by 1760 there were more than 1,200 (Feijoo 1763; Mogrovejo 2006) (Figure 5.4). While Spaniards and slaves occupied haciendas, indigenous people mostly lived and worked elsewhere in planned towns under the supervision of religious orders. Indeed, various rules and regulations specifically stated that native peoples should live apart from Africans and Spaniards (see O'Toole 2012).

As discussed in Chapter 1, in the 1560s, following a policy enforced throughout Peru, Chicama Valley natives were forced out of their homes into six reducciones, towns built on Spanish plans. As one of these communities, Magdalena de Cao was first built in a flood-prone location near the mouth of the Chicama River, but subsequently it was relocated to the El Brujo terrace due to floods brought by a massive El Niño event in 1578 (Huertas Vallejos 1987; Quilter 2011).

Magdalena de Cao was supposed to be occupied only by Andeans under the supervision of Dominican friars. But the degree to which Africans and Indians were separated is open to question. Recorded cases of close associations between groups and our discovery suggest that social boundaries between valley inhabitants were more porous than official rules demanded.

The remains of this unfortunate person are nevertheless a testament to the importance of Africans and people of African descent born in the New World in the making of the colonial world. Although the majority came involuntarily, their labors and services were essential to the colonial economy and, eventually, the social and economic transformations that led from colony to republic to today.

REFERENCES CITED

Álvarez-Iglesias, P., B. Rubio, and J. Millos
  2012 Isotopic Identification of Natural vs. Anthropogenic Lead Sources in Marine Sediments from the Inner Ría de Vigo (NW Spain). *Science of the Total Environment* 437:22–35.

Andrews, Richard M., Iwona Kubacka, Patrick F. Chinnery, Robert N. Lightowlers, Douglas M. Turnbull, and Neil Howel
  1999 Reanalysis and Revision of the Cambridge Reference Sequence for Human Mitochondrial DNA. *Nature Genetics* 23(2):147.

Bandelt, Hans J., Juliana Alves-Silva, Pedro E. Guimarães, Magda da Silva Santos, Antonio Brehm, Luisa Pereira, Alfredo Coppa, José M. Larruga, and C. Rengo
  2001 Phylogeography of the Human Mitochondrial Haplogroup L3e: A Snapshot of African Prehistory and Atlantic Slave Trade. *Annals of Human Genetics* 65(6):549–563.

Bastos, Murilo Q. R., Sheila M. F. Mendoça de Souza, Ricardo Ventura Santos, Della C. Cook, Claudia Rodrigues-Carvalhoe, and Roberto Ventura Santos
  2011 Da África ao Cemitério Dos Pretos Novos, Rio de Janerio: Um estudo sobre as orgens de escravos a parirda análise de isótopos de estrôncio no esmalte dentário. *Revista de Arqueologia (Brazil)* 24(1):66–81.

Bentley, R. Alexander
  2006 Strontium Isotopes from the Earth to the Archaeological Skeleton: A Review. *Journal of Archaeological Method and Theory* 13(3):135–187.

Bowser, Frederick
  1974 *The African Slave in Colonial Peru, 1524–1650.* Stanford, CA: Stanford University Press.

Bronk Ramsey, Christopher
  2009 Bayesian Analysis of Radiocarbon Dates. *Radiocarbon* 51:337–360.

Buikstra, Jane, and Douglas Ubelaker (editors)
  1994 *Standards for Data Collection from Human Skeletal Remains.* Arkansas Archaeological Survey Research Series No. 44. Fayetteville, AR: Arkansas Archaeological Survey.

Etayo-Cadavid, Miguel F., C. Fred T. Andrus, Kevin B. Jones, Gregory W. L. Hodgins, Daniel H. Sandweiss, Santiago Uceda-Castillo, and Jeffrey Quilter
  2013 Marine Radiocarbon Reservoir Age Variation in *Donax obesulus* Shells from Northern Peru: Late Holocene Evidence for Extended El Niño. *Geology* 41:599–602.

Feijoo de Sosa, M.
  1763 *Relación descriptiva de la ciudad y provincia de Truxillo del Perú.* Madrid: Imprenta Real.

Gnirke, Andreas, Alexandre Melnikov, Jared Maguire, Peter Rogov, Emily M. LeProust, William Brockman, Timothy Fennell, Georgia Giannoukos, Sheila Fisher, Carsten Russ, Stacey Gabriel, David B. Jaffee, Eric S. Lander, and Chad Nusbaum
  2009 Solution Hybrid Selection with Ultra-Long Oligonucleotides for Massively Parallel Targeted Sequencing. *National Biotechnology* 27(2):182–189.

Gonder, Mary Katherine, Holly M. Mortensen, Floyd A. Reed, Alexandra de Sousa, and Sarah A. Tishkoff
  2006 Whole-mtDNA Genome Sequence Analysis of Ancient African Lineages. *Molecular Biology and Evolution* 24(3):757–768. https://doi.org/10.1093/molbev/msl209.PMID 17194802.

Goodman, A. H., J. Jones, J. Reid, M. E. Mack, M. L. Blakey, D. Amarasiriwardena, P. Burton, and D. Coleman
  2009 Isotopic and Elemental Chemistry of Teeth: Implications for Places of Birth, Forced Migration Patterns, Nutritional Status, and Pollution. In *The Skeletal Biology of the New York African Burial Ground*, Part I, edited by M. L. Blakey and L. M. Rankin-Hill, pp. 95–118. Washington, D.C.: Howard University Press.

Hefner, Joseph. T.
  2009 Cranial Nonmetric Variation and Estimating Ancestry. *Journal of Forensic Sciences* 54(5):985–995.

Hodell, David A., Rhonda L. Quinn, Mark Brenner, and George Kamenov
  2004 Spatial Variation of Strontium Isotopes (^{87}Sr/^{86}Sr) in the Maya Region: A Tool for Tracking Ancient Human Migration. *Journal of Archaeological Science* 31:585–601.

Hogg, Alan G., Quan Hua, Paul G. Blackwell, Mu Niu, Caitlin E. Buck, Thomas
P. Guilderson, Timothy J. Heaton, Jonathan G. Palmer, Paula J. Reimer, Ron W. Reimer,
Christian S. M. Turney, and Susan R. H. Zimmerman

    2013 SHCal13 Southern Hemisphere Calibration, 0–50,000 Years cal BP. *Radiocarbon*
       55(4):1889–1903.

Huertas Vallejos, L.

    1987 *Ecología e historia. Probanzas de indios y españoles referents a las catastróficas lluvias de*
       1578, en los corregimientos de Trujillo y Saña. Edited by Francisco Alcocer. Chiclayo:
       CES Solidaridad.

IBM Corp.

    2011 IBM SPSS Statistics for Windows, Version 20.0. Armonk, NY: IBM Corp.

Jones, Kevin B., Gregory L. Hodgins, David L. Dettman, C. Fred T. Andrus, April Nelson,
and Miguel F. Etayo-Cadavid

    2007 Seasonal Variations in Peruvian Marine Reservoir Age from Pre-Bomb *Argopecten*
       purpuratus Shell Carbonate. *Radiocarbon* 49(2):877–888.

Kamenov, George, Andrew W. Macfarlane, and Lee Riciputie

    2002 Sources of Lead in the San Cristobal, Pulacayo, and Potosi Mining Districts, Bolivia, and
       a Reevaluation of Regional Ore Lead Isotope Provinces. *Economic Geology* 97:573–592.

Kamenov, George. D., and Brian. L. Gulson

    2014 The Pb Isotopic Record of Historical to Modern Human Lead Exposure. *Science of the*
       Total Environment 490:861–870.

Knudson, Kelly J., William J. Pestle, Christina Torres-Rouff, and Gonzalo Pimentel

    2012 Assessing the Life History of an Andean Traveler Through Biogeochemistry: Stable and
       Radiogenic Isotope Analyses of Archaeological Human Remains from Northern Chile.
       International Journal of Osteoarchaeology 22(4):435–451.

Knudson, Kelly J., Emily Webb, Christine White, and Fred J. Longstaffe

    2014 Baseline Data for Andean Paleomobility Research: A Radiogenic Strontium Isotope
       Study of Modern Peruvian Agricultural Soils. *Archaeological and Anthropological Sciences*
       6:205–219.

Laffoon, Jason E., Gareth R. Davies, Menno L. P. Hoogland, and Corinne L. Hofman

    2012 Spatial Variation of Biologically Available Strontium Isotopes ($^{87}Sr/^{86}Sr$) in an
       Archipelagic Setting: A Case Study from the Caribbean. *Journal of Archaeological Science*
       39:2371–2378.

Li, Heng, and Richard Durbin

    2009 Fast and Accurate Short Read Alignment with Burrows-Wheeler Transform.
       Bioinformatics 25(14):1754–1760.

Li, Heng, Bob Handsaker, Alec Wysoker, Tim Fennell, Jue Ruan, Nils Homer, Gabor
Marth, Goncalo Abecasis, and Richard Durban (1000 Genome Project Data Processing
Subgroup)

    2009 The Sequence Alignment/Map Format and SAMtools. *Bioinformatics*
       25(16):2078–2079.

Macfarlane, Andrew W., and Heather N. Lechtman

    2014 Andean Ores, Bronze Artifacts, and Lead Isotopes: Constraints on Metal Sources
       in their Geological Context. *Journal of Archaeological Method and Theory* 23:1–72.

Meyer, Matthias, and Martin Kircher

    2010 Illumina Sequencing Library Preparation for Highly Multiplexed Target Capture and Sequencing. *Cold Spring Harbor Protocols* 2010(6). https://doi.org/10.1101/pdb.prot5448.

Mogrovejo, Toribio

    2006 *Libro de visitas de Santo Toribio Mogrovejo (1593–1605)*. Edited by José A. Benito. Lima: Pontificia Universidad Católica del Perú.

Montgomery, Janet

    2010 Passports from the Past: Investigating Human Dispersals using Strontium Isotope Analysis of Tooth Enamel. *Annals of Human Biology* 37(3):325–346.

O'Toole, Rachel S.

    2012 *Bound Lives: Africans, Indians, and the Making of Race in Colonial Peru*. Pittsburgh: University of Pittsburgh Press.

Ogburn, Dennis. E.

    2012 Reconceiving the Chronology of Inca Imperial Expansion. *Radiocarbon* 54(2):219–237.

Ousley, Stephen D., and Richard L. Jantz

    2005 FORDISC 3.0. Personal Computer Forensic Discriminate Functions. Knoxville: University of Tennessee.

Ozga, Andrew T., Raul Y. Tito, Brian M. Kemp, Hugh Matternes, Alexandra Obregon-Tito, L. Neal, and Cecil M. Lewis Jr.

    2015 Origins of an Unmarked Georgia Cemetery Using Ancient DNA Analysis. *Human Biology* 87(2):109–122.

Price, T. Douglas, James H. Burton, Andrea Cucina, Pilar Zabala, Robert Frei, Robert H. Tykot, and Vera Tiesler

    2012 Isotopic Studies of Human Skeletal Remains from a Sixteenth to Seventeenth Century AD Churchyard in Campeche, Mexico: Diet, Place of Origin, and Age. *Current Anthropology* 53(4):396–433.

Price, T. Douglas, Clark M. Johnson, Joseph A. Ezzo, Jonathan Ericson, and James H. Burton

    1994 Residential Mobility in the Prehistoric Southwest United States: A Preliminary Study Using Strontium Isotope Analysis. *Journal of Archaeological Science* 21:315–330.

Pritchard, Jonathan K., Matthew Stephens, and Peter Donnelly

    2000 Inference of Population Structure Using Multilocus Genotype Data. *Genetics* 155(2):945–959.

Quilter, Jeffrey

    2011 Cultural Encounters at Magdalena de Cao Viejo in the Early Colonial Period. In *Enduring Conquests: Rethinking the Archaeology of Resistance to Spanish Colonialism in the Americas*, edited by Matthew Liebmann and Melissa Scott Murphy, pp. 103–125. Santa Fe, NM: SAR Press.

Reimer, Paula J., Michael G. L. Baillie, Edouard Bard, Alex Bayliss, J. Warren Beck, Paul J. Blackwell, Christopher Bronk Ramsey, Caitlin E. Buck, Hai Cheng, R. Lawrence Edwards, Michael Friedrich, Pieter M. Grootes, Thomas P. Guilderson, Haflidi Haflidason, Irka Hajdas, Christine Hatté, Timothy J. Heaton, Dirk L. Hoffmann, Alan G. Hogg, Konrad A. Hughen, K. Felix Kaiser, Bernd Kromer, Sturt W. Manning, Mu Niu,

Ron W. Reimer, David A. Richards, E. Marian Scott, John R. Southon, Richard A. Staff, Christian S. M. Turney, and Johannes van der Plicht

    2013   IntCal13 and Marine13 Radiocarbon Age Calibration Curves, 0–50,000 Years cal BP. *Radiocarbon* 55:1869–1887.

Rhine, Stanley

    1990   Nonmetric Skull Racing. In *Skeletal Attribution of Race*, edited by G. Gill and S. Rhine, pp. 9–20. Maxwell Museum of Anthropology Papers No. 4. Albuquerque: Maxwell Museum of Anthropology.

Santos Zalduegui, J. F., S. Garciá de Madinabeitia, J. I. Gil Ibarguchi, and F. Palero

    2004   A Lead Isotope Database: The Los Pedroches–Alcudia Area (Spain): Implications for Archaeometallurgical Connections Across Southwestern and Southeastern Iberia. *Archaeometry* 46(4):625–634.

Scheuer, Louise, and Sue Black

    2000   *Developmental Juvenile Osteology*. New York: Academic Press.

Schroeder, Hannes, Tamsin C. O'Connell, Jane A. Evans, Kristina A. Shuler, and Robert E. M. Hedges

    2009   Trans-Atlantic Slavery: Isotopic Evidence for Forced Migration to Barbados. *American Journal of Physical Anthropology* 139(4):547–557.

Skoglund, Pontus, Jan Stora, Anders Götherström, and Mattias Jakobsson

    2013   Accurate Sex Identification of Ancient Human Remains Using DNA Shotgun Sequencing. *Journal of Archaeological Science* 40(12):4477–4482.

Smith, B. Holly

    1991   Standards of Human Tooth Formation and Dental Age Assessment. In *Advances in Dental Anthropology*, edited by M. A. Kelly and C. S. Larsen, pp. 143–168. New York: Wiley-Liss.

Spradley, M. Katherine, and Richard L. Jantz

    2011   Sex Estimation in Forensic Anthropology: Skull Versus Postcranial Elements. *Journal of Forensic Sciences* 56(2):289–296.

Stuiver, Minze, and Henry A. Polach

    1977   Discussion: Reporting of ^{14}C Data. *Radiocarbon* 19:355–363.

Turner, Bethany L., George D. Kamenov, John D. Kingston, and George J. Armelagos

    2009   Insights into Immigration and Social Class at Machu Picchu, Peru based on Oxygen, Strontium, and Lead Isotopic Analysis. *Journal of Archaeological Science* 36:317–332.

Valentine, Benjamin, George D. Kamenov, Jonathan M. Kenoyer, Vasant Shinde, Veena Mushrif-Tripathy, Erik Otarola-Castillo, and John Krigbaum.

    2015   Evidence for Patterns of Selective Urban Migration in the Greater Indus Valley (2600–1900 BC): A Lead and Strontium Isotope Mortuary Analysis. *PLoS ONE* 10(4): e0123103.

White, Tim D., Michael Black, and Pieter A. Folkens

    2012   *Human Osteology*. 3rd ed. Boston: Academic Press.

6

Textiles and Clothing

Carrie Brezine

THE TEXTILES EXCAVATED from Magdalena de Cao Viejo show that assembling an ensemble of clothing in colonial Peru was a complicated endeavor: through what they wore, people could present multiple, even conflicting messages. The collection has more than 3,200 pieces and includes examples of indigenous cotton cloth, imported European silks, and heavy wool fabrics probably made in colonial *obrajes* (workshops). Several knitted stockings are among the artifacts, the first archaeological evidence of knitting in the Americas. Many of the existing fragments include seams or eyelets that give clues to the construction and fastening of garments, even when only a small scrap remains. The quality of the textiles varies from coarse cloth such as would be used for blankets or sturdy bags to fine white linen and elaborate silk trims.

At the time of culture contact, a Spaniard and an Andean would have been instantly distinguishable by their clothing. Andean people wore loose, simple garments woven from the fibers indigenous to the Andes: camelid and cotton. Most Spanish clothing was made of wool or linen. A complete European ensemble involved multiple layers of different fabrics, textures, and patterns. To be fully dressed, a person had to don many garments, some of which were fitted to the body and required intricate fastenings. Legs and feet were covered with stockings and shoes, hands with gloves. Face-to-face, an indigenous Andean and a Spaniard would have known that the other was completely foreign. To a Spaniard, an Andean body was one incompletely clothed—a state that had connotations of ignorance, immorality, and heathen beliefs. It is less easy to summarize what Spanish clothing indicated to Andeans, though once the Spaniards gained control, their habits of dress became associated with political and economic power.

Beginning almost immediately, both Spaniards and Andeans began to adjust their clothing in reaction to colonial institutions. Adapting some Spanish styles was essential for social mobility; Andeans used traditional materials to recreate European-style garments, often while still retaining some aspects of indigenous dress. Spaniards who had no access to or could not afford imported fabrics were forced to use locally produced cloth when they needed new garments. Thus far, the intricate manipulations of dress in the colonial era have come down to us primarily through wills (Graubart 2007, 2009), court cases (Earle 2001), and illustrations such as those by Martínez Compañón (1978). The textiles of Magdalena de Cao provide an unprecedented opportunity to study the actual clothing worn in a colonial reducción.

In addition to garments and clothing fabrics, the Magdalena collection contains a variety of textile artifacts that were used for other purposes, notably scraps of knotted fishing nets and cords of vegetal fiber. However, in this analysis I concentrate on fabrics that were, or could have been, worn on the body. These make up by far the largest part of the collection. Textiles embody many of the fundamental practices of any community. A textile may bear evidence of agricultural habits, botanical knowledge (e.g., in the use of dyes), animal husbandry, dominant spinning and weaving technologies, trading patterns, labor organization, and design preferences. As part of a garment, fabrics take on additional meanings. Clothing may reflect gender, age, wealth, status, profession, ethnicity, religion, attitude, and any number of other things. Faced with new fibers and unfamiliar ways of perceiving and enclosing the human form, indigenous Andeans adapted some garments, rejected others, and reinterpreted new items with the materials and tools at hand. Forced to adapt to the climate of the Andes and to local resources, Europeans found ways to continue their habits of dress but sometimes had to come up with creative combinations of local fabrics and imported materials.

In order to understand how indigenous and Spanish dress changed in the colonial situation, it is necessary first to identify the salient characteristics of precolumbian textiles and clothing. To that end, I briefly explain Andean and European textile practices and dress. I then discuss the overall composition of the collection, highlighting the most common fabrics and structures and describing several of the more unusual pieces. With European and Andean characteristics in mind, it is possible to classify most of the artifacts as indigenous, European, or hybrid. Examples of each are explained. Finally, I describe how people dressed in Magdalena de Cao and how their clothing demonstrates an intricate and subtle manipulation of social and ethnic categories.

Precolumbian Textile Practices

Fiber

Natural fibers are classified broadly as plant (cellulose) or animal (protein) fibers. The fibers relevant to the study of Magdalena textiles are cotton, camelid, linen, silk, and sheep's wool.

The cotton plant has been grown in Peru since at least 3500 B.C. (Bird et al. 1985). In precolumbian Peru, several natural colors of cotton were cultivated, including off-white, beige, pale green, light brown, and a darker reddish brown. Cotton is difficult to dye with vegetable dyes, and dyed colors often appear muted on cotton. Camelid fiber comes from any of the camelid species native to the Andes: llamas, alpacas, vicuñas, or guanacos. Camelid fiber is fine and smooth, and the fabric made from it is very warm. Because it is a protein fiber, camelid hair takes dye very well, and brilliant saturated colors can be achieved. The only camelid fiber found at Magdalena is alpaca.

Linen and wool were the fibers most commonly used in Europe for clothing in the sixteenth century (Arnold 1964, 1985). Neither was known in the Andes in precolumbian times. Throughout this chapter, "wool" refers only to the wool of sheep. Linen fiber comes from the stem of the flax plant, which is grown throughout Europe. Unlike cotton, linen does not have a range of naturally occurring colors, but its undyed shade can vary from beige to grayish depending on the preparation of the fiber. Sunshine will bleach linen close to white. Until the 1800s, Europeans preferred linen fabric for shirts and other undergarments.

Wool fiber varies widely depending on the breed of sheep. It is warm, elastic, and water-resistant. The wool trade was fundamental to the medieval European economy. By the late 1400s Spain was overtaking England as the primary producer of fine wool; the fleece from Spain's merino sheep was edging out the coarser fleeces produced in England (Chorely 1997; Coleman 1969; Munron 1997, 2003, 2005). Spain exported both fleece and woven cloth. Sheep were imported into the Andes shortly after the Spanish arrived. Like camelid fibers, wool takes dye well and also occurs in a range of natural colors. By the mid-1500s, people in Peru would have had access to fleece and fabric from domestically raised sheep as well as wool cloth imported from Europe.

The rarest of fibers found in the Magdalena collection is silk. Silk has long been considered precious for its sheen and strength. Silkworms originated in China, and the secrets of silk production were closely guarded for centuries, but silk cultivation was well established in Italy by the 1400s. Silk is an animal fiber and so can take brilliant color, which is enhanced by the fiber's luster. Silk weaving was established in Puebla, Mexico, soon after the arrival of the Spanish (Bazant 1964), but I have not yet encountered references to silk weaving in colonial Peru. The silk fabrics found at Magdalena de Cao were almost certainly imported.

Spinning

Spinning is the process of adding twist to fiber. Twist is necessary to bind the fibers together and create long, continuous pieces of yarn. Twist can be imparted to fibers in one of two directions: S or Z. The direction of twist can be seen by examining the way the fibers lie in relation to the lengthwise axis of the yarn. If their direction is like the midstroke of the letter S, the yarn is S-spun; if they lie in the opposite direction, like the midstroke of the letter Z, the yarn is Z-spun.

In collections of precolumbian textiles, usually one spin direction occurs more frequently than the other. The dominant spin direction may be different for different fibers; for instance, at Magdalena, most cotton thread is spun S, but alpaca yarns are spun Z and then plied two together in the S direction. The choice of whether to spin S or Z is not random; new spinners tend to spin the same direction as the more experienced spinners they emulate. Generally, most people in a given community will spin singles (the first step in creating yarn, before strands are plied together) in the same direction. Distinct spinning practices may correlate to different communities of practice; for instance, spin direction might vary by ethnicity. Spin direction can also correlate to technology. In most wool fabrics at Magdalena de Cao, the warp yarns are spun Z and the weft yarns are spun S. This may indicate that warp yarns were wheel spun and weft yarns were spun on a drop spindle, as depicted by Martínez Compañón.[1]

Weaving

A woven fabric is made of two sets of yarns: one set, the warp, is held under tension, with all the threads parallel to one another, and the second set, the weft, interlaces over and under those (Emery 1994). A loom is a machine that keeps the warp taut and organized. Looms often include some mechanism to make the insertion of the weft easier and faster. Precolumbian and European weaving have been explained in many excellent publications.[2] The details of Andean and European looms are not essential here; what is important is that weaving methods inevitably leave traces in the finished fabric. By examining the cloth, it is possible to determine whether it was woven on an Andean body-tensioned loom or a European-style floor loom.

Andean fabric was woven to size. A piece of Andean cloth has four finished edges, called selvedges. There are no raveling threads, and in precolumbian times woven cloth was never cut. When Andean cloth is patterned, the design may change along the length of the cloth, because the patterning is not restricted by the working of the loom but depends on the weaver's mind and fingers (see Franquemont 2004). Andean looms do not include any way of spacing the warp threads, so the warps tend to pack together. The resulting fabric is warp-emphasis or warp-faced. Almost all of the cotton cloth at Magdalena is warp-dominant.

Cloth woven on a floor loom has only two selvedges, at the weft edges of the cloth. The warp ends ravel. The maximum length of the fabric is limited by the loom's capacity but is typically many meters. Most cloth woven on a floor loom is produced as yardage, under the assumption that it will be cut and reassembled into garments. Floor-loom woven cloth in a finished artifact such as a garment will usually show evidence of cutting, seams, or stitching. When yardage is produced, most of the patterning is defined by the setup of the loom at the beginning of the process. Pattern repeats in floor-loom fabric are regular, consistent, and usually fairly small.

Extremely complex and ornate floor-loom-woven fabrics were created in Europe at least as early as the thirteenth century. Italy was the center of silk weaving, producing damasks, velvets, brocades, and innumerable other intricate and ornate materials that were exported throughout Europe. Many of these textiles had large-scale flowing patterns in multiple colors (Schneider 1978). Such cloth was greatly desired by Spaniards in the New World and requested by name (Boyd-Bowman 1973; Voss 2008a). Although indigenous Andeans may not have seen the machines that produced these fabrics, they quite likely would have seen the fabrics' textures and designs on clothing worn by Europeans.

Precolumbian Dress

Andean Dress

Guaman Poma (et al. 2002) provides many drawings of Andeans from the preconquest and early colonial era wearing indigenous clothing. There are also many archaeological remains of garments that were preserved in burials on the coast. The basic male garment in Inca times, immediately before the arrival of the Spanish, was a tunic made of two panels of cloth (Rowe 1995–1996). The warp of the panels extended from the front hem up over the shoulders and down to the back hem. The total length varied according to how long the tunic was to be. The two panels were sewn together up the middle with an opening left in the seam for the neck. The sides were sewn together with an opening left near the shoulders for the arms. The neck slit and armholes were both vertical. Guaman Poma often depicts men wearing a large mantle tied across the body over the tunic.

Inca influence did not spread to the North Coast of Peru until around 1470. The Chimu, the pre-Inca culture of the North Coast, wore clothing made primarily of cotton. Because the

Chimu were independent of Inca control for so long, the clothing traditions of people on the North Coast at the time of Spanish invasion may still have been strongly influenced by Chimu practices. Chimu cotton plainweaves are distinct from plainweaves of the Central and South Coasts because Chimu weavers used paired warps and single wefts, unlike the single warps and wefts of other styles (Rowe 1984:9). Chimu tunics have a distinct shape: they are short, ending around the waist, often very wide, and usually have square sleeves set into the arm slits. Male garments were often made in matching sets of tunic, loincloth, and turban.

Unfortunately, no identifiable female Chimu clothing has survived. Rodman and Fernandez Lopez (2005) briefly describe dresses found in tombs near Magdalena de Cao Viejo dating to between 900 and 1100 A.D. These dresses were apparently large rectangles sewn up the sides, with horizontal slits left at the top for the head and arms. It is unclear how long this style persisted on the North Coast. There is, however, good evidence for female Inca-style dress. Inca women's ensembles had two components: a square dress and a shawl. The dress was a wide piece of fabric wrapped around the body and pinned over the shoulders. A tightly wrapped belt, often with complex patterning, held the dress around the waist. The shawl was an approximately square piece of fabric smaller than the dress. It was wrapped over the shoulders and pinned in front over the chest. The pins, called *tupu*, had large and distinctive spoonlike heads.

Because Andean cloth was woven to the desired dimensions, seaming pieces of fabric usually involved joining two finished edges. The selvedges were butted together and sewn with whipstitch or herringbone stitch (Figure 6.1). This created a flat seam that, with care, could look the same on both sides, and it involved no waste of fabric. Often points of stress, such as the bottom of a neck slit, were reinforced with overcasting or blanket stitch.

Precolumbian clothing was held in place with belts and pins. Garments were loose enough to pull over the head or were of the kind that wrap around the body. Some, such as loincloths, had ties incorporated into the garment. Others, such as the dresses described earlier, depended on separate belts to help hold the garment in position. There were no formfitting garments, and therefore no need for plackets and shaped openings with buttons, laces, or other fastenings that would hold them in place precisely. Buttons are unknown on precolumbian garments. There is no evidence of eyelets or lacing of any kind. Hemming was unknown because fabrics were woven to size, and there were no raw edges.

Spanish Dress

Describing European fashions from the sixteenth through the eighteenth century in detail would take far more space than is available here. By the 1500s fashion was already a motivating force of dress, and styles could change quickly. Dress also varied dramatically by region and according to the status of the wearer. Here I focus on general aspects of clothing that can help clearly distinguish European from Andean garment fragments.[3] In this chapter I use modern terminology for garments to minimize confusion.

European ensembles were composed of many pieces. Men typically wore a shirt, pants, a jacket, stockings, shoes or boots, a hat, and a cloak. The forms of all these items changed over the centuries. For instance, the full short breeches of the 1500s had by the late 1700s become tight trousers ending just below the knee. Shirts were made of linen, as were accessories such as neck ruffs and separate cuffs. Shirts were sewn out of a variety of rectangles and triangles to

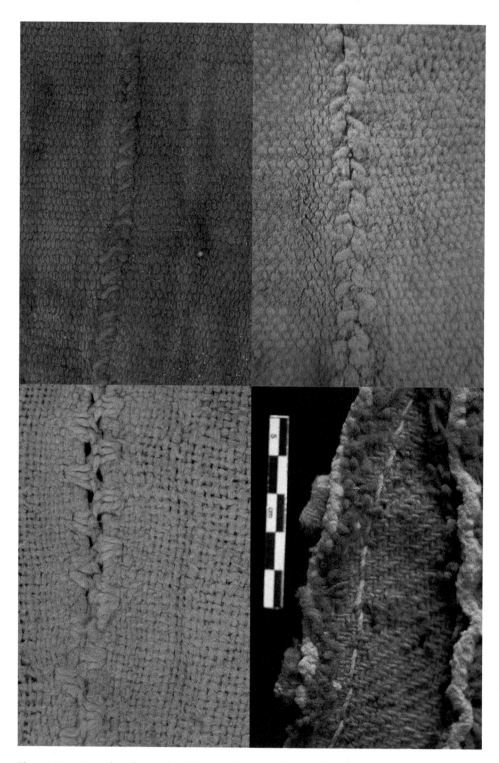

Figure 6.1 Examples of seams found at Magdalena. Top left: Andean plainweave cotton cloth, selvedges butted together and whipstitched. Top right: Andean plainweave cotton cloth, selvedges butted together and joined with herringbone stitch. Bottom left: plainweave linen. Edges brought together and joined with a fancy stitch that makes a lacy seam. Bottom right: inside of a garment of coarse wool twill, showing cut edges and seam backstitched in blue thread.

conserve cloth (Arnold et al. 2008; Burnham 1997). When necessary, excess fabric was gathered to fit—for instance, sleeves were gathered into a cuff at the wrist. Jackets and trousers, on the other hand, were constructed out of multiple complex shapes to create the desired form and were usually of wool (Arnold 1985; Baumgarten 2002). Tailoring such garments required cutting yardage and sewing it together again to form a tapered body and sleeves that followed the natural curve of the arm. Even the simplest jacket usually required a variety of materials: the outer stuff, lining to neaten the inside, interlining for stiffness, and possibly padding for shape. If the jacket was at all decorative, it might well require more materials, such as contrasting fabric for piping the seams or silk thread for embroidery. Because garments followed the shape of the body they could not simply be pulled on over the head or stepped into. It was essential to have secure fastenings to hold the edges of clothing together. Lacings, buttons, and hooks and eyes were the most common.

Europeans viewed clothing not just as something to cover the body but as a tool to shape it. Garments emphasized or minimized different parts of the anatomy. Women's clothing was purposely restrictive. Dresses were worn over boned stays (an early form of corset) that were laced tightly to decrease the waist circumference (Cunnington and Cunnington 1992). Bodices were generally cut very close to the form of the stays, allowing little room for freedom of movement. Full-length skirts and underskirts added weight to the total costume. The skirts of the outer gown were often open in front, showing the underskirt, which might be quilted, embroidered, or decorated with ribbons. The vast amount of material used in gathered floor-length skirts was ideal for showing off fabrics with large-scale designs such as elaborate and expensive Italian silks. Ribbons were a favorite embellishment. They could be used in loops or bows on the sleeves or gathered or pleated along the edges of the neckline and skirt opening (Fukai and Suoh 2004:12–15, 32–33; Hart et al. 1998:132, 138, 140). As with men's clothing, wool was the most common material for European gowns for those who could not afford silk. Women wore linen next to the skin in the form of a shift: a loose, low-necked undergarment that was cinched under the stays (Arnold et al. 2008:13; Baumgarten et al. 1999:67). The wealthy wore silk stockings; those not so fortunate wore wool or went without stockings altogether.

These descriptions give only the most general outline of European practices of dress during this time period. For the purposes of this study, the most important points are:

- European ensembles included several different garments.
- In this period there was a distinction between inner wear and outerwear, and they were usually made of different fibers.
- The tailoring of European clothing depended on cutting large expanses of cloth into intricate shapes and reassembling them into volumetric forms.
- The close-fitting shapes required a variety of fastenings to hold the edges in place.
- Because of the way they were cut, European garments required more yardage than simple rectangular tunics or dresses.
- Rather than clothing taking the shape of the body beneath it, clothing was used to impose a certain shape on the body.

From this summary, it is apparent that European clothing required construction techniques that were significantly different from those used in Andean garments. Seaming was done by placing the fabrics to be joined face-to-face, with the cut edges aligned (Figure 6.1). When the pieces were stitched and then opened out, the raw cut edges would be with the wrong side of the fabric, on the inside of the garment. The two most common stitches used for joining pieces were running stitch and backstitch (Baumgarten et al. 1999). Unfinished cut edges have a tendency to ravel, and over time, raveling could jeopardize the stability of the seam. Most jackets, trousers, and bodices from this time period were lined. A full lining will enclose all raw edges between the inner and outer fabrics, protecting them from abrasion and raveling.

Because European garments were made of cut pieces, even the edges that were not seamed together had to be finished somehow for neatness and durability. Typically edges such as the bottom of a skirt were turned under and stitched to the wrong side of the garment. It is possible to do this almost invisibly on most fabrics. On linen, tiny rolled hems of no more than 1.5 mm were possible. Hems on linen could also be executed with stitches that pulled the threads together in decorative patterns, creating a line of openwork.

Lacing and eyelets were widely used to draw together garment edges that should meet but not overlap. Eyelets were made by punching a small hole through the garment near the edge and overcasting the hole with small stitches all around. Narrow tapes and strong ribbons were in much demand for laces. Buttons and buttonholes were used lavishly, especially in the 1700s. Spherical buttons were popular and were often closely spaced down the center front of a doublet or bodice. Arnold shows several variations of spherical buttons wrapped in silk cord (Arnold 1985:38, 41, 48). Buttonholes were slits cut perpendicular to the edge of the garment. They were finished with close stitching to prevent raveling. Often the inner and outer ends of the buttonholes would be finished with bars, which gave the buttonhole a rectangular appearance (Arnold 1985:41).

The characteristics described here were used to categorize the Magdalena textile artifacts broadly as indigenous, European, or hybrid (showing both indigenous and European characteristics). Assuming that the remaining fragments are indicative of what would have been worn in the town, the textile collection allows us to form a picture of how residents dressed when the town was occupied.

Magdalena Textile Artifacts

Of the more than 3,000 pieces in the Magdalena textile collection, about 2,890 are relevant to the study of dress. This number excludes numerous bagfuls of tiny, disintegrating scraps that are too small to study. It also excludes vegetal cordage and plaited cane or reeds. For the purposes of this research, textiles were assigned to one of three spatial categories: church, town, or cemetery. Because of widespread looting at the site, it is quite possible that for many artifacts, the place where they were found was not the place they were deposited. The classification of church, town, and cemetery permits an investigation of differences throughout the site without false precision.

Of the artifacts, 874 (30 percent) were found in the town, 1,276 (44 percent) in the church, and 459 (16 percent) in the cemetery. Location is unclear or missing for about 10 percent of the items. More than 90 percent of the artifacts are woven cloth; the remainder are knotted, felted, raw fiber, spun thread, or textile tools such as spindles. There are 11 knitted artifacts. While this is very few pieces given the overall size of the collection, they are the earliest known examples of knitting in South America.

It is notable that no net, felt, knitted items, or buttons were found in the cemetery. Except for net, all of these are European introductions. The absence of any such items in the cemetery indicates that the textiles associated with the people buried there are indigenous in character. Given the Spaniards' rigid Catholicism and feelings of superiority toward Andeans, it is unlikely that this cemetery includes any people who were considered Spanish. The lack of European textile items in the cemetery supports Quilter's description (Chapter 2) of this area as an indigenous burying ground.

Fiber and Structure

The structures that occur most frequently in the collection are plainweave (85 percent), twill (10 percent), basketweave (2 percent), doubleweave (less than 1 percent), and tapestry (less than 1 percent). A number of other structures such as satin and velvet are found in one or two examples. In the town and church, about 85 percent of the pieces found are plainweave; in the cemetery, 98 percent of the textiles are plainweave. Plainweave pieces are not necessarily undecorated. Many of the plainweaves from the cemetery are striped in different shades of brown and blue. Some have small warp-patterned stripes, and some have narrow tubular borders in alpaca. They also come in a variety of textures, from open, gauzy weaves to stiff fabrics similar to canvas. If the cemetery is indeed for indigenous burials, then plainweave appears to have been the fabric of choice for Andean-style grave wrappings. Plainweave also constitutes the majority of structures found in other areas, but in the church and town twills form a small but significant proportion of the total structures found. Doubleweaves and tapestries are quite rare, and all examples are indigenous in style and execution. Tapestries occur primarily as narrow borders with cotton warp and colored alpaca weft. They are usually ornamented with small creatures in multiple colors and are typically used to trim the bottom of tunics (Figure 6.2). Doubleweaves are executed in dark and light shades of undyed cotton and have geometric motifs. No complete examples of doubleweave survive, so it is difficult to say how they were used.

There is a high correlation between weave structure and the type of fiber used. Almost 80 percent of the plainweaves found are cotton (1,806 out of 2,288 plainweave pieces), with wool a distant second (316 artifacts, about 14 percent). Most of the twills are wool (238 pieces out of 258, 92 percent), though a handful are woven in cotton (18, about 7 percent). Linen is most commonly found as balanced plainweave, such as would have been used for shirts. There are a few examples of linen twill or damask. Complementary warp and weft structures, which are typical indigenous patterned weaves, are always woven of cotton or alpaca. Structures such as velvet, damask, and satin are found only in fibers introduced by the Spanish: silk and linen.

Most objects are made entirely or mostly from one fiber. Cotton is the primary fiber in about 71 percent of the artifacts. Twenty-one percent are made from wool, 6 percent are made from linen, and silk, alpaca, and other fibers make up about 2 percent of the textiles in the collection. Surprisingly, there is a significantly higher percentage of cotton textiles in the church (66 percent) than in the town (59 percent) and a higher percentage of wool fabrics in the town (31 percent) than in the church (23 percent). This seems to contradict the idea of the church as

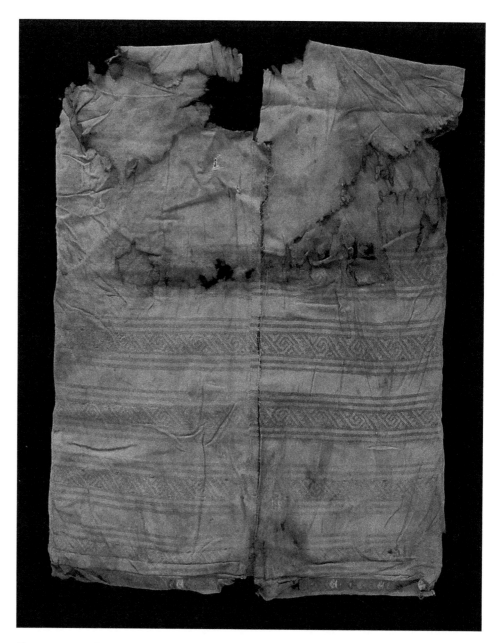

Figure 6.2 Andean cotton tunic, 70 cm × 90 cm. The tunic is decorated with weft stripes in dark brown cotton that show the twill patterning. The bottom border is a narrow band of tapestry weave with cotton warps and alpaca weft. It depicts fish of various colors on a red ground.

a place where Spanish, European, or hybrid materials would be dominant, and the town as a place where indigenous fibers would be more common. Possibly fine wools and imported silks were considered precious enough to remove from the church. The church may also have been subjected to more looting than the town after occupation ended. Fine wool and silk would be considered valuable enough to carry away, while the very heavy and worn woolen fabric found in the town would have little worth in trade or sale. It may also be the case that the items found in the church reflect grave goods and church furnishings rather than what people wore during life. If that is the case, the emphasis on cotton in the church could be because cotton was the preferred material for shrouds.

There is a small but significant percentage of linen artifacts. The number of different pieces of linen found—50 in the town and 89 in the church—suggests that European-style shirts were worn in Magdalena. Even supposing that some of the scraps of linen once belonged to the same item, there are enough remnants to indicate that linen was known and used in the colonial settlement. Many of the fragments of linen have seams, hemstitching, gathers, or embroidery similar to that on seventeenth-century garments (Figure 6.3). The fact that linen is more plentiful than alpaca suggests that it had become integral to the requirements of dress in colonial Magdalena de Cao, and that perhaps alpaca, being associated with indigenous decoration such as the figured tapestry borders, was being used less frequently as Spanish styles became dominant.

There are very few wool pieces that are not plainweave or twill. Most have cut edges. There is one weft-faced wool ribbon or band, and one narrow complementary warp band in indigenous style. In the complementary warp band, the wool is used with alpaca. This is one of the few examples at Magdalena of a fiber introduced by the Spanish being used in an indigenous technique. Most of the wool fabrics are heavy and are woven with threads much thicker than those found in cotton cloth. The most common color for wool cloth is dark blue. This blue is remarkably consistent between different artifacts and may indicate that Magdaleneros dressed in fabric produced in large quantities in colonial obrajes.

All of the remaining silk examples are small, less than 10.0 cm in any direction, and none have any stitching or construction details that would show how they were used (Figure 6.4). The plainweave silks may well correspond to the kinds of taffeta listed by Boyd-Bowman in a compilation of fabrics imported into Mexico from Spain between 1540 and 1562 (Boyd-Bowman 1973). There are a few fragments of plainweave silk not associated with other objects, but this fabric most frequently appears as the lining of a wool garment or as piping or binding on a piece of clothing. The tiny amounts of patterning visible on the scraps of damask suggest curvaceous floral designs. There is one example of a silk damask also being used as a lining. The silk ribbons found likely were used as trim, to lace together waistbands and bodices, or as garters to hold up stockings (Baumgarten et al. 1999:79). More elaborate trims in multiple colors with fancy edgings were known as passementerie and could be constructed in a myriad of intricate ways. They often incorporated threads of different thicknesses and decorative edges, such as interlocking loops forming scallops. One of the examples of silk passementerie has a twined structure that could be tablet woven, though it could also be done with finger-loop braiding (Sophie Desroisiers, personal communication). The other has a braided appearance and loops of weft on both edges.

One would expect to find silk only in small quantities, as it has always been an expensive fiber. However, the number of alpaca pieces found at Magdalena is surprisingly small. Based on surviving garment fragments, cloth of sheep's wool was a staple for European-style clothing: skirts, bodices, jackets, trousers, and pockets were all made from wool cloth. If camelid fiber was widely available, one might expect to find yardage of llama or alpaca, but only one scrap of plainweave alpaca has been found at the site so far. Otherwise, alpaca occurs only in indigenous-style weaving, such as in tapestry bands bordering cotton tunics.

Figure 6.3 Examples of linen fabrics found at Magdalena. Top left: corner of plainweave linen fabric showing turned-under hem and lacy hemstitching. Top right: linen cloth with structural checkerboard pattern. Bottom: fine linen closely pleated into a plain band; possibly a shirt cuff.

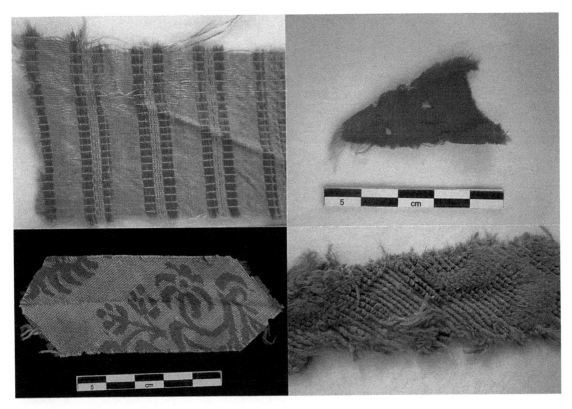

Figure 6.4 Silks found at Magdalena. Top left: gold-colored plainweave with supplementary warp stripes in red. Top right: scrap of red satin. Bottom left: brocade in blue and gold with floral design. Bottom right: scrap of figured velvet. This cloth has a gold ground with a design in blue. The figure is executed in both cut and uncut velvet. The artifact is too small to determine the nature of the design.

Dress in Magdalena de Cao

Although few entire garments survive, there are enough pieces to suggest the kinds of clothing that were worn in colonial Magdalena. The greatest number of examples are indigenous in style. Hints of European imports survive in some fancy seams and buttons. There is a significant selection of artifacts that combine indigenous and European styles and techniques, indicating that the adaptation of new forms of dress was not as straightforward as one might assume.

Indigenous Clothing

There are a few tunics that are almost complete or complete enough to clearly indicate their function. The existing tunics are made of cotton and frequently have trim around the bottom woven in dyed alpaca. They were woven in two panels, each 35 cm by 180 cm. Stitched together in the manner of Inca tunics, the panels produced a garment approximately 70 cm wide and 90 cm long. Magdalena tunics show no evidence of sleeves. Fancier tunics were ornamented with horizontal stripes, sometimes embellished with dots of colored alpaca. The tunic in Figure 6.2 is of natural beige cotton with horizontal woven pattern stripes. Alpaca yarns in blue, brown, gold, and red are inlaid in small dots. The colors echo the colors in the bottom tapestry band, which was woven separately and stitched to the garment. The ornamental bands frequently depict birds or fish and usually include multiple colors.

Shawls from Magdalena could be woven in two panels or in three panels. Shawls are made from cotton in warp-emphasis plainweave. They vary from plain pieces all in one color (usually beige, tan, or light brown) to those with colored stripes throughout. Most colors used were the natural colors of cotton: white, tan, reddish brown, dark brown, and pale green. The only dyed color present is blue. Blue seems to be associated with finer weaving and more patterning.

Three-part shawls have a wide center plainweave pattern, usually woven in reddish brown cotton (Figure 6.5). Few complete shawls remain. If those that survive are representative, the center panels were about 50 cm by 85 cm. The center was bordered lengthwise by two striped plainweave panels, each about 30 cm wide, making the entire shawl approximately 110 × 85 cm. There are enough fragments of these side panels with two surviving weft selvedges to suggest that their width did not vary much from garment to garment. The patterning on the side panels could be quite elaborate. They were usually striped in several different colors, and sometimes included patterned stripes in complementary warp weave. The designs were arranged to be

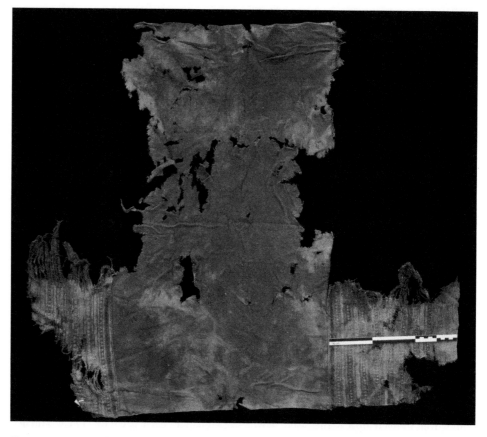

Figure 6.5   Example of a three-part cotton shawl: center panel in dark reddish brown cotton plainweave, side panels in striped cotton with small warp pattern. Colors in the side panels include blue, white, and light brown.

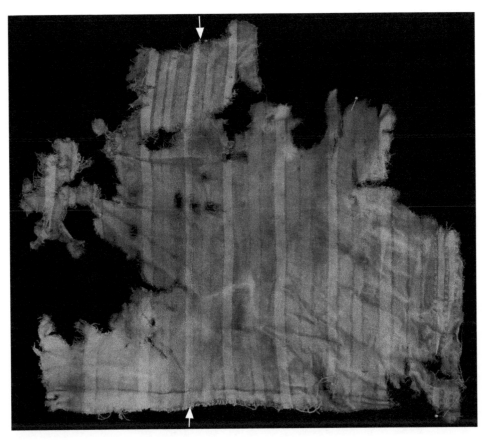

Figure 6.6 Incomplete two-part shawl. The right-hand panel has both weft selvedges and is 35 cm wide. The white arrows indicate the center seam; the left panel is incomplete. The shawl is warp-emphasis cotton plainweave striped in natural colors of cotton and blue cotton. In this shawl the stripe pattern is not symmetrical around the center.

symmetrical around the lengthwise center of the shawl. Based on the number of surviving patterned side panels, the three-part shawl was common at Magdalena.

Two-part shawls were made from two panels of equal width. The most complete two-part shawl measures 100 cm × 125 cm; each panel is 50 cm wide. The stripe patterns of two-part shawls could be symmetrical around the center seam, but there are also examples of irregular stripe patterns that are different in each half of the shawl (Figure 6.6).

Most of the cotton plainweave fragments are of a quality similar to that found in the few large cloths. If these fragments were once a part of tunics or shawls, then it is likely that such indigenous-style garments were still in frequent use in Magdalena.

European

There are few surviving artifacts at Magdalena that are definitively European without indigenous influence. The correlation between linen and shirts is suggested by one linen artifact that includes a square gusset between two seams. Gussets were a common way of adding ease to the underarm of a shirt sewn from rectangles (Burnham 1997). One piece of linen is

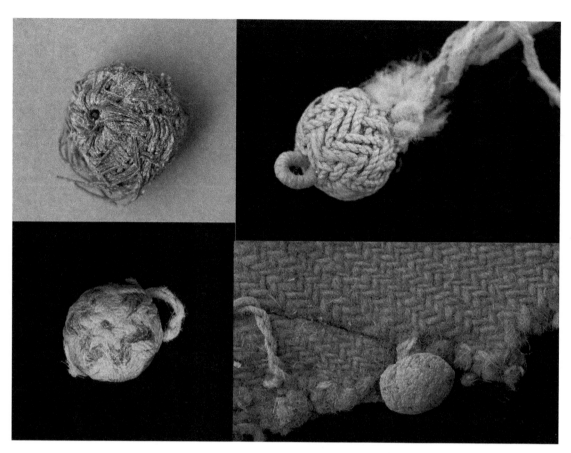

Figure 6.7 Buttons excavated at Magdalena de Cao. Top left: undetermined material woven over a spherical core. Top right: silk cord in light green and gold woven over a spherical core. From the sides the colors make a zigzag pattern; seen from the top, the colors form a star. Bottom left: silk cord in dark brown and light brown woven over a spherical core. The star pattern shown here, on the top of the button, is similar to that on the top right. Bottom right: spherical button still attached to wool twill garment fragment. The button has been abraded but included at least two colors, brown and blue. Material uncertain. All buttons are approximately 1 cm in diameter.

embroidered in indigo thread in a style similar to blackwork, which was fashionable in Europe in the fifteenth century. Shirt collars and cuffs were sometimes ornamented with blackwork, suggesting that the surviving linen fragment may once have been part of such a garment. There is also an example of what may have been a shirt cuff. As can be seen in Figure 6.3, a width of linen was gathered tightly to a narrow band. This would have been typical of shirt cuffs in the seventeenth century, when sleeves were very wide (Arnold et al. 2008).

A few spherical buttons wrapped in silk cord were found in the excavations (Figure 6.7). The buttons were wrapped to form a starlike pattern opposite the shank. Most of the surviving buttons included at least two colors, making the pattern more distinct. Buttons were needed only on European-style garments, which required precise fastening. No buttons were found associated with indigenous cloth.

New Forms of Expression

Andean and Spanish practices of dress were combined in many different ways and, probably, for many different reasons. There is not space here to discuss every variation. Instead, I present a few artifacts that are typical of the collection and show a blending of indigenous and European traditions.

Many of the wool pieces found in the collection incorporate a rich combination of materials and techniques. Based on the curve in the fabric and the position of the blue patch, the garment fragment in Figure 6.8 looks as though it might have covered a leg, but the size makes it more likely that the patch is an elbow patch and that this is a portion of a sleeve. The piece is 47 cm long and 28 cm wide at the widest point. The brown color is probably the natural color of fleece. The patch, on the other hand, is of fabric that has been dyed blue. There are seven buttonholes near one edge. If this is a sleeve, the buttonholes would have been at the outer edge of the wrist when the piece was worn. The buttonholes are slits in the fabric finished with close buttonhole stitching around all edges. Rather than curving the stitching around the ends of the slits, the ends are reinforced with bars of close stitching that extend beyond the width of the buttonhole stitching. This is one way of relieving stress on an opening that will take some strain. One button remains, stitched to the edge of the cuff opposite the buttonholes. It is a spherical button about 1 cm in diameter covered with interlaced red and blue cord.

The inside of this piece shows a lot of wear. The surface of the fabric is matted and felted, as happens when wool fabrics are subjected to heat, moisture, and abrasion. The buttonholes and surviving button are very finely done, but the fabric is relatively coarse, and the patch, being a different color from the rest of the fabric, is quite obvious. Together the various features of this artifact suggest a garment that was originally well made out of sturdy cloth and was used enough to wear through in places. It was valuable enough to be worth mending, as shown by the patch, and may have undergone alterations, if the facings along the cuff were not original. The fiber and construction details clearly show this to be a garment copying European styles.

Knitting was a textile technique unknown in the Andes before the arrival of the Spanish. There are several knitted artifacts among the colonial textiles at Magdalena de Cao. All of them appear to be socks or stockings. In Europe, leg and foot coverings would have been knit out of wool or silk (Thirsk 2003). The example in Figure 6.9 is knit with cotton yarns in two colors: natural white or tan and natural dark brown. It is 22.0 cm long and 9.5 cm wide. The S-spun singles are indistinguishable from the cotton singles used in the warp and weft of indigenous cloth, but they are held four together for the knitting. The leg of the stocking has regular stripes: four rows brown, four rows white. It is knit in the round and is slightly tapered toward the ankle. There is a heel flap in white that is knit back and forth in garter stitch over about half the stitches of the leg. The other live leg stitches are held on a scrap of yarn with large knots at both ends to keep them from unraveling. This suggests that the stocking was abandoned in progress. The technique is certainly European, but the fiber and spinning are firmly within the indigenous tradition of cotton yarn production. The stripe pattern is also intriguing—as previously noted, stripes were common in indigenous textiles, but most known European stockings were in a single color. They would have been ornamented with lace or textural stitches or embroidery rather than with horizontal stripes. This artifact is a clear example of the blending of European and Andean technologies and design.

Figure 6.8
Example of
a European-style
garment fragment,
probably a sleeve.
Top: outside as
garment was worn.
Bottom: inside
of garment.

Martínez Compañón pictures a *mulata* (woman of mixed Spanish and African heritage) of Trujillo wearing a scarf or stole of white cloth draped over her shoulder. One of the ends of the cloth falls to the front of her skirt; it appears to have two lace bands near the end and is trimmed with scalloped lace. A similar cloth was found in the church at Magdalena (Figure 6.10). It is 33 cm wide and 72 cm long, but the length is not complete. The scarf is off-white warp-emphasis cotton plainweave. The end is finished with fringe. There are five bands of openwork patterning near the end: two narrow bands of gauze, a wide band of woven mesh, and another two bands of gauze. The gauze is created by twisting groups of warps together

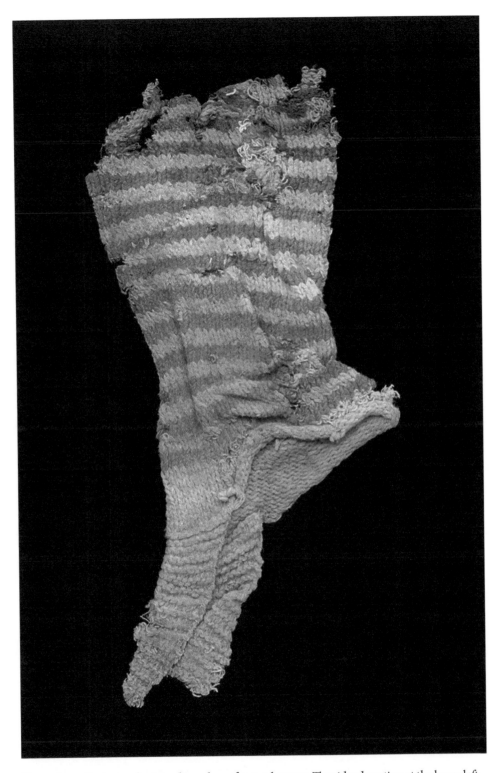

Figure 6.9   Cotton sock, striped in colors of natural cotton. The ridged portion at the lower left is the heel flap, from which stitches would be picked up to work the foot.

Figure 6.10
White cotton scarf or shawl
with fringe and border
of gauze and openwork.

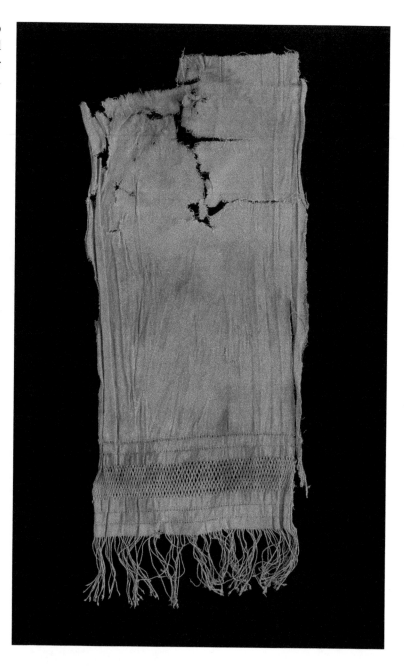

and passing a weft to keep them in place (O'Neale and Clark 1948). The twists create open spaces in the fabric. The meshwork band is done with many separate wefts, each weaving a very narrow portion of the warp, as if it were split up into separate ribbons. The "ribbons" join and separate again several times through the length of the band, creating an openwork pattern of diamonds.

Other women in Martínez Compañón's drawings are shown with white scarves like the one found here, but such scarves are never shown on Indian women, only on those with some Spanish ancestry. It seems safe to suppose that this was not a garment that communicated indigenous identity. The weaving style and spinning, however, are like that of indigenous cloths such as the mantles and tunics previously described. The use of gauze and openwork weaving techniques suggests that the maker was trying to imitate the lacy bands at the ends of a Spanish scarf. Rather than applying imported European lace, she chose to use bands of gauze. The most famous Andean gauzes are from Chancay, but this weaving technique was also used in Chimu cloth (Rowe 1984:36). This scarf suggests that the maker was aware of a fashion for such scarves and was intentionally trying to replicate one with easily available materials. By wearing such a scarf, a Magdalenera of mixed parentage might have been consciously emphasizing the Spanish part of her identity. It is also possible that a *mestiza* (woman of mixed Spanish and indigenous heritage), mulata, or Spanish woman commissioned an indigenous woman to weave such a scarf.

Conclusions

Dress can be used not only to differentiate but also to erase distinctions (Voss 2008b). The evidence of male colonial dress at Magdalena seems to discourage individuation. Similar wool fabric was used for all European-style garments, and the range of colors was strictly limited. It could be that Magdaleneros were encouraged (or required) to dress in a way that minimized distinctions between groups of *indios* (indigenous people) and fostered the creation of a new unified colonial identity for town residents. The similarity of ensembles might indicate a form of submission to colonial institutions and social order.

The composition of the town's population is not known for certain, but most of the human remains have been identified as Andean (see Chapters 4 and 5). It is of course possible that impoverished Spaniards and mestizos as well as indios and Africans lived in Magdalena and dressed in coarse woolen cloth. Even if this is the case, I believe that much of the textile production and clothing construction was done by indigenous Andean people. As a reducción, Magdalena may well have included indios from distinct ethnic groups and disparate areas. The two-part and three-part shawls suggest that different weaving practices coexisted; such practices may correlate to different ethnicities (Figure 6.11). The presence of different indigenous ethnic groups in Magdalena could also be supported by the fact that among the indigenous-style cotton plainweaves there are fabrics with paired warps and single wefts and examples with both warp and weft paired. The first is a Chimu method of construction. The second may indicate another weaving tradition practiced by a separate group of people. It is also possible that weavers simply chose whether or not to pair wefts depending on what they were weaving, how much yarn they had, or other considerations. Future work on the stripe sequences, colors, and iconography of a larger selection of cotton cloth might illuminate this issue.

What is evident from the textile remains at Magdalena is that household weavers—probably women, given what is known about gendered labor divisions in the colonial era (Graubart 2000)—were able to use local tools and materials to emulate imported styles. This is seen in the scarf described in the previous section and in the cotton socks. The overwhelming amount of cotton cloth at Magdalena decorated in Andean styles indicates that weavers were still producing textiles with traditional indigenous Andean aesthetics. At the same time, they were adapting their techniques to recreate fabrics that showed they also had command of European structures and were able to deploy them as desired. It is not known who cut and sewed the garments found in the colonial town, but from the widespread use of cotton thread I suspect

Figure 6.11　An illustration of a man working on a European-style loom from Martinez Compañón's book on life on the North Coast of Peru in the mid-eighteenth century.

many of the garments were made by non-Spanish residents (Europeans most likely would have used wool, silk, or linen). If this is the case, they very quickly learned how to cut and shape cloth to imitate complicated European garment styles. They mastered techniques such as piping, plackets, and buttonholes, and were able to improvise button fastenings out of cloth when needed. They were creative in combining materials, using linen to face waistbands and silk to bind the edges of wool cloth. All of these examples indicate that Magdaleneros actively manipulated the raw materials of their clothing, and quickly learned how to create garments that would help them navigate life in a colonial town.

Although a single garment might be easily classified as indigenous or European, when worn it could form part of an ensemble that included both indigenous and European garments. For instance, indigenous women frequently continued to wear shawls that indicated their ethnic identity, even when dressed in a Spanish-style skirt or dress. The cotton shawls found at Magdalena may have been worn with woolen skirts. Such an ensemble would combine cloth woven on an Andean body-tensioned loom with yardage from a colonial workshop, and the draped, rectangular garments of prehispanic times with clothing that was cut and fitted and required fastenings. The wearer would be displaying her ethnic identity and her own weaving skill along with her understanding of Spanish styles and competency in European dressmaking.

The weavers and garment makers of Magdalena show themselves to have been flexible and creative in using textiles to create new identities within colonial society. Although remote, Magdalena was touched by the global fashion network, which determined acceptable garment shapes and desirable colors and trims. Residents recognized the social and political value of small items such as fancy buttons and ribbons: appropriate use of these accents showed that the wearer was conversant with wider trends. At the same time, indigenous bodies were constrained by unfamiliar garment shapes, foreign fibers, and new strictures on which parts of the body could or could not be revealed. The textiles of Magdalena demonstrate the persistence of indigenous weaving, the reach of European imports, and various hybridizations of materials and techniques. They also represent a new way of physically being in the world: habits of movement, posture, and gesture are all affected by clothing. Manipulating one's image through clothing requires not only wearing the right garments but also wearing them in the correct way. Textiles are inextricably linked to diverse arenas of human endeavor—self-representation, technological adaptability, trade networks, virtue, and bodily practices of making and wearing clothes. The Magdalena collection presents an opportunity to investigate each of these at a time of intense cultural change.

NOTES

1 See Martínez Compañón 1978, vol. 2. For example, Illustration 82 shows an indigenous woman tending sheep and spinning wool from a distaff on a drop spindle. Illustration 89 depicts men carding fleece outside a church. Illustration 90 shows men spinning rolags of wool on a great wheel under supervision by an overseer. Illustration 91 shows a warp being wound for a floor loom directly from spindles. The sequence of pictures and appearance of the spindles suggest that it is the wheel-spun yarns that are being used as warp. Additional pictures of indigenous women spinning are found in Illustration 98, in which four women are cleaning and spinning white wool, and Illustration 99, which shows a woman spinning blue cotton from a rolag held in a distaff while a child plays nearby.

2 A sampling of work explaining Andean weaving includes C. Franquemont 1986; E. Franquemont 1991, 1997, 2004; O'Neale 1946; Rowe 1974, 1975, 1995–1996; Stone-Miller 1994. Methods of weaving some of

the elaborate European fabrics of the sixteenth through eighteenth centuries are given in Becker 1997. A variety of European fabrics are described in Jenkins 2003.

3 Sources on the history of European clothing include Arnold 1964, 1985, 2008; Baumgarten et al. 1999; Burnham 1997; Cunnington and Cunnington 1992; Harte 1997; Harte and Ponting 1983; Hollander 1975; and Jenkins 2003, among many others.

REFERENCES CITED

Arnold, Janet
   1964   *Patterns of Fashion: Englishwomen's Dresses and Their Construction.* London: Wace.
   1985   *Patterns of Fashion: The Cut and Construction of Clothes for Men and Women c. 1560–1620.* London: Macmillan.

Arnold, Janet, Jenny Tiramani, and Santina M. Levey
   2008   *Patterns of Fashion 4: The Cut and Construction of Linen Shirts, Smocks, Neckwear, Headwear and Accessories for Men and Women c. 1540–1660.* Hollywood, CA: Quite Specific Media Group.

Baumgarten, Linda
   2002   *What Clothes Reveal: The Language of Clothing in Colonial and Federal America.* New Haven, CT: Yale University Press.

Baumgarten, Linda, John Watson, and Florine Carr
   1999   *Costume Close-Up: Clothing Construction and Pattern 1750–1790.* Williamsburg, VA: Colonial Williamsburg Foundation.

Bazant, Jan
   1964   Evolution of the Textile Industry of Puebla 1544–1845. *Comparative Studies in Society and History* 7(1):56–69.

Becker, John
   1987   *Pattern and Loom: A Practical Study of the Development of Weaving Techniques in China, Western Asia, and Europe.* Copenhagen: Rhodos.

Bird, Junius Bouton, John Hyslop, and Milica D. Skinner
   1985   *The Preceramic Excavations at the Huaca Prieta Chicama Valley, Peru.* Anthropological Papers Vol. 62, Pt. 1. New York: American Museum of Natural History.

Boyd-Bowman, Peter
   1973   Spanish and European Textiles in Sixteenth Century Mexico. *The Americas* 29(3):334–358.

Brezine, Carrie
   2009   Algorithms and Automation: The Production of Mathematics and Textiles. In *The Oxford Handbook of the History of Mathematics,* edited by Eleanor Robson and Jacqueline A. Stedall, pp. 468–494. Oxford: Oxford University Press.

Burnham, Dorothy K.
   1997   *Cut My Cote.* Toronto: Royal Ontario Museum.

Chorley, Patrick
   1997   The Evolution of the Woollen, 1300–1700. In *The New Draperies in the Low Countries and England, 1300–1800,* edited by N. B. Harte, pp. 7–34. Oxford: Oxford University Press.

Coleman, D. C.

    1969 An Innovation and Its Diffusion: The "New Draperies." *Economic History Review* 22(3):417–429.

Cunnington, C. Willett, and Phillis Emily Cunnington

    1992 *The History of Underclothes.* New York: Dover.

Earle, Rebecca

    2001 "Two Pairs of Pink Satin Shoes!!": Race, Clothing and Identity in the Americas (17th–19th Centuries). *History Workshop Journal* 52:175–195.

Emery, Irene

    1994 *The Primary Structure of Fabrics: An Illustrated Classification.* Washington, DC: Textile Museum.

Franquemont, Christine R.

    1986 Chinchero Pallays: An Ethnic Code. In *The Junius B. Bird Conference on Andean Textiles,* edited by A. P. Rowe, pp. 331–338. Washington, DC: Textile Museum.

Franquemont, Edward M.

    1991 *Cloth, the Andean Art.* Ithaca, NY: Awasqa Cultural Constructions.

    1997 The True Treasure of Andean Textiles. In *Traditional Textiles of the Andes,* edited by L. A. Meisch, pp. 28–37. San Francisco: Thames and Hudson.

    2004 Jazz: An Andean Sense of Symmetry. In *Embedded Symmetries, Natural and Cultural,* edited by D. K. Washburn, pp. 81–94. Albuquerque: University of New Mexico Press.

Fukai, Akiko, and Tamami Suoh

    2004 *Fashion: The Kyoto Costume Institute: From the 18th to the 20th Century.* Koln: Taschen.

Graubart, Karen

    2000 Weaving and the Construction of a Gender Division of Labor in Early Colonial Peru. *American Indian Quarterly* 24(4):537–561.

    2007 *With Our Labor and Sweat: Indigenous Women and the Formation of Colonial Society in Peru, 1550–1700.* Stanford, CA: Stanford University Press.

    2009 The Creolization of the New World: Local Forms of Identification in Urban Colonial Peru, 1560–1640. *Hispanic American Historical Review* 89(3):471–499.

Guaman Poma de Ayala, Felipe, Rolena Adorno, and Ivan Boserup

    2002 *Guaman Poma: El Primer Nueva Corónica y Buen Gobierno.* Copenhagen: Royal Library.

Hart, Avril, and Susan North

    1998 *Historical Fashion in Detail: The 17th and 18th Centuries.* London: V & A Publications.

Harte, N. B., ed.

    1997 *The New Draperies in the Low Countries and England 1300–1800.* Oxford: Oxford University Press.

Harte, N. B., and K. G. Ponting (editors)

    1983 *Cloth and Clothing in Medieval Europe: Essays in Memory of Professor E. M. Carus-Wilson, Volume 2.* London: Heinemann.

Hollander, Anne

    1975 *Seeing Through Clothes.* Berkeley: University of California Press.

Jenkins, David, ed.

    2003 *The Cambridge History of Western Textiles,* vol. 1. Cambridge: Cambridge University Press.

Martínez Compañón y Bujanda, Baltasar Jaime

    1978   *Trujillo del Perú a Fines del Siglo XVIII*, vol. 2. Madrid: Ediciones Cultura Hispánica.

Munro, John H.

    1997   The Origin of the English "New Draperies": The Resurrection of an Old Flemish Industry, 1270–1570. In *The New Draperies in the Low Countries and England, 1300–1800*, edited by N. B. Harte, pp. 35–128. Oxford: Oxford University Press.

    2003   Medieval Woollens: Textiles, Technology and Organisation. In *The Cambridge History of Western Textiles*, edited by D. Jenkins, pp. 181–227. Cambridge: Cambridge University Press.

    2005   Spanish Merino Wools and the Nouvelles Draperies: An Industrial Transformation in the Late Medieval Low Countries. *Economic History Review* 58(3):431–484.

O'Neale, Lila

    1946   Mochica (Early Chimu) and Other Peruvian Twill Fabrics. *Southwestern Journal of Anthropology* 2(3):269–294.

O'Neale, Lila, and Bonnie Jean Clark

    1948   *The Gauze Weaves.* Textile Periods in Ancient Peru, vol. 3. Berkeley: University of California Press.

Rodman, Amy Oakland, and Gioconda Arabel Fernandez Lopez

    2005   North Coast Style After Moche: Clothing and Identity at El Brujo, Chicama Valley, Peru. In *Us and Them: Archaeology and Ethnicity in the Andes*, edited by R. M. Reycraft, pp. 115–133. Los Angeles: Cotsen Institute of Archaeology, University of California.

Rowe, Ann Pollard

    1974   *Peruvian Costume: A Weaver's Art.* Washington, DC: Textile Museum.

    1975   Weaving Processes in the Cuzco Area of Peru. *Textile Museum Journal* 4(2):30–46.

    1977   *Warp-Patterned Weaves of the Andes.* Washington, DC: Textile Museum.

    1984   *Costumes and Featherwork of the Lords of Chimor.* Washington, DC: Textile Museum.

1995/96   Inca Weaving and Costume. *Textile Museum Journal* 34–35:4–53.

Schneider, Jane

    1978   Peacocks and Penguins: The Political Economy of European Cloth and Colors. *American Ethnologist* 5(3):413–447.

Stone-Miller, Rebecca

    1994   *To Weave for the Sun: Ancient Andean Textiles in the Museum of Fine Arts, Boston.* New York: Thames and Hudson.

Thirsk, Joan

    2003   Knitting and Knitware, c. 1500–1780. In *The Cambridge History of Western Textiles*, edited by D. Jenkins, pp. 562–584. Cambridge: Cambridge University Press.

Voss, Barbara L.

    2008a *The Archaeology of Ethnogenesis: Race and Sexuality in Colonial San Francisco.* Berkeley: University of California Press.

    2008b Poor People in Silk Shirts. *Journal of Social Archaeology* 8(3):404–432.

7

Beads

Alexander Menaker

Introduction

WITH THEIR DIVERSE USES, values, and meanings, beads have played many important roles through time and space. They have been used for everything from simple adornments to delight an individual to money that affected the course of empires. The desire for beads was a cultural impulse that did not have to be translated when the Old World met the New—it was a common heritage extending to the most remote times of human antiquity. Yet bead use in Europe and the Americas had diverged enough that when Europeans encountered people of other traditions, new responses and innovations in cultural and social roles occurred. This was as true in the New World as in any other place.

Excavations at Magdalena de Cao Viejo yielded a rich collection of beads, including notable varieties of native and European forms. These were found throughout the town as well as within and around the church. In this chapter I will discuss the Magdalena beads within larger contexts and at the site itself, as well as some of the general characteristics of beads occurring throughout the Americas and Europe, their varied manufacturing techniques, and analytical methods for studying them. Following this, I will review the collection of beads recovered from Magdalena de Cao, particularly their archaeological contexts and interpretations of them.[1]

Beads Across the Andes and Beyond

Likely due to their portability, beads are among the first examples of human adornment for highly mobile early hunter-gatherers and foragers, and the tendency for them to be made in relatively durable materials means that they have been found at early archaeological sites. Such is the case for Peru, where a necklace of coarse greenstone beads interspersed with nine tubular gold beads was found in a grave at Jiskairumoko (ca. 2100–1900 B.C.), an intermittently occupied pithouse community in the Titicaca Basin. The find is not only one of the earliest complete necklaces in the Andes but also the earliest discovered example of metalworking (Aldenderfer et al. 2008).

The most notable bead type for early Peru is a biconvex, double-holed bead commonly made of red diatomite stone during the Late Preceramic Period (ca. 3000–2000/1500 B.C.) (Greider et al. 1988; Quilter 2014:104). Examples also are known made of the red *Spondylus princeps* shell. They appear to have been elements of high-status regalia, and reported findings tend to be at large Central Coast ceremonial centers such as Aspero and La Galgada. Other bead types are known for the era from findings at Caral, one of the most intensively studied Late Preceramic complexes, and include examples made of bone, wood, shell, quartz, and semiprecious stones (Shady 2006:52).

Beads of many different sorts were being made by the time of the Chavín culture (Burger 1992), circa 1000–200 B.C., including spectacular large gold ornaments such as found at Kuntur Wasi in the northern highlands (Kato 1979, 1993). No systematic study of the varieties of beads and their significance has been carried out for any of these early prehistoric eras, but it seems certain that there were various sumptuary laws at many times and places regarding who had rights to wear beads of particular materials or forms (Deagan 2002).

The greatest scholarly attention to ancient Central Andean beads is closely associated with the role of *Spondylus princeps* and *Spondylus calcifer* with their red, orange, and purple exterior and interior rims. Interest is particularly strong because the nearest sources to Peru of the mollusk are the warm waters of Ecuador, with other sources continuing northward (Carter 2011). The shell appears to have increasingly become more widely used in Peru, Bolivia, and Chile through time, suggesting intensified long-distance trade between these regions. There appears to have been a distinct increase in the importation of *Spondylus* late in the Early Intermediate Period (see Carter 2011; Paulsen 1974; Pillsbury 1996).

By the Late Intermediate Period the Lambayeque Culture (ca. A.D. 800–1350) (Shimada 1990), based in the northern valley of the same name, appears to have engaged in a vigorous importation of *Spondylus* to Peru, a practice continued by the succeeding Chimu culture, which expanded from its capital of Chan Chan in the Moche Valley to take over the former territory of Lambayeque. The Inca, who reportedly conquered the Chimu in 1470, also highly valued *Spondylus*. They may have attempted to monopolize or at least control its acquisition, distribution, and use, although how successful they were at doing so is not clear (see Besom 2010; Carter 2011). The large trading raft that encountered one of Pizarro's scouting expeditions may have been on its way north to obtain *Spondylus*.

We know that by late prehistory the Inca name for *Spondylus* was *mullu* and that, traditionally and to the present, the term *chaquira* is used to refer to *Spondylus* beads or, sometimes, beads in general.

During Pizarro's fateful journey to Cajamarca in 1532 Atahualpa sent a messenger bearing gifts to him. In return, Pizarro presented the Inca envoy and his men with presents that included glass beads (Estete [1535] and Trujillo [1571] quoted in Donnan 2011:368, 136). Additionally, throughout the northern Andes *Spondylus* shells and possibly beads made from them may have been used as a form of currency (D'Altroy 2002:255).[2]

European glass beads along with *Spondylus* shell beads have been recovered from indigenous burials dating to the time of the earliest Spanish intruders (1530–1560), including from significant prehispanic huacas at the site of Chotuna (Donnan 2011). One of our workers reported that a local huaquero told him that a burial was found on the eastern side of the Magdalena church complex that had been entirely wrapped in strings of *Spondylus* beads; if this is true, the numbers of chaquira would have been in the thousands. The church locale rests on top of a Moche or Lambayeque adobe structure, but descriptions of the find suggest that the burial was colonial or even later, inserted into the talus slope of the mound of soil of the crumbled church complex walls.

European Beads

We know much more about the history of beads in Europe and nearby regions than in the ancient Andes, due to the availability of documents and the link between glass beads and industrial and economic history. Even so, there are various aspects of the history of European beads, especially regarding their entry into the New World, that still are quite unclear.

Moravia and Bohemia supported glass workshops as early as the tenth century, but it was Venice and nearby Murano that played key roles in the production of the type of glass beads found in the New World (Durbin 2009:111–112). Venice's proximity to the Iberian Peninsula and the intertwined political and economic relations between Italian principalities and Spain were key to the island nation's commercial success. The complex political economies of Early Modern Europe complicate tracing the origins of glass beads found at early historical sites in the New World, however.

Venetian-style beads were so admired and in such high demand that competitors quickly established themselves in many other places. By the middle of the sixteenth century Venetian glassmakers weary of low wages had set up workshops in the Iberian Peninsula, and in 1549 the Venetian government enacted statutes to penalize those who refused to return from abroad (Frothingham 1963:34). Such attempts at control were likely not entirely successful given that during the same period workers from Murano, Altare, and Brescia set up successful industries in France and the Netherlands as well as in Iberia.

Deagan believes that the earliest beads in the Spanish colonies were made in Spain but that by the mid-sixteenth century these had been largely replaced by Venetian beads (1987:159). But the popularity of glass was great enough that local production began relatively early in the New World. Glass workshops were founded in Puebla, New Spain, as early as 1542 and exported their products throughout the Spanish colonies in the Americas, including Peru. Not much is known, however, about the specific items that were made or the frequency of trade that occurred (Smith and Good 1982; Soldi 2005).

One of the earliest accounts of glass production in Peru comes from the Spanish chronicler Antonio Vásquez de Espinosa. In 1617 he passed by the town of Ica, south of Lima, and noted "two furnaces for making fine glass" (Soldi 2005:335).[3] Glass production continued in Ica throughout the seventeenth and eighteenth centuries, including a workshop at a Jesuit hacienda, but was periodically disrupted by earthquake damage, debt, and other challenges (Soldi 2005).

Many aspects of bead making within the larger glass industry in Spanish colonial America are uncertain. It seems likely that a glass workshop would not ignore an apparently lucrative industry (Goggin 1960, quoted in Deagan 1987:159), but specific patterns of where and when glass beads were made and how they were distributed remain largely unknown. Detailed studies, including chemical and physical analyses, can discern different bead sources, but the amount of research still needed far exceeds current resources.

Glass Bead Fundamentals

At the time of early Spanish colonialism, which covers the main occupation of Magdalena de Cao, there were two predominant methods for manufacturing glass beads: the drawn cane method and the wire-wound method. Each leaves traces—wound beads have stress lines and bubbles encircling the string hole, while drawn cane beads have elongated bubbles and stress lines that parallel the perforation (Deagan 1987:160)—so identification is relatively easy for larger beads. For small beads, however, it can be difficult to discern the manufacturing method (Kidd and Kidd 1970:50).

Modifications of these primary manufacturing methods created a vast array of bead varieties. Twisting a glass rod with multiple stripes while it was being drawn produced spiraling stripes (Kidd and Kidd 1970:49; Smith and Good 1982:16). A mold with a square cross section produced a form similar to that seen in Nueva Cádiz beads, which were highly popular in early colonial times; another type of mold produced beads with a distinctive star-shaped cross section. The use of many rods of glass arranged around a core was another technique in both drawn and wound beads. After the initial formation, faceting, inlays, and other treatments produced a diversity of finished products.

The Magdalena de Cao European glass beads generally are similar to those found at other Spanish colonial sites in the Americas (Deagan 1987; Donnan 2011; Smith et al. 1994; Smith and Good 1982). Beads recovered at Magdalena de Cao include the diagnostic Nueva Cádiz style, named for the site in Venezuela where it was first found archaeologically. While the term "Nueva Cádiz" has been used to refer to a variety of tubular beads made by the drawn cane method and the use of molds with a square cross section, the most distinctive type is composed of three layers of glass, usually with interiors and exteriors of varying shades of blue and turquoise, with a white middle layer (Deagan 1987; Smith and Good 1982). Like other types of beads, Nueva Cádiz could be modified in several ways, including by twisting and faceting; both kinds of modification are present in the Magdalena de Cao collection (Smith and Good 1982). Moreover, historical archaeologists have usually identified Nueva Cádiz beads with sites dating to the sixteenth century, assigning them to before 1550 (Deagan 1987:163; Smith et al. 1994:36). The Magdalena de Cao Nueva Cádiz beads demonstrate that this type of bead was still in circulation beyond that time.

Chevron beads found at Magdalena de Cao have their origins around Venice and Murano and have been found throughout Spanish colonial sites beginning with those from the early sixteenth century (Smith and Good 1982). Deagan suggests that chevron beads might have been produced and used as paternoster rosary beads as early as the fourteenth century in France, where the glass industry has its origins in the medieval era (Deagan 1987:158). Because chevron beads were historically used for rosaries, it is no great surprise that such beads were found in the church at Magdalena de Cao. With their colorful multiple layers of blue, red, and green formed in star-shaped molds, these beads also offer temporal resolution, since the number of layers of glass used decreased over time (Smith and Good 1982). Chevron beads recovered from Spanish colonial sites from the sixteenth century consist of seven layers of glass and are faceted, while those of the later seventeenth century most often have five layers and are tumbled, and eighteenth-century beads have four layers of glass (Deagan 1987:164–165; Smith et al. 1994:36).

Another common type of colonial glass bead that occurs at Magdalena de Cao is the gooseberry bead, found in association with faceted chevron beads but rarely associated with Nueva Cádiz beads. Gooseberry beads are a composite construction, made up of multiple layers of glass, with a colorless interior core, applied stripes that are actually linear air bubbles, and then a final exterior layer of glass. These beads have been recovered among sites throughout North America associated with Spanish and Dutch occupations from the sixteenth, seventeenth, and eighteenth centuries (Deagan 1987). Deagan suggests that gooseberry beads were most commonly used by the Spaniards for "trade or gifts rather than as rosary beads or adornments" (Deagan 1987:168). The presence of a gooseberry bead at Magdalena de Cao also provides evidence extending previous dates marking the occurrence of this bead back to the first half of the sixteenth century (Smith and Good 1982; Deagan 1987).

Small wire-wound and drawn cane beads (commonly referred to as seed beads) are ubiquitous at European colonial sites, and also occur at Magdalena de Cao. These beads were often used in embroidery, and given their small sizes, they were probably most easily kept together by thread, which is further evident at Magdalena de Cao. In a few cases these small beads were further modified with faceting, making them subspherical in shape (Smith et al. 1994). Both wire-wound and drawn cane beads are found among the Peruvian bead collection analyzed by Smith and Good, though Deagan asserts that wire-wound beads are less common at sixteenth-century sites and appear more frequently later (Deagan 1987; Smith and Good 1982).[4]

There are also a couple of bead types that are rare among assemblages and so far documented only among Spanish colonial sites in Peru dating to the sixteenth and seventeenth centuries: crumb beads and red melon beads. Most often occurring in a dark blue or purple color, the crumb bead is made from a manufacturing process, still poorly understood, in which a spherical piece of glass is heated and rolled in a container of small pellets that adhere to the hot glass, making the bead look like a blackberry or as though it is covered in crumbs. The red melon bead is a wire-wound bead, distinct for its pressed flute molding (Menaker 2011; Smith and Good 1982).

Given the paucity of studies of Spanish colonial bead collections in South America, and given the large number of bead varieties manufactured at the time of Spanish colonialism, it is no surprise that the assemblage from Magdalena de Cao includes numerous beads that do not fit into existing known types. Because there are so many combinations of techniques, colors, and modifications, it is useful to mention the criteria by which I categorized and analyzed the bead collection.

Study of the Magdalena Bead Assemblage

My analysis encompassed the entire collection of beads recovered from Magdalena de Cao. I began by visually inspecting the beads now housed at the Museo de Cao and identifying their general characteristics. I quickly separated shell (mostly *Spondylus*) beads from glass beads, which generally distinguished indigenous from introduced materials. I recorded basic dimensions of all beads, including diameter, length, perforation diameter, weight, and color.[5]

My analysis of the European glass beads draws primarily from the foundational classification systems of Smith and Good (1982) and Deagan (1987). In addition, other classic studies and systematic analyses were used to identify select materials (Karklins 1982, 1985; Kidd and

Kidd 1970). The classificatory system employed for studying the glass beads recovered from Magdalena de Cao identifies central characteristics of European glass beads, including the specific manufacturing method, construction type (number of layers of glass), shape, and any modifications.

The classification system used follows the one elaborated by Smith and Good, which uses letters and numerals. Classification begins with the manufacturing method of the beads: drawn cane, wire-wound, blown, or crumb (Smith and Good 1982:19). Drawn cane beads are divided into five classes based upon their cross section: round, molded, twisted cross section, chevron with round cross section, and chevron with molded cross section (Smith and Good 1982:19). Subsequently, beads are categorized into series based upon their finishing—untumbled, tumbled, or faceted. They are further classified by type of construction, based on the number of layers of glass and then appliqués or inlays: (1) simple—a single layer of glass; (2) compound—two or more layers of glass; (3) complex—simple beads with an appliqué or inlaid design; and (4) composite—compound beads with an appliqué or inlaid design (Deagan 1987:161; Smith and Good 1982). Wire-wound beads are categorized depending on whether they were modified in any way; this includes mold-pressing (e.g., melon bead with pressed flutes) or any sort of finishing.

All of the beads are subdivided based upon shape: spherical, subspherical, donut, olive, and tubular forms. Diaphaneity was documented by holding the glass bead in the air and noting transparence, translucence, or opacity (Deagan 1987; Smith and Good 1982).

Results of Analysis

Approximately 347 beads were recovered from Magdalena de Cao Viejo throughout the various field seasons of excavations.[6] Beads were found both in the colonial town and within and around the church itself, with more than two-thirds (242 beads; 70 percent) recovered from the town and the remainder (105 beads) found associated with the church. The beads were made from a wide variety of materials, with the majority consisting of *Spondylus* shells and European glass beads, along with a small number of beads made from other shell varieties (such as mother of pearl), wood, and stone. Of the 120 European glass beads from the site, 37 were recovered from the church, while 83 glass beads (69 percent) were found in the town; of the 179 *Spondylus* beads, 49 were found in the church and 130 (73 percent) in the town.

Beads and the Church at Magdalena de Cao

This section will primarily review the beads recovered from the church, providing necessary contextual descriptions and details; additional contextual information and significant interpretations will be left until the later discussion.

Many of the beads found in the church were recovered through initial surface collections or while cleaning looter holes. A majority of the remaining beads were recovered in the first levels of excavations, though there were some recovered at lower levels more closely associated with the earliest phase of occupation.

The beads recovered from the colonial church provide important evidence of the convergence of enduring indigenous materials and more recent European imports. Of the

105 beads recovered from the church, there were 37 European glass beads and 52 shell beads (49 *Spondylus* beads and 3 mother-of-pearl shell varieties), with the remaining collection consisting of 11 stone beads, 1 metal bead, 2 beads made from treated wood, and 2 beads of unidentifiable organic material. These material remains were scattered throughout the church.

The *Spondylus* shell beads were mostly small and medium-sized circular beads ranging in color from red to orange to purple, most likely indicative of *Spondylus princeps* and *S. calcifer* (Figure 7.3: FF) (Donnan 2011). There were 44 *Spondylus* beads with diameters that ranged from 2.71 mm to 5 mm, including two tubular *Spondylus* beads (Figure 7.3: EE), while 5 substantially larger beads had diameters greater than 5 mm; the largest diameter was 9.35 mm. One of the mother-of-pearl beads was distinct in that it was a long, pendant-style bead (Figure 7.3: AA).

Although it is known that beads were used in dress and strung together with thread for various purposes, at many archaeological sites any associated textiles, thread, and other organic materials that might have provided further contextual insight have been lost to decay. Fortunately, the great environmental conservation at Magdalena de Cao meant that many beads were recovered with threads still intact, providing critical contextual evidence. For example, 7 *Spondylus* beads with an intact thread remained strung together; these were recovered from a looter hole (Figure 7.1). Also found in the same pit were 12 other small circular *Spondylus* beads (one of which, as mentioned earlier, was tubular), 2 glass beads (a chevron bead and an interesting wire-wound bead of simple construction, consisting only of black glass, but which is composed of multiple wound coils still connected and fused, thus resulting more in a tubular shape [Figure 7.3: X]), and a possible metal bead. The only beads recovered from Unit 17 in the church were two similar chevron beads, one of which had a thread preserved inside its perforation (Figure 7.3: A, B).

Six *Spondylus* beads held together by string were the only beads found in Unit 18. Recovered from another area of excavation (Trench 1) was an intact thread strung with 10 beads: 6 tubular shell beads (diameter range 3.72 mm to 4.63 mm, length range 4.38 mm to 7.63 mm) and 4 black stone beads (possibly shale) of circular disc shape (diameter range 2.03 mm to 3.09 mm, length range 1.17 mm to 1.85 mm) (Donnan and Silton 2011). Three similar black stones were

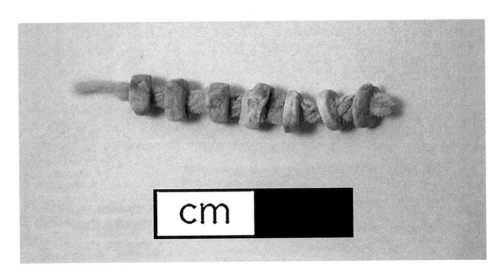

Figure 7.1
Spondylus shell beads with thread intact.

recovered in the same archaeological context, while 2 other similar *Spondylus* beads were found in contexts resting a little closer to the surface than the other beads.

Unique and interesting beads and fragments were recovered from Unit 12, at the northwest edge of the church. This excavation unit revealed a wealth of European-influenced materials, including paper with writing, colonial ceramics, and more. There were 16 beads collected there (minimum bead count, fragments of large wire-wound). This included 12 glass beads, 1 mother-of-pearl bead, and 2 *Spondylus* shell beads, along with a bead made from wood. All of the glass beads were simple construction, with one layer of glass, except for a broken teardrop-shaped glass bead with an appliqué indicative of complex construction. Remains of three wire-wound beads with large diameters were found within this area; as far as I am aware, wire-wound beads of this size have never been documented before in Peru (Figure 7.3: Y). There were also three identical small wire-wound, olive-shaped (with round cross sections) cobalt-blue beads, with diameters of 3.57 mm to 3.66 mm and lengths of 3.95 mm to 4.94 mm. Another notable bead was a quite weathered and worn clear glass spherical bead, with traces of metal remaining in its perforation (Figure 7.3: Z). The other glass beads included olive- and donut-shaped beads of dark blue and sky blue, as well as a similar bead of cream or tan, along with a tubular cobalt-blue bead molded with long protruding lines parallel to the perforation, similar to other beads found at the site (Figure 7.3: E).

There were seven beads recovered from Unit 5, including three glass beads, three *Spondylus* shell beads, and one stone bead. The glass beads included a flake of Nueva Cádiz bead along with two small glass beads, one a green drawn cane donut-shaped and tumbled bead with a diameter of 3.39 mm and length of 2.49 mm, the other a purple wire-wound olive-shaped bead with a diameter of 3.45 mm and length of 2.93 mm. Another assemblage of 15 beads (5 *Spondylus* shell beads and 10 glass beads) was excavated from Unit 7. This included a chevron bead, a Nueva Cádiz bead, a weathered compound bead composed of three layers of glass (an interior cobalt blue, a very thin layer of white, and an exterior layer of cobalt blue), and seven small, simple wire-wound beads, olive and donut-shaped, in green ($N=1$) and various shades of blue and purple ($N=6$) (diameter range 2.79 mm to 3.52 mm, length range 2.19 mm to 4.9 mm).

There were 15 beads recovered from Unit 32 (not including flake), which included a variety of glass ($N=5$) and shell beads (five *Spondylus*, two mother-of-pearl). During excavations, a twisted Nueva Cádiz bead and a small simple drawn cane sky blue bead were recovered in contexts associated with a burial, the only remaining and preserved mortuary context containing beads at the site. The three other glass beads, found in adjacent stratigraphy levels, included two small drawn cane and wire-wound beads, one teal and one cobalt blue, along with a cream-colored drawn cane tumbled bead. The two mother-of-pearl beads were primarily spherical in shape and ranged in diameter from 7.96 mm to 8.88 mm, though the larger bead is broken neatly in half along the perforation. A distinctively crafted oblong black stone bead with a diameter of 11.57 mm and length of 13.4 mm has one perforation running its length, with another hole perpendicular that intersects it at midpoint. There are also five small *Spondylus* beads that are red, orange, and purple. Also present in the collection were a black stone circular bead, an amber-brown spherical stone, and a well-crafted spherical organic bead (possibly wood).

Beads Throughout the Town

There were 242 beads recovered from the colonial town, including 83 glass beads and 130 *Spondylus* shell beads. Most of the beads were found in excavations of structures; and in one intriguing case, beads were recovered at the fringes of the residential area.

Just northeast of the plaza, Unit 28 provided plentiful evidence, with 65 beads recovered, including 26 *Spondylus* shell beads and 29 European glass beads (not including glass flake). For instance, there was a molded red melon bead with pressed flutes, which was broken in half, as well as a crumb bead—neither of which is commonly found in other Spanish colonial sites in the Americas (Figure 7.3: M, N) (Smith and Good 1982). Another bead that has not been presented in previous studies is a small wire-wound faceted red bead (one of two found at the site; Figure 7.3: P). There was also a glass bead of complex construction, which consisted of alternating red and white stripes parallel to the perforation and inlaid on a dark navy blue base layer (Figure 7.3: J). Four Nueva Cádiz beads with molded cross sections were found throughout the structure, with diameters of 3.31 mm to 5.88 mm and available lengths of 5.07 mm to 8.14 mm, along with a fragment of a twisted Nueva Cádiz bead (diameter 5.88 mm, length 4.39 mm). One of these Nueva Cádiz beads had a faceted finishing, which Fairbanks termed Peru Corner Faceted, but this finish has been found outside of Peru in recent years (Figure 7.3: D) (Deagan 1987:164; Smith et al. 1994:35). Three chevron beads, with varying quality of faceting finishes leading to unevenly crafted subspherical forms, were further found scattered in the structure. There were also two rare small donut-shaped compound beads composed of a colorless interior layer of glass and a green exterior (Figure 7.3: R). There were nine other drawn cane and wire-wound beads recovered from the structure, included a variety of small glass beads (such as the purple wire-wound beads in Figure 7.3: R, S). Worth mentioning is the presence of four tubular drawn cane beads of simple construction, cobalt blue, which exhibit very narrow linear protrusions running parallel to the perforation; these are most likely indicative of a mold (Figure 7.3: E). Other beads present in the collection included five small circular disk black stone beads (similar to those already discussed, Figure 7.3: CC), three unidentifiable organic beads, and one treated wood bead.

Moving from Unit 28 to the western edge of the plaza, we arrive at Units 1 and 2. Unit 2 seems to be a structure composed of multiple rooms, or at least composed of certain interior spatial divisions and entryways. Material culture of distinct Andean importance and artifacts with European influences were recovered from Unit 2, including a decorated gourd and a metal knife with a handle made of algarrobo. A substantial collection of beads was recovered from these two units, accounting for a significant proportion of the total number of beads found at Magdalena de Cao.

Specifically, there were 58 beads recovered from Unit 2, consisting of 48 *Spondylus* shell beads, 2 mother-of-pearl beads, 2 stone beads, and 6 glass beads (5 drawn cane, 1 wire-wound). One of the drawn cane beads was of complex construction, consisting of a base layer of black glass with inlaid white stripes parallel to the perforation (Figure 7.3: H). There were also fragments of a twisted Nueva Cádiz (Figure 7.3: C). A rare colorless spherical glass bead with white stripes and a third layer of colorless glass (Figure 7.3: L) is indicative of gooseberry beads recovered not just in a variety of Spanish colonial areas but throughout North America. As noted previously, the presence of this gooseberry bead at Magdalena de Cao provides compelling evidence extending previous dates marking the occurrence of this bead back to the first half of the sixteenth century (Deagan 1987:167–168; Smith and Good 1982). Another drawn cane composite bead was composed of three layers; navy blue, white, and blue with alternating white and red stripes (Figure 7.3: G). Two remaining beads were of simple construction, one a small green wire-wound bead and another a drawn cane turquoise bead. Thanks to meticulous excavations, a significant quantity of *Spondylus* beads were found *in situ* in Unit 2, and were indicative of having been formerly strung together. Once exposed to the current environment, the delicate remains that held these small beads together disintegrated, and the oranges, reds, and purples of the shells faded. The *Spondylus* shell beads ranged in diameter from 3.64 mm to 5.30 mm and in length from 1.36 mm to 2.9 mm.

Excavations of Unit 1, located in an adjacent structure north of Unit 2, yielded an assemblage of 76 beads, making it the largest of the groups recovered at Magdalena de Cao, and included 55 *Spondylus* shell beads and 13 glass beads. The *Spondylus* shells were all similar small circular beads of varying purple, orange, and red combinations, and with a diameter range of 3.23 mm to 4.93 mm and lengths of 0.80 mm to 2.11 mm. Additionally, there were five white shells with three remaining together on a thread and the other two also still connected by thread. There was one stone bead, one treated wood (or seed) bead (Figure 7.3: DD), and another shell bead. The collection included nine glass beads of simple construction and varying colors, and some with interesting and unique modifications, such as a faceted blue bead (Figure 7.3: Q), a red faceted drawn cane bead with a diameter of 3.84 mm and length of 7.11 mm (somewhat similar to another red faceted bead, Figure 7.3: P), and an intriguing green molded bead with an unidentifiable geometric design (Figure 7.3: O). Other simple-type beads were small olive- and donut-shaped beads, three purple, one white, and one gray-blue. There were two compound drawn cane beads—a Nueva Cádiz bead and a spherical bead composed of an interior layer of dark navy blue glass, a middle layer of white, and a cobalt-blue exterior (Figure 7.3: K). There was a bead of composite construction with multiple layers of blue and white glass and alternating red and white stripes running parallel to the perforation (Figure 7.3: F). There was an interesting complex bead, most likely twisted, with a white base layer, spiraling green bands, and white stripes (Figure 7.3: I).

Small wire-wound and drawn cane glass beads were the only beads recovered from Unit 24 (Figure 7.2). They were amazingly well preserved, with 22 small glass beads still connected by thread, and an additional fragment of thread with 8 beads together.[7] The colors of the beads include white, varying shades of blue (sky blue, blue, navy blue), red/maroon, and green. The range in diameter of these beads was 2.09 mm to 3.4 mm, with length ranges of 1.24 mm to 2.44 mm, along with a larger misshapen bead with a diameter of 3.6 mm and length of 4.32 mm.

The last context of beads discussed here, Unit 19, very much exists in the space of the reducción, yet also was possibly at its fringes. Nine beads were recovered from this area: two small *Spondylus* circular disk beads; three glass beads; two small stone circular disk beads, one dark green and one black; two wood beads (one spherical, similar to Figure 7.3: DD, and another in the form of a circular disk), and additional material including a *Spondylus* shell along with considerable faunal and vegetable remains that are most likely representative of food preparation or its resulting waste. The archaeological evidence was suggestive of multiple

Figure 7.2 European glass beads strung together with original threads. Drawn cane and wire-wound glass beads, all simple construction, some tumbled and some untumbled.

possibilities for the area—perhaps once the site of a residence and subsequently a trash pile. In this ambiguous context of refuse and remains a revealing find was uncovered—the presence of a chevron glass bead nestled in a gourd filled with burned materials (discussed below). The other two glass beads found were a fragment of a Nueva Cádiz bead and a dark sky blue olive-shaped wire-wound bead (diameter 3.5 mm, length 4.38 mm). Interestingly, all of the glass beads were broken.

Although, beads did not figure critically in dating the occupations of Magdalena de Cao, because of the variety of other chronological sources, it is worth quickly presenting a summary of the beads used as chronological indices, such as Nueva Cádiz and chevron varieties. For instance, the chevron beads recovered from Magdalena de Cao all had seven layers and faceted finishings (Figure 7.3: A, B). Smith identifies these chevron beads as indicative of sixteenth-century varieties, and notes that the ones with green layers were unique to Peru (Smith et al. 1994). However, given the known occupations of Magdalena de Cao, it is most likely that we can date the use of chevron and Nueva Cádiz beads, along with the other glass bead varieties, to the late sixteenth century and at least throughout the early part of the seventeenth century. Nueva Cádiz beads are also present at Spanish colonial sites in the Americas, such as Malata, throughout the sixteenth century, and their presence at Magdalena de Cao indicates their continued usage and circulation among the Andes at least throughout the early seventeenth century (Figure 7.3: C, D) (Menaker 2011; Wernke 2011). These dates extend previous studies, which usually only attribute the usage of these glass beads to the sixteenth century (Deagan 1987; Smith et al. 1994; Smith and Good 1982). Ultimately, the evidence from Magdalena de Cao suggests that Nueva Cádiz and certain chevron bead varieties, among others, continued to be used among local communities longer than previously thought.

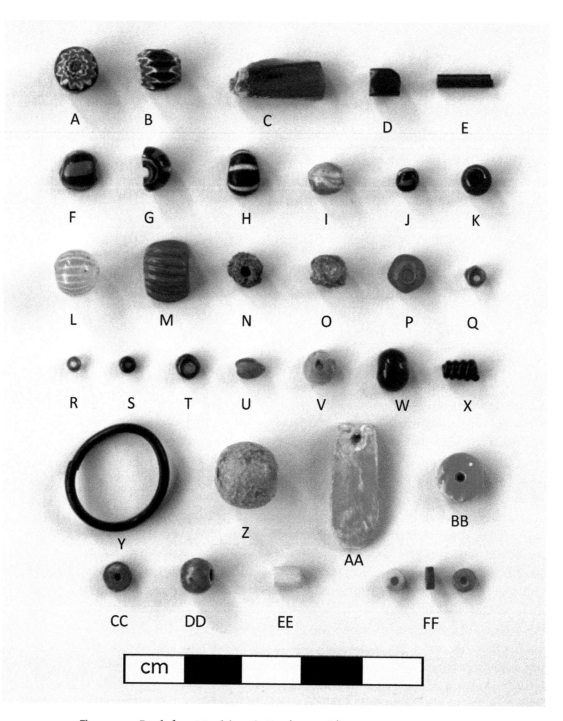

Figure 7.3 Beads from Magdalena de Cao (see guide).

GUIDE TO BEADS IN FIGURE 7.3

Classification criteria: quantity, manufacturing method, cross section, type, shape, modifying decoration, color (number of glass layers, from inside out), diaphaneity, diameter (range), length (range), number, corresponding classification types from Smith and Good 1982 where applicable, additional notes.

First row (from left to right):

A, B: Chevron beads; drawn cane; round cross section; compound; sub-spherical; faceted; opaque; 7 layers: green, white, green, white, red, white, blue; diameter range: 4.77–9.55 mm; length range: 4.68–10.07 mm; $N = 8$. Smith and Good classification: Class IV (chevron), Series C (faceted), Type 2 (compound construction).

C: Nueva Cádiz twisted; drawn cane; molded cross section; compound; tubular; untumbled (at least observable); opaque; 3 layers: blue, white, turquoise; diameter: 6.33 mm; length: 15.47 mm; perforation diameter: 2.39 mm; $N = 3$. Smith and Good classification: Class III (Nueva Cádiz twisted), Series A (untumbled), Type 2 (compound construction), Variety A.

D: Nueva Cádiz; drawn cane; molded cross section (square); compound; tubular; faceted corners; opaque; 3 layers: navy blue, white, cobalt blue; diameter: 4.28 × 4.53 mm; length: 5.08 mm; $N = 1$. Smith and Good classification: Class II (Nueva Cádiz plain), Series C (faceted), Type 2 (compound construction), Variety A.

E: Drawn cane; molded cross section (with linear protrusions running parallel to perforation); simple; tubular; cobalt blue; translucent; diameter range: 1.85–2.58 mm; length range: 7.92–10.42 mm; $N = 5$.

Second row (from left to right):

F: Drawn cane; round cross section; composite; tumbled; spherical; 3 layers: navy blue, white, navy blue; 2 inlaid white stripes running in a slight twisted orientation to perforation, with a thick red stripe/band running parallel in between the two white stripes in a similar orientation parallel to the perforation; opaque; diameter: 6.61 mm; length: 6.14 mm; $N = 1$.

G: Drawn cane; round cross section; composite; tumbled; spherical; 3 layers: navy blue, white, blue with alternating white and red inlaid stripes running parallel to the perforation; opaque; diameter: 7.23 mm; length: 5.67 mm; $N = 1$.

H: Drawn cane; round cross section; complex; tumbled; spherical; black with 3 white stripes parallel with perforation; opaque; diameter: 7.62 mm; length: 7.5 mm; $N = 1$.

I: Drawn cane; round cross section; composite; tumbled; olive-shaped; 2 layers: white base layer with green bands and white stripes running parallel to the perforation; diameter: 5.2 mm; length: 5.72 mm; $N = 1$.

J: drawn cane/wire-wound; round cross section; complex; dark blue with 3 alternating white and red stripes running parallel to the perforation; spherical/olive-shaped; translucent; diameter: 3.98 mm; length: 3.73 mm; $N = 1$.

K: Drawn cane; round cross section; compound; 3 layers: dark navy blue, white, cobalt blue; tumbled; spherical; opaque; diameter: 5.10 mm; length: 4.50 mm; $N = 1$.

Third row (from left to right):

L: Drawn cane; round cross section; composite; 3 layers: colorless, white stripes running parallel to perforation, additional exterior layer of colorless glass; tumbled; spherical; diameter: 7.81 mm; length: 7.47 mm; $N = 1$. Indicative of gooseberry beads (Deagan 1987:168).

M: Wire-wound; simple; modified (pressed flutes); red; opaque; diameter range: 8.16–10.15 mm; length range: 6.57–7.53 mm; $N = 2$.

N: Crumb bead; exterior is poorly preserved, most likely originally blue or purple; diameter: 6.21 mm; length: 3.77 mm; $N = 1$.

O: Drawn cane; simple; molded, unidentifiable geometric design; green; translucent; diameter: 5.42 mm; length: 5.95 mm; $N = 1$.

P: Wire-wound; round cross section; simple; faceted; sub-spherical; red; diameter: 6.17 mm; length: 4.26 mm; $N = 1$

(continued)

Q: Drawn cane; round cross section; simple; faceted; subspherical; sky blue; diameter: 3.79 mm; length: 2.73 mm; $N=1$.

Fourth row (from left to right):

R: Drawn cane; round cross section; compound; 2 layers: clear interior core, green; tumbled; donut-shaped; diameter: 1.91 mm–2.54 mm; length: 1.27–1.73 mm; $N=2$.

S: Wire-wound; round cross section; simple; purple; donut-shaped; diameter: 2.94 mm; length: 1.91 mm; $N=6$.

T: Wire-wound; round cross section; simple; purple; donut-shaped; diameter: 3.97 mm; length: 2.52 mm; $N=6$.

U: Wire-wound; round cross section; simple; green; olive-shaped; diameter: 3.16 mm; length: 4.9 mm; $N=4$.

V: Drawn cane; round cross section; simple; turquoise/sky blue; slightly translucent; circular disk; diameter: 5.55 mm; length: 2.57 mm; $N=1$

W: Drawn cane; round cross section; simple; dark blue; tumbled; spherical; translucent; diameter: 7.05 mm; length: 5.22 mm; $N=1$

X: Wire-wound coil; round cross section; simple; composed of 5 circular coils, thus making it tubular in form; unmodified; black; opaque; diameter: 3.55 mm at wider end, 2.91 mm at narrower end; length: 6.04 mm; $N=1$.

Fifth row (from left to right):

Y: Wire-wound; simple; unmodified; dark navy blue/black; opaque; large circular diameter: 18.34 mm; diameter of the tubular glass: 1.92 mm; $N=3$.

Z: Drawn cane; round cross section; simple; cloudy clear; tumbled; spherical; transparent; diameter: 10.8 mm; length: 10.27; perforation diameter: 2.31 mm; $N=1$.

AA: Mother-of-pearl pendant; diameters/lengths: 8.09 mm × 20.28 mm; thickness 3.33 mm; $N=1$. Additional notes: A 90-degree perforation with the opening at one part of the large face; the other opening is at the top side of the pendant.

BB: *Spondylus* shell beads; circular; range of colors: orange/red; diameter range: 6.74–9.35 mm; length range: 2.52–4.17 mm; $N=4$.

Sixth row (from left to right):

CC: Black stone (shale?); circular disk shape; diameter range: 2.03–6.77 mm; thickness range: 1.17–3.79 mm; $N=17$. (Donnan and Silton 2011:223).

DD: Wood (seed or organic material); spherical; diameter: 5.89 mm; length: 5.20 mm; perforation: 2.12 mm; opaque; tan/red and mottled, with black throughout; $N=1$.

EE: *Spondylus* shell beads; tubular; colors: orange; diameter range: 3.38–3.54 mm; length range: 3.64–6.47 mm[1]; $N=3$.

FF: *Spondylus* shell beads; circular[2]; range of colors: red, purple, pink/red, orange/red, all with scattered presence of white throughout; diameter range: 2.71–5.30 mm; length range: 0.80–3.70 mm; $N=173$.

---

1 The lowest measurement is of a tubular *Spondylus* shell bead fragment.

2 Some of the *Spondylus* shell beads are uneven circles and "rounded squares," though this could be due to erosion and wear. It is also a somewhat subjective characterization. Therefore I have grouped such beads within the larger category of "circular."

Interpreting Beads from the Archaeological Record at Magdalena de Cao Viejo

The varied assemblage and rich preservation of beads and associated materials found at Magdalena de Cao provide important evidence of the uses and significances of beads during Spanish colonialism. For example, preserved threads that still hold together several of the beads are highly suggestive of their use in dress and adornment, as necklaces or bracelets, or perhaps woven into textiles. At the same time, beads could have been strung together for a whole host of other purposes; held together by thread, beads could have been more easily traded and kept track of. Moreover, the juxtaposition of *Spondylus* shell beads and European glass beads in contexts and assemblages, along with other materials, is revealing of cultural and colonial encounters. The varied distribution of beads with extensive pasts and usages in prehispanic contexts alongside distinctly European glass beads throughout the site of Magdalena de Cao suggests that the uses and meanings of the numerous different beads did not conform to a uniform pattern, or at least one that would indicate a clear dialectic of domination and resistance (Wernke 2011). Instead, in accordance with recent studies of colonial encounters, Magdalena de Cao exemplifies the complicated nature of colonial situations, which are filled with ambiguity, mutual appropriation, ambivalence, and contestation (see Liebmann and Murphy 2011). As Quilter suggests, the materiality of the social processes of the Conquest and Colonial Period is difficult to identify clearly (Quilter 2011). Additionally, the various disturbances throughout Magdalena de Cao due to ecological and historical factors provide certain challenges and limitations to the interpretive resolution of the archaeological contexts. Nonetheless, we are still afforded certain interpretive lenses as we consider the distinct locations and areas where these beads were recovered. The site of Magdalena de Cao, born from imperial violence and articulated with enduring indigenous relations and traditions, pulsed with meaning.

The Spanish colonial contexts, both social and religious, in which beads were used were quite dynamic. But amid such cultural convergence, beads may have signified in ambiguous and fluid ways. For instance, burned matter found in an overturned gourd at the fringes of the reducción is suggestive of long-standing Andean practices and offerings, but this instance included a European glass bead (see Figure 2.27 in Chapter 2). If this was in fact a ritual, it was carried out in an area away from the symbol and locus of Spanish colonial power, the church. Of course, it is also possible that the entire context might be refuse, deposited at the edges of domestic occupations. Given a colonial situation in which indigenous and European material culture mixed amid eclectic and changing beliefs and practices, it can be difficult to use material remains to ascribe hints of resistance to colonial encounters. What is more certain is that the archaeological contexts of beads further support a dynamic and flexible negotiation of European and indigenous influences.

The remains of *Spondylus* bivalves neatly placed beneath the level of the floor in Unit 2, with the surrounding sand floor revealing traces of burning, appears to be an offering reminiscent of important and ubiquitous prehispanic domestic rituals and practices. Yet in this "world turned upside down," colorful glass beads complemented the oranges, reds, and purples of *Spondylus* beads. One might ask whether the glass beads that circulated alongside shell beads also came to be considered *mullu*, a powerful object able to invoke and satisfy suprahuman powers of the universe (Carter 2011). The negotiation of these European materials and Andean meanings contributed to the shaping of new cultural identities as local indigenous meanings were matched to colonial objects (van Dommelen 2005:136).

One must also consider whether the impressive assemblages of beads recovered from the domestic units on the plaza (Units 1, 2 and 28) might strongly reflect certain residents' higher status within the community, which offered privileged access to the plaza and possession of rare and coveted objects. Although interpreting the archaeological record is fraught with ambiguity, the presence of materials wrought and acquired through a great investment of human energy does suggest possible hierarchical social positions and relations, along with potentials for exchanges within the community and elsewhere.

Just as shell beads were used in burial practices throughout the prehispanic Andes, shell beads continued to adorn the dead during Spanish colonialism, except this time they were buried in churches. Although the contextual disturbances throughout the church at Magdalena de Cao prevent conclusive interpretations of their specific uses and significances in that setting, the sheer fact of the continued use of shell beads associated with the space of the church—a distinctly Spanish colonial political and religious structure—provides a compelling framework for a range of possible uses, much as at Chotuna, where both shell and glass beads adorned the dead. Recent historical archaeological work conducted nearby on the North Coast at the Spanish colonial church site of Ñoquique, dating to the sixteenth and seventeenth centuries, allows for an important contextual comparison. The European beads recovered from the surface collection of the church nave at the site of Ñoquique are diverse, including jet beads most likely originally composing part of a rosary, and various types of glass beads—many similar to those recovered at Magdalena de Cao (Deagan 1987:183).[8] At the site of Mocupe Viejo (1572–1652), in the nave of the church there are looted burials with scatterings of bones exposed from where they were originally entombed beneath the church. Here *Spondylus* shell beads were also extensively recovered in association with European beads (VanValkenburgh 2012). It is evident that shell beads, in particular *Spondylus*, remained an important material among the living and the dead, along with the more recently circulating European glass bead varieties. Ultimately, at this intersection of the familiar and unfamiliar, glass and shell beads "were more than just simple adornment as they were used to evoke other memories and associations meaningful to constructing early colonial identities" (Loren 2008:104).

At the site of Magdalena de Cao beads were used in an array of activities that crisscrossed the economic, political, social, and religious spheres of colonial Andean life—a fact that in many ways complicates dichotomies of colonizer and colonized. In lived realities, colonial Andean beliefs and practices were constantly being negotiated and reformulated in the reducciones, where European glass beads were used to invoke ancient Andean powers and *Spondylus* shells were interred with the dead in newly constructed Christian churches built in the shadows of earlier temples and shrines. Central to many of these meaningful activities, beads were not merely a backdrop to human action but were intricately involved in shaping cultural identities and negotiating structures of power.

NOTES

1 My analysis of the Magdalena bead assemblage occurred in two separate visits to the collection in 2010 and 2013, respectively. In total, my studies at the Museo de Cao were carried out during four weeks with subsequent library and other research in the preparation of this chapter.

2 Carter (2011:79–80) argues that the presence and use of *Spondylus* shells and beads at the time of the arrival of the Spanish have been overestimated.

3 "Hay en ella dos hornos de vidrio muy buenos," Vásquez de Espinosa, quoted in Soldi (2005:335).

4 It is important to note that the bead collection analyzed by Smith and Good (1982) is considered to correspond to the sixteenth century, though it comes from private collections and consists of materials removed unsystematically, so it cannot be relied upon for archaeological context, further making its chronological accuracy dubious. Therefore, this analysis provides foundational archaeological contexts to the study of European glass and shell beads in Peru and Latin America more broadly.

5 Given the productive insight gained from analyzing certain manufacturing features and modifications, and given the distinct variations of colors, a Munsell color chart was not used.

6 This count is based upon a minimum bead count. In certain cases, beads are extremely fragmented, thus limiting their analytical and typological resolutions.

7 In order to preserve the thread stringing these beads together, I chose not to adequately analyze all of these beads, and thus was not able to identify all of the manufacturing methods.

8 It is also worth noting that no beads made from jet were recovered from Magdalena de Cao.

REFERENCES CITED

Aldenderfer, Mark, Nathan M. Craig, Robert J. Speakman, and Rachel Popelka-Filcoff
    2008 Four-Thousand-Year-Old Gold Artifacts from the Lake Titicaca Basin, Southern Peru. *Proceedings of the National Academy of Sciences of the United States of America* 105(13):5002–5005.

Besom, Thomas
    2010 Inca Sacrifice and the Mummy of Salinas Grandes. *Latin American Antiquity* 21(4):399–422.

Burger, Richard
    1992 *Chavin and the Origins of Civilization.* London: Thames and Hudson.

Carter, Benjamin
    2011 *Spondylus* in South American Prehistory. In *Spondylus in Prehistory: New Data and Approaches,* edited by Fotis Ifantidis and Marianna Nikolaidou, pp. 63–89. Oxford: Archaeopress.

D'Altroy, Terence
    2002 *The Incas.* Cambridge, MA: Blackwell.

Deagan, Kathleen
    1987 *Artifacts of the Spanish Colonies of Florida and the Caribbean, 1500–1800,* vol. 1, *Ceramics, Glassware, and Beads.* Washington, DC: Smithsonian Institution Press.
    2002 *Artifacts of the Spanish Colonies of Florida and the Caribbean 1500–1800,* vol. 2, *Portable Personal Possessions.* Washington, DC: Smithsonian Institution Press.

Donnan, Christopher
    2011 *Chotuna and Chornancap: Excavating an Ancient Peruvian Legend.* Los Angeles: Cotsen Institute of Archaeology, UCLA.

Donnan, Christopher, and Jill Silton

2011 Colonial Period Beads. Appendix 5 in Christopher Donnan, *Chotuna and Chornancap: Excavating an Ancient Peruvian Legend.* Los Angeles: Cotsen Institute of Archaeology, UCLA.

Durbin, Lois

2009 *The History of Beads: From 100,000 BC to the Present.* New York: Abrams.

Earle, Timothy

1994 Wealth Finance in the Inka Empire: Evidence from the Calchaqui Valley, Argentina. *American Antiquity* 59(3):443–460.

Frothingham, Alice

1963 *Spanish Glass.* New York: Thomas Yoseloff.

Goggin, John

1960 *Spanish Trade Beads and Pendants.* Gainesville: Florida State Museum.

Greider, Terence, Alberto Mendoza, C. Earle Smith, and Robert Malina

1988 *La Galgada, Peru: A Preceramic Culture in Transition.* Austin: University of Texas Press.

Karklins, Karlis

1982 *Glass Beads.* History and Archaeology Series No. 59. Ottawa, ON: National Historic Parks and Sites Branch.

1985 Early Amsterdam Trade Beads. *Ornament* 9(2):36–41.

Kato, Yasutake

1979 Chullpas at Tornapampa. In *Excavations at La Pampa in the North Highlands of Peru,* edited by Kasuo Terada, pp. 163–167. Tokyo: University of Tokyo Press.

1993 Resultados de las excavaciones en Kuntur Wasi, Cajamarca. In *El mundo ceremonial andino,* edited by Luis Millones and Yoshio Onuki, pp. 203–228. Senri Ethnological Studies, no. 37. Osaka: National Museum of Ethnology.

Kidd, Kenneth, and Martha Ann Kidd

1970 *A Classification System for Glass Beads for the Use of Field Archaeologists.* Occasional Papers in Archaeology and History No. 1. Ottawa, ON: National Historic Sites Service.

Liebmann, Matthew, and Melissa Scott Murphy

2011 Rethinking the Archaeology of "Rebels, Backsliders, and Idolaters." In *Enduring Conquests,* edited by Matthew Liebmann and Melissa Scott Murphy, pp. 3–18. Santa Fe, NM: School for Advanced Research Press.

Loren, Diana DiPaolo

2008 *In Contact: Bodies and Spaces in the Sixteenth- and Seventeenth-Century Eastern Woodlands.* Lanham, MD: Altamira Press.

Menaker, Alexander

2011 Beads Throughout the Peruvian Andes: An Archaeological Examination of Meaning and Value During Spanish Colonialism. Master's thesis, Program in the Social Sciences, University of Chicago.

Paulsen, Allison

1974 The Thorny Oyster and the Voice of God: *Spondylus* and *Strombus* in Andean Prehistory. *American Antiquity* 39(4):597–607.

Pillsbury, Joanne

1996 The Thorny Oyster and the Origins of Empire: Implications of Recently Uncovered *Spondylus* Imagery from Chan-Chan, Peru. *Latin American Antiquity* 8(1):313–340.

Quilter, Jeffrey

    2011   Cultural Encounters at Magdalena de Cao Viejo in the Early Colonial Period. In *Enduring Conquests*, edited by Matthew Liebmann and Melissa Scott Murphy, pp. 103–125. Santa Fe, NM: School for Advanced Research Press.

    2014   *The Ancient Central Andes.* London: Routledge.

Sandweiss, Daniel

    1999   The Return of the Native Symbol: Peru Picks *Spondylus* to Represent New Integration with Ecuador. *SAA Bulletin* 17(2):1, 8–9.

Shady Solís, Ruth

    2006   America's First City? The Case of Late Archaic Caral. In *Andean Archaeology III: North and South*, ed. William Harris Isbell and Helaine Silverman, pp. 28–67. New York: Springer.

Shimada, Izumi

    1990   Cultural Continuities and Discontinuities on the Northern Coast of Peru, Middle-Late Horizons. In *The Northern Dynasties: Kingship and Statecraft in Chimor*, ed. Michael Moseley and Alana Cordy-Collins, pp. 297–392. Washington DC: Dumbarton Oaks.

Smith, Marvin, and M. E. Good

    1982   *Early Sixteenth-Century Glass Beads in the Spanish Colonial Trade.* Greenwood, MS: Cottonlandia Museum.

Smith, Marvin, Elizabeth Graham, and David M. Pendergast

    1994   European Beads from Spanish-Colonial Lamanai and Tipu, Belize. *Beads: Journal of the Society of Bead Researchers* 6:21–48.

Soldi, Ana María

    2005   Obrajes de vidrio en Ica en los siglos XVII y XVIII: El caso de Macacona. In *Esclavitud, economía y evangelización*, edited by Sandra Negro and Manual Marzal, pp. 333–344. Lima: Pontificia Universidad Católica del Perú.

van Dommelen, Peter

    2005   Colonial Interactions and Hybrid Practices. In *The Archaeology of Colonial Encounters: Comparative Perspectives*, edited by Gil Stein, pp. 109–141. Santa Fe, NM: School of American Research Press.

VanValkenburgh, Nathaniel P.

    2012   Report from Dissertation Field Research 2009–2010. Proyecto Arqueologico Zaña Colonial, Zaña River Valley, Perú.

Wernke, Steven A.

    2011   Convergences: The Origins of Colonial Hybridity at an Early *Doctrina* in Highland Peru. In *Enduring Conquests*, edited by Matthew Liebmann and Melissa Scott Murphy, pp. 77–101. Santa Fe, NM: SAR Press.

8

Colonial Ceramics

Commerce and Consumption

Parker VanValkenburgh

Introduction

I N AN ARTICLE WRITTEN more than 70 years ago, art historian George Kubler (1946:363) observed that no aspect of Spanish colonial life in the Andes had been so poorly studied as its material culture (quoted in Tschopik 1950:199). Today, we could justifiably echo his lament. While the study of colonial plastic and visual arts has flourished in recent years (e.g., Acevedo et al. 2004; Stastny 1981; Stastny and Acevedo 1986), scholars of colonial Peru still know very little about quotidian material culture of the sixteenth through eighteenth centuries. Yet we might also be forgiven for our ignorance, given how seldom the stuff of daily life is preserved in museum collections or described in archival documents.

The recent growth of historic-site (postcontact) archaeology in the Andes is providing a wealth of new data to address these questions. At Magdalena de Cao Viejo, exceptional conditions for organic preservation have permitted the recovery of basketry, textiles, wooden tools, gourd vessels, animal skins, paper, candles, and other perishable materials discarded by the site's former residents, generating a uniquely detailed picture of material life at the site. However, ceramics, that most ubiquitous of inorganic archaeological materials, still provide what are arguably the richest indices of daily praxis at Magdalena, mapping out activities through their formal qualities as well as their spatial distribution. Moreover, their chemical characterization provides a means of charting connections between communities of producers and consumers, allowing us to shed light on how household economies articulate with interregional exchange networks.

In this chapter, I argue that the use and exchange of ceramics at Magdalena de Cao Viejo played an active role in the construction of social and spatial distinctions at the site—most saliently, between commoners and clergy and between sacred and profane areas. I present the results of two types of analysis: chemical characterization of a small sample of decorated ceramics, and macroscopic examination of functional and decorative characteristics. Chemical characterization provides insights into Magdalena's connections with distinct spheres of production and circulation in the colonial economy, demonstrating that its occupants were (despite their ostensible social marginalization) tied into interregional trade networks. In turn, the macroscopic data map out significant differences in the spatial distribution of nonlocal ceramics within Magdalena de Cao, primarily between the church and town sectors. I interpret these patterns as evidence of clergy's greater access to nonlocal goods, and I suggest that the display of these materials in daily consumption events would have reinforced the social divide between clergy and commoners at the site.

The Assemblage

Over five field seasons at Magdalena de Cao Viejo, surface collection and excavation recovered 69,267 ceramic sherds. Following recovery and labeling, ceramic analysis began with the systematic study of diagnostic materials—whole vessels, decorated fragments, and sherds with enough evidence of form to allow reasonable reconstruction of vessel shape and function. The subset of diagnostic materials contained 12,918 sherds, or 18.6 percent of the total sample. Each was coded using a 45-part scheme initially developed to analyze materials from survey and excavations in the lower Zaña Valley (Torres 2011; VanValkenburgh 2012), which brought together elements of Wernke's (2013) schema for classifying colonial ceramics from the Colca Valley, Tschauner's (2001) typology of late prehispanic materials in the Lambayeque Valley, and references provided by the Florida Museum of Natural History Historical Archaeology Digital Type Collections. The vast majority of variation observed in the Magdalena sample was accurately described using attributes from the Zaña Valley typology, but as analysis progressed the team also added codes for new formal and decorative elements recorded in the Magdalena collection.

In addition to metrics (weight, vessel thickness, rim thickness, rim diameter, neck height), the coding scheme included classified values for ware, function, surface treatments, decoration, weathering, and multiple elements of rim, body, and basal forms. Major wares are discussed in detail below. Functional categories were assigned based on vessel form, surface treatment, and archaeological context—storage,[1] serving, cooking, transportation, cooking/storage, food processing (e.g., *rayadores*), and ceramic or metallurgical production (e.g., paddles or crucibles). The categories are discussed at greater length later in this chapter. Where vessel function could not be inferred based on these characteristics, it was listed as unknown.

Of the total sample population, including nondiagnostic materials, approximately 85 percent are thin-walled low-fired earthenwares, most lacking decoration. Macroscopic paste characterization and formal comparisons suggest that these ceramics were manufactured locally (see Chapter 9). Although most are undecorated, 6.5 percent contain paddle-stamped (*paleteado*) designs, and a subset of paddle-stamped wares are also slipped or painted. Together, plain and slipped paddle-made wares constitute nearly 40 percent of the sample of diagnostic materials, and are scarcely distinguishable from prehispanic ceramics produced in the Chicama Valley. The remaining 60 percent of the decorated ceramics from Magdalena have distinctive colonial forms and/or decorations, and they are dominated in counts and volume by fragments of *botijas* (olive jars). However, the sample also includes Ming Dynasty porcelain, a wide range of glazed earthenwares (including majolica of likely Panamanian manufacture), lead-glazed Early Green Glazed (EGG) Ware, and tin-enameled wares of unidentified provenance.

Paddle-Stamped Earthenwares (*Cerámica Paleteada*)

A total of 27.8 percent of diagnostic ceramics recovered in excavations at Magdalena de Cao Viejo are paddle-stamped earthenwares (*cerámica paleteada*), produced through paddle-and-anvil construction and decorated with simple motifs impressed into their surface by decorated paddles (see Chapter 9). As part of this technique, the potter forms a mass of clay around a rounded stone or ball of fired clay, gradually thinning it out by turning the mass around the stone and using a smooth wooden paddle to slap against its exterior (Stastny 1981:110). After molding the vessel, the potter may add decorations to its exterior using engraved paddles or stamps. At Magdalena, paddle-stamped decorations are diverse but dominated by simple crosshatched patterns and parallel lines. Paddle-stamped wares from the site are relatively thin, with a mean thickness of .6 cm.

According to Cleland and Shimada (1998), paddle-stamped wares first appeared in Late Moche (A.D. 700–800) contexts from the La Leche and Reque Valleys, and became nearly ubiquitous in sites within the Lambayeque Valley complex during Middle Sicán/Lambayeque (A.D. 800–1350) times. Throughout this period, the pastes, forms, and decorations of paddle-stamped wares were highly variable, and Cleland and Shimada interpret this variation as evidence that the type was produced in small, dispersed workshops. The history of paleteada production within the Chicama Valley is not as well known, but the type seems to first appear during the period of Lambayeque/Sicán expansion into the valley in the twelfth century. Diversity in macroscopic paste characteristics among paddle-stamped wares at Magdalena suggests that they continued to be produced in dispersed workshops in the lower Chicama Valley after the Spanish conquest, with few notable changes either in technical or decorative characteristics.

Slipped and Decorated Wares

While a majority of the paleteada fragments in the Magdalena de Cao Viejo diagnostic ceramic collection are unslipped and unpainted, a small number are decorated with red and brown slips or with post-fire white paints (referred to as "cream-slipped ware"). The associated vessel shapes are globular, but the necks are narrow, signaling their primary usage as storage vessels. Pastes among these wares are diverse as well, again suggesting that they were produced in a series of dispersed workshops.

Three dozen fragments of decorated redware were recovered in excavations at Magdalena de Cao Viejo. The type shares significant characteristics with Panama Redware, a form of ceramics with a well-fired brick-red paste and a fine red slip, which Jamieson and Hancock (2004:579–580) source to Panama la Vieja (see also Deagan 1987; Long 1967), but preliminary sourcing suggests that they were more likely made in Peru (Kelloway 2015). Other samples have been recovered from sixteenth- and seventeenth-century contexts in the Zaña Valley, Peru (VanValkenburgh 2012) and Cuenca, Ecuador (Jamieson and Hancock 2004). At Magdalena, only one decorated redware sherd was well preserved enough to allow its form (a brimmed plate) to be discerned.

Olive Jars (Botijas)

After paddle-stamped wares, fragments of *botijas* constitute the largest portion of the sample of diagnostic ceramic fragments recovered from Magdalena de Cao—22.4 percent by count and a considerably larger percentage by weight, due to their bulk. Labeled "olive jars" by North American archaeologists since the early twentieth century, botijas are the archetypal liquid storage and transport vessels of the Spanish Empire in the Americas (Goggin 1960:3) (see Figure 9.27 in Chapter 9). Their shapes are typically oblong, 20 to 30 cm across (following an axis parallel to vessel rim), and 50 to 60 cm long (perpendicular to the axis of the vessel rim), leading them to resemble olives in profile—the basis of their English name. Botija body fragments are relatively easy to recognize, due to their well-fired and sorted pastes (which are consistently pale orange with occasional light gray firing cores) and the deep wheel marks on the interior, which were impressed into them during turning. Goggin (1960:10) suggests that botija bodies were thrown in two separate sections (top and bottom) and that the rim was also thrown before all three portions were joined together. In contrast, Marken (1994:107) argues that botija bodies were fashioned in a single throwing, with only rims added later.

The relative flatness of the lower portion of their bodies would have allowed botijas to be stacked and laid flat on ships. Their size struck a balance between their ultimate purpose (storing and shipping considerable quantities of liquid) and the necessity of using human labor to move them on and off ships and the backs of beasts of burden—much like Greek or Roman amphorae, which were likely their forebears (Goggin 1960:5). Their narrow rim diameters (an average of 6.72 cm among 42 botija rim sherds in the Magdalena sample) and carinated rims allowed them to be sealed with plugs to prevent leakage, while thick walls (an average of 1.2 cm among the Magdalena sample) provided resistance against breakage. The fact that whole botijas are considerably larger than locally manufactured cooking pots may imply that recovered numbers of botija sherds overrepresent their importance in Magdalena's social life. However, the greater durability of botijas (which would not have been as easily broken as thinner cooking pots, and therefore not discarded as often) would have mitigated this problem.

Based on excavations of remains at circum-Caribbean sites, Goggin (1960) suggests that the shapes and rim forms of olive jars varied systematically over time, and that vessels can be arranged into one of three chronological types—Early (1500–1580), Middle (1580–1800), and Late (after 1800). Only Middle-style olive jar rims have been found in excavations at Magdalena de Cao Viejo, reinforcing the dates of foundation and abandonment for the site suggested by archival research (Castañeda 2006; see also Chapter 1 and Chapter 12). Sourcing studies show that some botijas found in New World archaeological sites were manufactured in Spain, while others were produced in metropolitan centers in Spanish America (e.g., Panama la Vieja) and wine-producing regions (Kelloway et al. 2014; Rice 1994, 2012). To date, we have not conducted chemical characterization of botija fragments from Magdalena de Cao Viejo, but future studies should allow for more precise understandings of their locations of manufacture and usage.

Panamanian Majolica

Between the second half of the sixteenth century and 1671, when the city was sacked and subsequently abandoned, Panama la Vieja was home to a community of potters that produced

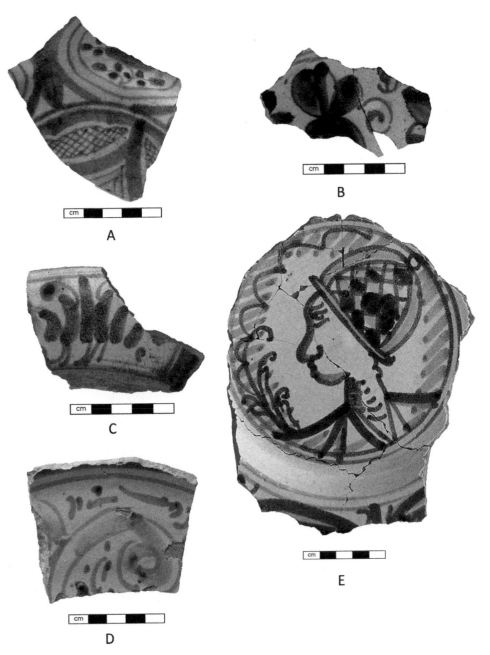

Figure 8.1 Panamanian majolica. A. Church, Unit 31, Level 3: flanged bowl interior fragment; B. Town, Unit 28, Capa A, Level 1: interior (?) body sherd; C. Town, surface find: exterior bowl rim; D. Church, Unit 12, Level 11: plate interior; E. Church, Unit 12, Level 2a: plate or bowl interior.

great quantities of tablewares that were traded extensively within the Viceroyalty of Peru (Deagan 1987; Lister and Lister 1974; Rovira 2001) (Figure 8.1). The city was strategically situated near the end of the portage that trading parties would have made when they crossed the isthmus of Panama en route to Peru from Spain or its Caribbean colonies, oftentimes carrying enslaved Africans from the market at Portobello, on Panama's Caribbean coast. Its position within the Viceroyalty of Peru meant that trade between Panamanian and Peruvian agents was less affected by the periodic prohibition against trade between viceroyalties, legislated at various times in the late sixteenth and early seventeenth centuries (Skowronek 1992). Chemical characterization studies have identified tin-enameled wares of Panamanian origin in highland Ecuador and in the Moquegua Valley, on Peru's South Coast (Rice 1997, 2012, 2013, 2016), and as far afield as the Solomon Islands (Kelloway et al. 2016). In addition, macroscopic paste characterization suggests that Panamanian wares were abundant in seventeenth-century households in the city of Lima (Miguel Fhon, personal communication).

Potters in Panama la Vieja produced a wide variety of wares, but it was their tin-enameled earthenwares (majolicas) that seem to have generated the greatest demand within the viceroyalty. These materials are consistently fired, with a well-sorted brick red paste and no firing cores visible in cross section. Their surfaces are covered with a thin white glaze, made opaque through the inclusion of tin—a technology developed by at least the ninth century in the Middle East and popularized in Spain and Italy during later centuries (Goggin 1968:5). Long (1964, 1967) distinguishes between four subtypes of Panamanian majolica, based on surface decoration: Panama Plain, whose glaze is undecorated; Panama Blue-on-White, which includes decorations in light blue; Panama Polychrome A, whose decorations are rendered in light blue, green, and manganese-brown paint; and Panama Polychrome B, with light blue, light green, and occasional yellow or orange accents. Pottery so decorated included various forms of tablewares (and chamber pots), but the brimmed *plato*—a relatively deep-bodied plate, with a wide decorated brim—appears to have been the most popular.

Mogrovejo (1996) argues that scholars have overestimated the ubiquity of Panamanian wares in Andean sites—and, indeed, that much tin-glazed earthenware labeled "Panamanian" may in fact have been produced in Lima. Although his contestation that far too little is known about the production of glazed pottery in Peru still rings true, several lines of evidence suggest that vast quantities of majolica were indeed produced in Panama la Vieja, and that a great deal of this material ended up in Peruvian sites. While large kilns at Panama la Vieja appear to have been destroyed in the 1950s (Long 1964, 1967), spacers and saggars have been recovered from the site, and its domestic contexts contain prodigious amounts of majolica (Rovira 2001; Rovira et al. 2006). Moreover, the mineralogy of these materials is consistent with the andesitic geology of the region around Panama la Vieja (VanValkenburgh 2009).

The majority of tin-enameled fragments recovered from Magdalena de Cao Viejo— upward of 90 percent of 760 total glazed fragments—possess pastes, decorations, and morphological characteristics that fit within the parameters of Panamanian majolica. Of these, brimmed plates dominate identifiable forms, and nearly 70 percent (530 fragments) have blue-on-white decoration. Later in this chapter I present characterization data that reinforce this interpretation; however, it is clear that additional types of tin-glazed earthenwares (many of them likely produced in the central Andes) were also employed at Magdalena.

Porcelain

With its fine, completely vitrified paste and delicate build, the porcelain in the Magdalena de Cao Viejo assemblage is easily distinguished from the tin-glazed earthenwares whose white surfaces and floral decorations were ultimately (if distantly) inspired by it. The technical and material requirements for producing porcelain—sustained high temperatures (1300–1450 degrees C) and refined kaolinite clays (Rice 1987)—were beyond the achievement of both Middle Eastern and European potters for hundreds of years, and long-distance trade with China proved the only way of gaining access to porcelain until the late eighteenth century. Portuguese traders in the early sixteenth century provided an inroad into Chinese markets, and early Chinese export porcelain is sometimes known as Kraak ware, purportedly in reference to Portuguese ships called carracks (Rinaldi 1989) It was not until the Spanish conquest of the Philippines and the establishment of the yearly galleon trade between Manila and Acapulco, however, that porcelain became widely available in the Spanish colonies (Deagan 1987:96). During the Ming (to 1644) and Qing (1644–1911) dynasties, producers in the Pearl River delta region crafted porcelain specifically for export, and it is these varieties were widely circulated in the Spanish Americas.

In Peruvian coastal sites dating to the late sixteenth and seventeenth centuries, archaeologists have found modest amounts of porcelain in domestic assemblages, including among remains of reduccións in the Zaña and Chamán Valleys and at the site of Piura la Vieja (Astuhuamán 2016; Fhon 2016; VanValkenburgh 2012). At Magdalena de Cao Viejo, excavations recovered only 38 fragments of porcelain, which were nearly evenly divided between the church (20 fragments) and town (18 fragments) sectors of the site—a percentage of the total assemblage roughly comparable to that recovered in the Zaña Valley sites (Figure 8.2). While fragments of Ming-period vessels predominate, several fragments of Qing-period porcelain are also present, and all identifiable vessel types are plates with narrow brims and thin-walled cups.[2]

Early Green Glazed (EGG) Ware

Early Green Glazed (EGG) Ware vessels are a unique variety of ceramics produced in Peru's North Coast region during the sixteenth century. The vessels have primarily prehispanic forms with surfaces covered with a thin lead glaze. Among complete vessels from museum collections, the most common forms are double-bodied whistling jars, with smaller numbers of animal-shaped pitchers, eccentric forms, and flat-bottomed pitchers with no prehispanic precedents (Acevedo et al. 2004; Bushnell 1959). Glaze color ranges from light yellow to dark green, and this appears to result from impurities in the lead ores that were ground up to produce glaze paints, rather than additional colorants. Our chemical analysis of EGG Ware glazes from Magdalena de Cao Viejo, presented in this section, indicates that they are composed of 70–85 percent lead oxide.

At Magdalena, excavations in the town sector recovered 121 fragments of EGG Ware, exclusively in strata corresponding to the site's earliest decades of occupation, in the late sixteenth (and perhaps early seventeenth) century (Figure 8.3). Research at colonial sites in the lower Zaña Valley has similarly recovered EGG Ware exclusively from contexts with termini post quem before the seventeenth century (VanValkenburgh 2012). The fact that EGG Ware was recovered from middens and domestic fills at Magdalena de Cao Viejo and sites in the lower Zaña Valley demonstrates that the type was used in domestic settings. However, whole vessels in museum collections (such as those held at the Museo Rafael Larco Herrera and the Museo de la Nación) were likely recovered from mortuary contexts, which may imply either that vessels were used in domestic settings before being interred with burials or that different EGG Ware vessel types were designated for use in domestic and burial contexts.

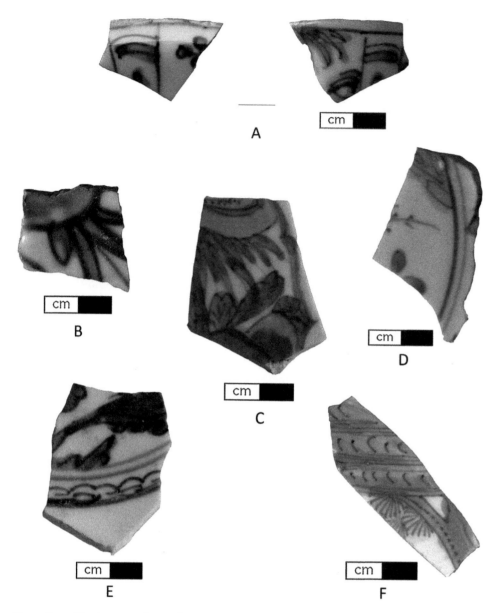

Figure 8.2 Kraak ware and porcelain. A. Town, Unit 2, Capa B, Level 3, exterior (left), interior (right); B. Town, Unit 28, Capa A, Level 3; C, D, E, and F. Surface finds from the town.

While EGG Ware vessels frequently have been displayed in museum exhibits, where they typically serve as iconic representations of the Spanish conquest's effects on native material culture and lifeways, the type has never before been subject to systematic study, and the technologies employed to produce it are poorly understood. Because glazes are unknown among ceramics from precolumbian Andean contexts, several authors have speculated that the production of EGG Ware might have been spawned by direct technology transfer from Spanish potters to native artisans, where the former instructed the latter in how to produce lead-glazed vessels (Bushnell 1959; Mayer 1983; Mogrovejo 1996). A corollary assumption is

Figure 8.3
Sherds of Early Green Glazed (EGG) Ware often are small and fragmentary, but the bird whistle shown here (Unit 28, Capa A, Level 2) still bears traces of the glaze on its surface.

that EGG Ware was fired in kilns—a technology unknown in late prehispanic workshops on the North Coast (though see Wagner et al. 1999 for a description of North Coast kilns dating to 2700 B.C.). However, given its heavily lead-based composition, EGG Ware glaze could have achieved pseudo-vitrification at temperatures as low as 800 degrees C—well within the range of the open bonfires used in the production of late prehispanic ceramics in North Coast workshops (Cleland and Shimada 1998; VanValkenburgh et al. 2017; Yamunaqué 1979).

Macroscopic study of whole vessels and fragments make it clear that the producers of Early Green Glazed Ware had yet to fully master the process of firing lead-glazed pottery. Of two dozen examples of whole vessels that the author has examined in museum collections in Peru and the United States, virtually all display evidence of potters' imperfect mastery of the firing process—pinholing (a product of under- or overfiring), crawling (glaze recession, leaving behind bare clay, which may be the result of differential expansion of the underlying ceramic fabric during a single firing episode), and running and pooling (evidence of over- or underfiring). Together with their conservation of prehispanic vessel forms, these defects suggest that the producers of EGG Ware were experimenting with glaze compositions and firing conditions and may not have been directly supervised by European potters. Still, further research is necessary to assess the firing technology employed in the production of EGG Ware.

Chemical Composition of EGG Ware and Tin-Enameled Wares

Chemical characterization of the glazes of both tin-enameled wares and EGG wares from Magdalena de Cao Viejo has offered further insight into how these two major types of ceramics were used at the site. Following excavation, project researchers selected 41 ceramic samples from Magdalena de Cao Viejo for study using laser ablation inductively coupled plasma mass spectrometry (LA-ICP-MS)—19 EGG Ware sherds and 22 samples of tin-enameled wares. In addition, the project selected two sets of samples from other sites to allow for interregional comparisons—25 samples of EGG Ware excavated at sites in the Zaña Valley and 19 samples of majolica from Panama la Vieja, collected by Long (1964, 1967) and made available for study by the Florida Museum of Natural History. Characterizing glazes allowed us to shed light both on the organization of ceramic production (through the identification of chemical groups through trace elemental composition) and on technological requirements for glaze production.

Sampling was carried out at the Elemental Analysis Facility at the Field Museum of Natural History, using an Analytik Jena inductively coupled plasma mass spectrometer connected to a New Wave UP213 laser for direct introduction of solid samples, with guidance from Dr. Laure Dussubieux. Helium was used as a gas carrier in the laser, and scan line analysis mode was selected. To clean the surface of the glaze, a pre-ablation was conducted with a laser beam diameter of 100 μm, a speed of 70 μm/s, and a pulse frequency of 20 Hz. The beam diameter for the actual ablation was 65 μm, and it was used with a speed of 5 μm/s and a frequency of 15 Hz. For each glaze sample, the average of four measurements corrected from the blank was considered for the calculation of concentrations. A total of 48 element concentrations were determined: Li, Be, B, Sc, Ti, V, Cr, Fe, Mn, Ni, Co, Cu, Zn, As, Rb, Sr, Zr, Nb, Ag, In, Sn, Sb, Cs, Ba, La, Ce, Pr, Ta, Au, Y, Pb, Bi, U, W, Mo, Nd, Sm, Eu, Gd, Tb, Dy, Ho, Er, Tm, Yb, Lu, Hf, Th. For additional details, see procedures outlined in Dussubieux et al. 2009.

EGG wares and tin-enameled wares were studied separately, with four to five samples loaded into the sampling chamber at a time. Surface areas with the thickest observable glaze were targeted for sampling, in order to increase the chances that readings would be obtained from glazes rather than underlying pastes. While this strategy registered very high levels of lead oxide in a majority of the sample glazes, several outlier data points with a relatively high percentage composition of silicon oxide (EGG Ware samples MDC2011-54-05, MDC2011-46-08, MDC2011-126-13) suggest that it was not perfect. For tin-enameled wares, sampling targeted the glaze background rather than decorated glaze areas. Calculation of elemental concentrations followed the protocol outlined by Gratuze (1999).

The resulting data were subjected to principal components analysis (PCA). PCA and elemental bivariate plots were used to determine chemical groupings. Statistical analyses were performed using Statistica (v. 7.0), MURR GAUSS routines (v. 8), and Microsoft Excel 2007, with JMP (v. 10.0.0) used to create figures. Zn, As, Ag, In, Sb, and Bi were excluded from the analysis, due to their high variability in concentration and their tendency to associate with lead, which was excluded due to its overwhelming concentration in some samples (up to 80 percent). In some cases, high Pb concentrations may have swamped trace elemental patterns in the data. Gold (Au) was also excluded due to low concentrations and detection limits. Further details regarding LA-ICP-MS data processing are available in VanValkenburgh et al. 2015.

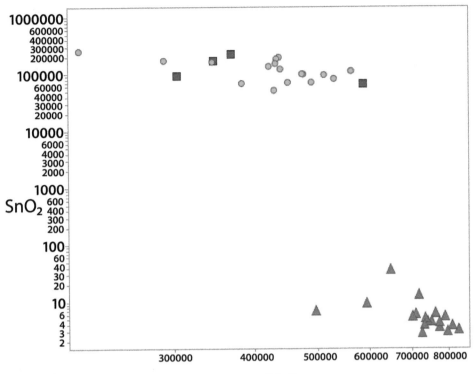

Figure 8.4
Biplot of tin oxide
and lead oxide
composition (in
ppm) in EGG Ware
and tin-enameled
wares.

Glazed Ceramic Type
▲ Magdalena de Cao - EGG Ware
■ Magdalena de Cao - Other Majolica
● Magdalena de Cao - Panamanian Majolica

The results demonstrate an expectedly wide separation between the EGG wares and the tin-enameled wares, but also reveal intragroup variation (Figure 8.4). The sampled tin-enameled ware glazes register between 3.65 and 21.2 percent tin oxide by composition, while lead oxide (PbO_2) composition of EGG Ware glazes ranges from 70.2 to 83.1 percent. A biplot of parts-per-million lead oxide and tin oxide in the composition of EGG Ware and tin-enameled wares displays broad differences between the two types (Figure 8.4). Ultimately, the high lead composition of EGG Ware glazes would have allowed this material to vitrify at much lower temperatures than tin-enameled wares—as low as 500 degrees C, well below the temperature required to fire clay to maturation. The idea that EGG Ware was kiln-fired is thus problematic, and EGG Ware fabrics should be subject to systematic study in order to further describe the technology used to fire them.

Analysis of trace elemental composition of glazes from these two types of ceramics offers a number of insights into their patterns of production and circulation. EGG Ware from Magdalena displays some heterogeneity in trace elemental composition, but broad separation between these and samples from sites in the Zaña Valley. A biplot of magnesium and calcium oxides outlines this separation, demonstrating minimal overlap between the 95 percent confidence ellipses of the Magdalena and Zaña samples (Figure 8.5). In PCA, the first seven principal components can be used to explain 89.2 percent of the total variation in the sample (Figure 8.6). Overall, less variation is present in the composition of the samples from

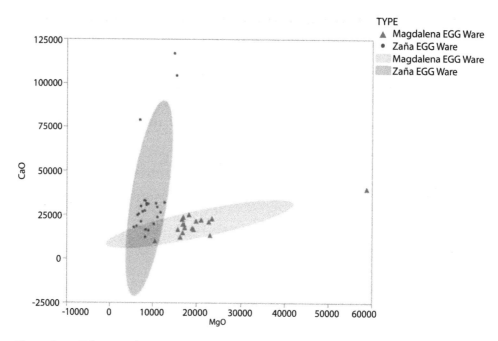

Figure 8.5 Calcium and magnesium oxide concentrations (in ppm) in EGG Ware from Magdalena de Cao Viejo and sites in the Zaña Valley.

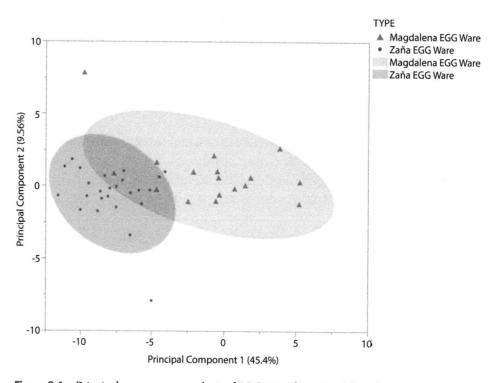

Figure 8.6 Principal-components analysis of EGG Ware from Magdalena de Cao and sites in the Zaña Valley.

Magdalena de Cao, suggesting that the recipes and/or raw materials used to produce them were more consistent than those present among the Zaña Valley samples. Notably, the two sets of samples also fall into two compositional groups, which align with geography, with separation between glazes on samples from the Zaña Valley and glazes from samples from Magdalena de Cao. These patterns suggest that diverse materials and/or recipes were used to produce the ceramic glazes, perhaps because the lead ore exploited to produce them was procured from two distinct regional sources. It is worth noting, however, that two samples from the Zaña Valley fall within the 95 percent confidence ellipse of the Magdalena sample group, suggesting that either ceramics themselves or raw materials were circulated between the two valleys during early colonial times (see also VanValkenburgh et al. 2015).

Trace elemental composition of the glazes of tin-enameled ware samples from Magdalena de Cao Viejo suggests that most of these ceramics were produced at Panama la Vieja. Of 19 samples selected for characterization, 15 were categorized as Panamanian, based on macroscopic characteristics of pastes and glazes. A further four samples were assigned to the category "other majolica" based on deviations in paste and glaze characteristics from Panamanian standards. Statistical analysis of trace elemental data shows some differences in composition between the two types. A biplot of magnesium oxide (MgO) and calcium oxide shows some enrichment in MgO within the Magdalena samples compared to the samples from Panama la Vieja (Figure 8.7), and PCA reveals that two "non-Panamanian" samples, MDC2011-113-54-23/PVV025 and MDC2011-135-49-18/PVV027, are outliers (Figure 8.8). Comparison with ceramics recovered from the Solomon Islands and Panama la Vieja suggests that these sherds may be fragments of tin-glazed vessels produced in Peru (Kelloway et al. 2018). Elsewhere, Rice (2012) has identified tin-enameled wares from Colonial Period sites in the Moquegua Valley that group separately from Panamanian majolica, and interprets them as being Peruvian-made. However, these outlier

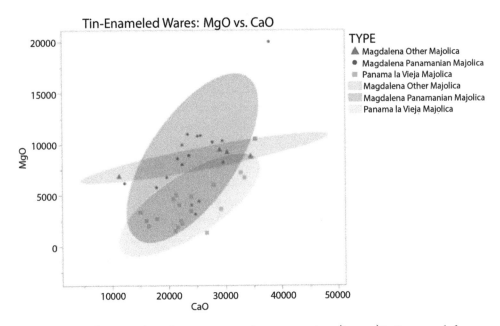

Figure 8.7 Calcium oxide and magnesium oxide concentrations (in ppm) in tin-enameled wares from Magdalena de Cao Viejo and Panama la Vieja.

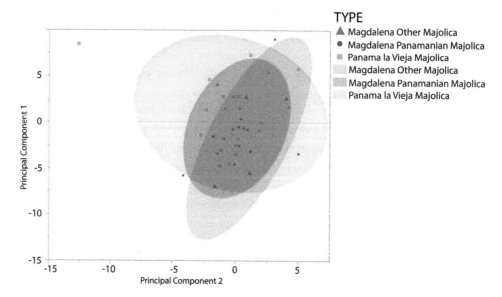

Figure 8.8   Principal-components analysis of tin-enameled wares from Magdalena de Cao Viejo and Panama la Vieja.

samples appear typologically distinct from Rice's Peruvian-made tin-enameled wares, and additional characterization of tin-enameled ceramics from Peruvian metropolitan centers is necessary before more specific conclusions can be drawn about where they may have been produced.

Intrasite Distribution Patterns

As Quilter outlines in Chapter 2, excavations at Magdalena de Cao Viejo concentrated on two primary areas of the site—the church sector (comprising the church itself, the atrium, the cemetery, and the cloister) and the town (where three separate structures and one isolated midden were targeted for investigation). Excavations in the church sector produced 60 percent of all ceramics in the sample—largely from middens, cooking areas, and storage areas in the cloister. In the town sector, materials were recovered from diverse domestic contexts, including smaller middens immediately associated with houses. Based on typological associations and stratigraphy, the vast majority of the collection dates to the site's occupations in the seventeenth through the early eighteenth century occupations, rather than its earliest decades.

Virtually all of the ceramic types in the collection are present in both the church and town sector assemblages (Figure 8.9)—plainwares, slipped wares, porcelain, olive jars, and tin-glazed earthenwares. Only one type (EGG Ware) was limited to a single site sector (the town), where it was recovered in lower levels of each of three substantial horizontal excavation units (Units 1, 2, and 28).

Despite these continuities, significant differences appear in the proportions of wares recovered from the town and church sectors. While plainwares constitute the largest percentage of materials from both sectors of the site, they constitute a much larger portion (68.1 percent) of the material recovered from the town sector than the church sector (48.5 percent). Conversely, greater numbers of both tin-glazed earthenwares and olive jars are found in the church precinct.

Distribution of Wares by Sector and Unit

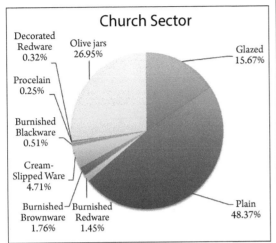

Church Sector

Decorated Redware 0.32%
Olive jars 26.95%
Glazed 15.67%
Procelain 0.25%
Burnished Blackware 0.51%
Cream-Slipped Ware 4.71%
Burnished Brownware 1.76%
Burnished Redware 1.45%
Plain 48.37%

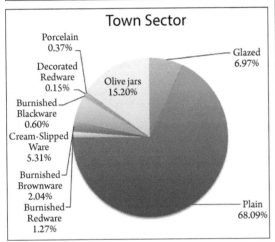

Town Sector

Porcelain 0.37%
Decorated Redware 0.15%
Olive jars 15.20%
Glazed 6.97%
Burnished Blackware 0.60%
Cream-Slipped Ware 5.31%
Burnished Brownware 2.04%
Burnished Redware 1.27%
Plain 68.09%

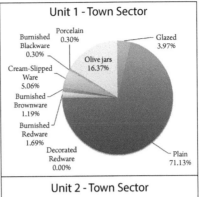

Unit 1 - Town Sector

Porcelain 0.30%
Burnished Blackware 0.30%
Glazed 3.97%
Olive jars 16.37%
Cream-Slipped Ware 5.06%
Burnished Brownware 1.19%
Burnished Redware 1.69%
Decorated Redware 0.00%
Plain 71.13%

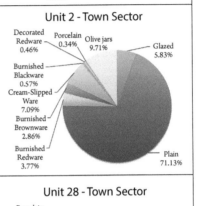

Unit 2 - Town Sector

Decorated Redware 0.46%
Porcelain 0.34%
Olive jars 9.71%
Glazed 5.83%
Burnished Blackware 0.57%
Cream-Slipped Ware 7.09%
Burnished Brownware 2.86%
Burnished Redware 3.77%
Plain 71.13%

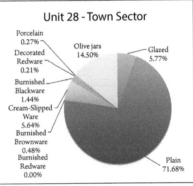

Unit 28 - Town Sector

Porcelain 0.27%
Decorated Redware 0.21%
Olive jars 14.50%
Glazed 5.77%
Burnished Blackware 1.44%
Cream-Slipped Ware 5.64%
Burnished Brownware 0.48%
Burnished Redware 0.00%
Plain 71.68%

Figure 8.9
Distribution of wares by sector and major town units.

While glazed earthenwares account for 15.7 percent of the ceramics recovered from the church sector, they make up only 7 percent of material from the town. Similarly, olive jars constitute 27 percent of all church sector ceramics but only 15.2 percent of the town sector assemblage. By implication, because neither olive jars nor glazed earthenwares appear to have been produced near Magdalena de Cao Viejo, ceramics from the church sector include a much greater percentage of nonlocal materials than ceramics from domestic units in the town. Notably, however, both sectors contained equal (but minimal) amounts of porcelain.

Comparison of the ceramic assemblages from the three major domestic units in the town sector reveals minimal differences in the relative proportions of wares. The assemblage from Unit 2 has a smaller percentage of olive jars (9.7 percent) than Unit 1 (16.4 percent) and Unit 28 (14.5 percent). Moreover, Unit 1 contains a slightly smaller percentage of glazed earthenwares (4 percent) than Unit 2 (5.8 percent) and Unit 28 (5.8 percent).

Proportions of functional types also differ between the town and church precincts (see Figure 8.10). The church assemblage contains higher percentages of both serving vessels

Distribution of Functional Types by Sector and Unit

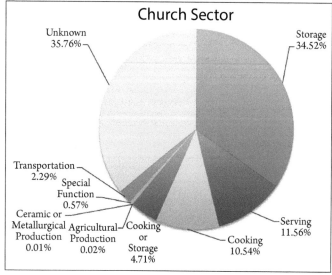

Church Sector

- Unknown 35.76%
- Storage 34.52%
- Transportation 2.29%
- Special Function 0.57%
- Ceramic or Metallurgical Production 0.01%
- Agricultural Production 0.02%
- Cooking or Storage 4.71%
- Cooking 10.54%
- Serving 11.56%

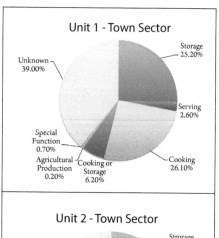

Unit 1 - Town Sector

- Unknown 39.00%
- Storage 25.20%
- Serving 2.60%
- Cooking 26.10%
- Cooking or Storage 6.20%
- Agricultural Production 0.20%
- Special Function 0.70%

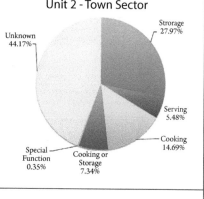

Unit 2 - Town Sector

- Unknown 44.17%
- Strorage 27.97%
- Serving 5.48%
- Cooking 14.69%
- Cooking or Storage 7.34%
- Special Function 0.35%

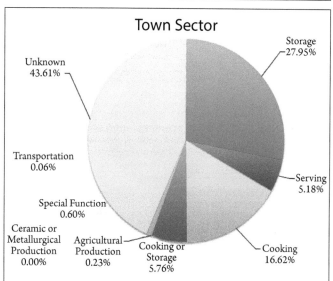

Town Sector

- Unknown 43.61%
- Storage 27.95%
- Transportation 0.06%
- Special Function 0.60%
- Ceramic or Metallurgical Production 0.00%
- Agricultural Production 0.23%
- Cooking or Storage 5.76%
- Cooking 16.62%
- Serving 5.18%

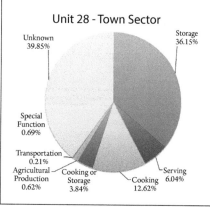

Unit 28 - Town Sector

- Unknown 39.85%
- Storage 36.15%
- Special Function 0.69%
- Transportation 0.21%
- Agricultural Production 0.62%
- Cooking or Storage 3.84%
- Cooking 12.62%
- Serving 6.04%

Figure 8.10 Distribution of functional types within site sectors and major domestic units.

(11.6 percent) and storage vessels (34.5 percent) than the town sector (5.2 percent serving vessels and 28 percent storage vessels, respectively) (see Figure 8.9). In contrast, cooking pots constitute a greater percentage of the town sector assemblage (16.1 percent) than the church collection (10.5 percent). The grinding stone and two large ovens in the eastern church sector leave little doubt that a good deal of food was prepared in this precinct during its latter phases, but the differences in the ceramic assemblage suggest that display and storage were more central to food practices in the church sector than in the town. Nevertheless, vessels themselves seem to differ little between the two sectors. Cooking pots from both the church and the town are thin-walled locally made vessels, and a two-tailed student's t-test of the rim diameters[3] of cooking vessels from the church ($M = 12.96$ cm, $SD = 6.58$ cm) and town ($M = 13.62$ cm, $SD = 7.4$ cm) is not statistically significant, at $t(1715) = 1.929, p = .0539$.

The functional characteristics of ceramics also vary between domestic units in the town sector. Unit 1's assemblage includes a greater percentage of cooking vessels (26.1 percent) and a smaller percentage of serving vessels (2.6 percent) than assemblages from Unit 2 (14.7 percent cooking, 5.5 percent serving) and Unit 28 (12.6 percent cooking, 6 percent serving). In addition, the Unit 28 assemblage includes a greater percentage of storage vessels (36.2 percent) than collections from Unit 1 (25.2 percent) and Unit 2 (28 percent)—a pattern that is paralleled by the recovery in Unit 28 of several large in-situ storage vessels covered with carved gourd tops (see Chapter 9).

I interpret the variation in distribution of wares and functional types in the town sector as evidence of differences in household subsistence. In addition to yielding fewer glazed ceramics and a greater percentage of cooking vessels than other units within the site, ceramic materials from Unit 1 are also generally smaller. The mean rim diameter of cooking vessels recovered from Unit 1 ($M = 12.73$ cm, $SD = 6.22$ cm) is significantly less than that of cooking vessels from Unit 28 ($M = 16.37$ cm, $SD = 8.04$ cm; $p < .05$) and also less than that of cooking vessels from Unit 2 ($M = 13.53$ cm, $SD = 8.75$ cm; $p = .058$). Similarly, storage vessels from Unit 1 average 15.23 cm in diameter ($SD = 8.47$ cm), compared to 18.11 cm in Unit 28 ($SD = 8.64$ cm), $t(459) = 3.0694$. Inversely, cooking and storage vessels from Unit 28 are significantly larger, on average, than those from Unit 1, and cooking vessels from Unit 28 are significantly larger than cooking vessels from both Unit 1 and Unit 2. The fact that the floor areas of each of these houses are comparable suggests that differences in average vessel size cannot be interpreted as straightforward evidence of scalar differences in households. Therefore, variation in vessel size may reflect different patterns of food preparation and subsistence strategies, with Unit 28's residents preparing larger meals and storing greater amounts of food over time than the household(s) in Unit 1.

Discussion and Conclusions

The chemical characterization and spatial distribution of ceramics within Magdalena de Cao Viejo suggest that ceramics played an active role in the establishment of social networks between Magdalena and distant communities, as well as the production of distinction within it. For members of a supposedly marginal indigenous community, Magdalena's families acquired a wide range of foreign goods—and not simply as curios that enhanced the prestige of one or two elite individuals but as items that were central to daily consumption events across all of the households whose remains have been sampled to date. In the seventeenth and early eighteenth centuries, Magdalena's indigenous residents ate meals on locally made serving vessels, Chinese porcelain, and Panamanian majolica, and they stored foods and liquids in both locally produced containers and Spanish-made olive jars. While the forms and dimensions of cooking vessels from the town sector suggest that Magdalena's residents did retain aspects of prehispanic traditions of food preparation (see Chapter 3 and Chapter 9), the rapid incorporation of foreign materials into domestic assemblages and the presence of a wide range of new foods in the local diet make it clear that the town's domestic sphere was not more culturally conservative than its public sphere (cf. Deagan 1974). Magdalena's households gained access to nonlocal materials because, rather than being insulated from the colonial economy, they were integral to it. Magdaleneros performed a wide variety of economic roles, from laboring on nearby haciendas to working as porters and muleteers delivering agricultural and pastoral goods to markets in the nearby city of Trujillo (see Chapter 12).

At the same time, characterization of Early Green Glazed Ware suggests that not all nonlocal ceramics at Magdalena de Cao were purchased from Spanish markets. Minimal overlap between the chemical composition of EGG wares from Magdalena and from sites in the Zaña Valley suggests that at least a small amount of this material may have moved back and forth between these two regions (VanValkenburgh et al. 2015). The recovery of EGG Ware from sites as distant from the North Coast as Laguna de Los Cóndores, in Chachapoyas (Guillen 1999), leaves little doubt that the type was widely circulated during the late sixteenth century and that it was entailed in the perpetuation of indigenous burial practices and rituals. However, characterization of a larger number of EGG Ware samples from North Coast sites will be necessary in order to chart regional patterns of production and circulation in more detail.

Ceramics also contributed to the construction of social and spatial distinctions between clergy and commoners, and between the church and town sectors of Magdalena de Cao Viejo. The monumentality of the church and its placement atop the plaza of a Moche period huaca immediately differentiated it from the town, but daily consumption events in the cloister would have reinforced the separation between these two areas of the site. Our analysis suggests that Magdalena's Dominican priests prepared food, ate meals, and stored goods using a range of ceramics similar to those found in the town sector, but they seem to have eaten more frequently on imported glazed plates than Magdalena's indigenous townspeople. The high numbers of storage vessels recovered from the church sector demonstrates that they also stored more goods than their parishioners—perhaps because the town's indigenous people were legally required to provide priests with comestibles in exchange for their ministry.

NOTES

1 Olive jars were coded as "storage" rather than "transportation" vessels, based on the expectation that the majority of olive jar fragments found in middens and domestic contexts in the church and town sectors at Magdalena de Cao Viejo came from vessels that were retained and reused in or near these contexts to store foods, rather than being continually reused for transporting goods.

2 Images of porcelain fragments recovered from excavations at Magdalena de Cao Viejo are available on the project website at https://www.peabody.harvard.edu/Magdalena.

3 I assume here that rim diameter size correlates with vessel volume, if ware and functional type are consistent.

REFERENCES CITED

Acevedo Basurto, Sara, Fernando Torres, and Pedro Pablo Alayza
    2004 *La loza de la tierra: cerámica vidriada en el Perú.* Lima: Universidad Ricardo Palma.

Astuhuamán Gonzalez, Cesar
    2016 Fundación, esplendor y colapso de la Iglesia de San Miguel de Piura (1534–1578), primer templo del Perú. *Boletin de Arqueología PUCP* 21:39–58.

Bushnell, Geoffrey
   1959   Some Post-Columbian Whistling Jars from Peru. *Actas del XXXIII Congreso de Americanistas*, pp. 416–420 (San José, Costa Rica: Lehmann).

Castañeda Murga, Juan
   2006   Etnohistória de Magdalena de Cao, informe de investigación. Report prepared for Jeffrey Quilter. On file in Peabody Museum of Archaeology and Ethnology, Cambridge, MA.

Cleland, Katherine M., and Izumi Shimada
   1998   Paleteada Potters: Technology, Production Sphere, and Sub-Culture in Ancient Peru. *MASCA Research Papers in Science and Archaeology* 15:111–152.

Deagan, Kathleen A.
   1974   Sex, Status and Role in the Meztizaje of Spanish Colonial Florida. Unpublished Ph.D. dissertation, Department of Anthropology, University of Florida, Gainesville.
   1987   *Artifacts of the Spanish Colonies of Florida and the Caribbean, 1500–1800*, vol. 1, *Ceramics, Glassware, and Beads*. Washington, DC: Smithsonian Institution Press.

Dussubieux, Laure, Peter Robertshaw, and Micheal D. Glascock
   2009   LA-ICP-MS Analysis of African Glass Beads: Laboratory Inter-Comparison with an Emphasis on the Impact of Corrosion on Data Interpretation. *International Journal of Mass Spectrometry* 284(1–3):152–161.

Fhon Bazán, Miguel
   2016   Espacios públicos y domésticos: Transformaciones de la casa bodega y quadra en relación a la traza urbana de Lima (siglos XVI–XIX). *Boletín de Arqueología PUCP* 21:147–166.

Goggin, John M.
   1960   *The Spanish Olive Jar: An Introductory Study*. Yale University Publications in Anthropology 62. New Haven, CT: Yale University Press.
   1968   *Spanish Majolica in the New World: Types of the Sixteenth to Eighteenth Centuries*. Yale University Publications in Anthropology 72. New Haven, CT: Yale University Press.

Gratuze, Bernard
   1999   Obsidian Characterization by Laser Ablation ICP-MS and Its Application to Prehistoric Trade in the Mediterranean and the Near East: Sources and Distribution of Obsidian Within the Aegean and Anatolia. *Journal of Archaeological Science* 26(8):869–881.

Guillen, Sonia E.
   1999   Arqueología de emergencia: Inventario, catalogación y conservación de los materiales arqueológicos de los mausoleos de la Laguna de Los Cóndores. Archaeological Research Report. Instituto Nacional de Cultura, Lima, Peru.

Jamieson, Ross W., and R. G. V. Hancock
   2004   Neutron Activation Analysis of Colonial Ceramics from Southern Highland Ecuador. *Archaeometry* 46(4):569–583.

Kelloway, Sarah J.
   2015   PAZC 2015 PXRF Report. Analytical Report. University of New South Wales, Sydney, Australia.

Kelloway, Sarah J., Steven Craven, Mark Pecha, et al.
   2014   Sourcing Olive Jars Using U-Pb Ages of Detrital Zircons: A Study of 16th Century Olive Jars Recovered from the Solomon Islands. *Geoarchaeology* 29(1):47–60.

Kelloway, Sarah J., Timothy J. Ferguson, Javier García Iñañez, Parker VanValkenburgh, Cody Roush, and Michael Glascock

    2016   Sherds on the Edge: Characterisation of Spanish Colonial Pottery from the Solomon Islands. *Archaeometry* 58(4):549–573.

Kelloway, Sarah, Parker VanValkenburgh, Javier Iñañez, Laure Dussubieux, Jeffrey Quilter, and Michael D. Glascock

    2018   Identifying Andean-Made Majolica from 16th–18th Century Sites on Peru's North Coast. *Journal of Archaeological Science: Reports* 17:311–324.

Kubler, George Alexander

    1946   The Quechua in the Colonial World. In *Handbook of South American Indians*, vol. 2, edited by Julian H. Steward, pp. 331–410. Washington, DC: Smithsonian Institution.

Lister, Florence C., and Robert H. Lister

    1974   Maiolica in Colonial Spanish America. *Historical Archaeology* 8(1):17–52.

Long, George A.

    1964   Excavations at Panama la Vieja. *Florida Anthropologist* 17(2):104–109.

    1967   Archaeological Investigations at Panama la Vieja. Unpublished M.A. thesis, Department of Anthropology, University of Florida, Gainesville.

Marken, Mitchell W.

    1994   *Pottery from Spanish Shipwrecks, 1500–1800*. Gainesville: University Press of Florida.

Mogrovejo Rosales, J. D.

    1996   *Arqueología urbana de evidencias coloniales en la ciudad de Lima*. Cuadernos de Investigación. Lima: Pontificia Universidad Católica del Perú, Instituto Riva-Agüero.

Rice, Prudence M.

    1987   *Pottery Analysis: A Sourcebook*. Chicago: University of Chicago Press.

    1994   The Kilns of Moquegua, Peru: Technology, Excavations, and Functions. *Journal of Field Archaeology* 21(3):325–344.

    1997   Tin-Enameled Wares of Moquegua, Peru. In *Approaches to the Historical Archaeology of Mexico, Central and South America*, edited by Janine Gasco, Greg C. Smith, and Patricia Fournier García, pp. 173–180. Los Angeles: Institute of Archaeology, UCLA.

    2012   *Vintage Moquegua: History, Wine, and Archaeology on a Colonial Peruvian Periphery*. Austin: University of Texas Press.

    2013   Political-Ecology Perspectives on New World Loza (Majolica). *International Journal of Historical Archaeology* 17(4):651–683.

    2016   Algunas perspectivas político-ecológicas sobre la loza andina. *Boletín de Arqueología PUCP* 20:51–66.

Rinaldi, Maura

    1989   *Kraak Porcelain: A Moment in the History of Trade*. London: Bamboo Publishers.

Rovira, Beatriz E.

    2001   Presencia de mayólicas panameñas en el mundo colonial: Algunas consideraciones acerca de su distribución y cronología. *Latin American Antiquity* 12(3):291–303.

Rovira, Beatriz E., James Blackman, Lambertus van Zelst, et al.

    2006   Caracterización química de cerámicas coloniales del sitio de Panamá Viejo. *Canto Rodado* 1:101–131.

Skowronek, Russell K.

    1992 Empire and Ceramics: The Changing Role of Illicit Trade in Spanish America. *Historical Archaeology* 26(1):109–118.

Stastny, Francisco

    1981 *Las artes populares del Perú.* Madrid: Ediciones Edubanco.

Stastny, Francisco, and Sara Acevedo

    1986 *Vidriados y mayólica del Perú.* Universidad Nacional Mayor de San Marcos, Facultad de Letras y Ciencias Humanas, Museo de Arte y de Historia, Lima, Peru.

Torres Mora, Rocío

    2011 Cerámica colonial en el valle bajo y medio de Zaña: Tecnología, formas y comercio. Unpublished *licenciatura* thesis, Department of Archaeology, Pontificia Universidad Católica del Perú.

Tschauner, Hartmut

    2001 Socioeconomic and Political Organization in the Late Prehispanic Lambayeque Sphere, Northern North Coast of Peru. Unpublished Ph.D. dissertation, Department of Anthropology, Harvard University.

Tschopik, Harry

    1950 An Andean Ceramic Tradition in Historical Perspective. *American Antiquity* 15(3):196–218.

VanValkenburgh, Parker

    2009 Thin Section Analysis of Majolica from Panama La Vieja. Unpublished Report.

    2012 Building Subjects: Landscapes of Forced Resettlement in the Zaña and Chamán Valleys, Peru, 16th–17th Centuries C.E. Unpublished Ph.D. dissertation, Department of Anthropology, Harvard University.

VanValkenburgh, Parker, Sarah J. Kelloway, Laure Dussubieux, Jeffrey Quilter, and Michael D. Glasock

    2015 The Production and Circulation of Indigenous Lead-Glazed Ceramics in Northern Peru During Spanish Colonial Times. *Journal of Archaeological Science* 61:172–185.

VanValkenburgh, Parker, Sarah J. Kelloway, Karen L. Privat, Bill Sillar, and Jeffrey Quilter

    2017 Rethinking Cultural Hybridity and Technology Transfer: SEM Microstructural Analysis of Lead Glazed Ceramics from Early Colonial Peru. *Journal of Archaeological Science* 82:17–30.

Wagner, U., R. Gebhard, W. Häusler, et al.

    1999 Reducing Firing of an Early Pottery Making Kiln at Batán Grande, Peru: A Mössbauer Study. *Hyperfine Interactions* 122:163–170.

Wernke, Steven A.

    2013 *Negotiated Settlements: Andean Communities and Landscapes Under Inka and Spanish Rule.* Gainesville: University Press of Florida.

Yamunaqué B., José Luis

    1979 La cerámica: Técnicas tradicionales. *Historia y Cultura* (Lima) 12:151–171.

9

Indigenous Pottery

Jennifer Ringberg

THIS CHAPTER EXAMINES the role of indigenous pottery containers used in daily household tasks at Magdalena de Cao through the relationship of vessel form to function. By "indigenous" I refer to pottery produced by local, native manufacturers during the Colonial Period occupation of Magdalena de Cao Viejo using materials, forms, and techniques that display continuity with prehispanic products. I reconstruct the links between the vessel assemblage and foodways in a sample of three town residences, Units 1, 2, and 28, and the domestic areas of the church that served the needs of the Dominican friars in residence. The first goal of this analysis was to determine the functions and relative frequencies of different vessel categories at Magdalena de Cao. The assessment of vessel function is based mainly on the physical characteristics of the necks and rims of pottery containers as well as evidence for actual use. The second goal was to compare vessel assemblages within and between the three town residences and the church residence to explore how, where, and when culinary practices may have varied in the colonial settlement. Finally, I compare the indigenous pottery assemblage of colonial Magdalena de Cao to precontact domestic assemblages on the North Coast, especially Late Intermediate Period and Late Horizon pottery assemblages in the Chicama and other valleys on Peru's North Coast to explore how people used domestic pottery in their daily lives and how these practices changed or endured through time.

Background

Continuity and change in the daily activities of households on the North Coast of Peru provide an excellent perspective from which to view the lives of indigenous Magdaleneros and their Spanish and mestizo neighbors. This is especially true since this area of the coast (the Chicama Valley and the El Brujo terrace in particular) has a potentially uninterrupted record of domestic occupation from the Formative through the Colonial Period. Of particular interest for the purposes of this study are the century-and-a-half periods both before and after Spanish entry into Peru (roughly the fifteenth century to the late seventeenth century) and how households maintained or innovated their foodways during Chimu through Spanish colonial times.

Pottery on the North Coast has historically served as a time marker, but archaeologists increasingly look to assemblages for insights into household economy and culinary practice. Archaeologists of the Central Andes now use culinary pottery assemblages to interpret the interactions of smaller sociopolitical groups within the ebb and flow of large-scale political organizations (Bray 2003; Hayashida 1999; Hildebrand and Hagstrum 1999). The interpretation of culinary function works well for late precontact assemblages, especially for the Inca, because we know much of their culinary and material practice through ethnohistorical accounts. Fewer such accounts exist for North Coast culinary practices. The Codex Martínez Compañón is an exception (Figure 9.1). Ethnoarchaeological studies also provide evidence for continuity of practices surrounding chicha beer production (Hayashida 2008; Shimada 1994). However, the further removed we are from these examples, the more challenging interpretations become. Therefore, household pottery forms with their potential and actual uses are better understood through direct, contextualized evidence, including residue and use alteration analysis, as well as careful study and interpretation of the shapes, technical properties, and mechanical performance characteristics of each pottery form in an assemblage. These contextual and material studies of practices can then combine with studies of foodways (see Chapter 3).

Methods of the Functional Analysis

This study connects the shapes and mechanical performance characteristics of pottery vessels to foodways by drawing upon a body of work in the archaeology of precontact pottery assemblages in the Old World and North America (Braun 1980; Hally 1983a, 1986; Henrickson and McDonald 1983; Rice 1987) as well as a growing number of studies in the Central Andes (Bray 2003; Cutright 2009; Gamarra and Gayoso 2008; Mehaffey 1998). The food remains and pottery assemblage at Magdalena de Cao provided excellent preservation and good archaeological contexts; complete botanical and faunal studies, bioarchaeological evidence of diet, and pottery residue analysis help to directly connect the culinary vessel assemblage to the processing, storage, and consumption of food in daily household practice.

The functional categories used in this study mainly follow those used by Torres (2011) for the Zaña Valley. I identified three functional categories related to culinary activity for the Magdalena de Cao vessel assemblage. These include food processing (mainly cooking), storage of liquids or dry goods, and food or beverage serving and consumption. Figure 9.2 presents reconstructions of the most common forms of the indigenous culinary vessel assemblage from Magdalena.

I based my functional analysis of pottery on the assumption that pots of similar shapes were used in similar ways in both prehistoric and ethnographic contexts and that these associations are not significantly different cross-culturally (Pauketat 1987:3). Inferences about function, therefore, can be supported both by archaeological and ethnographic evidence. Although whole vessels are the ideal basic unit of analysis, these are rare in most archaeological collections. In fact, the Magdalena de Cao domestic assemblage contained few whole or nearly complete indigenous pottery vessels ($N = 4$). However, Braun (1980), Hally (1983a, 1983b, 1984, 1986), and others (Egloff 1973; Ericson and De Atley 1976; Fitting and Halsey 1966; Plog 1985; Walsh 1979; Whallon 1969) demonstrate that form and function can be assessed accurately even when only fragments (potsherds or sherds) of the rim represent the whole vessel.

Figure 9.1 Image of Indian women in the eighteenth century using pottery vessels of varying sizes for straining and skimming chicha during its preparation. From the Codex Martinez Compañón.

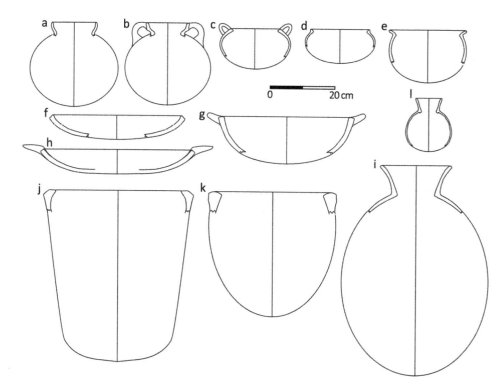

Figure 9.2 Reconstruction of common indigenous vessel forms at Magdalena Viejo. a. Cuello convexo olla; b. C-rim olla. c and d. Neckless ollas; e. Angled-neck olla; f, g, and h. Open bowls; i. Cántaro; j and k. Tinajas; l. Bottle.

I assigned functional categories based on a set of mechanical performance characteristics connected with the physical and morphological features of different kinds of vessels. These mechanical performance characteristics and physical features are based largely on Hally's (1986) research in North America. In addition to being guided by previous research, I established my functional categories based on a combination of characteristics including the relative frequencies of different vessel classes as well as vessel morphology and technology related to intended and actual vessel use (vessel shape, surface treatment, and evidence for use alteration—especially the presence of soot and its location on the vessel). In this study, I established relative frequencies of vessel classes through identification of rim segments by context.

The Magdalena Household Pottery Assemblage and Sample Selection

Many domestic contexts at Magdalena de Cao underwent archaeological sampling, but three compounds (Units 1, 2, and 28) and the eastern sector of the church complex received the most complete excavation. I drew my sample from the indigenous pottery found in these contexts. Although I examined diagnostic and nondiagnostic potsherds from vessel bodies, my analyses included only indigenous vessel rims, which totaled 1,355 (Table 9.1). This is approximately an 11 percent sample of the 12,918 fragments of diagnostic pottery described by VanValkenburgh in Chapter 8. Further, I did not include diagnostic material from prehispanic time periods, nor

Table 9.1 Raw Count, MNV, and Metric Data Assemblage Counts for Magdalena
Viejo Pottery

RAW COUNT OF VESSEL RIMS		STUDY ASSEMBLAGE COUNT (MNV)		METRIC DATA ASSEMBLAGE COUNT	
1,355	100%	831	61% of raw ct.	785	94% of MNV

did I include diagnostic pottery from the ground surface; rather, I concentrated on excavated contexts below level 1 in order to make more secure interpretations of material and activity associated with the households.

This analysis followed criteria established by others for arriving at a minimum number of vessels (MNV) (Chase 1985; Holley 1989; Orton 1993; Schiffer 1985; Wilson 2005). For reasons summarized by Chase (1985), I did not use simple potsherd counts to establish MNV for the Magdalena de Cao indigenous pottery study assemblage. Rather, I identified single or conjoining rim segments in feature and nonfeature contexts and counted these as individual vessels. When I could make such identifications with certainty, individual vessels included numerous nonfitting rim and body sherd segments. I also made every attempt to identify cross-mends between contexts and included all refits along with the single initially identified vessel. Cross-mends sometimes occurred between contexts within a residential compound, but never between residential compounds or between houses in town and the eastern sector of the church complex.

My sample for the MNV included only vessel rims that I could readily sort into categories by type and functional class and that provided a suite of other information about vessel function. Bases were also not included in the MNV unless as part of a vessel represented by a rim. This avoids counting a rim and a base that may be from the same vessel as two vessels and inflating the MNV. In spite of careful control, discrete vessel identification is subject to analyst error, not only because of the size and condition of the collection but also because surface and rim morphology often varies circumferentially for an individual vessel (Holley 1989:9).

The sample set for metric data analyses constituted a relatively large proportion of the MNV. The criterion for this selection was the presence of 5 percent or more of the orifice diameter for all functional classes. These vessel fragments also had to have a complete lip in order to determine shape and thickness. Most composite vessels such as jars had the neck juncture present, but many vessels had broken above the neck-body juncture. Few vessels with long necks were intact from the lip past the neck-body juncture. These criteria provided me with a 94 percent sample ($N = 785$) of the MNV to work with for analyses of metric variables from vessel necks and rims related to vessel size and capacity, or other functional, technological, or chronological information.

An accurate representation of the relative frequencies of vessel classes derived from the MNV provides essential information on the food preparation, storage, and consumption activities important to the residents of Magdalena de Cao. It also helps to envision the in-use assemblage for each household (Skibo 2014). The in-use assemblage was the typical suite of vessels for cooking, storing, and serving food on a day-to-day basis and was an essential element of household social reproduction (Sillar 2000:31; Wilson 2005:147).

Pottery gathered from residential spaces at most archaeological sites does not represent the in-use assemblage for any given point in time in the occupation of a typical household. Rather, it is a discard assemblage, largely composed of secondary refuse accumulated through occupation, abandonment, and post-abandonment processes (Schiffer 1996). Ethnoarchaeological studies have shown that because different vessel classes have varied but have reasonably predictable breakage and replacement rates, archaeologists can make approximations of the in-use vessel assemblage (David 1972; DeBoer 1974; Foster 1960). Factors such as frequency of use, heat exposure, amount of handling or movement, and lower replacement cost make cooking pots (*ollas*) appear much more frequently in discard assemblages when compared to large, immovable, harder-to-replace storage jars (Foster 1960).

Results of the Functional Analysis

Table 9.2 shows the breakdown by primary function and form of the sample. The presentation of data for the vessel assemblage is organized by intended activity and includes (1) cooking or food processing, (2) storage, transport, or fermentation, and (3) food serving and consumption. I describe indigenous pottery with nonculinary primary functions at the end of this section.

In general, the shape and size of a vessel's rim and neck vary according to the need for containment security (wherein the shape of a vessel's walls and mouth reduce spillage and decrease the angle at which one can access its contents) and access frequency (the number of times people add, remove, or manipulate a vessel's contents in a given time period) (Braun 1980:172). Table 9.3 indicates that residents of the town and church chose indigenous pottery forms that provided a high degree of containment security with a zone of restriction in the walls around the vessel mouth. Reducing spillage or evaporation, controlling the amount of material flowing into or out of a vessel, and facilitating the application of a cover to keep out debris and pests or to slow heat loss are the main reasons household members chose vessels with restricted profiles. While restricted orifice forms occurred in roughly the same relative frequencies in clerical residence

Table 9.2 Indigenous Vessel Forms in the Town Units and Clerical Residence

FORM	UNIT 1	%	UNIT 2	%	UNIT 28	%	CLERICAL RESIDENCE	%	TOTAL
C-rim olla	35	49.3%	59	42.4%	93	37.7%	96	25.7%	283
Angled-neck olla	5	7.0%	5	3.6%	16	6.5%	89	23.8%	115
Neckless olla	13	18.3%	34	24.5%	43	17.4%	62	16.6%	152
Convex-neck olla	8	11.3%	10	7.2%	23	9.3%	42	11.2%	83
Tinaja	7	9.9%	9	6.5%	20	8.1%	21	5.6%	57
Cántaro	2	2.8%	10	7.2%	35	14.2%	15	4.0%	62
Bottle	0	0.0%	6	4.3%	10	4.0%	19	5.1%	35
Jarra	1	1.4%	2	1.4%	2	0.8%	7	1.9%	12
Bowl	0	0.0%	4	2.9%	5	2.0%	23	6.1%	32
Total	71	100.0%	139	100.0%	247	100.0%	374	100.0%	831

Table 9.3 Indigenous Vessel Mouth Complex Categories in the Church and Town

MOUTH COMPLEX	CLERICAL RESIDENCE		TOWN		TOTAL	
	COUNT	%	COUNT	%		
Necked, restricted	374	75.86	504	79.62	878	77.98%
No neck, restricted	87	17.65	121	19.12	208	18.47%
No neck, unrestricted	32	6.49	8	1.26	40	3.55%
	493	100.00	633	100.00	1126	100.00%

and town contexts, the clerical residence contained a different suite of restricted-orifice food processing vessels and greater frequencies of unrestricted forms (mainly open bowls). I address the discrepancies within and between functional categories in the indigenous assemblage in more detail under each vessel shape subcategory and in the discussion section.

Cooking, Food Processing

The food processing category includes mainly wet cooking or toasting activities in pottery containers suspended over fire. The most common container for these tasks was the classic cooking pot or olla (refer to Figure 9.2). Ollas in the Magdalena assemblage were globular and thin-walled, and had relatively coarse nonplastic inclusions to facilitate heat transfer. Judging from the few whole or partially complete specimens, ollas were about as tall as they were wide, although vessels with no necks were probably wider. They were stable with minimal support, had a relatively low center of gravity, and were small enough to be movable when full. The rounded base provides effective heat transfer and handles the stress of repeated heating and cooling better than a pot with a flat base. Necked, restricted-orifice vessels would have been especially useful for many food processing tasks because covers easily could have been affixed to reduce spills, evaporation, and pests. Other food processing activities involving ollas may have included reheating leftovers, soaking, steaming, and pickling. Boiling or stewing foods with a liquid or semiliquid consistency, such as soups, stews, gruels, or beverages including chicha, likely would have been the most common activities for which people at Magdalena used indigenous pottery. Toasting or parching likely also took place in ollas as part of the processing of maize or legumes. A vessel form specifically for toasting, such as a shallow open bowl or pan, was not identified in household contexts in the town. The shallow bowl with tab handles discussed below was the only vessel tentatively identified as being used for toasting or parching of foods in the clerical residence.

Seventy-eight percent of this assemblage comprised olla forms primarily intended for cooking or processing liquid or semiliquid foods over fire. Ollas showed the highest incidence of soot (89 percent) of all vessel forms. Not all ollas had direct evidence for use over fire. Since the olla is the quintessential multipurpose vessel, a wide variety of uses (culinary and otherwise) were probably common. However, my goal was to identify trends in intended function based on shape and other technical characteristics and infer secondary uses primarily from evidence for use alteration or ethnographic and ethnohistorical sources.

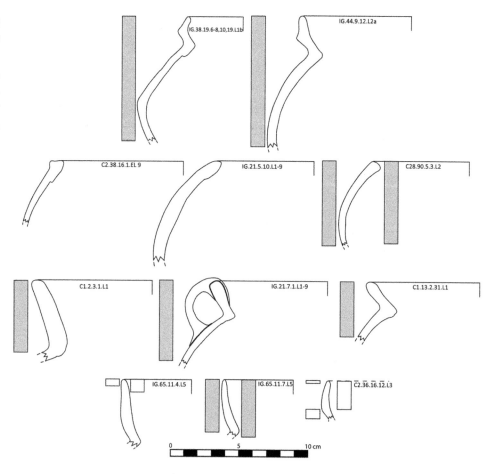

Figure 9.3
Olla subtypes
(top to bottom):
c-rim, neckless,
angled-neck, and
convex-neck. Gray
bars indicate soot.

OLLAS. I identified four main shape categories of olla at Magdalena: (1) the cambered- or c-rim olla, (2) the angled-neck olla, (3) the neckless olla, and (4) the convex-neck olla (Figure 9.3). The variety of shapes of olla vessel openings, both with and without necks, in the Magdalena household pottery inventories was higher than expected. This variety could be attributed to a number of causes, including primary vessel function, access to different manu-facturers over time, or personal preference for technical or aesthetic reasons. Each category of olla differed in the mean and range of sizes for vessel opening (Figure 9.4). These differences in neck shape and size could be related to variation in food processing techniques and conduct-ing residue analysis for each subtype could be informative. Each olla subtype also contained a significant number of rim fragments with evidence for use over fire.

The c-rim (cambered-rim) olla accounts for the greatest number of cooking pots at Magdalena. Neck profiles vary in shape and size (Figure 9.5). C-rim ollas with measurable ori-fice diameters had a mean of 12.8 cm. Excavators recovered only one whole c-rim vessel, buried in the floor of Room 2 in Unit 28 (Figure 9.6). Although it has a relatively small opening, an adult woman's hand or a ladle or spoon could easily fit through the opening for manipula-tion of contents. Vessel strength varies inversely with orifice diameter (Skibo 2013, fig. 3.28), likely giving c-rim ollas reasonable strength. The relatively small orifice diameter, combined with thin, textured walls that enabled quicker heat transfer and lessened stress during repeated

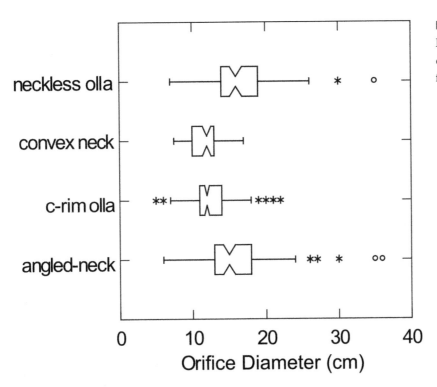

Figure 9.4
Boxplot of orifice diameters (cm) for the four olla forms.

heat-cool cycles, made c-rim ollas reasonably durable vessels (Skibo 2013). The number of rim sherds that had enough of the body below the neck present to determine surface treatment was relatively low. However, the indigenous potsherd sample contained a number of paddle-stamped body sherds, many of them with exterior soot ($N = 1{,}564$ of 9,551 indigenous sherds, or 16.4 percent). This suggests that paddle stamping remained common for smaller food processing vessels long after North Coast potters began using the technique between the ninth and tenth centuries (Cleland and Shimada 1998).

C-rim ollas often had thick accumulations of soot on their exteriors ($N = 146$; 51 percent). At least 22 c-rim fragments also had carbonization built up on the interior vessel wall near the lip. Only the whole vessel from Unit 28 provided evidence for carbonization on the entire vessel (for exterior soot, this mainly reflects the last use over fire). For the exterior of the olla, carbon was thick all over except for a diffuse patch of oxidation offset slightly from the base, indicating that the vessel was tilted slightly when propped over the cooking fire. The interior had light carbonization throughout. This may indicate that the vessel was full of liquid when over the fire, since a heavier ring of carbonization would be present just above a partial fill line, and soot would be thick on the interior surface if the vessel was used for dry roasting or toasting. The olla contained fish bones as well as maize and manioc starch grains and phytoliths, providing support for the hypothesis of wet cooking (Chapter 3). However, this single vessel provides only anecdotal evidence for cooking activity. Although heavily used over fire, the vessel had been covered with sheep's wool and partially buried, thus converting it to a storage function.

Neckless ollas were the next most numerous category of cooking vessel in the indigenous vessel assemblage, at 18.3 percent of the total study assemblage (Figure 9.7). Neckless ollas had a mean orifice diameter of 17 cm, larger than the mean for all ollas, and were found in a broader

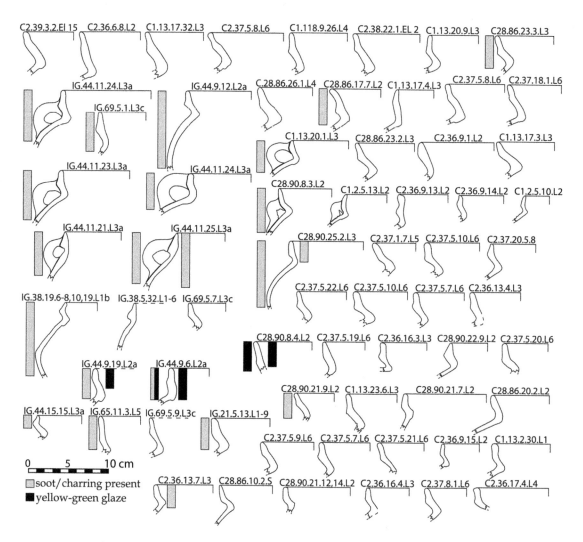

Figure 9.5 C-rim olla forms.

range of sizes than c-rim ollas (7 to 35 cm). A variety of lip shapes were common. Neckless ollas commonly had large, vertical strap handles on the shoulder near the lip. Handles would have provided a way to lift or tip a vessel that lacked an outflaring neck. Donnan (1997) refers to this form as a restricted bowl, but because of the prevalence of soot on neckless ollas in the Magdalena study assemblage, I consider it appropriate to categorize the form as a variety of olla. Eighty-five of the 152 neckless ollas in the study assemblage (56 percent) had exterior soot, often heavily encrusted on the vessel fragments. Twelve had interior carbonization near the lip.

The lack of neck and larger mouth on this olla subtype is a strong indicator for functional difference when compared to the necked olla subtypes. Necks on pots serve as funnels and spouts, as well as places for holding, tipping, or attaching a cover to a vessel. One can easily imagine the difficulty and mess of pouring liquid or semiliquid foods into or out of an

Figure 9.6   Whole c-rim olla from house floor, Room 2, Unit 28.

incurved, neckless vessel. If neckless ollas held such contents, the cook may have ladled contents into or out of it. Scooping and then scraping on the lip with a spoon, small gourd, or even fingers (once food had cooled) may have been an effective way to avoid drips or spills. It is also possible that cooks prepared larger pieces of solid food, such as potatoes, manioc, or larger pieces of meat, in neckless ollas, either by roasting or by steaming with less liquid. However, drier cooking techniques appear less likely with the Magdalena neckless ollas because the incidence of internal carbonization near the lip (an indicator of cooking with less liquid) is equal to or lower than that in the necked olla subtypes in the assemblage.

The neckless olla had many rim sherds with evidence of a yellow-green glaze on the vessel lip (Figure 9.8). Potters created a similar-colored glaze and used it on traditional-style finewares (VanValkenburgh 2012; see also Chapter 8), but it is unknown how these were related. Potters applied glaze to neckless ollas in thin and uneven fashion. They applied it

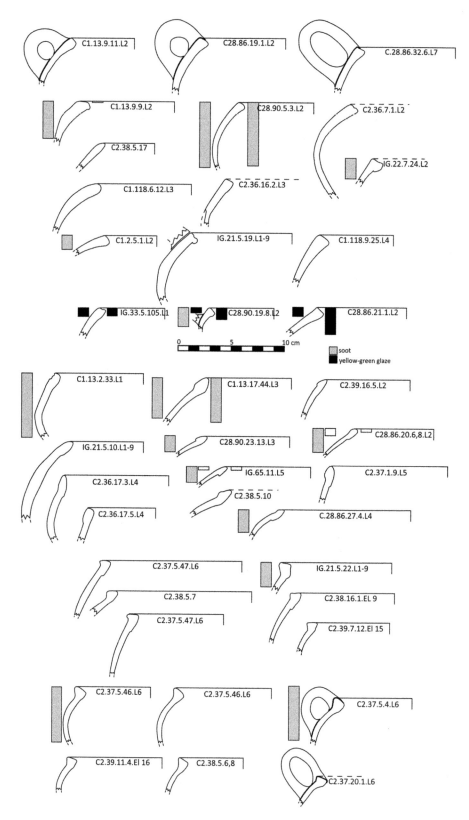

Figure 9.7 Neckless olla forms.

Figure 9.8 Vessel fragments with interior yellow-green glaze from Units 1, 2, and 28 in the town.

mainly to the exterior and interior lip of the pot, and sometimes the glaze exhibits dripping, or very incomplete coverage in the vessel interior. It is possible that potters experimented with using glaze as either a decorative element or possibly as a surface treatment to strengthen the vessel lip and reduce the risk of impact damage. The thin, incomplete interior glaze coverage on neckless ollas does not indicate the use of glaze to decrease the permeability of vessel walls.

The angled-neck olla accounts for 13.8 percent of vessels in the Magdalena assemblage (Figure 9.9). Angled-neck ollas had a mean orifice diameter of 16.5 cm and a slightly broader range of sizes than neckless ollas (6 to 44 cm). Sixty-five percent of angled-neck ollas ($N = 75$) exhibited exterior soot, while 19 (16 percent) had interior carbonization near the lip. The angled-neck olla's incidence of interior carbonization (25 percent) was greater than each of the other three subtypes of ollas (14 percent). This could indicate that cooks used a lower liquid level or drier cooking methods in angled-neck ollas than in the other subtypes.

Finally, the convex-neck olla made up 9.6 percent of the Magdalena sample assemblage (Figure 9.10). Roughly half of these ollas (52 percent, $N = 168$) had exterior soot, while five (3 percent) also had soot on the interior by the lip. These vessels had a mean orifice diameter of 11.7 cm, the smallest of the olla subtypes, and a range of sizes very similar to that of the more ubiquitous c-rim olla. In fact, many of the neck profiles in this category as well as the angled-neck olla type exhibit a much less pronounced camber (an "almost c-rim" shape), indicating a very similar forming technique for the two types of ollas. However, the convex-neck olla usually had oxidized pastes and often had a band of thin white slip at the lip or neck, whereas the

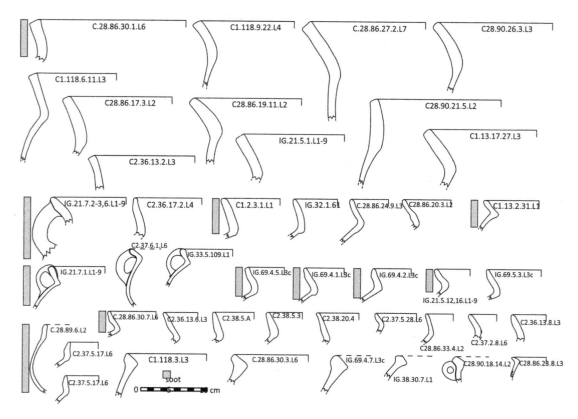

Figure 9.9 Angled-neck olla forms.

c-rim was a mix of oxidized and reduced pastes and often had paddle-stamped, mold-made, or stamped surfaces. The fact that many of the convex-neck ollas were slip-painted may indicate that this vessel, though very similar in shape to the more common c-rim, may have had another primary or intended use besides cooking. The slip paint and bright pinkish orange oxidized paste could also represent a distinct group of manufacturers.

LID. A single example of a possible lid had an estimated diameter of 14 cm (Figure 9.11). Soot was located on the concave side (the underside) of the piece. The fragment is uniquely shaped, but it could have served as a cover for many different varieties of cooking vessels, especially for the smaller c-rim or convex-neck ollas. Excavators recovered the fragment from the clerical residence. No other similar pieces were found.

OPEN BOWLS. The open, shallow bowl is not a common form in the Magdalena indigenous pottery assemblage, accounting for 3.9 percent of the functional assemblage. The majority of bowls were recovered from the domestic contexts of the clerical residence (6.1 percent of the clerical residence indigenous assemblage) (Figure 9.12). When bowls with measurable orifice diameter are divided between the town and the clerical residence, the clerical residence appears to have two size classes (Figure 9.12, top four rows). Many larger shallow bowls in the clerical residence ($N = 8$) had soot on the exterior and interior. These ranged in size from 19 to 28 cm at the orifice, which was also the maximum diameter of the bowl. At least three of the vessels also had traces of yellowish green glaze either on the lip, on the interior body, or near the tab handles, possibly for aesthetics or to reduce vessel wall permeability (Figure 9.13).

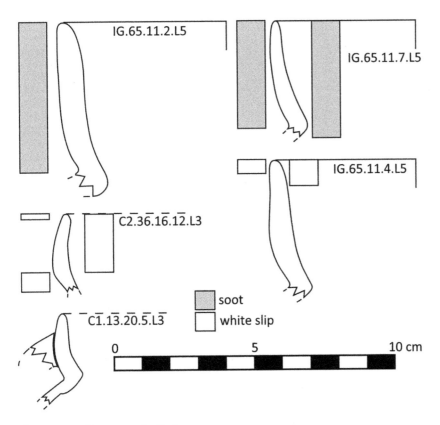

Figure 9.10   Convex-neck olla forms.

The majority of bowl fragments with yellow-green glaze were recovered from the clerical residence. The hypothesized culinary function of large, sooted, shallow bowls in the clerical residence is toasting or parching, but residues, if present, might be tested to verify this. The other possibility is a nonculinary function, which at this point is unknown. Parching or toasting was a common food processing activity in Peruvian households (Gillin 1947; Hildebrand and Hagstrum 1999), but it is also possible that cooks in indigenous households chose to use a multipurpose cooking olla for this activity.

Food Storage, Transport, and Fermentation

Transporting and storing beverages, especially chicha, in pottery vessels is well documented both archaeologically and ethnographically in the Central Andes and shows great longevity ethnohistorically (Bray 2003; Cutler and Cardenas 1947; Goldstein 2003; Hayashida 2008; Jennings and Chatfield 2009; Moore 1989). However, changes that occurred in indigenous communities after the Spanish reorganized them into reducciones probably had some effect on the scale of production, storage, and transport of the beverage. The Spanish documented subterranean storage of dry goods such as maize by the original Magdalena residents, but no mention was made of the type of vessels used, or if vessels were used at all (López 1994). Unlike the *aríbalo* (chicha storage vessels carried with a tump line) introduced by the Incas, prehispanic vessels as containers specifically for transport are not well documented on the North Coast.

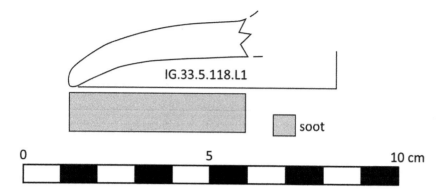

Figure 9.11 A possible lid form.

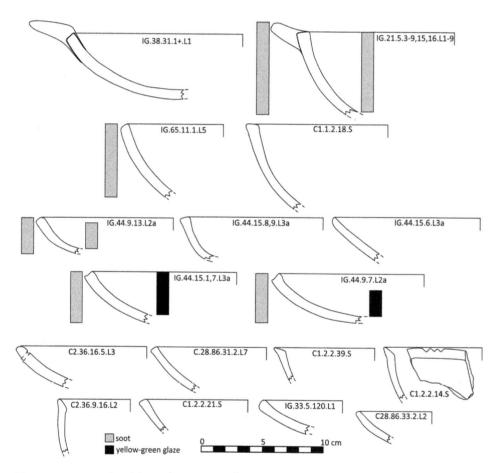

Figure 9.12 Large bowl forms (top four rows) and small, individual serving bowls (bottom two rows).

Figure 9.13 Vessel fragments with yellow-green glaze from the clerical residence.

TINAJAS. *Tinajas* are large containers with slightly constricted openings typically used on the North Coast of Peru for water, chicha, or dry goods storage (Figure 9.14). Such vessels had a maximum height much greater than maximum diameter, with rounded bases requiring support or partial burial for stability. Tinajas were so large as to have been immovable when full. Access to vessel contents was likely frequent and facilitated by the large and only slightly restricted opening. Vessel walls were relatively thick, and pastes were coarse and porous, allowing for airflow or evaporative cooling. Tinajas were presumably the largest-capacity vessels in the Magdalena assemblage, but no whole or partially complete specimens were recovered from excavations.

Tinaja fragments have the smallest relative frequency of vessels at Magdalena (6.5 percent of indigenous assemblage) and at archaeological sites generally, due to their relatively low breakage and replacement rates. The total number of specimens with measurable orifice diameters was 27. The mean orifice diameter was 42.5 cm, ranging between 32 and 58 cm. Lip form is consistently thickened interiorly and beveled, a possible deterrent to impact damage from frequent access to contents. Tinajas appear to have been constructed with slabs, large coils, and paddling. At least two appeared to be paddle-stamped below the exterior lip. A few of the Magdalena tinajas had

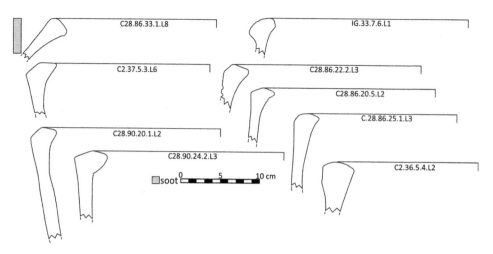

Figure 9.14 Tinaja forms.

plastic surface treatment or decoration, including stamping and broad incisions below the lip ($N=2$) and coil appliqué ($N=1$). The difficulty of transporting such large vessels makes it likely that tinajas were built and fired not very far from their permanent use locations.

Ten tinaja vessel rim fragments exhibited light soot or carbonization on the interior below the lip. There are several possible explanations for this pattern. First, this could be related to the vessel's original firing, being inverted over a fire. Or the vessel may have had a second fire built inside to "cure" or refire the vessel so it could withstand holding liquid. Secondary uses apart from storage are also a possibility. Fires could have been built inside the large vessel for activities related to food processing or possibly for tasks totally unrelated to foodways. No other use alteration evidence was present on any of the tinaja fragments in the Magdalena assemblage to indicate patterns of use.

CÁNTAROS. The cántaro has a relatively long flared or everted neck and a globular body, and it has a smaller capacity than the tinaja (Figure 9.15). The cántaro vessel form is most typically associated with fermentation and short-term storage of liquids, especially chicha, on the North Coast of Peru. In general, longer, flared necks would have provided containment security but also aided in pouring (when contents were being removed) or funneling (when vessels were being filled). Covering was also facilitated by the neck and opening in order to keep out debris and pests. Vessel bodies were either globular, with maximum height and width nearly equal, or taller than they were wide, with rounded bases that required a depression or support for vessel stability. Cántaros from other North Coast assemblages frequently have burnished or slipped and burnished surfaces, presumably to reduce permeability and slow evaporation. Although excavators at Magdalena recovered many large cántaro neck fragments, they did not recover any whole vessels of this shape category. Forms for liquid storage constituted 7.4 percent of the indigenous diagnostic assemblage at Magdalena. Mean orifice diameter for cántaros was 22.8 cm, with a median of 21 cm. Because of the longer, more outcurved necks for cántaros in this assemblage, the typical breakage pattern occurred above the neck-shoulder juncture, making definitive identifications less common. The total number of cántaros identified may reflect this.

Because of the low frequency of vessel rim fragments with body below the neck juncture for the Magdalena cántaros, I could not determine shape or patterns in surface treatment.

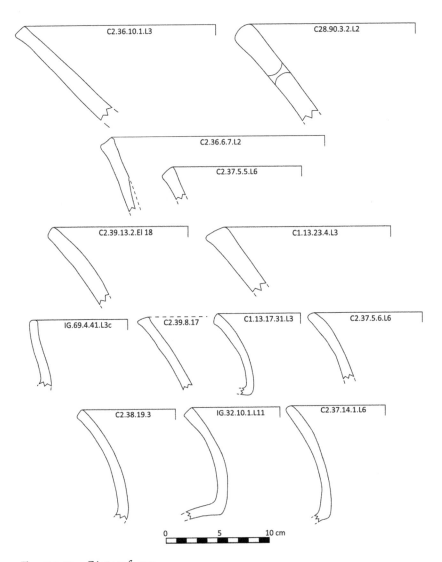

Figure 9.15 Cántaro forms.

However, judging from the great quantities of plain, medium-thick, paddle-made body sherds in the Magdalena indigenous assemblage, the cántaro was a simple, undecorated vessel. The incidence of decoration on cántaro necks and rims was low. Three cántaros had a wash of white slip painted in a band at the lip or neck-body juncture, and two had appliquéd dots of clay around the neck. Use alteration was minimal for the cántaro specimens and included one rim sherd with possible burnt residue, four fragments with exterior and interior soot (possibly secondary use or postdiscard burning), and one vessel rim fragment with abrasions on the superior and interior part of the lip, probably from dragging the empty inverted vessel on the ground in order to move it.

Serving, Consumption

Vessels specifically for serving, eating, or drinking food and beverages were a relatively minor component in the total indigenous vessel assemblage at Magdalena. The *jarra* (pitcher or jug)

Figure 9.16
Jarra and
bottle forms.

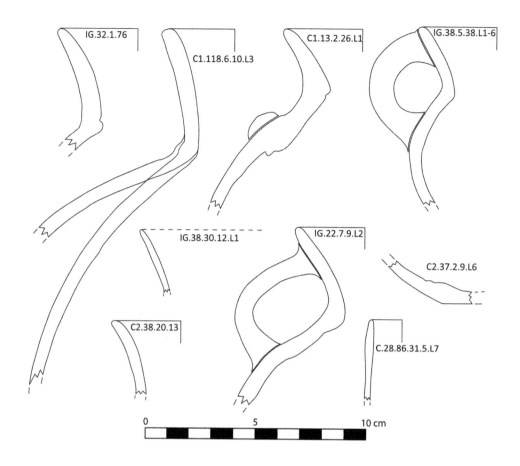

IG.32.1.76

C1.118.6.10.L3

C1.13.2.26.L1

IG.38.5.38.L1-6

IG.38.30.12.L1

IG.22.7.9.L2

C2.37.2.9.L6

C2.38.20.13

C.28.86.31.5.L7

0   5   10 cm

and the bottle, both used for short-term storage and serving of liquids, accounted for roughly 6 percent of the total vessel assemblage in both clerical and town residences (Figure 9.16). These share many mechanical performance characteristics, including a relatively small size and volume capacity for relatively easy lifting and pouring when filled, constricted but straight or slightly outflared necks to aid pouring and reduce spilling, stable bases (usually flat, but if the vessel was globular, it had a low center of gravity), and a minimal to significant investment in surface treatment depending on degree of permeability desired or context of use (higher-visibility items tending to have greater attention to surface treatments or decoration (Braun 1991)). The main difference between jarras and bottles was the size and capacity of each vessel category, jarras being larger, for serving larger groups of people, and bottles having a smaller capacity, for individual or small group serving events. Perhaps due to their smaller size, a single whole vessel (Figure 9.17) and a few large rim fragments in the jarra and bottle category made up part of the Magdalena indigenous serving vessel assemblage.

JARRAS. A very low percentage of the assemblage was devoted to short-term liquid storage and serving vessels (1.2 percent). The mean orifice diameter for jarras was 9 cm (Figure 9.16a). The maximum vessel volume for the jarra is larger than for the bottle, though the categories comprise a largely continuous range of sizes. The range of orifice diameters for both comprises a continuum of very small to medium sizes. The jarra and the bottle are distinct from the larger liquid storage and fermentation vessel, the cántaro, not only because of size but also because of the greater variety of firing effects and amount of finishing or decoration applied to them.

Figure 9.17
Whole jarra from clerical
residence. Height: 12.2 cm.

Jarras were generally fired in oxidizing atmospheres, but a few examples of blackwares were present in the assemblage. Decoration or surface treatments consisted of simple modeled or incised facial features or abstracted "ear" lugs on vessel necks as well as burnishing on the blackware examples and thin white slip bands around neck and lip on oxidized redware jarras. Vessel necks are longer than ollas and slightly everted to facilitate pouring.

BOTTLES. Bottles (3.9 percent) account for a greater proportion of the indigenous vessel assemblage than jarras (Figure 9.16b). The mean orifice diameter, 6 cm, was smaller than for the jarra. Most bottles appear to have been globular, but one vessel from Unit 1 had a lozenge-shaped body. Eleven bottle bases were part of the diagnostic vessels assemblage. The collection contained eight examples of flat bases and three annular (ring-shaped) bases. Again, oxidized and reduced examples were about equal. Three flat bases showed signs of use wear in the form of parallel fine abrasions along the edge of the base caused by dragging across a surface. One flat base exhibited pitting, and a single flat base fragment bore soot. The relative frequencies of oxidized and reduced wares were more or less equal for bottles, and surface treatments were similar to those of jarras. A larger bottle fragment had mold-impressed designs on the body close to the neck (Figure 9.18, left), and a single example had a bright red slip (Figure 9.18, right).

SMALL OPEN BOWLS. Bowls made with indigenous pastes and styles were somewhat complex to parse out in terms of function. In the serving and consumption category, I categorized individual serving bowls as those with an orifice or maximum diameter smaller than 20 cm and lacking soot or tab handles (see Figure 9.12, bottom two rows). Due to the presence

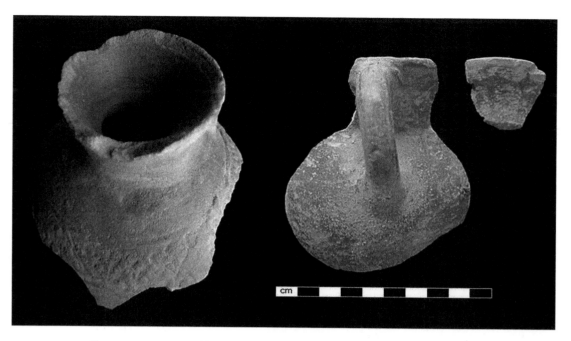

Figure 9.18　Press-molded, reduction-fired bottle fragment (left) and red-slipped, oxidized bottle fragment (right) from the clerical residence.

of soot, the larger tab-handled bowls discussed in the cooking and food processing section likely served a toasting function. Small open bowls are seen at very low frequencies in the indigenous vessel assemblage. Serving bowls of a size suitable for individuals or small groups of people ranged from 8 to 20 cm in orifice diameter.

Small open bowls bore a range of surface treatments and firing effects that fell in line with the jarras and bottles already described (five oxidized redware, four gray or black reduced wares, and three tan or brown oxidized paste bowls). Some of the small redware bowls are extremely thin-walled with fine pastes. Burnishing occurred on all the interior surfaces of black- or grayware bowls. Vessels with the largest orifice diameters may have been plates, but not enough of the rim or body was present to make that distinction. Neither the clerical residence nor the town houses in this sample contained fragments of the flat-based reduced-ware plates typical of Chimu and Chimu-Inca pottery assemblages.

Unknown or Other Primary Function

Agricultural Production

RAYADORES. The sample assemblage at Magdalena contained 17 *rayador* ("grater" bowl) fragments, distinctive bowls with wide, deep, parallel or cross-hatched incisions made on the interior while the clay was still moist (Figure 9.19). Excavation also recovered seven body fragments from the town, eight from the clerical residence, and two from the refuse heap. Some sherds exhibit faint grid-design paddle marks on their exteriors. Two distinct rayador rims were recovered from the town, in Units 1 and 28 (Figure 9.20). Excavation in the uppermost level of Unit

Figure 9.19
Rayador rim
and body
fragments from
town contexts.

1 recovered a thick-walled shallow rayador with deep, cross-hatched interior incisions and an exterior circular stamp design below a thick squared lip. In Unit 28 the rayador rim from an incurved bowl seemed similar to a neckless olla in form. The interior incisions trail diagonally down from just below the vessel's mouth. The form is similar in appearance to a larger fragment of a rayador from the archaeological site of Lambayeque One (Bennett 1939:115, fig. 22C). Interestingly, the fragment from Unit 28 has soot on the exterior, but soot is not reported for other rayador bowls found in archaeological contexts elsewhere on the North Coast. Although there is not much of the body present below the rim on this particular fragment, it would be worth considering the specimen for residue analysis. Apart from soot, I observed no other evidence of use alteration, including attrition in the form of scratches, abrasion, or pitting, especially along the raised edges of the incisions, where such wear might be expected to occur.

Clearly the rayador or "grater" form was intended to be a container, but to date little direct evidence exists for a specific function. The coarse, deep incisions could have served to mash or break up cooked and softened tubers, or perhaps they could have helped strain or catch food particles in suspension in liquids. There is no reported evidence on the North Coast of wear or residues on the deeply incised interior surfaces of these bowls. These vessels appear in low

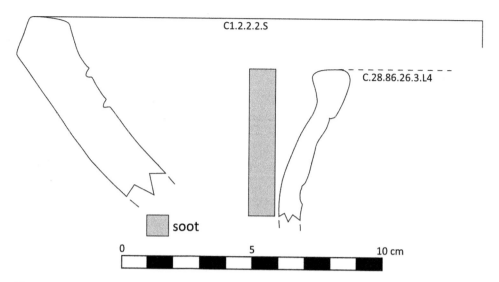

Figure 9.20   Rayador forms from house compounds in the town: Unit 1 (left) and Unit 28 (right).

numbers in household and other contexts throughout the North Coast from at least the Early Intermediate Period (ca. A.D. 1–650) into the Colonial Period, but there are no modern correlates or ethnohistorical descriptions of rayador forms in use in households.

Non-Food-Related Use

Although people likely used pottery vessels for a variety of nonculinary activities at Magdalena, only a few indigenous pottery forms had a non-food-related intended function in the colonial households there. This short section describes the few indigenous fired clay objects apart from containers present in the Magdalena pottery assemblage.

FIGURINES. Unit 1 in the town yielded a clay figurine of a mother nursing a child, although the appliquéd baby had broken or eroded off the figure after it was discarded (Figure 9.21), and a fragment of a hollow figurine, also probably female (Figure 9.22). Both fragments were recovered from the uppermost excavation level of each unit. Both display simple, minimal detail from molding, modeling, and fine incisions made in wet clay.

MUSICAL INSTRUMENTS. In addition to a whistle (Figure 8.3), two small fragments of fired clay instruments were found, one in level 3 of an excavation in Unit 28, the other in level 1 of Unit 12 in the church. Each fragment was an oxidized red ware covered on the exterior with a dark-pigmented slip. The piece from the clerical residence had three small holes made in the clay before firing. Both had relatively coarse temper. The fragments may belong to wind instruments of some variety. A third fragment resembles a tube but does not appear to have been a bottle neck or spout. The piece was crudely made and measures 1 cm in diameter. Both ends were broken, so I could determine neither a complete length nor whether one or both ends were closed or open. Excavators found the piece in the first excavation level of Unit 12 in the church. The fragment may be the remains of a musical instrument, such as a flute.

Figure 9.21
Figurine fragment.

Figure 9.22   Figurine fragment, in context (Unit 1, Level 1) and front and back views.

Spatial Comparisons of Magdalena Indigenous Vessels

A breakdown of the vessel rim sample by general functional category, including both colonial and indigenous pottery, shows that cooking outweighs other functional categories in both church and town, and that serving food and drink in ceramic containers played a more significant role in the clerical residence, while houses in town devoted more containers to storage (Figure 9.23). The distribution of cooking vessel subtypes revealed possible differences in cooking practices between church and town. While the proportions of olla subtypes among the three residential units in the town showed no significant difference ($\chi^2 = 4.8$, df $= 6$, $p > .05$), the difference between the town and the clerical residence was significant ($\chi^2 = 64.65$, df $= 3$, $p < .01$). The Figure 9.24 bar graph indicates that the clerical residence favored the angled-neck olla subtype far more than the three town households, which preferred c-rim and neckless ollas.

A boxplot (Figure 9.25) of orifice diameters for all olla subtypes in church and town shows that mean orifice sizes differed very little between the town and church household contexts. The smaller-mouthed c-rim may have been preferred by households in the town for several reasons. Its mechanical properties, including small capacity, thin walls, and restricted opening, would have brought liquids quickly to boil with relatively little fuel and slower rates of evaporation and cooling than larger-mouthed vessels. The buried vessel in Unit 28 (see Figure 9.6) also demonstrates that the c-rim's small, globular form and coarse but compact vessel paste withstood repeated heat-cool cycles very well. Based on a volume estimate for the whole vessel from Unit 28 (whose orifice diameter of 12 cm is the median for c-rims from the town), c-rim

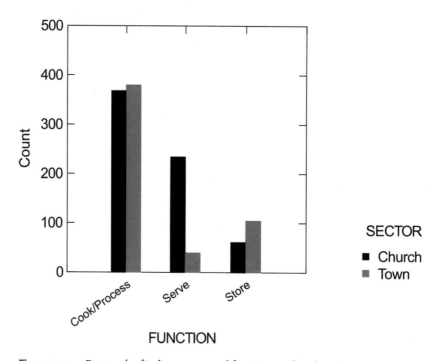

Figure 9.23 Bar graph of indigenous vessel function in church and town.

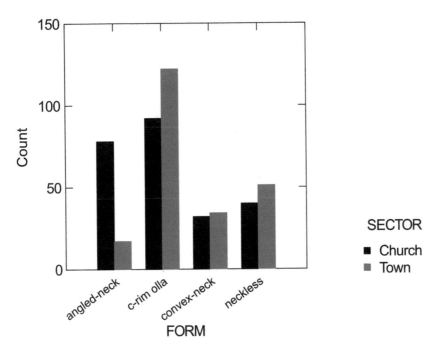

Figure 9.24 Bar graph of olla subtypes in church and town.

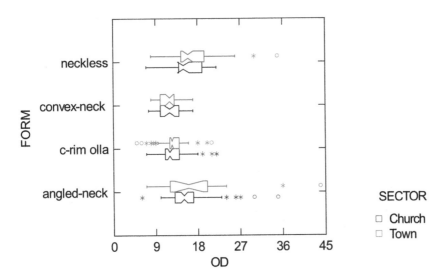

Figure 9.25 Boxplot of orifice diameters (cm) for olla subtypes in church and town.

vessel capacity suggests servings for smaller numbers of people, flexible meal schedules, and easy application of a cover for keeping leftover food.

It is notable that differences between cooking vessels in church and town focused mainly on the larger-mouthed olla subtypes, the angled-neck and neckless ollas. Residents of the church area possessed nearly equal proportions of c-rim and angled-neck ollas. A marked preference for the angled-neck olla in the clerical residence could be due to a number of culinary and economic differences between the clerical residence and town households, including the preparation of more food in a single event, different types of food, or different preparation techniques. Faunal studies at Magdalena (Chapter 3) indicate that the clerical household probably ate more and better-quality meats as well as different varieties of fish. These may have been prepared in greater quantities and larger cuts per person in the clerical residence. The wider-mouthed vessel also more closely resembled the Spanish olla or *cazuela*, better suited to Spanish-style cooking and serving of meals eaten more formally. Vessels for simmering frequently have larger openings and sit a little above the fire, rather than in it (Rice 1997). The clerical household may have also had less concern for conserving water or fuel than people in town and chosen more open-profile cooking pots for easier manipulation and serving of vessel contents over reduced evaporation and cooling.

The clerical residence may have had a significantly greater number of angled-neck ollas, but contexts in the town contained a greater range of sizes, including the largest outlier sizes of any of the olla subtypes. In the case of the neckless olla, town contexts contained a higher proportion of this subtype, a larger-mouthed (and presumably larger-capacity) vessel. Town contexts also included several extra-large outliers of the neckless olla. Perhaps most significant, the largest cooking vessels in the town, for both the neckless and angled-neck olla categories, came from Unit 28. It seems clear that the broader range of sizes created an efficient and flexible inventory for Unit 28's expanded cooking and food processing activities. This flexible range of sizes shows that Unit 28 could prepare food or drink for either small or large groups of people, indicating the potential for production beyond the level of a single household. This supports VanValkenburgh's (Chapter 8) conclusions about Unit 28's status.

Unit 28's inventory of extra-large capacity cooking pots may relate to its greater proportion of liquid storage vessels, including tinajas and cántaros. The proportion of storage vessels among church and town, including the Spanish botija and indigenous tinajas and cántaros, is significant ($\chi^2 = 46.57$, df $= 2$, $p < .01$). The clerical residence contained more Spanish botijas, but again, the town contained more indigenous larger-capacity storage vessels (Figure 9.26). When only the units of the town are compared, Unit 28 had a significantly greater proportion of cántaros compared to the other residences. Cántaros represent from 2 to 6 percent of the vessel assemblage for the clerical residence and Units 1 and 2 in the town, while the proportion of cántaros was higher in Unit 28's vessel assemblage (13 percent) (Figure. 9.27). The greater proportion of liquid storage vessels could indicate that the Unit 28 household produced liquids such as chicha beer beyond what was needed for its own consumption.

It is not yet clear what overall impact the Spanish botija had on indigenous vessel assemblages on Peru's North Coast, but fragments of these thick, durable vessels clearly began to impact storage in Unit 28 in the town. Unit 28, Room 2, along the south and east perimeter walls of the compound, contained the only *in situ* evidence for vessel use in the town. Excavators uncovered three buried pottery vessels and one buried gourd container associated with floor 1 of Room 2. Two of the buried vessels were Spanish colonial botijas with their necks broken off. The two botijas contained residues of potato and manioc (Chapter 3). Archaeologists interpreted Room 2 as a storage room because of the limited accessibility through Room 1 and the buried containers. Floor 1 of Room 2 contained pottery, marine shell, and charred plant fragments embedded in its surface. The area also exhibited evidence of burning but no formal

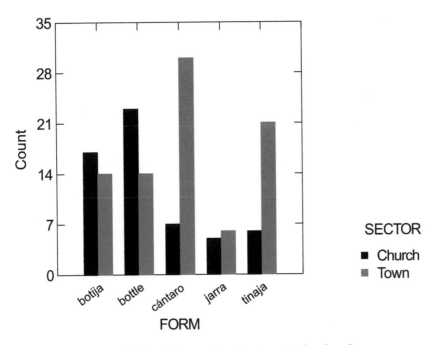

Figure 9.26 Bar graph of liquid storage/serving forms in church and town.

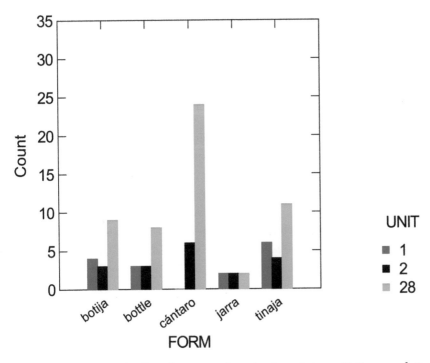

Figure 9.27 Bar graph of liquid storage and serving forms in town, Units 1, 2, and 28.

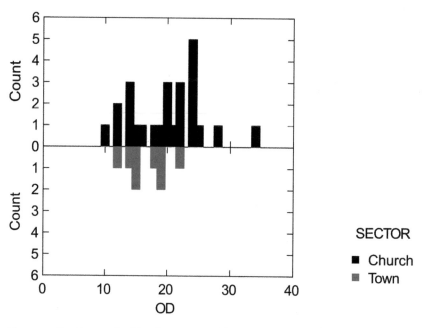

Figure 9.28 Bar graph of bowls categorized by orifice diameter (cm) for clerical residence and town compounds.

hearth. Clearly, household members intensively utilized the space around the buried vessels to prepare, cook, and store food. The decision to use botijas for buried, larger-volume storage in the Unit 28 storeroom instead of cántaros or tinajas is interesting. Did the botija's superior vessel strength or the smaller orifice provide better containment security than the indigenous alternatives? Only one of the pottery vessels buried in Unit 28 was an indigenous form—the single heavily sooted c-rim olla (see Figure 9.6).

Finally, the differences in the proportion of serving vessels between church and town was significant, even when considering only the indigenous forms of serving vessels—jarras, bottles, and bowls. Perhaps not surprisingly, the relative frequencies of vessels for serving and consumption of food and drink were higher for the clerical residence. The distribution of both large and small bowls indicated the use of different vessels for different tasks in the clerical residence and the town (Figure 9.28). Indigenous bowls may have two size classes, with only the smaller sizes being used for individual servings of food or drink. Large bowls, some with tab handles, were mainly used in the clerical residence and often had soot from use over fire. The sample of town residences contained few large pottery bowls, leading to the conclusion that perhaps larger ollas served multiple functions in the households of Magdalena.

Temporal Trends in Magdalena Indigenous Vessels

Domestic pottery assemblages on Peru's North Coast exhibit remarkable continuity from the Late Intermediate Period into the Colonial Period. However, changes occurred in assemblages that marked new introductions and influences as well as declines in the distribution of certain forms. Archaeologists must infer how trends in material culture reflected alterations in the social and economic status of the households, their size, work schedules and tasks, or the contexts of eating and drinking together. Changes in pottery assemblages through time may involve alterations of vessel shapes, the relative proportions of different functional vessel types making up a household's assemblage, or vessel manufacturing technology. Here I highlight continuity and change in the Magdalena indigenous pottery assemblage by examining trends several generations before and after the Spanish arrival on the North Coast of Peru. Again, I discuss trends in order of the three main functional categories presented in this chapter—cooking/processing, storage, and serving/consumption.

Vessels for cooking show broad continuity in pottery assemblages from at least the early part of the Late Intermediate Period (A.D. 1100–1450) in the Lambayeque to Virú Valleys. Ford (1949) and Collier (1955) both note the emergence of the c-rim olla form out of earlier Castillo series necked vessel forms for the Virú Valley. C-rim neck shapes occur with great variation across the North Coast throughout the Late Prehispanic Period (Cutright 2009; Donnan 1997; Hayashida 1999; Keatinge 1973; Tate 2007; Tschauner 2006). One possible trend may be in mean orifice diameter of c-rim ollas. In Tate's sample at the Chimu and Chimu-Inca elite residences at the El Brujo complex, the mean rim diameter is between 8 and 9 cm, while the mean at Magdalena is 12.5 cm. This change in size of the opening of a c-rim olla may have reflected an increase in mean vessel size or changes in access to vessel contents. Changes to the c-rim olla neck form could also have affected heat loss and boil-over or impacted the way a person lifted, moved, tipped, or covered a container to protect the vessel's contents.

Households continued to use other olla forms, such as the convex-neck olla and the angled-neck olla, but in general residential contexts have far fewer of these than c-rim ollas. These forms appear as a smaller proportion of household assemblages at a fairly consistent rate from the Late Intermediate Period into the Colonial Period. Neckless ollas appear more commonly in household assemblages during the latter part of the Late Intermediate Period and the Chimu-Inca Period. Donnan (1997) hypothesized that local potters developed this neckless olla form as a product of Inca influence. Neckless ollas appear in the household inventories reported by many archaeologists during Chimu times (Cutright 2009; Tate 2007; Tschauner 2006) and later Chimu or Chimu-Inca contexts (Collier 1955; Keatinge 1973).

During the Late Intermediate Period, farther north in the La Leche–Lambayeque region, Cleland and Shimada (1998; see also Tschauner 2006) note changes to the form of large storage vessels (*porrones* or tinajas) from squared rim/lip shapes with exterior thickening to an interiorly thickened lip profile. Such seemingly minor changes in forms may have produced insignificant effects on vessel function, but they also could have affected mechanical performance. Changes in tinaja lip and neck shapes could have impacted the way a person lifted, moved, or tipped a container or how a cover was placed on the vessel.

Changes also occurred in serving pieces present at household and cemetery sites. A variety of mold-made bowls and plates begin to appear, and in general, the quantities and varieties of mold-made forms increase in late prehispanic times. Early in the North Coast Late Intermediate Period, bowls show influences from Cajamarca, with white or cream slips and pedestal or tripod bases (Collier 1955:161). But later on, black or gray reduction-fired plates and bowls quickly come to dominate assemblages of serving wares throughout Chimu and Chimu-Inca occupations. Small and large oxidized bowls with rounded bases made up small portions of North Coast assemblages. At Medaños de la Joyada, a Late Horizon and Colonial Period occupation

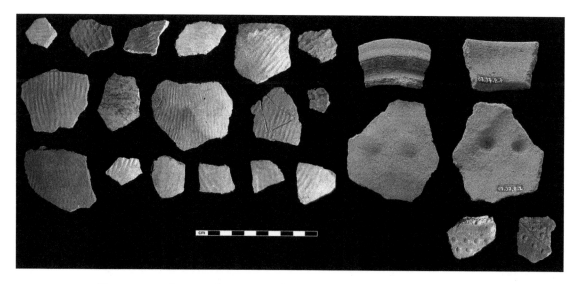

Figure 9.29 Common decorative techniques on Magdalena ollas: carved paddles (left), two-finger impressions (right), and mold-impressed designs (bottom right).

approximately 9 km north of Chan Chan, Keatinge (1973) reported the larger, oxidized bowls as well as a number of the classic Chimu-style reduced bowls and plates. The presence of plates and bowls at Medaños de la Joyada decreased compared to sites from earlier periods in Keatinge's study. The large, tab-handled bowls in the Magdalena clerical residence are distinct from popular indigenous forms on the North Coast. One possible origin could be an Inca-influenced form (Hayashida 1998; Rowe 1946 [form G]; also see Meyers 1975:F13, cited in Bray 2005).

Finally, the changes in vessel forms broadly coincide with changes in manufacture and decoration from the Late Horizon to the Colonial Period. Trends include an increase in paddle and anvil manufacture and decoration, a postcontact decline in use of molds for fine and everyday vessel forms, and a decrease in the use of reduction firing techniques (which produce blackwares). The paddled "waffle," grid, or net pattern (Figure 9.29) is by far more common than mold-impressed stipple and line designs at Magdalena, contrasting with Tate's observation at El Brujo, where mold-made design predominated in Chimu-Inca times. White or cream bands of slip-painted decoration on ollas remained fairly common. Keatinge (1973) and others (Collier 1955, Tate 2007) note the perfunctory or sloppy application of lines at neck and lip and other simple designs painted on the shoulder of oxidized redwares. These slip-painted decorations, and the simple, two-finger bump-out on olla bodies noted by Tate, continued in use from the Late Intermediate Period into the colonial occupation at Magdalena de Cao.

Conclusions

Domestic spaces in the town at Magdalena de Cao were similar in size and constructed according to a similar general plan that, like the indigenous pottery assemblage, followed a blueprint for domestic life on the North Coast since at least the Middle Horizon and Late Intermediate Period (ca. A.D. 650–1450) (Bawden 1977; Billman 1996; Lockard 2009; Shimada 1994; Topic 1982). However, Magdalena was a refugee community loosely following a Spanish reducción plan (Quilter 2013; VanValkenburgh 2012; Wernke 2012). While there were continuities in indigenous domestic pottery and its use in household cooking activities on the North Coast of Peru after the arrival of the Spanish, the introduction of new forms and technologies by the Spanish had a growing impact on indigenous storage and serving behaviors and assemblages. By the time people had arrived at the refugee community of Magdalena de Cao, a modest amount of replacement in these functional categories had occurred.

At Magdalena both the town and the clerical residence used only indigenous-made ollas for cooking. However, cooks chose vessels with different neck shapes—the cambered-rim olla predominating in the town assemblages and the angled-neck olla in the clerical residence. Why these differences existed is not yet entirely clear, but the data presented in this chapter suggest that different daily habits existed in the processing and cooking of different types, qualities, and possibly quantities of daily meals. Differences probably existed between friars and townfolk in the timing and frequency of meals as well as who ate together. These differences may have reflected distinctions of culture, class, and economic circumstances between the occupants of the clerical residence and the town. Residue analysis of the vessels in town contexts at Magdalena indicates that residents used indigenous and Spanish vessels for in-ground storage of native tubers and maize, suggesting that foodways and storage practices remained conservative and focused on basic indigenous staples after the conquest and well into the Colonial Period.

Major differences existed between the clerical residence and the town in storage and serving activities. That the church had ample storage vessels and a greater proportion of Spanish botijas than houses in the town is not surprising, given that it was likely a depository for tribute from the surrounding community. Indigenous families tried and selectively adopted new forms and technologies (especially the botija and the use of lead glaze) where they proved efficient, affordable, and beneficial to daily practice. However, the significant difference in cooking and storage capabilities between Unit 28 and the other two households sampled in the town is important. As household members ducked obligations, pursued opportunities inland or in cities, or turned to muleteering as an alternative to local farming, it is likely that the number of people regularly taking meals together at home diminished and cooking for large gatherings became rare. A range of smaller cooking vessels and fewer storage and serving pieces is a logical consequence of this trend. However, the greater quantities of cooking and storage vessels in Unit 28, plus the presence of extra-large-capacity cooking/food processing vessels, indicate a supra-household function. Perhaps Unit 28 residents provided food or drink to people who did not have enough time or family members at home to warrant daily meal preparation.

Indigenous families may have considered Spanish fineware ceramics as status items, perhaps even more affordable than books or clothing (Chapter 12) but less practical to accumulate in homes without furniture or shelves. Small indigenous serving bowls and Chimu-style blackware plates became rare to nonexistent in household assemblages, replaced by gourd and majolica forms. Perhaps the decline or disappearance of the local lord as an administrator of craft production and distribution caused the sharp decline in fine serving pieces as well as a decline in the occasions on which they would have been distributed and used (Ramírez 1996). As social and economic conditions changed in the Colonial Period, indigenous households at Magdalena may have preferred common-pot-style meals, or they may have shifted to gourd bottles and bowls for individual serving. All households in the town possessed a few majolica plates, but not in abundance, as the clerical residence did.

Technologies such as lead glaze increased the value of indigenous pottery. VanValkenburgh (2012:147; see also Chapter 8) describes early green-glazed Chimu-Inca-style fineware bottle fragments recovered from Magdalena. Interestingly, glaze occurs not on other indigenous serving pieces such as individual serving bowls or jarras, but rather on vessels with a food processing function, many of which have evidence for use over fire. Indigenous potters clearly experimented with this introduction, indicating that in spite of difficulties and alongside shifts in household economies, residents showed interest in new things and sought ways to incorporate them into their daily lives. These everyday vessels may have had a limited distribution and constituted objects of higher status. That might explain why Units 1 and 2 have fewer of these potsherds than Unit 28. Occupants of the clerical residence also likely had easier access to such pieces, and it is evident that they had accumulated a greater variety of glazed everyday forms compared to the town's household assemblages, mainly limited to neckless ollas.

As Delibes (Chapter 12) makes clear, over time things got more difficult for the indigenous residents of Magdalena de Cao Viejo. The decrease in indigenous serving pieces, fancy blackwares, and mold-made vessels might have been related to a pauperization of the community compared to better times in the prehispanic era. Continual shortages of water and fuel, as well as ever-increasing numbers of family members leaving town temporarily or for good, made it increasingly difficult for those who stayed behind to invest in, much less expand or embellish, a household economy. Those who could improve their household economies may have been drawn to new items and technologies as much as Spanish colonial importers/producers encouraged their distribution. In material ways, continuity characterized the community of Magdalena, but families had become accustomed to change too, especially since the arrival of the Inca. The people of Magdalena saw new opportunities and innovations and incorporated what they could. In the process they simultaneously strove to maintain traditional culinary practices.

REFERENCES CITED

Bawden, Garth
    1977 Galindo and the Nature of the Middle Horizon in Northern Coastal Peru. Unpublished
          Ph.D. dissertation, Harvard University.

Bennett, Wendell C.
    1939 *The Archaeology of the North Coast of Peru.* Anthropological Papers Vol. 37, Pt. 1.
          New York: American Museum of Natural History.

Billman, Brian R.
    1996 The Evolution of Prehistoric Political Organization in the Moche Valley, Peru.
          Unpublished Ph.D. dissertation, University of California, Santa Barbara.

Braun, David P.
    1980 Experimental Interpretations of Vessel Use on the Basis of Rim and Neck Formal
          Attributes. In *The Navajo Project: Archaeological Investigations, Page to Phoenix 500 KV
          Southern Transmission Line*, edited by D. C. Feiron, S. M. Wilson, D. C. Fiero, R. W.
          Munson, M. T. Mcclain, and A. H. Zier, pp. 171–231. Flagstaff: Museum of Northern
          Arizona.
    1991 Why Decorate a Pot? Midwestern Household Pottery, 200 B.C.–A.D. 600. *Journal of
          Anthropological Archaeology* 10:360–397.

Bray, Tamara
2003 Inka Pottery as Culinary Equipment: Food, Feasting, and Gender in Imperial State Design. *Latin American Antiquity* 14(1):3–28.

Chase, Philip G.
1985 Whole Vessels and Sherds: An Experimental Investigation of Their Qualitative Relationships. *Journal of Field Archaeology* 12(2):213–218.

Cleland, Kate M., and Izumi Shimada
1998 Paleteada Potters: Technology, Production Sphere, and Sub-Culture in Ancient Peru. In *Andean Ceramics: Technology, Organization, and Approaches*, edited by Izumi Shimada, pp. 111–150. MASCA Research Papers in Science and Anthropology, Vol. 15 Supp. Philadelphia: University of Pennsylvania Museum of Archaeology and Anthropology.

Collier, Donald
1955 *Cultural Chronology and Change as Reflected in the Ceramics of the Virú Valley, Peru*. Fieldiana Anthropology 43. Chicago: Natural History Museum.

Cutler, Hugh, and Martin Cardenas
1947 Chicha, a Native South American Beer. *Botanical Museum Leaflets, Harvard University* 13:33–60.

Cutright, Robyn E.
2009 Between the Kitchen and the State: Domestic Practice and Chimu Expansion in the Jequetepeque Valley, Peru. Unpublished Ph.D. dissertation, University of Pittsburgh.

David, Nicholas
1972 On the Life Span of Pottery, Type Frequencies, and Archaeological Inference. *American Antiquity* 37:141–142.

DeBoer, Warren
1974 Ceramic Longevity and Archaeological Interpretation: An Example from the Upper Ucayali, Peru. *American Antiquity* 39(2):335–343.

Donnan, Christopher B.
1997 A Chimu-Inka Ceramic-Manufacturing Center from the North Coast of Peru. *Latin American Antiquity* 8(1):30–54.

Egloff, B. J.
1973 A Method for Counting Rim Sherds. *American Antiquity* 38(3):351–353.

Ericson, Jonathan E., and Suzanne P. De Atley
1976 Reconstructing Ceramic Assemblages: An Experiment to Derive the Morphology and Capacity of Parent Vessels from Sherds. *American Antiquity* 41(4):484–489.

Fitting, James E., and John R. Halsey
1966 Rim Diameter and Vessel Size in Wayne Ware Vessels. *Wisconsin Archaeologist* 47:208–211.

Ford, James A.
1949 *Cultural Dating of Prehistoric Sites in the Virú Valley, Peru*. Anthropological Papers Vol. 43, Pt. 1. New York: American Museum of Natural History.

Foster, George M.
1960 Life Expectancy of Utilitarian Pottery in Tzintzuntzan, Michoacan, Mexico. *American Antiquity* 25:606–609.

Gamarra Carranza, Nadia, and Henry Gayoso Rullier

2008 La cerámica doméstica en huacas de Moche: Un intento de tipología y seriación. In *Arqueología Mochica: Nuevos Enfoques*, edited by Luis Jaime Castillo Butters, Hélène Bernier, Gregory Lockard, and Julio Rucabado Yong, pp. 187–202. Lima: Fondo Editorial de la Pontificia Universidad Católica del Perú.

Gillin, John

1947 *Moche: A Peruvian Coastal Community.* Institute of Social Anthropology, Publication No. 3. Washington, DC: Smithsonian Institution.

Goldstein, Paul

2003 From Stew Eaters to Maize Drinkers. In *The Archaeology and Politics of Food and Feasting in Early States and Empires*, edited by Tamara L. Bray, pp. 143–172. New York: Springer.

Hally, David J.

1983a Use Alteration of Pottery Vessel Surfaces: An Important Source of Evidence for the Identification of Vessel Function. *North American Archaeologist* 4:3–26.

1983b The Interpretive Potential of Pottery from Domestic Contexts. *Midcontinental Journal of Archaeology* 8:163–196.

1984 Vessel Assemblages and Food Habits: A Comparison of Two Aboriginal Southeastern Vessel Assemblages. *Southeastern Archaeology* 3:46–64.

1986 The Identification of Vessel Function: A Case Study from Northwest Georgia. *American Antiquity* 51:267–295.

Hayashida, Frances

1998 New Insights into Inka Pottery Production. In *Andean Ceramics: Technology, Organization, and Approaches*, edited by Izumi Shimada, pp. 313–335. MASCA Research Papers in Science and Anthropology, Vol. 15 Supp. Philadelphia; University of Pennsylvania Museum of Archaeology and Anthropology.

1999 Style, Technology, and State Production: Inka Pottery Manufacture in the Leche Valley, Peru. *Latin American Antiquity* 9(4):337–352.

2008 Ancient Beer and Modern Brewers: Ethnoarchaeological Observations of Chicha Production in Two Regions of the North Coast of Peru. *Journal of Anthropological Archaeology* 27:161–174.

Henrickson, Elizabeth F., and Mary M. A. McDonald

1983 Form and Function: An Ethnographic Search and Archaeological Application. *American Anthropologist* 85(3):630–643.

Hildebrand, John A., and Melissa Hagstrum

1999 New Approaches to Ceramic Use and Discard: Cooking Pottery from the Peruvian Andes in Ethnoarchaeological Perspective. *Latin American Antiquity* 9(1):25–46.

Holley, George R.

1989 *The Archaeology of the Cahokia Mounds ICT-II: Ceramics.* Illinois Cultural Resources Study No. 11. Springfield: Illinois Historic Preservation Agency.

Jennings, Justin, and Melissa Chatfield

2009 Pots, Brewers, and Hosts: Women's Power and the Limits of Central Andean Feasting. In *Drink, Power, and Society in the Andes*, edited by Justin Jennings and Brenda J. Bowser, pp. 200–231. Gainesville: University Press of Florida.

Keatinge, Richard W.

    1973 Chimu Ceramics from the Moche Valley, Peru: A Computer Application to Seriation. Unpublished Ph.D. dissertation, Harvard University.

Lockard, Greg.

    2009 The Occupational History of Galindo, Moche Valley Peru. *Latin American Antiquity* 20(2):279–302.

López, Luis Francisco Rodríguez

    1994 *Costa Norte: Diez mil años de prehistoria*. Lima: Ministerio de la Presidencia, Consejo Nacional de Ciencia y Tecnología.

Mehaffey, Douglas T.

    1998 Broken Pots and Life in Two Rural Moche Villages: Pottery Analysis, Interpretation, and Comparisons. Unpublished M.A. thesis, University of Arizona, Phoenix.

Meyers, Albert

    1975 Algunos problemas en la clasificación del estilo incaico. *Pumapunku* 8:7–25.

Moore, Jerry

    1989 Pre-Hispanic Beer in Coastal Peru: Technology and Social Context of Prehistoric Production. *American Anthropologist* 91(4):682–695.

Orton, Clive

    1993 How Many Pots Make Five? An Historical Review of Pottery Quantification. *Archaeometry* 35(2):169–184.

Pauketat, Timothy

    1987 A Functional Consideration of a Mississippian Domestic Vessel Assemblage. *Southeastern Archaeology* 6:1–15.

Plog, Stephen

    1985 Estimating Vessel Orifice Diameters: Measurement Methods and Measurement Error. In *Decoding Prehistoric Ceramics*, edited by Ben A. Nelson, pp. 243–253. Carbondale: Southern Illinois University Press.

Quilter, Jeffrey

    2013 Interpreting the Colonial Experience at Magdalena de Cao Viejo, Chicama Valley, Peru, 1578–1770. Annual Report, NEH Collaborative Research Grant RZ511509.

Ramírez, Susan

    1996 *The World Upside Down: Cross-Cultural Contact and Conflict in Sixteenth-Century Peru*. Stanford, CA: Stanford University Press.

Rice, Prudence

    1997 Wine and Brandy Production in Colonial Peru: A Historical and Archaeological Investigation. *Journal of Interdisciplinary History* 27(3):455–479.

Rowe, John H.

    1946 Inca Culture at the Time of the Spanish Conquest. In *Handbook of South American Indians*, vol. 2, *The Andean Civilizations*, edited by Julian Steward, pp. 183–330. Washington, DC: Bureau of American Ethnology.

Schiffer, Michael B.

    1985 Is There a "Pompeii Premise" in Archaeology? *Journal of Anthropological Research* 41(1):18–41.

    1996 *Formation Processes of the Archaeological Record*. Albuquerque: University of New Mexico Press.

Shimada, Izumi

    1994 *Pampa Grande and the Mochica Culture.* Austin: University of Texas Press.

Sillar, Bill

    2000 *Shaping Culture: Making Pots and Constructing Households, An Ethnoarchaeological Study of Pottery Production, Trade and Use in the Andes.* BAR International Series 883. Oxford: Archaeopress.

Skibo, James M.

    2013 *Understanding Pottery Function: Manuals in Archaeological Method, Theory and Technique.* New York: Springer.

Smith, Marian J. Jr.

    1988 Function from Whole Vessel Shape: A Method and an Application to Anasazi Black Mesa, Arizona. *American Anthropologist* 90:912–922.

Tate, James P.

    2007 The Late Horizon Occupation of the El Brujo Site Complex, Chicama Valley, Peru. Unpublished Ph.D. dissertation, University of California, Santa Barbara.

Topic, John R.

    1982 Lower-Class Social and Economic Organization at Chan Chan. In *Chan Chan: Andean Desert City,* edited by Kent C. Day and Michael E. Moseley, pp. 255–284. Albuquerque: School of American Research Press.

Torres Mora, Rocío de María

    2011 Cerámica colonial en el valle bajo y medio de Zaña: Tecnología, formas y comercio. Unpublished *licenciada* thesis, Pontificia Universidad Católica del Perú, Lima.

Tschauner, Hartmut

    2006 Socioeconomic and Political Organization in the Late Prehispanic Lambayeque Sphere, Northern North Coast of Peru. Unpublished Ph.D. dissertation, Harvard University.

VanValkenburgh, Parker

    2012 Building Subjects: Landscapes of Forced Resettlement in the Zaña and Chamán Valleys, Peru, 16th and 17th Centuries C.E. Unpublished Ph.D. dissertation, Harvard University

Walsh, M. R.

    1979 From Sherds to Pots: Deriving the Volumes of Broken Vessels. Unpublished M.A. thesis, Department of Anthropology, University of California, Los Angeles.

Wernke, Steven A.

    2012 Andean Households in Transition: The Politics of Domestic Space at an Early Colonial *Doctrina* in the Peruvian Highlands. In *Decolonizing Indigenous Histories: Exploring Prehistoric/Colonial Transitions in Archaeology,* edited by Maxine Oland, Siobhan M. Hart, and Liam Frink, pp. 201–229. Tucson: University of Arizona Press.

Whallon, Robert

    1969 Rim Diameter, Vessel Volume, and Economic Prehistory. *Michigan Academician* 11(2):89–98.

Wilson, Greg

    2005 Between Plaza and Palisade: Household and Community Organization at Early Moundville. Unpublished Ph. D. dissertation, University of North Carolina at Chapel Hill.

10

Metals

Andrew Z. Lorey and Jeffrey Quilter

Introduction

T HE MAGDALENA DE CAO excavations yielded a diverse collection of 105 metal objects, ranging from inlaid finger rings to utilitarian nails. Magdaleneros likely used these artifacts on a daily basis at the site, either within the domestic area populated by the settlement's laborers and craftspeople or within the confines of the site's church complex. We found 39 metal artifacts in and close to the church compound and 66 others in depositional association with the town. A few artifacts were small pieces of scrap metal or fragments of larger objects, and most items clearly exhibit European styles or forms. We successfully identified a majority of the artifacts in the Magdalena assemblage, such as horseshoes, straight pins, and bells, but others resisted straightforward categorization and appeared to represent components of composite artifacts used for purposes we cannot determine. Others may have existed as possible decorations for furniture or clothing. Several notable metal artifacts do, however, exhibit indigenous styles. Many of these materials also hint at the possible coexistence of indigenous and European production methods.

As with other material assemblages at the site, we do not fully know how the nature and quantity of metal artifacts at Magdalena de Cao compare to those at other colonial settlements. Poor chronological controls for our items further complicate our archaeological interpretations, since some artifacts may date to early in the occupation and others to later periods. Because of the general scarcity of published literature concerning sixteenth- and seventeenth-century metallurgy, we also possess little knowledge regarding the production and use of quotidian metal objects in Europe. This fact, in turn, prevents us from drawing absolute comparisons between indigenously produced and imported objects. Despite these obstacles, we present observational and compositional descriptions for our metal objects as a means to advance archaeological understandings of the complex interactions between European and Andean people, production regimes, and metallurgical objects that occurred at colonial and religious settlements such as Magdalena de Cao Viejo.

Metallurgy in the Central Andes has a long history (Quilter 2011). The earliest cold-hammered gold beads in the Titicaca Basin date to between 2155 and 1936 cal. B.C. (Aldenderfer et al. 2008), and archaeologists have discussed at length the widespread and elaborate work in precious metals dating to subsequent Initial Period cultures throughout Peru (Burger and Gordon 1998; Lechtman 2014). The Chavín culture and the later Moche, in particular, created spectacular crowns and other personal adornments (Alva and Donnan 1994; Burger 1995; Donnan 2012; Stone-Miller 2002). During the Early Intermediate Period, the Moche also used various copper alloys to create utilitarian items such as pointed spikes on two-handed clubs, and their highland Recuay neighbors frequently utilized copper as a preferred material for mace heads (Lau 2011; Quilter 2008). By the Late Intermediate Period (ca. 1100–1450), Lambayeque metalsmiths produced an impressive array of metal items that included not only costume elements and ritual paraphernalia but also weapons and agricultural tools (Lechtman 2014; Merkel and Velarde 1998; Shimada 2013; Shimada and Griffin 1994).[1] These trends continued with the florescence of the Chimu and Inca Empires (Bray 2012; Stone-Miller 2002). The actual quantities of these artifact types in antiquity are difficult to assess, however, due to issues such as tool deterioration and the ease with which craftspeople could repurpose metals for reworking them into new items.

Prior to Spanish contact with Andean communities, metal objects undoubtedly had value as tools, if only for the physical advantages they could provide in comparison to stone and wood. Metallic materials also carried value as ornaments because of their reflective and transformative properties, often interpreted by archaeologists as material markers of ideological and social power (Cummins 2002; Lechtman 1993; Saunders 2003). As such, traditions of both fine and functional metallurgy possessed rich histories in Peru prior to Spanish conquest and colonization, although European contact brought new design forms and production technologies, notably the introduction of refined iron and steel (Lechtman 2014). Still, we know little about the ways in which indigenous Peruvians received, resisted, or transformed European tools, technologies, and concepts during the early years of the encounter. The Magdalena metals assemblage thus offers an intriguing glimpse into the roles that metal objects played within day-to-day life in Colonial Period Peru.

Overview of the Magdalena de Cao Metal Objects

For classificatory purposes, we define the main categories of our assemblage as straight pins, bells, ornaments, and hardware/tools (Table 10.1). Although the pins could be included as a subtype of hardware and tools, they are so numerous and common that separation into a distinct category helps to clarify our analysis. A fifth category consists of items that do not easily fit within our four aforementioned artifact types.

Raw object counts illustrate that straight pins and small bells represent the most plentiful types of metal artifacts found at Magdalena. Pins probably served a wide variety of purposes during the early Colonial Period, functioning as clothing fasteners or sewing implements and aiding in engraving, puncturing, and other tasks. Our compositional and observational analyses suggest that the pins found at Magdalena de Cao Viejo were manufactured in Europe, produced in a relatively cheap and large-scale fashion, and shipped to Peru in bulk (see the section on straight pins in "Artifacts by Category"). The nearly even distribution of straight pins throughout the site's church and town sectors suggests that pins were likely accessible

Table 10.1 Metal Objects Found during Excavations at Magdalena de Cao Viejo

OBJECT TYPE	TOTALS	TOWN	CHURCH COMPLEX	pXRF TESTED	pXRF SCANS COMPLETED
Bells	19	13	6	2	5
Hardware/tools	19	14	5	11	38
Ornaments	13	10	3	8	28
Straight pins	42	19	23	2	6
Other items	12	10	2	7	24
Totals	105	66	39	30	101

to most, if not all, segments of the community's population. This fact also implies that pins served multiple purposes and possessed flexible functionalities. Archaeologists in Peru have not yet found any local equivalents to the sturdy copper alloy pins that circulated in Europe during this time period, so indigenous inhabitants at Magdalena de Cao may have eagerly sought them.

Local populations likely mined the collapsed church complex for useful objects during the Colonial Period (see Chapter 2), and this practice may have artificially distorted the frequencies of materials unearthed during our excavations at Magdalena de Cao Viejo. Consequently, any interpretations based on object distribution should be treated with due caution. For this reason, we do not consider the relatively high number of bells excavated from the town significant even though it is more than double the number found in the church. A larger sample size might confirm, for example, a hypothesis that higher artifact counts occurred in the town due to friars' distributions of goods to community members, but such a conclusion represents a matter for future research.

Either of two possible explanations may account for the relatively high quantity of metal objects found in the town compared to the quantity found in the church. First, townspeople may have engaged more frequently in activities that required metal objects than did the friars, possibly in the form of manual labor. Second, local metalworking traditions may have made metal objects more accessible to townspeople than to friars. As previously mentioned, we acknowledge that the observed disparity between town and church may also simply have resulted from the colonial-era mining of the church complex.

Compositional Analysis of Magdalena Metal Artifacts

We conducted our compositional analyses using a Bruker Tracer III-SD portable X-ray fluorescence (pXRF) spectrometer.[2] The spectrometer collected compositional data from each artifact at two to four discrete locations, depending on artifact size, and for each analytical trial we positioned the tested object under a covered housing and oriented it to expose its flattest surface to the X-ray beam. This precaution minimized the unwanted effects of scattering and improved the accuracy of the spectrometer's readings. Each sample was analyzed at settings of 40 kV and 30 μA in an air path for a count period of 200 seconds live time, and the instrument used a 2,048-channel configuration. Lastly, we employed S1pXRF and ARTAX computer software packages to calculate our quantitative data and produce spectral graphs. We will present our pXRF results within the discussions of artifacts by category (see Table 10.4).[3]

Upon preliminary visual inspections, Magdalena artifacts appeared to consist of iron and copper alloys. A characteristic green patina often seemed to indicate the presence of copper, but it is widely known that different chemical alloys may exhibit similar visual appearances (Killick 2014; Notis 2014). Determining the compositions of alloys in the Magdalena metals through the use of pXRF spectrometry allowed us to differentiate between objects of possible European manufacture and those likely to be of local origin. Although our results should be regarded as the starting point for more conclusive analyses or source determinations in the future, our readings are at the very least internally consistent and demonstrate that patterns of compositional differentiation exist within the metals assemblage at Magdalena. The following discussion considers the Magdalena de Cao Viejo metals assemblage in reference to the object categories outlined above, though we include artifacts of special interest within a separate section, regardless of their category membership.

Artifacts by Category
Straight Pins

Round-headed straight pins (Figure 10.1; Table 10.2) represent the most abundant metal artifact type within the colonial deposits at Magdalena de Cao, a pattern that also is typical of archaeological sites in Europe that date to the Late Medieval (ca. 1300–1500) and Early Modern (ca. 1500–1750) periods (Beaudry 2006:10).[4] In Early Modern Europe, people used straight pins for various practical purposes—as fasteners for their clothing and as sewing or puncturing implements—and we infer that pins served similar ends in contemporary colonial settings, primarily because of their small size, their portability, and their flexible functionalities. Given that pins were more difficult to procure and replace in the New World than in more proximal colonies, consumers may have used them for even more varied purposes in settlements such as Magdalena de Cao.

Representing 40 percent ($N=42$) of Magdalena de Cao's metal assemblage, straight pins probably played important roles during the daily lives of inhabitants at the site. Of the 42 pins, 34 range between 2.7 and 3.6 cm in length and between .1 and .3 g in weight. The other eight pins vary between 4.2 and 6.3 cm in length and weigh between .2 and 1.1 g. For practical reasons, colonial people may have used larger pins to secure heavier fabrics or garments of greater size. Alternatively, pins of different sizes may have served as indicators of differing statuses or wealth. Of the total number of pins, eight were bent to an interior angle less than or equal to 150 degrees, but none were broken. Though the bending could have resulted from taphonomic actions at the site, it may represent a direct marker of use, indicating either the stresses placed on the pins by heavy fabrics or the preferred angle at which a clothing item was fastened.

Our pXRF analyses of two pins, 07-M-21 and 07-M-22, revealed that both contained seemingly identical copper-zinc alloys. Beyond this important similarity, pXRF analysis did not record any other elements in measurable concentrations.

Mechanized pin production in the Old World began as early as the late Middle Ages and developed through distinct phases of manufacturing improvement (Beaudry 2006; Coovadia

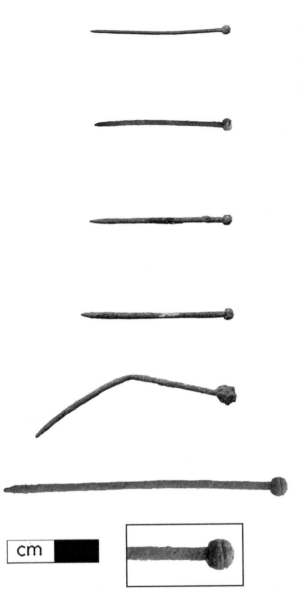

Figure 10.1
Straight pins. Detail shows the wire-wound head of the largest pin. Top to bottom: 05-M-02, 07-M-07, 05-M-06, 05-M-05, 07-M-14, 07-M-08.

2008; Harskamp 2010). By the fifteenth and sixteenth centuries, craftspeople were producing thousands of pins per day, although production methods still required a multistage process in order to create finished items (Beaudry 2006:15–21). Early production methods drew brass wire to create the pointed shank and required a laborer to add the head separately, by hand. At this stage in the development of European metalworking, brass had become the material of choice for functional metallic items. As a result, many different items exemplified brass's characteristic copper-zinc composition, an alloy easily differentiated from those autochthonous to the Andes (Lechtman 1996, 2014). Subsequent mechanization enabled manufactories to create pinheads by coiling wire two or three times to form a spherical head at a shank's proximal end (Beaudry 2006:19).

Table 10.2 Straight Pins of Magdalena de Cao Viejo

OBJECT NUMBER	PROVENANCE	LENGTH (cm)	WEIGHT (g)
05-M-02	Church	3.0	.10
05-M-03	Church	3.0	.10
05-M-04	Church	3.3	.20
05-M-05	Church	3.2	.20
05-M-06	Church	3.0	.20
05-M-08	Church	3.3	.30
06-M-07	Town	3.0	.20
06-M-11	Town	3.3	.20
06-M-12	Town	5.2	.60
07-M-07	Church	2.9	.20
07-M-08	Church	6.3	1.10
07-M-10	Town	3.6	.20
07-M-14	Church	4.3	.40
07-M-17	Town	3.2	.20
07-M-20	Town	2.9	.10
07-M-21	Town	4.5	.40
07-M-22	Town	4.2	.40
07-M-26	Town	2.9	.10
07-M-27	Town	3.3	.20
07-M-28	Town	3.3	.30
07-M-29	Town	3.0	.10
07-M-30	Town	3.3	.20
08-M-04	Town	4.6	.30
08-M-05	Town	3.1	.10
08-M-07	Town	4.6	.20
08-M-08	Town	5.7	.80
08-M-12	Town	3.0	.10
08-M-16	Church	3.0	.10
08-M-17	Church	3.3	.30
08-M-18	Church	3.2	.10
08-M-19	Church	3.3	.20
08-M-20	Church	3.0	.10
08-M-21	Church	3.2	.30
08-M-22	Church	3.2	.30
08-M-23	Church	3.4	.20
08-M-26	Church	3.0	.20
08-M-27	Church	3.2	.30
08-M-29	Church	3.3	.20
08-M-30	Church	2.7	.10
08-M-31	Church	3.3	.30
08-M-32	Church	3.2	.20
12-M-02	Town	3.2	.20

Although some of the smallest pins from Magdalena exhibit corrosion that obscures the details of their heads, in many cases preservation is good and the distinctive wire-wound head can be seen (Figure 10.1, detail). This indicates that the Magdalena pins are the products of mechanization and that the site's inhabitants likely imported them from Europe. However, the presence of wire-wound heads does not correspond to an exact date in the New World, as objects from La Isabela, the settlement founded by Christopher Columbus and occupied between 1493 and 1498, also possess wire-wound heads (Deagan 2002; Deagan and Cruxent 2002). Manufacturers continued to use the technique well into the eighteenth century, further complicating the issue of dating the pins at Magdalena (Tylecote 1972, cited in Beaudry 2006:21).

Beaudry (2006:16–17) notes the inferiority of British pins during the fifteenth century due to problems with brass wire production in England. Given this, many fifteenth-century consumers preferred French pins manufactured in Paris, and scholars note that the British imported large quantities of foreign pins, especially from France and Spain (Beaudry 2006:16–17; Beck 1995:24). Low-quality raw materials contributed to much of the issue with British manufacturing. Given the history of raw metal processing in Spain since antiquity and our historical knowledge concerning the site's colonial inhabitants (see Chapter 12), it is quite possible that Magdalena's pins originated there.

Bells

The next most abundant category of metal artifacts at Magdalena de Cao, bells, accounted for 18 percent ($N = 19$) of the objects considered within our study. Interestingly, one bell bears what appears to be its original clapper (Figure 10.2; Table 10.3). Even though most of the small bells are fragmentary or deformed to various extents, all possess intact shoulders. In addition, many still retain their crowns.

We found two distinctive styles of bells at the site, hemispherical and pyramidal. All 19 bells fall into these two categories, with ten being hemispherical and nine being pyramidal. The bells were made from sheet metal and possess diameters or widths ranging from 1.1 to 3.5 cm. Overall, pyramidal bells generally exhibit larger dimensions than their hemispherical counterparts. Metalworkers appear to have created the hemispherical bells by pounding sheet metal on a form to produce the rounded shape, a time-consuming and laborious process involving hammering and the use of anneals (Lechtman 2014). Workers may have manufactured the pyramidal bells more expeditiously, evident in the fact that they resemble crimped pieces of sheet metal. Whether or not these different shapes indicate the presence of two distinct populations of craftspeople at the site, perhaps one more adept at metalsmithing than the other, cannot be determined from archaeological evidence alone.

Artisans may have used the same sheet metal stock to create both types of bells, as the thicknesses of all bells fall within the same range, regardless of form (.40–2.40 mm). Evidently these thicknesses functioned equally well within the two very different production methods used to create the bells, pounding in the case of the hemispherical form and crimping in the case of the pyramidal. Both techniques imply a considerable amount of metalworking knowledge and dexterity on the part of their makers, because transforming thin metal base sheets into such delicate forms required careful manipulation and precision.

Eight of the ten hemispherical bells present an identical pattern of engraving, with two parallel lines running around the circumference of each bell near its crown. Conversely,

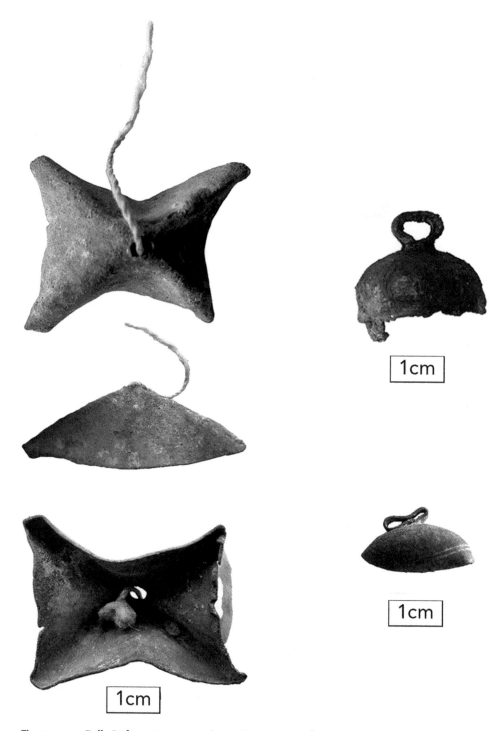

Figure 10.2 Bells. Left: 07-M-05, top, side, and bottom views (original string). Right, top: 07-M-01. Right, bottom: 06-M-02.

Table 10.3   Bells of Magdalena de Cao Viejo

OBJECT NUMBER	FORM	PROVENANCE	DIAMETER (cm)	SHEET METAL THICKNESS (mm)	WEIGHT (g)
05-M-01	Hemispherical	Church	1.2	1.60	1.7
05-M-07	Hemispherical	Church	1.1	.87	1.9
06-M-02	Hemispherical	Town	1.1	.80	1.1
06-M-06	Pyramidal	Town	2.7	2.40	6.8
06-M-08	Hemispherical	Town	2.4	1.10	2.1
06-M-10	Hemispherical	Town	1.6	.71	.9
07-M-01	Hemispherical	Town	2.5	1.38	4.0
07-M-05	Pyramidal	Church	3.2	.75	6.2
07-M-11	Hemispherical	Church	1.6	.40	0.6
07-M-13	Pyramidal	Church	2.2	.80	0.9
07-M-18	Pyramidal	Town	2.3	1.20	6.6
07-M-19	Hemispherical	Town	1.2	.70	1.3
08-M-09	Pyramidal	Town	2.1	2.10	5.7
08-M-10	Hemispherical	Town	2.7	2.00	2.1
08-M-11	Hemispherical	Town	3.3	1.90	1.4
08-M-13	Pyramidal	Town	2.6	.87	3.6
08-M-14	Pyramidal	Town	2.7	1.30	5.4
08-M-24	Pyramidal	Church	3.5	1.00	15.8
08-M-33	Pyramidal	Town	2.0	1.60	4.1

the nine pyramidal bells bear no apparent decorations but are quite uniform in their forms and dimensions. Similar to the standardized sizes and shapes of the straight pins, the presence of the same decorative motif on so many of the rounded bells suggests that they were mass-produced.

Whether the two types of bells fulfilled different purposes or satisfied different groups of consumers cannot be definitively determined from archaeological or compositional analyses. We frequently discovered bells of both styles within the same excavation units, however, and this may suggest that the Magdalena community used the different forms together or interchangeably. Only three bells appeared in contexts without at least one other associated bell, and this could mean that individuals at the site often used bells in groups. Frequent bell use in Catholic services may offer one explanation for bell groupings and quantities at the site (e.g. Herrera 2004).

While Catholic rites and rituals may have initially inspired bell use at Magdalena, it seems likely that colonial townspeople used metal bells in additional ways. It is widely accepted that indigenous peoples throughout the Americas made and eagerly sought bells and rolled sheet metal tinklers for their acoustic and visual properties, frequently attaching them to clothing (Brown 1979:201; Donnan 2012:191; Stone-Miller 2002:117). The round bells from Magdalena may or may not have produced a good, clear ringing sound, but it seems likely that the pyramidal forms would have produced effective sounds only when used in groups. Furthermore, two or more pyramidal bells striking one another surely would have produced better ringing than clappers operating within the crimped metal objects.

Previous analyses (Cummins 2002; Donnan 2012; Hosler 1994) have suggested that the metallic and sound-producing qualities that appealed to other precolumbian populations also encouraged metal use among indigenous people in colonial Peru. Excavations at Magdalena, however, did not reveal clothing or textile fragments in direct association with our bells. Thus, whether townspeople used the bells strictly for liturgical purposes or for decoration is not clear at present. The reasons noted here do, however, tend to suggest ceremonial rather than decorative uses of bells and tinklers at Magdalena de Cao.

We analyzed one each of the hemispheric and pyramidal bells (06-M-02 and 08-M-24, respectively) using pXRF spectrometry. Both possessed significant copper and zinc concentrations, but analysis of the crimped bell revealed a detectable quantity of lead. Such a fact may indicate that metalworkers used multiple metal stocks during the manufacture of the bells, but more bells should be examined before drawing any decisive conclusions. Interestingly, the hemispherical bell exhibits a compositional profile strikingly similar to that of the straight pins. Given the presumed European origin of the straight pins, this similarity suggests that these bells, or the metal sheets from which they were made, were imported European objects.

Our semi-quantitative application of pXRF spectrometry cannot conclusively prove that the hemispherical bell and the two analyzed straight pins were created using the same metal alloy, but the results of our study strongly support this notion (see Shackley 2012 for a comprehensive assessment of pXRF and its limitations). If colonists, traders, priests, or colonial administrators brought the pins to Magdalena, then they may have brought bells to the site as well. Alternatively, European colonists could have brought sheet metal to a New World urban center or to Magdalena itself, where it was then made into various items such as bells of different shapes and forms. From an economic perspective, it would certainly have been easier to ship metal in unrefined sheets and then make the bells according to local needs and desires.

Ornaments

Decorative ornaments constitute another easily identifiable category of metal artifacts at Magdalena (Figure 10.3). Broadly, this artifact group contains objects whose aesthetic qualities seem to overshadow their practical uses. They include simple starlike objects (07-M-16 and 07-M-32) and a more elaborate starburst (07-M-02) that might have been attached to a piece of furniture or clothing; a flat object resembling a badge or cockade, perhaps worn as part of a uniform (06-M-09); finger rings (08-M-36 and 08-M-37); and crucifixes and other religious medallions. Given their unique aesthetic qualities, these items may have been highly personal in nature. Out of the 13 artifacts classified as ornaments, 8 underwent pXRF testing to determine their elemental compositions.

Our pXRF analysis of ornamental artifacts yielded several interesting results. One of the less ornate star-shaped objects, the five-pointed star (07-M-16; Figure 10.3A) was almost pure copper, suggesting a high degree of processing and refinement. The six-pointed star (07-M-32), on the other hand, exhibited an arsenical copper alloy (Figure 10.3B). The eight-pointed star-like ornament (07-M-02; Figure 10.3C) possesses a compositional profile similar to that of the

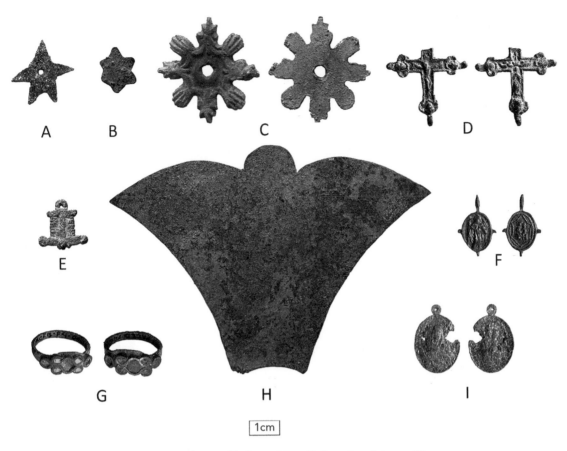

Figure 10.3 Ornaments. A. Star with central hole, 07-M-16; B. Six-pointed star, 07-M-32; C. Eight-pointed starlike ornament, 07-M-02; D. Crucifix, 07-M-36; E. Anchor-like pendant, 07-M-09; F. Small medallion, 13-M-01; G. Rings, left: 08-M-36, right: 08-M-37; H. Ornament, 05-M-09; I. Large medallion, 13-M-02.

pyramidal bell. Finally, the badge or cockade (06-M-09; Figure 10.3H) was made from what appears to be the same copper-zinc alloy as the straight pins and hemispherical bell.

Contrary to what one might expect given its likely associations with priestly elites and religious conceptualizations of the divine, the crucifix (07-M-02; Figure 10.3D) did not exhibit any traces of precious metals. Rather, it contains a copper alloy that possesses elevated zinc and lead concentrations. The composition of this alloy is similar to the alloys found in the straight pins and bells, particularly the pyramidal bell. One ornament, a small pendant, exhibited a significant proportion of silver within its composition (07-M-09; Figure 10.3E). The presence of arsenic within the composition of 07-M-32 (Figure 10.3B), the six-pointed star, is notable because Andean populations manufactured arsenical bronze alloys prior to European contact (see the discussion of 08-M-03 later in this chapter). These results do not reveal any significant patterns concerning the composition of ornamental metals at Magdalena de Cao, but they do demonstrate that townspeople used a wide variety of alloys and raw materials at the site.

Hardware and Tools

The fourth grouping of Magdalena de Cao's metal objects represents 18 percent of the total assemblage and consists of 19 hardware items and tools. For our purposes, we define any metallic component whose use is primarily functional in nature as a hardware item. Similarly, we consider any handheld implement designed to complete a specific task a tool. This group includes one clearly identifiable nail or stud (07-M-06; Figure 10.4B), suggesting that European methods influenced at least some proportion of the construction episodes undertaken at the site. Further evidence of European materials within this object category comes in the form of two horseshoe fragments (06-M-05 and 08-M-28; Figure 10.5) that indicate the presence of horses, donkeys, or mules at the site. Another artifact (06-M-04; Figure 10.6) consists

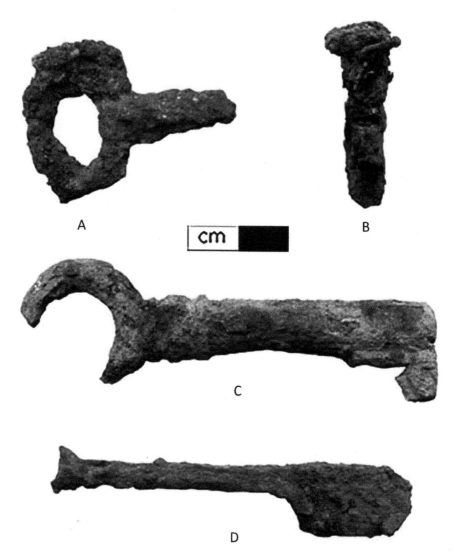

Figure 10.4 Iron objects. A. Key or handle, 12-M-01; B. Stud or nail, 07-M-06; C. Key, 05-M-09; D. Flanged rod, 08-M-02.

Figure 10.5
Possible horseshoe
and fragment.
Top: 06-M-05.
Bottom: 08-M-29.

cm

of relatively thick wire bent into a unique and distinctive shape. It may have formed part of a spur, stirrup, or other piece of riding equipment. Taken together, the horseshoe fragments and this intriguing wire artifact represent some of the earliest traces of equine husbandry in the Andean archaeological record.

Keys, cutting implements, and several other large objects form the remainder of this artifact group, and many of these items are composed entirely of iron. That said, a few of the more uniquely shaped objects exhibit complex compositional profiles and illustrate the wide range of metal objects used by the people of Magdalena de Cao Viejo. One of the most striking objects (08-M-34; Figure 10.7) is composed of iron or an iron alloy (not tested through the use of pXRF). Its highly corroded surface obscures details of its original shape, but the presence of a small hole at one end suggests that the object attached to something else via the use of a small

Figure 10.6
Two views of
a bent wire artifact,
06-M-04.

cm

Figure 10.7
Possible hammer
of a flintlock gun,
08-M-34.

cm

bolt or pin. To our knowledge, the object that this artifact best resembles is the hammer of a flintlock pistol or musket (see Wilkinson 1971). If it is indeed part of a gun, then it represents one of only two examples of authentic or stylized weaponry in the entire Magdalena material suite. The other is a paper cutout of a spearhead (Figure 13.12 in Chapter 13). It is possible that 08-M-02 (Figure 10.4D), another corroded iron artifact, might also be part of a weapon, although this is highly speculative.

Figure 10.8 Copper alloy candlewick trimmer or snuffer, 08-M-25.

Another hardware item (08-M-25; Figure 10.8) is one of only a few Magdalena de Cao objects made using what appears to be mostly copper. A cast object that may represent part of a larger device, its basic form is that of a rectangular box, 3.2 cm wide, attached to a bar 12.6 cm long at its side. Both ends of the bar have decorative knurls, and the proximal end, farthest from the box, may represent a handle. A hole in the bar's flange suggests possible attachment to another physical component to form a composite artifact. This boxlike construction indicates that the object received or housed other materials or items, and a small break in the box's rim may imply that the object could be handled in such a manner so as to deposit the box's contents into another container below it. Despite these observations, the exact purpose of the item remains uncertain.

The artifact resembles a type of composite candlewick trimmer or snuffer that became popular in wealthier European households in the eighteenth century (Eveleigh 1985:14–16; McGreggor 1776). These tools usually consisted of a box attached to a device that resembled a long pair of scissors. The Magdalena object seems to have been too heavy to have served this function, however, and does not possess the finger holes typical of this type of wick trimmer or snuffer. Nonetheless, it is possible that this object could represent an early Spanish or Peruvian version of this type of implement.

In compositional terms, the bronze alloy used in 08-M-25 appears to be unique within our assemblage. It consists mostly of copper with a notable concentration of lead, as opposed to the more prevalent copper-zinc combination typical of other artifacts at Magdalena de Cao. Two of the four pXRF readings associated with this object did, however, reveal trace quantities of zinc, so the definitive composition of this object is not entirely certain. As noted earlier, copper-zinc bronzes were typically European in origin, so the observed presence of zinc within this artifact implies that it was brought to Magdalena de Cao or composed of metallic material that was not local to the site (Table 10.4).

We have classified other copper alloy artifacts as hardware, but many are too fragmentary or perplexing to discuss here. These include such things as a beveled edge fragment from a platelike object (08-M-06; Figure 10.9A) and a rectangular object in the form of a box with open, beveled ends (08-M-01; Figure 10.9E) that may have served as a sleeve for some other object. Object 07-M-04 (Figure 10.9F) likely represents a crude knife or perhaps an ingot of copper reserved for later use. Interestingly, this object was found wedged between the bases of cane posts that formed part of a quincha wall in Unit 2 (Figure 10.10). This may suggest a conscious effort to hide the object for safekeeping—perhaps a townsperson hid a metal knife from an inspector or tax collector. Alternatively, the placement of this knife or ingot within the quincha wall could bespeak a deliberate ritual act, making this object not unlike the apotropaic devices or warding items uncovered by archaeologists at other New World sites dating to the Colonial Period (e.g., Beck 2016; Manning 2014).

The most elaborate tool found at Magdalena was a folding knife with a carved wooden handle and iron alloy blade (07-M-38; Figure 10.11). This artifact was found in the uppermost level of Unit 2 in the surface dust and straw fragments alongside the eastern wall of the quincha compound. It is intricately carved, with a stylized lion's head at the proximal end of the wooden handle, architectonic motifs on its handle, and an encircling band of small circles about three-fourths of the way toward the blade. In the spaces between architectural forms that continue along the knife's handle, the initials "A.I." are carved on both sides of the handle, oriented to be visible when the knife is gripped from the bottom. The initials may refer to the knife's owner and imply that a high degree of sentimental value was assigned to the object. The knife's characteristic architectonic ornamentation dates it to between the sixteenth and eighteenth centuries (see Moore 1988). Its discovery in the upper levels of the house compound may indicate that it dates to relatively late in the occupation of the site, but it could just as easily have been curated for some time before it finally reached its observed depositional context.

Objects 05-M-09 and 12-M-01 (Figure 10.4A & C) appear to be fragments of keys. Because keys can be used to regulate access to objects and spaces, these artifacts probably played significant roles during daily life at the colonial site. Object 05-M-09 was found within the church, while 12-M-01 was excavated from within the town complex. These artifacts exhibit differing degrees of structural completeness and possess differences in terms of their physical dimensions as well. Both display certain characteristics that are consistent with sixteenth-century keys: circular handles, cylindrical shafts, and, in the case of 05-M-09, large rectangular teeth (Monk 1999). It could merely be a coincidence that the more robust key (presumably used with a more robust lock) was discovered within the confines of the church, but its presence in that location could also confirm that authorities at Magdalena de Cao controlled access to the church, its interior rooms, or its storage chests more strictly than they controlled access to other areas at the site.

Despite their structural similarities, the two incomplete keys show pronounced compositional differences. Object 05-M-09 is composed almost purely of iron, but pXRF analysis of 12-M-01 revealed significant copper, zinc, and calcium concentrations in addition to a dominant presence of iron. We cannot fully explain why this artifact possesses such a markedly different composition, but its chemistry could indicate that 12-M-01 served a more ornamental purpose than the other key fragment, that it originated at a different location, or that it was created during a different time period than the other. Alternatively, these chemical differences may simply demonstrate the different ways in which taphonomic processes have altered the compositions of two similar objects.

Although the formal and compositional characteristics of 05-M-09 and 12-M-01 reveal much concerning their functions and origins, the greatest revelation provided by these objects comes from their cultural significance. If metal keys existed at Magdalena de Cao, then metal locks did as well, and such a fact suggests that some inhabitants were concerned with keeping things secure from theft and with regulating access to certain spaces. The degree to which this concern existed in the town versus the church is unclear. The sizes of the keys appear to be in the middle of the expected range, not so small to suggest that they opened small caskets nor so large that they might have been keys to large doors. Their midrange sizes suggest that they served to lock storage chests, perhaps implying that individuals or groups at Magdalena took active steps to safeguard material items from cohabitants at the site. The presence of such protective measures indicates that conflicting social or ideological beliefs may have existed at Magdalena de Cao during the Colonial Period, although further archaeological and historical analyses may help to clarify this notion. Another example of colonial hardware at Magdalena de Cao, 08-M-03 (Figure 10.12), came from a depositional context within the town complex. Weighing 419.6 g, the object measures 10.5 by 14.5 cm with an average thickness of 1.0 cm. Its crescentlike shape appears to have been inspired by a specific prehispanic form of knife sometimes referred to as a *tumi* (Barrenechea 1967; Rutledge and Gordon 1987; Waszkis 1993). This tumi-like implement, however, possesses a relatively rare, though not completely unknown, handle form that runs parallel to the blade's cutting edge. Few examples of this prehistoric-style knife exist, but one is housed in the collections of the Peabody Museum of Archaeology and Ethnology at Harvard University, where it is labeled as a "semi-oval metal axe blade" (cat. no. 39-83-30/1877). This object came to the museum in 1877 with little information as to its origins except for an early catalogue entry of "Inca; Late Coastal." Today, we cannot be certain of this "axe blade's" cultural

Table 10.4   Summary Results of pXRF Analysis

OBJECT TESTED	NUMBER OF pXRF SCANS	OBJECT CATEGORY	OBJECT DETAILS	
05-M-09	4	Hardware/tools	Large fragment of key	
06-M-01	3	Hardware/tools	Triangular base for composite object	
06-M-02	2	Bell (hemispherical)	Hemispherical bell with two parallel lines running along shoulder	
06-M-09	4	Ornament	Possible cockade in ornamental design	
06-M-13	4	Other	Square sheet metal piece with small hole in middle	
07-M-02	3	Ornament	Ornate floral or star-shaped decoration	
07-M-04	3	Hardware/tools	Possible knife, ingot, or blank	
07-M-09	3	Ornament	Pendant displaying anchorlike motif	
07-M-16	4	Ornament	Star-shaped ornament	
07-M-21	3	Straight pin	Long straight pin with wound head	
07-M-22	3	Straight pin	Straight pin with wound head	
07-M-31	4	Hardware/tools	Tweezers in indigenous style	
07-M-32	2	Ornament	Six-pointed starlike decoration	
07-M-33	3	Other	Soft, light-colored, curved metal fragment; possibly slag	
07-M-34	2	Other	Crimped metal fragment; possibly slag	
07-M-35	4	Other	Three metal fragments; possibly slag	
07-M-36	4	Ornament	Crucifix with upper portion broken off	
08-M-01	3	Hardware/tools	Boxlike object with beveled edges on two sides	
08-M-02	3	Hardware/tools	Possible key fragment; possible spoon	
08-M-03	4	Hardware/tools	Large tumi-like implement with handle	
08-M-06	3	Other	Possible plate fragment with beveled edge	
08-M-15	3	Hardware/tools	Fragment of sewing needle	
08-M-24	3	Bell (pyramidal)	Crimped tinkler in sheet metal not dissimilar to 06-M-13	
08-M-25	4	Hardware/tools	Possible candlewick trimmer or snuffer	
08-M-35	4	Ornament	Metal ring with inlaid stones	
08-M-36	4	Ornament	Metal ring with inlaid stones	
12-M-01	3	Hardware/tools	Handle fragment of a key or other implement	
12-M-03	4	Other	Coin	
12-M-04	4	Other	Coin	
12-M-05	4	Hardware/tools	Possible knife or ingot	
Total	101			

PRIMARY ELEMENTS PRESENT	TRACE ELEMENTS PRESENT	PRESUMED ORIGIN OF OBJECT BASED ON CU ALLOY	PRESUMED ORIGIN OF OBJECT BASED ON FORM
Fe	NA	NA	European
Cu, Zn	Ca, Fe	European	European
Cu, Zn	Fe, Ni	European	European
Cu, Zn	Fe	European	European
Cu	Fe, Ni	Ambiguous	Ambiguous
Cu, Zn	Ca, Fe	European	European
Cu	Fe	Ambiguous	Ambiguous
Cu	Fe, Ag	Ambiguous	European
Cu	Fe	Ambiguous	European
Cu, Zn	Fe	European	European
Cu, Zn	Fe	European	European
Cu, Zn	Fe, Pb	European	Peruvian
Cu, As	Ca, Fe	Peruvian	Ambiguous
Pb	NA	NA	Ambiguous
Pb	NA	NA	Ambiguous
Pb	NA	NA	Ambiguous
Cu, Zn	Fe, Pb, Ni	European	European
Cu, Zn	Ca, Fe, Pb	European	Ambiguous
Fe	NA	NA	European
Cu, As	Ca, Fe	Peruvian	Peruvian
Cu, Zn	Fe, Pb	European	European
Cu, As	Ca, Fe	Peruvian	European
Cu, Zn	Ca, Fe, Pb	European	Ambiguous
Cu	Zn, Ca, Fe, Pb	Ambiguous	European
Cu, Ag	Ca, Fe	Ambiguous	European
Cu, Ag	Ca, Fe	Ambiguous	European
Fe	Ca, Cu, Zn	NA	European
Ag	Cu, Pb, Fe	NA	European
Ag	Cu, Fe	NA	European
Fe	NA	NA	Ambiguous

Figure 10.9 Copper alloy objects. A. Plate (?) fragment, 08-M-06; B. Worked sheet metal, 06-M-13; C. Washer (?),06-M-03; D. Smashed stud through sheet metal, 07-M-03; E. Four views of an open-ended box, 08-M-01); F. Knife or ingot, 07-M-04.

Figure 10.10 Copper knife or ingot, 07-M-04 (see Figure 10.9F), wedged in the *quincha* in the interior side of a wall in Unit 2.

Figure 10.11 Folding knife, 07-M-37.

Figure 10.12 Crescent-shaped, *tumi*-like knife, 08-M-03. Inset shows similar knife from the Peabody Museum, Harvard (cat. no. 39-83-30/1877).

affiliation, but the entry hints that it may have been found on Peru's coast, a fact that—along with its size (10.7 × 11.3 × .7 cm)—reveals a close similarity to the Magdalena specimen.

In compositional terms, the tumi-shaped implement is one of only three tested objects that contained significant arsenic levels (the others were 07-M-32 and 08-M-15). This observation is important because Andean populations manufactured copper-arsenic alloys prior to

Figure 10.13
Three cubes of
lead, 07-M-35;
left to right:
A, B, C.

1cm

European contact (Lechtman 1996, 2014). This object may thus represent the handiwork of
Peruvian metallurgists using autochthonous raw materials. If indigenous metalworkers produced this knife, then its production may conform to a larger pattern in which functional and
utilitarian objects were produced using Andean materials and methods, while luxury goods
or objects associated with European belief systems and customs were imported or produced
using European materials and techniques. Whether or not this pattern existed at Magdalena
de Cao Viejo, this object remains an important testament to the persistence of indigenous
material culture during the Colonial Period. We also found three lead fragments at Magdalena
(collectively labeled as 07-M-35; Figure 10.13). Their heavy weight, density, and color immediately provided insights into their composition, and pXRF spectrometry confirmed that these
small objects were pure lead. Only slightly more than 1 cm wide and about 2 cm in maximum
height, these items may have served the inhabitants of Magdalena de Cao Viejo in a variety of
ways, possibly as weights, or simply as the waste products of other manufacturing activities at
the site. Given the trace presence of lead in several of the metal artifacts at Magdalena de Cao
Viejo (e.g., 06-M-01, 08-M-01, and 08-M-25), it is possible that such fragments represent material markers of localized metalworking activities at the site.

We also note that a site guard brought a candlestick to the Museo de Cao laboratories
in 2013 claiming that he had found it in the colonial sector of the El Brujo complex (13-M-03;
Figure 10.14). No details were provided as to the object's specific location or context, and we
did not examine the object in great detail. Its general appearance conforms to styles of candlesticks or candelabra used throughout a considerable period of time. Candles were likely
expensive and rare early on in Peru's Colonial Period, and the only traces of candle use we
found were in the church. For all of these reasons, we cannot speculate about the particular
role that this candlestick played at Magdalena de Cao.

Distinctive and Unique Items

Several metal artifacts from Magdalena de Cao resist classification within the categories outlined above, and many others are distinctive enough that they deserve extended commentary.
These one- or two-of-a-kind artifacts elucidate some of the subtler aspects of daily life as it
existed during Magdalena's colonial occupation.

Figure 10.14
Candlestick,
12-M-06.

TRIANGULAR BASE

Found within the town, 06-M-01 (Figure 10.15) possesses a unique triangular shape. Measuring 12.1 cm along all three of its sides and 4.5 cm high, this artifact may represent a fragment of a larger, composite object that may have belonged to the hardware or ornamental categories.

We first considered 06-M-01 to be a candlestick base. A stem fragment rising from its platform, however, appears too thin to support a candle. Perhaps it supported something else, such as a crucifix or another religious icon. The flat base with raised feet suggests that the object originally rested on a flat surface such as a desk or table. Traditional Andean interiors did not possess tables, so Magdalena de Cao's colonial inhabitants may have used this item in the context of the church and then later removed it after the collapse of the nave.

Compositionally, the base exhibits an elemental fingerprint that closely resembles those of 08-M-01 and 08-M-25, the box of unknown function and the possible candlewick trimmer or snuffer described earlier. All three items are made of zinc-based copper alloys with trace lead concentrations. Consistent utilization of compositionally similar, or even identical, bronze alloys implies that many of the colonial-era objects were manufactured at the same location(s) using the same source material(s). As with several of the other metal artifacts, standardized material composition and a distinctly European decorative style suggest that this object was imported from abroad.

TWEEZERS

Measuring approximately 3.6 cm in length and 2.1 cm in width, 07-M-31 is a pair of tweezers that exhibits a traditionally and distinctively Andean style (Figure 10.16). Our pXRF analysis revealed that this artifact was created using a copper-zinc alloy. This suggests that colonial-era smiths made the tweezers using imported, or at least European-style, metal to make an object of Andean form. Despite this interesting juxtaposition of Andean aesthetics and European material composition, the independent invention of tweezers in both the Old World and the New leaves the question of this object's design influences open to further study.

ORNATE RINGS

Two finger rings, 08-M-36 and 08-M-37 (Figure 10.3G and Figure 10.17), were found lying near each other on an occupation surface in Unit 28. The floor on which they were found dates to

Figure 10.15
Top and oblique
view of triangular
base, 06-M-01.

relatively late in the use life of the house but before the town economy shifted primarily to goat pastoralism. In absolute terms, the occupation surface probably dates to sometime in the mid-seventeenth century.

The rings are similar in terms of size and decoration. Each measures about 1.8 cm in diameter—fairly large even for modern fingers. Nearly identical inlays decorate each ring in guilloche patterns bordered by circles on the sides.

Figure 10.16
Tweezers of
Andean style
(07-M-31).

Both rings also appear to have been manufactured in the same manner. Colonial-era metallurgists would have first pounded the circular bands on one side to expand a particular section. Next, they would have attached bent wire forms to the flattened oval surfaces. Two pieces of bent wire set together form a guilloche on each ring in order to form a complex decorative motif. Each separate wire creates a curvilinear W-shape with the ends bending back to create a circular shape for a central inlay with four bordering inlays, two on each side (Figure 10.17). The two circles flanking either side of the guilloche are also pieces of bent wire formed to hold inlays. All these features appear obvious to the naked eye because none of the created circles are continuous—they are clearly bent wires. Whether the wires were attached to the ring through soldering or some other adherence mechanism is less clear.

Many of the rings' inlaid stones, especially on 08-M-37, are of irregular shape and do not perfectly conform to the circular enclosures of the guilloches. Nor were all the inlays preserved in place. On 08-M-36 the central inlay and one of the flanking inlays are missing, while on 08-M-37 only one of the flanking inlays is absent. The absence of loose stones within Magdalena de Cao's excavation contexts suggests that these losses must have occurred before the rings reached their final depositional locations.

We did not perform pXRF analyses on the inlays, so their material compositions remain unknown, though inlays still present are green or blue in color. The green inlays in the two different rings may represent different materials, but it is also possible that they are the same material and that the darker green inlays have changed color due to some process that diminished their original luster. The bright green material exhibits characteristics similar to those of chrysocolla, a copper-based mineral related to malachite and sometimes mischaracterized as "turquoise" when found in prehistoric and other Peruvian artifacts. The blue inlays may be glass or possibly lapis lazuli, a blue stone with sources in Chile. Lapis lazuli appears in some prehistoric jewelry, and consumers in the Colonial Period may have used it as well.

Judging from their archaeological co-association, the two rings seem to unambiguously represent a pair expressing complementary opposition. Ring 08-M-36 has four green inlays in the outer circles of its guilloche and a blue inlay in one of the flanking circles. Ring 08-M-37, on the other hand, possesses three blue inlays in its outer guilloche circles, a green inlay in one of its flanking circles, and a green inlay in the center of its guilloche. It seems likely that both rings exhibited inverse decorative motifs when complete, with each ring following the opposite pattern of the other—for example, having inlays of one color in the four circles of the guilloche and inlays of the other color in the center and flanking circles of the guilloche. The use of a green stone in one of the bordering inlays in 08-M-37 suggests that the jewelsmith or wearer may have deviated from the originally desired pattern due to the lack of a blue inlay to perfectly complete the pattern.

The manifestation of dualism within the arrangement of the rings' inlays echoes indigenous ideological concepts throughout the Andes but may have appealed to European sensibilities as well. The overall design of a central element bordered by four at the corners conforms to well-documented Andean concepts of organization and symmetry also found in textiles and on ceramics throughout prehistory. In and of itself, the creation of paired ornamental objects follows long-term Andean patterns. That the rings are quite large in size, even by today's standards, suggests that they may have been worn by the same person.

Figure 10.17 Detail of finger rings. Left: 08-M-37. Right: 08-M-36.

Semi-quantitative pXRF analysis confirmed that the rings possess significant concentrations of silver, in addition to the expected presence of copper (Table 10.4). As is the case with modern consumers, sixteenth-century inhabitants of European metropoles and colonies highly prized silver as a decorative material and status symbol, and these rings likely represented a special gift and required a considerable investment of wealth or capital to purchase or procure.

PENDANTS

Part of a crucifix (07-M-37; Figure 10.3D) likely worn as a pendant was found within occupational deposits in Unit 1 that date to the early-to-mid-seventeenth century. The artifact bears raised imagery along its axes that is consistent with objects cast in sand-cast molds or through similar production processes. On the obverse side, the crucified Christ is portrayed. We struggled to observe exact details on the reverse side, but it may hold images of the instruments of the Passion. A smaller pendant (07-M-09; Figure 10.3E) appears to represent an anchor, a traditional Christian symbol dating to Roman times.

Curators at the Museo de Cao also brought two other metal pendants to our attention during labwork in 2013. Museum personnel discovered both at surface level while walking across the site and provided no specific details regarding the contexts of their collection. One (13-M-01; Figure 10.3F) was made of extremely thin metal and was highly corroded. A barely legible outline of a front-facing person with long hair, probably Jesus, appears on one side of the object. A faint image of two standing individuals with an avian figure or angel above appears on the other side of the object. This iconography may allude to the baptism of Jesus by John the Baptist. There appears to have been an outer band running around this image on the rim of the oval object and the letters *SCAP* are still legible. The object may represent a scapular medal associated either with a confraternity of the church or with the promulgation of indulgences by Magdalena's friars (Chapters 2 and 12).

The second pendant (13-M-02; Figure 10.3I) is a small oval medallion probably made of a low-grade alloy—possibly containing tin or zinc—that may have been covered in a thin wash of gold. One side portrays Mary and the Christ Child, and the other portrays either the risen Christ or a saint.

SEWING NEEDLE

We also found a sewing needle at the site (08-M-15, Figure 10.18). This object comes from the same excavation unit as the *tumi* described earlier, albeit from a slightly older depositional level. The tip has fragmented, but the remaining portion of the shank measures 3.1 cm in length with a diameter of about .2 cm. We may infer that the original needle likely was at least 4 to 5 cm long and probably quite longer. Corrosion on this artifact limits the accuracy of observational analysis, but the 2.5 mm eyelet appears to be beveled, a common feature of sewing needles. On the scale of sewing needles published by Beaudry (2006:53 [table 3.1]), the Magdalena example would rank among the top three heaviest forms and was likely used to sew relatively heavy materials.

The needle's composition, a copper-arsenic alloy, resembles that of the tumi-like implement. As discussed above, the presence of arsenic suggests that the needle was created locally by metalworkers who used locally sourced ores. This also makes sense inasmuch as Europeans preferred steel needles beginning in the early eras of fabric production and use. For these reasons, this needle represents yet another intriguing linkage between Magdalena's inhabitants and Andean traditions of material culture production and use.

Discussion

The assemblage of metal artifacts uncovered during excavations at Magdalena de Cao offers preliminary insights into the economic, political, and social forces at play in the settlement and in the Peruvian colonial world at large. Many of the metal goods exhibit copper-zinc compositions consistent with European origin, while a few notable examples exhibit copper-arsenic alloys more typical of Andean manufacture. In some cases, Europeans may have brought raw materials such as metal sheets to the site for local fabrication into bells and other items. Why colonizers would have employed such an economizing strategy is difficult to assess: was it out of necessity, or was it somehow advantageous? Our observational and compositional research regarding the metals assemblage at Magdalena de Cao Viejo reveals some interesting ideas that may prompt further research, but it also leaves many questions unanswered. Who had access to metallic materials or objects at the site? How and where were metals manufactured and distributed in the community? Why did some traditional forms endure while objects of European origin seem to have supplanted others?

Our general impression is that the number of metal objects found during excavations at Magdalena de Cao Viejo (and possibly in use during its occupation) is quite low for a site of its time period, especially when compared to contemporaneous towns in Europe or even among

Figure 10.18
Needle fragment, 08-M-15, shown at twice actual size.

1cm

other indigenous New World populations that were in contact with Europeans. For example, the density of metal trade goods at sites and found in burials during the Peabody Museum's lower Mississippi Valley Tunica project in the 1970s seems far greater than the metal from Magdalena (Brain 1988). Several factors may explain these differences, including the fact that the Tunica sites date only to the eighteenth century. It seems more important, however, that French traders supplied metal and other products to Amerindians in a context of mutual trade and exchange, while the Magdaleneros were subjugated peoples under Spanish rule.

In conjunction with previous scholarship concerning the development of Andean alloys (see Lechtman 1996), our compositional analysis suggests that only a small proportion of the metal objects used at Magdalena de Cao Viejo during its colonial occupation were produced locally. Only 3 of the 30 objects tested using pXRF spectrometry exhibit profiles consistent with Andean manufacture, and the vast majority of compositionally analyzed and unanalyzed artifacts exhibit European stylistic or formal characteristics (Table 10.4). This disparity may imply that European inhabitants of Magdalena de Cao regulated access to metal objects at the site and restricted the expression of indigenous metalworking practices. Such an interpretation is also supported by the fact that excavations at the site's church and town complexes did not reveal any obvious traces of production centers or workshops.

While the metal objects at Magdalena de Cao Viejo provide insights into the lives of the townspeople and friars and offer preliminary data through which to examine trade patterns and production, the overall impression provided by the inventory of the metal objects is one of poverty. This is most strikingly brought home by those most quotidian of objects, the straight pins. European manufactories produced thousands of pins as early as the Middle Ages, and Adam Smith referred to them as "a very trifling manufacture" in his *Wealth of Nations* (Smith 2008 [1776]). Pins are ubiquitous at Late Medieval and Early Modern sites in Europe, often numbering in the hundreds or thousands even in sites of modest means (Beaudry 2006). Yet the total for the whole of Magdalena's excavated contexts is a mere 42. Perhaps the clothing styles at Magdalena simply did not demand as many pins as contemporaneous European fashions (see Chapter 6), but they clearly would have served many purposes for the inhabitants of Colonial Period sites in Peru. This scarcity at Magdalena could indeed indicate the community's lack of access to common material goods, but such a conclusion must be tempered with the consideration that complicated political and social issues may have existed at the site. Consumers may have reutilized or reforged metal objects over long periods, thereby diminishing the absolute quantities of certain material forms over time. Furthermore, use practices may have resulted in fewer materials being present archaeologically than we would otherwise expect. Whatever the case, it is clear that metal objects and metalworking were important aspects of life at Magdalena and included use of imported, locally made, or locally refashioned objects (Figure 10.19).

The analysis of Magdalena de Cao's metals assemblage reveals a number of preliminary insights into material-cultural continuities, hybridities, and resilience as illustrated through the diverse suite of metal artifacts used by its colonial-era inhabitants. Copper-arsenic alloys appear in objects that may express local production and aesthetic traditions, and standardized copper-zinc alloys exist in European-style objects that likely were imported to the site. For the most part, European forms and alloys dominate this relatively small assemblage. Further research regarding

Figure 10.19 Illustration from Martínez Compañón's book on the North Coast of Peru in the mid-eighteenth century showing a couple working metal.

metal objects in early Colonial Period Peru will help to clarify the patterns documented in this study, and continued inquiry at sites such as Magdalena de Cao Viejo will also help to elucidate the complex social and economic considerations at work in Colonial Period Peru.

NOTES

1 Lambayeque also is known for copper alloy "proto-money," commonly known as *naipes*. The production and use of these items appears to have diminished later in the Late Intermediate Period, however.

2 The X-ray tube within the machine featured a 40-kV/60-μm power supply with a Rh target, and a filter composed of .0254 mm of Ti foil layered over .3048 mm of Al foil. Cooled using a thermoelectric mechanism, the detector had a resolution of 145 eV at 100,000 counts per second.

3 Full presentation of the pXRF spectra is on the project website: https://www.peabody.harvard.edu /Magdalena.

4 Much of the following discussion on the history of pins is derived from Beaudry's (2006) discussion of these matters.

REFERENCES CITED

Aldenderfer, Mark, Nathan M. Graig, Robert J. Speakman, and Rachel Popelka-Filcoff
    2008 Four-Thousand-Year-Old Gold Artifacts from the Lake Titicaca Basin, Southern Peru. *Proceedings of the National Academy of Sciences of the United States of America* 105(13):5002–5005.

Alva, Walter, and Christopher B. Donnan
    1994 *Royal Tombs of Sipán*. Los Angeles: Regents of the University of California.

Barrenechea, Raúl Porras
    1967 Introduction. In Miguel Mujica Gallo, *The Gold of Peru: Masterpieces of Goldsmith's Work of Pre-Incan and Incan Time and the Colonial Period*, pp. 9–36. Recklinghausen, Germany: Verlag Aurel Bongers.

Beaudry, Mary C.
    2006 *Findings: The Material Culture of Needlework and Sewing*. New Haven, CT: Yale University Press.

Beck, Robin A.
    2016 The Iron in the Posthole: Witchcraft, Women's Labor, and Spanish Folk Ritual at the Berry Site. *American Anthropologist* 118(3):525–540.

Beck, Thomasina
    1995 *The Embroiderer's Story: Needlework from the Renaissance to the Present Day*. Newton Abbott, UK: David and Charles.

Brain, Jeffrey P.
    1988 *Tunica Archaeology*. Papers of the Peabody Museum of Archaeology and Ethnology Vol. 78. Cambridge, MA: Peabody Museum Press, Harvard University.

Bray, Tamara L.
    2012 From Rational to Relational: Reconfiguring Value in the Inca Empire. In *The Construction of Value in the Ancient World*, edited by John K. Papadopoulos and Gary Urton, pp. 392–405. Los Angeles: Cotsen Institute of Archaeology, UCLA.

Brown, Ian

    1979   Historic Artifacts and Sociocultural Change: Some Warnings from the Lower Mississippi Valley. In *The Conference on Historic Site Archaeology Papers 1978, Vol. 13*, pp. 109–121. Columbia: Institute of Archaeology and Anthropology, University of South Carolina.

Burger, Richard L.

    1995   *Chavín and the Origins of Andean Civilization*. London: Thames and Hudson.

Burger, Richard L., and Robert B. Gordon

    1998   Early Central Andean Metalworking from Mina Perdida, Peru. *Science* 282:1108–1111.

Coovadia, Imraan

    2008   A Brief History of Pin-Making. *Politikon* 35(1):87–105.

Cummins, Thomas B. F.

    2002   *Toasts with the Inca: Andean Abstraction and Colonial Images on Quero Vessels*. Ann Arbor: University of Michigan Press.

Deagan, Kathleen

    2002   *Artifacts of the Spanish Colonies of Florida and the Caribbean, 1500–1800*, Vol. 2, *Portable Personal Possessions*. Washington, DC: Smithsonian Institution Press.

Deagan, Kathleen, and José María Cruxent

    2002   *Archaeology at La Isabela: America's First European Town*. New Haven, CT: Yale University Press.

Donnan, Christopher B.

    2012   Dressing the Body in Splendor: Expression of Value by the Moche of Ancient Peru. In *The Construction of Value in the Ancient World*, edited by John K. Papadopoulos and Gary Urton, pp. 186–196. Los Angeles: Cotsen Institute of Archaeology, UCLA.

Eveleigh, David J.

    1985   *Candle Lighting*. Haverfordwest, UK: Shire Publications.

Harskamp, Jaap

    2010   In Praise of Pins: From Tool to Metaphor. *History Workshop Journal* 70(1):47–66.

Herrera, Matthew D.

    2004   *Sanctus Bells: History and Use in the Catholic Church*. San Luis Obispo, CA: Tixlini Scriptorium.

Hosler, Dorothy

    1994   *The Sounds and Colors of Power: The Metallurgical Technology of Ancient West Mexico*. Cambridge, MA: MIT Press.

Killick, David

    2014   From Ores to Metals. In *Archaeometallurgy in Global Perspective: Methods and Syntheses*, edited by Benjamin W. Roberts and Christopher P. Thornton, pp. 11–45. New York: Springer.

Lau, George F.

    2011   *Andean Expressions: Art and Archaeology of the Recuay Culture*. Iowa City: University of Iowa Press.

Lechtman, Heather

    1993   Technologies of Power: The Andean Case. In *Configurations of Power: Holistic Anthropology in Theory and Practice*, edited by John S. Henderson and Patricia J. Netherly, pp. 244–280. Ithaca, NY: Cornell University Press.

1996 Arsenic Bronze: Dirty Copper or Chosen Alloy? A View from the Americas. *Journal of Field Archaeology* 23(4):477–514.

2014 Andean Metallurgy in Prehistory. In *Archaeometallurgy in Global Perspective: Methods and Syntheses*, edited by Benjamin W. Roberts and Christopher P. Thornton, pp. 361–422. New York: Springer.

McGreggor, Malcolm
1776 *Ode to Mr. Pinchbeck, upon His Newly Invented Patent Candle-Snuffers.* London: J. Almon.

Manning, M. Chris
2014 The Material Culture of Ritual Concealments in the United States. *Historical Archaeology* 48(3):52–83.

Merkel, John F., and Maria Ines Velarde
1998 Naipes (Axe Moneys): A Pre-Hispanic Currency in Peru. *Archaeology International* 2:57–510.

Monk, Eric
1999 *Keys: Their History and Collection.* Princes Risborough, UK: Shire Publications.

Moore, Simon
1988 *Penknives and Other Folding Knives.* Haverfordwest, UK: Shire Publications.

Notis, Michael R.
2014 Metals. In *Archaeometallurgy in Global Perspective: Methods and Syntheses*, edited by Benjamin W. Roberts and Christopher P. Thornton, pp. 47–66. New York: Springer.

Quilter, Jeffrey
2008 Art and Moche Martial Arts. In *The Art and Archaeology of the Moche*, edited by Steve Bourget and Kimberly L. Jones, pp. 215–228. Austin: University of Texas Press.

2011 The Shining Dawn of American Gold: Metallurgy in Ancient America. In *To Capture the Sun: Gold of Ancient Panama*, edited by Carol Haralson, pp. 44–77. Tulsa, OK: Gilcrease Museum.

Rutledge, John W., and Robert B. Gordon
1987 The Work of Metallurgical Artificers at Machu Picchu, Peru. *American Antiquity* 52(3):578–594.

Saunders, Nicholas J.
2003 "Catching the Light": Technologies of Power and Enchantment in Pre-Columbian Goldworking. In *Gold and Power in Ancient Costa Rica, Panama, and Colombia*, edited by Jeffrey Quilter and John W. Hoopes, pp. 15-47. Washington, DC: Dumbarton Oaks Research Library and Collection.

Shackley, M. Steven
2012 *X-Ray Fluorescence Spectrometry (XRF) in Geoarchaeology.* New York: Springer.

Shimada, Izumi
2013 The Style, Technology and Organization of Sicán Mining and Metallurgy, Northern Peru: Insights from Holistic Study. *Chungara Revista de Antropología Chilena* 45(1):3–31.

Shimada, Izumi, and Jo Ann Griffin
1994 Precious Metal Objects of the Middle Sicán. *Scientific American* 270(4):80–91.

Smith, Adam

    2008 [1776] *An Inquiry into the Nature and Causes of the Wealth of Nations: A Selected Edition.* New York: Oxford University Press.

Stone-Miller, Rebecca

    2002 *Art of the Andes from Chavín to Inca.* London: Thames and Hudson.

Waszkis, Helmut

    1993 *Mining in the Americas: Stories and History.* Cambridge, UK: Woodhead Publishing.

Wilkinson, F.

    1971 *Flintlock Guns and Rifles: An Illustrated Reference Guide.* London: Garden City Press.

11

Colonial Period Coins

Richard L. Burger

T HE EXCAVATIONS AT Magdalena de Cao Viejo recovered two silver coins. This discovery is noteworthy because few if any early colonial coins have been published from systematic archaeological excavations. A large literature exists on the colonial coinage of the Viceroyalty of Peru, but most of it is oriented to a numismatic rather than academic audience, and it is almost exclusively based on coins from hoards and material from sunken ships as well as coins without any provenance at all. In recent decades coins salvaged from colonial shipwrecks have become a particularly significant source of information as a result of the vast amount of material recovered. For example, the Spanish galleon *Atocha*, which sank off the coast of the Florida Keys in 1622, produced more than 100,000 silver coins when it was salvaged; most of these had been struck in Potosí, Bolivia (Sedwick and Sedwick 2007:155).

Both coins were found associated with Unit 28, a house compound northeast of the town plaza (see Chapter 2). The smaller coin (Mag-12-M-4) was not recognized as a coin until it was cleaned in the laboratory, while the larger coin (Mag-12-M-3) was found in surface dust on the northern edge of the perimeter wall of the compound (Figure 11.1).

The two coins recovered in the excavations at Magdalena de Cao have irregular shapes and incomplete decorations. Crude coins such as these as are widely known as *macuquinas* in Peru and "cobs" in the English-speaking world. Many scholars believe that the etymology of the word "macuquina" comes from the Quechua term *makkaikuna* or *makkay*, meaning "something that was hammered or hit." Others believe that the term may derive from the Arabic *mahquq*, which means "something assured or demonstrated to be true" (Sedwick and Sedwick 2007:10). Whatever the etymology, the term "macuquina" is still applied to early colonial coins among Quechua-speakers in Cuzco.

The English term "cob" has an even more elusive etymology than its Quechua equivalent. While some have tried to derive the word from the Old English term for a small mass of something, such as a cob of dirt or a cob of coal, others believe that it comes from the Spanish *cabo de barra*, "end of the bar" (Sedwick and Sedwick 2007:2007). After considering the alternatives, historian Alan Craig (2000:200) rejected these hypothetical derivations and concluded: "There is nothing more to be gained from etymology of the word 'cob.'" In this chapter I will refer to these coins by the Peruvian term *macuquina* rather than the English numismatic term.

Figure 11.1　Coin Mag-12-M-3. Silver 2-real coin. This macuquina was minted in Potosí between 1608 and 1617 under the reign of Philip III. The two faces of the coin are oriented differently to show the image on them right side up.

Figure 11.2　Coin Mag-12-M-4 showing both faces. Silver half-real coin. It is a macuquina minted in Potosí between 1598 and 1617 under the reign of Philip III. Top: uncleaned. Bottom: cleaned.

Macuquinas were mostly made prior to the mid-eighteenth century. Workers at a mint created thick rods or straps of high-quality silver that were then cut into thin slabs of uneven thickness. These blanks were trimmed down to a fixed weight using steel shears or chisels. The trimmed blanks, known as planchets, were annealed to make the silver less brittle. Each planchet was individually inserted into a die, and while a worker held it with tongs, a second worker struck it with another die using a sledgehammer, thereby decorating the coin's obverse and reverse at once. The precise weight of the coin, which was officially established by the Spanish Crown, was then checked and, if necessary, modified to the desired weight using shears; as a consequence of this process, the final form of macuquinas is often irregular and rarely circular. Given the artisanal nature of the production, there was variability in the thicknesses and diameters of the coins in order to achieve the officially mandated weight. A high degree of variability is also reflected in where and with what force the imprint of the die fell on the irregular planchet, and it is common for portions of the decoration and inscriptions to be illegible or completely absent.

The low quality standards made it possible to produce an enormous volume of coinage with a very simple technology and nonspecialized labor. It also has been suggested that crude coins were minted primarily to facilitate payment of the tribute levied by the Spanish Crown on all mining operations, and that many of them were sent to Spain to be melted down or exchanged with lands to the east, rather than circulated within the Viceroyalty of Peru (Sedwick and Sedwick 2007:11). Given this, the fineness of the silver and the weight of the coins would have been of much greater interest than their appearance.

Only four mints were established in the Viceroyalty of Peru. Two of these, one in Cuzco and the other in La Plata, functioned for only a year and were of little significance; they will not be considered here in any detail. The two major mints in the viceroyalty were the one in Lima and the one in Potosí. Prior to the establishment of the mints, the Spanish invaders introduced the use of precious metals for commercial purposes in the form of weighed gold dust and silver ingots stamped with the symbol of the assayer. In order to better control the mining activities, King Philip II approved the establishment of a mint in Lima on August 21, 1565, and the first coins were produced in 1568. As a result of scandals and political conflicts, the Lima mint was closed after three years. This mint was eventually reopened, but it continued to be plagued with problems, and production there was quite limited. There were complaints that no coins from the mint were found outside of a radius of 10 miles (16 km) from Lima (Grunthal and Sellschopp 1978:14). The Lima mint, undermined by political opposition and accusations of corruption, was closed again in 1588 and not reopened until 1621.

A more successful mint was opened in Potosí to take advantage of the growing volume of silver coming from the adjacent mines. The first coins were produced there in 1575. These coins strongly resemble those minted in Lima, since the design of dies was under the control of the Spanish Crown for all centers of coin production in this and the other viceroyalties. For nearly a century Potosí was the dominant mint in the Viceroyalty of Peru. Despite or perhaps because of this dominance, the mint at Potosí was undermined by a series of scandals, and by 1652 the quality of macuquina production had declined to the point where monetary reform was necessary to ensure the continued acceptance of this currency. To highlight the reform, the Spanish Crown introduced new decorative imagery to renew confidence in the beleaguered currency and make the new coinage immediately recognizable.

Although every macuquina was unique because of the production process, the quality of the precious metal utilized was prescribed by the Spanish Crown. Macuquinas dating to before 1652 were supposed to have a silver content of 93.1 percent. Judging from the historical documentation resulting from the investigations into the irregularities at the Potosí and Lima mints, the silver composition was sometimes diluted by dishonest assayers and other mint officials (Craig 2000:22–38).

Most of the early coinage minted in Lima and Potosí during the late sixteenth and early seventeenth centuries featured the arms of the kingdom of Spain on the obverse and the arms of the House of Hapsburg on the reverse, thus representing both kingdom and empire on the same coin.

The Spanish monarchical arms originated with John II of Castile (1405–1454) and was continued under Isabella I (1451–1504). It was composed of a quartered shield with a three-towered castle, upper dexter and lower sinister (proper upper right and lower left), symbolizing the kingdom of Castile, and a crowned lion rampant, upper sinister, lower dexter (proper upper left, lower right), representing the kingdom of León.

The coat or shield of arms of the Hapsburg Empire contained dense imagery because of the many principalities within it, thus presenting difficulties for representation in small images (Figure 11.3). Its clearest features were the supporters: a double-headed eagle behind the shield

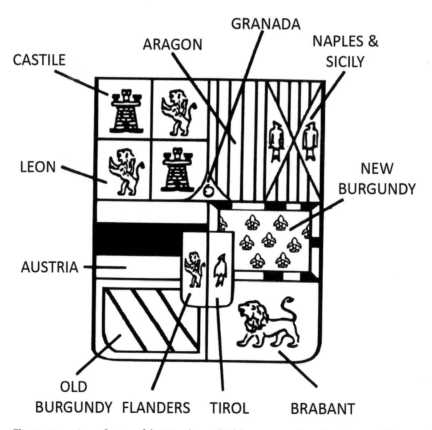

Figure 11.3 A rendering of the Hapsburg shield represented on the obverse of the 2-real coin illustrated in Figure 11.1. The supporters, the Pillars of Hercules, are not shown here but may be seen in the right-hand image in Figure 11.6. Redrawn from Sedwick and Sedwick 2007:23.

and the Pillars of Hercules on either side of it. Probably in order to simplify the design field, in the mid-seventeenth century coins from Potosí and Lima began to carry new imagery, with the Hapsburg escutcheon replaced by a representation of the Pillars of Hercules over the Atlantic waves. The Pillars of Hercules had been an important royal emblem since the time of Charles V, symbolizing entrance into the world beyond the Mediterranean and emphasized by the inscription *plus ultra* (meaning "further" or "beyond") on ribbons draped around the pillars.

About a century later, a more sophisticated and mechanized minting procedure for Peruvian viceroyal coinage was adopted, which used milled planchets of fixed size and thickness. As a consequence of this shift in technology, beginning in 1752 in Lima and 1773 in Potosí, macuquinas ceased being manufactured.

The Denomination of the Magdalena de Cao Coins

The denomination of coins produced in the Viceroyalty of Peru was defined on the basis of weight. Between 1435 and 1728 six kinds of high-grade silver coins were minted; these correspond to the 8-, 4-, 2-, 1-, half-, and quarter-real denominations (Table 11.1) (Craig 2000:16). There apparently was a tolerance for slightly underweight and overweight coins despite mint regulations (e.g., 0.3 grams variance for an 8-real piece) (Sedwick and Sedwick 2007:12).

Using these prescribed weights, it is possible to identify the denominations of the two coins recovered at Magdalena de Cao. The larger of the coins (Mag-12-M-3) weighed 6.8 grams and thus is a 2-real coin (Figure 11.1). The smaller coin (Mag-12-M-4) weighed 1.4 grams, indicating that it is a half-real coin (Figure 11.2).

It is noteworthy that Mag-12-M-4 is .3 grams less than the prescribed legal weight. Whether this difference is due to post-depositional erosion, heavy use wear from when the coin was in circulation, intentional lightening of the coin by shaving its edge, or some other illegal but common Colonial Period practice cannot be determined. Its pitted condition suggests that natural post-depositional forces most likely are to blame for its reduced weight (see Craig 2000; Sedwick and Sedwick 2007:12).

The two coins unearthed at Magdalena de Cao were both found in a corroded state. I conducted an analysis of their metallurgical content using a portable XRF instrument and confirmed that the coins were predominantly of silver, although a significant amount of copper was also present (Figure 11.4). Corrosion was due to the oxidation of the copper in the coin metal. The other element evident in the XRF analysis beside Ag and Cu was Br (bromine). Its

Table 11.1   Coins of Magdalena de Cao Viejo

REALES COINS	WEIGHTS (GRAMS)
8	27.468
4	13.734
2	6.867
1	3.4435
1/2	1.7167
1/4	0.8584

Figure 11.4
Half-real coin better
preserved than the
Magdalena example but
roughly the same age.
Private collection.

presence is probably due to the incorporation of ocean salts in the corrosion product covering the coins (Tom Fenn, personal communication), derived from the site's proximity to the
Pacific. The confirmation that the two coins from Magdalena de Cao are high-grade silver is
not surprising because copper coins were not produced in the Viceroyalty of Peru, and while
gold coins were minted in Cuzco and Lima, they were of great value and quite rare.

The Archaeological Context of the Magdalena de Cao Coins

The coins found at Magdalena de Cao Viejo were recovered in the excavations of Unit 28 in
the residential section of the site, rather than the church complex. This is significant because
it suggests that the coins encountered were not the by-product of church activities but rather
a reflection of daily household activities by the Magdalena de Cao townsfolk. The 2-real coin
was found on the northern edge of what is likely the yard of the house compound. Both coins
came from layer A, which is the surface stratum rich in domestic artifacts. Since this area of the
site had been heavily looted, the layer probably included some remains from deeper strata as
well as the materials from the final use of the site.

It seems reasonable to suggest that these coins came from the household refuse associated with the colonial habitations. There is no evidence that they originally were part of an
intentionally buried hoard or a tomb context. Given the small size of the coins, it is not unrea-
sonable to speculate that they may have been lost during daily activities. Significantly, the two
Magdalena de Cao coins are of low denominations. Neither 8-real nor 4-real coins were recovered during the excavations. According to Sedwick and Sedwick (2007:11), "Depending on

the period, a typical Spanish seaman was paid about a ½ real a day, hence about two 8 reales a month." While a farmer or fisherman living in Magdalena de Cao may have earned less than a Spanish seaman, the low denominations of the silver coins are consistent with the low economic level of indigenous townsfolk during the Colonial Period.

The Production Date of the Magdalena de Cao Coins

When and where were the coins produced? Are the coins contemporary with the occupation of the houses adjacent to where they were found? Given the relatively detailed available knowledge of colonial numismatics in the Viceroyalty of Peru, a more detailed study of the coins has the potential of providing an estimate of when and where the coins were minted. Toward this end I will offer a description of each coin and discuss the implications of the features that can be identified.

Mag-12-M-3 is a 2-real coin that measures 2.3 cm in diameter and has a thickness of 22 mm (Figure 11.1). The coin has a generally round shape, but there are four straight cuts along the perimeter of the artifact that give the coin an irregular, angular shape. As described previously, these cuts were made at the time of minting to achieve the prescribed coin weight and are typical of coinage prior to the mid-eighteenth century.

The obverse of the coin is decorated with a simple cross. Unlike the unbalanced form of a conventional crucifix, the four arms of this cross are of equal length; they form four quadrants of the same size. The equal size of the arms of the cross symbolized the union of the Catholic Church and the Spanish state. Decoration of coinage with this type of cross began with the reign of Philip II (1554–1598). It appears on the 2-real coins produced at the Lima mint between 1572 and 1588 and those produced by the Potosí mint between 1575 and 1652. After this time, short perpendicular bars were added at the extremities to produce what is sometimes known as a Jerusalem cross.

In the upper left and lower right quadrants of the cross on the 2-real coin from Magdalena de Cao it is possible to identify the frontal representation of a castle, shown with three towers or turrets, two windows, and a central entryway (Figure 11.1, left). In the upper right and lower left quadrants are profile representations of lions that are shown rearing upright. This pose is known as rampant (in contrast to passant or statant), and it is interpreted as representing a lion whose trunk and forepaws are raised as if fighting (Sedwick and Sedwick 2007:22). The two castles and two lions symbolized the unification of the kingdoms of Castile and León as the core of the Spanish state. One distinctive feature of the coin under consideration is that the lion's head is shown raised as if looking upward and the tail is similarly curved upward. Enclosing the cross are a series of converging arcs forming what is known as a quatrefoil or tressure. On this coin, the tressure is formed by two parallel lines encircled by a ring of large round dots. On well-struck 2-real coins, a legend occurs outside the ring of dots specifying the date and other information, but on the coin in question, none of the legend fit on the coin's planchet.

The reverse of Mag-12-M-3 (Figure 11.2, right) features the Hapsburg shield. The shield imagery is typical of 2-real coins struck in Potosí and Lima between 1556 and 1700 (Figure 11.3). Also, as previously noted, the escutcheon is partitioned into numerous fields, each symbolizing a different principality linked to the House of Hapsburg. Among these symbols represented are the lion and castle of Castile and León. Adjacent to them are vertical lines representing

Aragon, followed by the symbol for Naples and Sicily on the upper right. In the central register of the shield were symbols representing Austria and New Burgundy. In the lower register of the shield are the symbols for Old Burgundy, Flanders, Tirol, and Brabant (Sedwick and Sedwick 2007:23–24). Many, but not all, of these components of the Hapsburg shield can be recognized on the 2-real coin from Magdalena de Cao. Nonetheless, the overall layout and the details that are identifiable leave no doubt that it is the Hapsburg shield that was being represented on the coin's reverse. A single line of large round dots encircles the shield. The legend should appear outside the dots, and although there is space for a portion of the legend, since the coin was struck off center, none is legible.

Based on the above description, the 2-real coin could have been struck either in the Lima mint sometime between 1572 and 1588 or at the Potosí mint between 1575 and 1652. Fortunately, the style and details of macuquinas varied over time and between mints, and this information permits a more precise estimate of when the coin was minted. When the details of the obverse and reverse of Mag-12-M-3 are compared to the published 2-real pieces and other cobs, the coins most similar to Mag-12-M-3 were those produced at the Potosí mint between 1608 and 1617 by an assayer (possibly Gaspar Ruíz) during the reign of Philip III, whose identity was signified by an "R" on coins (Grunthal and Sellschopp 1978:159–164; see also Sellschopp 1964). Among the features used to reach this conclusion are the position of the lion, the details of the castles, the form of the symbols for Austria and Granada, and the large circular dots that encircle the central imagery on both sizes of the coin. At the present time the coin has not been cleaned, and it is possible that this procedure would reveal additional features.

Mag-12-M-4 (Figure 11.1) is a silver half-real coin, known as a *medio* in Spanish. It was heavily corroded and almost completely illegible until it was cleaned. Even after cleaning, details of the coin are unclear due to the pitting of the surface as a result of the corrosion. Nonetheless, it is possible to make out the general decoration of the coin and offer suggestions about its likely date and mint. Like Mag-12-M-3, the obverse of this coin (Figure 11.2, left) features a simple cross with no elaboration of the extremities. There is no evidence of a quatrefoil or tressure, and the cross was apparently encircled by dots. The coin's obverse was struck off center, but the legend that should have been outside the line of dots is illegible.

The reverse of this half-real coin (Figure 11.2, right) features the monogram of the Latin spelling of the name of the king rather than the Hapsburg shield. Decoration featuring the royal monogram was only used to decorate half-real coins, and in 1652 it was replaced by the pillar and wave imagery referred to earlier. The royal monograms are difficult to describe (see Figure 11.5 for a better-preserved example), but the one on Mag-12-M-4 has a prominent *P* and *S* traversed by a central horizontal line. When compared to other half reales, the coin's monogram appears to be closest to the form used on coins minted in Potosí during the reign of Philip II, III, or IV. The possibility that the coin was produced at the Potosí mint is also consistent with the size and spacing of the circle of dots on both sides. The absence of adornment at the end of the cross on the obverse is consistent with coins struck during the reign of Philip II or III. Based on the above information, I suggest that the medio coin Mag-12-M-4 was minted in Potosí sometime between 1598 and 1617.

Of course, these estimates for the dating of the coins from Magdalena de Cao refer only to when the coins were minted (1608–1617 for the 2-real coin and 1598–1617 for the half-real coin). It is likely that the coins continued in circulation for many years after they were produced. On

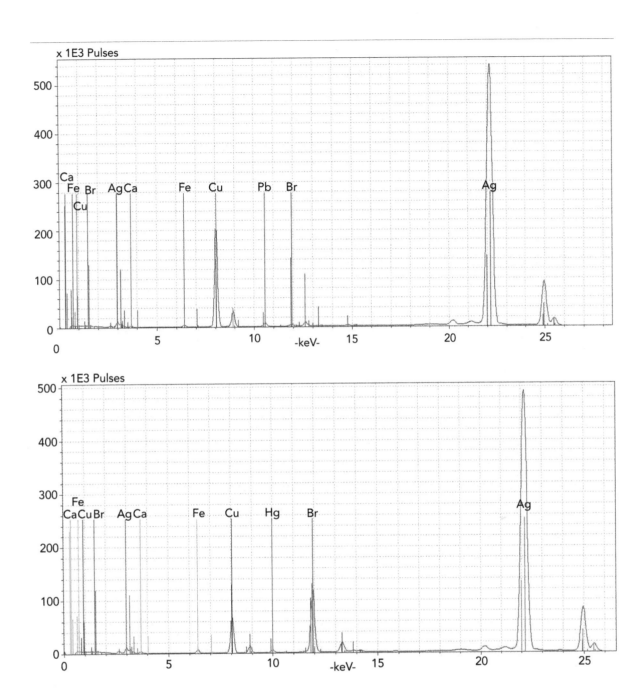

Figure 11.5 Spectra of elements in the two macuquina coins made using a pXRF. Top: 12-M-03. Bottom: 12-M-04. Note the high spikes, at right, reflecting their high silver content.

the other hand, it is unlikely that the coins would have remained in circulation for long after the monetary reform of 1652. The estimates suggested for when the two coins were produced fit well with Quilter's conclusion that the residential area was established in the late sixteenth century and changed dramatically in character after the 1680s (see Chapter 2 and Chapter 12). Based on this chronology, the two coins would have been struck during the period when the town of Magdalena de Cao was thriving.

Figure 11.6 Silver 1-real coin produced in Lima in 1776 under the reign of Charles III and recovered from the site surface. It is a milled coin using more sophisticated minting technology than the older macuquinas from the Magdalena de Cao excavations.

A third coin (Mag-14-M-1; Figure 11.6) was found by a Peruvian archaeologist traversing the colonial sector of El Brujo during the archaeological off-season. He turned it in to the proper authorities but did not report details of the discovery location. The small 1-real silver coin is made using the more sophisticated minting technology that involved the use of a circular blank rolled to a fixed thickness and then cut with a press to a standard diameter. The resulting milled coins were round, had well-centered images on both obverse and reverse, and had serrated edges to discourage the removal of silver shavings. The obverse bears the image of Charles III dressed in Roman armor and facing to the right. Its legend reads *CAROLUS.III. DEI.GRATIA.1776*. The reverse is decorated with a crowned shield between the two Pillars of Hercules. Its legend reads *HISPAN.ET.IND.REX.ME.1R.M.I.* In this inscription, *M.I.* stands for the coin's assayers, Manuel Iglesia Abarca and Ignacio Zenón Gálvez. In contrast to the two macuquinas recovered at the site, the coin was minted in Lima rather than Potosí (Grunthal and Sellschopp 1978:108–114). The coin's date, 1776, indicates that it was lost quite late in the occupation of Magdalena de Cao Viejo. Similar to the macuquinas from the earlier colonial occupation, the coin's denomination, 1 real, is of low value.

Conclusions and Discussion

Analysis of the two coins excavated at Magdalena de Cao Viejo revealed that they are low-denomination coins of high-grade silver from early colonial times. Such coins, known in Peru as macuquinas, have irregular forms and were fabricated by a crude technique. For reasons discussed in detail earlier in this chapter, I suggest that the two coins were probably produced in the early seventeenth century at the mint in Potosí. The context where the coins were found at Magdalena de Cao Viejo suggests that they come from the domestic trash produced by the colonial town at the site.

The discovery of these coins is significant because they represent one of the few instances of early colonial coins that have been documented in an archaeological context other than from shipwrecks and hoards. More important, the coins constitute evidence that by the first half of the seventeenth century, coinage produced under the authority of the Spanish Crown had penetrated the everyday life of farmers and fisherfolk living in this shoreline town in the Chicama drainage.

It should be noted that neither of the two coins (nor the 1-real coin found at El Brujo) was perforated. Perforation of coinage was common in early colonial times in order for coins to be sewn as ornaments on textiles, leather pouches, and other materials. The absence of such perforations on the Magdalena de Cao Viejo coins reinforces the thesis that these coins represent a money form of value, something that was absent in the Central Andes prior to the invasion of the Spaniards (Burger 2013; Rowe 1946).

Thomas C. Patterson has observed in his work on the eighteenth-century Chumash of Southern California that the introduction of money into a society produces a profound transformation not only in the way daily economic activity is conducted but also in the very manner that social labor is conceived. As a consequence, the worldview of people who choose to adopt the use of money becomes radically transformed. As Patterson (2014) writes, "Money is a measure of value—the social incarnation of human labor whose magnitude is gauged in units of time." As a measure of value, money converts the value of all commodities into prices, which are then expressed in terms of quantities of a particular commodity, in this case silver reales of officially prescribed purity.

The adoption of money throughout the Central Andes was a crucial element in the entanglement of indigenous peoples with the larger socioeconomic and political system known as the Viceroyalty of Peru. Historical sources rarely provide a sense of how and when the integration of money occurred at the level of rural communities, and thus archaeological evidence from sites such as Magdalena de Cao have an important role to play in our understanding.

If one accepts Patterson's perspective and the thesis that the coins from Magdalena de Cao were used as money, rather than for some other purpose, then their presence is much more significant than simply representing the appearance of a new artifact class previously absent on the Peruvian coast. It would imply that the people of Magdalena de Cao had begun to conceptualize commodities and labor in a fundamentally different way or that they were being imposed upon to think so. Although earlier economic patterns such as barter and reciprocity continued, these townsfolk had begun to be integrated into the money-based market system promoted by the Spanish invaders and their descendants. The process of how this occurred is barely known. The small silver coins discussed in this chapter, mined and minted at 4,050 m above sea level some 2,600 km to the south of where they were found offer an eloquent testament to this powerful historical process and a small contribution to understanding how it occurred.

REFERENCES CITED

Burger, Richard L.

2013 In the Realm of the Incas: An Archaeological Reconsideration of Household Exchange, Long-Distance Trade, and Marketplaces in the Pre-Hispanic Andes. In *Merchants,*

Markets and Exchange in the Pre-Columbian World, edited by Kenneth Hirth and Joanne Pillsbury, pp. 319–334. Washington, DC: Dumbarton Oaks Research Library and Collection.

Craig, Alan K.

2000 *Spanish Colonial Coins in the Florida Collection.* Gainesville: University of Florida Press.

Grunthal, Henry, and Ernesto Sellschopp

1978 *The Coinage of Peru.* Frankfurt: Verlag P. N. Schulten.

Patterson, Thomas C.

2014 Shell-Bead Money and the Mission Period Economy of Alta California. *Journal of Social Archaeology* 14(1):112–127.

Rowe, John Howland

1946 Inca Culture at the Time of the Spanish Conquest. In *Handbook of South American Indians*, Vol. 2, edited by Julian H. Steward, pp. 183–330, pls. 77–84. Washington, DC: Smithsonian Institution.

Sedwick, Daniel, and Frank Sedwick

2007 *The Practical Book of Cobs.* Winter Park, FL; Daniel Sedwick and Frank Sedwick.

Sellschopp, Ernesto

1964 *Las acuñaciones de la ceca de Lima.* Lima: Novagrafica.

Appendix 11.1
Details on Magdalena Coins

All measurements are in centimeters unless otherwise noted.

CATALOGUE #	MAG-12-M-3
Site area	Town
Max L/H	2.3
Max W/dia	2.3
Max thick	2.2
Metal thick (mm)	22
Weight	6.8 g
Excav unit	28.12 (Unit 28)
Natural level (Capa)	A
Arbitrary level (Nivel)	—
Y coordinate	348
R coordinate	394

Note: This coin was found on the northern edge of what is likely the yard of the house compound.

CATALOGUE #	MAG-12-M-4
Site area	Town
Max L/H	1.5
Max W/dia	1.4
Max thick	.18
Metal thick (mm)	1.8
Weight	1.4 gr
Excav unit	28.12 (Unit 28)
Natural level (Capa)	A
Arbitrary level (Nivel)	—
Y coordinate	348
R coordinate	394

12

A Historical Approximation of Santa María de Magdalena de Cao Through the Written Sources

Rocío Delibes Mateos

Introduction

IN 1724, AFTER LONG MONTHS crossing the Atlantic Ocean, a letter arrived in Madrid, the city of the royal court, and finally reached the Council of the Indies, the supreme governing body for the administration of Spanish territories in the New World. The letter had been written in a small town on the North Coast of Peru, Santa María de Magdalena de Cao, and signed by the members of the *cabildo* (town council) and the *alcalde ordinario* (mayor), Juan Panira Zaman, a "principal Indian" (Archivo General de Indias [AGI], Lima, 495).[1] The recipient of the letter was Don Vicente de Mora Chimo, "attorney general of the Indians and the first chief of four towns in the Chicama Valley: Santiago, San Pedro y San Pablo de Chocope, San Sebastian, and Santa María de Magdalena de Cao."[2]

It had been many years since Don Vicente had left his lands to defend his community in front of Spanish authorities, first in the *audiencia* (royal appellate court) of Lima and then, after years of failed efforts in the viceroyalty's capital, in Madrid (Mathis 2017).[3] The Magdaleneros complained in their letter that there now remained very few Indians in their town and that it had been more than a decade since their church had been "ruined and completely fallen in, with our having hope of seeing it once more as it used to be and not just as a Calvary."[4] The Magdaleneros were complaining that their church had been reduced to a *calvario*, a wooden cross on a pile of rubble and bones.

It had been only 150 years since the catastrophic flood of 1578 forced the population of Magdalena de Cao to flee their town in the valley for the terrace, where they reestablished their town. And only a few decades before that flood had the first Spaniards arrived in the valley. Within the space of just a few generations the population had gone from living in relatively independent communities spread across the landscape to living in a European-style town, from practicing their own religion to worshiping a new god, from building a church to watching it fall into ruin.

From an archaeological perspective, 150 years is a relatively short period of time. But from a historical view it is a very long time, a period that can easily see drastic political, economic, social, and environmental transformations. This chapter seeks to use documentary sources to present a general view of some salient features of the life and times of Magdalena de Cao that can contextualize and clarify the archaeological record presented in other chapters of this book.

From a *Parcialidad* to a *Pueblo de Indios*

It is clear that the colonial sector of the El Brujo complex is the second Magdalena de Cao, established there in 1578 after the Chicama River overflowed its banks and sent residents of the first Magdalena de Cao fleeing (Huertas 2001:201). But we have scant evidence as to who those people were who moved to the high terrace after days of rain and flooding.

The meaning and significance of different terms used in documents pose challenges to interpreting historical records. For example, Spaniards often used the Caribbean Taino term *cacique* (chief) interchangeably with the Quechua *curaca* to refer to local leaders in Peru. In the earliest documents "Cao" or "Caux" is presented as one of the main indigenous communities (*parcialidades*) of the *cacicazgo* (chiefdom) of Chicama. In the Colonial Period the center of regional power shifted to Trujillo, in the Moche Valley. Founded in 1534, Trujillo was one of the earliest Spanish communities in Peru; the king bestowed upon it the rank of city only three years later. The Chicama Valley, 48 km to the north, was under its jurisdiction, as implemented through the colonial system of *repartimientos* (repartitions) or encomiendas. In exchange for tribute, labor, and personal service, the encomendero was to protect his native charges and provide them with religious instruction by arrangement with clerics (de la Puente Brunke 1992).

Don Alonso Caxa Guamán had been the *cacique principal*—the lord of the entire valley—and was the first indigenous leader of the valley to be baptized. His successor, Don Juan de Mora, took the surname of his baptismal godfather and encomendero, and this name continued to be used by his family in subsequent years, as seen in the letters from Madrid signed by Don Vicente de Mora Chimo two centuries later.

Under Spanish governance the native population of the Chicama Valley was divided into two repartimientos: Licapa in the north, under the encomienda of Don Francisco de Fuentes, and Chicama in the south, with Don Diego de Mora as its *encomendero* (Ramírez 1986; Zevallos 1996). Mora exercised his substantial power by establishing the first sugar mill in the region (AGI, Justicia 458).

Native hierarchical classifications usually were defined in relation to a principal chief or lord in charge of a cacicazgo or *señorio*.[5] The señorio was divided into parcialidades. In contrast to the sierra, where the Quechua term *ayllu* prevailed, Spanish administrators used the term parcialidad to refer to the different subdivisions of indigenous groups on the coast. Today this term carries a neutral sense of simply "part of a whole," but in colonial Spanish documents it could refer to groups at different hierarchical levels within indigenous communities (Rostworowski 1981). The ethnohistorian Patricia Netherly (1974, 1978, 1984, 1990) traced a quadripartite sociopolitical scheme for the Chicama Valley that followed these principles in the prehispanic and early Colonial Period, as described in the 1566 census carried out by Gregorio González de Cuenca (AGI, Justicia 458).

Table 12.1 Caciques of Magdalena de Cao During the Sixteenth and Seventeenth Centuries

NAME	DESCRIPTION	DATE MENTIONED
Xachaminchan Collatnamo	Principal cacique of Cao when the Spaniards arrived in the valley	Around 1550 (mentioned in 1604)
Don Antonio Panira Zaman	Cacique of Cao	1590
Don Andrés Zachumxarca	Cacique of the Pueblo de la Magdalena de Cao	1604
Don Gaspar Panira Zaman	Governor and cacique of the Pueblo de la Magdalena de Cao	1616
Don Diego Timón	Cacique of the Pueblo de Cao	1644
Don Andres Panira Zaman	Principal cacique of the Pueblo de Cao	1674

Sources: ARL, Co, Leg. 160, 383; ARL, Co, Leg. 237, 2187; ARL, Leg. 273, 3397; ARL, Co, Leg. 199, 1358; ARL, Co, Leg. 192, 1199.

As Netherly points out, the organization of the Chicama Valley reflected two concepts that defined the prehispanic political organization of the coast: hierarchy and duality. The cacicazgo was divided into two large parcialidades, one under the authority of the cacique principal and the other under a person or office defined by the Spaniards as the *segunda persona* (Second Person). In turn, these two parcialidades also were divided in two, each with its respective leader. Below that there was another level, also so organized. In this system, Cao was one of four principal parcialidades that made up the cacicazgo of Chicama.

When the Spaniards arrived in the valley, Xacchiminchan Collatnamo was the cacique of the parcialidad of Cao and subject to the cacique principal of Chicama (Table 12.1). Consequently, he was considered an important authority and is said to have "governed his people quietly and peacefully."[6]

Like other caciques, Collatnamo had to serve as an intermediary between his Indian followers and the encomendero, a difficult task that in the end cost him his life. An account of his dramatic death was recorded decades later by his grandson, the cacique of Magdalena de Cao. During the unstable years of civil wars and uprisings in early colonial Peru, Don Diego de Mora had ordered the Indians of Cao to escort his wife, Doña Ana Pizarro, a cousin of Francisco, to the more secure Zaña Valley, reached by crossing the Pampa de Paiján desert. Although the escorts began the journey, they abandoned Doña Ana in the middle of their flight. Collatnamo paid for this disobedience by being hanged from an algarrobo tree in front of the other caciques and principales of the valley. This execution, ordered by Diego de Mora, was carried out to demonstrate what could happen to native leaders if they did not obey orders, and it served to express the absolute power of encomenderos during the first decades after the conquest (ARL, Co, Leg. 160, 383).

Prior to the arrival of the Spaniards, the people of the Cao parcialidad lived in settlements scattered throughout the valley. While over the millennia some places were completely abandoned, and others abandoned and then reoccupied, many settlements were maintained over long periods of time, up through the first three decades after the arrival of the Europeans.

But in the 1560s the Reducción General de los Indios began to be enforced. At first, under Viceroy García de Castro, the relocation of natives was haphazardly carried out, but it was implemented more systematically soon after Francisco de Toledo became Peru's fifth viceroy in 1569.

Details of pre-reducción settlement patterns are only slowly emerging for some areas of the Andes (Saito and Rosas 2017; VanValkenburgh 2012; Wernke 2013), and we do not have such information for the Chicama Valley. It is highly likely that the native population had been arranged across the landscape in small settlements, ranging from a single farmstead to a few houses. The reducción program was to end this dispersed settlement and gather together populations in larger towns organized on Spanish plans. Each settlement was to be laid out in an orthogonal grid system of intersecting streets around a central plaza. Places were designated on the plaza for a church with its resident priest and for a building to house an elected cabildo (Rappaport and Cummins 2012; Mumford 2012; Toledo 1986).

The reducción process began on the North Coast when Gregorio González de Cuenca was sent there on an official visit in 1566. According to reports from Cuenca's visit, fourteen or fifteen dispersed communities were reduced to four towns in Chicama and two in Licapa (AGI, Justicia, 458; Ramírez 1996:32). We have little information as to how the reducción process actually occurred, the precise locations of all the old and new settlements, and the way in which the indigenous parcialidades were distributed among them. We also do not know how it was decided where the new towns would be located or how the actual movements of people were carried out—whether they were forced or if they took place after negotiations between Spaniards and native peoples. We do know, however, that the population of the first town called Santa María de Magdalena de Cao, established in 1567, were members of the parcialidad of Cao, because in 1603 Don Andrés Zachumxarca, the cacique of Magdalena de Cao, said that he had been told his grandfather Collatnamo had been the principal chief of the Cao people when the Spaniards arrived.[7]

Considering the strong emphasis on concepts of duality and hierarchy, we might expect that the Cao parcialidad had been divided into two units. But the documents indicate that there were three of these lower parcialidades in Magdalena: Cao, Topquem, and Bechop. The townspeople identified themselves with these units while at the same time recognizing that they were members of the larger community. They made statements such as "Francisco Guamán, native Indian of the town of Cao of the parcialidad of Topquem" (ARL, Co, Leg. 176, 835), or "Juan Ciparán, native of the town of Cao of the parcialidad of Bechop" (ARL, Co, Leg. 242, 2375).[8] Although the three groups lived together in the town, there were more than a few confrontations between their leaders over internal power and the use and distribution of communal resources.

We do not know the exact location of the first Magdalena de Cao, established in 1567 and abandoned eleven years later in 1578. We do know that it had a church building that was ruined by the deluge and that it was located "near the mouth of the river" (AGI, Justicia, 458; Huertas 2011).[9] This suggests that it was not too distant from the terrace. Furthermore, in 1577, Don Juan de Mora, the cacique of Chicama, stated that its lands were limited by the town of Chocope and on the south by the "swamp that is on the town of Cao road."[10] This swamp is not present in the landscape today, likely because of natural or cultural land alterations and subsequent drainage changes. In 1728, however, the Cao townspeople affirmed that their cattle were pastured in this swamp, which abutted the lands of Soloque. Soloque no longer exists but is shown on Feijoo de Sosa's map of 1760 to the south of the El Brujo terrace and north of the river in roughly the same location as modern-day Nazareno, which may be the same place. Whatever the specifics, it is likely that the original Magdalena was relatively close to the El Brujo terrace and between it and the mouth of the river. The scale of available early maps and changes in the configuration of the river mouth make it difficult to attempt to locate these places.

The Population of Magdalena de Cao and Daily Life There

The Spanish chroniclers stated that the Chicama Valley was greatly populated during the times of the Inca (Feijoo de Sosa 1763:100), but European diseases and social dislocations due to the conquest rapidly diminished the population. In 1565, slightly more than three decades after the arrival of the Spaniards, various reports described the Chicama Valley as semi-abandoned and noted that the majority of the land was not cultivated (ARL, Co, Leg. 146, 46; Cook 1981) (Table 12.2).

According to Miguel Feijoo de Sosa, who wrote a mid-eighteenth-century report on Trujillo and its region, the town had more than 3,000 inhabitants subject to the cacique of Cao immediately after the Conquest Period, although how accurate this number is remains uncertain (Feijoo de Sosa 1763:106). The census of 1549 stated that in the entire cacicazgo of Chicama there had been some 1,000 or 2,000 Indians (Rostworowski 1984:88). Sixteen years after the second Magdalena was established, Archbishop Toribio de Mogrovejo visited the region and counted 715 people living in Magdalena de Cao, of which 169 were *tributarios* (tribute payers), adult men who paid taxes, did communal labor, and provided personal service to the encomendero (Ramírez 1986:72; Toledo 1986:89).[11] Only six years after this visit, however, the number of tributarios was reported to have dropped to 150 (Mogrovejo 2006). This declining trend continued until the mid- to late eighteenth century, by which time the Magdalena at El Brujo had been abandoned and the townspeople relocated 4 km north to the present town.

While the reported population figures show a clear demographic decline during the seventeenth century, they cannot be taken as a precise number, because they count only tributarios; they do not include indigenous authorities (curacas), women, children, the aged, or the infirm. Furthermore, while sixteenth- and seventeenth-century legislation strictly prohibited non-indigenous people, including Spaniards, blacks, mestizos, or mulattos, from living in Indian towns (*pueblos de indios*), the enforcement of this regulation appears to have relaxed over time.[12] The archaeological discovery of the remains of at least one African suggests that there indeed may have been a considerable number of other kinds of residents (see Chapter 5).

Table 12.2 List of the Population and Tribute Payers (Adult Men) of Magdalena de Cao

Year	1550	1594	1599	1651	1723	1760	1785	1860
Population	2000	715	630*	243*	139*	125	184	500
Tributarios		169	150	58	33			

Sources: ARL, Co, Leg. 286, 4341; Feijoo de Sosa 1763; Martínez Compañón 1978; Mogrovejo 2006; Raimondi 1876; Zevallos Quiñones 1992.

The types of differences noted by the Spanish authorities included not only racial categories but also place of origin. For example, a 1688 report states that 270 of 384 tributarios living in Santiago, Chocope, Magdalena, and the surrounding area were *indios forasteros*, or "foreign Indians"—that is, people who were not natives of Chicama (ARL, Real Hacienda, Leg. 131, 161).[13] In 1723 the Indians of Magdalena stated that only 33 tributarios were living there, but we do not know how many non-tribute-paying residents were present (AGI, Lima, 495). In 1760, Feijoo de Sosa (1763:106, 107) emphasized race when he noted that of the 125 residents living there, 69 were Indians and 56 were mestizos.

Magdalena's loss of population over the years may have been due to a number of factors. The pressure of being forced into tribute service often encouraged Indians to leave their small towns for the anonymity of large cities, especially Trujillo and Lima for North Coast populations. Another tactic was to work as an indentured servant (*yanacona*) in a distant hacienda. Some set up small houses and *ranchos* (herding farmsteads) in out-of-the-way places such as valley bottoms or abandoned fields.

The caciques had to assume the difficult role of tribute collector and undertake journeys to find "hidden" Indians, with the goal of rounding up a sufficient quantity to meet the labor requirements set for their communities. In 1616, Hernando Cosco Guamán, described as "a very bellicose Indian who always had quarrels with other Indians," fled Cao for Lima, where he hid for "more than six or seven years"; "the tribute overseers had trouble because of this" (ARL, Co, Leg. 241, 2294).

The problem of "hidden" Indians was not the only one caciques faced. Another issue was the counting of those who could be called upon for "labor and personal services" (ARL, Co, Leg. 191, 1184).[14] Communities constantly asked for recounts of their populations, to try to reduce the number of their members called for service and to reduce the amount of payments demanded if the labor could not be provided. In the recounts, Indian communities would name the men from the community who had been absent for more than ten years (and so could no longer be made to pay tribute), those who could no longer be found, and those who had died.

In 1642, Don Diego Isla Guamán, a *principal* (that is, member of a prominent native family) and collector of the Magdalena tributes, was accused of falsifying the list of dead and absent tributarios of the town. The judge in the case complained that he lacked faith that those Indians said to have died were truly deceased, nor was it certain that Indians supposedly in Lima or elsewhere had been away for the ten years required before being taken off the tributary rolls. For example, he asserted that "Mechor Quispe is one of those absentees whose whereabouts are supposedly unknown yet he is in the town of Chancay with his father and brothers . . . and that for the same reason Don Diego [Isla Guamán] should go to Lima every year and collect their tribute and present it so that the tribute will not be lost" (ARL, Co, Leg. 191, 1184).[15]

The forced movement of Indians into new towns resulted in many communities losing access to different resource zones that had been available to them in their former residences, including access points to draw water from major canals. In 1617, members of the Sacop parcialidad, who had been moved to the town of Santiago de Cao, claimed that the majority of their absentees were gone because they "could not plant their crops and so are lost, distracted, and absent, and have left the reducción to find places to grow crops to sustain themselves" (ARL, Co, Leg. 110, 2050).[16] These sorts of strategies were means by which Indian populations resisted, violated, or ignored regulations that the Spaniards tried to enforce.

In 1643, a confrontation occurred in Magdalena de Cao that highlighted the interactions of personal interests, conflicts between parcialidades, and administrative edicts meant to maintain populations in the Indian towns. Don Juan Chumbi Guamán, principal Indian of Magdalena town, brought suit against Alonso Jaratán, a member of the Bechop parcialidad and the mayor of Magdalena. Chumbi Guamán claimed that Jaratán had stolen important papers and other objects from a house in his fields, a league from town, and then burned the house down. Jaratán, who was jailed in Trujillo, never denied the charges, but instead based his defense on his need to fulfill his duties as mayor. He took this drastic action and others because "the said Indians are in rebellions and out in their fields without coming to help in the town or be in attendance there for Mass nor any of their other obligations" (ARL, Co, Leg. 246, 2541).[17]

On November 19, Don Alonso, together with Fernando Cachi, the other alcalde ordinario of the town, dictated to the recording secretary of the cabildo a command that was to be sent to all the Indians who were officially listed as residents of the town but had been too long absent: they must return to the town or else the mayors would burn down their homes. Specific reference was made to Juan Chumbi Guamán, who "had never wanted to obey the rules and justice as he should" (ARL, Co, Leg. 246, 2541).[18] Subsequently it was reported that the two mayors did gather together their followers and went to burn the ranchos of the dispersed townspeople.

In another case that shows how townspeople attempted to avoid obligations in the towns, in 1731, the corregidor complained that the Indians of Magdalena who worked as mule drivers in neighboring Spanish haciendas "did not attend [religious] feast days nor hear Mass nor the Christian doctrine, nor their other obligations"; this not only resulted in great spiritual harm to them but, furthermore, was a great detriment to those who remained in the town, for they had to work doubly hard to make up for the others' absence (ARL, Co, Leg. 269, 3265).[19]

The documents show that life in Magdalena de Cao was not an Eden of native peoples under the tutelage of benevolent friars. Neither was it a harsh penal camp, however. Rather, it was a community that was directly interconnected with surrounding communities and social networks, for better or worse. Rules and regulations attempting to control the townspeople were often ignored or violated, and the stresses of living under the Spanish regime not only resulted in conflict between foreigner and native but also caused severe strains within indigenous communities themselves as people attempted to respond to a multitude of demands, both individually and collectively.

The Stuff of Daily Life at Magdalena de Cao

The administrative records, petitions, and other documents of the Colonial Period occasionally offer information about objects that people used in their everyday lives as well as some of their valued possessions and the contexts in which they were used. Although information is not always as extensive or complete as we might wish, these references may be of particular value when presented in relation to archaeological research, as has occurred at Magdalena de Cao. Examples of the capacity of the Magdalena residents to obtain various goods and their circulation within various economic spheres include possession of breeches of new cloth from Quito, blue cloth breeches from Castile, a black *lliquilla* adorned with purple Castile taffeta, silk from China, or books printed in Madrid (see Appendix 12.1).

Similarly, although the documentation is not detailed, we can find references to the plan of the town and the uses of different spaces within it. Following the stipulated plan for reducciones, the plaza was the heart of the community, the site of religious and civil authorities. It was also the location of the *casas de cabildo*, the town hall. All major events took place in the plaza. Every visit by officials was formally staged in it, and new rules and regulations were proclaimed there. Every Sunday after Mass, all of Magdalena's inhabitants were expected to be in the plaza along with laborers from nearby haciendas as well as their Spanish masters, united—at least in physical presence—in one place at one time.

After Mass one Sunday in 1646, with the community together in the plaza, the town crier announced the forced public auction of the possessions of the principal Don Juan de Paypay Chumbi, to be held next to the doors of the casas de cabildo. The items to be sold included a red shirt, various tablecloths, and a cloak or cape (*capa*) of blue taffeta of great value bought by a Spanish foreman from a nearby hacienda. The documents describe how the protagonists of this event were positioned, and how the textiles were placed on a stone bench outside the casas de cabildo while the auction took place (ARL, Co, Leg. 192, 1230).

Other interactions with Spanish neighbors were violent. Many years before, on a Sunday night in 1609, a fight occurred in the same plaza between Pedro de Santiago, a Spanish laborer, and the cacique of Chicama, Don Pedro de Mora, in front of the cacique's house on the plaza. Witnesses described how the Spaniard repeatedly punched the cacique as well as the mayor of Magdalena, who had come to the cacique's aid. In the document about the case, the Magdalena authorities stated that they were preventing the Spaniard from taking María Chayan, a resident of Magdalena, to his farm, where he claimed her husband was residing. According to the cacique, María had been moved to the town in the reducción, and it was therefore forbidden by royal decree to remove her from it. This confrontation between native authorities and a Spaniard resulted in the latter being found in the wrong. Don Pedro de Mora pardoned Pedro de Santiago, however, on the condition that he was not to set foot in Magdalena de Cao for the following two years under pain of being sent into exile in Chile (ARL, Co, Leg. 238, 2214).

The houses of the cabildo members should have been placed on one of the sides of the plaza, according to the ordinances specifying how reducciones were to be organized. As noted in Chapter 2, archaeological investigations have not been able to distinguish these residences from others in the town, although work has been limited in investigating these issues. The cabildo comprised one or two *alcaldes ordinarios* or *principales* (principal mayors), the *alcalde de aguas* (mayor of waters), the *alcalde de campo* (mayor of the fields), two sheriffs (*alguaciles*), two aldermen or councilmen (*regidores*), a town crier (*pregonero*), and a town scribe (*escribano*) (ARL, Co, Leg. 269, 3265). The ordinances established that these officials were to be elected from members of different parcialidades, not all from the same one. This rule was not always followed, however, and at times the cacique or members of the cabildo challenged election results (ARL, Co, Loose Pages). Don Juan de Mora, cacique of Chicama, contested the election of Don Diego Sicha Guamán of the Bechop parcialidad as alcalde ordinario of Cao because he "had done many notorious injuries to the Indians of the town due to his bad nature," and petitioned for the election to be declared null and void, for the peace and good governance of the town (ARL, Co, Loose Pages).[20] The post of cacique, an inherited position, coexisted with these new elected authorities inside the reducciones, and the responsibilities and powers of each were not always clear. Over time, however, caciques did lose power; by the beginning of the nineteenth century they were no longer recognized as political officials (Delibes 2016; O'Phelan 1997).

Unfortunately, there are not many descriptions of the architectural features of Magdalena or the arrangement of houses and streets. One account that touches on this dates from 1616, when numerous witnesses related how Don Hernando Cosco Guamán had spent many nights roaming the streets of Magdalena. Specifically, they saw him walking in the street where the house of Don Andrés de Silva was located, and that he said he "wasn't going to stop until he could kill him."[21] This eventually led to the killing of Cosco Guamán by Andrés de Silva in de Silva's fields on the road to Santiago de Cao; de Silva claimed that he had acted in self-defense (ARL, Co, Leg. 241, 2294).

While the cabildo was the representation of civil power, the church was the representation of religious power, and it occupied the most important place on the town plaza. Each Indian town was required to support a priest, who could be either a secular minister (that is, not a member of a religious order) or a friar from a religious order. The three towns in the repartimiento of Chicama—San Pedro y San Pablo de Chocope, Santa María de Magdalena de Cao, and Santiago—were under the Dominican order, also known as the Order of Preachers (Orden de Predicadores). The Dominicans had arrived quite early in the Chicama Valley, where their legendary leader Domingo de Santo Tomás founded the Convent of Santo Domingo around 1540 in the *tambo* of Chicama, a former way station on the Inca coastal road. It was one of the first Dominican monasteries in Peru (Cieza de León 2005:190, 296), and its establishment led to the Dominicans serving as the priests for parishes of the reducción towns.

Each *curato* (parish) was assigned a priest from the Santo Domingo convent, although they apparently were moved from service in one community to another over time.[22] In 1580, Fray Bartolomé de Vargas was the vicar of the Chicama convent when he testified in the investigations of the 1578 flood.[23] Fourteen years later, in 1594, Santo Toribio de Mogrovejo, archbishop of Lima, visited Magdalena de Cao while Vargas was the priest of the town and wrote of him that he was a "good speaker of the languages of the fisherfolk" (Mogrovejo 2006:52).[24] Almost a century later, however, in 1681, the Dominican chronicler Juan de Meléndez wrote a history of the Order of Preachers in Peru and described Fray Bartolomé de Vargas as the priest of Chocope (Huertas 2011:200; Meléndez 1681:38). Meléndez may have been in error, or perhaps Vargas was serving as priest to both communities.

The fortunes of the Chicama evangelization project were in trouble by 1681 as economic hard times affected the entire valley. Meléndez wrote:

> In our times almost the entire valley is depopulated and of the many towns once in it only three remain and they have very few people, being Chocope, Cao, and Santiago, with each one having a religious who administers the sacraments, and all subject to the prior living with two or three others in the Chicama convent, a place completely depopulated. (Meléndez 1681:613)[25]

While the reducciones were losing populations, the haciendas were growing in both population and economic power, thanks to the expanding haciendas and sugar cane fields, which needed Indian and slave workers; there are records that the curate of Cao administered the sacraments at the haciendas of Sonolipe and San Jacinto in 1750.

By 1725 there were only a few members of the Chicama convent left. In 1760 there remained only one, a prior who served there and in Santiago de Cao, as his home monastery fell into ruin (Feijoo de Sosa 1763:102). This was around the time when Magdalena's fortunes were waning as well.

The indigenous inhabitants of the valley appear to have accepted conversion to Christianity in fairly large numbers from early on, including the baptism of the cacique Alonso Caxa Guamán. In 1577 his successor, Don Juan de Mora, in recognition of the friars having saved him from being an infidel, donated pastures as well as enough land to plant 10,000 vine arbors. In exchange for this, the friars were requested to pray every week for the souls of Don Juan's parents and for the "conversion of the Indians of the valley" (Zevallos 1992:16).[26]

There were many priests who served at Magdalena de Cao during its two centuries of occupation. We do not know the names of many of them, although some are listed in documents (Figure 12.1; Table 12.3). And we have added one name, Fray García de Haro, from a fragment of a document found during our archaeological research (Figure 13.19 in Chapter 13).

The documents also provide us with information about the daily lives of the priests and friars. In addition to officiating at the Mass and other religious services, they were obliged to provide religious instruction to the Indians. As the designated religious and moral authority of the community, the priests and friars were expected to be present for key events in the life of the town outside of strictly religious events. Thus, in 1609 the friars Diego de Montoya and Joseph de Santa María signed as witnesses to the pardoning of Pedro de Santiago by the

Figure 12.1   Letter fragment: "To the Reverend, my Father, Friar García de Haro, curate of the *doctrina* of Magdalena de Cao of the Order of Preachers." Photographed shortly after its discovery.

Table 12.3 List of Preachers of Magdalena de Cao from the Written Sources

DATE MENTIONED	NAME
1580	Fray Bartolomé de Vargas
1609	Fray Diego de Montoya y Fray Joseph de Santa María
1616	Fray Alonso Ramírez
1628–1632	Fray Alonso de Çea
1643	Fray Diego de Vera
1661	Fray Agustín de Oviedo
1728–1741	Fray Félix de Moncada

Sources: ARL, Co, Leg. 238, 2214; ARL, Co, Leg. 241, 2294; ARL, Co, Leg. 176, 835; ARL, Co, 246, 2541; ARL, Co, Leg. 196, 1312; ARL, Co, Leg. 286, 4341; ARL, Leg. 223, 1852; Huertas 2011; Melendez 1681; Mogrovejo 2006.

cacique Don Pedro de Mora (ARL, Co, Leg. 238, 2214). In 1616, after stabbing Don Hernando Cosco Guamán to death, his brother had to pay 20 coins to Fray Alonso Ramírez, "teacher of Cao, that the father of the deceased owed to the Cofradía de Nuestra Señora del Rosario of the town of Cao" (ARL, Co, Leg. 241, 2294).[27] In 1632, Father Alonso de Çea assisted in the inventory of the goods of the late Francisco Guamán and gave guarantees that the account was accurate and honest (ARL, Co, Leg. 241, 2294). And in 1643, when Alonso Jaratán burned outlying ranchos to force people back to Magdalena de Cao, Fray Diego de Vera, priest of Magdalena, accompanied him as a symbol of legitimacy and moral authority (ARL, Co, Leg. 176, 835).

Some of the main priestly duties were to offer the sacraments of baptism, matrimony, and, above all, the funeral and burial of the dead. In February 1632, Fray Alonso de Çea certified the deaths of two girls, Juana and María, seven and eight years old, respectively, noting that they had been buried in the town church for less than a year (ARL, Co, Leg. 176, 835). The importance to the townspeople of proper funerals is clearly expressed in the 1670 testament of Don Diego Isla Guamán of the Topquem parcialidad, who desired that his body be buried and preserved in the "church for this, my town, in the sepulture of my parents." Don Diego described the precise way in which he wanted his funeral to be carried out (ARL, Co, Leg. 199, 1358):

> I request and supplicate the Father of this town to accompany my body from my lodging to my tomb with the Cross high, a sexton, and double bells . . . and if there is sufficient time, to say Mass, that a sung Requiem Mass be done with singing and responses with a vigil over my body, present, and if there is no time then the following day such a Mass will be held and that alms be paid with twelve goats, this is my will.[28]

Given the importance of the church building in the life of the community, and especially its role as the place of ancestral burials, the Magdaleneros' preoccupation with the ruined state of their church in their 1723 letter to Don Vicente de Mora Chimo is understandable. They complained that it was still in ruins, much as he had last seen it when he left on his voyage years before, and that the Holy Sacrament was now kept in a simple hut (*ramada llana*) in the middle of the plaza. In their letter, they pleaded with Don Vicente to ask the king to offer alms for the rebuilding of their church.

Five years later, in 1728, a letter was sent from Magdalena to Spain complaining that the priest Felix de Moncada, "having forgotten his pastoral duties, . . . must work with his parishioners to get the Indian boys of Magdalena de Cao and the Hacienda Trapiche, who are their brothers, to work to fix the church." Despite the fact that the church had been in ruins for so long, it was never rebuilt. Don Vicente reported that the Magdaleneros intended to repair the church but that Moncada stole the lime and bricks to use for his sugar mill (Mora Chimo 2003:190–191).

Another important aspect of religious activities in early colonial Peru is the role of confraternities (*cofradías*). These are voluntary societies devoted to specific religious personages, pious devotions, and, today, charitable activities. In the colonial world of seventeenth-century Peru they took on specific responsibilities for the good of the community as well, although we do not know how their organizations related to the parcialidades.

Various cofradías are mentioned as present in Magdalena, but documents do not discuss them in any detail. The cofradías for Nuestra Señora del Rosario, Santa Bárbola, San Pedro, San Isidro, and Nuestro Amo are mentioned, as well as the fact that payment was required for membership. The presence of five or more cofradías in a relatively small population suggests that a good many Magdaleneros were members of them (AAL, Cofradías, Leg. 4; Herrera Calderón 1988). Membership in cofradías could crosscut the boundaries imposed by the parcialidades, although Don Diego Isla Guamán stated in his testament that the Santa Bárbola cofradía was specifically of the Topquem parcialidad (ARL, Co, Leg. 199, 1358). The cofradías also may have been quite politically active. Documents report that the cofradía of Nuestra Señora de la Consolación of the church of the town of Chocope fought a court case over the rights to access water from a specific canal to irrigate its fields. This suggests that cofradías actively owned lands and had interests concerning rights for water, critical issues in the Chicama Valley.[29]

Conflicts over Resources

The environment of the Chicama Valley underwent great changes after the arrival of the Spaniards. In 1565, at about the same time as the founding of the first Magdalena, witnesses testified that much of the valley land was abandoned and had been taken over by swamps and *montes* (secondary forest vegetation) due to lack of maintenance and repairs to irrigation canals (ARL, Co, Leg. 148, 46). Because the encomiendas granted to Spaniards by the Crown did not give them title to land but only entitled them to the labor of indigenous people, the Spanish overlords had little incentive to maintain or make improvements; rather, they sought to extract as much as possible from the Indians, who had to support themselves as well as supply tribute (Ramírez 1986:17). Consequently, for the first few decades after the conquest the lands in Chicama continued mostly in the hands of indigenous groups, who were required to bring tribute and provide personal service to their encomendero, Don Diego de Mora, but the presence of Spaniards in the valley was relatively light.

As the decades passed, the few conquistadors and their immediate families were joined or replaced by new Spaniards seeking their fortunes, creating a new upper class in the region (Marchena 1996:485). The distant Spanish Crown's original concern to maintain the indigenous inhabitants' rights and customs was outweighed by local authorities' need to find ways to support these new Spanish residents. In a slow but steady process, usufruct rights were replaced with ownership. Since the end of the sixteenth century, royal officials had occasionally made *visitas de tierras* (visits to lands) to review and adjudicate land disputes. The land gradually became commoditized, as the rights to land considered abandoned or to unworked fields could be bought by payment to the Crown. In other cases, Spaniards paid for titles to land that had been cultivated or occupied without permission (Ramírez 2006). These kinds of machinations were carried out by the Magdaleneros' Spanish neighbors from the late sixteenth century until the town was abandoned.

Quite soon after the conquest, wheat and other Old World domesticates were introduced into Peruvian valleys to support Spanish populations with products that they liked and were familiar with, such as bread, wine, and sugar, as well as with alfalfa for feeding newly introduced animal stocks. In the first decades of European occupation of the Chicama Valley the majority of the haciendas near Magdalena de Cao dedicated themselves principally to growing wheat and vegetables and raising cattle. The role of the Chicama as a breadbasket soon grew beyond the valley—by the middle of the seventeenth century it was of vital importance for supplying wheat not only to Trujillo and Lima but also to distant Panama City (ARL, Co, Leg. 220, 3327). Sugar production started early, with the installation of one of the first sugar mills in the valley by the encomendero Diego de Mora around 1540, but it took more than a hundred years before it came to dominate agriculture in the Chicama Valley. Interestingly, while wheat is present in the plant remains found at the site, sugar cane is not commonly present; it was grown exclusively in the haciendas.

Sugar requires great amounts of water to grow and labor to cut and process the cane. Consequently, African and African-descended slaves were brought to work in the fields at a very early time, given the relative scarcity of Spaniards and Indians available to serve as laborers. In 1594 there were more than 230 slaves working in the sugar fields and mills in Chicama, but by 1760 there were more than 1,200, demonstrating how sugar had come to dominate local agriculture (Feijoo 1763:108–126; Mogrovejo 2006:51–64). Given the distance of Chicama from Trujillo and the relative lack of Spaniards in the valley, the area soon came to be known as a refuge for escaped slaves, known as *cimarrones*, who often resorted to banditry to survive. Indians as well as Spaniards traveling through the region reported that they had been assaulted by cimarrones, although peaceful interchanges between them and indigenous groups also occurred (Castañeda 1998; Lavallé 1999).[30]

Interactions between the hacienda slaves and the reducción Indians most commonly took place when both worked together in labor service (*mita*) on haciendas and ranches or when they crossed paths on the roads around the towns (O'Toole 2012:74). In 1623, Alonso "El Cuchara," a mulatto, violated the wife of Don Andrés de Silva Paypay Chumbi, principal of Cao, and was condemned to be hanged, drawn, and quartered, with his head mounted on a pole at the entrance to the town. In 1626, Mateo, slave of a Spanish laborer (and said to have been from the Congo), attacked Juan Ciparán, an Indian resident of Magdalena de Cao of the Bechop parcialidad, stabbing him seven times and killing him. Ciparán had been to Trujillo to denounce Mateo, who he claimed had stolen a horse from him. Both attacks occurred on the road between Magdalena and Santiago, and although they emphasize negative relations, they show that there were frequent interactions between hacienda slaves and reducción Indians.

Relations between the new neighbors of the haciendas and the pueblos de indios generally were not easy. The Cao community, like others in the valley, had to repeatedly deal with disputes and court cases to defend their rights to water and land, and they had to learn how to appeal to the Crown to defend their "natural rights" (*derechos naturales*) as vassals of the king of Spain.

As in other Peruvian coastal valleys, water and land were essential resources for the inhabitants of the Chicama Valley. According to Patricia Netherly (1984:240), in prehispanic times the lands of the Cao parcialidad were watered by a canal that today is still known as the Cao Canal.[31] In the early Colonial Period, the population of the parcialidad decreased, and the people were concentrated in the single settlement of Magdalena de Cao; at the same time, new hacendados and laborers were entering the valley, and they had interests in water and land. These changes led to conflicts not only on the local level but throughout the valley. On September 2, 1665, representatives of the Cao and Bechop communities declared that their people were critically short of water because of their location in the lower valley; upriver communities could too easily divert water, leaving the downstream communities parched. The alcalde de aguas, Don Mateo de Villalobos, noted that many harvests had been lost and that there had been many disturbances and fights in the valley over water (ARL, Ca, Aguas, Leg. 111, 2087).[32]

In 1681, the *procurador* (attorney) of Cao, Pedro Mache, stated that the situation was desperate: not only were people losing the crops, but they did not have "a single drop of water to drink." He remarked on the "poor and miserable people who have been obligated to leave their town and look in other places to sow their seeds to sustain themselves, their wives, and children and pay the royal tributes."[33] Magdalena de Cao received a judgment in its favor in this case, but, as on other occasions, this was insufficient to preserve their rights. In 1683 the protests continued, this time with the Magdaleneros allying themselves with neighboring hacendados against those upstream. On other occasions, however, the Magdalena community was positioned against those same lower valley neighbors, given its location at the very end of the Cao Canal.

Responding to the severe lack of water and the Indian communities' petitions, in 1699 the Spanish official Don Antonio de Saavedra, in Trujillo, reorganized the distribution of the waters of the Cao Canal so that they were apportioned by the amount of land to be watered, not by the number of those claiming use rights. Furthermore, Saavedra stated that the Magdalena lands should be the first to be watered because they were at the end of the system (Saavedra 1915:99–104). But his orders were not obeyed, and the hacendados continued to usurp the water and send their slaves to damage the canals that serviced Indian lands. As late as 1723, the Magdaleneros were complaining to Don Vicente that despite the royal decrees issued for their benefit and protection, the whites ignored them as they wished (AGI, Lima, 495).[34]

When Don Vicente de Mora Chimo petitioned the king, he noted in particular, the abuses that Fray Felix de Moncada had heaped upon his flock. The priest of Magdalena not only had stolen the bricks that were supposed to be used to repair the church but also had made members of his flock work in his *trapiche* (mill) and treated them like slaves. He even appropriated natural resources that were the common property of the Magdalena community, such as firewood from the forest of Soloc (or Soloque). He diverted water into his own fields to raise grain to feed the mules he used to carry the firewood to Trujillo for sale, not allowing "those miserable Indians to cut one tree for use in their own houses" (Mora Chimo 2003:191).

At about the same time that Moncada was abusing the Magdaleneros, they were involved in another dispute with a local hacendado, Don Eusebio de Villalobos. Don Eusebio had sent his slaves to cut Magdalena's firewood and also wild cane (*caña brava*), which the Indians used for house construction. His cattle were pastured in Cao lands, and his slaves were diverting water for their own fields. Part of the issue was that by this time there apparently were few people still living in the town, for Don Eusebio defended his actions on the basis that he "knew that there were abundant fertile lands while weeds were blocking the entrance to the town and were in the town itself and even growing in the church where they had buried their dead, for there were so few Indians in the town because they were all away serving as porters" (ARL, Co, Leg. 286, 434).[35]

The statement that townspeople were away serving as porters is intriguing, but being "muleteers" (*arrieros*) seems to be a common activity for the Indians of the valley in the 18th century (O'Toole 2017). Presumably the shift to these roles had occurred at least in part because agriculture was made difficult or impossible by conflicts over water—a push factor. But we may also wonder to what degree new economic roles and opportunities drew people away from agriculture—a pull factor. The issue of economic roles extends into the past as well. Given the town's location so near the ocean, we might expect that a principal economic activity of the townspeople would have been fishing. We may also surmise that at least some of the people at Magdalena spoke one or more of the languages of the fishing peoples, as noted earlier. Nevertheless, based on historical documents, fishing does not appear to have been as important as we might expect.

The tribute lists of 1549 state that the Indians of Chicama were required to provide an annual tribute of 600 pesos of gold, a large quantity of cotton textiles and clothing (Table 12.4), and 800 fanegas each of wheat and beans, as well as birds, eggs, dried fish, and salt, and to provide personal service (Rostworowski 1984:88).[36] We do not know if all the parcialidades participated equally in accruing these items, but it is probable that one or more specialized in fishing, perhaps a continuance from prehispanic times. In 1643, Juan Antonio, principal and scribe of Cao, stated at a trial that he had left his fields and residence to go to the beach to "collect shellfish" (*a mariscar*) (ARL, Co, Leg. 246, 2541), suggesting that, at least by this time, agriculturalists may have engaged in shellfish collecting.

It seems that the Indians of Cao began to grow wheat primarily in order to pay the tribute demanded of them. In 1599, the cabildo of Trujillo proposed that the Chicama Indians should grow more wheat and not just maize, as they had been doing, because the Old World grain would benefit the entire city (Actas de Cabildo, vol. 3, fol. 59). The same cabildo stated that "the Indians should pay their tributes by renting out their horses and mantles because in the Chicama Valley there is much wheat but no means to bring it [to Trujillo]" and that "the Chicama Indians in Santiago and Cao have a great many horses and so could profit, though their mantles are old, so that the wheat [brought by them] would be of great benefit to the town."[37] This statement and others emphasize the importance of horses and mules for transportation, cattle and goats for food, and sheep for wool. Perhaps these new economic endeavors were undertaken because agriculture was not successful. As noted throughout this book, the second Magdalena became a goat herders' camp after the townspeople relocated to the third Magdalena, the one still occupied today.

The inventory of the goods of Francisco Guamán, of the Topquem parcialidad, upon his death included a corral with 76 head of cattle, 43 goats (*cabrios*), 7 mules with their gear (saddles, bridles, etc.), and 40 more goats that were about to be sold at 7 reales a head to pay a debt (ARL, Co, Leg. 176, 835). Another example of how wealth was valued may be found in the

Table 12.4 Annual Tribute Required of the Indians of the Chicama Repartimiento in 1549

Seiscientos pesos de oro de ley perfecta en oro o en plata
Y seiscientos vestidos de ropa de algodón, la mitad de hombre y la mitad de mujer deste tamaño, la manta del indio y el anaco de la india de dos varas en ancho y dos varas y cuarta en largo, y la camiseta del indio de una vara y ochava en largo y en el ancho del ruedo dos varas menos ochava e la liquilla de una vara y media en ancho y una e tres cuartas en largo, puesto en Trujillo
Y seis toldos de algodón los tres medianos y los tres grandes
Y seis colchones de algodón
Y seis tablas de manteles y sesenta pañizuelos de algodón
Y diez y ocho mantas para caballos con diez e ocho mandiles para caballos
Y sesenta costales de algodón
Y tres arrobas de algodón hilado basto
Y treinta libras de hilo para pavilos
Y de xaquimas con sus cabestros e çinchas con sus látigos de algodón e de cabuya, de cada destas treinta en casa del encomendero
Y mil doscientas fanegas de maíz
Y ochocientas fanegas de trigo, de la cuales ponen en Trujillo las quinientas fanegas y las demás dan en sus tierras
Y cincuenta fanegas de frisoles en sus tierras
Y cincuenta puercos
Y un mil aves, la mitad hembras
Y sesenta arrobas de pescado seco
Y treinta fanegas de sal
Y cada semana cuatro cargas de comares y alguna fruta de la tierra en el tiempo que lo hay
Y todos los viernes y días de pescado cada un dia 30 huevos
Y cada año ochenta lampas de madera para cavar los cañaverales en sus tierras

Source: Rostworowski 1984:88.

possessions left by the principal Don Diego Isla Guamán in 1670: 200 head of sheep and goats, a pair of oxen, a mule, a mare with two foals, another mare with one foal, and a cow (ARL, Co, Leg. 199, 1358). This is the same person, mentioned above, who asked to be buried in the church. Payment for his funeral was in the form of 12 goats.

The degree to which the Magdaleneros were forced into or chose to partake in new economic roles may be hard to assess, but by 1728 they were described by Villalobos as arrieros. In 1760, Feijoo de Sosa said the same of most of the Chicama Indians: "They generally serve as muleteers bringing the fruits of the valley to the city of Lima and other places, [and] in the valley may be found more than 2,000 mules to conduct this business" (Feijoo de Sosa 1763:103).[38]

The Final Years of Magdalena de Cao Viejo

The problems with water that the Magdalena community continually confronted may have been one of the factors that led to the abandonment of the town, but we cannot be sure of all

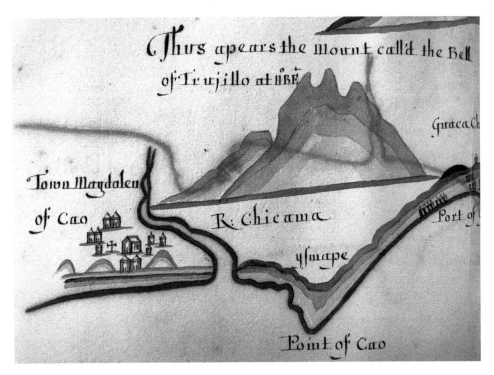

Figure 12.2 Detail of a 1682 map showing Magdalena de Cao. "An Accurate Description of all the Harbours . . . in the South Sea of America," undated manuscript, Sharp's South Sea Waggoner.

the causes, nor of the moment at which they decided to abandon it. The new town, the one still occupied today, is only 4 km north of El Brujo, and we may wonder why such a short distance made such a difference. This is especially so because the lands around modern Magdalena do not appear to be substantially better than elsewhere in the valley: until quite recently the water table there was very high, making it often too wet to sustain agriculture. Nevertheless, the move was made, and reference to various historical maps of the region can aid us in investigating when and how the event transpired.

The archaeological investigations have found evidence to suggest that an earthquake may have destroyed the church, though whether this was the cause of the abandonment is not completely certain (see Chapter 2). A map captured and copied by an English pirate around 1682 appears to show Magdalena on the littoral (Figure 12.2).[39] It was around this time that the Cao community was in disputes over water. As has been described, documents note that they had to leave their houses to grow crops elsewhere, but this was a temporary abandonment.

The dramatic population losses at Magdalena do not substantially differ from those in other communities from the late sixteenth through the early eighteenth centuries. Many historical documents refer to absent Indians and the abandonment of fields due to lack of workers and water. In 1580, a witness stated that the Indians of Cao had not one *ganado*, or domestic animal (Huertas 2001:201), although, as noted, two centuries later the valley was supposedly well stocked with animals and its residents were characterized as "muleteers."[40]

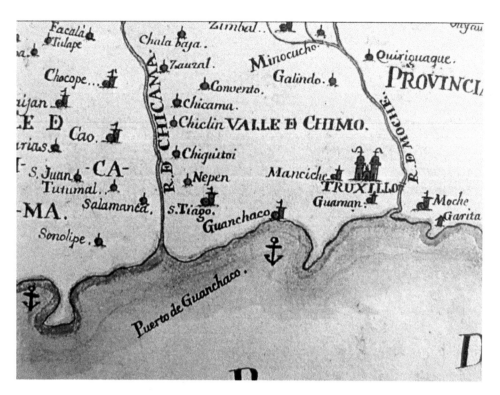

Figure 12.3 Detail of a map commissioned between 1780 and 1790 by Martínez Compañón, showing Magdalena de Cao inland.

In 1760, Miguel Feijoo de Sosa described Cao as a town with only one Dominican friar and a few inhabitants tilling just 161 of the 914 fanegas of their lands, and he produced a map showing it on the coast. Shortly afterward, in 1785, Cao is clearly shown as away from the coast on a map commissioned by the archbishop of Trujillo (Figure 12.3). This might lead us to conclude that the abandonment of the town occurred sometime between 1760 and 1785. The scale of these maps, however, raises the question of how precise their locations are. Furthermore, a comparison of a copy commonly in use and the original map of 1760 shows an important difference between the two. Both maps depict houses and, importantly, churches marked by a cross, but in the copy the cross for Cao has disappeared and only the name of the town, "P[ueblo] Cao" can be read. The original map seems to mark the Cao church clearly inland. This leaves open the possibility that the town at El Brujo could have been abandoned earlier than 1760.

What was occurring in the early to mid-eighteenth century in terms of the location of the town is difficult to assess. As the opening of this chapter recounted, in 1723 the residents of Magdalena wrote to Don Vicente de Mora Chimo saying that they wanted to rebuild their church, which had been in ruins for more than ten years, with important church goods being kept in a hut in the town plaza. Whether this town plaza was in Magdalena at El Brujo or a new location is uncertain, however.

It was not until 1732 that Mora Chimo appeared before the Council of the Indies and told of the grave abuses of the Indians by Fray Felix de Moncada and others. And, as noted, whatever attempts were made to address these issues were of no avail, for in 1740 the Indians of Cao once again complained that they had not even enough water to drink and were losing their crops for lack of it (ARL, Co, Leg. 286, 4403). This was when the church was overgrown with weeds and few people remained in town. We do know with certainty that by 1791 the Magdaleneros were in their new town, although they still did not have a new church there and petitioned the archbishop in Trujillo to help them build a new one, because the sacrament was being administered in a "narrow and indecent ramada that doesn't have enough room for the faithful to enter to hear Mass or the explication of the doctrine."[41]

Given these issues, the abandonment of Magdalena at El Brujo may not have been a sudden event. That settlement may have been abandoned or nearly so by 1728, but the writers of the letter make no mention of a new town, nor do any other sources currently known. Eusebio de Villalobos's remarks suggest that no services were held in the church in his time. It is quite possible that both towns coexisted for a time, with the old one inhabited by few people, mostly goat herders, and the new town closer to the main canal and perhaps closer to better roads. It was farther from the sea, however, suggesting that fishing may not have been important as in earlier times. It was certainly warmer and a more pleasant place, as it was farther inland and thus not subject to the nearly constant cold ocean winds. Eventually the new church was built and the old town finally abandoned for the most part. Now it is archaeologists and tourists who spend time at El Brujo.

NOTES

1 *Principal* was a Spanish term applied to all members of important native families. Members of the cabildo would have been *indios principales*, not *indios communes* (common Indians).

2 *Procurador general de indios y cacique principal de los pueblos de Santiago, San Pedro y San Pablo de Chocope, Santa María Magdalena de Cao y San Esteban en el valle de Chicama.*

3 On the figure of Don Vicente de Mora Chimo and his defense of the Indians of Chicama and other places in Peru in front of Spanish authorities, see Mathis 2008 and 2017.

4 *... arruninada y toda caída, sin que haya esperanzas de que la volvamos a ver como estaba si no tan solamente verla hecha un calvario.*

5 *Cacique principal* or *mandón principal*. The Spanish term *señorío* has come into common English usage in discussing these matters. It may be translated as "lordship" but refers to the sense of rulership, both in terms of the rank held by a person and in the sense of the domain over which the lord (*señor*) ruled. It will be used here interchangeably with *cacicazgo*, which refers to a chiefdom but also more generally to rulership and the territory or people ruled.

6 *... gobernó a su gente quieta y pacíficamente ...*

7 *... cacique principal que era del dicho mi pueblo al tiempo que los españoles entraron en este reino.*

8 *Francisco Guamán, indio natural del pueblo de Cao, de la parcialidad de Topquem* and *Juan Ciparán, natural del pueblo de Cao de la parcialidad de Bechop.*

9 *... junto a la boca del río ...*

10 *... cienega que está camino del pueblo de Cao.* From a document transcribed in the Appendice Documental (Zevallos 1992:28).

11 The age at which a man was considered an adult and thus required to pay tribute varied from place to place until Viceroy Toledo standardized it to the range between 18 and 50 years.

12 This was Ley XXI from the Recopilación de Leyes de Indias: *Que en pueblos de indios no vivan españoles, negros, mestizos, o mulatos.*

13 *... 384 indios tributarios y un cacique, los 114 de ellos originarios y los 270 restantes forasteros residentes en ellos y en las chacaras de su distrito con el título de yanaconas alcabaleros y mitmas ...*

14 *... las mitas y servicios personales.* The mita was the traditional reciprocal labor service between communities, a system that was appropriated by the Spanish and then changed to their advantage.

15 *Melchor Quispe es de los ausentes que no se sabe donde está y está en el pueblo de Chancay y con su padre y hermanos ... y la misma razón militan los demás y el dicho don Diego (Isla Guamán) va todos los años a Lima y cobra de ellos su tributo y de presente esta de partida para hacer viaje a la ciudad de los Reyes a hacer lo mismo, para que no se pierdan los tributos.*

16 *... por no tener con que sembrar están perdidos y distraídos y se ausentan y van fuera de su reducción a buscar donde sembrar para sustentarse.*

17 *... los dichos indios estanse rebeldes en dichas a sus chacaras sin venir ni asistir en su pueblo ni acudir a oír misa ni a las demás cosas de sus obligaciones.*

18 *... jamás ha querido obedecer los mandatos de la justicia como debería ...*

19 *... no concurrían en los días de fiesta a oír misa ni la Doctrina Cristiana, ni a otras obligaciones.*

20 *... había hecho muchos y notorios agravios a los indios del pueblo por tener mal natural ...*

21 *... no iba a parar hasta matarlo ...*

22 The documentary sources use the term *parroquia* (parish) and *curato* (roughly "curateship") interchangeably, and so those terms will be used the same way in the text.

23 A vicar in the Roman Catholic Church is a representative of the archbishop, who in the case of Chicama would have been resident elsewhere, at first Lima and later Trujillo.

24 *... un buen lenguaraz de las lenguas pescadoras ...* See Chapter 13 on the issue of the "languages of the fishermen."

25 *(E)n nuestro tiempo está casi despoblado todo el valle y de muchos pueblos que tenía, han parado en solo tres, estos de muy poca gente que son Chocope, Cao y Santiago, que cada uno tiene un religioso que administra sacramentos y todos están sujetos al prior, que con otros dos o tres habita en el convento de Chicama, sitio despoblado del todo ....*

26 *... por la conversión de los naturales del valle.*

27 *doctrinero de Cao que su padre del difunto debía a la Cofradía de Nuestra Señora del Rosario del pueblo de Cao.* The payment was for 20 *patacones*, a type of colonial silver coin.

28 *Iglesia deste dicho mi pueblo en la sepultura de mis padres ... pido y suplico al padre cura vicario deste dicho pueblo me acompañe el cuerpo desde mi posada hasta mi sepultura con Cruz alta, sacristán y dobles de campanas ... y si fuere hora suficiente de decir misa se me diga una misa de réquiem cantada y responsos y vigilia al cuerpo presente, y si no fuere hora de otro día siguiente se mi diga la dicha misa y se le pague la limosna con doce cabezas de cabras, esto es mi voluntad.* In the first quote, the mention of *sepultura de mis padres* suggests that there were designated areas of the church for family tombs.

29 The information on the Chocope cofradía was supplied to the author by Juan Castañeda who is gratefully acknowledged. Sources on the cofradías of Magdalena are AAT, Cofradías, Leg. 4 and Herrera Calderón 1988.

30 See Chapter 5 for a discussion of the single individual of African descent found in the archaeological studies of Magdalena.

31 The 1699 reorganization of the canal, discussed below, noted that the Cao Canal was also knowns as *Ojanap*, likely an aboriginal term.

32 *Y porque el dicho río tiene a esta parte de abajo donde está nuestra acequia mucha distancia que correr el agua después de la mita de los de arriba y muchos pozos y arena en que se entretiene dicha agua todo un día para llegar abajo nuestra acequia.* (ARL, Ca, Aguas, Leg. 111, 2087).

33 *... gota de agua ninguna para beber ... son personas pobres y miserables que se han visto obligadas a dejar su pueblo y buscar en otros lugares donde hacer sus sementeras para poder sustentarse, y a sus mujeres e hijos, y pagar los Reales Tributos a que están obligados.* (ARL, Ca, Aguas, Leg. 111, 2087).

34 *... sabe usted las desdichas y necesidades que passamos por estos Reinos de por acá, que aunque hay cédulas Reales en nuestro abono, amparo y defensa las sepultan y no parecen sino aquellas que son de conveniencias para los blancos.*

35 *... siendo las tierras fértiles abundan sus montes e impidieran aun las entradas de dicho pueblo, pues el recinto de él se halla lleno de montes y aun la Iglesia, en que se entierran los difuntos, por no haber indios en dicho pueblo porque están en el ejercicio de arrieros.*

36 A fanega is a dry unit of measurement used in Spain and its colonies. Its measurement varied but commonly was about 1.6 bushes (56 liters or 51 dry quarts). The term also was used for areas of land in Mexico and Perú.

37 *... los indios pagaban sus tributos con el alquiler de sus caballos y mantas porque en el valle de Chicama hay mucho trigo pero no como traerlo (...) y que los indios del valle les sigue gran provecho traer a esta ciudad el trigo con sus mantas que son viejas.* Actas de Cabildo, vol. 3.

38 *... estos generalmente se aplican a ser arrieros que llevan los frutos del valle a la ciudad de Lima y a otros lugares para su expendio, hallándose en dicho valle más de 2000 mulas para esta conducción.* (Feijoo de Sosa 1762:103).

39 The map is supposedly a copy of a Spanish version captured by the pirate Bartolome Sharp in 1680. The English copy was drawn by William Hack, and it is known as Hack's Manuscript. There are several copies in different libraries around the world.

40 Although *ganado* commonly refers to cattle, some colonial sources use it to refer to cattle, sheep, and goats, often modifying it (*ganado cabrío*: goat). Thus, the meaning is not clear in this citation as to whether it refers to any of these domestic animals or only cattle.

41 *... una estrecha e indecente ramada, que ni permite campo para que los feligreses entren a oir missa ni explicación de doctrina."* (AAT, Fábrica de Iglesias, Leg. 1; cited in Castañeda 2006). A *ramada* is usually an open-sided structure protected only by a roof, often of thatch or cane.

GUIDE TO ARCHIVAL SOURCES

Example: ARL, Co, Leg. 241, 2294

Refers to: Archivo Regional de La Libertad, Sección Corregimiento, Legajo 241, Cuadernillo 2294

ACRONYMS AND ABBREVIATIONS

AAT: Archivo Arzobispal de Trujillo (Perú)

AGI: Archivo General de Indias (España)

ARL: Archivo Regional de la Libertad (Perú)

Ca: Cabildo

Co: Corregimiento

Leg: Legajo

MP: Mapas y Planos

REFERENCES CITED

Castañeda, Juan

1998   Relaciones entre negros e indios en el Valle de Chicama, 1565. In *Actas del IV Congreso Internacional Etnohistoria*, vol. 3. Lima: Pontificia Universidad Católica del Peru.

2006   Etnohistoria de Magdalena de Cao. Informe de investigación. Unpublished ms., Universidad Nacional de Trujillo.

Cieza de León, Pedro

2005   *Crónica del Perú. El señorío de los Incas.* Caracas: Biblioteca Ayacucho.

Cook, Noble D.

  1981 *Demographic Collapse: Indian Peru 1520–1620*. Cambridge: Cambridge University Press.

de la Puente Brunke, José

  1992 *Encomienda y encomenderos en el Perú*. Seville: Diputación Provincial de Sevilla.

Feijoo de Sosa, Miguel

  1763 *Relación descriptiva de la ciudad y provincia de Truxillo del Perú*. Madrid: Imprenta Real.

Herrera Calderón, Ángel Américo

  1988 Magdalena de Cao: Origen milenario y despojo. *Alternativa* 8:53–71.

Huertas, Lorenzo

  2001 *Diluvios andinos a través de las fuentes coloniales*. Lima: Pontificia Universidad Católica del Perú.

Lavallé, Bernard

  1999 *Amor y opresión en los Andes coloniales*. Lima: Institut français d'études andines, Instituto de Estudios Peruanos.

Marchena Fernández, Juan

  1996 Complejidad y textura de las relaciones de dominación: Orden y sistema colonial en el mundo andino (s. XVI). In *Actas del I Congreso de Investigación Social. Región y sociedad en Latinoamérica, su problemática en el noroeste Argentino*, edited by Alfredo Bolsi, Julia Patricia Ortiz, Cristina López, et al., pp. 485–491. Tucumán: Universidad Nacional de Tucumán.

Martínez Compañón, Baltasar Jaime

  1978 [1780–1790] *Trujillo del Perú*. Madrid: Ediciones de Cultura Hispánica.

Mateos Delibes, Rocío

  2016 Y no soltó la vara de justicia: Conflictos, crímenes y autoridad real en las reducciones indígenas del Valle de Chicama (1590–1616). In *Poder y conflictividad social en América Latina*, edited by Sigfrido Vázquez Cienfuegos, pp. 13–26. Prague: Karolinum.

Mathis, Sophie

  2008 L'Amérique espagnole: Vicente Mora Chimo, ou l'itinéraire original d'un cacique hispanisé de la côte nord du Pérou à la cour d'Espagne au début du XVIII siècle. Unpublished Ph.D. dissertation, Centre de Recherches Latino-Américaines, Université de Poitiers.

  2017 *Una figura de la primera globalización de la América Española. Vicente Mora Chimo. El itinerario original de una cacique ladino*. Lima: Universidad Nacional Agraria La Molina.

Meléndez, Juan de

  1682 *Tesoros verdaderos de las Indias*. Rome: Imprenta de Nicolás Angel Tinassio.

Mogrovejo, Toribio

  2006 *Libro de visitas de Santo Toribio Mogrovejo (1593–1605)*. Edited by José Antonio Benito. Lima: Pontificia Universidad Católica del Perú.

Mora Chimo, Vicente

  2003 [1732] Manifiesto de los agravios, bexaciones, y molestias, que padecen los Indios del reyno del Peru. *Letras* (Lima) 105–106:171–194.

Mumford, Jeremy

  2012 *Vertical Empire: The General Resettlement of Indians in the Colonial Andes*. Durham, NC: Duke University Press.

Netherly, Patricia Joan

    1974 Los señores tardíos en la costa y sierra norte. *Alternativa* 2: 59–74.

    1978 Local-Level Lords on the North Coast of Peru. Unpublished Ph.D. dissertation, Cornell University.

    1984 The Management of Late Andean Irrigation Systems on the North Coast of Peru. *American Antiquity* 49(2):227–254.

    1990 Out of Many, One: The Organization of Rule in the North Coast Polities. In *The Northern Dynasties Kingship and Statecraft in Chimor*, edited by Michael E. Moseley and Alana Cordy-Collins, pp. 461–487. Washington, DC: Dumbarton Oaks Research Library and Collection.

O'Phelan, Scarlet

    1997 *Kurakas sin sucesiones: Del cacique al alcalde de Indios (Perú y Bolivia, 1750–1835)*. Cuzco: Centro de Estudios Regionales Bartolomé de Las Casas.

O'Toole, Rachel Sarah

    2012 *Bound Lives: African, Indians and the Making of Race in Colonial Peru*. Pittsburgh: University of Pittsburgh Press.

    2017 Mobilizing Muleteer Indigeneity in the Markets of Colonial Peru. In *To be Indio in Colonial Spanish America*, edited by Mónica Díaz, pp. 95–122. Alburquerque: University of New Mexico Press.

Quilter, Jeffrey, Marc Zender, Karen Spalding, Régulo Franco Jordán, César Gálvez Mora, and Juan Castañeda

    2010 Traces of a Lost Language and Number System Discovered on the North Coast of Peru. *American Anthropologist* 112(3):357–369.

Ramírez, Susan E.

    1986 *Provincial Patriarchs: Land Tenure and the Economics of Power in Colonial Peru*. Alburquerque: University of New Mexico Press.

    1996 *The World Upside Down: Cross-Cultural Contact and Conflict in Sixteenth Century Peru*. Stanford, CA: Stanford University Press, 1996.

    2005 *To Feed and Be Fed: The Cosmological Bases of Authority and Identity in the Andes*. Palo Alto, CA: Stanford University Press.

Rappaport, Joanne and Tom Cummins

    2012 Beyond The Lettered City. Indigenous Literacies in the Andes. Durham and London: Duke University Press.

Rostworowski, María

    1975 Algunos comentarios hechos a las ordenanzas del Doctor Cuenca. *Historia y Cultura* 9:126–154.

    1981 La voz parcialidad en su contexto de los siglos XVI y XVII. In *Etnohistoria y antropología andinas*, edited by Amalia Castelli, María Koth de Paredes, and Mariana Mould de Pease, pp. 35–45. Lima: Museo Nacional de Historia.

    1984 La tasa ordenada por el licenciado Pedro de La Gasca (1549). *Revista Histórica* 34:53–102.

Saavedra, Antonio de

    1915 [1700] *Repartición general de las aguas de Trujillo y sus valles*. Trujillo: Imprenta Comercial Progreso No. 629.

Saito, Akira, and Claudia Rosas

2017 *Reducciones: La concentración forzada de las poblaciones indígenas en el virreinato del Perú.* Lima: National Museum of Ethnology of Osaka and Pontificia Universidad Católica del Perú.

Toledo, Francisco de

1986 [1569–1574] *Disposiciones gubernativas para el virreinato del Perú.* Seville: Consejo Superior de Investigaciones Científicas.

VanValkenburgh, Nathaniel Parker

2012 Landscapes of Forced Resttlement in the Zaña and Chamán Valleys, Peru, 16th and 17th Centuries C.E. Unpublished Ph.D. dissertation, Department of Anthropology, Harvard University.

Wernke, Steven A.

2013 *Negotiated Settlements: Andean Communities and Landscapes Under Inka and Spanish Colonialism.* Gainesville: University Press of Florida.

Zevallos Quiñones, Jorge

1973 La ropa tributo de las encomiendas trujillanas en el siglo XVI. *Historia y Cultura* 7:107–121.

1990 Pretendientes a la encomienda de Chicama. *Boletín del Instituto Riva Agüero* 17:373–381.

1992 *Los cacicazgos de Trujillo.* Trujillo: Gráfica Cuatro S.A.

1996 *Los fundadores y primeros pobladores de Trujillo del Perú.* Trujillo: Fundación Alfredo Pinillos Goicochea.

Appendix 12.1

Material Culture Mentioned in Documents

This appendix presents a list of references to material culture found in documents by the author while conducting the research for Chapter 12.

OBJECT	MATERIAL	DATE	SOURCE	DESCRIPTION OF CONTEXT
Reins of horse leather (*riendas de caballo de cuero*)	Textile	1590	ARL, Co, Leg. 237, 2187	Don Pedro Mache, cacique of the town of Santiago and Second Person of the Valley, ordered Juan Guamán, scribe of the town of Cao, to be whipped with these reins
Shirt (*camiseta*)	Textile	1590	ARL, Co, Leg. 237, 2187	Don Pedro Mache, cacique of the town of Santiago and Second Person of the Valley, ordered Juan Guamán, scribe of the town of Cao, to remove this shirt to be beaten with the reins
Rod of justice (*vara de justicia*)	Wood	1590	ARL, Co, Leg. 237, 2187	Don Pedro Mache, cacique of the town of Santiago and Second Person of the Valley of Chicama, received a stick and said that it had the job of the "rod of justice" and ordered whipping
Rope to lead a horse (*soga para llevar el caballo*)	Textile	1590	ARL, Co, Leg. 237, 2187	Juan Guamán, scribe of the town of Cao, took the robe and the horse in one hand and with the other clutched his injured stomach when he returned to Magdalena de Cao after being beaten in Santiago by Cacique Don Pedro Mache
Book and account of the Indians	Paper	1590	ARL, Co, Leg. 237, 2187	Book brought by Juan Guamán, scribe of the town of Cao, of the account of the third tribute of the Chicama Valley, June 1589
Thick-soled boots	Textile	1590	ARL, Co, Leg. 237, 2187	Thick boots worn by the cacique of Santiago Don Pedro Mache, which gave many kicks (and whips and punches) to the scribe of Magdalena de Cao, Juan Guamán
50 kg box sealed with a key (*caja quintaleña sellado con llave [cabe un quintal]*)	Wood and metal	1609	ARL, Co, Leg. 238, 2214	Property of the Spaniard Pedro Santiago, a resident of the sugar mill San Francisco in Chicama, confiscated by the sheriff for having abused the cacique of Chicama, Don Pedro de Mora, and the mayor of Magdalena de Cao, Don Antonio Jalca Guamán
A Rouen mattress (*un colchón de ruan*)	Textile	1609	ARL, Co, Leg. 238, 2214	Property of the Spaniard Pedro Santiago, a resident of the sugar mill San Francisco in Chicama, confiscated by the sheriff for having abused the cacique of Chicama, Don Pedro de Mora, and the mayor of Magdalena de Cao, Don Antonio Jalca Guamán

(continued)

OBJECT	MATERIAL	DATE	SOURCE	DESCRIPTION OF CONTEXT
Two pillows (*dos almohadas*)	Textile	1609	ARL, Co, Leg. 238, 2214	Property of the Spaniard Pedro Santiago, a resident of the sugar mill San Francisco in Chicama, confiscated by the sheriff for having abused the cacique of Chicama, Don Pedro de Mora, and the mayor of Magdalena de Cao, Don Antonio Jalca Guamán
A Rouen pillow in wrought blue silk (*una almohada de ruan labrada de seda azul*)	Textile	1609	ARL, Co, Leg. 238, 2214	Property of the Spaniard Pedro Santiago, a resident of the sugar mill San Francisco in Chicama, confiscated by the sheriff for having abused the cacique of Chicama, Don Pedro de Mora, and the mayor of Magdalena de Cao, Don Antonio Jalca Guamán
Two Rouen sheets (*dos sabanas de ruan*)	Textile	1609	ARL, Co, Leg. 238, 2214	Property of the Spaniard Pedro Santiago, a resident of the sugar mill San Francisco in Chicama, confiscated by the sheriff for having abused the cacique of Chicama, Don Pedro de Mora, and the mayor of Magdalena de Cao, Don Antonio Jalca Guamán
One colorful brocade bed cover (*una sobrecama de borrachera labrada de colores*)	Textile	1609	ARL, Co, Leg. 238, 2214	Property of the Spaniard Pedro Santiago, a resident of the sugar mill San Francisco in Chicama, confiscated by the sheriff for having abused the cacique of Chicama, Don Pedro de Mora, and the mayor of Magdalena de Cao, Don Antonio Jalca Guamán
One new suede jerkin with gold trim (*un coleto de ante nuevo con sus pasamanos de oro*)	Textile	1609	ARL, Co, Leg. 238, 2214	Property of the Spaniard Pedro Santiago, a resident of the sugar mill San Francisco in Chicama, confiscated by the sheriff for having abused the cacique of Chicama, Don Pedro de Mora, and the mayor of Magdalena de Cao, Don Antonio Jalca Guamán
Dagger (*daga*)	Metal	1609	ARL, Co, Leg. 238, 2214	Property of the Spaniard Pedro Santiago, a resident of the sugar mill San Francisco in Chicama, confiscated by the sheriff for having abused the cacique of Chicama, Don Pedro de Mora, and the mayor of Magdalena de Cao, Don Antonio Jalca Guamán
Knife (*cuchillo*)	Metal	1616	ARL, Co, Leg. 241, 2294	Hernando Cosco Guamán, Indian of the Topquem parcialidad, attacked Don Andrés de Silva, principal Indian of the same parcialidad, with a knife and a garrote
Club (*garrote*)	Wood and metal	1616	ARL, Co, Leg. 241, 2294	Hernando Cosco Guamán, Indian of the Topquem parcialidad, attacked Don Andrés de Silva, principal Indian of the same parcialidad, with a knife and a garrote

OBJECT	MATERIAL	DATE	SOURCE	DESCRIPTION OF CONTEXT
A book entitled "A Temporal Death" (*un libro intitulado "De la muerte temporal"*)	Paper	1616	ARL, Co, Leg. 241, 2290	Property of Don Andrés de Silva, Indian of the Topquem parcialidad, seized for having killed Don Hernando Cosco Guamán
Some breeches of light blue cloth with three silver buckles (*unos calzones de paño azul de castilla claro con tres hevillas de plata*)	Textile	1616	ARL, Co, Leg. 241, 2290	Property of Don Andrés de Silva, Indian of the Topquem parcialidad, seized for having killed Don Hernando Cosco Guamán
A black lliquilla adorned with purple Castile taffeta and black trim (*una lliquilla negra atornada en tafetan morado de castilla trae un pasamanos negros*)	Textile	1616	ARL, Co, Leg. 241, 2290	Property of Don Andrés de Silva, Indian of the Topquem parcialidad, seized for having killed Don Hernando Cosco Guamán
Another lliquilla of black satin, old and broken (*otra lliquilla de raso negro vieja y rota*)	Textile	1616	ARL, Co, Leg. 241, 2290	Property of Don Andrés de Silva, Indian of the Topquem parcialidad, seized for having killed Don Hernando Cosco Guamán
Some old cotton tablecloths (*unos manteles viejos de algodón*)	Textile	1616	ARL, Co, Leg. 241, 2290	Property of Don Andrés de Silva, Indian of the Topquem parcialidad, seized for having killed Don Hernando Cosco Guamán
A purple blanket with wrought edges (*una manta morada labrada las puntas*)	Textile	1616	ARL, Co, Leg. 241, 2290	Property of Don Andrés de Silva, Indian of the Topquem parcialidad, seized for having killed Don Hernando Cosco Guamán
A red shirt (*una camiseta encarnada*)	Textile	1616	ARL, Co, Leg. 241, 2290	Property of Don Andrés de Silva, Indian of the Topquem parcialidad, seized for having killed Don Hernando Cosco Guamán
Two old silk sashes, one from China (*dos chumbes de seda viejos, uno de la China*)	Textile	1616	ARL, Co, Leg. 241, 2290	Property of Don Andrés de Silva, Indian of the Topquem parcialidad, seized for having killed Don Hernando Cosco Guamán
Two silver spoons (*dos cucharas de plata*)	Metal	1616	ARL, Co, Leg. 241, 2290	Property of Don Andrés de Silva, Indian of the Topquem parcialidad, seized for having killed Don Hernando Cosco Guamán
A cedar box (*una caja de cedro*)	Wood	1616	ARL, Co, Leg. 241, 2290	Property of Don Andrés de Silva, Indian of the Topquem parcialidad, seized for having killed Don Hernando Cosco Guamán

(*continued*)

OBJECT	MATERIAL	DATE	SOURCE	DESCRIPTION OF CONTEXT
Some papers of minor importance that were not inventoried (*unos papeles de poca importancia que por serlo no se inventarían*)		1616	ARL, Co, Leg. 241, 2290	Property of Don Andrés de Silva, Indian of the Topquem parcialidad, seized for having killed Don Hernando Cosco Guamán
A denim hat with a false gold braid (*un sombrero de mezcla con su trencilla de oro falso*)	Textile	1616	ARL, Co, Leg. 241, 2290	Property of Don Andrés de Silva, Indian of the Topquem parcialidad, seized for having killed Don Hernando Cosco Guamán
Lance (*lanza*)	Metal and Wood	1620	ARL, Co, Leg. 241, 2329	Spear with which the mulatto Alonso "El Cuchara" attacked the principal of Cao, Don Andrés de Silva Paypay Chumbi, to steal his wife Ana, Indian
Short sword (*terciado [espada corta]*)	Metal	1620	ARL, Co, Leg. 241, 2329	Short sword with which Don Andrés de Silva Paypay Chumbi defended himself from the attack of the mulatto Alonso el "Cuchara", at the entrance of Magdalena de Cao
Shotgun (*escopeta*)		1620	ARL, Co, Leg. 241, 2329	Belonged to Joan de la Carrera, Spaniard, and taken by the other Spaniards when leaving to defend Don Andrés de Silva Paypay Chumbi, principal of Cao, who, in the midst of a brawl, asked for help "giving the voice of the king" (pleading for royal justice)
Horsehair chair (*sillon de caballo*)	Textile	1625	ARL, Co, Leg. 242, 2375	From the horse of Mateo, a black slave from the Congo, when he was murdered on the road to Cao from Santiago by Juan Ciparán, an Indian from the town of Magdalena de Cao
Butcher knife (*cuchillo carnicero*)	Metal	1625	ARL, Co, Leg. 242, 2375	The knife that killed Mateo, a black slave from the Congo (from seven stab wounds with the knife and his intestines came out), by Juan Ciparán, an Indian from the town of Magdalena de Cao
A hawthorn club three quarters long (*garrote de palo de espino de tres cuartas de largo*)	Wood	1625	ARL, Co, Leg. 242, 2375	Stick with which Juan Ciparán, an Indian from the town of Magdalena de Cao, chased Mateo, a black slave from the Congo
Saddle tack and ropes (*aparejo de enjalmas y sogas*)		1628	ARL, Co, Leg. 176, 835	Probate inventory of Francisco Guamán, deceased native of the town of Cao in the parcialidad of Topquem
Cedar box with lock and key, purchased at 16 pesos (*caja de cedro con su chapa y llave, la compro en 16 pesos*)	Wood and metal	1628	ARL, Co, Leg. 176, 835	Probate inventory of Francisco Guamán, deceased native of the town of Cao in the parcialidad of Topquem

OBJECT	MATERIAL	DATE	SOURCE	DESCRIPTION OF CONTEXT
Cape (*capa*)	Textile	1628	ARL, Co, Leg. 176, 835	Probate inventory of Francisco Guamán, deceased native of the town of Cao in the parcialidad of Topquem
Pants of Quito cloth (*calzones de paño de Quito*)	Textile	1628	ARL, Co, Leg. 176, 835	Probate inventory of Francisco Guamán, deceased native of the town of Cao in the parcialidad of Topquem
Vicuña hat (*sombrero de vicuña*)	Textile	1628	ARL, Co, Leg. 176, 835	Probate inventory of Francisco Guamán, deceased native of the town of Cao in the parcialidad of Topquem
Medium-sized silver tumbler (*tembladera de plata mediana*)	Metal	1628	ARL, Co, Leg. 176, 835	Probate inventory of Francisco Guamán, deceased native of the town of Cao in the parcialidad of Topquem
Bridle seat/stand (*silla a brida*)	Leather	1628	ARL, Co, Leg. 176, 835	Probate inventory of Francisco Guamán, deceased native of the town of Cao in the parcialidad of Topquem
Small silver spoon (*cuchara pequeña de plata*)	Metal	1628	ARL, Co, Leg. 176, 835	Probate inventory of Francisco Guamán, deceased native of the town of Cao in the parcialidad of Topquem
New cedar box with lock and key (*caja de cedro es nueva con cerradura y su llave*)	Wood and metal	1640	ARL, Co, Leg. 245, 2514	Property of Gabriel Pérez, native of the town of Olmos and died in the town of Magdalena de Cao. The box was confiscated and broken open with a blow from the mayor of Magdalena de Cao, Don Gonzalo
Silver tumbler (*tembladera de plata*)	Metal	1640	ARL, Co, Leg. 245, 2514	It was inside the cedar box owned by Gabriel Pérez, native of the town of Olmos and died in the town of Magdalena de Cao. The box was confiscated and broken open with a blow from the mayor of Magdalena de Cao, Don Gonzalo
Another silver tumbler (*otra tembladera de plata*)	Metal	1640	ARL, Co, Leg. 245, 2514	It was inside the cedar box owned by Gabriel Pérez, native of the town of Olmos and died in the town of Magdalena de Cao. The box was confiscated and broken open with a blow from the mayor of Magdalena de Cao, Don Gonzalo
Glass tumbler (*tembladera de vidrio*)	Glass	1640	ARL, Co, Leg. 245, 2514	It was inside the cedar box owned by Gabriel Pérez, native of the town of Olmos and died in the town of Magdalena de Cao. The box was confiscated and broken open with a blow from the mayor of Magdalena de Cao, Don Gonzalo
Silver spoon (*cuchara de plata*)	Metal	1640	ARL, Co, Leg. 245, 2514	It was inside the cedar box owned by Gabriel Pérez, native of the town of Olmos and died in the town of Magdalena de Cao. The box was confiscated and broken open with a blow from the mayor of Magdalena de Cao, Don Gonzalo

(continued)

OBJECT	MATERIAL	DATE	SOURCE	DESCRIPTION OF CONTEXT
Half pound of carved or worked wax (*media libra de cera labrada*)	Wax	1640	ARL, Co, Leg. 245, 2514	It was inside the cedar box owned by Gabriel Pérez, native of the town of Olmos and died in the town of Magdalena de Cao. The box was confiscated and broken open with a blow from the mayor of Magdalena de Cao, Don Gonzalo
Two new shirts of Rouen, unused (*dos camisetas de ruan nuevas sin estrenar*)	Textile	1640	ARL, Co, Leg. 245, 2514	It was inside the cedar box owned by Gabriel Pérez, native of the town of Olmos and died in the town of Magdalena de Cao. The box was confiscated and broken open with a blow from the mayor of Magdalena de Cao, Don Gonzalo
One pair of new Rouen pants (*unos calzones de ruan nuevos*)	Textile	1640	ARL, Co, Leg. 245, 2514	It was inside the cedar box owned by Gabriel Pérez, native of the town of Olmos and died in the town of Magdalena de Cao. The box was confiscated and broken open with a blow from the mayor of Magdalena de Cao, Don Gonzalo
Two and a half yards of Rouen (*dos varas y medio de ruan*)	Textile	1640	ARL, Co, Leg. 245, 2514	It was inside the cedar box owned by Gabriel Pérez, native of the town of Olmos and died in the town of Magdalena de Cao. The box was confiscated and broken open with a blow from the mayor of Magdalena de Cao, Don Gonzalo
One pair of new pants from Quito with wraps and buttons (*unos calzones de paño nuevo de Quito con sus aforros y botones*)	Textile	1640	ARL, Co, Leg. 245, 2514	It was inside the cedar box owned by Gabriel Pérez, native of the town of Olmos and died in the town of Magdalena de Cao. The box was confiscated and broken open with a blow from the mayor of Magdalena de Cao, Don Gonzalo
Two new pairs of armbands with garnets (*dos pares de brazales de granates nuevos*)	Textile	1640	ARL, Co, Leg. 245, 2514	It was inside the cedar box owned by Gabriel Pérez, native of the town of Olmos and died in the town of Magdalena de Cao. The box was confiscated and broken open with a blow from the mayor of Magdalena de Cao, Don Gonzalo
Two thousand beads (*dos millares de chaquiras*)	Bead	1640	ARL, Co, Leg. 245, 2514	It was inside the cedar box owned by Gabriel Pérez, native of the town of Olmos and died in the town of Magdalena de Cao. The box was confiscated and broken open with a blow from the mayor of Magdalena de Cao, Don Gonzalo
Three account books (*tres libros de cuentas*)	Paper	1640	ARL, Co, Leg. 245, 2514	It was inside the cedar box owned by Gabriel Pérez, native of the town of Olmos and died in the town of Magdalena de Cao. The box was confiscated and broken open with a blow from the mayor of Magdalena de Cao, Don Gonzalo

OBJECT	MATERIAL	DATE	SOURCE	DESCRIPTION OF CONTEXT
Handwritten documents, vouchers, and cards (*escrituras, vales, y cédulas*)	Paper	1640	ARL, Co, Leg. 245, 2514	It was inside the cedar box owned by Gabriel Pérez, native of the town of Olmos and died in the town of Magdalena de Cao. The box was confiscated and broken open with a blow from the mayor of Magdalena de Cao, Don Gonzalo
Pins and needles (*agujas y alfileres*)	Metal	1640	ARL, Co, Leg. 245, 2514	It was inside the cedar box owned by Gabriel Pérez, native of the town of Olmos and died in the town of Magdalena de Cao. The box was confiscated and broken open with a blow from the mayor of Magdalena de Cao, Don Gonzalo
Soap (*jabón*)	Soap	1640	ARL, Co, Leg. 245, 2514	It was inside the cedar box owned by Gabriel Pérez, native of the town of Olmos and died in the town of Magdalena de Cao. The box was confiscated and broken open with a blow from the mayor of Magdalena de Cao, Don Gonzalo
Candlestick (*candelero*)	Metal	1640	ARL, Co, Leg. 245, 2514	It was inside the cedar box owned by Gabriel Pérez, native of the town of Olmos and died in the town of Magdalena de Cao. The box was confiscated and broken open with a blow from the mayor of Magdalena de Cao, Don Gonzalo
A new cape of brown cloth with blue taffeta trimming (*una capa de paño pardo nueva guarnecida con tafetán azul*)	Textile	1647	ARL, Co, Leg. 192, 1230	Clothing belonging to Don Juan de Paypay Chumbi, principal Indian from Cao, seized by Mayor Don Diego Isla Guamán to pay off a debt and sell at public auction in the square, at the gates of the cabildo, on Sunday after Mass
A yard and a half of tablecloths (*vara y media de manteles [tabla de manteles]*)	Textile	1647	ARL, Co, Leg. 192, 1230	Clothing belonging to Don Juan Paypay Chumbi, principal Indian from Cao, seized by Mayor Don Diego Isla Guamán to pay off a debt and sell at public auction in the square, at the gates of the cabildo, on Sunday after Mass
A bobble red shirt (*una camiseta colorada de motilla*)	Textile	1647	ARL, Co, Leg. 192, 1230	Clothing belonging to Don Juan Paypay Chumbi, principal Indian from Cao, seized by Mayor Don Diego Isla Guamán to pay off a debt and sell at public auction in the square, at the gates of the cabildo, on Sunday after Mass
Team of oxen for plowing with rig (*yunta de bueyes de arado con su aparejo*)		1661	ARL, Co, Leg. 196, 1312	Probate inventory of Don Lorenzo Guamán, Indian widower, who died intestate at the age of 60 years
Old hat (*sombrero viejo*)	Textile	1661	ARL, Co, Leg. 196, 1312	Probate inventory of Don Lorenzo Guamán, Indian widower, who died intestate at the age of 60 years

(continued)

OBJECT	MATERIAL	DATE	SOURCE	DESCRIPTION OF CONTEXT
Pocket or bag (*faltriquera [bolsa]*)	Textile	1661	ARL, Co, Leg. 196, 1312	Probate inventory of Don Lorenzo Guamán, Indian widower, who died intestate at the age of 60 years
Dish (*trastes*)	Ceramic	1661	ARL, Co, Leg. 196, 1312	Probate inventory of Don Lorenzo Guamán, Indian widower, who died intestate at the age of 60 years
Maize "jar" (*maiz "embotijado"*)	Ceramic	1661	ARL, Co, Leg. 196, 1312	Probate inventory of Don Lorenzo Guamán, Indian widower, who died intestate at the age of 60 years
Shovels (*lampas*)	Metal and wood	1661	ARL, Co, Leg. 196, 1312	Probate inventory of Don Lorenzo Guamán, Indian widower, who died intestate at the age of 60 years
Oak box with closure (*caja de roble con su cerradura*)	Wood and metal	1670	ARL, Co, Leg. 199, 1358	Testament of Don Diego Ysla Guamán, principal of the town of Magdalena de Cao, of the parcialidad of Topquem
A team of oxen with all their gear, including yoke and plow (*Una junta de bueyes con todo su aparejo, "yugo y arado"*)	Wood and metal	1670	ARL, Co, Leg. 199, 1358	Testament of Don Diego Isla Guamán, principal of the town of Magdalena de Cao, of the parcialidad of Topquem
Sedan chair for sitting (*silla de mano de sentar*)	Leather	1670	ARL, Co, Leg. 199, 1358	Testament of Don Diego Isla Guamán, principal of the town of Magdalena de Cao, of the parcialidad of Topquem
Desk (*bufete*)	Wood	1670	ARL, Co, Leg. 199, 1358	Testament of Don Diego Isla Guamán, principal of the town of Magdalena de Cao, of the parcialidad of Topquem
Tumbler (*tembladera*)	Metal	1670	ARL, Co, Leg. 199, 1358	Testament of Don Diego Isla Guamán, principal of the town of Magdalena de Cao, of the parcialidad of Topquem
Spoon (*cuchara*)	Metal	1670	ARL, Co, Leg. 199, 1358	Testament of Don Diego Isla Guamán, principal of the town of Magdalena de Cao, of the parcialidad of Topquem
Quincha house in this town with two plank doors with keys (*casa de quincha en este mi pueblo con sus dos puertas de tabla con sus llaves*)		1670	ARL, Co, Leg. 199, 1358	Testament of Don Diego Isla Guamán, principal of the town of Magdalena de Cao, of the parcialidad of Topquem
Plank door (*puerta de tabla*)	Wood	1670	ARL, Co, Leg. 199, 1358	Testament of Don Diego Isla Guamán, principal of the town of Magdalena de Cao, of the parcialidad of Topquem
Keys to the house (*llaves [de casa]*)	Metal	1670	ARL, Co, Leg. 199, 1358	Testament of Don Diego Isla Guamán, principal of the town of Magdalena de Cao, of the parcialidad of Topquem

OBJECT	MATERIAL	DATE	SOURCE	DESCRIPTION OF CONTEXT
Two axes (*dos hachas*)	Metal	1670	ARL, Co, Leg. 199, 1358	Testament of Don Diego Isla Guamán, principal of the town of Magdalena de Cao, of the parcialidad of Topquem
Cart with two screws (*carretón con sus dos tornillos*)	Metal and Wood	1670	ARL, Co, Leg. 199, 1358	Testament of Don Diego Isla Guamán, principal of the town of Magdalena de Cao, of the parcialidad of Topquem
Shovel (*una lampa*)	Metal and Wood	1670	ARL, Co, Leg. 199, 1358	Testament of Don Diego Isla Guamán, principal of the town of Magdalena de Cao, of the parcialidad of Topquem
Two flagons (*dos limetas*)	Ceramic	1670	ARL, Co, Leg. 199, 1358	Testament of Don Diego Isla Guamán, principal of the town of Magdalena de Cao, of the parcialidad of Topquem
An earthenware saucer (*un platillo de barro*)	Ceramic	1670	ARL, Co, Leg. 199, 1358	Testament of Don Diego Isla Guamán, principal of the town of Magdalena de Cao, of the parcialidad of Topquem
An earthenware cup (*una tacilla de barro*)	Ceramic	1670	ARL, Co, Leg. 199, 1358	Testament of Don Diego Isla Guamán, principal of the town of Magdalena de Cao, of the parcialidad of Topquem
Two old hoes (*dos barretas viejas*)	Metal and wood	1670	ARL, Co, Leg. 199, 1358	Testament of Don Diego Isla Guamán, principal of the town of Magdalena de Cao, of the parcialidad of Topquem
Land titles (*papels de tierras*)	Paper	1670	ARL, Co, Leg. 199, 1358	Testament of Don Diego Isla Guamán, principal of the town of Magdalena de Cao, of the parcialidad of Topquem
Batons of royal justice (*varas de la real justica*)	Wood	1716–1761	ARL, Co, Leg. 269, 3265	Batons granted to the mayors of Magdalena de Cao after being elected and sworn into office

13

Papers

Jeffrey Quilter, Karen Spalding,
and Nicholas E. Brown

O F ALL OF the artifacts found at Magdalena de Cao, the ones that most surprised us by
their presence were the remnants of paper documents. They were found in our very first
excavations in 2004 at the northwestern corner of the complex, and their discovery was an
important stimulus to us to continue work at the site. For although we had a vague notion of
the kinds of things that we might discover in our excavations of the colonial sector, we had not
reckoned that we might find paper, even though the logic of the good preservation at the site
would have led us to such a conclusion had we thought the matter through.

The development of writing marks the end of prehistory and the beginning of history. It
is generally considered one of the great leaps forward in human progress, as is the invention of
the printing press, which vastly improved the production and circulation of texts. Western historians tend to emphasize that writing had a profound impact on indigenous societies, which,
not possessing recording systems of their own, were impressed by "talking papers." But how
writing and documents were received seems to have varied from people to people, including
those who had their own writing system, such as the Maya (Coe 2012) and the Inca with their
khipu (e.g., Quilter and Urton 2002). In some places writing per se impressed native peoples,
but in other cases it seems that it was the role of documents in serving the larger European
purposes of empire, colonialism, and domination that impressed, baffled, or dismayed peoples
working from very different cultural assumptions.

This chapter discusses paper documents as artifacts, in terms of their nature as things,
as well as what they state in writing or print. The Magdalena de Cao papers offer unique
views into how everyday people may have felt about paper and documents in a society that
had experienced European domination by the use of such instruments for two generations.
Scholarship on the history of books, manuscripts, and printing is a well-established and extensive field unto itself, and we do not claim to have deep knowledge of these subjects. The corpus
of Magdalena documents available to specialized scholars is being made available on a website, https://www.peabody.harvard.edu/Magdalena. We hope that such scholars will benefit
from having the Magdalena materials available for their research, and we, in turn, will learn
more about the site and its occupants from the contributions experts will make regarding the

details of the manuscripts. In the meantime, our project has taken advantage of its members' expertise regarding some of the documentary materials. Rocío Delibes references some of our papers in Chapter 12, and Sarah Quilter discusses playing cards in Chapter 14. Here we present a general overview of the paper collection, followed by discussion of several categories of papers and fragments or pages of special interest.

The papers are currently stored in stable conditions at the Museo de Cao at the El Brujo Archaeological Complex. While much of the dirt on the papers has been removed with soft paintbrushes, some need further cleaning to remove embedded fine-grained soil; we await conservation experts (and funding) to help us with this task. We have developed a cataloguing system for the collection to reference individual papers, though at the time of writing we are still refining it, so no numbers are presented here. The specific papers discussed in this chapter, however, are distinctive enough that they will eventually be posted on the project website.

As previously noted, we first discovered paper fragments in 2004, when we placed a small test pit, Unit 4, at the north face of the northwest corner of the church atrium. After our initial surprise at finding any paper at all, we were intrigued by the discovery of smoked cigarette ends (butts); it seemed the cigarettes had been made by rolling what we presumed to be tobacco in pieces of old manuscripts. Because we were uncertain as to the age of the deposits, we at first hesitated in considering these artifacts as pertaining to the colonial settlement. Indeed, several Peruvian archaeologists in attendance noted that in the 1960s and 1970s they used to roll marijuana in Bible pages because they were so thin.

Samples of the cigarette ends were exported and then examined by personnel at the Harvard University Herbaria, who identified the smoking mixture as tobacco. Unrolling the cigarette papers confirmed that they were colonial and not of more recent date, and subsequently we sent the contents for radiocarbon dating. The resulting dates, from the seventeenth century, confirmed that they likely had been rolled and smoked in that era after the church was abandoned.[1]

In addition to cigarette ends, we found examples of other paper fragments in the 2004 excavations. It was only in 2005 and in subsequent years, however, that great numbers of paper fragments were unearthed. These were found in both church and town and in almost every excavation context imaginable. Papers were most numerous in the archaeological deposits along the outside of the church compound wall; we also found several large fragments against the outside western wall of the baptistry. We found virtually no paper fragments on living surfaces in house compounds in the town, but we did encounter them at the bases of quincha walls and similar locations. This suggests that some of the papers were blown into town by prevailing winds.

We cannot know with certainty how looting of the site after its abandonment in the Colonial Period affected the amount of paper there. Members of our excavation crew told us that there is a local person of some means who sponsored looting of colonial contexts prior to the early 1990s when the site came under the protection of the Fundación Wiese. Those rumors also suggested that at least one and possibly more entire books were recovered during that time. We have not been able to follow this lead to determine if the claims are true and what kinds of documents may be available in one or more private collections.

After primarily serving as letters and official documents, paper generally was used at Magdalena for its functional value. We have one clear case of a sheet being used as toilet paper, while other papers appear to have been used for personal amusement (see the section on cutouts, later in this chapter) after serving their initial purposes of documentation and communication.

General Features of the Magdalena Papers Corpus

Paper documents can be—and usually are—studied for what they state in handwriting or print, but they also can be treated as we do here: as artifacts considered in terms of what their physical characteristics and contexts can tell us about their uses and about the behaviors and beliefs of the people who used them. Treating them as artifacts, however, presents challenges as well as opportunities.

The overwhelming majority of the papers that we found were fragments of larger documents, manuscripts, and books. As is the case with pottery sherds, number counts of paper fragments are not highly informative: just as big pots produce many sherds and small pots few, big documents produce many scraps and small ones few. Thus, interpretative considerations about the nature of original materials in relation to the archaeological remnants found must be taken into account when treating papers as artifacts. But when approached cautiously, simple counts of basic types of documents may serve as general indicators of various cultural and social facets of their original uses. Paper fragments can easily tear after their excavation, increasing total counts, but thanks to cautious handling such damage in our sample was low. The numbers presented in the following discussion, therefore, are general indications of quantities, and future studies may result in somewhat higher counts.

We found slightly more than 2,500 separate pieces of colonial-era paper at the site. There also were a few score examples of modern papers, but most of these were recovered from superficial or looted deposits. Examples of the modern papers include scraps of newspapers and schoolchildren's chemistry homework. These appear to be of relatively recent vintage, such as a fragment of the *Expreso* newspaper dating to June 3, 1986. Within archaeological strata, modern paper was nonexistent except for the occasional scrap found in the uppermost levels.

Table 13.1 provides a breakdown of the types of papers and their distribution at the site. As might be expected, more paper was found in the church area than in the town. With many of the papers pertaining to ecclesiastical matters and with the church as the center of European activity within the colonial establishment, it makes sense that the majority of documents recovered were from excavations of the church compound. It is hard to assess whether the presence of papers in the town indicates use or ownership by indigenous townspeople or if papers were blown or brought into the town after the church collapsed, as noted earlier. Given this, it is difficult to determine the degree to which paper was a part of the everyday lives of townspeople. We must also keep in mind that the friars may have taken a selection of books and manuscripts with them when they abandoned the church, though we have no way to know the quantity of items they may have removed. This may bias our sample to an unknown degree.

All of the documents found at the site and studied in some detail consist of laid paper, with its distinctive ribbed texture resulting from the paper pulp drying on mesh or chains. Paper quality varies, as would be expected. Printing typefaces and handwriting styles also vary considerably. Although these styles generally appear to accord with early and mid-seventeenth-century forms, handwriting styles varied greatly over the 200-year occupation of the town, and typefaces probably persisted. The majority of documents are in Spanish, but one example in

Table 13.1 Distribution of Papers in Church and Town

CATEGORY	CHURCH	TOWN	TOTALS
Printed, 1 side	236	71	307
Printed, 2 sides	258	117	375
Handwritten, 1 side	433	103	536
Handwritten, 2 sides	289	59	348
Music	94	27	121
Cutouts	27	0	27
Cigarettes	59	0	59
Cards	7	6	13
Blank	299	116	415
Totals	**1,702**	**499**	**2,201**

Italian has thus far been identified. Many of the printed religious documents are in Latin or in both Latin and Spanish.

Even though earlier handwriting and printing styles may persist to later times, we should be able to employ the principle of a *terminus ante quem* to the paper collection as a whole to generate information on the use life of the church compound. We could use the latest known printing or the latest dated handwritten document as a means to indicate that the church compound was still in use at that date, currently estimated as the mid-seventeenth century. We require the contributions of experts on early publishing, however, to help us find the latest printed document.

We presume that the majority of the papers we encountered were originally in the possession of the Dominican friars in the church compound. Most of the handwritten papers appear to be concerned with the administration of the church and town, and most of the printed papers seem to be related to ecclesiastical matters. Many fragments clearly are related to religious matters and even to religious services, such as remains of musical scores for plainchant (*cantus planus*), a type of chant used in Catholic liturgies. But we also found pages from the first volume of Giovanni Battista Ramusio's famous *Delle navigationi et viaggi*, a 1550 compilation of exploration tales and travelogues, as well as a page from Bernardino de Mendoza's 1592 history of the Eighty Years' War between Spain and the Netherlands (Figure 13.1), suggesting that perhaps the friars' library included reading materials for both work and pleasure.[2]

The majority of papers at the site are presumed to have come from the church compound, perhaps even from a library of some sort. We do not understand why so many documents were apparently left in the church after its abandonment, presumably after a destructive event, but this seems to have been the case. We might expect that, living so far removed from sources of new books and paper, the friars would have spent time to retrieve documents from the ruins of their church. Perhaps they did so, prioritizing only their most important and valued manuscripts and leaving the rest. It is possible that a few paper documents were in the possession of townspeople, as discussed in the section on indulgences later in this chapter. As indigenous people were drawn into the entanglements of the imperial legal world, they likely would have come into ownership of documents of various kinds, which they safeguarded in their homes.

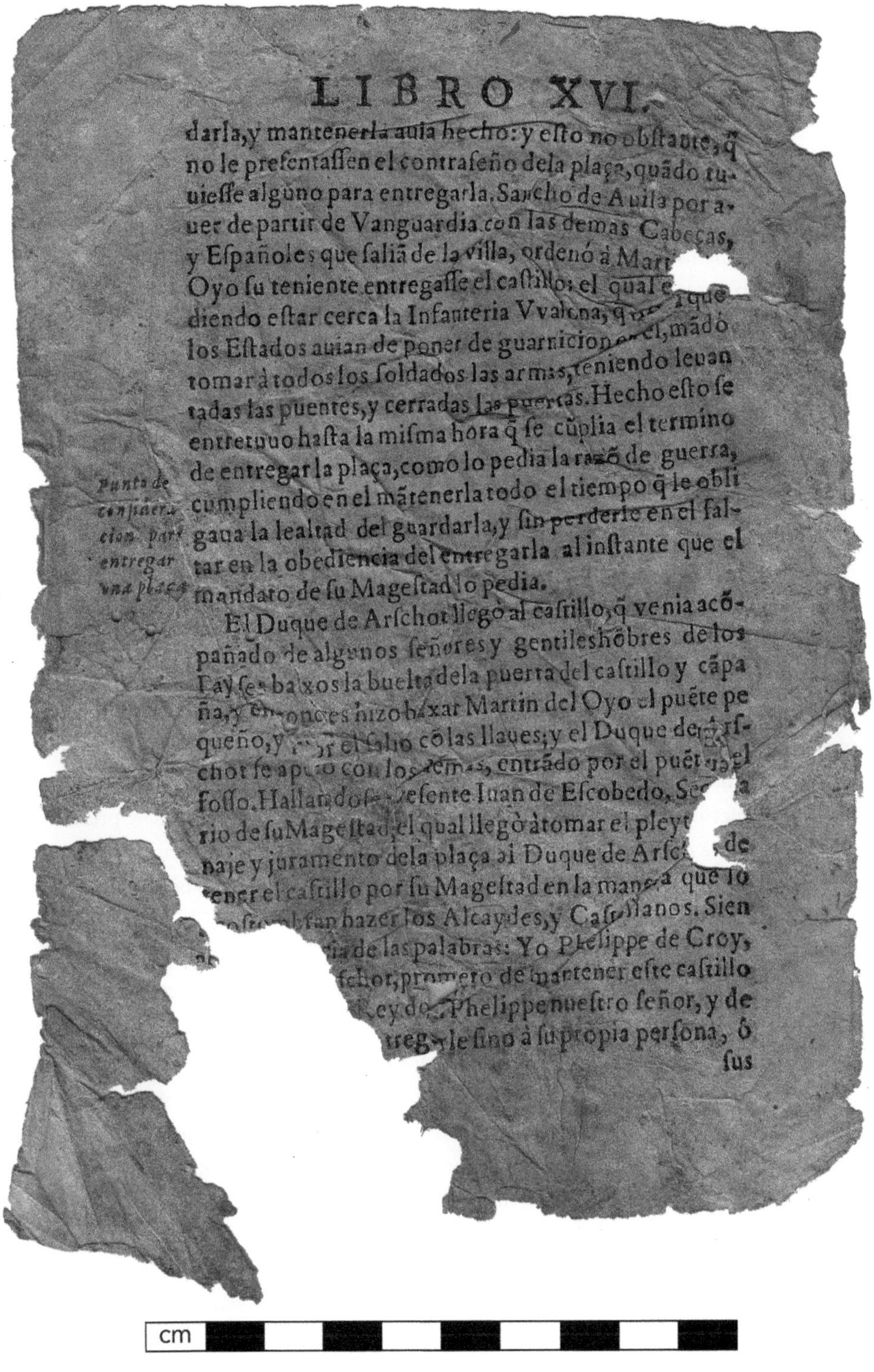

LIBRO XVI.

darla,y mantenerla auia hecho: y esto no obstante, q̃
no le presentassen el contraseño dela plaça, quãdo tu-
uiesse alguno para entregarla. Sancho de Auila por a-
uer de partir de Vanguardia con las demas Cabeças,
y Españoles que saliã de la villa, ordenó à Mart[illegible]
Oyo su teniente entregasse el castillo: el qual e[illegible] que-
diendo estar cerca la Infanteria Vvalona, q[illegible]
los Estados auian de poner de guarnicion [illegible]el, mãdó
tomar à todos los soldados las armas, teniendo leuan
tadas las puentes, y cerradas las puertas. Hecho esto se
entretuuo hasta la misma hora q̃ se cũplia el termino
de entregar la plaça, como lo pedia la razõ de guerra,
cumpliendo en el mãtenerla todo el tiempo q̃ le obli
gaua la lealtad del guardarla, y sin perderle en el fal-
tar en la obediencia del entregarla al instante que el
mandato de su Magestad lo pedia.

Punto de consideracion para entregar una plaça

El Duque de Arschot llegò al castillo, q̃ venia acõ-
pañado de algunos señores y gentileshõbres de los
Payses baxos la buelta dela puerta del castillo y cãpa
ña, y entonces hizo baxar Martin del Oyo el puẽte pe
queño, y [illegible] el salio cõ las llaues; y el Duque de Arschot se apeo con los demas, entrãdo por el puẽte [illegible]el
fosso. Hallandose presente Iuan de Escobedo, Se[illegible]a
rio de su Magestad, el qual llegò à tomar el pleyt[illegible] de
naje y juramento dela plaça al Duque de Arsc[illegible]
tener el castillo por su Magestad en la man[illegible]a que lo
[illegible] hazer los Alcaydes, y Castellanos. Sien
[illegible]de las palabras: Yo Phelippe de Croy,
[illegible]schot, prometo de mantener este castillo
[illegible]Rey do[illegible] Phelippe nuestro señor, y de
[illegible]tregarle sino à su propia persona, ó
sus

cm

Figure 13.1
Page from a book on the Spanish invasion of the Netherlands.

For initial analyses, the collection was examined on the basis of nine major categories (Table 13.1). These categories were based on clear differences in purposes or uses of paper, such as musical scores, playing cards, and cigarette ends. Handwritten and printed documents were also separated, since these pertain not only to different activities but possibly to different sources: handwritten papers tend to relate to local activities and subject matter, and printed materials were presumably received or brought in from elsewhere, likely Lima or even Spain. We also distinguished between documents with handwriting or printing on only one side of a page and documents with inscriptions on both sides. We did this on the very general assumption that documents with words on both sides of a page tend to be in books or other compilations, such as ledgers, whereas those with text on only one side tend to be formal, official documents. Of course, there are likely exceptions in both cases.

Handwritten documents make up the largest set of paper artifacts in the collection, with a total of 729 fragments. Some appear to be letters related to personal matters, while others seem to pertain to legal or business affairs of the church or town. Presumably, many of these were documents sent from elsewhere and received by the friars (or, later in the Colonial Period, perhaps the townspeople) and kept on file. The only complete letter is a handwritten document concerning the purchase of fabric for the church, the back of which was later used to note the words for numbers in a native language, possibly Quingnam (Quilter et al. 2010). A wide variety of other kinds of documents are attested to in the Magdalena materials.

It is difficult to determine whether differences in the quantities of documents with writing or printing on one side and those with writing or printing on both sides are meaningful or not. The fact that blank paper fragments are fairly numerous ($N = 510$) also may or may not be significant. Perhaps this is a general indication that paper was not scarce at Magdalena, though it is possible that access to paper varied across time. As in the case of books, we presume that the nearest source of paper would have been Lima. We have only a few examples of papers in which writing was crammed onto the page, suggesting that the paper had been used more than once; this might imply that while paper may have been generally available most of the time, it could have been sporadically in short supply.

Many of the one-sided printed fragments are likely pieces of indulgences (discussed later in this chapter), while double-sided pages are probably from books. These books could have been texts for performing religious ceremonies (missals), compilations of Bible passages, accounts of the lives of saints, texts to be read aloud to monks while they worked or ate (lectionaries), or similar kinds of volumes. Red ink was commonly used in printed books of the time to highlight important passages or for decorative effect. We believe that most double-sided pages with both red and black printing are likely from lectionaries or missals, but many of the double-sided fragments with only black printing are also probably from such volumes, as red ink is used sparingly throughout such publications. Some of the printed pages were illustrated, and we have also found fragments of printed illustrations unaccompanied by text. There were only four examples of single-sided papers printed in both red and black ink, two each in town and in the church, all likely fragments of indulgences.

The following sections describe some of the papers that we have studied in detail and for which we have some information of interest, demonstrating the range of types of papers in the overall corpus. Future work will surely add to our knowledge.

Missal and Lectionary Fragments

We found many pages from missals (books containing texts used in the Mass and other rites throughout the year) and lectionaries (compilations of scripture to be read at church services or other gatherings). In many monastic orders, readings were done while friars were gathered outside of Mass or other rites—while eating, for example. There is a variety of these kinds of documents with varying degrees of elaboration in regard to the size of volumes, the quality of printing, and whether or not they are illustrated. As previously noted, many are printed with red and black ink, the former being used to highlight important passages of text.

There are two examples of illustration fragments portraying St. Martin of Tours cutting his cloak in half in order to give a piece to a beggar, who reveals himself as Jesus (Figure 13.2). The story of the Roman military commander performing this act of charity, which served as a catalyst for his later conversion to Christianity, was particularly popular in France, though El Greco, who was working in Italy and Spain during the early years of Magdalena de Cao, rendered the scene as well. The fact that we found two versions of the print suggests that more than one copy of this document was present at the site. At present, we don't know the nature of the larger text of which this print was a part. It may have been in a printed book of which there was more than one copy at the site. Another possibility is that these prints appeared on indulgences, although none was preserved on any fragments of those documents that we have recovered and were able to identify, as noted later in this chapter. The double-line border on these fragments, however, resembles a similar border on fragments of indulgences that we do have.

Other prints in the collection include one of the Ascension of Jesus (Figure 13.3). One of the few complete printed pages is from a missal for the solemn Maundy Thursday evening Mass held to commemorate the Last Supper, during which Jesus washed the feet of the disciples (Figure 13.4), as recounted in John 13:1–17, 31–35.[3] This page has a small printed image at the beginning of the text depicting that event. There also are a number of fragments of printed images of scrolls or floral elements. These likely were decorative borders to title pages of books or similar documents.

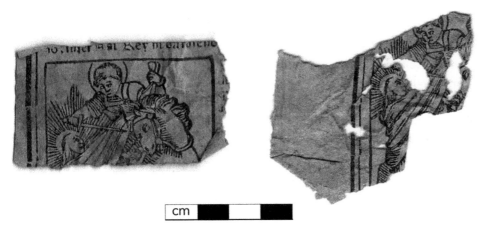

Figure 13.2
Two examples of a print of St. Martin of Tours cutting his cloak.

Figure 13.3
Fragment of a print
of the Ascension.

cm

Indulgences

In the Roman Catholic Church an indulgence is the remission of temporal punishment of souls detained in purgatory for their sins. It can be plenary, forgiving all of the punishment due for sins, or partial, forgiving any sin committed during a specific period of time expressed in weeks, days, or months. An indulgence was expressed on a printed piece of paper sold by authority of the Pope. Many fragments of indulgences were found in our excavations. Only a few pieces, however, are large enough to be easily read.

An important means by which indulgences were obtained by parishioners was through cofradías (confraternities), "salvation cooperatives" run by the laity and serving as a link between priests or friars and the parish community. According to Juan de Meléndez (1681:[2]82), the Pope granted the Dominicans the right to establish cofradías of the Holy Rosary (Cofradía del Santissimo Rosario), whose members were authorized to grant indulgences to the faithful, including the group's own members, in exchange for contributions, labor, and other acts of piety and good work.

Cofradías were voluntary organizations whose members devoted themselves to pious acts that supplemented the devotional practices of the parish. They gave alms to the poor, provided burial rites for their members, scheduled Masses to honor their patron saints, and acted to ensure good opportunities for their members by reducing their time in purgatory. The chief means for achieving the last of these was through the accumulation of indulgences, which could be accomplished by various means, including purchase of a document.

In Peru, sermons were given in Quechua urging the faithful to obtain indulgences; one such was preached by Juan Martínez de Ormachea and preserved in folios printed in Lima in

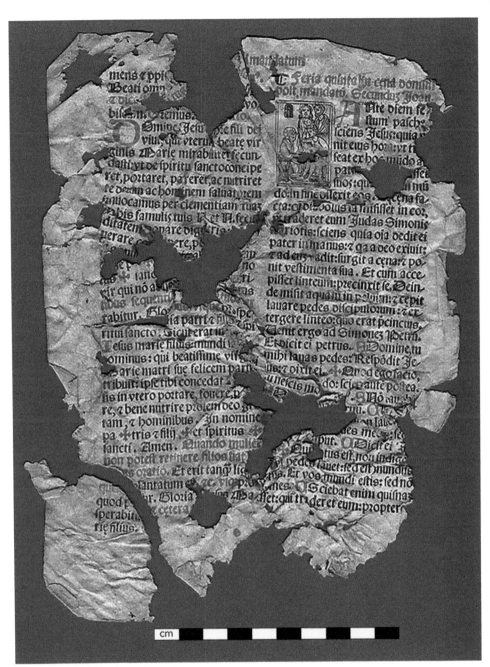

Figure 13.4
Page of a missal
with a print of
Jesus washing the
disciples' feet at
the Last Supper.

1600 (Cummins 2011:221–223). Specific alms (prices) were prescribed for these indulgences, though the amount varied based on social position. Thus, principal caciques and other members of the native elite were charged one silver peso, while lesser caciques and ordinary people, men or women, were assessed a lesser amount, two *tomines* (a *tomín* was one-eighth of a minted gold coin).

Two of the largest fragments of indulgences found at Magdalena are presented here. One (Figure 13.5) is a fragment of the upper left-hand section of an indulgence, judging by the

Figure 13.5
Fragment of the
upper section
of an indulgence.

vertical double-line border on one side of the fragment. Near the top of the document the line of largest letters reads *Sumario de las indulgencias y estaciones de Roma* (Summary of the indulgences and stations of Rome). The second fragment (Figure 13.6) is from a very similar document and consists of most of the bottom right side of the indulgence (based on the margin and finish of the vertical edge of the page); it includes a printed seal, a signature, and a section of an image in the page's bottom margin. Based on the text available to us, these two fragments appear to be plenary indulgences.

Indulgence papers are rare because they were used and then usually discarded or destroyed. Indeed, the pardon from most sins had a limited-time warranty, so new indulgences had to be purchased after the old ones expired. We can infer from the fragments we found that the indulgences held at Magdalena were documents that consisted of an extensive text at the top of the page followed by a list of days of the week and the devotions to various saints and other venerations to be carried out as part of the rites of penance. Both fragments seen here exhibit columns of these day lists and related devotions.

Figure 13.6
Fragment of the lower section of an indulgence.

The holder of the paper that represented the indulgence would have kept it to invoke it when needed—in most cases, near the end of life. A "good death" was one in which the dying person had time to make arrangements for departure from this world and entrance into the next, and indulgences were needed to escape time in purgatory. Meléndez (1681:[2]129) described the death of a Dominican father, Nicolás de Aguero, who, after the doctors confirmed that nothing more could be done for him, asked for his plenary indulgence and died with it displayed at the head of his bed.

The holder of a paper indulgence would have kept it among his or her personal possessions so that it could be invoked by a confessor after the dying person received the sacrament of extreme unction (often called "last rites"). The indulgence—particularly if it was a plenary indulgence—would guarantee the remission of sin at death before any new transgressions could be added to the holder's spiritual account.

What became of paper indulgences once they were used or expired, or once the person who held them died? We do not know, but we might presume that they would have been destroyed to prevent them from being falsely reused by someone else. Perhaps this is why so few examples are to be found in archives. In 1894, the archaeologist Adolph Bandelier excavated burials on the north coast of Chile, and one of the "mummies" he found was buried with a copy of Pope Gregory's bull (Cummins 2011:222). Although not technically an indulgence, this is clearly a case where a document relating to the remission of sins was deemed important enough to be taken to the grave. Attitudes regarding indulgences likely varied throughout the

Andes during the Colonial Period, and we remain uncertain why a seemingly great number of indulgences was found at the Magdalena site. Did the indigenous townspeople retain indulgences after their family members died? Did they perhaps not take the practice of using indulgences seriously? Or did the remains of the indulgences that we found come from a stockpile of these documents that were in the church when it collapsed and were not subsequently retrieved?

Bravo Thesaurus

We found a large fragment of a page from a Latin–Spanish dictionary (Figure 13.7) in the church refuse at Magdalena. At first we thought this was from the dictionary by Antonio de Nebrija (1441–1552), who is famous for standardizing and organizing the Spanish language and for various humanistic writings. Byron Hamann, however, advised that while superficially similar to the Nebrija dictionary, our page more closely matches the 1611 printing of the *Thesaurus verborum* by Bartolomé Bravo, a thesaurus designed to aid in the elaboration of Latin speeches from Spanish.[4] While mass and other church services would have been conducted in ecclesiastical Latin, Spanish likely was the native language of most friars at Magdalena de Cao. The presence of this book can be explained by the possibility that these friars needed assistance

Figure 13.7
Fragment of a page from the Bravo Thesaurus.

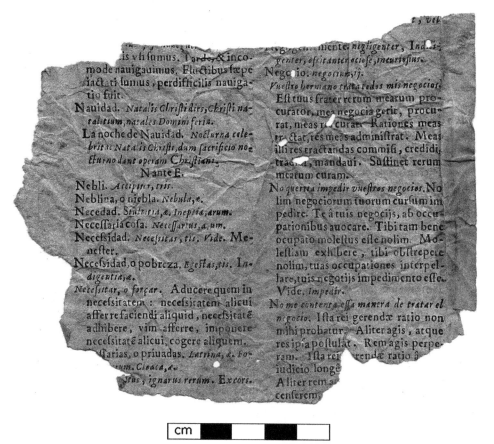

to render their Spanish into Latin for official church matters. This thesaurus may have been a general work kept in Spanish colonial churches as a matter of course.

Trilingual Confessionary

The fragment shown in Figure 13.8 is the lower half of the first page of a section of a book titled *Confessionario para los curas de indios. Con la instruction contra sus ritos: y exhortacion para ayuda a bien morir, y suma de sus privilegios: y forma de impedimentos del matrimonio* (Confessionary for priests of Indians. With instruction against their rites: and exhortations to help them have a good death, and a sum of their privileges: and the forms of impediments of marriage). It was first printed in Lima in 1583 and then reprinted in Seville in 1603. At the time of this writing we have not been able to determine the edition of the Magdalena fragment.[5]

The section or chapter that this page begins is an exhortation to be said by the priest or other person attending a dying Indian. On the top part of the full page is printed the title: *Exhortacion breve para los indios que estan ya muy al cabo de la vida para que el sacerdote, o algun otro les ayude a bien morir* (Brief exhortation for the Indians that are very close to the ends of their lives so that the priest or someone else can aid them in a good death). Below the title is the exhortation, written in Spanish (here translated):

> My brother, our Lord Jesus Christ is with your soul and saves you in this hour from your enemies. Now is the time that you get right with God and call for him in your heart so that he will aid you. You see how your parents and friends cannot save you from death nor will the things of this earth benefit you.

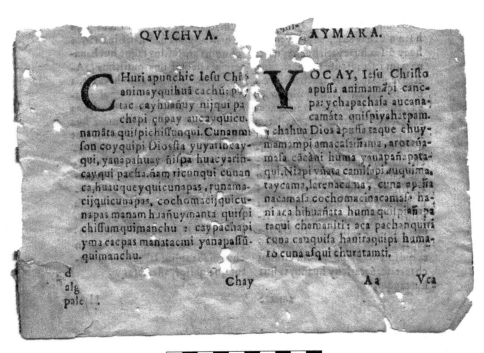

Figure 13.8
Fragment of a page from a confessionary bearing Quechua and Aymara texts.

Beneath this text the same exhortation is printed in Quechua in the left-hand column and in Aymara in the right-hand column; it is this lower section that we found.

The practice of shriving, in which a person confessed to and was absolved of sins as close to death as possible so that time in purgatory would be reduced, was documented in medieval and early modern Europe. This page is an expression of that belief and suggests that shriving was practiced at Magdalena.

Musical Scores

There were 126 examples of musical scores found at Magdalena, 104 in the church and 22 in the town. This count is larger than the total number of unique scores in the collection, since fragments of the same document were counted individually during our initial inventory; there probably are a hundred or so unique sheets of music represented in the Magdalena corpus. Seventy of these fragments are handwritten on both sides of the page, 30 are handwritten on only one side, 1 is printed on one side, and 26 are printed on both sides. There appears to be a great variety of hands that wrote the musical scores; some scores include words, while others are solely musical notations. Many of the scores are examples of plainchant used in the Mass and other rituals.

An interesting aspect of the music is that the majority of fragments are of handwritten scores, with only a few examples of printed sheet music. There are also a few finely rendered documents that appear to be the work of highly trained scribes; these display beautifully rendered capital letters and even an example of the use of gold leaf or ink (Figure 13.9). The greater amount of handwritten music suggests that the friars at Magdalena were actively involved in preparing music to be sung or played in their church. The handwritten music shows varying degrees of concern for the appearance of the final work (Figure 13.10). Some of the documents

Figure 13.9
Two sides of a
fragment of a finely
produced religious
musical text.

Figure 13.10 Examples of musical scores. Upper left: printed plainchant. Upper right: finely handwritten plainchant. Bottom: rough score.

look either like original pieces composed by the person who wrote them or like hastily made copies of other works. These documents include plainchant and music for voice.

In the eighteenth century, the bishop of Trujillo, Baltasar Jaime Martínez Compañón, included 20 musical scores in his compendium of more than a thousand images documenting life in his diocese. Although the dating (ca. 1782–1785) is toward the end of the Magdalena town occupation and long after the church collapsed, the bishop's inclusion of music in his report is a testament to how important this artistic form was to the early church on the North Coast of Peru and to missionization efforts in general.

A Letter and a Number List

In 2008, we recovered one of the few complete handwritten documents at the site (Figure 13.11). Although it has been discussed in detail elsewhere (Quilter et al. 2010), a brief summary of it and its importance is presented here.

The letter was written on a sheet of paper measuring 21 cm in width by 12 cm in height. The main text flows across the width of the page and is signed by one Lope Fernández de Vaqueta. The text concerns the failed attempt by Lope Fernández to purchase two *varas* of cloth because the price was too high.[6] The writer suggests that the padre to whom he is writing should decide whether or not he wishes to make the purchase.[7]

One interesting aspect of the letter is its indication that the purchase of fine goods may have occurred relatively near to Magdalena de Cao. If the writer had traveled to Lima, he would not have been able to suggest to the padre that he could still make the purchase if he was willing to meet the price of 14 reales and have a boy bring the goods to him. Such a possibility suggests that the source of the textile was close enough to Magdalena town—perhaps within the Chicama Valley itself—that a boy could be entrusted to serve as a porter for the cloth.

The handwriting in the letter is in a style common to the seventeenth century. The paper was folded horizontally and vertically: possibly twice from left to right from the writer's perspective, and then once from the top down to produce a folded paper one-eighth the size of the opened document. This may have occurred after the letter was written for ease of carrying by the messenger who delivered it.

At some later time, the letter was unfolded into a half sheet, and the blank back was used to jot down (with the fold side at bottom and the open end at top) a list of numbers in a column on the left-hand side of the page, with occasional dashes followed by one or more words. We have interpreted this to be a record of the terms for numbers in an indigenous language, quite possibly Quingnam, which was spoken in the region from Chicama through several valleys to its south.

As noted in Chapter 2, the Chicama Valley was at the margin of the realms of two native languages: Muchik, spoken north of the Pampa de Paiján, and Quingnam, spoken south of it. The former language survived into the nineteenth century, so we know it fairly well thanks to various word lists (Salas 2002). There is no Quingnam dictionary available, however. To complicate matters, colonial sources also refer to the Pescadora (fisherfolk) language and the Yunga ("warm region," i.e., middle valley) language, but it is uncertain whether these designations refer to separate tongues or to Quingnam, Muchik, or both. It is quite likely that there was more than one fisherfolk language: in 1594, Santo Tomás wrote that the presiding priest

Figure 13.11   Two sides of the letter and number list.

at Magdalena de Cao was a "good speaker of the languages of the fisherfolk" (see Chapter 12), with the use of the plural form suggesting more than one tongue.

We know that the words written on the back of the letter are not Muchik; they may be Quingnam, Pescadora, Yunga, or some other, unknown language. Analysis of the words by Marc Zender suggests that the language may be a version of Quechua or that it may have borrowed words from Quechua. Many issues regarding the nature and distribution of prehispanic languages are still under discussion at present, and likely will remain so for some time to come.

The numbers recorded by the note are clearly part of a base-10 system, as was found among the Inca and, most likely, the Moche and Chimu as well (Ascher 1986; Donnan 2007:199–202; Urton 1997). The digits from 1 through 10 are listed, followed by 21, 100, and 200, suggesting an acute intelligence at work in posing appropriate questions to learn the principles of the number system.

Although many questions remain regarding the language and number system recorded on this document, this single piece of paper has already told us much about the larger world of Peru in the Colonial Period. The casual way in which the notes appear to have been recorded on the back of a letter also offers us a glimpse of an intimate moment of contact between the Old World and the New at Magdalena de Cao many centuries ago.

Cutouts

We use the term "cutouts" to refer to paper fragments that usually are bilaterally symmetrical reused papers that were folded and trimmed through cutting or other methods (Figure 13.12). The most striking of the cutouts were formed to produce a recognizable image, though these are relatively rare. Only three were found: a butterfly, a lance or spear point, and, less certainly, a face or mask. The butterfly was made out of a missal page with choral parts from a Christmas Eve Mass.[8]

Other cutouts are geometrics, including a sheet with three diamond-shaped holes, one with two triangular shapes, and another with complex shapes (Figure 13.12). The last of these may be a decorative endpiece to a document and not a reused piece of paper at all, but of this we are not sure. We found a total of 34 papers that we labeled cutouts, but this count definitely includes some papers that took on such forms simply because they had been folded and subsequently torn. The geometrics and representational images tend to have crisp edges that suggest they were cut with very sharp implements, likely knives, and perhaps scissors. The edges of the butterfly are scorched, indicating that fire was employed to shape it.

In addition to the categories of images and geometrics, a third category is that of pieces that may or may not have been deliberately formed, which we refer to as "erratics." Quite a few papers display a sort of mirror image because they were folded and then torn, thus exhibiting bilateral symmetry when opened. It is very difficult to determine how many of these were the product of deliberate manipulation of the paper and how many are simply the result of accidental tearing or other damage to paper that had been folded. Erratics tend to have frayed edges, which increases the difficulty of determining if the manipulation of the paper was deliberate.

The purposes or roles of cutouts are uncertain. Were the papers to be cut selected with consideration of the relationship between the original document's contents and the cutout design?

Figure 13.12
Examples of cutouts. Scales vary and centimeter bars apply only to two bottom examples.

Our sample size is small, making inferences tentative at best, but it is interesting to note that some cutouts are made on blank or lightly inscribed papers, while others are oriented so that the cutout is rectilinearly positioned in relation to the printed page. For example, the text on the butterfly is in the same position as it was in the original document, so the words can be read when the butterfly is viewed with its head up and wings outstretched. The same is true for the paper with three diamond holes. The text on the spearhead, however, is diagonal to the axis of the image whether the shape is held point up, point down, or on its side; the masklike cutout has the text running at a right angle to the viewing position of the mask. In some but not all cases, then, it appears that either for aesthetic or other reasons an important aspect of the integrity of the original document was maintained when the paper was transformed into a cutout.

With so few images, it is hard to interpret meaning in the portrayal of a butterfly, a spear, and a mask or face. A few examples are known of cloth formed into butterflylike objects for adornments to Andean textiles (Thomas Cummins, personal communication), and the butterfly was a very popular motif in Inca art. No overtly symbolic messages or intentional links to decorative functions are in evidence from our paper cutouts, however, and their recovery contexts shed no light on their possible roles or uses. It is all too easy for archaeologists to retreat to the "ritual purposes" explanation for objects that they cannot easily explain and that have no clear utilitarian functions, but based on the evidence we can only say that although cutouts may have had some kind of ritual use, it is equally likely that they were created for personal amusement or simple enjoyment in passing the time.

We initially assumed that the cutouts were made by townspeople who retrieved papers from the church after it collapsed and then used them for various purposes. In conducting our initial review of the distribution of the papers, however, we determined that of the 34 cutouts, only one was found in the town. Of course, it is still possible that the townspeople made the cutouts on the grounds of the church after the structure collapsed, but the distribution pattern opens up the possibility of alternative interpretations—though it is hard to imagine that religious clerics would treat their own documents in this way.

It is difficult to assess whether the idea of paper cutouts was independently invented by the Magdaleneros, perhaps borrowing from textile traditions, or if it was a European import. There is a long and vigorous tradition of paper cutting in Mexico that would have been well known to any Spaniard who had spent time there, but the Magdalena examples are much simpler than the elaborate paper art of the Aztecs and their neighbors. Whatever their origins or meaning, these paper cutouts suggest that the Magdaleneros felt quite comfortable in altering colonial documents for uses other than their intended purposes.

Papers with Dates

We found three papers with dates on them, all from handwritten documents (Figure 13.13). Only one of these papers has a clear date, 1612; the other two are somewhat problematic. The second fragment reads 2 *de Julio de 609* (2 of July of 609). This likely is either a reference to a historical event a thousand years before Magdalena or a case in which the writer forgot or considered it unnecessary to add the *1* for a date intended to be 1609. The third paper fragment is from a list. At the top of the fragment is an incomplete word followed by *de 41* (of 41), all underlined. Near the bottom is written *Año de 4* . . . (year of 4 . . .) with an additional digit

Figure 13.13
Papers with dates.

incomplete but likely a 2 or 3, so it would have been intended to read "Año de 42" or "Año de 43." This, then, is probably a list of some sort; it may track calendrical years, such as 1641 through 1642 or 1643, or indicate some other sequence, such as the number of years since the founding of the church or reducción. The text between the year notations is hard to interpret but appears to be part of a list. At the far right-hand edge of the document there appears to be the number 6 followed by a stroke, which may be part of an account of some sort. Before it is the word *alcance* (scope), with a period after it.

All of these papers confirm evidence known from historical records that Magdalena was a functioning community and church in the early seventeenth century. We cannot fully rely on the latest date of this group as an indicator that the church was still functioning in the 1640s, as the evidence is too problematic. As Rocío Delibes discusses in Chapter 12, we know that the town was in operation into the eighteenth century, but the critical issue of when the church collapsed is not resolved by these papers with dates.

Cigarette Ends

We found the first few smoked cigarette ends in our 2004 excavations on the exterior of the northwest corner of the church atrium (Figure 13.14). Subsequently, we found other cigarette remains in excavations; not all of them contained tobacco. Only a few had burnt ends, indicating that they had been smoked, and others had no tobacco in them but had been formed into tubes. Some cigarette ends were clearly pieces of written documents, while others showed no external signs of printing or writing (we did not unroll them). Two butts had improvised holders made of twisted pieces of paper, one of which had handwriting on it. This may indicate that tobacco was scarce enough for at least some Magdaleneros to make holders in order to obtain the maximum amount of smoking pleasure.

There are a number of different ways to interpret the cigarette remains as artifacts, and our thinking about them developed as the work continued. Our first question was if these were early Colonial Period artifacts at all, because some of the (older) Peruvian archaeologists

Figure 13.14
Cigarette ends.

noted that in the 1960s and 1970s a popular casing for marijuana "joints" was Bible paper—in many editions, the paper in Bibles was thin and easily rolled. We thought this modern explanation unlikely, given that the cigarettes looked so old. Nevertheless, the critical question of the age of the butts needed to be addressed.

As noted in Chapter 2, two examples of the cigarette remains were exported from Peru and brought to the United States, where personnel at the Harvard Herbaria identified the smoking mixture as tobacco. Since we were concerned that the papers could have been made into cigarettes quite recently, we dated the tobacco and not the paper, which we already knew to be old. By dating the tobacco, we could determine if the cigarettes had been made relatively recently or in the past. We sent a sample of the tobacco to the AMS Laboratory of the University of Arizona under an NSF-sponsored program. The result presented to us was 442 ± 76 B.P. (AA68059, Sample ID #3, tobacco leaves; $\delta^{13}C = -25.9‰$). Subsequently, Darden Hood of Beta Analytic recalibrated the date for us at 440 ± 80 B.P. The 2-sigma calibration had two intercepts for conversion to calendar years: 1320–1350 and 1390–1640. We can eliminate the first intercept, as it is prehistoric and we know that the paper and tobacco are historic. Regarding the remaining range, we know that the earliest possible date for the paper is when the Brujo terrace was first occupied in the Colonial Period. Therefore, we can propose that the cigarettes date to between 1578 and 1640.

Having determined that the cigarettes had been made and smoked in the distant past, our interpretations of exactly when they were smoked and who smoked them were influenced by the fact that they were rolled in ecclesiastical papers. Under the assumption that the friars would not have treated their own documents in this way, we interpreted these cigarettes as having been made by townspeople after the church had collapsed and been abandoned by the Dominicans. If so, it would follow that the dates for the cigarettes would be late in the ranges, closer to the 1630s and 1640s than to 1578.

The scenario that we conceived was of townspeople making cigarettes to smoke from papers retrieved from the ruins of the church. Another hypothesis was of townspeople's ceremonial smoking in the church ruins. In the Andes, it is a common practice to visit ruins and picnic there on Good Friday as a way to get in touch with ancestors, much like the Mesoamerican festivities for the Day of the Dead, which is commonly observed in the Christian calendar from All Saints' Day Eve to All Souls' Day.

In all of the scenarios we imagined, we thought of tobacco smoking as a European practice adopted by local Andean peoples in the Colonial Period or later. Tobacco was a New World plant and its consumption an American practice, but one that was not common in the coastal and highland Andes. As with other New World domesticates such as chocolate, Europeans used tobacco in ways that accorded with indigenous traditions of the particular region of the Americas where they first encountered it. British and Continental Europeans took up pipe smoking from North American Indians, and Iberians adopted snuff, cigars, and similar nicotine delivery systems from Central and South American Indians (Goodman 1994:67).

Snuff inhaling has been documented as practiced by Spanish priests in Peru as early as 1588; in the same year, a synod in Lima announced, "It is forbidden under penalty of eternal damnation for priests to administer the sacraments, either to take the smoke of sayri [an Aymara term for tobacco] or tobacco, into the mouth, or the powder of tobacco into the nose, even under the guise of medicine, before the service of the mass"—a prohibition that would be repeated in other parts of Spanish America and Spain (Dickenson 1954:150). There was much ecclesiastical controversy over the status of tobacco: whether the Blessed Sacrament left the body through the sneeze after inhaling snuff or the spitting out of tobacco juice (Corti 1931:132); whether tobacco counted as food consumption during periods of fasting, such as in Lent; and whether it was a substance invented by the devil himself and therefore inappropriate for Christian use (Philaretes 1936:F4). While tobacco use was condemned by some authorities, others recommended that it be taken by clerics to combat lust, and Pope Benedict XIII, himself addicted to tobacco, even declared an ordinance in 1725 permitting use of snuff in St. Peter's Basilica in the Vatican (Tedeschi 1987:112).

Given these considerations, it may be (and, indeed, we consider it quite likely) that it was the friars and not the townspeople who were smoking at Magdalena, contrary to what we first assumed. The importance of where cigarette remains were found in the colonial sector thus comes into play, following standard archaeological concerns of the contexts of the discovery of artifacts. Seventy cigarette papers were found in the church and only two in the town, thus strengthening the hypothesis that the friars were smokers. However, as previously noted, alternative explanations are feasible, and we cannot be conclusive in our analysis. The issue remains intriguing.

As a final note on this topic, we return to the point that before tobacco was introduced widely in Europe in the seventeenth century, its consumption was a Native American practice—though one not widely followed in the Andes. Thus, the cigarettes at Magdalena demonstrate that the complex interactions of indigenous Americans and Europeans elsewhere in the New World had profound cultural effects in Peru. In this early period of the colony, it is quite likely that if the friars smoked and introduced the practice of smoking to the coast of Peru, they themselves had learned of it from indigenous peoples in some other region of the Americas.

A Name List

Perhaps some of the people who smoked these cigarettes, or their ancestors, are listed in the documents of folded paper. We found a few fragments that list names of indigenous individuals, apparently all men, such as Baltasar Perguaman.

On the largest example (Figure 13.15), but on others as well, the names are written in a column, and the paper on which they are written was folded in a long, narrow form. Most names are preceded by a *v*-like motif over a dash, and each name is followed by a long dash and then the numeral *1, 2, 3,* or *4* followed by a *p* with the superscript *a*, apparently an abbreviation. It seems possible that this is an accounting list for money owed either to or by the men listed. Perhaps the *v*-like figure is a check mark for the presence of the person listed and the numbers followed by p^a refer to some unit of value. The paper may have been folded to make it easier to write up the list or to refer to it in a standing position, perhaps in the open air.

Sabine Hyland (personal communication) agrees that the *v*-like symbol is a check mark or proof of performance—that is to say, someone did something (perhaps appearing at a gathering for payments), and this was accounted for by the mark.[9] Account books of this general form were used for festival contributions in the early twentieth century in central Peru. Hyland also notes that the p^a could indeed refer to money. The peseta was not introduced as official Spanish currency until the nineteenth century, but from the fifteenth century onward

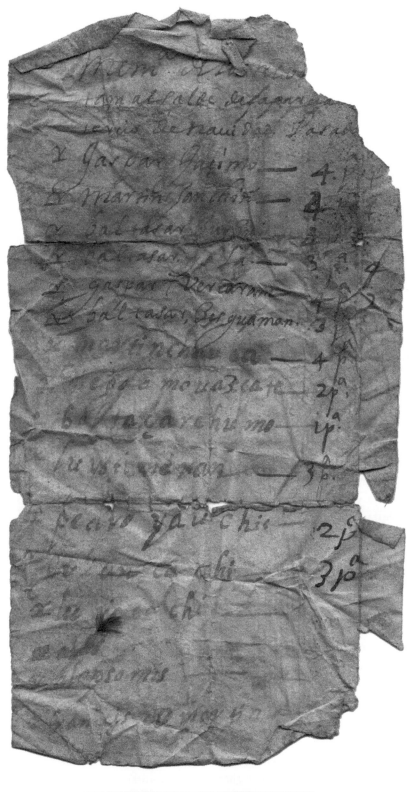

Figure 13.15
Name list.

the word *peçeta* occasionally was used to denote 2 reales, or one-quarter of a piece of eight (see Chapter 11). While the p^a might refer to something else, such as *piezas* (pieces), the fact that every entry on the list falls within the narrow range between 1 and 4 suggests that it might be money. If so, and if this paper dates to between 1578 and 1619, it is one of the earliest pieces of material evidence that Andean peoples were being incorporated into a monetized economy.

Another possibility is that the document relates to social matters rather than economic affairs. Given that all the individuals listed are men, perhaps this document lists the heads of families, with the p^a standing as shorthand for *personas* (persons) and relating to the number of people in a household.

Writing Practice and Penmanship

In some of Magdalena's paper artifacts it is apparent that an individual was practicing the art of writing (Figure 13.16), suggesting that illiterate friars, townspeople, or both were being taught to write or were practicing their penmanship. We have four different examples. One (Figure 13.16, top left) clearly is writing practice because each line in the preserved fragment consists of repeated letters. It is interesting to note that on one line, pairs of the lowercase letter *g* are written, separated by commas. On lines below this are pairs of the letter *h*, also separated by commas, followed by a line of commas and then a line of lowercase *u*'s, each separated by a comma. Another fragment (Figure 13.16, top right) shows flowing script from a practiced or seasoned hand, with the text reading "... municación y co ..." In English, this would be "... munication and co ..."—possibly a fragment of "... communication and co ..."

A third example again shows writing done by someone who had mastered cursive script. On one side (Figure 13.16, middle left) the text reads "... *maior dicha que tienen puesto sena ...*," while on the other side is written "... *aunque vinieron el aussio muchas ...*," with the final letters harder to discern but possibly reading either *canciones* or *cantan*. All the words are the same as in modern Spanish except *auccio*, which may be a version of *aviso* (likely "announcement," in this case). Possible translations are "Although the announcement came many letters not ..." or "Although the announcement came many songs ..."

The fourth paper fragment with handwriting on it contrasts with those discussed earlier, as it displays the crude lettering of someone unskilled in writing (Figure 13.16, bottom). On one side the person apparently was writing to distinguish between *B*'s and *P*'s, with possibly an occasional *R*. On the other side, in reversed direction, mostly large capital letters are arranged, possibly with small letters as well, to spell out *AiMiCno*, and there are smaller letters underneath an X that is apparently not meant to denote a letter. The letters below the X are hard to discern but may include *u*, *s*, and an *i* or an *n*.

The first and last fragments discussed in this section both appear to be examples of the practice of writing by hand. The first, with letters separated by commas, is an expression of disciplining a hand already fairly well schooled in the art. The second example is highly disorganized and might have been done by a child or by someone untrained in writing, possibly in a casual attempt to replicate the shape of letters. The other examples are clearly exercises in the art of penmanship. The hands at work were highly skilled and working to produce smooth, flowing, elegant letters. The fragments of the phrases written that we can discern suggest that they may be aphorisms chosen to exercise the hand.

Figure 13.16 Examples of writing practice.

The original manuscripts from which these fragments came may have been produced at very different times in the life of the Magdalena de Cao community. The circumstances of who wrote them and when are critical to understanding something about how instruction in writing and its practice were transmitted within the clerical and secular communities at the site, but we cannot approach those issues based on the papers alone. And even though there is a suggestion that there may have been a schoolroom or something of the equivalent in the church complex (see Chapter 2), no direct physical links between that space and the papers exist. We can say, however, that some people at the site learned to write, or at least to improve their penmanship, while they were there. The fact that one or more individuals had time to practice the art of writing gracefully is an indication that some leisure time was available to community members at some point during the life of the church and town.

Other Papers

Within the collection we found two small folded pieces of paper with sharpened reed fragments piercing them (Figure 13.17). We removed the reed from one of these to find that the paper likely had come from a musical score, judging by the four parallel inked lines running across one end of the opened paper. This operation also revealed that the paper fragment had been shaped into a rectangular form by being folded twice along its short axis and then once on its long axis, and was then pierced once. The unopened example appears to have been folded and pierced in the same manner.

There are two other papers that may also have been folded and pierced. One is an incomplete fragment of a small but narrow rectangle; it appears to have been folded along its narrow axis four times, then pierced, and later was opened or fell apart. Another was a similar piece of paper that was folded on its long axis and then apparently pierced three times. In these two cases the implements used to pierce the papers were not found. We might speculate that these pierced objects were used to seal an oath, a promise, or a curse: similar piercing rites are attested to ethnographically in syncretic "voodoo" belief systems like *Longanis,* which developed within African slave communities in colonial Mauritius (Seetah 2015:241). Indeed, the practice of "nailing" materials as part of a promise or curse seems to be widespread throughout time and space.

Figure 13.17
Folded and pierced papers.

cm

Figure 13.18
Scratch paper.

What appear to be short notes—such as reminders that one jots down at a meeting—are present, and even examples of what appear to be doodles, possibly done in idleness, in preparation for work, or as a break from more serious work. One example (Figure 13.18) is particularly interesting because it appears to be made on what today we would call scratch paper. In one section of the page there is a long continuous string of loops that suggests the writer was either idly doodling or warming up his quill pen for writing. Another wavy line seems to have been produced by a wide-nib quill or a brush. Four conjoined circles are present near a dark stain close to the middle of the paper, and elsewhere on the page is a carefully rendered lobed design made of triangular elements with rounded ends.

We found a small fragment of paper with the names of the site and one of its priests or friars, García de Haro (Figure 13.19). This person is not present in the lists available in archives of resident priests at Magdalena de Cao (see Chapter 12). He is addressed in this fragment as "of the order of preachers" (*del orden de predicadores*), a term used to refer to Dominicans (see Chapter 12).

Discussion

Printing using movable metal type was a little over a hundred years old in Europe at the time of the establishment of Magdalena de Cao at El Brujo, but the Spaniards had been waving papers in the faces of the people they were encountering in the New World for some time. By the time Magdalena's church collapsed in the early seventeenth century, Andean residents not

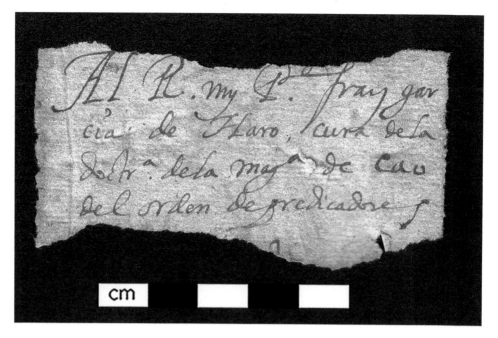

Figure 13.19 Letter fragment addressing García de Haro, curate of Magdalena de Cao.

only had seen plenty of paper documents but had had sheets thrust upon them in the form of indulgences that they were urged to purchase. We may surmise that the Magdaleneros' attitudes toward paper and what was written or printed on it likely varied to a great degree. As in so many other cases of indigenous experiences with new cultures and technologies as they entered into a world they co-created with Europeans, attitudes toward introduced practices and things probably differed depending on individual personalities and circumstances.

The collection of papers we recovered at Magdalena has barely been studied at present. There are many issues that need the attention of experts, including the production of paper, its sources, and its accessibility for friars on the North Coast of Peru. We look forward to the comments and advice of such scholars as the paper and other collections from Magdalena de Cao are made available for study. The potential for these scraps to inform us of life within the Magdalena community is immense indeed, ranging from lists of workers to the reading preferences of friars in their leisure time to many more topics.

NOTES

1 Upon returning to the United States, Quilter tried to contact several cigarette companies to see if they would be interested in learning of this discovery and perhaps help in analysis of the materials. The websites were impenetrable in regard to contacting scientists at those companies; they did, however, consistently direct the viewer to pages on how to quit smoking.

2 Giovanni Battista Ramusio, *Primo volume delle navigationi et viaggi nel qual si contiene la descrittione dell'Africa, et del paese del Prete Ianni, con varii viaggi, dal mar Rosso a Calicut & infin all'isole Molucche, dove nascono le Spetierie, et la Navigatione attorno il mondo* (The first volume of navigations and travels, in which is contained the description of Africa, and of the country of Prester John, with various

travels, from the Red Sea to Kozhikode, and finally to Maluku Islands, where the Spetiere are born, and Navigation around the world) (Venice: Giunti, 1550); Bernardino de Mendoza, *Comentarios de Don Bernardino de Mendoça de lo sucedido en las Guerras de los Payses baxos, desde el año de 1567 hasta el de 1577* (Commentaries of Don Bernardino of Mendoza of what happened in the Wars of the Netherlands, from the year 1567 till that of 1577) (Madrid: Pedro Madrigal, 1592).

3 Thanks to Tom Cummins for research on this page.

4 *Thesaurus verborum, ac phrasium, ad orationem ex Hispana Latinam efficiendam, & locupletandam. Authore Bartholomaeo Bravo Societatis Iesu sacerdotea pud Ioannem de la Cuesta typographi* (A thesaurus of words and phrases to make and adorn Latin speech from Spanish. Author Bartholomaeo Bravo, a priest of the Society of Jesus with Ioannem de la Cuesta typography).

5 We gratefully acknowledge the research assistance on this item rendered by Anne Marie Creighton and Bridget Gazzo of the Dumbarton Oaks Library.

6 A vara is a colonial measurement roughly a yard in length, though exact lengths may vary.

7 The text reads, *Mi Padre agora fuy a buscar los dos baras de Bramante floresti y no lo quieren darme nos de a catorce reales bea buesa Paternidad si lo quiere que luenbo al Punto le llevara el muchacho y todo lo mas q.e buesa Paternidad mandase a quien guarde m.s. De buesa Paternidad mandase a quien guarde m.s. De buesa Paternidad, Lope Fernández de Vaqueta* (My Father, I just went to get the two varas of fine cloth, and they do not want to give them to me for 14 reales; your Fatherhood should decide if you wish the boy to bring it later to the Punto together with anything else that your Fatherhood who cares for us commands. From your Fatherhood, Lope Fernández de Vaqueta).

8 Thanks again to Tom Cummins for this reference. The text may be found online at the Saint Louis University Medieval Liturgy Database, http://libguides.slu.edu/c.php?g=185812&p=1227880, Item No. MO669.

9 Quilter is grateful to Sabine Hyland for her commentary on this paper, made via email on May 29, 2015.

REFERENCES CITED

Ascher, Marcia
> 1986 Mathematical Ideas of the Incas. In *Native American Mathematics*, edited by Michael P. Closs, pp. 261–289. Austin: University of Texas Press.

Coe, Michael D.
> 2012 *Breaking the Maya Code*. 3rd ed. London: Thames and Hudson.

Corti, E. C.
> 1931 *A History of Smoking*, London: G. G. Harrap.

Cummins, Thomas B. F.
> 2011 The Indulgent Image: Prints in the New World. In *Contested Visions in the Spanish Colonial World*, edited by Ilona Katzew, pp. 200–223. Los Angeles: Los Angeles County Museum of Art.

Dickson, S. A.
> 1954 *Panacea or Precious Bane: Tobacco in Sixteenth Century Literature*. New York: New York Public Library.

Donnan, Christopher B.
> 2007 *Moche Tombs at Dos Cabezas*. Los Angeles: Cotsen Institute of Archaeology, University of California, Los Angeles.

Goodman, Jordan
> 1994 *Tobacco in History: Cultures of Dependence*. London: Routledge.

Meléndez, Fray Juan de

    1681 *Tesoros verdaderos de las Indias. Historia de la 1ª provincia de San Juan Bautista del Perú, del orden de Predicadores.* 3 vols. Rome: Imprenta de Nicolas Angel Tinassio.

Philaretes

    1936 [1602] *Work for Chimny-sweepers; or, A Warning for Tobacconists.* Oxford: Oxford University Press.

Quilter, Jeffrey, and Gary Urton (editors)

    2002 *Narrative Threads: Accounting and Recounting in Andean Khipu.* Austin: University of Texas Press.

Quilter, Jeffrey, Marc Zender, Karen Spalding, Régulo Franco Jordán, César Gálvez, and Juan Castañeda Murga

    2010 Traces of a Lost Language and Number System Discovered on the North Coast of Peru. *American Anthropologist* 112(3):357–369.

Salas, José Antonio

    2002 *Diccionario Mochica–Castellano/Castellano–Mochica* [Mochica–Spanish/Spanish–Mochica Dictionary]. Lima: Universidad San Martín de Porres.

Seetah, Krish

    2015 Objects Past, Objects Present: Materials, Resistance and Memory from the Le Morne Old Cemetery, Mauritius. *Journal of Social Archaeology* 15(2):233–253.

Tedeschi, J.

    1987 Literary Piracy in Seventeenth-Century Florence: Giovanni Battista Neri's *De iudice S. inquisitionis opusculum. Huntington Library Quarterly* 50:107–118.

Urton, Gary

    1997 *The Social Life of Numbers: A Quechua Ontology of Numbers and Philosophy of Arithmetic.* Austin: University of Texas Press.

14

Playing Cards

Sarah McAnulty Quilter

Introduction

BOTH COMPLETE AND FRAGMENTARY remains of twelve playing cards were found during the field research at Magdalena de Cao. In this chapter I provide details on these remains and contextualize them in relationship to the other paper artifacts at the site and their larger cultural and social roles. The cards, or *naipes*, as they are called in Spanish, are a subcategory of a larger group of paper artifacts found during excavations, including printed and handwritten or drawn documents.

As cards originated in the Old World, I will begin by discussing the origins of cards and card playing there. I follow this with some general information on Early Modern playing card styles and production techniques. Then I will describe the cards and fragments of Magdalena de Cao and their archaeological contexts. This is followed by a discussion of cards from other Peruvian sites as a guide to dating and as the basis for a proposal for the age of the Magdalena cards. I then broaden the discussion by reviewing evidence for gambling in prehispanic Peru followed by card games of sixteenth- and seventeenth-century Spain and Peru, with final comments on how this information contributes to understanding cards and gambling at Magdalena de Cao.

Playing cards were found in both the church and the town. Based on my analysis, the naipes date to circa 1580–1680, the period of primary occupation and use of the site. The cards were very likely made in Spain and brought to the site by settlers or by native people who had had previous contact with the colonists.

Historical Background and Cultural Contexts of Cards in Europe

Some of the earliest references to playing cards and gaming in Europe are from Spanish and Italian sources. It is likely that the idea of playing cards came into these regions via trade or occupation by Muslims, and some scholars believe that card playing arrived via the Nasrid Emirate of Granada (thirteenth through fifteenth centuries). Playing cards were generally known in Spain and Catalonia by 1370, after which references to them appear fairly frequently in documents and edicts banning public card playing and games of chance (Demming 1996:18).

Spain was fertile ground for card games. As early as 1283, King Alfonso X of Castile, Galicia, and León commissioned the creation of a handwritten and illuminated manuscript titled *Libro de juegos* (Book of games). This manuscript was a translation of an earlier Arabic document with additions and changes by the king himself. This book discussed and illustrated three types of games: chess, which emphasizes strategy; dice, a game that depends on chance; and tables, a game akin to backgammon that combines strategy and chance. These games had been imported into Spain from the Arab lands and played by the Islamic rulers of southern Iberia. Even though chess, dice throwing, and backgammon were known in Spain by the time of King Alfonso, card playing apparently either was not known or was not very popular. In *A History of Card Games* David Parlett writes, "Cards are first mentioned in Spain in 1371, described in detail in Switzerland in 1377" (1991:35).

In the beginning, playing cards were large and hand-painted, and they mainly belonged to the upper classes and well-to-do scholars and clerics. Card playing had limited influence on the general population, as did the other aforementioned games, with the possible exception of dice, which date to Roman times. This may be due in part to the fact that some of the games required special boards or tables to play upon. Most people would not have had the money needed to procure this equipment. Dice and cards, on the other hand are extremely portable and do not require much in the way of equipment.

The portability of cards and the variety of different kinds of games that can be played with them likely explains why they became popular in Spain and elsewhere in Europe. Their growing popularity probably was aided by the ability of *naiperos* (card makers) to do a type of mass production after printing became established in Spain around 1472, when printers from Germany and the Low Countries were invited into Spain by the bishop of Segovia and encouraged to set up shop in Spain (Agudo Ruiz 2000:42). By 1532, when the Spanish arrived in Peru, the business of producing cards and playing games with them was well established in Spain and in its other colonies, such as Mexico and Panama.

A sign of the popularity of cards and card playing in Spain and its colonies was the institution of a licensing fee on the workshops that produced cards. This occurred during the reign of King Philip II (1556–1598) and was enforced by the government of Spain throughout the home country and colonies. A great deal of money was being made on the sale and manufacturing of cards, and the government wanted its portion of the profits. The Crown set up a monopoly and established protectionist measures to control card production. Trying to enforce these fees and regulations was more difficult in the far-flung regions of the empire, including the viceroyalty of Peru. Such was the Spanish fondness for card playing and the great quantity of cards produced that in 1553 the viceroy of New Spain, Luis Velasco, prohibited natives and Spaniards from possessing the woodblock forms for producing cards, under pain of being whipped and exiled (Cardenas 2002:82).

Deck Styles

The cards from the site are all in what is generally referred to as a Latin Deck style. This was the card style popular in Italy, Spain, Portugal, and early Colonial Period Peru, although it was also used in some areas of western France. This style of cards is still in use today in Latin

Figure 14.1   Examples of Latin Deck cards from Copacabana, Bolivia. Top (left to right): caballero (horseman) of swords, rey (king) of clubs, sota (valet) of cups, and caballero of coins. Bottom: six of cups, swords, coins, and clubs. The deck was accessioned by the Peabody Museum in 1875. PM 75-20-30/8385.

America and parts of Europe for playing certain games, although northern European (Anglo-American/French) decks also are used.

The Latin Deck is different from the northern European decks in the number of cards per deck and the symbols used on them. A standard deck had 48 cards, similar to a northern European style deck save for the lack of a ten in each of the suits. The suits were *bastos* (clubs), *copas* (cups), *espadas* (swords), and *oros* (coins). The face cards in the Spanish Latin deck were the *rey* (king), *caballero* (horseman), and *sota* (valet) (Figure 14.1). A deck of 48 cards was used for some games, while the eights and nines were removed to produce a deck of 40 for other games (Demming 1996:4). In the early days of card production, no numerals were printed on the cards; this practice was introduced after 1800.

While the Latin Deck style refers to widely shared commonalities, there are national variations. Italian decks are stylistically distinct from Spanish decks in several ways. In Italian cards, swords are curved and interlaced as in latticework. The swords in Spanish decks are straight-sided, are laid out separately, and are shrunk to the size of daggers on higher-count cards in order to fit them onto the card face. The clubs in Italian decks resemble polo sticks and are slim and plain. In Spanish decks, they appear to have been recently hacked off a tree and look as if a cartoon caveman could have carried them (Parlett 1991:31). All of the Magdalena cards that had enough diagnostic traits on them to be recognizable exhibited elements of the Spanish style.

Card Production Methods

The arrival of woodblock printing in Spain from Germany around 1370 to 1380 made it possible to produce multiple decks of cards in short order (Demming 1996:14). Cards produced in this manner quickly replaced the hand-painted cards of earlier times and made them accessible to the less wealthy. In *Los naipes de España* Agudo Ruiz illustrates several scenes of card production and provides images of some stencils, woodblocks, and other equipment used in the production of playing cards (2000:37–63).

All of the cards found at Magdalena de Cao were printed from woodblocks, likely in sheets of twelve cards. Layered sheets of laid paper provided the necessary stiffness for printing and use and remained the standard stock until the nineteenth century, when they were replaced by woven paper.

After printing, if the cards were to be colored, a stencil was laid over them and paint was brushed over the printed images. The tints used were likely enhanced by the addition of some form of glue that helped colors to adhere better and last longer. The earliest colors used were yellow and red; blue and green were added slightly later. Cards were cut out individually from the sheets by naiperos in small workshops all over Spain.

The Magdalena Cards

Twenty-six paper fragments that might have been the remains of cards were among the papers found at Magdalena, but many were so poorly preserved that identification as cards was highly speculative. Twelve were well preserved enough to identify with a reasonable degree of certainty, and it is those that are discussed here. Six card fragments came from Unit 4, located at the northwestern corner of the church complex and just outside the low-walled atrium. The fragments were mixed with numerous other paper artifacts, mostly torn, that appear to have been dumped outside of the church walls at some point in the past. Most of these fragments seem to have had a direct relationship to church business, as they include printed indulgences, prayer cards, sections of holy writ, samples of musical notation for plainchant, and letters addressed to priests. Card fragments are the only set of paper artifacts at the site that were specifically made for secular use (see Chapters 2 and 13).

The cards from Unit 4 are all fragmentary and incomplete. They consist of two unidentifiable fragments as well as a three of swords, a three of clubs, a four+ of coins, and a two+ of coins.[1] For the examples with enough of the card remaining to be measured, the three of swords is approximately 3.8 cm in width and the three of clubs measures close to 3.7 cm in width, but the four+ of coins is nearly double that width. This size discrepancy indicates the presence of at least two decks (Figure 14.2).

A single example of a playing card was found in Unit 8 near the western wall of the church's baptistry (Figure 14.3). It is another three of swords. It too measures approximately 3.7 cm in width and is quite similar to the other three of swords except that its colors are red and blue instead of red, green, and yellow. It is therefore likely to have come from yet another deck.

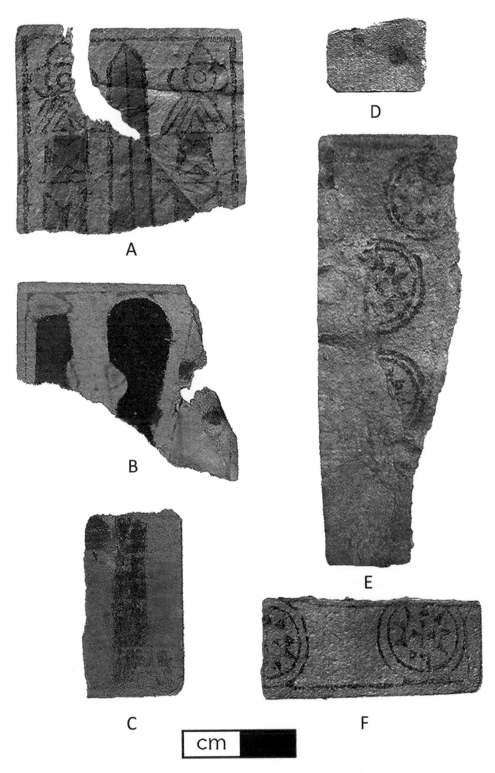

Figure 14.2 Unit 4 card fragments: A. Three of swords; B. Three of clubs; C. Unknown, possibly a face card; D. Unknown; E. Four+ of coins; F. Two+ of coins.

Figure 14.3
Unit 8 card fragment,
a three of swords.

cm

The paper found in Unit 8 tended to be less fragmentary than in other locales. Whole pages of printed religious texts or handwritten letters were preserved in readable condition. Some of the papers in this unit had bird droppings on them, suggesting that they may have lain uncovered on the ground surface for a time, after the church collapsed and people left the vicinity, before the wind blew sand and dirt over them and sealed them in the ground.

Four card fragments were discovered on the floor of Unit 1, a domestic compound in the town. In this group, there is a clubs card, a cups card, an unidentifiable card, and a nearly complete but extremely faded king of coins (Figure 14.4). The king of coins measures 3.7 cm in width and is approximately 7 cm in length.

Unit 2, another residence, contained only one fragment of a card (Figure 14.5). It is the lower left-hand corner of a face card. Lack of preserved detail inhibits further identification.

The remaining card is from Unit 28, yet another house site (Figure 14.6). It was found on an occupation surface, the dirt floor of the residence, in association with other artifacts including indigenous-style textiles. Excavators estimated that the floor on which this artifact lay was occupied when the town was relatively prosperous, in the first half of the seventeenth century. Shortly after we removed this card from the ground surface, the back sheet separated from the front sheet with the printed image. This card is the valet of cups and measures 3.5 cm wide by 6.9 cm tall.

The card remains show the presence of at least three decks at the site. The fact that there are two differently colored three of swords cards and an extremely wide card supports this conclusion. Except for the valet of cups, we have virtually no evidence of the cultural contexts of the cards beyond their locations in either the church or town, although some tentative inferences on the uses of cards at Magdalena will be offered below. The total number of card remains is relatively low, but it is noteworthy that evidence of them was encountered in each of the three domestic occupations excavated as well as in the church. This is a testament to the importance of cards and their uses in Colonial Period Peru as well as in contemporary Europe.

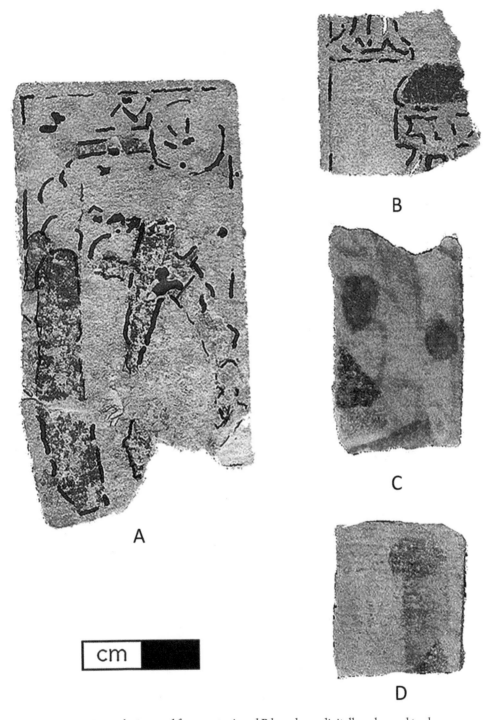

A

cm

B

C

D

Figure 14.4 Unit 1 playing card fragments. A and B have been digitally enhanced to show outlines of the rey of coins and a cup, respectively. C is unidentifiable but may be a face card. D appears to be a club card.

Figure 14.5
The single card fragment found
in Unit 2, likely a sota.

cm

Figure 14.6
The card from Unit 28,
a sota of cups.

cm

Cards from Other Peruvian Sites

Magdalena de Cao is not the only archaeological site in Peru to yield playing cards. Excavation recovered 33 cards and card fragments in the late 1960s at Huaca Tres Palos, part of the Maranga archaeological complex in the northern part of Lima (see Figure 14.8). A Spanish colonial building had been constructed on top of a huaca, and the cards and other documentary fragments were found in a nearby trash heap. Gilda Cogorno Ventura (1970a, 1970b) subsequently analyzed and published reports on these cards. She describes two basic types of cards found at Huaca Tres Palos. Her Type A card was printed only in black and white and not colored. It had three-dimensional, Renaissance-style renderings of human figures and objects with strongly hatched borders. These cards typically measure 8–9 cm in length and 4–5 cm in width. Additionally, some Type A cards were made by pasting the Renaissance-style image onto another card used as a backing to strengthen it. This group bears little resemblance to the Magdalena de Cao cards.

The cards from Magdalena are more similar to Cogorno's Type B cards. These are slightly smaller, are tinted with colors (usually red and blue), and have a single line as a border. The artwork on these cards is more linear and two-dimensional and is in a more Gothic style, as is the case with the Magdalena de Cao cards. The images have a flatter and more cartoon-like appearance than the Type A cards.

Cogorno also refers to other finds of playing cards in Peruvian archaeological sites. She mentions that Alberto Bueno discovered playing cards during excavations at Pachacamac, a large ceremonial complex south of Lima occupied by the Inca and earlier cultures. In addition, a stone box is reported to have been found containing a deck of Spanish playing cards in a tomb in the region of Ocucaje, on the South Coast, and both container and cards eventually were included in the Soldi Collection, although details of its present state are not available (Cogorno 1970a:2).

More recently, I was informed by David Earle that playing card fragments were found among the ruins at Tambo Viejo near the town of Acarí, in southern Peru, when it was excavated in the 1980s by Francis Riddell and Alina Aparicio. At that site there was a tower that, when it was built or rebuilt, incorporated various classes of fill, including a layer of thatched roofing material with bits of paper in it, several pieces of which appear to have been playing cards. The roofing and paper may have come from the *tambo* structure adjacent to the church, which was used by the Spanish in the 16th and early 17th centuries (David Earle, personal communication).

Dating the Cards

It is difficult to date the cards and fragments from Magdalena de Cao with any precision because styles were used over long periods of time. But there are certain clues that can assist in setting time ranges. The site was first occupied by Spaniards in 1578, while final abandonment occurred in the mid-1700s. In general, then, our cards were likely made in Spain and imported into Peru sometime between the conquest of Peru in 1532 and 1740, more likely between 1578 and 1740.

The cards belong to the Spanish National Pattern style, a variant of the Latin Deck that was produced during the seventeenth century, possibly slightly earlier. As already noted, these cards were not very elaborate, nor was much care put into their production. This lack of subtlety may have been because naiperos in Spain began to be taxed and licensed by the Spanish

Figure 14.7 Comparison of sword pommels from Sevillian deck (left) and a card from Magdalena (right). Not to scale.

government during the reign of Philip II (1554–1613). Also around this time, card makers were attempting to respond quickly to the great demand both in Spain and in its colonies for decks of cards, rather than catering exclusively to the upper classes.

A narrower date range can be considered for the Magdalena cards because there are design similarities between our cards and naipes produced in Seville in 1647 and later in the seventeenth century. The forms of the handles on the sword cards from two Sevillian decks and the three of swords from Unit 4 (Figure 14.7) are very similar. The pommels on the sword cards have an eared aspect with a downturned fringe or basket shape below them. The manner of rendering coins is also quite similar in the Magdalena and Sevillian decks. In addition, an archaeological contextual clue to the age of the cards was provided by the paper rubbish found in Unit 4. The card fragments in this trash heap were mixed with documents that occasionally had dates written on them, and these dates ranged between 1612 and 1665.

The Magdalena de Cao cards are quite similar to some examples found at the Huaca Tres Palos near Lima, as has already been mentioned. Cogorno suggests in her report that some of these cards, her Type A (Figure 14.8, bottom), date to the sixteenth century. The earliest date found written on other Huaca Tres Palos documents is 1582. In reporting to me about card fragments found at Tambo Viejo in southern Peru, David Earle stated that the known Spanish presence at that site was approximately between 1570 and 1670. These dates fit nicely with the known Magdalena de Cao dates.

Taking all of these dates into consideration, I suggest that the cards and fragments found at Magdalena de Cao were likely manufactured in Spain. Furthermore, it is possible they were made by naiperos in Seville, based on stylistic similarities and because over the course of time Seville became the major base of operations for Spanish explorations in the New World.

A conservative range for the date of the manufacture of the cards is between 1580 and 1700, while a more speculative one is between 1590 and 1690. The narrower range is based on

Figure 14.8 Cards from Huaca Tres Palos, Lima. Bottom row is Style A and top row is Style B. The Style A cards may be of Italian origin based on stylistic elements in them.

our knowledge of the history of site use and the presumed date of the church collapse. Several factors remain uncertain, of course. We do not know how long cards may have stayed in use. In the colonies their use lives may have been longer than in Spain, where replacement decks were more readily available. On the other hand, cards do tend to wear out quickly, so while it is possible that a late-sixteenth-century deck would still have been in use several decades later, it seems unlikely.

Games and Game Playing in Prehispanic Peru

Games (and, quite likely, gambling) existed in the Andean region prior to the arrival of the Spanish, but research on the topic is scant. Those who have worked on this include Anne

Marie Hocquenghem (1987), who explored the question of games among the Moche (ca. A.D. 350–900); noted Andeanist John Rowe (1946); and Thierry Depaulis (1998), a games authority. All three investigated Inca games using both archaeological findings and reports by early chroniclers. Investigation of the games of the earlier Moche mostly are based on examining prehistoric art but also rely upon chroniclers' reports about Inca games as analogies for earlier practices.

To date there is very little concrete evidence of game playing from the archaeological record. The strongest evidence comes from Machu Picchu and was found by Hiram Bingham during his excavations in the early twentieth century. He found several cubes and small pyramidal objects, all made of pottery, in the vicinity of Snake Rock and the City Gate area of the site. The cubes were differently marked on each of their six sides. Bingham identified these small forms as counters and related them to the famous khipu cords (Bingham 1915). John Rowe identifies these small objects as likely gaming pieces and suggests they may have been used similarly to Western dice, especially in a game he identifies as *picqana* (1946:288). Richard Burger and Lucy Salazar agree with Rowe that the objects were likely used in gaming but suggest that they may have been used in divination as well (2004:155, plate 82).

These archaeological finds tally nicely with information gleaned by Depaulis in his studies of the writings of early chroniclers, dictionary writers, and ethnographers. Sixteenth- and seventeenth-century writers all mention *pichqa* (with various spellings) as referring to the die itself or to a game played with dice. Depaulis (1998:28) quotes Father Murrua, writing in 1590:

> The Indians play with one die, called *pichca*, with 5 points one side, one on the other, two on the other and three on the other, plus side four: the crossed top is five and the bottom of the die is twenty.

The die was used in simple throwing games or as counters for moving pieces in the course of a board game.

An alternative name for dice among the Inca was *wayru*. Interestingly, the term *wayru* or *huayru* also refers to bicolored beans grown in Peru (*Erythrina americana*). This may be the type of bean that is shown in use on much earlier painted Moche ceramics. Anne-Marie Hocquenghem (1987) devotes a section of her book *Iconografía Mochica* to a detailed study of scenes on such vessels that seem to show a game being played by two seated players and involves each of them taking a turn throwing beans in the air while holding a bundle of sticks in the other hand. An auspicious landing of a bean or beans may have been the goal of this game. Hocquenghem suggests that the sticks may have been a way of keeping score, and that the beans and how they landed may have been a way of foretelling the future.

It is likely that this game is similar to *mancala* (the general name for a group of African games). Mancala games are played by throwing a die and then, based on the number thrown, moving seeds or pebbles across a board with circular depressions or cups in it. The possible similarity comes from the likelihood that the board for the African games represents an abstracted version of a plowed field or holes dug in the ground for planting, and the Moche scenes show the players seated on furrowed ground similar to a plowed field.

The Inca played a bean game, known as *appaytalla*, for several reasons and at specific occasions. One such occasion was upon the death of an individual, when a game was played by the deceased's relatives as a way of dividing up that person's belongings or letting the game winner distribute the goods—in essence, allowing chance or perhaps the spirit of the deceased person decide who won.

Another possible use for this game was as a means of divining the wishes of the spirits or gods at the beginning or end of the harvest season. Hocquenghem quotes Guaman Poma, the Andean chronicler, writing about celebrations held by the Inca Raymi Quilla in April, around harvest time, near the austral autumn equinox, in the highlands of Peru. He describes large gatherings of celebrants eating, drinking, dancing, and singing in a large public plaza as the population was treated to the Inca's stored provisions. This would have been a harvest festival or preparation for going into the leaner winter months and the waning of the sun's power. As Guaman Poma noted:

> This is the month of harvest; all ate and drank courtesy of the Inca. And this is the month that the birds of the sky and the mice must eat. All month the principal men played *ruichoca (tejo), uayro de ynaca, hilancala,* and *challcochima*; they played other games and gathered across the realm during April. (Guaman Poma 1980:171, author's translation)

One of the games mentioned by Guaman Poma, hilancala, was briefly described by Ludovico Bertonio in 1612 as a race game somewhat akin to backgammon and played with the pichqa die on a board called *aucattana*. Another game, ruichoca, involved throwing *bolas* (round stones connected by a cord, used for hunting) as far as possible (Depaulis 1998:39). *Uayro* (possibly *wayru*?) *de ynaca* may refer to a dicing game played by noble ladies. *Challcochima* was the name of an Inca warlord and supporter of Atahualpa who may have had a game named after him (Depaulis 1998:31, 39–40).

The only other evidence from ancient Peru that could possibly be interpreted as related to gaming involves what look like models of buildings made of ceramic or stone found at various sites throughout Peru. These have been variously interpreted as gaming boards, abacuses, or building models. They may be *yupana*, or Inca "abacuses," mentioned by early chroniclers, or perhaps they are the aucattana boards just mentioned. The native peoples of Peru likely had other games about which we know little from the chroniclers, dictionary writers, and ethnographers.

Some of the games described herein and elsewhere indicate that the Andeans did have a concept of chance, given that the use of dice, by their very nature, introduces an element of uncertainty as to outcome. "Chance," of course, is an English word and thus a specific cultural concept, but Quechua has a similar word and concept: *sami* (good fortune, luck) (Quechua Web 2014). How luck or chance enters into human affairs often leads to issues of religion, spiritualism, and fate controlled by forces other than human volition. How much these factored into Inca thought, especially in terms of games, is not completely clear. The records imply that many games may have been played only on special occasions as at festivals, funerals, or at specified times of the year. Rowe (1946:289) states, "The Inca gambled lightly on games of skill and chance, betting such things as clothing, llamas and guinea pigs, but amusement rather than winnings was the main purpose of their games." Given the paucity of evidence available, I conclude, along with Depaulis and Rowe, that while the Inca played games and had a concept of chance, gaming was not an everyday practice. According to Depaulis, there is strikingly less evidence for it among the Incas than in groups such as the Aztecs and North American Indians.

Card Playing and Gambling in Sixteenth- and Seventeenth-Century Spain and Peru

By the time of the conquests of Mexico and Peru, card playing in Spain had become increasingly associated with gambling and corruption, especially among the lower classes. Cervantes discussed and described card playing and cheating in his 1613 novella *Rinconete y Cortadillo*, part of his series Novelas Ejemplares (Exemplary Novels). The story gives the reader a view into the life and times of two scamps, Rinconete and Cortadillo, who wend their way through southern Spain pickpocketing and cheating at cards. They end up in Seville, where a wide-open attitude prevailed and many gathered to get their share of the riches and spoils coming from the New World or to ship out on expeditions. Cervantes colorfully describes the motivations and skills of his character Rinconete:

> "I did not fail to include this pack of cards among them"—here the speaker exhibited that oviform specimen already mentioned—"and with these I have gained my bread among the inns and taverns between Madrid and this place, by playing at Vingt-et-un. It is true they are somewhat soiled and worn, as your worship sees; but for him who knows how to handle them, they possess a marvelous virtue, which is, that you never cut them but you find an ace at the bottom; if your worship is then acquainted with the game, you will see what an advantage it is to know for certain that you have an ace to begin with, since you may count it either for one or eleven; and so you may be pretty sure that when the stakes are laid at twenty-one, your money will be much disposed to stay at home." (Cervantes 1881:795)

Gambling, including card playing, was an integral part of the Spanish conquest of the New World. One of the most famous incidents among the Spanish from the early days of the conquest of Peru involved gambling. One of the conquistadors, Mancio Serra de Leguizamón, received a large gold disk from the Temple of the Sun in Cuzco as his share of the spoils and quickly lost it gambling that night. The story spread all the way back to Spain, leading to a popular saying, "gambling away the sun before it rises" (*juega el sol antes que amanezca*) (de la Vega 1991:163).

Dice and cards were on the list of needed items that the Spanish sent back home. A letter from about 1540 by Hernando Pizarro asking for supplies to be sent from Panama expressed Spanish priorities: 176 bottles of wine, 60 shirts of Holland lace, 26 pairs of velvet hose, 71 pairs of shoes and velvet slippers, 18 spectacles, 56 pairs of leather gloves from Cordoba, 12 habits of the Order of Santiago, 80 hats, 6 jars of anchovies, and 386 packs of playing cards (Stirling 1999:77).

After the colonial administration was established, gambling remained popular in the viceroyalty. Felipe Guaman Poma de Ayala wrote a 1,200-page letter of complaint to the king about Spanish behavior and policies toward the native Peruvians, and one of his 400 illustrations of cruelties and hypocrisies illustrates card playing. It shows a priest and a Spanish soldier engaged in a card game, with coins on the table (Figure 14.9). Guaman Poma not only saw gambling as an evil that robbed natives but also as morally corrupting:

Figure 14.9   Guaman Poma's rendering of a card game between a priest and a corregidor
(chief magistrate of a town), 1615.

Those said head chiefs make themselves great cheats and liars and loafers. Their vice is to be continuously drunk and loose with tribute money. And they learned to play cards and dice like the Spanish; they played *axedres, hilancula, chalco chima, uayro, ynaca, riui, pampas, runa, yspital, uayro ynaca.* They played with Spanish and mestizos, mulattos, negroes, sharecroppers, and Indian shamans. And when they got drunk, they killed each other and robbed the poor. They give offense to the service of God and Your Majesty and evil and damage to the Indians and the poor and destroy the kingdom through their drunkenness. (Guaman Poma 1980:714, author's translation)

Some authorities do appear to have been concerned about abuses brought about by gambling, although their solution was to punish players already in vulnerable positions and hard circumstances. An ordinance in the *Libros cabildos de Lima* describes the legal difficulties of native persons who had been convicted of playing cards in public:

> Another remembered that his experience when Indians and sharecroppers played cards was that they became vicious and miscreants. The Justice ordered that all who played would lose their *mantas* [wearing blankets] and if they didn't have any wearing blankets they would lose their shirts.[2]

In Trujillo, closer to the site of Magdalena de Cao, throughout the seventeenth century there are various references to difficulties over playing cards and gambling involving native people, mestizos, and blacks. A 1730 entry in the *Asuntos de gobierno* of Trujillo discusses a mandate from the corregidor in charge prohibiting gaming tables, dice, tabu, and cards (Rocío Delibés, personal communication). That there were so many and such forceful commentaries about gambling suggests that it was highly popular.

The presence of playing cards at Magdalena and other Peruvian Colonial Period sites that have received archaeological study clearly indicates that card gaming was popular in these places: the cards retrieved from excavations probably are few in comparison to the numbers that were played and not discarded to be found by archaeologists. Many questions about the cards and their social roles remain, however, especially at Magdalena. Do the few cards found in the town indicate that native people played them, or did only friars play? Or did friars invite natives to play in the church so that they could be swindled, as in Guaman Poma's commentary? Were cards in the town prior to the collapse of the church, or were they mined from church ruins? Were cards used by townspeople to play games, or did they serve as talismans or for fortune telling? Although these questions may never be satisfactorily answered, the presence of the cards throughout the site demonstrates the great attraction that cards and gaming had to both Spaniard and native alike at Magdalena de Cao in the early Colonial Period.

NOTES

1 The plus sign (+) indicates that the complete card originally may have had a higher number of suit markings on it.

2 Archivo Regional de la Libertad (Perú), Corregimiento, Legajo 269, Cuadernillo 3274, dated February 13, 1730; author's translation. Thanks to Rocío Delibes for advising me on this citation.

REFERENCES

Agudo Ruiz, Juan de Dios
   2000 *Los naipes en España*. Vitoria-Gasteiz, Spain: Diputación Foral de Alava, Departamento de Cultura.

Bingham, Hiram
   1915 The Story of Machu Picchu. *National Geographic* 27:172–217.

Burger, Richard L., and Lucy C. Salazar (editors)
   2004 *Machu Picchu: Unveiling the Mystery of the Incas*. New Haven, CT: Yale University Press.

Cardenas, Ricardo Estabridis
   2002 *El grabado en Lima virreinal (siglos XVI al XIX)*. Lima: Fondo Editorial Universidad Nacional Mayor de San Marcos.

Cervantes Saavedra, Miguel de
   1881 [1612] *Rinconete and Cortadillo in the Exemplary Novels of Cervantes*. Translated by Walter K. Kelly. London: George Bell and Sons.

Cogorno Ventura, Gilda
   1970a Documentos y naipes hallados en las excavaciones de la Huaca Tres Palos, Pando (Lima). *Boletín de Seminario de Arqueología* 5:1–39.
   1970b Hallazgos ultimos de dos naipes en la Huaca Tres Palos. *Boletín de Seminario de Arqueología* 6:84–89.

de la Vega, Garcilaso
   1991 *Comentarios reales de los Incas*, vol. 1. 3rd ed. Caracas, Venezuela: Miró Quesada Sosa.

Demming, Trevor
   1996 *The Playing Cards of Spain*. London: Cygnus Arts.

Depaulis, Thierry
   1998 Inca Dice and Board Games. *Board Game Studies* 1:26–49.

Guaman Poma de Ayala, Felipe
   1980 [1615] *El primer nueva coronica y buen gobierno*. 3 vols. Edited by John V. Murra and Rolena Adorno. Mexico, DF: Siglo Veintiuno.

Hocquenghem, Anne-Marie
   1987 *Iconografía mochica*. Lima: Fondo Editorial de la Pontificia Universidad Católica del Peru.

Parlett, David
   1991 *A History of Card Games*. Oxford: Oxford University Press.

Quechua Web
   2014 English-Quechua Dictionary. https://en.glosbe.com/en/qu.

Rowe, John Howland
   1946 Inca Culture in the Time of the Spanish Conquest. In *The Handbook of South American Indians*, vol. 2, edited by Julian Steward, pp. 183–330. Washington, DC: US Government Printing Office.

Stirling, Stuart
   1999 *The Last Conquistador*. Gloucestershire: Sutton Publishing.

15

Other Inscriptions

Gourds, Marked Adobes, and Burial Textiles

Jeffrey Quilter

Introduction

THREE CHAPTERS IN this book discuss the remains of papers found at Magdalena de Cao Viejo. But there were other ways that people made meaningful marks on materials that have been preserved through to the present. This chapter discusses three of them: gourds, adobe bricks, and painted textiles.

Gourds

Gourds played a key role in the daily lives of Andean peoples. They were the everyday ware for eating and drinking, and given that soups and stews were the main ways food was consumed, they were in constant use. Those uses stretched back quite far, as bottle gourds were already domesticated when the earliest peoples entered the New World from Asia (Erickson et al. 2005). One reason ceramics came into use relatively late in Peru may be due to the fact that gourds were so easy to grow and so useful as containers. Junius Bird (1963; Bird et al. 1985) found the most famous early Peruvian gourds during his 1946–1947 excavations at Huaca Prieta; the gourds' elaborate decorations drew much attention and contributed to defining the Preceramic Period as a chronological concept.

In Peru, the bottle gourd (*Lageneria siceraria*), which grows on a vine on the ground, was more favored for containers than the tree calabash (*Crescentia* spp.). The natural shape of the bottle gourd is a pear with a long thin neck, and the forms for plates, bowls, ladles, and other basic utensils can all be produced by cutting it at different angles (see Lathrap 1980). Gourds must be dried for use, their exteriors turning a caramel-brown color that reveals a lighter shade when scratched. For most common folk, undecorated gourd containers were the norm, although gourds are so easily decorated that many received some simple adornment. There are, however, many highly decorated prehispanic gourds that took hours to make (see Vergara 2015). Gourds still remain the hallmark Andean craft today, ranging from simple, low-priced items displayed in big baskets for tourists to pick from to expensive artworks displayed in glass cases in art galleries and awarded prizes in shows.

Pyroengraving is the decorative technique mostly commonly associated with Andean gourds. The artist uses a heated pointed tool or a smudging method to make black lines or areas, respectively, on the gourd's surface. This method was employed in prehispanic times, but simple engraving also was used without recourse to heat. Gourds also were sometimes carved in relief or, at the other extreme, simply scraped and polished. Elaborate pieces sometimes were colored with pigments, including rubbing one or more colors into the inscribed lines. Some gourds were inset with shiny shells or stones.

We found hundreds of fragments of gourd containers at Magdalena and several complete gourd bowls, most of which were undecorated. Perhaps the most impressive evidence of the domestic use of gourds was in the kitchen area of Unit 28, where we found ceramic jars half buried in the adobe floor (Figure 15.1; see Chapter 2). These jars had gourd bowls placed over their mouths as protective lids. There also was a very large gourd sunk into the ground like the jars. None of the gourd bowls were decorated. In other areas of the site we found cut gourd containers that were filled with various vegetal items and other small organic objects, such as one found on a floor in Unit 1 (Figures 2.25 and 15.2). We often found these filled gourds buried under floors, indicating that they likely were offerings, and in most cases these gourds too were undecorated.

Figure 15.1   Vessels in the food preparation area of Unit 28. At left, two pottery jars sunk into the floor retaining their gourd bowl lids. The one at far left has a textile between the gourd and the jar mouth. At rear, a jar sits in an adobe stand in the floor. At right, a large gourd jar was buried in the floor, like the ceramic ones, and still retains a textile cover.

Figure 15.2
A gourd vessel
found on a floor
in Unit 1. It is
filled with seeds
and small pieces
of cloth. See also
Figure 2.25.

There are 55 examples of decorated gourds in the Magdalena collection. Most of these are single sherds, a handful are joins of two or more sherds, and there are four examples of complete or near-complete (half or more) gourds. In addition, there are several large fragments that allow for a fairly reliable interpretation of their original decorative program. Of the total, 22 were found in the town and 32 were found in the church, although the latter includes the large trench, Unit 5, that ran from the northern edge of the church mound down to the level of the town. Most of these gourd fragments are more related to the town than the church, as the trench was largely on the exterior of the compound. A few other gourd fragments were found in or close to the nave of the church, although post-occupational disturbances easily could have moved them there. In the town, five decorated gourd sherds were found in Unit 19 (the trash deposit), four were found in Unit 1, and eleven were recovered in Unit 28. Notably, both the Units 1 and 28 house compounds were richer in artifacts than Unit 2, in which no decorated gourd fragments were found and that compound was the poorest of the three in terms of artifacts, as noted in Chapter 2.

It is possible that some prehistoric gourds or fragments of them were picked up and kept by colonial-era peoples or that post-occupational activities including looting and archaeology moved prehistoric items into colonial-era archaeological contexts. Our excavations were careful enough, however, that we are fairly confident that most of the decorated gourds here under discussion date to the time of the colonial occupation.

Since, to the best of my knowledge, no study of Colonial Period gourds has heretofore been carried out, I make interpretations tentatively. Proceeding with this in mind, most of the collection consists of gourds or fragments of them decorated in "traditional," prehispanic styles. Three examples, including two very large segments of the original vessels, were decorated in styles that appear to have been greatly influenced by European artistic conventions. Five gourds are decorated in styles that seem to have been influenced by European conventions but exhibit some characteristics that suggest hybridity. There are 10 gourd fragments that cannot be assigned to any distinct style. Some of the "traditional style" gourd fragments that we found could easily fit into the collection of gourd fragments recovered from excavations by Tom Dillehay (2017) and Duccio Bonavia at preceramic Huaca Prieta and Paredones while others clearly are quite different. Style apparently differed, perhaps by site or community, even in the Preceramic Period, however (Dillehay and Bonavia 2017: 440–446).

Gourd fragments were identified as decorated in prehispanic styles if they included broad bands and lines, geometric motifs, and highly stylized animals, especially birds. It is interesting to consider that the styles of representation found on gourds, even in prehispanic times, generally have few correlates in ceramic decorations. Although birds and fish were popular motifs during the Late Intermediate Period and the Late Horizon on the North Coast, and although some sharing occurs between gourds and ceramics in the way these animals as well as geometric motifs were rendered, in general, gourd art is distinct unto itself.

There is a wide range of styles of geometric motifs in the Magdalena gourd assemblage. A nearly complete vessel (Figure 15.3) consists of a simple rim band with two rows of circles below. In each row the circles are alternately dark and light. Both the black rim band and darkened circles were made through the use of a pyroengraving technique.

Gourd sherds with geometric techniques include cross-hatching and delicately rendered zoned punctuation (Figure 15.4 A, B). Four sherds (Figure 15.4 C–F) were decorated by creating incised bands framing dense imagery. Two of these sherds (Figure 15.4 D, E) appear to have had some kind of fill added to the incisions that likely produced a colorful effect on the original gourd, and this may also be the case with another example (Figure 15.4 I) as well. All

Figure 15.3
A complete pyroengraved gourd vessel. Maximum width approximately 15 cm.

Figure 15.4
Gourd vessel fragments showing various techniques. G has traces of applied pigment.

of these sherds appear to have been engraved without the use of fire. A sherd with curvilinear designs was painted in more than one color (Figure 15.4 G), while another (Figure 15.4 H) has an engraved geometric design that may be part of a stylized, likely mythological animal, as may be depicted on two other sherds (Figure 15.4 C, I).

The great variation in the kinds of geometric motifs employed in decorating gourds at Magdalena is further emphasized by a complete gourd bowl with a "wandering" line running around its exterior (Figure 15.5). The design was made through the use of fire, as can be seen by the separate marks made to produce the lines on the vessel.

Figure 15.5
Shallow gourd
bowl with
wandering line
design on
exterior.
Maximum width
approximately
25 cm.

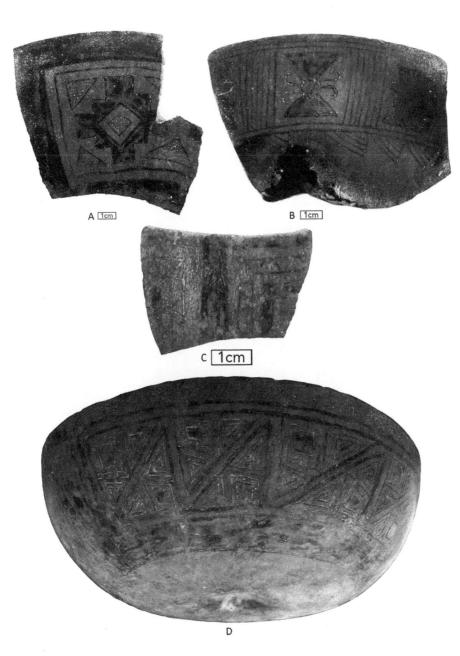

Figure 15.6
Gourd fragments
and gourd bowl
with tocapu design
elements.

A 1cm

B 1cm

c 1cm

D

There also are examples of elaborate geometric designs resembling *tocapu*, an Inca term for rectangular designs usually consisting of geometric motifs (Cummins 2011; Rowe 1996). Although the term derives from weaving, tocapu designs are also found on a wide variety of other media, including murals and, in the Colonial Period, *keros*, wooden tumblers for drinking chicha (Cummins 2002). It is generally believed that tocapu carried meaning, although exactly what was conveyed is uncertain. Some may have been emblems of place, ethnicity, or social position, and a few have been interpreted as to specific symbolic referents such as one that is in the form of a military tunic.

There are six examples of tocapu designs among the Magdalena gourds. One (Figure 15.6 A) is a square-shaped cross (sometimes known as a *chakana* or Andean cross),

Figure 15.7
Gourd fragments
with images of
animals.

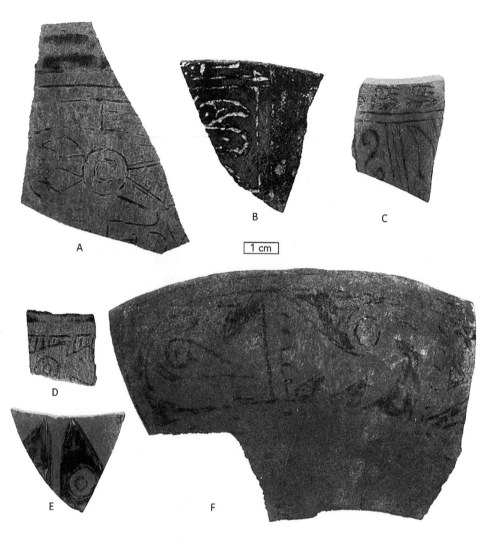

A

B

C

1 cm

D

E

F

a motif of great antiquity. The Magdalena example is rendered in a common form that includes a diamond center and four triangle fillers in the corners. One tocapu-like motif is of an hourglass shape made by two equilateral triangles with a curvilinear design at their juncture (Figure 15.6 B). Another gourd fragment shows what appear to be three nested squares or rectangles that may or may not be a tocapu motif, while a complete gourd bowl has a panel with square elements made up of nested triangles and large diagonal bands (Figure 15.6 C, D).

Along with geometric designs, stylized animals are fairly common on the Magdalena gourds, mostly birds and fish (Figures 15.7–15.9). These animals also were the most commonly used motifs in Late Intermediate Period and Late Horizon art on the North Coast of Peru. As best as can be judged, even in prehispanic times these images of animals appear to have been decorative, with relatively low symbolic values. Birds are more frequently depicted than fish, although our sample is small. The avifauna appear to be highly stylized, so it seems that no particular species are represented.

Figure 15.8
Gourd fragments
with images of
birds.

A

1 cm

B

C

There are four examples of bird depictions that do not follow traditional representational styles but instead may have drawn on European modes. One (Figure 15.8, A) consists of two large sherds that join together depicting two engraved birds in profile and a third, at right, with body in profile but facing the viewer. Only the central bird is complete. It appears that the carver did some initial work on the head of the bird at viewer's right that was not satisfactorily rendered at first, judging by lines to the left of the head. The final version shows the head with two eyes, facing the viewer. The birds are rendered with few details that might help identify the species represented. The distinctive clawed feet are suggestive of passerines (perching birds) rather than shore waders, and the short, sharp beak of the central bird suggests an Andean flicker (*Colaptes rupicola*), although that bird's habitat is the highlands. At rest, a bird's wing feathers are aligned with its body, but the central and left birds on this gourd have slightly raised wings, suggesting that they are about to take flight.

Whether the nuances noted above were in the mind of the carver is impossible to know. It seems quite likely that these are generic birds carved without great consideration of the species represented or the bird's pose. Indeed, the central bird is not even completely rendered, as its back and wing feathers are unfinished.

Figure 15.9
Fragments of
a repaired gourd
engraved with
images of birds
and fish.

A second sherd (Figure 15.8 B) is small and appears to have been part of a gourd that had been repaired, judging by the cords on its edge. There was a wide, cross-hatched frame within which the body of a bird and apparently part of a second one, also cross-hatched, were rendered. A third sherd (Figure 15.8 C) may have shown birds in profile and in a line, as if walking from the viewer's left to right. The head of one bird is on the far left, while the tail, body, wing, and a leg are on the right. As in the case of the first example, these birds appear to be generic avians rather than specific species.

The fourth example is an almost complete gourd bowl (Figure 15.9) that still retains a repair made with string. Here birds alternate with stylized fishes. The fish are rendered in a

Figure 15.10
Gourd fragment with
fine-line depiction
of human figures.

1 cm

prehispanic style of joined triangles, while the birds were engraved with large semicircular bodies, minimal or no wings, and, in two cases, long, thin necks, beaks, and legs. The use of a simple circle to depict the heads on these two birds harks back to prehispanic styles, but the rest of the animals do not. A third bird is curiously rendered upside down in relation to the others and with a short beak and no distinctive neck. In addition to the animals, a stylized sun was placed between a fish and a bird. The missing section of the gourd is to the viewer's right, after the bird and to the right of the sun, so we cannot know if a moon, another fish, or some other animal was in the missing piece. Another interesting feature of this gourd is that burning was used within the outlines of all of the animals and the sun, with a few marks also occurring outside of the engravings near the sun.

The fish on this gourd clearly are generic fish, given their highly stylized forms. While the birds may not be referencing distinctive species, it seems noteworthy that one bird has a large,

Figure 15.11   Three fragments of a gourd bowl showing animals and human figures with a stacked tocapu border.

wide, down-curving beak and the other has a long, thin, up-curving one. The upside-down bird's features suggest that a finch, sparrow, or similar avian is depicted.

In addition to gourds that seem to show hybrid artistic conventions, there are three examples of renderings that much more strongly follow European conventions. The clearest example of this is a single engraved sherd (Figure 15.10) depicting two human figures walking to the viewer's right. The right-hand figure wears a long tunic with alternating plain and hatched stripes, cross-hatched thighs that may indicate breeches, clear lower legs perhaps indicating hose, and rounded feet that might indicate shoes. A protuberance on the right side of the figure may indicate a penis, although it is not in an anatomically correct location. Less of the figure on the viewer's left is preserved, but the crooked left arm may sport the sleeve of a close-fitting jacket in European style; here again, cross-hatched thighs, clear lower leg, and rounded feet may portray breeches, hose, and shoes, respectively. A cross-hatched border is below both figures. It is tempting to interpret the more complete figure as representing a native person wearing a hybrid costume of both Andean and European clothing and the less complete figure as dressed in European garb.

The remains of part of an engraved gourd bowl were found in three fragments (Figure 15.11). The preserved section consists of a portion of a panel that depends from a band that likely encircled the entire circumference of the bowl immediately below its lip. The band consists of two parallel smaller bands with triangular motifs between them. All are hatched so as to give the impression of twisted ropes. At the viewer's far left, four roughly square units, each with the same imagery, are stacked in a column and serve as a border to the panel. From the bottom of this column another band serves as a border and ground line for the images above them. Interior tick marks cut from the upper line of the border at an angle emphasize the ground line effect.

The segment of gourd that had the other end of the imagery has not been preserved, but we might assume that a similar column of stacked squares served to define it and create a panel in which images were rendered. The carvings likely encompassed half or more of the circumference of the bowl when it was complete.

The images within the panel appear to be representations of animals and an anthropomorph, possibly a human, interspersed between motifs. Each of these motifs has the same central element: a T-shaped form with its base resting on or in the ground as formed by the lower border of the panel. The two images to the viewer's right are virtually the same. From the cross of a T-shaped element, two S-shaped elements rise. In the space near the top of the S-shaped elements, a short upside-down V-shape suggests that the space between them is meant to be viewed as solid or containing materials, and from this point three marked lines emerge depicting foliagelike elements. The image on the far left has a different pattern, however, consisting of between ten and twelve elements that resemble the S-shaped elements, or fragments of them, and two elements with V-shaped marks inside them emerge below and near the base of the T-shape.

The animals depicted between the motifs discussed above seem to be highly stylized or generic creatures, and no easy identifications can be made. The creature at far left appears to be a quadruped of some sort, judging by the location of its legs in relation to its body and tail. The next image, to the right, has a generally quadrupedlike body, but its head is hard to discern and its tail is incomplete. The anthropomorph is highly stylized and appears to be unclothed but with no indications of its sex. Next, the arched wings of a bird in profile suggest that it might be a raptor of some kind. The last image shows an eared creature that may be eating one of the branches rising from the object below.

Interpreting this scene is challenging. From a formalist approach there are both Andean and European elements in the engraving. The use of the panel as a frame for the images is present in prehispanic gourd decoration (see Vergara 2015), while the relative looseness of the way images are placed within it has a European feel.

The geometric motifs in each of the four squares appear to be generally similar chakanas. The two uppermost chakanas have the most elaborated designs, and the third is less well executed, as it is missing the two lower filler triangles in the square. The fourth chakana is minimally rendered to the point that the cross is not accurately done and there are no filler squares whatsoever. This may indicate that this border was carved after the scene to the right and from the top down. The carver did not carefully plan so that all squares were of equal size and had the same details, resulting in simpler and smaller third and fourth squares. It is interesting to note that these chakanas have a central circle, different from the more standard central diamonds that can be seen in most prehistoric and early Colonial Period *keros* (flared wooden drinking vessels; Cummins 2002: figs. 4.1, 7.3, 8.2, 8.24, 8.25).

Narrative appears to be present in the imagery. The three figures at far right are moving to the left, as may the animal with the peculiar head. Perhaps the imagery is related to concepts of a garden in an earthly or divine paradise. The two motifs at the right are suggestive of elaborate plants or urns with plants in them. The curvaceous elements might signify water, and the motif at far left is perhaps is a fountain or other water source with new growth rising from its base. It is interesting to note that the ground line of this panel is almost identical to that of the two human figures discussed in the last example. This may indicate that the same artist carved both gourds, or that two artists used similar conventions.

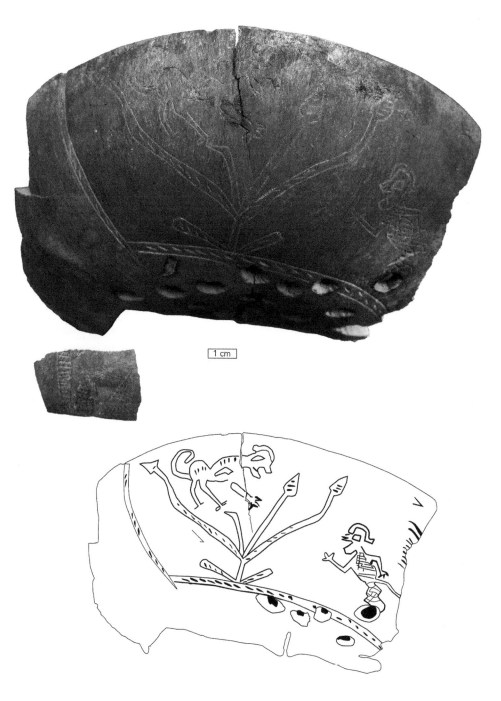

1 cm

The third and final decorated gourd employing European artistic conventions is a large section of a colander, judging by the holes in its bottom (Figure 15.12). It may be, however, that the vessel was first used as a bowl and then later converted to a colander, as some of the holes pierce the imagery engraved on it, such as in the lower border and the lower section of the anthropomorph at the viewer's far right.

The dominant image in the fragment and, we may suspect, in the entire panel, is a large plant or tree with an associated animal apparently in the tree. The plant is peculiar in that it consists of four long tendrils or branches emerging from a single stem. Three of the tendrils terminate in incised triangles, and one is foreshortened in order to portray the animal.

The animal appears to be a quadruped. It has a curved tail and tick marks on its body. Perhaps it represents a spotted feline of some sort; jaguars are known to climb trees to ambush prey. The mouth of this animal is shown open, as if roaring, and it has the same kind of crest or headwear as the anthropomorph to the right.

The anthropomorph, possibly a human, is rendered in a pose suggesting action through its bent stance, leaning forward toward the tree. The splayed hands and open mouth suggest that the figure is agitated, perhaps surprised, or otherwise highly active. As the one preserved foot is also (curiously) splayed too, this may simply be the artist's style, one that represents anthropomorphs in a notably different fashion than in the other two gourds just discussed.

The complete scene was more complicated than simply that of a person confronting an animal in a tree. The figure at far right has what appears to be a belt or rope of some sort around its middle that extends outward, to the right, to intersect with a vertical line that appears to be the trunk of a tree or palm, judging by the diagonal hatched lines at the upper right edge of the gourd fragment. It may be that the person is tied to the tree and in fear of the feline in the tree and about to pounce. Two other fragments that are likely part of the original vessel were found nearby. One is a small fragment of a border of the panel, and the other is a panel edge with cross-hatched cones, probably depicting more foliage or possibly maize, extending into the interior of the frame. Neither helps to clarify the imagery or to understand what is occurring in the scene portrayed.

It is quite likely that the same person who executed the designs on the two previous examples or someone who closely followed that artisan's style carved this bowl, judging by the use of a hatched panel in which the imagery is located. The arms of the anthropomorphic figures on all three gourds are shown bent at the same angles, and the two elements extending from the base of the plant in this gourd are quite similar to imagery in the gourd shown in Figure 15.11. Although details differ, the heads of the anthropomorphs on both gourds are similar in that each is rendered by a continuous line with an indentation serving to portray both the nose and mouth.

The most striking aspect of the Magdalena de Cao decorated gourd assemblage is the great range of stylistic variation within it. As noted, above, we have no comparative example of the range of gourd styles in a single community in late prehispanic Peru, a testament to the lack of detailed publications on quotidian material culture for the period in general. The community of Magdalena de Cao was an amalgamation of different groups of people from the region, and we must also confront the issue of possible changes through time at the site that may have influenced artistic conventions.

The three cases of representational or narrative art that we have from Magdalena might have been inspired by European imagery, but there are alternative explanations. There is a strong tradition of representational art on the North Coast, as in the Moche culture of circa A.D. 350–900, which produced narrative scenes in both modeled and painted ceramics (Quilter 2010). Some of the conventions in the Magdalena gourds resemble those of Moche painted ceramics, such as the full breadth of the human torso presented to the viewer but heads shown in profile. Representational art, though highly stylized, diminished in popularity after the Moche era, although we may assume that this was due to a change in the demands of what art was supposed to convey rather than to a loss of the capability to employ the style.

How much these issues are related to the three gourds with representational depictions on them is hard to assess, and the question of whether these gourds might be the products of European influences remains open. More examples might help to clarify the issue. All three of the representational gourds likely were made relatively quickly and spontaneously. The two with scenes on them do suggest that they are depicting parts of narratives, which, again, is something known in prehistory. The tales that they depict may have been old or recent, too, and there may have been one or more artists who produced all three of the representational scenes. Indeed, the hybrid styles depicting mostly birds and fish are perhaps greater testaments to the infiltration of European-influenced artistic conventions because they seem to represent a number of different hands at work rather than the oeuvre of one or two artisans.

The use of tocapu is intriguing. If these icons had once been restricted to items used by elites, that clearly was no longer the case in the Colonial Period, by which time the poor Magdalena townsfolk felt free to use them in decorating their lowly gourd bowls. How much these designs carried specific meanings for the Magdaleneros is hard to assess, and the same holds true for the depictions of birds and fish. The decorations on the Magdalena gourds seem to be more decorative than symbolic, as likely was the case for the use of birds and fish as design elements in late prehistory as well. If the friars in the church complex were aware of these images, they apparently did not prevent their use, perhaps because of the lack of overt (at least to Spanish eyes) symbolism linked to Andean religious ideas—although we must always wonder if native peoples were deceiving their Spanish masters in regard to how significant such representations were to them.

Marked Adobes

Unfired earthen bricks, usually referred to as adobes, were literally the building blocks of ancient civilizations on the coast of Peru, and much has been written about them. They come in various sizes and styles, and researchers often use changes in the styles of adobes as chronological or cultural markers. While adobes were used as early as the Late Preceramic Period, it seems that only in the Initial Period and Early Horizon did standardized adobes become common. By Moche times, adobes on the North Coast tended to be rectangular solids, and at Huaca Cao Viejo they were made in molds constructed of cut cane. Adobes continued in use throughout the Colonial Period and into the present day, although they are currently much less frequently used than in previous eras.

Not just any earth can be used for adobes; clean, clayey soils from riverbeds are required. It is commonly stated as a truism among archaeologists that prehistoric adobes contained no straw or other binder and Colonial Period adobes did contain straw, but our research suggests that it is not as simple as this. In our studies we found that early Moche bricks, such as at the Huaca Cortada, often contain fairly significant amounts of plant fibers, so much so that the plant material appear to have been deliberately included in the clay mix. Most of the later Moche adobes at Brujo have little to no plant inclusions, and none have plant materials in quantities that would suggest straw or similar material was being added in preparing the clay.

The latest prehistoric adobes are those associated with the montículos near the colonial occupation, and they have very few plant parts in them at all.

In Colonial Period Trujillo, fired red bricks were considered a status symbol. Because fired bricks were so hard to acquire, they were used sparingly and often reserved for the entrances of the houses of the wealthy, where they were left uncovered to display the owner's wealth. In some cases adobe was carved and painted to look like fired bricks in such locations.

Some Moche and later adobes were marked while the clay was still wet, and this has drawn scholarly efforts to interpret the markings and their larger significances (e.g., Cavallaro and Shimada 1988). The most common markings are lines, indentations, or combinations of them. Variations occur in the number, shape, and direction (diagonal, horizontal, vertical) of lines and the number and placement of indentations.

Although there is an extensive literature on marked adobes, there is no consensus about what they mean. Generally, most scholars think the markings were made as a way of accounting for something—perhaps to keep track of loads of bricks contributed by a social group to the construction of a huaca, or to account for some group activity involved with the building process itself, such as the construction of a section of huaca fill.

Adobes were one of the principal construction materials for the Magdalena population at El Brujo. Like their grandparents, the Magdaleneros may have "robbed" old prehispanic buildings of adobes in good condition to reuse in their own houses. These, in turn, may have been robbed again when the Magdalena houses were abandoned, since we found many walls in our excavations that were incomplete, most likely because adobes were removed for use elsewhere.

We found many adobes in the Magdalena town houses with little to no plant materials in them, suggesting that they may be reused prehistoric bricks, and we also recovered some adobes with high straw content, seemingly following the colonial practice of adding such materials to clay in preparing bricks. We also found two examples of fired red bricks. These are of interest particularly because of the historical documentation of a Magdalena priest using funds to buy bricks for his mill instead of the church (Chapter 12). Perhaps a few fired bricks eventually found their way to the church after all.

All of the church structure was built of adobes covered with a thin layer of adobe mud to create a seamless wall surface. In some interior places, such as in the baptistry and in low sections of walls in the sanctuary area of the nave, we found a smooth white surface that served as the base for mural painting. Although we have not analyzed this material, it looks like a thin coating of plaster.

We found marked adobes in the large section of wall fall that we uncovered to the east of the nave in 2008. Many of these were in poor states of preservation (Figure 15.13). Some had curving or straight lines reminiscent of Moche marks, although not as firmly and deliberately made, and one fragment bore what appears to be the place name "Cao." Another adobe fragment bore the clear image of a Christian cross, probably made with an index finger. Because these were in a jumble of collapsed wall, we could not be certain of how they were placed in the building, but they likely were placed so that they could be viewed, not hidden, judging by the surfaces of the adobes that suggested exposure to air. The fact that the Christian cross and the word "Cao" were written on the bricks suggests that at least some Magdaleneros were active and willing participants in the life of the church and supporters of its doctrines to some degree and in some ways.

Figure 15.13
Marked adobes in
the collapsed wall
found east of the
church nave
(see Figure 2.31).

Two remarkable adobes with complex images on them also were found in the rubble of the collapsed church wall. One was marked with two undulating lines running the entire length of the brick: one line dominates the center of the brick, and the other is near the left edge (Figure 15.14, right). Seven or eight diagonal slashes subsequently were made over the undulations. Whether these marks have meanings connected to them is hard to assess.

Another brick bears markings that seem to offer opportunities for interpretation (Figure 15.14, left). Although its original orientation may be debated, if the brick is viewed as shown in Figure 15.14, the markings appear as two short diagonal incisions extending downward at similar angles but in opposite directions from the top edge of the brick. The right-hand line may be extended farther than the left and crossed by a diagonal, although these are both faint marks. More prominent are a circle and a diamond shape toward the center of the brick. The diamond has what appears to be a cross at its apex (somewhat obscured by a spall of the surface of the brick on the left). Below this is a rectangle with vertical and horizontal internal lines producing a grid design.

This brick bears some resemblance to a drawing by Juan de Santa Cruz Pachacuti Yamqui Salcamaygua, a Christianized Indian of noble descent resident in or near Cuzco. Sometime in the first two or three decades of the seventeenth century he wrote an account of Inca traditions and history (Duviols and Itier 1993). The most famous of his illustrations is a cosmogram that depicts a universe ordered on dualistic principles with the sun and moon at the top, a man and woman in the middle, and a stylized representation of agricultural fields at the bottom, with other celestial and natural images also portrayed. Although the brick likely was inscribed casually, perhaps during a break from work, it is interesting to note that the top images appear to pair the circle with what appears to be a schematic image of a church, while the rectangular grid at the bottom of the brick is strikingly similar to Santa Cruz Pachacuti's image of fields.

Painted Burial Shrouds

We found several examples of large cotton textiles painted in distinct designs. Research on these textiles is still at an early stage, and all that can be presented here are some very preliminary observations. We still need to determine the exact number in the collection, clean them, and draw the designs. Given their large sizes, photographing them is difficult, and the complexity of the imagery makes analyzing them challenging. They are worth considering here, however, because—like gourds and adobes—they seem to combine both indigenous and European artistic conventions.

Presently we have three examples of these painted textiles (Figures 15.15–15.17). Two were found in the church cemetery area and one was found as part of the wrappings of burial 3, the

Figure 15.14 The two adobes with the most elaborate markings, photographed shortly after excavation. At right, the adobe with meandering lines measures 50 cm in length and between 25 and 30 cm in width. The adobe at left measures 50 cm in length and 25 cm in width.

Figure 15.15
A section of a
painted burial
shroud. The
painting has
completely faded
from the areas
bordering the
central square
design.

woman buried in prehispanic style in the church cemetery next to the outer wall of the atrium
(Chapter 4). All are fragmentary and in poor states of preservation and all are large, well over
1 m in their maximum dimension. Given the location of the finds as well as the association
of one of them with a burial, these appear to be shrouds or winding sheets for the deceased,
though it is possible they were also used in life.

The decoration programs for the three examples we have available share common features yet also exhibit differences. One shared feature is a complete filling up of all the available
space on the textile. Another is that the designs on the cloths appear to be readable from any
angle, or at least many angles. All the textiles used a pigment that is now a brown color. All
three examples for which we have substantial sections of the original textile exhibit decorations that could have been done relatively rapidly. These tend to consist of sections or panels
within the larger expanse of the textile that are filled in with repeating motifs. It is the variation
in the kinds of motifs in each of the three textiles that is of particular interest.

The large segment of preserved decoration in painted textile 1 (Figure 15.15) is dominated
by a large square filled in with parallel diagonal stripes, each of which includes an array of projecting triangles. This central element is bounded by rectangular panels that include opposed
L-shapes formed of squares and a row of nested triangles on one side. The opposite side of the
square is less well preserved but seems to exhibit similar motifs, though not exactly the same
as the other side. To the left of the textile as shown in Figure 15.15, several different rows are in
evidence. These, however, are made to seem in the rear of foregrounded large triangular elements with multiple lines for edges and complex interior imagery.

Figure 15.16
A section of a
burial shroud
with a blue glass
bead sewn into it
(shown in inset).

Textile 2 (Figure 15.16) is similar in some ways to the first example except that it is less complex in the ordering of its elements. It is also better preserved, so the individual elements are easier to read. As shown in Figure 15.16, it consists of a lower section comprised of a comparatively wide panel of crosslike designs with radiating circles behind them. On either side of this row are rows of a truncated diamond motif followed by a row of closely spaced parallel lines. Each one of these rows is separated from the adjoining row by a pair of horizontal lines. The repetition of the truncated diamonds and parallel lines on either side of the row of crosses

Figure 15.17 A section of another painted burial shroud. The style of the volutes terminating in animal heads and tasseled triangles is identical to imagery found in art of the Lambayeque Culture, which occupied the region ca. A.D. 800–1350.

brings a sense of order to a visually dense field. The bottom section of the textile differs, however, with a row of separate squares pendant from one of the pair of horizontal lines defining the row of parallel lines above it. A blue glass bead was sewn on a thread into this textile, confirming its use in the Colonial Period (Figure 15.16, inset).

The six rows just described border the main imagery that covers the rest of the textile preserved for us. Repeating V-shapes with rounded ends, bristling with triangles on both sides, and with pendant circles at their ends dominate this larger field.

The third textile (Figure 15.17) shares the same dense imagery filling the field but differs in decoration. The scheme is complicated by the presence of what appears to be a large patch of plain or highly faded textile sewn into in the middle of the larger fragment. Below this patch, a very poorly preserved textile has diagonal bands in alternating dark and light colors with contrasting design elements within them. Above the patch is a large motif that appears to be part of a stepped image filled with sections of two or three curving designs that end in isosceles triangles, two of which have pendants of two right triangles while the third, outer triangle is raised upward, supporting what appears to be a stylized boat with a figure in it. A broad band that has an extension that bends twice to form a motif like a Greek key frames the perimeter of the stepped space containing the triangles. The bend occurs in a larger design field of repeating motifs of a stylized bird head and neck.

The large design elements in this textile are particularly interesting. Although we only have a fragment available, if the main section was a stepped motif, it links directly with a prehispanic design that was used for millennia in Peru and very likely was symbolically linked to concepts associated with sacred mountains. More certainly, the interior elements of sinuous bands ending in isosceles triangles are prehispanic in origin. They are examples of a wave motif sometimes turned into an anthropomorphic wave design. The motif first appears in late Moche art, becomes prominent in Lambayeque (A.D. 800–1350) art, and continues, though apparently with less popularity, during Chimu hegemony (see McClelland 1990:84–88).

In the Magdalena case the upper sections of the wave motif are not preserved in the textile, so we cannot know if the wave was an anthropomorphic version or not. The design is securely prehistoric in concept and execution, however, leading to questions of how it was considered by the people who incorporated it into the burial wrappings of the woman buried in the town cemetery. The fact that a piece of textile with the stepped mountain and wave motifs was inserted into the burial shroud is intriguing because it raises the question of whether this was a prehistoric piece that was recovered from some other context. If it was, then we may wonder about the degree to which the imagery and its symbolism were known and appreciated by those who put together the textile. If the textile was not a reused prehispanic cloth but made in the Colonial Period, then we may ponder these issues in a different light. Resolving these questions, however, is an elusive task.

Discussion

As noted in Chapter 13, the paper artifacts found at the site suggest that the Magdaleneros' attitudes toward writing, printing, documents, and books varied. The three media discussed here provide us with other ways to think about how European modes of communication and representation were received by at least some Andeans. The corpus of gourds includes designs done in styles that would not have been out of place centuries before the arrival of the Spaniards, other designs that are apparently hybrids of native and European styles, and a few that appear to be done in styles directly borrowed from Europeans. We are hampered because we cannot tell when these different gourds were carved during the two centuries of site occupation, but as the heyday of Magdalena was from the late sixteenth century to the mid-seventeenth century, we may tentatively assume that the gourds were carved within the few generations corresponding to that time period. It is interesting, however, to note that a scratched design on an ancient pottery vessel is identical in style to the way birds were rendered on the Magdalena gourds.

Burial M-U1412 was excavated at the site of San José de Moro in the Jequetepeque Valley (Castillo 2006:68–70). The skeleton in an earthen grave was of an adult, likely female, flexed and buried on her back with four pottery vessels, three long bones, and wooden sticks. There were fragments of unidentified animal bones, other ceramics, and textiles in the grave. A small wooden spatula, possibly used for consuming lime to activate coca, also was in her grave. This woman lived during the time of the Lambayeque Culture, circa 800–1350, and because she was buried in front of the temple (huaca) at San José de Moro she likely was a person of some prestige. But she was not a member of the elite, judging by the artifacts in her grave. One of them was a large plate or very shallow bowl, an unusual form, with a handle that had been partly broken. On the underside of this plate, off center, a figure of a bird had been scratched into the clay when the vessel was still wet (Figure 15.18).

For our purposes, this image is of interest because it features an animal that was popular in the Magdalena gourd imagery. The general style is the same in each medium with the neck,

Figure 15.18   Underside of a Lambayeque handled plate from burial M-U1412 excavated at San José de Moro in the Jequetepeque Valley. (Detail from Castillo Butters 2006:54, fig. 38)

beak, long legs, and exaggerated feet rendered as single lines. A single line forms the neck, arcs downward to form the belly of the bird, and then sweeps upward to serve as the upper side of the tail, rendered sideways from its natural angle. The lower edge of the tail is another line that crosses the upper one to define the proximal end of the tail and continues on to serve as the line that defines the bird's back. The style of the image and the technique of rendering it are the same as bird images on the Magdalena gourds, notably fragment C in Figure 15.8. In the case of both graphic and textile arts, then, we can confidently state that the artistry of many of the Magdalena gourds were expressions of a folk art style of great antiquity on the North Coast of Peru, one of several hundred years that apparently continued without change into the early Colonial Period.

In contrast to the gourds, we can safely say that the adobes were all marked within a relatively brief period of time when the church was being built, probably in the late sixteenth century. All of the markings we have found either are rather abstract designs and hard to interpret or images that partake of European culture, such as the cross and the word "Cao." It is interesting to consider that all of the images we have encountered in the adobes are European-derived or appear to be so. Whether these images indicate sincere devotions to Christianity, viewing the church positively, and referencing images and writing as European modes of communication or were done because a European gaze was upon the makers of these marks is hard to assess.

We only have three good examples of the painted burial shrouds. They are strongly indigenous in style, using old techniques of painting and following generally prehistoric stylistic conventions of filling the entire design space with small repeating images. Indeed, both the general approach and specific details of textile painting extend back from colonial Magdalena to a thousand years earlier and from poor townspeople to Moche royalty.

As in so many other aspects of the material remains from Magdalena de Cao Viejo, what is left to us includes apparently contradictory indications that the residents of the town were devout Catholics and that they were devout Andeans; that they practiced old ways of doing things, new ways of doing things, and ways of doing things that combined the old, the introduced, and the locally and recently invented. All of these are probably true, because the reactions of individuals to their circumstances were as mixed as the opinions and behaviors of people at any time and at any place. Equally interesting and perplexing is the question of how the Spanish priests and other authorities dealt with the persistence of precontact beliefs and practices. Apparently those too were complicated and mixed in the complex world that was the Early Colonial Period.

REFERENCES

Bird, Junius B.
    1963   Pre-Ceramic Art from Huaca Prieta, Chicama Valley. Ñawpa Pacha 1:29–34.

Bird, Junius B., John Hyslop, and Milica Dimitrijevic Skinner
    1985   The Preceramic Excavations at the Huaca Prieta, Chicama Valley, Peru. Anthropological Papers Vol. 62, Pt. 1. New York: American Museum of Natural History.

Castillo Butters, Luis Jaime (editor)
    2006   Programa Arqueológico San José de Moro: Informe de Excavaciones Temporada 2006. Lima: Pontificia Universidad Católica del Perú.

Cavallaro, Raffael, and Izumi Shimada
    1988   Some Thoughts on Sican Marked Adobes and Labor Organization. American Antiquity 53(1):75–101.

Cummins, Thomas B. F.
    2002   Toasts with the Inca: Andean Abstraction and Colonial Images on Quero Vessels. Ann Arbor: University of Michigan Press.
    2011   Tocapu, What Is It, What Does It Do, and Why Is It Not a Knot? In Their Way of Writing: Scripts, Signs, and Pictographies in Pre-Columbian America, edited by Elizabeth Hill Boone and Gary Urton, pp. 277–317. Washington, DC: Dumbarton Oaks Research Library and Collection.

Dillehay, Tom D. (editor)
    2017   Where the Land Meets the Sea: Fourteen Millennia of Human History at Huaca Prieta, Peru. Austin: University of Texas Press.

Dillehay, Tom D., and Duccio Bonavia

    2017   Nontextile and Nonbasketry Material Culture. In *Where the Land Meets the Sea: Fourteen Millennia of Human History at Huaca Prieta, Peru,* edited by Tom D. Dillehay, pp. 434–457. Austin: University of Texas Press.

Duviols, Pierre, and César Itier (editors)

    1993   *Relación de las antigüedades deste reyno del Pirú.* Lima: Institut Français d'Etudes Andines.

Erickson, David L., Bruce D. Smith, Andrew C. Clarke, Daniel H. Sandweiss, and Noreen Tuross

    2005   An Asian Origin for a 10,000-Year-Old Domesticated Plant in the Americas. *PNAS* 102(51):18315–18320.

Lathrap, Donald W.

    1980   *Ancient Ecuador—Culture, Clay and Creativity, 3000–300 B.C.* Chicago: Field Museum of Natural History.

McClelland, Donna

    1990   A Maritime Passage from Moche to Chimu. In *The Northern Dynasties: Kingship and Statecraft in Chimor,* edited by Michael E. Moseley and Alan Cordy-Collins, pp. 75–106. Washington, DC: Dumbarton Oaks Research Library and Collection.

Quilter, Jeffrey

    2010   *The Moche of Ancient Peru: Media and Messages.* Peabody Museum Collections Series. Cambridge, MA: Peabody Museum Press.

Rowe, Ann Pollard

    1996   All-*T'oqapu* Tunic. In *Andean Art at Dumbarton Oaks*, vol. 2, edited by Elizabeth Hill Boone, pp. 457–465. Washington, DC: Dumbarton Oaks Research Library and Collection.

Rowe, John H.

    1979   Standardization in Inca Tapestry Tunics. In *The Junius B. Bird Pre-Columbian Textile Conference,* edited by Anne Pollard Rowe, Elizabeth P. Benson, and Anne-Louise Shaffer, pp. 239–264. Washington, DC: Textile Museum and Dumbarton Oaks.

Vergara Montero, Enrique

    2015   *Mates: Corpus Iconográfico Perú Prehispánico.* Lima: Imprente Gami.

16

Concluding Thoughts

Jeffrey Quilter

I N GRAPPLING WITH the issue of how to present some concluding thoughts at the end of this book, I decided that the only way I can effectively do so is by offering some personal reflections on issues that are explicitly or implicitly addressed in this tome. I begin by admitting that I came to this Colonial Period site with some ambivalence. I was one of those archaeologists who liked the "pure play" of past indigenous cultures "untainted" by European or any other influences. I was not alone in this view. A distinguished Peruvian archaeologist said to me as I was starting the Magdalena project, "Well, you know, Jeffrey, in Peru when we say 'archaeology' we mean *prehistoric* archaeology." That statement fed into my insecurities as to whether I was making a good choice for my interests and my career.

I decided to commit myself to excavating Magdalena de Cao Viejo (Figure 16.1) for two reasons, one practical and one theoretical. The practical reason was that Moche archaeology was well in hand at El Brujo. The Peruvian archaeologists were doing a fine job of excavating one of the major Moche temples at the site, Huaca Cao Viejo, and I did not see a role for me to play in that. I had already done some Moche archaeology anyhow. I had excavated around one of the ceremonial wells (Quilter et al. 2012) and also had helped to discover the Señora de Cao, the burial of a high-status woman found at the Huaca Cao Viejo. There were other Moche sites on the terrace, of course, as well as spectacular sites of other periods, and I contemplated excavating one of those instead.

The other reason that swayed me to dig in the colonial sector at El Brujo related to my experiences at Dumbarton Oaks (D.O.) when I was director of the Pre-Columbian Studies Program there, from 1995 to 2005. In fact, I began the work at Magdalena in 2004, while still in that role. I had hosted a wide range of scholars who studied cultures from Mexico to Chile. The Pre-Columbian Studies Program at D.O. tends to emphasize the more humanistic end of the research spectrum. While it does support some work that is more scientifically oriented, most of the scholars who use the institution's outstanding library and other resources tend to be art historians, historians, and archaeologists whose research interests focus on ritual, religion, and the arts rather than on soils and bone chemistry.

As I watched scholars troop in and out of D.O. and heard their offhand comments as well as formal talks, I got the overwhelming message of a sense of superiority among those who

Figure 16.1 Magdalena de Cao under excavation in 2007. The buildings at the foot of the Huaca Cao Viejo have since been replaced with a site museum, laboratories, and offices.

worked with documents—the historians and ethnohistorians. Granted, the Pre-Columbian Studies Program at D.O. did not generally support strictly Colonial Period projects, but those that drew upon written records in order to investigate prehistory as well as research on the New World society with the most elaborate written language, the Maya, seemed to get special attention and adulation from scholars, librarians, and other interested parties in the D.O. community and beyond.

This annoyed me, because I believe in the power of objects as tellers of stories, as sources of information as well as things we can appreciate aesthetically. Archaeology deals with artifacts, which do not yield their stories easily, but I was and remain a firm believer that they have interesting and important stories to tell. The challenge to anyone who attempts to learn those stories is to develop ways to hear them. Archaeologists and fellow travelers have employed a wide variety of methods to extract those stories, from statistics and flow charts at one extreme to near-séance-like attempts at communication at the other.

Every so often, there is a rise in academic concern over the "New Materialism," with scholars hailing a new era in which objects will be the focus of new ways to learn about the world. The *Journal of Material Culture*, first published in 1996 and still going strong, focuses on objects, yet the overwhelming majority of articles in that most valued journal tend to rely on texts to anchor discussions of the material world. The most recent voice for object-based research, Alfred Gell (1998), proposed an ambitious and promising project to engage with objects as active social agents, but the examples he used to promote his ideas all had links to written or oral sources to help explain them. His project was cut short by his untimely death, and it would have been interesting to see how far his proposed approach might have gone.

Perhaps it is my "pure play" nature at work, but I have been interested in exploring how we can get objects to speak to us when they have few to no ties with written or oral sources. This is one of the main reasons I have been attracted to the Moche, a highly complex ancient culture with sophisticated art and engineering but with no written language and remote enough in prehistory that few ethnographic or historical sources can be tied to them. What can we learn about them solely through studying their remains?

It was in this spirit that I decided that excavating the ruins of Magdalena de Cao at El Brujo might be a very interesting project. One trend among art historians is a drift toward Colonial Period topics. There actually are very few of them who stay with strictly precolumbian topics throughout their careers. I suppose the lure of the written sources associated with the objects they study is too strong to resist. So here was a case in which archaeology could serve as a counternarrative to history and art history. Excavating Magdalena de Cao would offer an opportunity to see what archaeology alone could say about a period much beloved by those other scholars. That is one of the main reasons I decided to excavate at the site. And then, of course, I wound up excavating documents.

It was those fragments of handwritten letters, musical scores, and notes and the pieces of printed books and indulgences that helped win the substantial grants funding the project. The discovery and analysis of the letter with the word list on the back (Figure 13.11) attracted great attention and secured a spot in *American Anthropologist*, the leading journal of my discipline (Quilter et al. 2010). The paper fragments certainly added an important extra dimension to our understanding of the site. While I had to chuckle at the fact that my attempt to find a purely archaeological project for the Colonial Period had been foiled, I also was happy to accept this unexpected source of information. In short, I yielded to the power of the written word, even if it came in fragments.

Yet at the same time, considering these documents has given me some insights into studying the past. And the great amount of information on Magdalena that Rocío Delibes (Chapter 12) has so skillfully found in archives has offered me a chance to reconsider my work: what would archaeology tell us compared to the stories from documents? Once I started finding the paper artifacts, I couldn't ignore them, and having both them and Delibes's work available offers opportunities to consider how these different modes of investigation do or don't inform each other, and how they might or might not combine to create a richer understanding.

Perhaps other sites and situations would be different, but my sense of the relationship of the archaeology and historical research on Magdalena de Cao is that they tell different stories that sometimes enrich each other. We would never know of Don Vicente de Mora Chimo's travails in Madrid, far from his homeland, without the written record; likewise, without the artifacts it is highly unlikely that we would have an inkling about the real attitudes of indigenous inhabitants of Cao toward documents (expressed by using them as everything from toilet paper to cutouts) or their use of both traditional Andean motifs and European conventions in decorating gourds. This insight is not particularly new or revelatory to many current scholars, but it has made an impression on me. Because most documents tend to be written by authorities in power about large issues in their world, they give us a picture of a different scale than artifacts do. The residues and lost items of everyday life that archaeologists tend to work with tell us smaller tales, the "small things forgotten," of James Deetz (1997).

Of course, it is worth emphasizing that the "big story versus little story" contrast between historical research and archaeology has many exceptions. Sarah Quilter (Chapter 14) found valuable information from texts about Spanish cards and card playing that enriched her study. Some of the metal objects that Andrew Lorey (Chapter 10) and I examined may have been imported from Spain or elsewhere, the Chinese porcelains clearly were imports; these objects can tell us about long-distance trade patterns and economic exchanges, giving us insights into how the poor indigenous Cao townspeople were swept into the great global system of early capitalism, a Chinese teacup in one hand and an indulgence in the other.

I arranged this book to focus on the artifacts. Whatever new theoretical trends may come and go in ensuing years, the artifacts will remain sources of data and inspiration. And one might consider how Chapter 12, the historical account, works in conjunction with the artifact chapters to give this book something of a dualistic layout, in keeping with an Andean tradition. As noted at the beginning of this book, while there is an extensive presentation of Magdalena artifacts here, there is much more to be offered and studied in publications, websites, and other media. As but one small example, the issue of footwear still remains to be addressed (Figure 16.2).

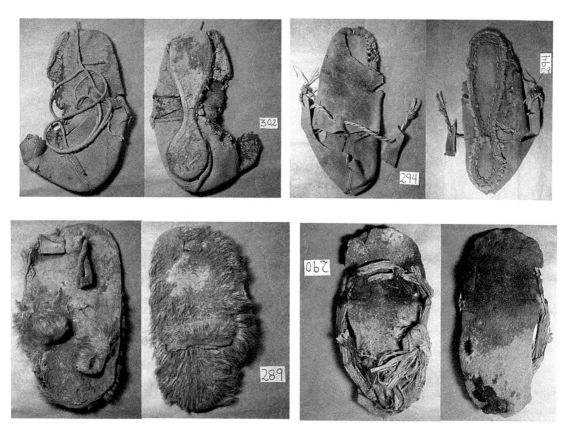

Figure 16.2   Work to be done: four examples of footwear (tops and soles) from more than a dozen found at the site.

As noted at the beginning of this book, the website for the Magdalena de Cao project (https://www.peabody.harvard.edu/Magdalena) can crowdsource identifications for many of the objects that were found during work at Magdalena that could not be presented in this book for lack of space or that are simply hard to identify, such as fragments of paper documents or the more peculiar metal object parts. The project already has found not only the remains of some of the earliest examples of cigarettes but also the first known examples of what may be the Quingnam language, the earliest physical remains of an African in South America, and one of the largest collections of quotidian Colonial Period clothing, among other finds. Engaging the help of a world community on the Web very likely will reveal more discoveries.

Since my attention was first drawn to the colonial sector at the end of the 2004 field season, there has been an impressive growth of interest and research in Colonial Period archaeology in Peru. The result has been a series of publications that include books (e.g., Wernke 2013), edited volumes (Traslaviña et al. 2016), and articles on special topics (deFrance et al. 2016; Kelloway 2018; VanValkenburgh et al. 2017; Weaver 2012). Andean archaeology is often (for reasons too complicated to discuss here) not included in compendiums on global issues, but the exciting research on the Colonial Period may finally mean that it will be more integrated into such discussions (e.g., Liebmann and Murphy 2010).

And somewhere along the way, I was converted; the Colonial Period in Peru and elsewhere now fascinates me. It was not an easy time—indeed, it was a time of tragedy for many—but it is a fascinating one. In the decade and a half since I began the Magdalena project it has become increasingly clear to me that there never was a "pure play" anywhere. Cultures and peoples were always mixing it up with other peoples and different ideas. Even in remote antiquity, something new was around the corner, frequently terrifying and occasionally wonderful. There was never unanimity about anything: there were as many contrarian Moche who didn't believe that those people dressed as gods and standing on the temple tops could control anything as there were congregants in the Magdalena church dubious about salvation or freeing the Holy Land from the Moors. It is the richness and diversity of everyday life as well as the grand sweep of historical narratives that make the study of the past so interesting and help us to try to comprehend and perhaps even endure our own tumultuous times.

REFERENCES CITED

Deetz, James
  1997 *In Small Things Forgotten: The Archaeology of Early American Life.* New York: Random House.

deFrance, Susan D. Steven A. Wernke, and Ashley E. Sharpe
  2016 Analysis of Faunal Remains from an Early Spanish Colonial Doctrinal Settlement in Highland Peru. *Latin American Antiquity* 27(3):300–317.

Gell, Alfred
  1998 *Art and Agency: An Anthropological Theory.* Oxford: Oxford University Press.

Kelloway, Sarah J., Parker VanValkenburgh, Javier G. Iñañez, Laure Dussubieux, Jeffrey Quilter, and Michael D. Glascock
  2018 Identifying New World Majolica from 16th–18th Century Sites on Peru's North Coast. *Journal of Archaeological Science: Reports* 17:311–324.

Liebmann, Matthew, and Melissa S. Murphy

2010 *Enduring Conquests: Rethinking the Archaeology of Resistance to Spanish Colonialism in the Americas.* Santa Fe, NM: School for Advanced Research Press.

Quilter, Jeffrey, Régulo Franco Jordán, César Gálvez Mora, William Doonan, Catherine Gaither, Victor Vásquez Sánchez, Teresa Rosales Tham, Jaime Jiménez Saldaña, Hal Starratt, and Michele L. Koons

2012 The Well and the Huaca: Ceremony, Chronology, and Culture Change at Huaca Cao Viejo, Chicama Valley, Peru. *Andean Past* 10:101–131.

Quilter, Jeffrey, Marc Zender, Karen Spalding, Régulo Franco Jordán, César Gálvez, and Juan Castañeda Murga

2010 Traces of a Lost Language and Number System Discovered on the North Coast of Peru. *American Anthropologist* 112(3):357–369.

Traslaviña, Abel, Zachary Chase, Parker VanValkenburgh, and Brendan J. M. Weaver (editors)

2016 Arqueología histórica en el Perú (primero y segunda partes). *Boletín de Arqueología PUCP,* Nos. 20 and 21. Lima: Fondo Editorial Pontificia Universidad Católica del Perú.

VanValkenburgh, Parker, Sarah J. Kelloway, Karen L. Privat, Bill Sillar, and Jeffrey Quilter

2017 Rethinking Cultural Hybridity and Technology Transfer: SEM Microstructural Analysis of Lead Glazed Ceramics from Early Colonial Peru. *Journal of Archaeological Science* 82:17–30.

Weaver, Brendan J. M.

2012 Perspectivas para el desarrollo de una arqueología de la diáspora africana en el Perú: resultados preliminarios del Proyecto Arqueológico Haciendas de Nasca. *Allpanchis* 43(80):85–120.

Volume Appendix
Correlation of Magdalena Project Artifact Numbers with Proyecto Arqueológico Complejo El Brujo (PACEB) Numbers

Jeffrey Quilter

Research on the artifacts recovered from Magdalena de Cao Viejo began shortly after they were excavated and continued as work proceeded. Magdalena project members created a numbering system for artifacts so that they could be referred to in publications; subsequently, Peruvian archaeologists at El Brujo numbered some of the same artifacts using a different system. In addition, some artifacts were never given specific numbers by one team or the other, although all retain field numbers and other information available in tags and other data sources in the collections stored at the Museo de Cao at the El Brujo Complex. Continuing work will rectify this situation, providing catalogue numbers for all artifacts.

The following list provides the Magdalena project numbers, the El Brujo numbers, or both as available. The list is incomplete, and it is hoped that a full accounting of all artifact numbers will be available in the future on the project website (https://www.peabody.harvard.edu/Magdalena).

The following list is organized by book chapter. The figure number in which the artifact is shown is given, followed by the Magdalena number and the PACEB number.

FIGURE NUMBER (MAGDALENA NUMBER)	PACEB NUMBER
Figure 3.3	PACEB_E1_173
Figure 7.1	PACEB_D1_0028
Figure 7.2 (both strings of beads)	PACEB_F6_00053
Figure 7.3A	PACEB_F6_55
Figure 7.3B	PACEB_F6_56
Figure 7.3 C	PACEB_F6_59
Figure 7.3 D	PACEB_F6_66
Figure 7.3 E	PACEB_F6_70
Figure 7.3 F	PACEB_F6_58
Figure 7.3 G	PACEB_F6_65
Figure 7.3 H	PACEB_F6_72
Figure 7.3 I	PACEB_F6_63
Figure 7.3 J	PACEB_F6_77
Figure 7.3 K	PACEB_F6_61
Figure 7.3 L	PACEB_F6_64
Figure 7.3 M	PACEB_F6_67
Figure 7.3 N	PACEB_F6_76
Figure 7.3 O	PACEB_F6_73
Figure 7.3 P	PACEB_F6_68

(continued)

FIGURE NUMBER (MAGDALENA NUMBER)	PACEB NUMBER
Figure 7.3 Q	PACEB_F6_74
Figure 7.3 R	PACEB_F6_69
Figure 7.3 S	PACEB_F6_78
Figure 7.3 T	PACEB_F6_79
Figure 7.3 U	PACEB_F6_75
Figure 7.3 V	PACEB_F6_60
Figure 7.3 W	PACEB_F6_62
Figure 7.3 X	PACEB_F6_71
Figure 7.3 Y	PACEB_F6_54
Figure 7.3 Z	PACEB_F6_57
Figure 7.3 AA	PACEB_D1_31
Figure 7.3 BB	PACEB_D1_32
Figure 7.3 CC	Not catalogued
Figure 7.3 DD	Not catalogued
Figure 7.3 EE, left	PACEB_D1_30
Figure 7.3 FF, center	PACEB_D1_29
Figure 7.3 FF, right	Not catalogued
Figure 8.1 E	PACEB_F1_062
Figure 9.6	PACEB_F1_0261
Figure 9.17	PACEB_F1_0260
Figure 9.22	PACEB_F1_0259
Figure 10.1 (05-M-02)	PACEB_F4_0118
Figure 10.1 (07-M-07)	PACEB_F4_0126
Figure 10.1 (05-M-06)	PACEB_F4_0119
Figure 10.1 (05-M-05)	PACEB_F4_0120
Figure 10.1 (07-M-14)	PACEB_F4_0132
Figure 10.1 (07-M-08)	PACEB_F4_0127
Figure 10.2 (07-M-05)	PACEB_F4_0123
Figure 10.2 (07-M-01)	PACEB_F4_0122
Figure 10.2 (06-M-02)	PACEB_F4_0102
Figure 10.3 (07-M-06)	PACEB_F4_105
Figure 10.3 (07-M-32)	PACEB_F4_107
Figure 10.3 (07-M-02)	PACEB_F4_106
Figure 10.3 (07-M-36)	PACEB_F4_096
Figure 10.3 (07-M-09)	PACEB_F4_133
Figure 10.3 (08-M-36)	PACEB_F4_094
Figure 10.3 (08-M-37)	PACEB_F4_095
Figure 10.3 (06-M-09)	PACEB_F4_101

FIGURE NUMBER (MAGDALENA NUMBER)	PACEB NUMBER
Figure 10.3 (13-M-01)	Not catalogued
Figure 10.3 (13-M-02)	Not catalogued
Figure 10.4 (12-M-01)	PACEB_F4_135
Figure 10.4 (07-M-06)	PACEB_F4_124
Figure 10.4 (05-M-09)	PACEB_F4_100
Figure 10.4 (08-M-02)	PACEB_F4_113
Figure 10.5 (06-M-05)	PACEB_F4_121
Figure 10.5 (08-M-28)	PACEB_F4_128
Figure 10.6 (06-M-04)	PACEB_F4_129
Figure 10.7 (08-M-34)	PACEB_F4_130
Figure 10.8 (08-M-25)	PACEB_F4_117
Figure 10.9 (08-M-06)	Not catalogued
Figure 10.9 (06-M-13)	PACEB_F4_115
Figure 10.9 (06-M-03)	PACEB_F4_131
Figure 10.9 (08-M-01)	PACEB_F4_113
Figure 10.9. (07-M-03)	PACEB_F4_124
Figure 10.9 (07-M-04)	PACEB_F4_104
Figure 10.11 (07-M-37)	PACEB_D1_022
Figure 10.12 (08-M-03)	PACEB_4_114
Figure 10.13, left (07-M-35A)	PACEB_F4_111
Figure 10.13, center (07-M-35B)	PACEB_F4_110
Figure 10.13, right (07-M-34C)	PACEB_F4_109
Figure 10.14 (12-M-06)	PACEB_F4_134
Figure 10.15 (06-M-01)	PACEB_F_103
Figure 10.16 (07-M-31)	PACEB_F4_108
Figure 10.17 (08-M-37)	PACEB_F4_095
Figure 10.17 (08-M-36)	PACEB_F4_094
Figure 10.18 (08-M-15)	PACEB_F4_112
Figure 11.1	PACEB_F4_136
Figure 11.2	PACEB_F4_137
Figure 13.1	PACEB_E3_005
Figure 13.2	PACEB_E3_014
Figure 13.3	PACEB_E3_012
Figure 13.4	PACEB_E3_006
Figure 13.5	PACEB_E3_025
Figure 13.6	PACEB_E3_045
Figure 13.7	PACEB_E3_015

(*continued*)

FIGURE NUMBER (MAGDALENA NUMBER)	PACEB NUMBER
Figure 13.8	PACEB_E3_009
Figure 13.9	PACEB_E3_040
Figure 13.10, upper left	PACEB_E3_026
Figure 13.10, upper right	PACEB_E3_035
Figure 13.10, bottom	Not catalogued
Figure 13.11	PACEB_E3_013
Figure 13.12, upper left	PACEB_E3_046
Figure 13.12, middle left	PACEB_E3_036
Figure 13.12, lower left	PACEB_E3_039
Figure 13.12, upper right	Not catalogued
Figure 13.12, middle right	PACEB_E3_037
Figure 13.12, lower right	PACEB_E3_048
Figure 13.13, top	PACEB_E3_027
Figure 13.13, others	Not catalogued
Figure 13.14, top left	PACEB_E3_031
Figure 13.14, top right	PACEB_E3_030
Figure 13.14, lower left	Not catalogued
Figure 13.14, middle left	PACEB_E3_032
Figure 13.14, middle right	PACEB_E3_033
Figure 13.14, far right	PACEB_E3_034
Figure 13.15	PACEB_E3_029
Figure 13.16, top left	Not catalogued
Figure 13.16, top right	PACEB_E3_028
Figure 13.16, middle	PACEB_E3_052
Figure 13.16, bottom	PACEB-E3_038
Figure 13.17, top left	PACEB_E3_021
Figure 13.17, top right	PACEB_E3_022
Figure 13.17, lower left	PACEB_E3_023
Figure 13.17, lower right	PACEB_E3_024
Figure 13.18	PACEB_E3_044
Figure 13.19	PACEB_E3_002
Figure 14.2A	PACEB_E3_016
Figure 14.2B	PACEB_E3_020
Figure 14.2C	PACEB_E3_050
Figure 14.2D	PACEB_E3_018
Figure 14.2E	PACEB_E3_019
Figure 14.2F	PACEB_E3_017
Figure 14.3	PACEB_E3_041

Volume Appendix *continued*

FIGURE NUMBER (MAGDALENA NUMBER)	PACEB NUMBER
Figure 14.4A	PACEB_E3_043
Figure 14.4B	PACEB_E3_054
Figure 14.4C	PACEB_E3_042
Figure 14.4D	PACEB_E3_053
Figure 14.15	PACEB_E3_047
Figure 14.6	PACEB_E3_011
Figure 15.3	PACEB_E3_143
Figure 15.4 A	PACEB_E1_156
Figure 15.4 B	PACEB_E1_168
Figure 15.4 C	PACEB_E1_160
Figure 15.4 D	PACEB_E1_158
Figure 15.4 E	PACEB_E1_159
Figure 15.4 F	PACEB_E1_144
Figure 15.4 G	PACEB_E1_155
Figure 15.4 H	PACEB_E1_152
Figure 15.4 I	PACEB_E1_153
Figure 15.15	PACEB_E1_171
Figure 15.6 A	PACEB_E1_147
Figure 15.6 B	PACEB_E1_148
Figure 15.6 C	PACEB_E1_157
Figure 15.6 D	PACEB_E1_146
Figure 15.7 A	PACEB_E1_164
Figure 15.7 B	PACEB_E1_149
Figure 15.7 C	PACEB_E1_165
Figure 15.7 D	PACEB_E1_172
Figure 15.7 E	PACEB_E1_169
Figure 15.7 F	PACEB_E1_154
Figure 15.8 A	Not catalogued
Figure 15.8 B	PACEB_E1_166
Figure 15.8 C	PACEB_E1_167
Figure 15.9	PACEB_E1_163
Figure 15.10	PACEB_E1_162
Figure 15.11	PACEB_E1_013
Figure 15.12	PACEB_E1_170

Contributors

CARRIE BREZINE conducted the research for her chapter while a graduate student in the Department of Anthropology at Harvard University. Much of her doctoral dissertation (2011) was based on the Magdalena textile collection. She is currently an independent scholar.

NICHOLAS E. BROWN is a Ph.D. candidate in the Department of Anthropology at Yale University, specializing in early Andean prehistory, at the time of the publication of this book.

RICHARD L. BURGER holds the Charles J. MacCurdy Professorship of Anthropology at Yale University. His research has focused on early Andean civilization, long-distance exchange, and the Incas, and he also has a lifetime interest in numismatics.

BRENDAN J. CULLETON was a postdoc in the Department of Anthropology at the Pennsylvania State University during the time of most of the work at Magdalena de Cao. He is currently a research associate in the Institutes of Energy and the Environment at Penn State, where he runs the Accelerator Mass Spectrometer Radiocarbon Laboratory.

ROCÍO DELIBES MATEOS joined the Magdalena project while a postdoctoral Fulbright fellow at Harvard University. She is currently a professor in the Department of the History of America at the University of Seville, Spain.

RÉGULO FRANCO JORDÁN was director of the El Brujo Archaeological Program for much of the work presented in this book. He is currently director of the Brujo Complex Archaeological Project and the Museo de Cao (Proyecto Arqueológico Complejo El Brujo–Museo de Cao), posts supported by the Fundacíon Wiese.

CATHERINE M. GAITHER was a faculty member at Metropolitan State University of Denver, Colorado, from 2002 to 2015. She currently serves as an online anthropology instructor for Upper Iowa University and consultant in forensic anthropology from her home in Costa Rica.

DOUGLAS J. KENNETT was at the University of Oregon (2001–2011) and Pennsylvania State University (2011–2019) during the Magdalena research. He is currently professor of Environmental Archaeology in the Department of Anthropology at the University of California, Santa Barbara.

JOHN KRIGBAUM is an associate professor in the Department of Anthropology at the University of Florida, Gainesville.

CECIL M. LEWIS, JR. is professor in the Department of Anthropology and co-director of the Laboratories of Molecular Anthropology and Human Microbiome Research at the University of Oklahoma.

ANDREW Z. LOREY analyzed the metals assemblage at Magdalena de Cao Viejo after completing a bachelor's degree in anthropology at Harvard University. He has since earned a master's degree from the University of Cambridge and worked in the Anthropology Department at Bernice Pauahi Bishop Museum.

ALEXANDER MENAKER joined the Magdalena de Cao research team while conducting M.A. research at the University of Chicago on beads in the Spanish Colonial Andes. At the time of the publication of this book he is a Ph.D. candidate in the Department of Anthropology, University of Texas, Austin.

MELISSA S. MURPHY collaborated with Catherine Gaither in the data collection and bioarchaeological analysis of the human remains at Magdalena de Cao Viejo beginning in 2008. She is currently an associate professor of Anthropology and the director of Graduate Studies in Anthropology at the University of Wyoming.

GEORGE H. PERRY is an associate professor of Anthropology and Biology at the Pennsylvania State University.

JEFFREY QUILTER began work at Magdalena while serving as director of Pre-Columbian Studies at Dumbarton Oaks, Washington, D.C., and continued at Harvard University, where he served as the William and Muriel Seabury Howells Director of the Peabody Museum of Archaeology and Ethnology (2012–2019) and is now a Research Associate of the museum.

SARAH MCANULTY QUILTER began work as a crew member on the Magdalena project in 2005, processing the paper artifacts as a research associate of the Peabody Museum, Harvard University.

JENNIFER RINGBERG had just completed her Ph.D. at University of North Carolina, Chapel Hill when she joined the Magdalena Project (2012–2013). She is now a lecturer in Anthropology and director of the Minor in Latin American Studies at California State University, Stanislaus.

TERESA ROSALES THAM is co-director of ARQUEBIOS, an independent laboratory for the investigation of Andean archaeobiology and paleoecology in Trujillo, Peru.

KAREN SPALDING was professor in the History Department of the University of Connecticut during the early stages of research at Magdalena. She is now retired.

RAUL Y. TITO is currently a postdoctoral fellow at VIB, Center for Microbiology, Belgium, and research affiliate of the Laboratories of Molecular Anthropology and Human Microbiome Research at the University of Oklahoma.

PARKER VANVALKENBURGH is assistant professor of Anthropology at Brown University and director of the Brown Digital Archaeology Laboratory, as well as the Proyecto Arqueológico Zaña Colonial and the Paisajes Arqueológicos de Chachapoyas project.

VICTOR VÁSQUEZ SÁNCHEZ is director of ARQUEBIOS, an independent laboratory for the investigation of Andean archaeobiology and paleoecology in Trujillo, Peru.

Illustration Credits

Unless otherwise noted, all photographs in this volume are by Jeffrey Quilter and copyright © President and Fellows of Harvard College.

Figure 1.1.	Copyright © the Board of Trustees of the Leland Stanford Jr. University. All rights reserved. Used by permission of the publisher, Stanford University Press, sup.org.
Figure. 2.2.	Courtesy of Jefa Institucional, Archivo General de la Nación, Colección Antonio Raimondi, Perú.
Figure 2.14.	Courtesy of Luis Jaime Castillo Butters and the San José de Moro Archaeological Project, Peru.
Figure 3.4.	Copyright © and Courtesy of Gabriel Prieto.
Figures 4.4 through 4.12.	Photographs by Catherine Gaither and copyright © Catherine Gather.
Figure 5.1.	Photograph by Catherine Gaither and copyright © Catherine Gaither.
Figures 5.4.	Copyright © Patrimonio Nacional de España.
Figure 6.11.	Copyright © Patrimonio Nacional de España.
Figure 9.1.	Copyright © Patrimonio Nacional de España.
Figure 10.12.	Courtesy of the Peabody Museum of Archaeology and Ethnology, Harvard University, PM 39-83-30/1877.
Figure 10.19.	Copyright © Patrimonio Nacional de España.
Figures 11.1, 11.2, and 11.6.	Courtesy of Fundación Wiese.
Figure 11.4.	Photograph by Richard Burger and copyright © Richard Burger.
Figure 12.2.	Courtesy of the John Carter Brown Library at Brown University.
Chapter 13.	All photographs by Meredith Keffer and copyright © Meredith Keffer.
Figure 14.1.	Courtesy of the Peabody Museum of Archaeology and Ethnology, Harvard University, PM 75-20-30/8385.
Figure 14.8.	Courtesy of the Museo de Arqueología Josefina Ramos de Cox, Instituto Riva-Agüero, Pontificia Universidad Católica del Perú.
Figure 14.9.	Courtesy of the Royal Danish Library, GKS 2232 42 ["quarto"]: Guaman Poma, Nueva Corónica y Buen Gobierno (1615).
Figure 15.18.	Courtesy of the Museo de Arqueología Josefina Ramos de Cox, Instituto Riva-Agüero, Pontificia Universidad Católica del Peru.

Index

Page numbers in **boldface** refer to illustrations.

A

achira, 70. *See also* foodways

adobe: altarlike construction, 45, **45**; baulks, 96, **97**; bricks, marked, 57, **58**, 416–418, **418**, **419**, 424–425; bricks, reuse of, 417; bricks of collapsed walls, 65–66, 69; deterioration of, 74n5; Early Horizon use, 416; grinding platform, 64–65, **65**; heat-reddened floor, **63**, **64**, 66; hide-processing bin, 55; long bench, 63, **63**, **64**; melted, 38–39, 92; production of, 416–417. *See also* walls, adobe; walls, *quincha*

African cranium: background, 121–122, 147; chart of light isotope analysis of Magdalena and other burials, **152**; dating of, 149–150; dental calculus analyses, 100, 155; genetics, 150–151; isotope analyses, 151–154; macroscopic analysis, 147–148; radiocarbon date for the cranium compared to the timing of slave importation to Peru, **149**; summary and discussion, 155–157, 431; views of, **148**. *See also* Africans; burial analyses; burials

Africans: in Barbados, 153; in Chicama Valley, 147, 157, 329–330; in colonial Mauritius, 378; escaped slaves (*cimarrones*), 329; games of (*mancala*), 394; in New World, 147, 155, **156**, 157. *See also* African cranium

Aguero, Nicolás de, 361

Alfonso X, 384

Almagro, Diego de, 1

Alonso "El Cuchara," 329

AMS Laboratory of the University of Arizona, 373

Ancient DNA Laboratory, University of Oklahoma, 150–151

Andean culture: beads, 189–191; beginnings, 2; clothing, 163–164, 166–167, **168**, **172**, 175, **176**, **177**, 181; cranial modification, 112, 119, 129, 132; design concepts, symmetry dualism, 294; designs, butterfly adornments, 370; designs, gourd decoration, 401–402; designs, wave motif, 422–423; games and game playing, 393–396; hierarchical classifications, 318–319; metals, 279, 290–291, 292, **294**, 297; money, adoption of, 313; mortuary practices, 55, **55**, 114, 127–128; political organization, 318–320; visits to ancestors, 373. *See also chicha* (maize beer); Chimú; foodways; Inca; Lambayeque; Moche; religion, indigenous

animal remains studies: animal and plant remains found (table 3.1), 82–86; in ash analyses, 97; birds, 85, 89, 94, 102; camelids, 89; cattle, 89, 101–102; church–town differences, 89, 258; column samples, 92; column samples, details, 94; details, 82–85; distortion of remains, 81; domesticated, 89–90, 101–102; faunal and plant remains from a column sample in Magdalena town (table 3.3), 94–95; fish, 84, 89, **90**, 94, 95, 97, 102; goats/sheep, 89–90, 96, 101, 101–102, 104, 105n1, 155; Guanay cormorants, 89; introduced species, 85, 89, 94, 101–102, 103; mammals, 85, 89, 94; percentages of animal remains in Magdalena church and town (table 3.2), 89; plant and animal remains from ashes in Unit 28 (table 3.4), 98; shellfish, 82–84, 86–89, 92–94, 95, 96, 97, 101. *See also* animals, raised; food remains; foodways; plant remains studies

animals, raised: cattle, 9, 320–321, 329, 331–332, 337n40; *ganado* (domestic animal), 333, 337n40; goats/sheep, 9, 59, 60, 69, 72, 73, 327, 331–332, 335; horses, 9, 280–281, **281**, 331–332; mules, 226, 263, 323, 330, 331–332; sheep, 9, 331

Antonio, Juan, 331

Aparicio, Alina, 391

Arab lands, games imported from, 384

archaeology: of Colonial Period, 29, 431; of Moche culture, 427, 429; shortcomings of, 155; and written history, 427–430

Arqueobios laboratory, 70, 81, 155

Ascope (town), 8

Ascope Aqueduct, 10

ashes: in food preparation area (Unit 28), 96–97, **97**; in inverted bowls, 52, **52**, 199, 203

Aspero (town), 190

Atahualpa, 1, 190

Atocha (Spanish galleon), 303

Aveggio, Marco, 27

Aymara language, trilingual confessionary, 363–364, **363**

Aztec: games, 396; paper art, 370

B

Baker, Brenda J., 132

Bandelier, Adolph, 361

baptistry (Unit 8): exterior western wall, 54, 79, 352, 386, 388, **388**; interior, 46–47, **47**, **48**, 75n9, 352, 417; photo montage, **71**. *See also* church; church compound

Barbados, 153

baskets, 80

baulks: church, 46, **63**, 64; town, 96, **97**

beads: analysis criteria, 193–194, 205n5; Andean, 189–191; bone, 190; as chronological indices, 199; in church, 108, 114, 194–196, 204; glass, in ashes, 52, **52**, 199, 203; glass, chevron style, 192–193, 194, 195, 196, 197, 199; glass, drawn cane and wire-wound, **199**; glass, gooseberry, 193, 197–198; glass, at Ñoquique, 204; glass, Nueva Cádiz 192–193, 196, 197, 198, 199; glass, beads (*continued*)

on shroud, **421**, **422**; glass production methods, 191–193; gold, 189, 269; guide to, **200**, **201–202**; interpretation of, 203–204; jet, 204, 205n8; metal, 195; shell, 198; shell, mother-of-pearl, 195, 196, 197; shell, *Spondylus* (*chaquira*), 190–191, 194, 195, **195**, 196, 197, 198, 203, 204; stone, 189, 195–196, 197, 198; with threads, 195, 198, **199**, 203; in town, 194, 197–199; unidentified organic material, 195, 197; wood, 195, 196, 197, 198. *See also* jewelry and ornaments

Beaudry, Mary C., 275, 296

Bechop (*parcialidad* in Magdalena), 320, 324, 330

bells, 271, 275, **276**, 277–278. *See also* metals

Benedict XIII, Pope, 374

Bertonio, Ludovico, 395

Beta Analytic, 373

Bingham, Hiram, 394

bioarchaeological studies. *See* burial analyses

bioarchaeological studies at other sites, 132

Bird, Junius Bouton, 13, 26, 401

Bonavia, Duccio, 404

bone beads, 190. *See also* beads

bones, whale vertebrae, 65, **65**, 79, 96

botijas (olive jars): assemblage, discussion of, 225; assemblage description, 210; church–town differences, 222–223, 258, 263; coding scheme, 226n1; description and dating of, 212; in Unit 28, 260. *See also* ceramics, colonial; pottery, indigenous

bottles, **234**, 249–250, **250**, 251, 252, **252**, 264. *See also* ceramics, colonial; pottery, indigenous

Boyd-Bowman, Peter, 173

Braun, David P., 232

Bravo, Bartolomé, 362–363

Bravo Thesaurus, 362–363, **362**

brick, fired, 417. *See also* adobe; walls, adobe

brushes, scrubbing, 49, **50**, 79. *See also* tools

Bueno, Alberto, 391

Burger, Richard, 394

burial analyses: achondroplastic dwarf, 122–123, **122**, **123**; actual and expected counts of porous cranial lesions in adults in El Brujo and Magdalena de Cao (table 4.5), 119; actual and expected counts of porous cranial lesions in non-adults at El Brujo and Magdalena de Cao (table 4.7), 120; age determinations, 111–112; ancestral classification, 112, 115, 128–129, 150–151; ancestral classification, 116–117; ancestry classification results (table 4.2), 116–117; comparison of D^{30+}/D^{5+} Ratios (table 4.9), 130; conclusions, 133; dental calculus, 98–100, 155; details, cemetery (chapter appendix), 139–140; details, nave, NE corner (chapter appendix), 140–143; details, nave, NW corner (chapter appendix), 143–146; frequencies of porous cranial lesions in adults at El Brujo and Magdalena de Cao (table 4.6), 120; frequency of pathological lesions other than NSIS (adults only) (table 4.3), 118; genetic, 132; hypotheses, 112; insect puparia in, 114; isotopic, 132, 149–150,

151–154; macroscopic analysis, 147–148; mortuary, 114, 125, 127–128, 133; nonspecific indicators of stress (table 4.4), 118; osteological, 112–113, 114–121, 128–132; osteological, special and disturbed remains, 121–124, **124**, **125**, **126**; porous cranial lesions in non-adults at El Brujo and Magdalena de Cao (table 4.8), 121; sample composition of intact and partially intact burials from Magdalena de Cao (table 4.1), 116; statistical, 113. *See also* African cranium; burials; burials at other sites

burials: African cranium, 121–122, **148**; with beads, 196; cemetery, 55–56, **55**, 107, 111; cemetery, details (chapter appendix), 139–140; cemetery, painted shrouds, 419–423, **420**, **421**, **422**, 425; cemetery, textiles and clothing, 171; church compound, 190–191; church compound, Lambayeque culture, 69; church nave, 44, 56–57, 62, **63**, 107–108, **108**, **109–111**, 111, **115**, 123, **124**, **125**, 147; church nave, details, NE corner (chapter appendix), 140–143; church nave, details, NW corner (chapter appendix), 143–146; church nave, Republican era, 44, 124–125, **127**; dating of, 72, 108; disturbed, 111, 114, 147; sacristy wall, human foot, 45–46, **46**; style, Catholic, 56–57, 108, **108**, **109**, 110, 111, **111**, 114; style, indigenous, 55, **55**, 114, 419–420. *See also* African cranium; burial analyses; burials at other sites

burials at other sites: Chile, north coast, 361; in Chotuna, 190; in Ecuador, 107; in Lambayeque Valley, 107; Mórrope, 132; San José de Moro, 423–424. *See also* African cranium; burial analyses; burials

Busch, Richard, **38**

C

cabildos (town councils): letter to Don Vicente de Mora Chimo, 317; members of, 335n1; powers of, 324; and town plan, 320; of Trujillo, 331. *See also* political organization of Chicama Valley

Cachi, Fernando, 323

cacicazgos (chiefdoms), 318–319, 335n5. *See also* political organization of Chicama Valley

caciques (chiefs): of Magdalena de Cao (table 12.1), 319; other terms for, 335n5; powers and duties of, 318–319, 322, 324–325; price of indulgences for, 359. *See also* political organization of Chicama Valley

Caesalpinia spinosa ([Molina] Kuntze), 57, 59

Cajamarca (town), 1, 190, 261

caliche (calcium carbonate crust), 42, 73, **93**

camelid fiber (alpaca), 164, 171, 173, 175. *See also* textiles and clothing; wool

camelids, 89. *See also* animal remains studies; camelid fiber (alpaca)

Campeche, Mexico, 154

candlesticks, 291, **292**. *See also* metals; tools

candlewick trimmer or snuffer, 283–284, **283**, 292. *See also* metals; tools

cane and fiber structures, 69

cántaros (large liquid storage vessels), 18n8, 96, 104, **234**, 248–249, **249**, 258, 260. *See also* ceramics, colonial; gourds; pottery, indigenous
Cao (*parcialidad* in Magdalena), 320, 330
Cao (town). *See* Magdalena de Cao
Cao Canal, 330, 336n31
Caral (site), 190
Cardal (site), 101
Cartavio (town), 8
Carter, Benjamin, 205n2
Casa Grande, 8
Casa Wiese, 31
Castañeda, Juan, 336n29
Castro, García de (Viceroy), 320
Catalonia, playing cards in, 383
cattle: in animal remains studies, 89, 101–102; in economy, 320–321, 329, 331
Caxa Guamán, Alonso, 318, 326
Çea, Alonso de, 327
cemetery: at abandoned temples, 15; burials, 55–56, **55**, 107, 111, 114, 128, 132; burials, details (chapter appendix), 139–140; perimeter walls search, 69; shrouds, 66, **421**, **422**; surface collection from, 66; textiles found in, 170–171. *See also* burial analyses; burials; church; church compound
censuses: of 1549, 321; of 1566, 318
ceramics, 61, 70, 80, 96–97. *See also* ceramics, colonial; gourds; pottery, indigenous; vessels, wood
ceramics, colonial, 39; overview, 209–210, 225–226; biplot of tin oxide and lead oxide composition in EGG Ware and tin-enameled wares, **219**; *botijas* (olive jars), 210, 212, 222, 223, 225, 226n1, 258, 260, 263; calcium and magnesium oxide concentrations in EGG Ware from Magdalena de Cao Viejo and sites in the Zaña Valley (figure 8.5), **220**; calcium oxide and magnesium oxide concentrations tin-enameled wares from Magdalena de Cao Viejo and Panama la Vieja, **221**; chemical composition, 218–222; church–town differences, 104, 215, 222–225, **224**, 226; coding scheme, 210, 226n1; distribution of functional types by sector and unit, 223–225; distribution of, 223, **223**, **224**; earthenwares, 210; EGG Ware (Early Green Glazed Ware), 215–217, **217**, 218–221, **220**, 222, 226; fineware, 263; functional type distribution, **224**; glazed earthenwares, 223; glazes, 216–217; Kraak ware (Chinese porcelain), 215, **216**; paddle-stamped wares (*cerámica paleteada*), 211; PCA (principal components analysis), 218–222, **220**, **221**, **222**; plainwares, 222; porcelains, 72, 214–215, **216**; principal-components analysis of EGG Ware from Magdalena de Cao and sites in the Zaña Valley (figure 8.6), **220**; principal-components analysis of tin-enameled wares from Magdalena de Cao Viejo and Panama la Vieja, **222**; redware, 211; slipped and decorated wares, 211; tin-enameled ware (*majolica*), 212–214, 221–222, **221**, **222**, 263; tin-enameled ware (*majolica*), Panamanian, **213**.

See also ceramics; gourds; pottery, indigenous; vessels, wood
Cervantes, Miguel de, 396
Chachapoyas (town), 226
Chamán Valley, 215
Chancay (town), 183
Chan Chan (site), 5, 262
chaquira (*Spondylus* beads). *See* shell(s), *Spondylus*
charcoal, 96
Charles III, 312, **312**
Charles V, Emperor, 128, 307
Chase, Philip G., 235
Chavín culture, 190, 270
Chayan, María, 324
Chicama (town), 8, 9
Chicama, *cacicazgo* of, 318–319
Chicama, *repartimiento* of Chicama Valley, 318, 325–328
Chicama Valley: ancestral classification, 129; background, 5, 8–9; cattle raising, 101–102; domestic occupation, 231; early studies of, 25–27; economy, 325, 328–331; enslaved Africans in, 147, 157, 329–330; environmental changes, 328–329; map, 6; political organization, 318–319; population of, 321; wheat cultivation, 102–103, 329, 331
chicha (maize beer): continuity of practices, 232; paddle for production of, 47, **48**, 51, 79; production and consumption of, 59, 232, **233**, 245, 258; vessels for, 98, 237, 245–249, **249**, 407; vessels for drinking, 407, 413. *See also* Andean culture
Chiclayo (city), 7
Chiclín (town), 8
Chile, north coast, 361
Chimú: Ascope Aqueduct, 10; beads, 190; chronology of prehistoric cultures, 11, **11**; clothing, 166–167, 183; kingdom of, 5; metals, 270; number system, 368; pottery, 252, 261; wall, 13; wave motif, 422–423. *See also* Andean culture; Chimú-Inca pottery; Inca; Lambayeque; Moche
Chimú-Inca pottery, 261, 262
China trade, 215
Chocope (town), 8, 325, 328
Chotuna (site), 190, 204
chronological control, 70–74, 269
chronology of Colonial Period, 17
chronology of prehistoric cultures, 11, **11**
Chumash of Southern California, 313
Chumbi Guamán, Juan, 323
church: abandonment and collapse of, 317, 327; abandonment of, 51, 54, 73, 92, 104, 333, 334; aerial photography of, sacristy, **45**; aerial photo map, **12**; animal remains, 89; archaeological features, 39, 40; atrium, 31, **31**, 33, 36, 54–55, 352, 372; baptistry, 46–47, **47**, **48**, 352, 417; beads, 194–196, **195**, 204; bell tower, 35, **63**; burial excavations of 2007, **108**; ceramics, colonial, **213**, 222–223; ceramics, functional type distribution, **224**; cigarettes, 352, 372; gourd fragments, 403; keys, 280, 285; marked

church (*continued*)

adobes, 58, 417–418, **418**; nave, clearance of to floor, 34; nave, collapse of, 72; nave, excavation of, **43**; nave, looter holes, 56–57, 108; nave, walls, **30**, 33, 42; nave, walls and plaster, 44, **44**; passageway, **30**, 33; planning of project, 28–29; porcelains, 223; sacristy, 44–45, **45**, **46**, 74n6; Unit 12, level 11, **213**; Unit 12 pottery musical instrument, 254; Unit 31, level 3, **213**; walls, 23, 29. *See also* beads; burials; cemetery; ceramics, colonial; church as institution; church compound; cigarettes; coins, colonial; gourds; metals; paper(s); playing cards (*naipes*); pottery, indigenous; religion, Catholic; textiles and clothing; Unit 12 (church nave); *specific unit numbers*

church as institution: *cofradías* (confraternities), 57, 128, 295, 327, 328, 358; Dominicans' role in Chicama *repartimiento*, 325–328; indulgences, 358–362, **360**, **361**. *See also* Dominican order; religion, Catholic

church compound: aerial photograph, eastern sector, **63**; area photograph, **34–35**; bin and scraper for hide processing, 55, 59, 79; eastern sector, 35, **36**, 37–38, **37**, 62, **63**; exterior western wall of baptistry (Unit 8), 54, 79, 352, 386, 388, **388**; food preparation area, 64–65, 79, 80; food preparation area, hearth, **63**, 64; food preparation area, ovens, **63**, 64, 80, 102–103; heat-reddened floor, **63**, **64**, 66; northwest corner Unit 4, 386, **387**, 392, **392**; patio, 64, 65; perimeter wall, search for, 47–48, **49**, 57, 69, **70**; photo map, **40**; pottery, indigenous, **247**; room with long bench (classroom), 63, **63**, **64**, 377; view of, **34**; western wall of baptistry (Unit 8), 386, 388, **388**. *See also* beads; burials; cemetery; ceramics, colonial; church; church as institution; coins, colonial; gourds; metals; paper(s); playing cards (*naipes*); pottery, indigenous; religion, Catholic; textiles and clothing; Unit 12 (church nave); *specific unit numbers*

cigarettes, **372**; church–town differences, 374; dating of, 72, 91–92, 352, 372–373, 380n1; earliest known, 105n2; other tobacco uses, 373–374

Ciparán, Juan, 329

Cleland, Katherine M., 211, 261

clothing. *See* textiles and clothing

coca, 91

cofradías (confraternities), 57, 128, 295, 327, 328, 358. *See also* church as institution; Dominican order; religion, Catholic

Cogorno Ventura, Gilda, 391, 392

coins, colonial: cobs, etymology, 303; conclusions, 312–313; denominations, 307, **308**; denominations of coins produced in the Viceroyalty of Peru (table 11.1), 307; excavated, 303, **304**, **306**; excavated, compositional analysis, 307–308, 311; excavated, context, 308–309; excavated, details, 315; excavated, production date, 309–311; Hapsburg shield, 306–307, **306**, 309–310; *macuquinas*, etymology, 303; *macuquinas*, production of, 305–306, 310; *medios*, 310; perforation of, 313; from shipwrecks, 303; spectra of elements in

the two *macuquina* coins made using a pXRF, 311; surface find, El Brujo, 312, **312**. *See also* coins, *peçetas*

coins, *peçetas*, 374, 376. *See also* coins, colonial

Colca Valley, 210

Collatnamo, Xacchiminchan, 319, 320

Collier, Donald, 261

colonialism: biocultural effects of, 107, 125; impact on indigenous populations, 132; indigenous attitudes toward documents, 429–430; writing systems' impact on indigenous societies, 351, 379–380

Colonial Period: *encomienda* system, 2–3, 318, 328; land ownership and use, 328–329; map of Colonial Peru, **4**; political organization, 318–320; study of, 16–18, 429; world events, 3–5. *See also* El Niño event of 1578; haciendas; Magdalena de Cao, written sources; *reducciónes*

Colonial Period archaeology, 29, 427–431

column samples: details, animal remains, 94; details, plant remains, 95–96; looter hole, 92, **93**; photo map, 40

Conquest Period, 1–3

Convent of Santo Domingo, 325–326

Conyers, Larry, 28, 38, **38**

Copacabana, Bolivia, **385**

copper, 278, 284, **288**, **289**, 307

copper alloys, 272–273, 278–279, 283–284, 292, **293**

copper alloys, arsenic, 278, 279, 290–291, 296, 297

copper alloys, prehispanic, 270, 290–291, 299n1

Cosco Guamán, Hernando, 322, 325, 327

cotton: Andean clothing, 163, **172**, 175–176, **176**, **177**; cultivation of, 164; fiber and structure, 171; knitted socks, 179, **181**, 183; plant remains studies, 95, 96, 97; scarves, 180, 182–183, **182**; seams, 168; shrouds, 55, **55**, 66, 108, 110, 111, **111**, 171, 173; shrouds, painted, 419–423, **420**, **421**, **422**, 425; as tribute, 331. *See also* textiles and clothing

Council of Lima, First, 128

Council of Lima, Second, 127

Council of the Indies, 334

Craig, Alan K., 303

crosses/crucifixes: crucifix pendant, 61, **279**, 295; on marked adobes, 417; wood crosses, 61, 124. *See also* jewelry and ornaments

Cuenca, Ecuador, 211

Cuenca, Gregorio González de, 318, 320

Cuphea sp. seeds, 96

Cupisnique Mound, **12**, 13, **27**

curacas (high-ranking natives), 61. See also *caciques* (chiefs); political organization of Chicama Valley

Cuzco, 1, 103, 305, 308, 418

D

Deagan, Kathleen, 191, 192

Deetz, James, 430

dental calculus analyses, 98–100, 155; starch grain analyses from dental calculus of colonial burials (table 3.6), 99–100

Depaulis, Thierry, 394, 395–396

de Vargas, Bartolomé, 71

Dillehay, Tom, 13, 14, 404

documentary sources, 17–18, 72, 104. *See also* Magdalena de Cao, written sources

Dominican order: abandonment of church, 72; in Cao in 1760, 334; church at Magdalena de Cao, 8, **9**, 37–38; indulgences and *cofradías*, 359; papers at church compound, 354; preachers, list of (table 12.3), 327; role in Chicama *repartimiento*, 325–328. *See also* church as institution

Don Antonio de Ribera, 103

Donnan, Christopher B., 261

Doonan, William, 28

Drake, Francis, 3–4

Dumbarton Oaks, 31, 427–428

Dussubieux, Laure, 218

E

Earle, David, 391, 392

Early Horizon, 101, 416

Early Intermediate Period, 190, 254, 270

Early Modern Europe, 272, 297

earthenware, 210. *See also* ceramics; ceramics, colonial; gourds; pottery, indigenous; vessels, wood

earthquakes, 11, 72, 333

Ecuador: burials, 107; Panamanian tin-enameled wares, 214

El Brujo: archaeological site, 8, 16–18, 19n11; background, 11–12; Chimú and Chimú-Inca elite residences, 261, 262; chronological chart of prehistoric cultures, **11**; early studies, 25–27, **26**; human remains on surface, 107–108. *See also* El Brujo terrace; Magdalena de Cao; Magdalena de Cao project

El Brujo terrace: aerial photo map, **12**; description of, 11, 12–16; domestic occupation, 231; environment, 73, 75n10; location in relation to original Magdalena, 321; view of, distant, **12**. *See also* El Brujo; Magdalena de Cao; Magdalena de Cao project

El Greco, 357

El Niño event of 1578: aftermath of, 7–8, 19n10; description of, 5–7, 18n8, 18n9; investigation of, 325; relocation of Magdalena de Cao, 157; waterborne deposit, 53–54, **53**, 81. *See also* Colonial Period

El Niño events, later, 46

encomienda system, 2–3, 318, 328. *See also* Colonial Period; *reducciónes*

equines, signs of husbandry, 280, **281**, 331

Eten (colonial church), 107, 132

ethnoarchaeological studies, 236

ethnographic evidence of pottery use, 232

Europe: glass production, 191; playing cards, 383–384

F

Fairbanks, 197

fauna. *See* animal remains studies

Feijoo de Sosa, Miguel, 25, 321, 322, 332, 334

Fernandez Lopez, Gioconda Arabel, 167

Field Museum of Natural History, Elemental Analysis Facility, 218

figurines, 254, **255**

fish, 70, 84, 89, **90**, 94, 95, 97, 102. *See also* animal remains studies; foodways

fisherfolk languages, 325, 366, 368

flora. *See* plant remains studies

Florida Keys, shipwreck, 303

Florida Museum of Natural History, 218

Florida Museum of Natural History Historical Archaeology Digital Type Collections, 210

food preparation areas: church compound, **63**, 64–65, 79, 80; church compound, hearth, **63**, 64; church compound, ovens, **63**, 64, 80, 102–103; milling station, **63**, 64–65; residences (Unit 1), 80; residences (Unit 2), 80; residences (Unit 28), 80, 96–97, **97**

food procurement equipment: *chicha* paddle, 47, **48**, 51, 79; fishing nets, 77–78, **78**; grinding stones, 79; metal tools, 78; nets as transportation equipment, 80; stone tools, 78; wooden objects, 79

food remains: overview, 81; microbotanical analysis, 155; starch grain analyses, 97–98; in vessel contents Unit 28, 70, 97–98, 239. *See also* animal remains studies; foodways; plant remains studies

foodways: church-town differences, 102–103, 104, 258; coca, absence noted, 91; cormorants and other shorebirds, 102; dental calculus analyses, 98–100; fish, 102; fruits, 91; goats/sheep, 104, 105n1, 155; indigenous staples, 263; introduced species, 101–102; isotopic analyses, 104, 152–153; manioc, 101; olive oil, 103; parching or toasting, 245; pottery usage and, 232; prehispanic, 102; prehistoric cultures, 89; soups and stews, 89, 96, 101; tomato, absence noted, 91. *See also chicha* (maize beer); maize; manioc; pottery, indigenous

footwear, 430, **430**

Ford, James A., 261

France: pin manufacturing, 275; popularity of St. Martin of Tours, 357; trade with Amerindians, 297

Franco Jordán, Régulo, 27

Fuentes, Francisco de, 318

Fundación Wiese, 27, 31, 81, 352

G

Gaither, Catherine M., 56–57, 62

Gálvez, César, 27

gambling games, 384

games, prehispanic, 393–396

Garcilaso de la Vega, 103

Gell, Alfred, 428–429

Gildemeister family, 8

glass: beads, 52, **52**, 108, 114, 190–199, **199**, 203, 204; production of, 191–193. *See also* beads

goats/sheep: in animal remains studies, 89–90, 96, 101–102, 104, 105n1, 155; in later economy, 59, 60, 69, 72, 73, 81, 90, 103, 335

Goggin, John M., 212

gold: beads, 189, 269; coins, 308. *See also* beads; coins, colonial; metals

Good, M. E., 193, 194, 205n4

gourds: bowls, 47, 49, **50**, 52, **52**, 80, **97**, 199, 203; colander, 414–415; decorated, 197; fragments, 80; jar covers, 68, 96, 225; plates, 65; storage jars, 70. *See also* ceramics; ceramics, colonial; earthenware; inscriptions on gourds; pottery, indigenous

Great Britain, pin manufacturing, 275

grinding stones, **63**, 64–65, **65**, 79

ground-penetrating radar studies: *recinto* (ceremonial precinct), 28; town, 38, **38**

Guamán, Francisco, 327, 331

Guaman Poma de Ayala, Felipe, 395, 396, 398

Guaman Poma de Ayala, Felipe, et al., 166

Guanay cormorants, 89, 102

H

haciendas: agriculture, 329; conflicts with, 330–331; glass production at, 191; growth of, 325; Indians working on, 226, 322, 323; relations with Magdaleneros, 324; relations with reducciónes and, 329–330; residents of, 157; towns as former haciendas, 8

hacienda San Jacinto, 325

hacienda Sonolipe, 325

Hacienda Trapiche, 328

Hack, William, 337n39

Hally, David J., 232, 234

Hamann, Byron, 362

Hancock, R. G. V., 211

hand broom, **80**. *See also* tools

Haro, García de, 326, **326**, 379, **380**

Harvard University Herbaria, 352, 373

Hefner, Joseph T., 147

Hocquenghem, Anne-Marie, 393–394, 395

Holy Rosary confraternity, 359

Hood, Darden, 373

House of Hapsburg, 306–307, **306**, 309–310

Huaca Blanca (Huaca Cao Viejo), 25, 26, 74n2. *See also* Huaca Cao Viejo

Huaca Cao Viejo: adobe use, 416; aerial photo map, **12**; archaeological site, 16; comparison of bones from, 118–119; early studies of, 26–27; Lambayeque burials, 15; orientation of burials with, 127–128; site photograph (2007), **428**; view of, distant, **24**

Huaca Cao Viejo plaza: architectural features, 42; architectural organization, 39–41; fieldwork of 2004, 29; photo map, **40**; view of, distant, **24**. *See also* Moche plaza

Huaca Cortada (Huaca El Brujo): adobe composition, 416; aerial photo map, **12**; burials, 15; formerly thought to be Lambayeque, 74n2; as shamanic center, 19n14; view of, **15**

Huaca El Brujo. *See* Huaca Cortada (Huaca El Brujo)

Huaca Prieta (Dark Huaca): aerial photo map, **12**; early sketch map, **26**; early studies of, 13, 25–26; gourds,

401, 404; shoreline transition zone, 89; view of, distant, **27**

Huaca Rosario, **10**

huacas: for burials, 127; early studies of, 25–26, **26**; link to past, 73–74; locations, 8; looting, 14–15; meanings of, 19n13; Moche, 15; Taki Onqoy movement (Dancing Sickness) movement, 2

Huacas de Moche, 5, 16

Huaca Tres Palos, Lima, 391, 392, **393**

Huanchaco (town), 102

Humboldt (Peru) Current, 4–7

Hyland, Sabine, 374

I

Iberia, glass production, 191

Ica (town), 191

Inca: beads, 190; butterfly motif in art, 370; ceremonial complex, 391; clothing, 166–167; dualistic principles, 418; games and game playing, 394–396; *khipu* recording system, 351; metals, 270, 285; number system, 368; pottery usage, 232; *tocapu* designs, 407–408, **407**, **412**, 416; vessels for transport, 245. *See also* Andean culture; Chimú; Lambayeque; Moche

Inca royal road, 8

indigenous people in Americas, 277–278

Initial Period, 11, 13, 15, 26, 101, 270, 416

inscriptions: discussion, 423–425; marked bricks, 57, **58**, 416–418, **418**, 419, 424–425; painted burial shrouds, 419–423, **420**, **421**, **422**, 425. *See also* inscriptions on gourds; paper(s)

inscriptions on gourds: animal designs, 408–409, **408**, **409**, 410–415, **410**, **412**, **414**; church-town differences, 403; classification of styles, 403–404; discussion, 423–424; European influence on designs, 409, 410–416, **411**, **414**; geometric designs, 403–405, **404**, **413**; geometric designs, *tocapu*, 407–408, **407**, **412**, 416; gourd use, 401–402; gourd use, storage jars and lids, 402, **402**; human/anthropomorph figures, **411**, 412–413, **412**, **414**; representational art tradition on North Coast, 415–416; techniques, 404, **404**, **405**. *See also* gourds; inscriptions; paper(s)

insects: crickets, 8, 19n10; puparia in burials, 114, 127; in sediment, 53–54

introduced species: animals, 85, 89, 94, 101–102, 103; plants, 81, 86–88, 91, 103–104, 329

iron and iron alloys, 270, 272, 281–282, 284, 285, **290**. *See also* metals

irrigation: Ascope Aqueduct, 10; breakdown of ancient system, 74, 328; evidence of lacking, 91; modern, 9, 75n10; prehispanic (Cao Canal), 330, 336n31

Isabella I, 306

Isla Guamán, Diego, 322, 327, 328, 332

J

Jamieson, Ross W., 211

Jaratán, Alonso, 323, 327

jarras (pitchers), 249–251, **250**, **251**, 260, 264. *See also* ceramics; ceramics, colonial; earthenware; gourds; pottery, indigenous; vessels, wood

Jequetepeque Valley, 423–424

Jesus, prints of, 357, **358**, **359**

jewelry and ornaments: crucifixes and Christian pendant, 61; crucifixes and Christian pendants, 278, 279, **279**, 295; finger rings, 68, **279**, 292–295, **295**; leather fleur-de-lis, 62, **62**; miscellaneous, 278–279, **279**; prehistoric, 270. *See also* beads

Jiménez Saldaña, Jaime, 33, 37, 55, 69

Jiskairumoko (site), 189

John II of Castile, 306

Journal of Material Culture, 428

K

Kealhofer, Lisa, 132

Keatinge, Richard W., 262

Kennett, Douglas, 72

keys, **280**, 285. *See also* metals

Klaus, Haagen D., 107, 132

knives: folding, 60–61, 197, **290**; tumi-like, 285, 290, **290**; in wall, 284, **288**, **289**. *See also* metals; tools

Kubler, George, 209

Kuntur Wasi (site), 190

L

La Caleta del Brujo (Brujo Cove), 25–26

La Galgada (site), 190

LA-ICP-MS (laser ablation inductively coupled plasma mass spectrometry), 218–222

La Isabela (town), 275

La Leche–Lambayeque region, 261

La Leche Valley, 211

Lambayeque: beads, 190; bird figure, 423–424, **424**; burials, 15, 69; chronological chart of prehistoric cultures, 11; *huaca*, 26; metals, 270, 299n1; wave motif, 422–423. *See also* Andean culture; Chimú; Inca; Moche

Lambayeque One, 253

Lambayeque Valley, 107, 132, 210, 211, 261

lapis lazuli, 294

La Plata (city), 305

Larco family, 8

Larco Hoyle, Rafael, 13

Larsen, Clark S., et al., 132

Late Horizon, 261–262, 404, 408

Late Intermediate Period: beads, 190; bioarchaeology, 118; decorative motifs, 404, 408; metals, 270, 299n1; pottery, 260, 261, 262

Late Medieval Europe, 272, 297

Late Moche, 211

Late Preceramic Period, 26, 102, 103, 190, 416

Late Prehispanic Period, 261

lead, 278, 291, **291**. *See also* metals

leather, 62, **62**

Leguizamón, Mancio Serra de, 396

Libro de juegos (Book of games), 384

Libros cabildos de Lima, 398

Licapa (*repartimiento* of Chicama Valley), 318, 320

Lima (city): coin mint, 305–306, 307, 308, 310, 312, **312**; coins, 309; "hidden" Indians in, 322; Panamanian wares in, 214; sermons preserved in, 359–360; wheat from Chicama Valley, 329

linen, 164–165, **168**, 171, 173, **174**, 177–178

Long, George A., 214, 218

looter holes: column samples, 92, **93**; as excavation unit, 51–52, **53**; nave, 56–57, 108; Unit 28, **14**, 67

looters: at church site, 37; destruction by, 39; at Paredones, 14

looting: in Colonial or early Republican Period, 51; human remains on surface, 107–108; sponsored, 352

M

Mache, Pedro, 330

Machu Picchu (site), 394

Magdalena (El Brujo). *See* Magdalena de Cao; Magdalena de Cao, written sources; Magdalena de Cao project

Magdalena de Cao: abandonment of, 332–333, 335; archaeological site, 16–18, 19n11; background, 5, 8; dating of, 71–74, 212, 311; early sketch map of ruins, 25, **26**; economic hard times, 264, 297, 325, 330–333; economy, adoption of money, 313; economy, foreign goods, 225–226, 430; economy, mixed subsistence, 100–101, 104–105; economy, work as muleteers, 226, 263, 323, 330, 331–332; economy, work on haciendas, 226, 322, 323; establishment of, 71, 157. *See also* El Brujo; El Brujo terrace; Magdalena de Cao, written sources; Magdalena de Cao project

Magdalena de Cao (modern town), 8, 19n12, 25–26, 74, 332–333

Magdalena de Cao (original), 5, 7–8, 19n11, 157, 320–321. *See also* El Niño event of 1578

Magdalena de Cao, written sources: introduction, 317–318; annual tribute required of the Indians of the Chicama Repartimiento in 1549 (table 12.4), 332; architectural features, 324, 325; *caciques* of sixteenth and seventeenth centuries (table 12.1), 319; church's role in, 325–328, **326**, 336n22, 336n23; church's role in, preachers (table 12.3), 327; conflicts over resources, 328–332; conflicts within, 323, 324; daily life, 323–325; economic hard times, 325, 330–333; final years, 332–335; labor service, 329, 336n14; list of preachers of Magdalena de Cao from the written sources (table 12.3), 327; list of the population and tribute payers (adult men) of Magdalena de Cao (table 12.2), 321; location of original town, 320–321; maps, 333–334, **333**, **334**, 337n39; material culture in documents (chapter appendix), 341–349; nomenclature in records, 318, 335n1, 335n5; political organization, 318–320; population, 321–323; population and tribute payers (table 12.2), 321; town officials, 324–325; tribute and labor service, 321–323, 335n11; tribute lists, 331, 337n36; tribute lists, details (table 12.4), 332. *See also* Magdalena de Cao; Magdalena de Cao project; paper(s)

Magdalena de Cao project: bones, surface finds, 42, 74n4, 107–108; chronological control, 70–74, 269; concluding thoughts, 427–431; correlation of artifact numbers with PACEB numbers (volume appendix), 433–437; documentary sources, 42, 72; early studies, 25–27, **26**; field methods, 32, 74n3; fieldwork of 2004, 29–31, **30**, **33**; fieldwork of 2004, church, 351; fieldwork of 2005, church, 33–38, **352**; fieldwork of 2005, town, 38–42, **352**; fieldwork of 2006, church, 42, **43**, **44**–48; fieldwork of 2006, town, 48–54; fieldwork of 2007, **428**; fieldwork of 2007, church, 54–57, **58**, **59**, 108, **108**, **109**, **110**, 111, **111**; fieldwork of 2007, church compound, **63**; fieldwork of 2007, town, 60–62, **60**, **62**; fieldwork of 2008, church, 108, **109**, 417; fieldwork of 2008, church compound, 62–66, **64**, **65**; fieldwork of 2012, church, 68–69, 70; fieldwork of 2012, church compound, 111; fieldwork of 2012, town, 70; funding for, 27; funding of, 31; map of excavation units, 41; middens, 33–34; organic materials preservation, 23; photo map, **40**; planning, 27–28, 74n3; processing of materials, 32; *recinto* (ceremonial precinct), 28; research 2009–2013, 68; research strategies, 23–25; site organization, 23; well, ceremonial, 28, **28**. *See also* Andean culture; animal remains studies; baptistry (Unit 8); beads; burial analyses; burials; ceramics, colonial; church; coins, colonial; El Brujo; El Brujo terrace; inscriptions; inscriptions on gourds; Magdalena de Cao; Magdalena de Cao, written sources; metals; paper(s); plant remains studies; playing cards (*naipes*); pottery, indigenous; textiles and clothing; town

maize: comparative studies, 152, **152**; dental calculus analyses, 100–101, 155; plant remains studies, 90, 96; storage of, 263; vessel contents Unit 28, 70, 97–98, 239. See also *chicha* (maize beer); foodways; plant remains studies

Malata (site), 199

Manco Inca Rebellion, 2

manioc: dental calculus analyses, 100, 155; foodways, 72, 101; plant remains studies, 90; vessel contents Unit 28, 70, 97, 98, 239, 258. *See also* foodways; plant remains studies

Mansiche (town), 71

maps: seventeenth and eighteenth centuries, 333–334; seventeenth century, **333**, 337n39; eighteenth century, 321, **334**; aerial photo, El Brujo terrace, **12**; Chicama Valley, **6**; Colonial Peru, **4**; early sketch map, El Brujo *huacas*, 25, **26**; excavation units, **41**; photo map, colonial town, **40**

Marken, Mitchell W., 212

Martínez Compañón y Bujanda, Baltasar Jaime, 25, 163–164, 180, 182, 185n1, 232, **298**, 334, 366

Martínez de Ormachea, Juan, 359–360

Martin of Tours, print of, 357, **357**

Mateo (enslaved man), 329

Mauritius, piercing rites, 378

Maya, 351, 428

Medaños de la Joyada, 261–262

Meléndez, Juan de, 325, 359, 361

Mendoza, Bernardino de, 354

Mesoamerican festivities, 373

metals: overview, 269–271, 296–297, 299; beads, 189, 269; bells, 271, 275, **276**, 277–278; bells, details (table 10.3), 277; bells of Magdalena de Cao Viejo (table 10.3), 277; box of unknown function, 284, **288**, 291, 292; bromine, 307–308; candlestick, 291, **292**; candlewick trimmer or snuffer, 283–284, **283**, 292; in church compound, 269; church–town differences, 270–271, 274, 277; compositional analysis (pXRF spectrometry), 271–273, 278–279, 284, 285, 299n2; compositional analysis (pXRF spectrometry), details (table 10.4), 286–287; continuity and hybridities, 297, 299; copper, 278, 284, **288**, **289**, 307; copper alloys, 272–273, 278–279, 283–284, 292, **293**; copper alloys, arsenic, 278, 279, 290–291, 296, 297; copper alloys, prehispanic, 270, 290–291, 299n1; crucifixes and Christian pendants, 61, 278, 279, **279**, 295; excavations (table 10.1), 271; fan-shaped object, 49, **50**; finger rings, 68, **279**, 292–295, **295**; gold, beads, 189, 269; gold, coins, 308; horseshoe fragments, 280, **281**; iron, 281–282, 285; iron alloys, 272, 284, 285, **290**; keys, 280, 285; knives, 60–61, 197, 284, 285, **288–290**, 290; lead, 278, 291, **291**; metal objects found during excavations at Magdalena de Cao Viejo (table 10.1), 271; ornaments, 278–279, **279**; plate fragment (?), 284, **288**; production of, **298**; sewing needle, 296, **296**; silver, coins, 303, **304**, 305–306, 307–308; silver, finger rings, 68, **279**, 292–295, **295**; silver, pendant, 279, **279**; straight pins, 270–271, 272–275, **273**; straight pins, details (table 10.2), 274; straight pins of Magdalena de Cao Viejo (table 10.2), 274; summary results of pXRF analysis (table 10.4), 286–287; tools and hardware, 78, 280–285, **280–283**, **288–290**; tools and hardware, details (table), 286–287; in town, 269; triangular base, 292, **293**; tweezers, 292, **294**; weapon parts (?), **280**, 281–282, **282**. *See also* coins, colonial

Mexico, paper art, 370

middens: near atrium wall, 33–34, 81; town, 42, 81

Middle Sicán/Lambayeque, 211

Milner, George R., 132

Mirabel, Danielle, 81

Mississippi Valley Tunica, 297

Moche: adobe use, 416–417; archaeology, 427, 429; *chicha* (maize beer), 59; chronological chart of prehistoric cultures, **11**; games, 394; Huaca Cao Viejo, 26; *huacas*, 15; metals, 270; number system, 368; Paredones, 14; representational art, 415–416; Señora de Cao, 27, 28, **29**, 427; temples, 40; wave motif, 422–423. *See also* Andean culture; Chimú; Huaca Cao Viejo plaza; Inca; Lambayeque

Moche plaza, **24**, 54–55. *See also* Huaca Cao Viejo plaza

Moche Valley, 5, 8, 16

Mocollope (site), 8

Mocupe Viejo (town), 204
Mogrovejo, Santo Toribio de, 321, 325
Mogrovejo Rosales, J. D., 214
Moncada, Felix de, 328, 330, 334
Montículo 2, 39, **40**
Montículo 3, 40, 42, 60
Montículo 5 (*huaca*), 13
montículos (mounds), 39
Montoya, Diego de, 326–327
Moquegua Valley, 214, 221
Mora, Diego de, 318, 319, 329
Mora, Juan de, 7, 318, 320, 326
Mora, Pedro de, 324, 326–327
Mora Chimo, Vicente de, 317, 318, 327, 328, 330, 334–335, 429
Mórrope (colonial church), 107
mortuary analyses of burials, 114
Muchik language, 366, 368
murals: in church, 31, **31**, 33, 46; at Huaca Blanca (Huaca Cao Viejo), 26
Murrua, Father, 394
Museo de Cao, 295, 352
Museo de la Nación, 215
Museo Rafael Larco Herrera, 215
musical instruments, **217**, 254

N

Nasrid Emirate of Granada, playing cards in, 383
National Endowment for the Humanities, 31
National Geographic Society, 27
National Institute of Culture of Peru, 26–27
National Science Foundation, 31
Nazareno (modern town), 321
Nebrija, Antonio de, 362
Netherly, Patricia, 318–319, 330
nets, 77–78, **78**, 80. *See also* textiles and clothing
net weights, 78
New Materialism, 428–429
Ñoquique (town), 204
Nuestra Señora de la Consolación cofradía, 328. See also *cofradías* (confraternities)

O

Ocucaje (town), 391
olive jars. See *botijas* (olive jars)
olives, 91
ornaments and jewelry. *See* jewelry and ornaments

P

Pachacamac (site), 391
paicas (jars), 59
Paiján, 11, 13
Paiján (town), 8
Pampa de Mocan, 9
Panama City, 329
Panama la Vieja, 211, 212–214, 218, 221–222
Panama Redware, 211

Panamerican Highway, 8
Papal Bull, 361
paper(s): overview, 351–353; Bravo Thesaurus, 362–363, **362**; church, 46–47; church–town differences, 353, 364, 370, 374; church–town differences, details (table 13.1), 354; cigarettes, 72, 91–92, 105n2, 352, 372–374, **372**, 380n1; classification, 356; classification (table 13.1), 354; colored ink, 356, 357, 364, **364**; corpus general features, 353–356; cutouts, 51, 282, 368, **369**, 370; discussion, 379–380; distribution of papers in church and town (table 13.1), 354; document fragments, 326, **326**, 379, **380**; documents, 25; ecclesiastical, 72; ecclesiastical paper fragments, 92, 386, 392; folded and pierced, 378, **378**; as "fossil index," 92; fragments, 31, 81; fragments with dates, 370–371, **371**; functional value, 352–353; indigenous attitudes toward documents, 429–430; indulgences, 356, 357, 358–362, 360, **361**; letter, complete, 66, 356, 366, **367**, 368, 381n6; missal and lectionary fragments, 357, **357**, **358**, **359**; modern papers found, 353; musical scores, 364, **364**–365, 366; name lists, 374, **375**, 376; notes and doodles, 379, **379**; trilingual confessionary, 363–364, **363**; writing practice, 376–378, **377**. *See also* inscriptions; inscriptions on gourds; Magdalena de Cao, written sources; playing cards (*naipes*)
parcialidades (indigenous communities), 318. *See also* political organization of Chicama Valley
Paredones (site), **12**, **14**, 404
Parlett, David, 384
Patterson, Thomas C., 313
Paypay Chumbi, Juan de, 324
Peabody Museum of Archaeology and Ethnology, 31, 285, **290**, 297
Penn State Huck Institutes of the Life Sciences Genomics Core Facility, 150–151
Penn State Human Paleoecology and Isotope Geochemistry Laboratory, 149–150
Philip II, 305, 309, 310, 384, 391–392
Philip III, **304**, 310
Philip IV, 310
Pillars of Hercules, 306–307, **306**, 312, **312**
Piura la Vieja (site), 215
Pizarro, Ana, 319
Pizarro, Francisco, 1, 2, 5, 190
Pizarro, Hernando, 396
plant remains studies: animal and plant remains found (table 3.1), 82–86; ash analyses, 97, 98; *Caesalpinia spinosa*, 57; column samples, details, 95–96; cotton, 95, 96, 97; details (table 3.1), 86–88; distortion of remains, 88; faunal and plant remains from a column sample in Magdalena town (table 3.3), 94–95; food, 90–91; fruits, 91, 95, 103, 104; industrial, 90, 91, 95, 96, 97; introduced species, 81, 86–88, 91, 103–104, 329; medicinal and stimulant, 90, 91, 96; oil-producing, 90; ornamentals, 90, 91, 104; *pacay* tree, 95; plant and animal remains from ashes in Unit 28 (table 3.4), 98; seaweed, 90; starch grain analyses, dental calculus, 98–100;

plant remains studies (*continued*)

    starch grain analyses, food remains, 97–98; starch grain analyses from dental calculus of colonial burials (table 3.6), 99–100; summary of starch grain analyses of Unit 28 vessels (table 3.5), 98; tobacco, 91; in vessel contents, 49, 50, 52, **52**, 97–98; wheat, 102–103. *See also* animal remains studies; food remains; foodways; gourds; inscriptions on gourds; plants, cultivated; textiles and clothing; tobacco

plants, cultivated: beans (*Erythrina americana*), 394; cotton, 164, 331; gourd cultivation and use, 401; sugar cane, 9, 10, 75n10, 325, 329; wheat, 102–103, 329, 331. *See also* cotton; plant remains studies; tobacco

plaster, 33, 44, **44**, 57, 417

playing cards (*naipes*): introduction, 383; card playing and gambling in Peru, 396, **397**, 398; deck styles, 384–386, **385**; history of in Europe, 383–384; licensing of workshops, 384; Magdalena cards, 386, **387**, 388, **388**, **389**, 390; Magdalena cards, dating, 391–393, **392**; from other Peruvian sites, 391, **393**; prehispanic games in Peru, 393–396; production methods, 386; in Unit 28 (town), 68. *See also* paper(s)

political organization of Chicama Valley, 318–320

Portugal, porcelain trade, 215

Potosí, Bolivia: coin mint, 305–306, **307**, 310; coins, 303, **304**, 309

pottery, indigenous: overview, 231, 262–263; background, 231–232; bar graph of bowls categorized by orifice diameter for clerical residence and town compounds, **260**; bar graph of indigenous vessel function in church and town, **256**; bar graph of liquid storage and serving forms in town, Units 1, 2, and 28 (figure 9.27), **259**; bar graph of liquid storage/serving forms in church and town (figure 9.26), **259**; bar graph of olla subtypes in church and town (figure 9.24), **257**; blackware, 251, 262, 263, 264; bowls, 237, 244–245, **246**, 251–252, 260, **260**; boxplot of orifice diameters for olla subtypes in church and town (figure 9.25), **257**; boxplot of orifice diameters for the four olla forms, **239**; *chicha* production, **233**; church–town differences, 236, 244–245, **247**, 252, 256–260, **256**, **257**, **259**, 260, 263, 264; decorative techniques, 239, 243–244, 247, 249, 251, **252**, **253**, 254, 261, 262, **262**; discard assemblages, 236; early styles, 11; functional analysis methods, 232, 234, **234**; functional analysis results, 236–237; glazes, 241, 243, **243**, 244–245, **247**, 264; grater bowls (*rayadores*), 252–253, **253**, 254; indigenous vessel forms in the town units and clerical residence, 236; indigenous vessel forms in the town units and clerical residence (table 9.2), 236; indigenous vessel mouth complex categories in the church and town, 236; indigenous vessel mouth complex categories in the church and town (table 9.3), 237; lids, 244, **246**; liquid serving vessels, bottles, **234**, 249–250, **250**, 251, 252, **252**, 264; liquid serving vessels (*jarras*), 249–251, **250**, **251**, 260, 264; liquid storage and serving forms, **259**; liquid storage vessels (*cántaros*),18n8, 96, 104, **234**, 248–249, **249**, 258, 260; liquid storage vessels (*tinajas*), **234**, 247–248, **248**, 258, 261; non-food-related use, 254, **255**; ollas, angled-neck, 243, **244**, 257–258, **257**; ollas, boxplot of orifice diameters, **239**; ollas, convex-neck, 243–244, **245**, **257**; ollas, C-rims, 237–239, **240**, **241**, 256–257, **257**; ollas, neckless, 239–241, **242**, 243, **243**; ollas, subtypes, **238**, 243–245; plates, 252, 261–262, **263**, 423–424, **424**; raw count, MNV, and metric data assemblage counts, 235; raw count, MNV, and metric data assemblage counts for Magdalena Viejo pottery (table 9.1), 235; redware, 251, **252**, 262; sample selection, 234–236; storage jars, 68, 402, **402**; storage jars (*paicas*), 59; temporal trends, 260–262; for transport, 245. *See also* ceramics, colonial; foodways; gourds; vessels, wood

Preceramic Period, 13, 15, 78, 401, 404

Prieto, Gabriel, 49, **51**

Prisoner Frieze, 54–55, 75n7

Proyecto Arqueológico Complejo El Brujo (PACEB) Numbers, 433–437

Puebla, New Spain, 191

Q

quartz beads, 190

Quechua language: concept of chance, 395; sermons in, 359–360; trilingual confessionary, 363–364, **363**; words on back of letter, **367**, 368

Quilter, Jeffrey: column samples, 92; dating of site, 311; identification of cemetery, 66; materiality of social processes, 203; planning of project, 27, 28

quincha (wattle-and-daub): church compound walls, 36, 37; knife in wall (Unit 2), 284, **288**, 289; town walls, 23, **24**, 38–39, 42, 60–61, **60**

Quingnam language, 66, 356, 366, **367**, 368, 431

R

radiocarbon dating: of African cranium, 149, **149**; limitations of, 72, 92; of tobacco, 352; of various materials, 75n9

Raimondi, Antonio, 25–26, **26**, 66

Ramírez, Alonso, 327

Ramusio, Giovanni Battista, 354

Raymi Quilla, 395

recinto (ceremonial precinct), 28

Recopilación de las Leyes de Indias, 128

Recuay, 270

reducciónes: establishment of, 3, 73, 320; plans of, 61; relations of Indians with hacienda slaves, 329–330; residency laws, 122, 157, 321, 335n12; resistance to regulations, 322–323; standards of living, 104

religion, Catholic: bell use in services, 277; burial with documents, 361; *cofradías* (confraternities), 57, 128, 295, 327, 328; conversion to, 326; funerals, 327, 332, 336n28; indulgences, 358–362, **360**, **361**; mortuary practices, 114, 125, 127, **127**–128; music, 364, **365**–366, **366**; shriving, 363–364; tobacco controversy, 373–374.

See also burial analyses; burials; church as institution; Dominican order; religion, indigenous

religion, indigenous: and colonization process, 23–24; divining, 394–395; mortuary practices, 55, **55**, 114, 127–128; ritual disinterment (*pacaricuc*), 127; ritual objects, bead in ashes bowl, 52, **52**, 199, 203; ritual objects, buried filled gourds, 49, 402, **403**; ritual objects, knife in wall, 284, **288**, **289**; sacred places, 73–74. *See also* Andean culture; burial analyses; burials; burials at other sites; religion, Catholic

repartimientos, 318. *See also* political organization of Chicama Valley

Republican era: burials, 44, 124–125, **127**; cut in Huaca El Brujo, **15**

Reque Valley, 211

Ricardo, Padre, 46

Rice, Prudence M., 221–222

Riddell, Francis, 391

ritual disinterment (*pacaricuc*), 127

Rodman, Amy Oakland, 167

Rowe, John, 394, 395

Ruiz, Agudo, 386

S

Saavedra, Antonio de, 330

Sacop parcialidad, 322

Salazar, Lucy, 394

San José de Moro (site), 59, 423–424

San Pedro de Mórrope (site), 132

Santa Barbola cofradía, 328. See also *cofradías* (confraternities)

Santa Cruz Pachacuti, Juan de, 418

Santa María, Joseph de, 326–327

Santa María de Magdalena de Cao. *See* Magdalena de Cao

Santiago, Pedro de, 324, 326–327

Santiago de Cao (town), 8, 322, 325, 329

Santo Tomás, Domingo de, 325, 366, 368

Sedwick, Daniel, 308–309

Sedwick, Frank, 308–309

seeds: in bag with burial, **56**; *Cuphea* sp., 96; in gourd bowl, 49, **50**, **403**. *See also* plant remains studies

Señora de Cao, 27, 28, **29**, 427

señorios, 318, 335n5. *See also* political organization of Chicama Valley

Seville, playing cards, 392, **392**

sewing needle, 296, **296**. *See also* metals

Sharp, Bartolome, 337n39

sheep, 165. *See also* camelid fiber (alpaca); goats/sheep; wool

shell, 190

shell, mother-of-pearl, 195, 196, 197

shellfish, 88–89, 92, 95, 96, 101, 331. *See also* animal remains studies; foodways

shell(s), *Spondylus*: beads, 190–191, 194, 205n1; in church, 44, 194, **195**; church–town differences, 194; at other sites, 204; placed under floor (Unit 2), 203; in town,

194, 203; trade in, 14, 190, 205n1. *See also* animal remains studies; foodways

Shimada, Izumi, 211, 261

Sicha Guamán, Diego, 324

silks, 163, 165, 171–172, 173, **175**, **178**

Silva, Andrés de, 325

Silva Paypay Chumbi, Andrés, 329

silver: coins, 303, **304**, 305–306, 307–308; finger rings, 68, **279**, 292–295, **295**; pendant, 279, **279**. *See also* coins, colonial; metals

Skoglund, Pontus, et al., 151

slaves/slavery. *See* African cranium; Africans

Smith, Marvin, 193, 194, 199, 205n4

soils: fine-grained sediment, 53; matrix of nave burials, 108; screening of, 32; waterborne deposit from 1578 El Niño event, 53–54, **53**, 81

Soldi Collection, 391

Solomon Islands, tin-enameled wares in, 214, 221

Soloque (town), 321, 330

Spain: coinage, 305; colonial power, 317; expansion of empire, 3; olive jar production, 211; pin manufacturing, 275; playing cards, history, 383–384; playing cards and gambling, 396; porcelain trade, 215; wool production, 165

Spondylus. *See* shell(s), *Spondylus*

starch grain analyses: dental calculus analyses, 98–100; in food remains, 97–98. *See also* foodways; plant remains studies

stone: beads, 189, 190, 195, 196, 197, 198; grinding stones, 63, 64–65, **65**, 79; tools, 78

St. Peter's Basilica, Vatican, 374

straight pins, 270–271, 272–275, **273**. *See also* metals

strata: *caliche* (calcium carbonate crust), 42, 73, **93**; Layer A, Unit 28, coins, 308; Level 1, Unit 1, pottery, 254, **255**; Level 1, Unit 12 (church nave), pottery, 254; Level 1, Unit 28, ceramics, **213**; Level 2, Unit 28, ceramics, **217**; Level 2a, Unit 12 (church nave), ceramics, **213**; Level 3, Unit 2, porcelain, **216**; Level 3, Unit 28, porcelain, **216**; Level 3, Unit 28, pottery, 254; Level 3, Unit 31 (church), ceramics, **213**; Level 10, Unit 19 (midden), radiocarbon dating, 75n9; Level 11, Unit 12 (church nave), ceramics, **213**; Level 11, Unit 19 (midden), radiocarbon dating, 75n9; Level 14, Unit 19 (midden), earliest town occupation, 81; melted adobe, 92; paper in, 92; prehistoric deposits, 92, **93**; surface find, town, ceramic, **213**; waterborne deposit from 1578 El Niño event, 53–54, **53**, 81. *See also* stratigraphy, horizontal; stratigraphy, vertical

stratigraphy, horizontal, 72. *See also* strata; stratigraphy, vertical

stratigraphy, vertical, 72–73, 92–95. *See also* strata; stratigraphy, horizontal

straw, 47–48

Sturm, Jennie, **38**

sugar cane, 9, 10, 75n10, 325, 329

swamps, 73, 75n10, 320–321, 328, 333

T

Taki Onqoy movement (Dancing Sickness), 2

Tambo Viejo (site), 391, 392

tanning equipment, 55, 57, 59, 73

Tate, James P., 261, 262

temples, abandoned as cemeteries, 15

textiles and clothing: overview, 163–164, 170–171; Andean clothing, 68, 164–167, **168, 172,** 175–177, 370; bags, 55, **56**; burial clothing, 124; burial palls, 44, 124, **127**; burial shrouds, 55, **55,** 66, 108, **110,** 111, **111,** 171, 173; burial shrouds, painted, 419–423, **420, 421, 422,** 425; camelid fiber (alpaca), 164, 171, 173, 175; from cemetery, 171; from church, 180, **182**; church–cemetery differences, 171; church–town differences, 171–173; conclusions, 183, 185; cords, 164; cotton, Andean clothing, 163, 175–176; cotton, as tribute, 331; cotton, cultivation of, 164; cotton, fiber and structure, 171; cotton, scarves, 180, 182–183, **182**; cotton, seams, **168**; cotton, shawls, **176, 177**; cotton, socks, 179, **181,** 183; cotton, spinning of, 165; cotton, tunic, **172**; cotton, weaving of, 166–167; dyeing, 164, 173, 176, **176, 177**; European clothing, 167, 169–170, 177–178; exotic, 72; fastenings, 167, 169, 170, 178, **178,** 179; fiber and cane structures, 69; fibers, European, 167, 169; fibers, prehispanic, 164–167; fibers and structures, 171–173, **172, 174, 175**; footwear, 430, **430**; fragments, 49, **50,** 179, 180, 402, **403**; hybrid clothing, 173, 179–180, **180, 181,** 182–183, 185; knitted, 163, 170–171, 179, **181**; linen, 164–165, **168,** 171, 173, **174,** 177–178; manufacture, spinning, 165, 185n1; manufacture, weaving, 165–166, 182–183, **184**; mention of in records, 323, 324, 356, 366, 381n6; nets, 77–78, **78,** 80, 164; scarves, 180, 182–183, **182**; seams, 167, **168,** 169–170; shawls, 176–177, **176, 177,** 185; silks, 163, 165, 171–172, 173, **175,** 178; tassels, 68; threads with beads, 195, **195,** 198, **199,** 203; twine, 55, **56**; with vessels, 68, 96, **402**; wool, button on, **178**; wool, European clothing, 163; wool, European-style clothing, 183; wool, fibers and structures, 171–172, 173; wool, production of, 165; wool, seams, **168**; wool, sleeve fragment, 179, **180**; wool versus camelid fiber, 164

tinajas (large liquid storage vessels), **234,** 247–248, **248,** 258, 261. *See also* ceramics; ceramics, colonial; earthenware; gourds; pottery, indigenous; vessels, wood

Titicaca Basin, 269

tobacco: church–town differences, 374; cigarettes, 72, 91–92, 105n2, **372,** 380n1; controversy over, 373–374; dating of, 372–373; European and indigenous uses of, 373; as introduced species, 91

Toledo, Francisco de (Viceroy), 2–3, 127, 320

tools: agricultural, 77; bolas, 79; brushes, scrubbing, 49, **50,** 79; *chicha* paddle, 47, **48,** 51, 79; hand broom, 80; stone, 78; tweezers, 292, **294**. *See also* food procurement equipment; knives; metals

Topquem (*parcialidad* in Magdalena), 320, 327, 328, 331

Torres Mora, Rocío de María, 232

town: animal remains, 89; archaeological features, 39; beads, 194, 197–199; boundaries, 39–40, **40**; ceramics, functional type distribution, **224**; colonial ceramics, 222–225; column samples, 92, **93,** 94–96; crucifixes and Christian pendants, 295; documentary sources, 42; fieldwork of 2005, town, 38–42; finger rings, 68, **279,** 292–295, **295**; jars, 70; keys, **280,** 285; knives, 60–61, 197, 284, 285, **288–290,** 290; map of excavation units, 41; middens, 42; numbering system, 74n3; playing cards, 386, 388, **389, 390**; porcelains, 223; residences, 42, 49, **50,** 60–61, 66–67; sewing needle, 296, **296**; streets, 41–42; surface finds, ceramics, **213, 216**; triangular base, 292, **293**; walls, adobe Unit 28, 68, **68**; walls, delineation of, 23, 38–39, **38**; walls, perimeter, 48–49; walls (*quincha*), **24**. *See also* beads; ceramics, colonial; coins, colonial; gourds; metals; paper(s); playing cards (*naipes*); pottery, indigenous; textiles and clothing; *specific unit numbers*

transportation equipment, sling, 80

Trench 1, beads, 195

Trujillo, Peru: clothing depiction, 180; establishment of, 5, 318; fired bricks at, 417; gambling prohibitions, 398; location of, 8; map of Colonial Peru, **4**; population of, 321, 322; wheat from Chicama Valley, 329, 331

Tschauner, Hartmut, 210

Tupac Amaru, 2

U

Ubelaker, Douglas H., 132

Unit 1 (town residence), 32, 42; beads, 198, 204; ceramics, functional type distribution, **224**; colonial ceramics, 222, 223, 225; cross and crucifix, 61, 295; figurine fragment (pottery), 254, **255**; food preparation area, 80; gourds, 403; hand broom, 80; house, 48–49, **50**; indigenous pottery, 236, 243, 251–253, **254,** 258, 264; liquid storage and serving forms, **259**; net bag, 78, **78**; numbering system, 74n3; photo map, **40**; playing cards, 388, **389**; ritual objects, buried filled gourds, 49, **50,** 402, **403**; scrubbing brush, 49, **50,** 79; streets, 41

Unit 2 (town residence), 32, 66; beads, 197–198, 203, 204; ceramics, functional type distribution, **224**; colonial ceramics, **216,** 222, 223, 225; food preparation area, 61, 80; gourds, 197, 403; indigenous pottery, 236, **243,** 258, 264; knife, folding, 60–61, 197, 284, **290**; knife in *quincha* wall, 284, **288, 289**; liquid storage and serving forms, **259**; numbering system, 74n3; photo map, **40**; playing cards, 388, **390**; sheltered area, 43; site selection, 60–61, **60**; storage vessels, 61; streets, 41

Unit 4 (church compound): cigarettes, 352, 372–373; paper fragments, 352; paper fragments, ecclesiastical, 386, 392; playing cards, 386, **387,** 392, **392**. *See also* cigarettes

Unit 5 (trench from church to town): beads, 196; gourd fragments, decorated, 403

Unit 6 (church), 123, **124**

Unit 7 (church compound), 32, 196

Unit 8 (church): papers, 388; playing cards, 386, **388**

Unit 12 (church nave), 32; beads, 196; burial analyses, details, 140–143; burials, 56–57, 107–108, **108**, 109–111, 111, 123, **125**, 147; colonial ceramics, 196, **213**; location, 34; musical instrument fragments (pottery), 254; paper, 196; view of, **36**. See also African cranium; burial analyses; burials; church: nave

Unit 14 (church compound), 37, **37**

Unit 17 (church), 195

Unit 18 (church): beads, 195; bin and scraper for hide processing, 55, 59, 79

Unit 19 (midden): overview, 49, 51–54; beads, 198–199; gourd fragments, decorated, 403; paper fragments, 54; photo map, **40**; radiocarbon dating, 75n9; ritual object, bead in ashes in bowl, 52, **52**, 199, 203; strata, 81; view of, **51**; waterborne deposit, 53–54, **53**, 81

Unit 24 (town), 198–199, **199**

Unit 26 (town), 62, **62**

Unit 28 (town residence), 32; aerial photograph, **67**; ash analyses, 96–97; ash analyses, details (table 3.4), 98; beads, 197, 204; ceramics, functional type distribution, **224**; charcoal, 96; coins, 303, **304**, **306**, 308–309; coins, details, 315; colonial ceramics, **213**, **216**, **217**, 222, 223–225, 258; cooking pots, 225, 238, 239, **241**, 256–257, 258, 263; finger rings, 68, 279, 292–295, **295**; food preparation area, 80, 96–97, **97**, 402, **402**; food remains, 97–98, 239, 258; food remains, details, 98; foodways, 104; gourds, 70, 402, 403; indigenous pottery, forms (table 9.2), 236; indigenous pottery, fragments, 243; indigenous pottery, glazed, 264; indigenous pottery, grater bowls (*rayadores*), 252–253, **254**; indigenous pottery, whole olla, 238, 239, **241**, 256–257; liquid storage and serving forms, **259**; liquid storage vessels, 258, 260; looter holes, 14; musical instrument fragments (pottery), **217**, 254; numbering system, 74n3; photo map, **40**; playing cards, 68, 388, **390**; site selection, 66–68; storage vessels, 68, 70, 96, 225, 258, 260, 263, 402, **402**; textiles, **402**; view of, **14**, **68**; view of, distant, **93**

Unit 31 (church), **213**

Unit 32 (church), 196

Universal Transverse Mercator (UTM) system, 32

University of Arizona, AMS Laboratory, 373

University of Oklahoma, Ancient DNA Laboratory, 150–151

V

VanValkenburgh, Parker, 32, 49, **51**, 60–61

Vaqueta, Lope Fernádez de, 366, 381n6

Vargas, Bartolomé de, 325

Vásquez, Segundo, 27, 75n10, 100

Vásquez de Espinosa, Antonio, 191, 205n3

Velasco, Luis, 384

Venice, bead production, 191, 192

Vera, Diego de, 327

Verano, John W., 132

vessels. See ceramics; ceramics, colonial; gourds; inscriptions on gourds; pottery, indigenous; vessels, wood

vessels, wood, 407, 413

Viceroyalty of Peru coinage, 303, 305–307, 308. See also coins, colonial

Vilcabamba (town), 2

Villalobos, Eusebio de, 330–331, 332, 335

Villalobos, Mateo de, 330

Virú Valley, 261

Virú Valley Project, 13

W

walls, adobe: collapsed (church compound), 57, **58**, 65–66, 69, 417–418; melted (town), 38–39; with murals, 26, 31, **31**, 33, 46; perimeter, church compound, 47–48, **49**, 57, 69, **70**; with plaster, 30, 44, 46, 57, 417; in town (Unit 28), 68, **68**. See also adobe; walls, *quincha*

walls, *quincha*: in church compound, **36**, 37; in town, 23, **24**, 38–39, 42, 60–61, **60**; in town, with knife, 284, **288**, **289**; in town, with paper at bases, 352. See also walls, adobe

Wars of the Netherlands (Mendoza), 354, **355**

water disputes, 330–331, 333, 335

weapon parts (?), **280**, 281–282, **282**. See also metals

well, ceremonial, 28, **28**

wetlands, 73, 75n10, 320–321, 328, 333

wheat, 102–103, 329, 331. See also plant remains studies; plants, cultivated

Wiese de Osma, Guillermo, 26–27

wood: beads, 190, 195, 196, 197, 198; *chicha* paddle, 47, 48, 51, 79; coffins, 124–125, **127**; crosses, 61, 124; drinking vessels (*keros*), 407, 413; hide scraper, 55, 59, 79; knife handle, 197, 284, **290**; pestles or mauls, 79; sharpened sticks, 49, **50**, 78; stick as symbolic barrier, 64; unidentified objects, 79

wool: button on, **178**; versus camelid fiber, 164; European clothing, 163; European-style clothing, 183; fibers and structures, 171–172, 173; production of, 165; seams, 168; sleeve fragment, 179, **180**. See also camelid fiber (alpaca); textiles and clothing

writing systems, impact on indigenous societies, 351, 379–380. See also paper(s)

www.peabody.harvard.edu/Magdalena, 351, 431

Z

Zachumxarca, Andrés, 320

Zaña Valley: ceramics, 211, 215, 218; ceramic typology, 210; during civil wars of early Colonial Period, 319; functional categories, 232; glazes, 219–221

Zender, Marc, 368